HANDBOOKS

D0805249

BELIZE

JOSHUA BERMAN

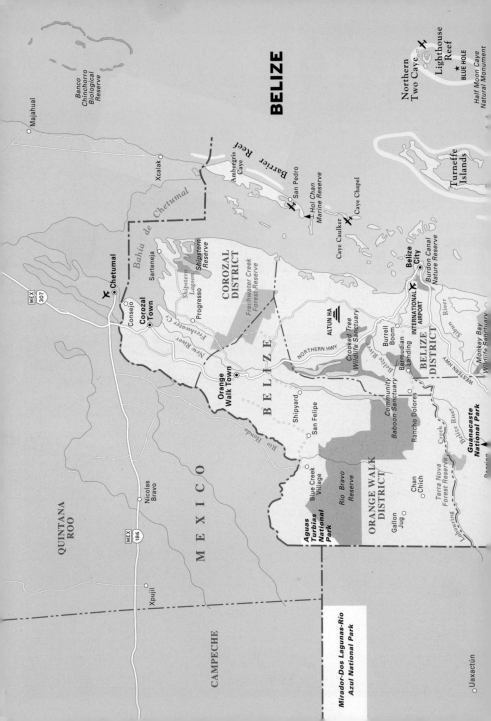

Contents

Discover **Belize**

The first morning I awoke in Belize, it was raining and warm. I got up before dawn and followed the crowds to the water's edge in Belize City. There, a gray dawn delivered a festooned flotilla of wooden dories to the dock in Haulover Creek. It was November 19, Settlement Day, the Garinagu people's annual reenactment of their ancestors' 1832 arrival to Belizean shores. Drums, smiles, and biting belts of *gífit,* a drink also known as "bitters," were on hand as I walked with the clump of celebrants through Belize City's narrow streets. People were singing and drumming, dancing and marching. There were shouts and umbrellas, black-and-yellow flags, babies crying. And the rain.

The parade marched across the old Swing Bridge. The first light of day had become a bright white suffused in a light drizzle, and masts of fishing boats were reflected on the water's glassy surface. The smell of low tide, fish, and gasoline completed the scene. As we turned onto Front Street, a man next to me beat on a string of turtle shells dangling from his neck, the drums thumping below him. When we arrived at the entrance to the church, I stepped aside and watched waves of wet, shiny people wash up the stairs with drums and flags, music never ceasing as they crammed inside for a blessing.

My first day in Belize delivered this damp, convivial experience. My

second day, driving inland, gave me a different experience entirely – river crossings, pyramids, and the roar of "baboons." On my fifth day, in the cayes, I saw Belize through a curtain of grouper fish and reef sharks.

If you've traveled in other parts of Central America or the Caribbean, forget them all. Belize is different: It is coconut shavings in your rice and beans. It is butter pooling in your conch soup – with a squirt of lime and a splash of Marie Sharp's hot sauce to make it bite. Belize is the hemisphere's largest barrier reef; it is massive forests of giant cohune palms and prehistoric tree ferns, some amid ancient Mayan plazas. There are birds, big cats, and strange rodents in Belize's ample backabush. And, of course, there are the Belizeans – about 300,000 of them, each family line hailing from a uniquely Creolized collection of cultures.

It's a country which is always new to me, as new as it was that first morning in the rain. Your experience will be just as personal. It will begin the moment you decide to go to Belize.

Planning Your Trip

▶ WHERE TO GO

Belize District

This stretch of coastline, islands, and swampy lowlands includes former capital Belize City. Scattered sights and events make it worth a quick visit. If you don't appreciate the city's unique grit and texture, focus on attractions like the Belize Zoo, Community Baboon Sanctuary, Crooked Tree Wildlife Reserve, and Altun Ha ruins.

The Northern Cayes

This group islands includes Ambergris Caye, with beach resorts on the swankiest side of Belize tourism. Caye Caulker, just down the reef, offers a slower pace with a cheaper, Rasta-tinted vibe. Turneffe Island and Lighthouse Reef Atolls offer spectacular wall diving and include Jacques Cousteau's old favorite, the Blue Hole.

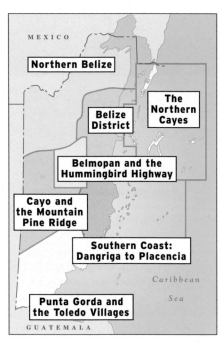

Belmopan and the Hummingbird Highway

For most travelers, Belize's capital, Belmopan, is nothing more than an annoying bus layover. The surrounding countryside, however—and the beautiful Hummingbird Highway that snakes through the district—is not to be missed. Some of the country's most famous adventure lodges occupy riverbanks in the area, as does one of Belize's only golf courses, along Roaring Creek.

Cayo and the Mountain Pine Ridge

Bordering Guatemala's Petén wilderness, Belize's interior offers a remarkable selection of lodges and camps. Sights include the Xunantunich and Caracol Archaeological Sites, the Belize Botanical Gardens, and the Mountain Pine Ridge. You can also float the interior's lazy rivers or wander its mountain trails, whether on foot, on horseback, or by mountain bike.

Southern Coast: Dangriga to Placencia

Stann Creek District offers hiking in several protected areas in the Maya Mountains, and kayaking, diving, and sailing out in the cayes. Dangriga is the cultural center of Belize's Garinagu population and a tranquil base for exploring surrounding islands and nature reserves. Just down the coast, lazy

IF YOU HAVE...

- **ONE WEEK:** Visit Caye Caulker and Cayo, three days each.
- **TWO WEEKS:** Add more days to each of the above.
- **THREE WEEKS:** Add Punta Gorda and the Toledo District.
- **FOUR WEEKS:** Add a side trip to the Mountain Pine Ridge or Tikal in Guatemala.

basketball on Caye Caulker

Hopkins Village and Sittee River are worthy beach and river areas, respectively.

Punta Gorda and the Toledo Villages

Think Belize is over-touristed? You've been spending too much time in San Pedro, amigo. Head south where forest, reef, river, ruins, and ridges await the handful of visitors who get off the beaten path and onto the "cacao trail." Consider signing up with a guesthouse or homestay program in the upcountry villages, where you can learn how to make a corn tortilla and speak a few phrases of the local Maya tongue.

Northern Belize

Orange Walk and Corozal Districts are not a focus for most travelers—unless, of course, they've heard about the Chan Chich or Lamanai Outpost Lodges, gorgeous accommodations amid remote, vast archaeological ruins. Both are set deep in the bush and are as popular with birders and naturalists as they are with archaeologists and biologists. You may also have heard about the sleepy streets of gentle and affordable Corozal, a possible launching pad to Ambergris Caye.

Chan Chich Lodge

▶ WHEN TO GO

High season is mid-December through May, a period many travel agents will tell you is the "dry season," in a vain effort to neatly contain Belize's weather patterns. In many years, this is true, with sunny skies and green vegetation throughout the country during the North American winter. However, November can be dry as a bone and sunny, while December, January, and even February can play host to wet cold fronts that either blow right through or sit around for days.

Don't forget your camera.

June, July, and August technically form the rainy season—which may mean just a quick afternoon shower or rain for days. This often means significantly discounted accommodations. August is the most popular with European backpackers, while December and February are dominated by North Americans. Some tourism businesses shut down completely during the months of September and October, the peak of hurricane season.

Your best bet? Be prepared for clouds or sun at any time of year. A week of stormy weather may ruin a vacation planned solely around snorkeling, but it could also provide the perfect setting for exploring the rainforests or enjoying a hot tub and fireplace in the Mountain Pine Ridge.

embarking on a tubing adventure

▶ BEFORE YOU GO

Opportunities for diving and snorkeling are plentiful.

Passports and Visas

You must have a passport that is valid for the duration of your stay in Belize. You may be asked at the border (or airport immigration) to show a return ticket or ample money to leave the country. You do *not* need a visa if you are a British Commonwealth subject or a citizen of Belgium, Denmark, Finland, Greece, Iceland, Italy, Liechtenstein, Luxembourg, Mexico, Spain, Switzerland, Tunisia, Turkey, the United States, or Uruguay. Visitors for purposes other than tourism must obtain a visa.

Vaccinations

Technically, a certificate of vaccination against yellow fever is required for travelers aged above one year arriving from an affected area, though immigration officials rarely, if ever, ask to see one.

In general, before traveling anywhere in Central America, your routine vaccinations—tetanus, diphtheria, measles, mumps, rubella, and polio—should be up to date. Hepatitis A vaccine is recommended for all travelers over age two and should be given at least two weeks (preferably four weeks or more) before departure. Hepatitis B vaccine is recommended for travelers who will have intimate contact with local residents or potentially need blood transfusions or injections while abroad, especially if visiting for more than six months. It is also recommended for all health care personnel and volunteers. Typhoid and rabies vaccines are recommended for those headed for rural areas.

Transportation

The vast majority of travelers arrive in Belize by air at Philip Goldson International Airport (BZE), located nine miles from Belize City. From there, short domestic connections are available around the country. A few travelers fly into Cancún, then rent a car and drive south through the Yucatan peninsula to get to Belize. Backpackers often include Belize on their extended tours of the Mundo Maya, which also includes Guatemala and southern Mexico. They most often cross into Belize at the western border at Benque,

Boats are an easy way to get around Belize.

or at Punta Gorda in the south, where travelers arrive by boat from both Honduras and Guatemala.

Belize is small and extremely manageable, especially if you fly the domestic airline from tiny airstrip to tiny airstrip. You can also get around by rental car, hired taxi, or public bus, experiences which make the country seem larger. Another option is to simply let your resort or lodge arrange your airport transfer and all tours.

Water taxis are another big way people get around in Belize, especially to and from Ambergris Caye and Caye Caulker; regular routes play the waters between Belize City and these islands.

What to Take

Pack for hot weather (80–95°F, both humid and dry), as well as the occasional cool front (60–80°F). At least one pair of pants and a light shell jacket are recommended, as rainy season can push all the way into February, and June through November are guaranteed to be damp. Long sleeves are helpful for avoiding mosquito bites and sunburn. Cayo and the Mountain Pine Ridge can drop to sweater weather in any part of the wet season. Bring a small first-aid kit, a flashlight or headlamp, and waterproof plastic bags for protection during rain or boat travel.

Explore Belize

▶ THE BEST OF BELIZE

A week and a half provides just enough time to see a few of Belize's major destinations and get a taste for just how much more there is to discover. Following is an active and mobile 10-day tour; you can double or triple the time allotted to any of the areas listed below and still stay busy. Feel free to follow this itinerary in any order and, when you tire, stop where you are and soak it in.

DAY 1

Arrive at Philip Goldson International Airport and transfer to Cayo on the San Ignacio shuttle. Settle into a family guesthouse and spend the evening strolling the mellow, misty village of San Ignacio. Or you can just as easily base yourself at one of the many area jungle lodges throughout Cayo and still hit all the best sights.

DAY 2

Rise early for a canoe trip up the Macal River. Depending on the water level, you may make it to Chaa Creek and duPlooy's Lodges, both with a number of attractions, including a nature center, a butterfly farm, and the Belize Botanic Garden. Float back downstream for another relaxed San Ignacio evening—book a massage for those well-worked shoulders.

DAY 3

Hit the Xunantunich or El Pilar archaeological sites, either by foot, mountain bike, or horseback. When you get back, ask your host to help plan a trip to Caracol the next day.

DAY 4

Enjoy the ride along the Mountain Pine Ridge to the ruins of Caracol, then try the swimming hole tour on the way back. Stop for an organic salad or gourmet pizza at Blancaneaux Lodge or a photo op at Thousand Foot Falls, one of the highest in Central America.

walkway at duPlooy's Lodges

THE MUNDO MAYA

There's a giddy, childlike feeling climbing thousand-year-old stone structures in the middle of the jungle – a fairy-tale, Tolkienesque mood of mystery as you scramble over winding, crooked staircases and tunnels while strange creatures howl from the surrounding forest canopy. Belize offers dozens of lushly vegetated archaeological sites to explore, some fully excavated and restored, others still hidden under ferns, trees, and orchids.

Archaeologists estimate that at one time, between one and two million Mayans lived in the area that is now called Belize (as compared to today's population of less than 300,000). They were part of a loose empire of city-states that extended far to the west and north, into present-day Guatemala and southern Mexico. New sites are discovered each year throughout Belize, and it's common for rural Belizean families to have ruins and mounds in their backyards without official archaeological knowledge.

Most Maya archaeological sites in Belize have simple visitor facilities that act as mini-museums and interpretive centers. Many provide guides to walk you through the ruins. Although many sites are quite accessible (especially Altun Ha, where the parking lot is on even ground with the main plaza), most require at least some level of physical activity to reach and can be explored by foot, horseback, canoe, or mountain bike.

You'll find that nearly every accommodation in every corner of Belize offers at least one day trip to a Maya archaeological site. Even if you're on San Pedro or Caye Caulker, you can take daily boat-bus commutes to and from **Altun Ha** or **Lamanai** – by nightfall, you'll be back in your beach chair. However, why not cut out all that travel time? Why not take your time in the ruins, stay the night in a jungle lodge nearby, and wake up to Maya dawn?

The most spectacular, extensive, and exciting sites in Belize are **Caracol, Xunantunich,** and **Lamanai,** where impressive ongoing excavations have made these ceremonial centers and tall, climbable pyramids more accessible to tourists. Other sites include **El Pilar,** whose main attraction is its *lack* of excavation, and the southern sites of **Nim Li Punit** and **Lubaantun,** each with a unique architectural flair.

To learn more about the history of the Maya empire, contact the **Belize Institute of Archaeology,** based in Belmopan and part of the government's **National Institute of Culture and History** (NICH; www.nichbelize.org). For archaeological fieldwork opportunities in ongoing excavations or archaeological cave projects, contact the **Belize Valley Archaeological Reconnaissance Project** (BVAR), a longtime scientific program in Belize, directed by esteemed national archaeologist Jaime Awe (www.bvar.org).

the royal residences at Lamanai

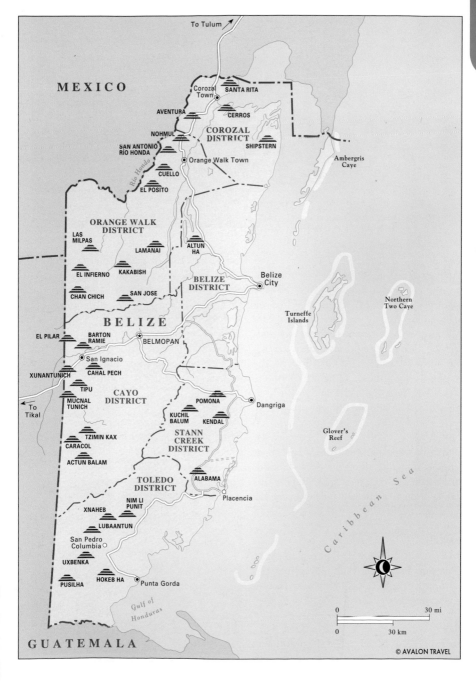

To Tulum

MEXICO

Corozal Town

SANTA RITA

AVENTURA

CERROS

NOHMUL

COROZAL DISTRICT

SHIPSTERN

SAN ANTONIO RÍO HONDA

Orange Walk Town

Ambergris Caye

CUELLO

Río Hondo

EL POSITO

ORANGE WALK DISTRICT

LAS MILPAS

LAMANAI

ALTUN HA

EL INFIERNO

KAKABISH

BELIZE DISTRICT

Belize City

CHAN CHICH

SAN JOSE

Northern Two Caye

BELIZE

Turneffe Islands

EL PILAR

BARTON RAMIE

BELMOPAN

San Ignacio

CAHAL PECH

XUNANTUNICH

TIPU

CAYO DISTRICT

POMONA

Dangriga

MUCNAL TUNICH

To Tikal

KUCHIL BALUM

KENDAL

TZIMIN KAX

STANN CREEK DISTRICT

Glover's Reef

CARACOL

ACTUN BALAM

ALABAMA

TOLEDO DISTRICT

Placencia

Caribbean Sea

NIM LI PUNIT

XNAHEB

LUBAANTUN

San Pedro Columbia

UXBENKA

HOKEB HA

Punta Gorda

PUSILHA

Gulf of Honduras

GUATEMALA

0   30 mi

0   30 km

© AVALON TRAVEL

the Altun Ha ruins

DAY 5

Transfer to Belize City in the morning, but be sure to stop for a hike at Guanacaste National Park or the Belize Zoo. When you arrive in the city, buy your water taxi ticket to Ambergris Caye for the last boat of the afternoon, then stash your bags at the water taxi terminal while you explore Fort George, the Image Factory, and the Museum of Belize. Get on the boat and arrive in San Pedro in time for a fancy seafood dinner.

DAY 6

Diving or snorkeling, anyone? How about window shopping along the dusty lanes or soaking in one of several spas? Repeat this day as often as needed, maybe even for the duration of your trip.

DAY 7

Two quick puddle-jumper flights plop you in Dangriga. From there, cruise out to Tobacco (or South Water) Caye for more sun, ocean, diving, and conviviality.

DAY 8

Back on the mainland, spend the morning at the Garinagu Museum and Marie Sharp's hot sauce factory, then ride south to Sittee River (or Hopkins) and arrange for a night canoe safari.

DAY 9

Stay put, or take a day trip to Cockscomb Basin Wildlife Sanctuary, where you can hike through the jungle and float the river under a sky of birdsong and green canopy.

DAY 10

Transfer to Philip Goldson International Airport for your departure. Plan on coming back next year to explore the southern and northern parts of Belize.

Cockscomb Basin Wildlife Sanctuary was created largely as a preserve for jaguars.

► THREE WAYS TO DIVING BLISS

Belize was a Western Hemisphere diving mecca decades before it became the romantic and trendy destination it is today. Hundreds of miles of reefs, atolls, caves, coral patches, and coastline harbor entire alien worlds to explore, as do shipwrecks with centuries of secrets. There's nothing like the raw excitement of swimming among the curious and brazen fish, combined with the sensation of zero gravity.

Belizean dive stories of yore include communing with wild dolphins, swarms of horse-eye jacks and massive tarpon, or dozens of spotted eagle rays at a time. Some divers go strictly to photograph the Dr. Seussian coral life or to get that elusive whale shark shot in March or April.

Dive shops exist everywhere there is access to the reef and cayes in Belize—this means San Pedro and Caye Caulker, Belize City, Sittee River, Placencia—and then there are more shops and dive resorts scattered throughout the islands and atolls. Options are much more limited in Punta Gorda, which means

you'll have the ocean to yourself when diving the southern hook of the Barrier Reef.

No matter which path to diving you choose, your first order of business is choosing a dive shop. You'll have no trouble finding a shop; in fact, you may have a difficult time choosing between so many options. In most cases, prices are more or less the same between shops, but it pays to do a bit of comparing. Expect to pay US$60–75 for a two-tank fun dive, possibly extra for gear rental or for longer boat trips. Know that the bigger a shop's boats, the more comfortable a long ride will be, but also the bigger your group will be, a serious consideration; small groups (6–10) assure more personalized attention from your dive masters. Also, to beat the crowds at more popular sights, choose a dive shop with early start times.

Certification Courses

The full menu of PADI- and NAUI-accredited courses are offered at most dive shops in Belize. Expect to pay about US$250–400

Belize has the largest barrier reef in the hemisphere.

BEST DIVE SITES

Phenomenal dives are abundant up and down the entire length of the **Belize Barrier Reef,** which begins off the northern tip of Ambergris Caye and extends southward to the Sapodilla Cayes in Belize's southernmost reaches. Except for a few overused or storm-damaged spots, the barrier reef's coral is in excellent condition.

Beyond the reef are Belize's three amazing atolls, or rings of coral and islands which rise up from deep water:

- **Glover's Reef:** The southernmost of Belize's atolls, Glover's Reef is a ring of beautiful coral reef that spans nearly 80 square miles.

- **Turneffe Islands:** Not far from Belize City, the Turneffe Islands are a diver's dream. Here you will find some of Belize's not-to-be-missed dive sites, such as The Elbow and Gales Point.

- **Lighthouse Reef:** Accessible from Belize City, Ambergris Caye, and Caye Caulker, the Lighthouse Reef atoll is a favorite diving destination – not to mention that it is home to the famous **Blue Hole,** as well

as the **Half Moon Caye Wall,** where the diving is second to none. While these dive sites might top the list, know that your options include literally hundreds of other opportunities that will keep you busy for a lifetime. Of particular note is the diving in **southern Belize,** where you'll find some of Belize's most exclusive and remote dive opportunities.

for Open Water or Advanced certification courses. Belize diving prices are roughly on par with diving prices in Roatán in the Honduran Bay Islands, but more expensive than they are in Utila, another of the Bay Islands.

Introductory Dive Courses

You're in Belize on vacation and want to dive— but you don't want to spend four precious days (and US$400) getting certified. What can you do? How about a "resort course"—a one-day introduction to scuba. Also called "discovery" courses, these usually include one tank of air and cost around US$75.

Live-Aboard Dive Boats

If you want to guarantee the most diving time possible, several live-aboard vessels based in Belize City are designed for serious divers, but can also accommodate an avid diver's companion if he or she is a sea lover or a casual angler. Your own luxury hotel and chef travel with you to some of the most scenic and best diving spots in the tropical world. Most of the following rates are weekly and all-inclusive (plus a few hundred dollars of extra charges, of course). Here are a few options: *Belize Aggressor III* (120-foot, U.S. tel. 800/348-2628, www.aggressor.com, US$2,295); the *Nekton Pilot* (78-foot, U.S. tel. 800/899-6753, www.nektoncruises.com, from US$1,495); and Peter Hughes Diving's *Sun Dancer II* (138-foot, U.S. tel. 800/932-6237, www.peterhughes.com, from US$2,195).

► BACKABUSH BELIZE

Even with Belize's increased name recognition around the world, it still doesn't take much to drop off the beaten path, and for those whose preferred "scene" is no scene at all, here are some ideas. The two-week adventure suggested below is an entirely mainland one. To add more Caribbean time to your trip, consider inserting several days on Caye Caulker, followed by Raggamuffin Tours' three-day sailing trip to Placencia, a unique fishing, snorkeling, and camping trip. From Placencia, you can visit Laughing Bird Caye National Park, spend a night in Monkey River Village, or hop a boat bound for Puerto Cortés, Honduras. Others figure out a way to get to Glover's Reef Atoll, an unparalleled Caribbean experience. Another alternative is to make it to Punta Gorda, as listed below, then instead of the village homestay, head for the Sapodilla Cayes or to Livingston, Guatemala, for a few nights.

Of course, the most important items you'll want to pack for any of these trips are an open mind, extra patience, and the ability to scrap the entire plan when you feel the adventure pulling you in its own direction.

howler monkey

DAY 1

Transfer to a riverside Belize City guesthouse and enjoy your first heaping plate of rice, beans, and stew chicken while reggae blasts all around you.

DAY 2

Catch a bus to the Community Baboon Sanctuary at Bermuda Landing, where you are guaranteed howler monkey sightings and can stay in a tent or cabin or with a local family.

kayaks on the beach in Placencia

BUTTERFLY SAFARI

A number of butterfly "farms" or "ranches" have been built around Belize, and a visit to one is always a pleasant, educational, and colorful experience. Many began as export businesses, to raise butterflies for foreign zoos and classrooms, but now feature screened-in rooms where you'll see the creatures fluttering about your head as you walk through.

Butterfly farms pay as much attention to the plants that provide the larval food as to the pupae and winged creatures. Different species often have different tastes and needs. Depending on where you are in the country, you'll see the intense **blue morpho** as well as the **white morpho,** which is white but shot with iridescent blue. Three species of the **owl butterfly** (genus *Caligo*) love to come and lunch on the overripe fruit. You'll also see tiny **heliconians** and large yellow and white **pierids,** among many, many more.

A butterfly goes from tiny teardroplike egg, to colorful caterpillar, to pupae, and then graceful adult. Butterfly farms gather breeding populations of typical Belizean species in the pupal stage, and then the pupae are carefully hung in what is called an "emerging cage" with a simulated jungle atmosphere – hot and humid (not hard to do in Belize). A short time later they shed their pupal skin, and a tiny bit of Belize flutters away to the amazement and joy of anyone who happens to be present.

Notable places to see butterflies include **Green Hills,** at Mile 8 on the Mountain Pine Ridge Road in Cayo District, a butterfly breeding, educational, and interpretive center. You'll find another small but diverse butterfly reserve at the entrance road to the Cockscomb Basin Wildlife Sanctuary. It's right across the creek from the Women's Craft Co-op in Maya Center. Another readily accessible butterfly farm, with one of the highest numbers of species, is **Tropical Wings,** located at the Trek Stop on the Western Highway, just outside San José Succotz. There's an excellent interpretive center, a guided tour, and a disk golf course and café for when you've finished.

Chaa Creek Lodge has the **Blue Morpho Butterfly Breeding Center.** Naturalists gladly explain the various stages of life the butterfly goes through, with a wonderful little flight room.

Depending on the species, butterflies live anywhere from seven days to six weeks. If you plan to visit a farm, or to go into the rainforest on a butterfly safari, you'll see much more butterfly activity on a sunny day than on an overcast day. If it's raining, forget it!

In many areas of Belize, butterfly populations have been almost totally depleted for many reasons, including habitat destruction (from logging, for instance) and changing farming practices, particularly the use of pesticides. Belize's steamy marshes, swamps, and rainforest have been a natural breeding ground for beautiful butterflies for thousands of years and hopefully will continue to be so.

Xunantunich archaeological site

DAY 3

After a morning hike, take a bus to the Western Highway and catch another ride to San Ignacio in Cayo District. Continue through town and stay at one of the budget places toward the Guatemala border, like the Trek Stop, where you should have time for a round of disk golf and a tour of the Tropical Wings Butterfly Farm before bedtime.

DAY 4

Spend the morning at the Xunantunich archaeological site, climbing pyramids and convening with the spirits. In the afternoon, arrange a pickup in Benque Viejo to take you to one of the funky places down the Hydro Road: Martz Farms or Chechem Ha.

DAY 5

Spend the day hiking, horseback riding, caving, and spouting poetry inspired by the awesome views of the upper Macal River Gorge. Spend a second night in your tent, cabin, or waterfall-enhanced tree house.

DAY 6

Get a ride back to Benque, then travel to Bullet Tree Falls via canoe or kayak—plan on five hours of easy paddling and mellow riffles down the Mopan River; when you arrive, have a cabin and meal waiting for you at the Cohune Palms or Parrot's Nest mini-resorts.

DAY 7

Roll into San Ignacio town and take a morning to enjoy the local vibe, and maybe the Cahal Pech ruins, then catch a southbound bus in Belmopan and get off in the village of Armenia for a cozy night with a mestizo family.

DAY 8

Make your way to Hopkins Village for a few beers and a Garinagu drumming workshop. You'll likely have to spend a few hours in Dangriga on the way, so feel free to get sidetracked out to Tobacco Caye for a night or two.

DAY 9

Spend the day hiking the trails and splashing in the waterfalls of Mayflower-Bocawina, Belize's newest national park.

DAY 10

Continue south to Punta Gorda and check into one of several lovely new

Garinagu drummers

accommodations, such as Hickatee Cottages or Coral House Inn. From PG, go on trips into the countryside and cayes, or arrange a homestay in the hills before dining on a vegetarian feast at Gomier's.

DAYS 11-13
Go deep into the Toledo bush, living among the Maya or Garinagu. Hire guides and listen to stories, music, and the river. On the last day, transfer back to PG. You can do this through the homestay program or based at one of the backabush accommodations in the area.

DAY 14
Fly back north to Philip Goldson International Airport and begin writing your memoirs as your return flight takes off.

► BIRDING IN BELIZE

Because of its extensive protected forests, varied wetland habitat, and location on a major migratory route, Belize is a minor mecca for both novice and experienced birders, who arrive throughout the year and from all over the world. The Belize Audubon Society (BAS, www.belizeaudubon.org) reports 587 recorded bird species in Belize, about 20 percent of which are migrants from other parts of North America. BAS helps manage many of the country's wildlife reserves and maintains updated checklists and field guides. Always check with BAS for the latest sightings, and you can purchase several bird guides in the central BAS office in the historic Fort George area of Belize City.

A number of lodges throughout the country cater specifically to birders. A sure sign is if they have downloadable bird checklists on their websites. Another is whether or not they employ guides; many inland resorts have brilliant Belizean birders on their staff for daily sunrise walks and other activities. Belizean park rangers also generally have excellent bird identification skills, notably Israel Manzanero, who works at St. Herman's Cave and St. Herman's Blue Hole National Park; his knowledge is legendary in birder circles.

Twitchers on a serious mission (motmot or death!) can choose from several bird-centric tour operators; this is for those who'd rather let someone else (someone who knows where the birds are) handle the logistics of a countrywide tour, so you can keep your eyes glued to those binocs. One option is Paradise Expeditions (www.birdinginbelize.com).

Bring binoculars; wear boots, a lightweight long-sleeved shirt, and lightweight trousers; and carry a copy of *Birds of Belize* by H. Lee Jones, illustrated by Dana Gardner.

For details about species you're likely to encounter, or to participate in the annual

rare khaki-breasted bird-watchers in Lamanai

Christmas bird count, consult the Belize Audubon Society's website, particularly the "Birds of Belize" section. Following are the most popular spots for birders:

- **Crooked Tree Wildlife Sanctuary:** Take a guided boat tour of these vast wetlands, host to a spectacular variety of wading birds, especially during the dry season (March through May). This is the last Central American stronghold of the jabiru stork—the tallest flying bird in the Americas, which can reach five feet in height, with up to an 11-foot wingspan.

- **Lamanai Archaeological Zone:** Enjoy the extensive river and lake sections as you travel to and from the jungle-encrusted, bird-choked ruins of Lamanai. All four species of trogon found in Belize can be seen here, along with many woodcreepers and woodpeckers. Be sure to watch for both blue-crowned and tody motmots, which burrow into unexcavated ruin walls to nest.

- **Mountain Pine Ridge:** Overlapping microclimates and habitats are favored by several species of extremely rare raptors, including the rare orange-breasted falcon, which nests near Thousand-Foot Falls. At the Caracol ruins, you can spot a keel-billed motmot, especially in March and April.

- **Cockscomb Basin Wildlife Sanctuary:** At Belize's preeminent birding destination, beginners will be overwhelmed by the abundance of wildlife and serious birders have a shot at a "big day"—spotting 100 species in a single day. Some of the less-traveled trails—like the Antelope or Gibnut Loops—may give you the chance of spotting a pheasant cuckoo. Also, swarms of army ants attract ground-dwelling species, such as tanagers and woodcreepers.

- **The Northern Cayes:** The mangroves and littoral forests of Caye Caulker and Ambergris Caye are disappearing, but these islands are still a stopover for many migratories,

northern jacana, a.k.a. "lily trotter," New River Lagoon

plus they are home to several threatened and endangered native species. Be sure to make a pilgrimage to the red-footed booby colony on Half Moon Caye National Monument.

- **Red Bank Village:** This small Maya settlement in southern Belize is the annual destination of one of Belize's last scarlet macaw populations (January through March). In March and April, various hawks can be seen over the peaks around the village, including swallow-tailed and plumbeous kites; the aplomado falcon lives in the surrounding pine savanna.

- **Aguacaliente Wildlife Sanctuary:** In Toledo District, near the village of Laguna, this reserve features breeding colonies of unique wading birds, as well as other species found nowhere else in Belize; most can be sighted within a half-hour drive from Punta Gorda.

BELIZE DISTRICT

This region of mangroves, pine savanna, marshes, and Caribbean cayes is the most populated district in the country, encompassing nearly a quarter of all Belizeans. The Mayan ruins of Altun Ha lie juxtaposed with the modern commotion of Belize City, where a unique cultural stew pot simmers in the sun.

In the middle of it all, on the tip of a small, jutting piece of land (land partly composed, some say, of centuries worth of rum bottles), Belize City is the hub of the nation. The city is ideally located for reaching any part of Belize within a couple hours' time. Because of this access, Belize City is where you'll find the headquarters of the bus lines, rental car agencies, and airlines, as well as water taxis to

the cayes. It used to be the capital of Belize as well, but the government now sits inland, in Belmopan.

For those wishing to avoid the bustle and traffic (and rising crime rate) of the city, the rest of Belize District offers a handful of destinations that feel utterly remote, even though they are less than an hour's drive from the city. Birders head straight to Crooked Tree Wildlife Sanctuary, others book a cabin in the Community Baboon Sanctuary, and still others do the half-day trip to the Altun Ha archaeological site. Offshore, a number of islands provide historical and ecological escapes; diving, snorkeling, and several marine reserves are a short boat ride away from downtown Belize City.

© JOSHUA BERMAN/THANKS TO ASTRUM HELICOPTERS

HIGHLIGHTS

(**Museum of Belize:** Housed in the old prison, this museum has rotating exhibitions and an incredible stamp collection that make it worth a visit (page 32).

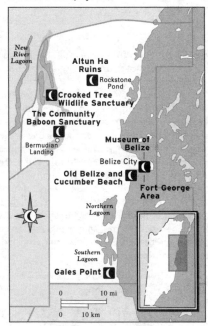

LOOK FOR (TO FIND RECOMMENDED SIGHTS, ACTIVITIES, DINING, AND LODGING.

(**Fort George Area:** Take a stroll through this breezy neighborhood with its ramshackle colonial homes and old wooden hotels (page 34).

(**Old Belize and Cucumber Beach:** Go for a meal, and stay for the beach, boats, waterslide, and zip line. This entertainment center is located a few miles down the Western Highway from Belize City and features a historical heritage tour and museum (page 34).

(**Gales Point:** The path less traveled lies to the south and leads to this peaceful fishing village in the middle of a vast, wild estuary, offering nature tours, Creole drumming, manatees, and more (page 43).

(**Altun Ha Ruins:** Head north to this ancient Maya trading center, the most extensively excavated ruins in Belize (page 45).

(**The Community Baboon Sanctuary:** The area is thick with black howler monkeys around a few simple Creole villages. This community-managed ecotourism venture offers an adventurous menu of wildlife hikes and canoe trips (page 49).

(**Crooked Tree Wildlife Sanctuary:** Drive an hour north of Belize City, to this habitat for hundreds of resident and migratory birds, for a full day of birding and a boat tour (page 52).

PLANNING YOUR TIME

You'll almost certainly pass through Belize District, whether just traveling between the cayes and the mainland, taking the time to plunge into Belize City, or exploring the region's nature reserves and ruins. A self-guided daytime walking tour of Belize City is a must for anyone interested in the bigger picture of the country—even if you have only a few hours between bus and boat connections. You can see all the sights in one rushed day or two relaxed ones. Although Belize City doesn't have the dining scene of some of the touristy parts of the country, there are a handful of decent restaurants and many more cheap local eateries to keep you stuffed. If you find the slow bustle of the streets and the daily swing of the bridge intriguing, stay a couple of extra days. There are dive, snorkel, bird-watching, and ruins trips from the city, which has a few quality accommodations.

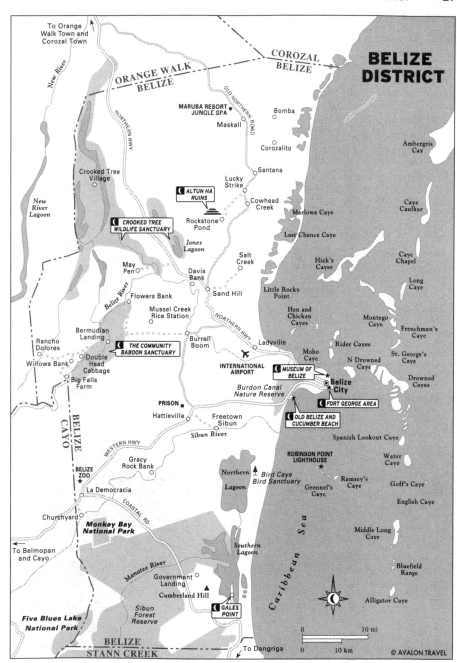

BELIZE
DISTRICT

To Orange
Walk Town and
Corozal Town

New River

ORANGE WALK
BELIZE

COROZAL
BELIZE

NORTHERN HWY

OLD NORTHERN ROAD

MARUBA RESORT
JUNGLE SPA

Maskall

Bomba

Corozalito

Ambergris
Cay

Crooked Tree
Village

New
River
Lagoon

Lucky
Strike

ALTUN HA
RUINS

CROOKED TREE
WILDLIFE SANCTUARY

Rockstone
Pond

Santana

Cowhead
Creek

Marlowe Caye

Last Chance Caye

Caye
Caulker

Caye
Chapel

Jones
Lagoon

Belize River

May
Pen

Davis
Bank

Salt
Creek

Hick's
Cayes

Long
Caye

Flowers Bank

Mussel Creek
Rice Station

NORTHERN HWY

Sand Hill

Little Rocky
Point

Hen and
Chicken
Cayes

Montego
Caye

Frenchman's
Caye

Bermudian
Landing

THE COMMUNITY
BABOON SANCTUARY

Burrell
Boom

Ladyville

Moho
Caye

Rider Cayes

N Drowned
Caye

St. George's
Caye

Rancho
Dolores

Wilfows Bank

Double
Head
Cabbage

Big Falls
Farm

INTERNATIONAL
AIRPORT

MUSEUM OF
BELIZE

Belize
City

Drowned
Cayes

BELIZE
CAYO

PRISON

Hattieville

Freetown
Sibun

Sibun River

Burdon Canal
Nature Reserve

FORT GEORGE AREA

OLD BELIZE AND
CUCUMBER BEACH

WESTERN HWY

Gracy
Rock Bank

Spanish Lookout Caye

BELIZE
ZOO

La Democracia

COASTAL RD

Churchyard

Monkey Bay
National Park

To Belmopan
and Cayo

ROBINSON POINT
LIGHTHOUSE

Northern
Lagoon

Bird Caye
Bird Sanctuary

Grennel's
Caye

Ramsey's
Caye

Water
Caye

Goff's Caye

English Caye

Middle Long
Caye

Southern
Lagoon

Bluefield
Range

Manatee River

Government
Landing

Cumberland Hill

Sibun
Forest
Reserve

GALES
POINT

Five Blues Lake
National Park

BELIZE
STANN CREEK

To Dangriga

Caribbean
Sea

Alligator Caye

0   10 mi

0   10 km

© AVALON TRAVEL

Belize City

Okay, so "city" might be stretching it, but there is no doubt that the biggest concentration of Belizeans in the world (about 70,000) live on a relatively small peninsula surrounded by the Caribbean Sea to the east and expanses of wetlands to the west. Belizeans throughout the country refer to Belize City, their former capital, as "Belize," which can be disorienting until you get used to it. And while there are no high-rises, only three traffic lights, and more faded paint and rotten wood than you'd expect, Belize City is an exciting cluster of cultures that throbs under tropical sun, wind, and rain.

The town straddles Haulover Creek (named when cattle were attached to one another by a rope around the horns and hauled across) and sprawls loosely north to the Belize River and the international airport. For tourists, Belize City is certainly no Caribbean paradise—not by a long shot. Indeed, the banks of the Belize River and Haulover Creek, meandering through the middle of the city, are often foul. The city is run-down and, though perched on the edge of the Caribbean, it is without beaches (except the artificial one at Old Belize, just outside town). Antiquated clapboard buildings on stilts—unpainted, weathered, tilted, and streaked with age—line narrow streets and are slowly being replaced by uninspired concrete structures. And even with the minor improvements, if Captain Lafitte, one of the founding buccaneers of old, came swaggering down a Belize City street today, he'd fit right in to some of these neighborhoods—and be grateful he had his sword.

The people, for the most part, are friendly—the hucksters who prey on cruise ship passengers may be a little too friendly. In general, Belize City residents are better off and more optimistic than those of many other cities in Central America—in large part because

The ground is too soggy to bury the dead at the Belize City Cemetery.

© JOSHUA BERMNA

CRIME AND THE CITY

Like other Central American countries, Belize has its share of problems with drugs, gangs, and violent street crime. Because of its extremely low population, however – 70,000 inhabitants, compared to millions in most Central American capitals – Belize City's problems are nowhere near as severe as those of El Salvador, Honduras, and Guatemala's cities. Still, over the last several years, violent crime has increased in Belize City, mostly in the form of petty theft, beatings, stabbings, and shootings. The government has taken steps to battle crime, including stiffer enforcement of the law and deployment of a force of tourist police, recognizable by their khaki shirts and green pants.

Most – but not all – violent crime occurs deep in the Southside part of the city, many blocks away from the traditional walking paths of tourists, but occasional sprees have occurred throughout the city and in broad daylight. Use the same common sense you would apply in any city in the world. Before you venture out, have a clear idea of how to get where you're going and ask a local Belizean – like your hotel desk clerk or a restaurant waiter – whether your plan is reasonable. At night, don't walk if you are at all unsure; taxis are plentiful. Only get in a taxi with a green license plate. Don't flash money, jewelry, or other temptations, and if threatened, hand them over. Report all crimes to the local police and your country's embassy.

Belize City is so much smaller. Schools and uniformed students are plentiful, little shops are everywhere (often referred to locally as the "Hindu," "Arab," or "Chinese" store, based on the ancestry of their proprietors), and some of the simplest bars are gathering places for truly interesting and important people.

ORIENTATION

The old **Swing Bridge** spans Haulover Creek, connecting Belize City's "Northside" to its "Southside," and it is the most distinct landmark in the city. North of the creek, Queen and Front Streets are the crucial thoroughfares. On this side of the bridge, you'll find the **Caye Caulker Water Taxi Terminal,** an important transportation and information hub. Across Front Street are the post office and library (with a quiet sitting room). Walking east on Front Street (toward the sea), you'll find several art galleries and shops before you come to "Tourism Village," the hopeful, Disneyesque name for the Cruise Ship Terminal area. The mini-malls and decorations that garnish this area of docks and shops are contrived and overpriced (and owned in part by the cruise ship companies). Tourism Village leads into the Fort George historic area and to the lighthouse.

On the Swing Bridge's south end, Regent and Albert Streets make a V-shaped split and are the core of the city's banking and shopping activity. There are a few old government buildings here, too, as well as Battlefield (Central) Park and a couple of guesthouses. Southside has a seedier reputation than Northside, which is monitored more closely by the police.

SIGHTS

An early morning stroll through the weathered clapboard buildings of Belize City gives you a genuine feel for this seaside population center. This is when people are rushing off to work, kids are spiffed up on their way to school, and folks are out doing their daily shopping. The streets are crammed with small shops (many operated by East Indian, Lebanese, and Chinese merchants), a stream of pedestrians, and lots of traffic.

There are decent art shops and galleries in and around the Fort George area and Tourism Village, including the **Fine Arts Gallery** (9:30 A.M.–4 P.M. Mon.–Fri.), on Front Street, which has a nice collection of paintings and crafts. Inside the Fort George compound is **Rachel's Art Gallery,** which carries prints and original art by various artists, including Rachel

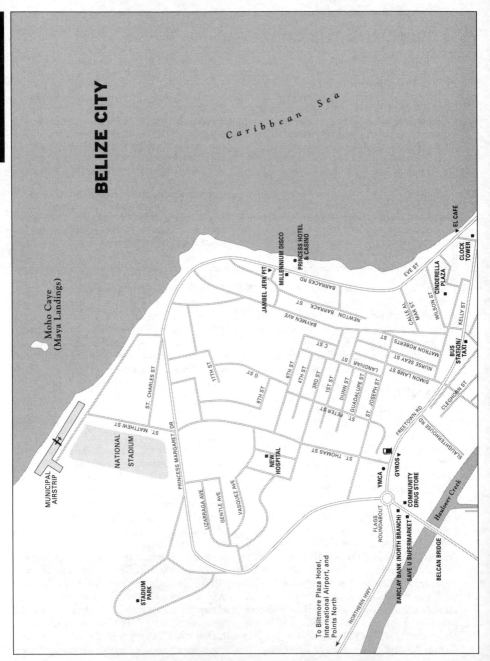

BELIZE CITY

Caribbean Sea

Moho Caye
(Maya Landings)

MUNICIPAL
AIRSTRIP

NATIONAL
STADIUM

STADIUM
PARK

LIZARRAGA AVE

GENTLE AVE

VASQUEZ AVE

PRINCESS MARGARET DR

ST. MATTHEW ST

ST. CHARLES ST

17TH ST

8TH ST

G ST

C ST

6TH ST

4TH ST

3RD ST

1ST ST

DUNN ST

GUADALUPE ST

ST. JOSEPH ST

PETER ST

ST. THOMAS ST

NEW
HOSPITAL

YMCA

GYROS

COMMUNITY
DRUG STORE

FLAGS
ROUNDABOUT

BARCLAY BANK (NORTH BRANCH)

SAVE U SUPERMARKET

BELCAN BRIDGE

Haulover Creek

NORTHERN HWY

To Biltmore Plaza Hotel,
International Airport, and
Points North

JAMBEL JERK PIT

MILLENNIUM DISCO

PRINCESS HOTEL
& CASINO

BARRACKS RD

NEWTON BARRACK ST

BAYMEN AVE

EVE ST

CALLE AL MAR ST

WILSON ST

KELLY ST

CINDERELLA
PLAZA

CLOCK
TOWER

EL CAFÉ

NURSE SEAY ST

SIMON LAMB ST

LANDIVAR

MATRON ROBERTS

BUS
STATION/
TAXI

CLEGHORN ST

FREETOWN RD

SLAUGHTERHOUSE RD

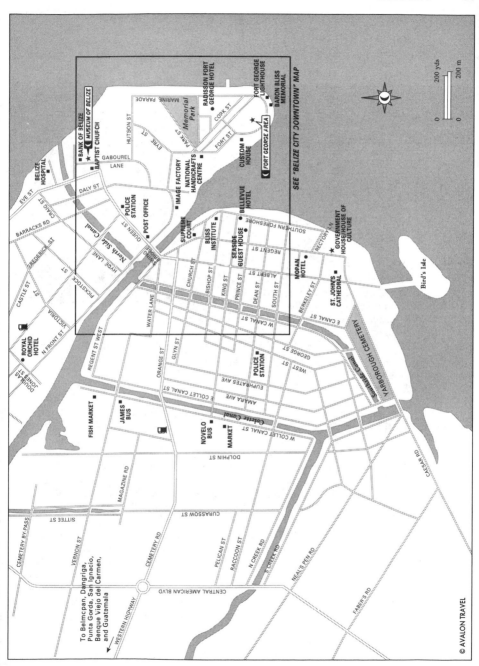

To Belmopan, Dangriga,
Punta Gorda, San Ignacio,
Benque Viejo del Carmen,
and Guatemala

SEE "BELIZE CITY DOWNTOWN" MAP

200 yds
200 m

© AVALON TRAVEL

herself. Around the corner, next to the park, look for the **National Handicrafts Center** (8 A.M.–5 P.M. Mon.–Fri., 8 A.M.–4 P.M. Sat.), an official Chamber of Commerce–sponsored shop with fine crafts purchased directly from artisans around the country.

As you cross to the Southside, you'll encounter even more traffic and local color. Vendors sell fruits, vegetables, clothing, incense, jewelry, and cold drinks along the southeast side of Swing Bridge. Bliss Promenade skirts the waterfront and brings you to the **Bliss Center for Performing Arts** (tel. 501/227-2110), which hosts social functions, seminars, arts festivals, and drama series. It is also the location of a theater, museum, and library, as well as the **Institute of Creative Arts.**

◖ Museum of Belize

Housed in the old city jail (Her Majesty's Prison was built in 1857 and served as the nation's only prison until the 1990s), this small but worthwhile museum includes city history artifacts, indigenous relics, and rotating displays, such as "Insects of Belize" and "Maya Jade." Philatelists will love the 150 years of stamps on display. Open 8 A.M.–5 P.M. Mon.–Thurs., till 4 P.M. on Fri. (tel. 501/223-4524. US$5.)

Supreme Court Building

Sitting in front of Battlefield (Central) Park, this structure is decorated with a graceful white metal filigree stairway that leads to the long veranda overlooking the square. An antiquated town clock is perched atop the white clapboard building.

St. John's Anglican Cathedral

This lovely old building, one of the only typically British structures in the city, is surrounded by well-kept green lawns and next to a lively school yard. In 1812, slaves helped erect this graceful piece of architecture, using bricks brought as ballast on sailing ships from Europe. Several Mosquito Coast kings from Nicaragua and Honduras were crowned in this cathedral with ultimate pomp and grandeur;

© JOSHUA BERMAN

clock tower atop the courthouse

the last was in 1815. It's usually okay to walk right in and take a moment; put something in the donation box on your way out.

Government House and House of Culture

Behind St. John's Cathedral, at the southern end of Regent Street and facing the Southern Foreshore, is the House of Culture museum in the old Government House, which, before Hurricane Hattie and the ensuing construction of Belmopan, was the home and office of the governor general, the official representative of the Queen of England. (Today's governor general can be found in Belmopan, at Belize House.) For a long time these grounds were used as a guesthouse for visiting VIPs and a venue for social functions. Queen Elizabeth and Prince Philip stayed here in 1994. The elegant wooden buildings (built 1812–1814) are said to have been designed by acclaimed English architect Christopher Wren. Government House is surrounded by sprawling lawns and wind-brushed palms

BELIZE DISTRICT

© AVALON TRAVEL

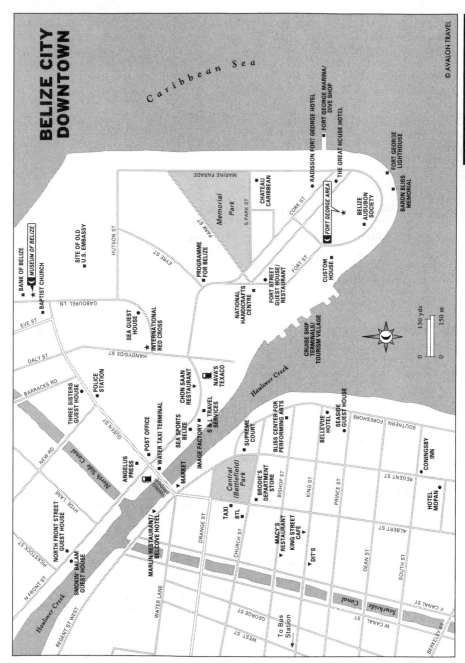

BELIZE CITY DOWNTOWN

Caribbean Sea

- BANK OF BELIZE
- MUSEUM OF BELIZE
- BAPTIST CHURCH
- SITE OF OLD U.S. EMBASSY
- SEA GUEST HOUSE
- INTERNATIONAL RED CROSS
- PROGRAMME FOR BELIZE
- NATIONAL HANDICRAFTS CENTRE
- FORT STREET GUEST HOUSE/ RESTAURANT
- CHATEAU CARIBBEAN
- MARINE PARADE
- FORT GEORGE MARINA/ DIVE SHOP
- FORT GEORGE HOTEL
- RADISSON FORT GEORGE HOTEL
- THE GREAT HOUSE HOTEL
- FORT GEORGE LIGHTHOUSE
- BARON BLISS MEMORIAL
- FORT GEORGE AREA
- BELIZE AUDUBON SOCIETY
- CUSTOM HOUSE
- CRUISE SHIP TERMINALS/ TOURISM VILLAGE
- THREE SISTERS GUEST HOUSE
- POLICE STATION
- POST OFFICE
- WATER TAXI TERMINAL
- SEA SPORTS BELIZE
- CHON SAAN RESTAURANT
- S & L TRAVEL SERVICES
- NAVA'S TEXACO
- IMAGE FACTORY
- ANGELUS PRESS
- MARKET
- SUPREME COURT
- BLISS CENTER FOR PERFORMING ARTS
- BELLEVUE HOTEL
- SEASIDE GUEST HOUSE
- CONINGSBY INN
- BRODIE'S DEPARTMENT STORE
- Central (Battlefield) Park
- TAXI
- BTL
- MARLIN RESTAURANT/ BELCOVE HOTEL
- NORTH FRONT STREET GUEST HOUSE
- SMOKIN' BALAM GUEST HOUSE
- MACY'S RESTAURANT
- KING STREET CAFE
- DIT'S
- HOTEL MOPAN

Memorial Park

Haulover Creek

North Side Canal

Southside Canal

Haulover Creek

HUTSON ST · EYRE ST · PARK ST · S PARK ST · CORK ST · FORT ST · GABOUREL LN · EVE ST · DALY ST · BARRACKS RD · HANDYSIDE ST · QUEEN ST · NEW RD · HYDE LANE · PICKSTOCK ST · N FRONT ST · REGENT ST WEST · WATER LANE · GEORGE ST · WEST ST · W CANAL ST · F CANAL ST · BERKELEY ST · SOUTH ST · DEAN ST · ALBERT ST · REGENT ST · PRINCE ST · KING ST · BISHOP ST · ORANGE ST · CHURCH ST · SOUTHERN FORESHORE

SWING BRIDGE

To Bus Station

0   150 yds
0   150 m

facing the sea; outdoor functions and ceremonies are still held here.

Wander through the wood structure and enjoy the period furniture, silverware, and glassware collections—plus a selection of paintings and sculptures by modern Belizean artists. There are special events, concerts, and art shows throughout the year. Stroll the grounds, on the water's edge, and enjoy the solitude. Open 8:30 A.M.–4:30 P.M. Mon.–Fri. (Admission US$5. More at www.nichbelize.org.) Also on site is the headquarters of the National Kriol Council, whose resource center you may find interesting; it includes a few Kriol language phrasebooks for sale.

Luba Garifuna Museum

This new house museum on Jasmine Street showcases Garifuna culture and history. Admission is US$5 and includes a guided tour. Opening hours vary, so it's best to call in advance (tel. 501/202-4331).

(Fort George Area

In general, the Fort George area is one of the most pleasant in Belize City (especially on days when it is *not* flooded with thousands of cruise ship passengers and their associated entourages of taxi drivers and would-be tour guides). Meander the neighborhood and you'll pass some lovely homes, including a few charming old guesthouses. The **Baron Bliss Memorial** and **Fort George Lighthouse** stand guard over it all.

The sea breeze can be pleasant here, and you can glimpse numerous cayes and ships offshore. Once you round the point, the road becomes Marine Parade and runs past the modern Radisson Fort George Hotel and **Memorial Park,** a grassy salute to the 40 Belizeans who lost their lives in World War I. The old U.S. embassy sits at the end of the block on the right; the house was built in New England, dismantled, and transported to Belize as ship's ballast. It was reconstructed in 1840 and served as the U.S. embassy until 2006, when operations were moved to Belmopan.

From the Radisson Fort George dock, you'll get a good view of the harbor. Originally this was Fort George Island; the strait separating the island from the mainland (the site of today's Memorial Park) was filled in during the early 1920s.

The Image Factory Shop and Gallery

A few doors down from the Water Taxi Terminal, the Image Factory Art Foundation (91 N. Front St., www.imagefactory.bz, 9 A.M.–5 P.M. Mon.–Fri., 9 A.M.–noon Sat.) is the official pulse of the Belizean art and literary scene. In addition to offering the best book selection in the country (both local authors and some foreign titles), the shop offers gallery space for semiregular art events, usually held on Friday evenings at happy hour.

RECREATION
Diving and Snorkeling

There are four cayes located just minutes away, all with excellent wall dives and idyllic snorkeling, and the main barrier reef and the Turneffe islands are accessible as well—perfect for anyone trapped in the city on business, but also for tourists who choose to base themselves here. Belize City has two dive shops: **Sea Sports Belize** (83 N. Front St., tel. 501/223-5505, www.seasportsbelize.com) is across from the post office; **Hugh Parkey's Dive Connection** (tel. 501/223-5086 or 223-4526, U.S. tel. 888/223-5403, www.belizediving.com) is based at the Radisson Fort George Marina and offers all manner of trips and certification courses. Hugh Parkey's has the newest and biggest day-trip boat fleet around and also runs Belize's first dolphin encounter program, at nearby Spanish Lookout Caye. At either shop, ask about group size and whether or not you'll be spending your day with cruise ship passengers.

(Old Belize and Cucumber Beach

It's hard to know where to list Old Belize (tel. 501/222-4153, www.oldbelize.com. US$2.50 for the museum tour, US$20 for

BARON BLISS, BELIZE'S BENEFACTOR

Henry Edward Ernest Victor Bliss, also known as the "Fourth Baron Bliss of the Former Kingdom of Portugal," was born in the county of Buckingham in England. He first sailed into the harbor of Belize in 1926, though he was too ill to go ashore because of food poisoning he had contracted while visiting Trinidad. Bliss spent several months aboard his yacht, the *Sea King*, in the harbor, fishing in Belizean waters. Although he never got well enough to go ashore, Bliss learned to love the country from the sea, and its habitués — the fishermen and officials in the harbor — all treated him with great respect and friendliness. On the days that he was able only to languish on deck, he made every effort to learn about the small country. He was apparently so impressed with what he learned and the people he met that before his death,

he drew up a will that established a trust of nearly US$2 million for projects to benefit the people of Belize.

More than US$1 million in interest from the trust has been used for the erection of the Bliss Institute, Bliss School of Nursing, and Bliss Promenade, plus contributions to the Belize City water supply, the Corozal Town Board and Health Clinic, and land purchase for the building of Belmopan.

An avid yachtsman, Bliss stipulated that money be set aside for a regatta to be held in Belizean waters, now a focal point of the gala Baron Bliss Day celebrations each March. The baron's white granite tomb is at the point of Fort George in Belize City, guarded by the Bliss Lighthouse and the occasional pair of late-night Belizean lovers.

the zip line)—in addition to a beach, a swimming lagoon, a zip line, a waterslide, and other water sports, Old Belize also features the impressive **Cultural and Historical Center** (open daily 10 A.M.–8:30 P.M.), a 45-minute tour through a thousand years of Belizean history. It's kind of like a walk-through museum, but with all kinds of fascinating relics and simulations. Some of the displays from the former Maritime Museum are now housed here and include models of boats used in Belize, as well as photos and bios of local fishermen and boat builders. On "Cruiseship Days" (usually Tuesday and Thursday), a Belizean cabaret showcases the dances and songs of Belize's cultural groups. There's also a boat marina, a helipad, and an excellent restaurant, bar, and grill (open daily 11 A.M.–10 P.M.). The whole complex is located five miles out of the city on the Western Highway and gets more Belizean clients than foreign tourists; it's definitely worth the trip. A snorkel pool containing ocean water, a manmade reef, and exotic fish is being planned. Bring a bathing suit and plan to spend half a day or more.

Sailing

Ask at any of the tour companies, marinas, or dive shops to see what's available; there should be a decent range of charters available, plus day trips and sunset cruises. Sailing/snorkeling trips to Caye Caulker (US$65) are offered, as well as sunset cruises to Ambergris Caye (US$35) on a "Belizean Authentic Gaff Rig Sloop" (tel. 501/610-3240 or 226-2340, ask for George Eiley).

Spectator Sports

The basketball court on Bird Isle used to be packed to the gills during local championship games. Ask around to see if any games are coming up. Catch a soccer (called "football" here) match at the stadium Sundays at 3:30 P.M. through mid-December or so. There's loud, booming pregame music and lots of security. The stadium is located across the street from the Princess Hotel.

Massage and Bodywork

If you're in a bind and can't make it to any of the resort spas around the country, try some "traditional Maya therapy" at the **Oltsil Day**

Spa (173 Juliet Soberanis St., tel. 501/223-7722, oltsil@yahoo.com), located just south of the Princess Hotel, which offers a long menu of treatments. Or put yourself in the strong hands of **Harold Zuniga**, a U.S.–trained physical therapist, masseur, and alternative medicine specialist (85 Amara Ave., tel. 501/227-6753 or 604-5679, haroldzuniga@yahoo.com).

NIGHTLIFE

Friday nights are big in Belize City, especially the ones that fall on payday. Ask around to find out where the best happy hours are being held—they often feature live music and free *bocas* (deep-fried something, probably). The bars at the Radisson, Biltmore, and Princess Hotels are popular and provide safe, contained venues—and some of the highest drink prices in the city.

There's nearly always some form of entertainment going on from Wednesday to Saturday, although serious dancing usually doesn't get started till after 11 P.M. If you go out dancing at Belize City's handful of nightclubs, you'll want to keep your wits about you and ask whether there have been recent shootings or stabbings before selecting a club. Seriously. **Eden's Nite Club** (35 Queen St.) is popular. Expect a loud mix of dancehall reggae, *punta* rock, and American pop. Most Saturday nights belong to the disco at the **Bellevue Hotel,** where views of the harbor are great at sunset and music often goes on until the wee hours of the morning.

SHOPPING

There are gift shops, craft stalls, and street vendors lining Front Street near Tourism Village, as well as just south of the Swing Bridge. In the Fort George area, check out the **National Handicrafts Center** (8 A.M.–5 P.M. Mon.–Fri., 8 A.M.–4 P.M. Sat.). It's near the Radisson. There is a **flea market** at the Catholic Church on North Front Street on Saturdays at 7 A.M. Seek out the **Mennonite Furniture Market** at 47 North Front Street, open Friday and Saturday during daylight hours. They won't arrange shipping, but you can get nice, basic handmade wooden furniture for reasonable prices.

ACCOMMODATIONS

Just a reminder: All room rates are for double occupancy in the high season. If you're traveling alone or between May and November, expect discounts at some (but not all) of the following hotels.

Under US$25

The **((Seaside Guest House** (3 Prince St., tel. 501/227-8339, seasidebelize@btl.net, dorms US$20 pp, private single rooms US$25, double rooms US$45, triples and quads available) is popular among budget travelers. The rooms are tiny, barely bigger than the beds, but the common spaces are good for meeting travelers from the world over. There is hot water in the community bathroom, a breeze on its ocean-facing porch, and a friendly, family-run atmosphere in this former Quaker house. A filling breakfast is available for US$4. If you know you're coming to town, make a reservation—the guest house can sometimes fill up fast.

On the Northside, just west of the Fort George neighborhood, **Sea Guest House** (18 Gabourel La., tel. 501/203-0043 or 605-0301, US$20) has nine funky old rooms in a rickety building with nice common space and a big Internet café downstairs. **Freddie's Guest House** (86 Eve St., tel. 501/223-3851) charges US$25 for a room with shared bath, US$30 for one of its three immaculate, very private rooms with private bath. It's like staying in your Grandma's basement, with no social scene at all.

North Front Street Guest House (124 N. Front St., tel. 501/227-7595, US$15) offers seven spartan rooms with shared basement bath. It's getting a bit decrepit, but it's worth considering if the other places are booked up. Across the street, the **((Smokin' Balam Guest House** (tel. 501/601-4510, smokinbalam2@yahoo.com, US$18–23) is a better choice. There are only four rooms, all airy with fans, two with private bathroom; all have access to a balcony overlooking Haulover Creek as well as the nice

The Seaside Guest House on Prince Street remains the best budget option.

café (meals from US$2). There's a gift shop, a pay phone, and Internet access downstairs. The guest house also offers weekly/monthly rates, bag storage, and laptop ports.

US$25-50

The **Belcove Hotel** (9 Regent St., tel. 501/227-3054, www.belcove.com, US$33–52), centrally located on the southern bank of Haulover Creek, two blocks west of the Swing Bridge, is well taken care of, clean and bright, and easy to recommend. There are 13 rooms on three stories; options include shared or private bath with fan or the works (a/c and TV). The porch over the creek is fun to watch boats from, and cheap, lively eats are right next door at the Marlin. Tour packages will keep you busy on the reef or at inland sights. The only downside is the seedy two blocks on Regent Street between the hotel and the Swing Bridge; take a cab to and from the hotel door. **Three Sisters Guest House** (tel. 501/207-3139 or 203-5729, US$30) has three big, clean rooms with private baths and fans, plus a massive, cavernous common

space, all on the second floor of an old building on Queen Street. It's good for groups, friendly, and has lots of beds. Additional rooms are also for rent in an annex on Albert Street.

US$50-100

The **Hotel Mopan** (55 Regent St., tel. 501/227-7351, www.hotelmopan.com, US$45–75) is an old standby. There are 14 rooms, some with ocean view, all with private bath, TV, free wireless Internet, phone, and optional air conditioning. Patio and balcony rooms cost slightly more. The bar has been a meeting place for locals and travelers for decades. Across the street, **Coningsby Inn** (76 Regent St., tel. 501/227-1566, www.coningsby-inn.com, US$60) has 10 rooms with TV, private bath, air conditioning, wireless Internet, and minibar. There's a second-story bar and restaurant; breakfast is US$6. Staff can help plan your tours as well as your wedding! Both of these hotels are in Southside, near the House of Culture.

Back in Northside, toward "the Flags" roundabout, the **Bakadeer Inn** (74 Cleghorn St., tel. 501/223-0659, www.bakadeerinn.com, US$55) has clean, well-kept rooms with comfy beds, private bath, ceiling fans, TV, and optional air conditioning in any of the rooms (singles, doubles, triples, and quads available), as well as laundry service, a dining area, high-speed Internet access, and a cozy common space. The family that runs the hotel is involved in tour guiding and archaeology (and owns a frame shop). Another functional place in this neighborhood is the **Royal Orchid Hotel** (153 New Rd., at the corner of Douglas Jones St., tel. 501/223-2783, wchang@btl.net, US$50), a four-story hotel across the street from a pizza shop; the 21 rooms have hot and cold water, private baths, air conditioning, and TV. The hotel is run by a second-generation Belizean-Chinese family.

Over in Fort George Radisson territory, the **Chateau Caribbean** (6 Marine Parade, tel. 501/223-0800, www.chateaucaribbean.com, from US$89) resides in an old wooden building with wide porches, ocean breezes, and plenty of character, but it is overall in need of some TLC. The 19 rooms are worn but have

© JOSHUA BERMAN

private baths, cable TV, fridges, and air conditioning. Carpet in the hallways is shabby, but the restaurant and bar have big east-facing bay windows.

Located in Belama, a residential area three miles north of downtown and seven miles south of the international airport, 〔 **D'Nest Inn** (475 Cedar St., tel. 501/203-0443 or 223-5416, www.dnestinn.com, US$65–75) is a two-story Caribbean-style bed-and-breakfast surrounded by an English garden and run by one of the sweetest, most accommodating couples in Belize. Gaby and Oty offer three comfortable rooms decorated with Belizean antiques, all with private bath, air conditioning, TV, and data ports for your laptop. Wonderful multicourse breakfasts feature lots of fresh fruit and conversation with your hosts. Also north of downtown, but closer to the sea, the **Villa Boscardi Bed & Breakfast** (6043 Manatee Dr., tel. 501/223-1691, www.villaboscardi. com, US$75 plus tax) is an excellent option, with six rooms boasting "European elegance" in Buttonwood Bay, a safe, quiet residential area a block away from the Caribbean (and the prime minister's residence). Rooms are spotless white tile and white paint, with bathtubs and secure parking; the place is popular with business travelers. There's easy access to the international airport, and it's a short ride to downtown Belize City. Several restaurants are within walking distance, including a mellow oceanfront bar. Full breakfast is included in the room rate.

US$100-150

The **Princess Hotel and Casino** (tel. 501/223-2670, U.S. tel. 800/233-9784, www. princessbelize.com, from US$120) has 170 concrete rooms, all with the same air conditioning, cable TV, and breakfast. Overall, you'll find much better value elsewhere, particularly at the B&Bs mentioned above. The Princess is more popular for having Belize's only cinema and bowling alley (there's also a pool, a gift shop, a beauty salon, a conference room, bars, restaurants, and a tour desk); an on-site marina has docking facilities and water sports and the popular casino is open from midnight–4 A.M.

Over US$150
The Great House (13 Cork St., tel. 501/223-3400, www.greathousebelize.com, from US$150) is a beautiful colonial-style boutique hotel, built in 1927 and recently renovated to show off its 16 unique, colorful rooms. Both tiled and hardwood floors offset the pastel walls and modern furniture; the rooms in back have more charm than the rest. Downstairs, you'll find car rental and tour services, plus a high-end real estate company, a business service center, and the Smoky Mermaid Restaurant.

After World War II, visiting dignitaries from England came to Belize with plans for various agricultural projects, but they couldn't find a place to stay. As a result, the **Radisson Fort George Hotel** (2 Marine Parade, tel. 501/223-3333, U.S. tel. 800/333-3333, www.radisson. com/belizecitybz, US$139–174 plus tax) was built, and it remains the premier accommodation in town. The Radisson's 102 nicely appointed, full-service rooms sport all the amenities you'd expect, including outrageously priced minibars. This grand resort-style hotel has two swimming pools, a poolside bar, the Stone Grill (an outdoor restaurant where you grill your own meat), and fine dining and a massive breakfast buffet in St. George's Dining Room. All the restaurants host special events and happy hours. Full catering facilities and banquet rooms are available. All kinds of tours, from diving to caving to golfing, are organized right out of the hotel. Renovation in the Villa Wing includes bathrooms, a new business center, a gym, and an expansion of Le Petit Café, connecting it to the Villa Lobby with expanded seating and wireless Internet.

The Belize Biltmore Plaza (tel. 501/223-2302, U.S. tel. 800/528-1234, www.belize-biltmore.com, from US$140) is the local Best Western branch, three miles north of the city center (seven miles south of the international airport) on the Northern Highway. The Biltmore is popular with business travelers; its 75 mid-size rooms surround a garden, pool, and bar and have cable TV, phones, and modern baths. There's also Internet service, an excellent gift shop, and an overpriced dining room (US$12–20 per entrée of mediocre international food) and lounge. The hotel may be convenient for flights, but the Biltmore is walking distance to nothing, so you may feel a bit trapped.

FOOD
Cafés
Southside's **King Street Café** (6:30 A.M.–4:30 P.M. Mon.–Sat.) is a low-key Belizean espresso bar, ice-cream shop, and tamale joint, with breakfasts from US$2. A bit more European in flavor is **Le Petit Café** (6 A.M.–8 P.M. daily), belonging to the Radisson right across the street. It offers delicious pastries, cakes, and ham-and-cheese croissants and possibly the best cup of fresh-brewed coffee in town.

The **Smokin' Balam** (59 North Front St., 7 A.M.–5 P.M.) is a café, gift shop, cigar room, and Internet hub. There are great views of Haulover Creek from their back porch. Up on Marine Parade, **Pandora Café** (daily lunch and dinner) has all sorts of coffee drinks, smoothies, teas, Chinese and Belizean plates (US$4–10 entrée).

Belizean, Bar & Grill
The cheapest food in Belize City comes from the taco vendors in the streets and the many fast-food stands and shacks scattered throughout the city.

Macy's Restaurant on the top floor of the public market, is a good bet for Creole food at reasonable prices. So is **Dit's** (on King St., 7 A.M.–7 P.M. Mon.–Sat., 8 A.M.–4 P.M. Sun.). It's always packed with Belizeans—a good sign.

Deep Sea Marlin's Restaurant & Bar (Regent St. West, 7 A.M.–9 P.M.) is located on Haulover Creek, next to the Belcove Hotel. It's a cheap and sometimes raucous fishermen's joint, with Belizean and American staples for US$4. The **Jam-Bel Jerk Pit** (164 Newtown Barrack St., tel. 501/223-1966, 10 A.M.–10 P.M. daily) combines Jamaican and Belizean recipes to produce a savory menu in

a great atmosphere. The breezy patio overlooks the ocean, just north of the Princess Hotel complex (the place used to be located in Southside). Entrées are US$8–15, appetizers about US$6.

The **Riverside Tavern** (2 Mapp St., tel. 501/223-5640, bar open all day, kitchen open 11 A.M.–2 P.M. and 6–9:30 P.M.) is an upscale sports bar whose massive "gourmet burger" is one of the best in Belize (US$9 for a 10-oz. patty, US$12.50 for the super-sized 16-oz. patty; Belizean beef from Barry Bowen's Gallon Jug Estate). Or go for the coconut-crusted shrimp or other bar foods. There's beer on tap, and the very convivial atmosphere is a popular meeting place for Belize's who's who crowd. The tavern is run by Belize's Belikin brewing family.

The **Sibun Bit Bar & Grill** (tel. 501/222-4153, www.oldbelize.com, open 11 A.M.–9 P.M. daily, a bit later on weekends) is part of the **Old Belize** complex, 10 minutes from downtown Belize City on the Western Highway. The tasty, varied menu and excellent service complement the open setting with lots of activities available.

Pizza
Not many options here, but try **Pepper's Pizza** (tel. 501/223-5000, 11 A.M.–10 P.M.), with free delivery within city limits. The same is true at **Carol's Pizza**, which offers "Love at First Bite" (tel. 501/203-0716, 10 A.M.–9 P.M.).

International Food
Jambel's Jerk Pit (150 Newtown Barracks Road) is the place for ribs, barbecue, burgers, and seafood, all served with a Jamaican and Caribbean flair. A nice outdoor deck with ocean view and live music on some Friday and Saturday nights add to the great atmosphere.

There is plenty of authentic Chinese food in Belize City. The place rated highest by expats is **Chon Saan Palace** on Kelly Street. **Chinatown** (in Cinderella Plaza) is one of the newer Chinese restaurants and features Taiwanese cuisine. **Mama Chen's** is fantastic for vegetarians, serving very inexpensive Chinese dishes (less than US$4); it's located on the corner of

Eve and Queen Streets. Choose from veggie chow mein, spicy beef dumplings, crispy spring rolls, sushi, and bubble tea (the "bubbles" are sweet seaweed balls that are slurped up through a thick straw).

Belize City's Arab community ensures a few authentic Lebanese restaurants in town; **Gyro and Crepe** (near "the Flags" traffic circle, 10 A.M.–10 P.M. daily) has Middle Eastern veggie and meat options, with US$6 gyros and falafel. There's also **Manatee Landing,** before the entrance to the international airport, about 15 minutes north of the city; watch dolphins swim by in the Belize River while you enjoy your hummus.

For authentic Italian dishes and home-made ice cream, go for **La Tavernetta** (tel. 501/223-7998), an Italian-run restaurant on the Northern Highway on the way out of the city.

For East Indian curries and dal, try **Sumathi** (190 Newtown Barracks Rd.). At **Natraj, Gateway of India** (5 Amara Ave.), you'll find a menu that includes chicken tikka, mutton egg fry, and fish biryani. The **Sea Rock Restaurant** (190 Newtown Barracks Rd.) also features a large selection of Indian dishes.

Fine Dining
The Smoky Mermaid (tel. 501/223-4759, 6:30 A.M.–10 P.M., entrées US$12–20) has a built-in smokehouse and specializes in smoked fish, meats, and assorted fresh breads. Breakfast, lunch, and dinner feature Belizean cuisine and fresh-baked Creole bread, served on a dining patio under thatch roofs surrounding a porcelain mermaid.

The restaurant at the **Radisson Fort George Hotel** serves a beautiful buffet with a multitude of tasty seafood delicacies, and its **Stone Grill** is a fun, meat-sizzlin' experience in the heavily vegetated outdoor patio bar.

INFORMATION AND SERVICES
Tourist Information
The central office of the **Belize Tourism Board** (BTB, 64 Regent St., tel. 501/227-

2420, toll-free 800/624-0686, info@travel-belize.org, www.travelbelize.org) is located in the Southside, near the Mopan Hotel. The **Belize Tourism Industry Association** (10 N. Front St., tel. 501/203-1969, or 10 N. Park St., tel. 501/223-3507) can also answer many of your questions and give you lodging suggestions, as can any tour company and many hotel front desks. You'll find hotel ads, brochures, and an information desk at the Water Taxi Terminal.

Money
Most of the city's banking is clustered in one strip along Albert Street, just south of the Swing Bridge, and includes **Atlantic Bank** (tel. 501/227-1225), **Bank of Nova Scotia** (tel. 501/227-7027), **Barclay's Bank** (tel. 501/227-7211), and **Belize Bank** (tel. 501/227-7132). Most banks keep the same hours: 8 A.M.–1 P.M. Monday–Thursday, 8 A.M.–1 P.M. and 3–6 P.M. Friday. **Casas de Cambio,** whose purpose is to change money in an effort to retain U.S. dollars in the country, only functions regularly in Corozal and San Pedro. In Belize City and other towns, its usefulness is questionable, as it offers a significantly lower rate than the oft-used black-market changers, easily found in most "Hindu shops" on Albert Street.

Health and Emergencies
For police, fire, or ambulance, dial 90 or 911. Another ambulance service is B.E.R.T (tel. 501/223-3292). **Belize Medical Associates** (5791 St. Thomas St., tel. 501/223-0302, 223-0303, or 223-0304, bzmedasso@btl.net, www.belizemedical.com) is the only private hospital in Belize City. The fairly modern 25-bed facility provides 24-hour assistance and a wide range of specialties. Or try **Karl Heusner Memorial Hospital** (Princess Margaret Dr., tel. 501/223-1548 or 223-1564).

Internet Access
As elsewhere in the country, an increasing number of hotels and guesthouses offer at least a single computer for guests or even

wireless Internet for your laptop. There are a few broadband Internet cafés in Belize City, though not nearly as many as in San Ignacio or San Pedro.

On the Southside, try the mothball-smelling **KGS Internet** (near the corner of King and E. Canal Sts., 8 A.M.–7 P.M. Mon.–Fri., reduced hours on weekends, US$3/hr.). It's a bit dark and dingy but has fast cable connections. The **Community Computer Center** (9 A.M.–5 P.M. Mon.–Fri., sometimes closed for lunch), located in a narrow, tucked-away room above the library, has nine speedy computers, but no laptop docks. Check **Angelus Press,** right around the corner on Queen Street, which has a few available machines. More expensive options are available in Tourism Village and in fancier hotels' business centers.

Library and Bookstores

A quiet reading room and two stories of books are found on Front Street at **Turton Library** (tel. 501/227-3401, 9 A.M.–7 P.M. Mon.–Fri., 9 A.M.–1 P.M. Sat.), a wonderfully quiet respite from the chaotic rush just outside. Stop in to enjoy the day's newspaper at one of the long, open tables, or dig into their archives for a look at the past.

A few stores have small but pertinent book selections, featuring several shelves of Belizean and about-Belize books. The newest is the **Image Factory** on Front Street. **Angelus Press,** right around the corner on Queen Street, has a complete corner of books and maps, back behind all the office supplies. Across the Swing Bridge, you'll want to hit the second-story **Book Center,** open 8 A.M.–5:30 P.M. Monday–Thursday and Saturday, 8 A.M.–9 P.M. Friday.

Groceries and Sundries

Brodie's (Albert and Regent Sts., tel. 501/227-7070, 8 A.M.–7 P.M., closes earlier on weekends) is a department store, supermarket, sub shop, drugstore, and more—a Belizean institution. Across the street is another supermarket, **Ro-Macs.**

Stock up on your way into or out of the north edge of town at **Sav U Supermarket.**

This modern, air-conditioned market sells everything any supermarket in the United States would carry, and it's reasonably priced. There's also a new, massive Brodie's on the Northern Highway, just before you reach the Biltmore Hotel.

Post Office

The old post office in the Paslow Building (at the corner of Queen and Front Sts., by the north end of the Swing Bridge) was burned down in 2002 by an embezzling employee trying to hide the evidence (he's now serving time in the "Hattieville Marriott" for his efforts), but the new one is right next door to the razed lot (tel. 501/227-2201, 8 A.M.–5 P.M. Mon.–Fri.). There is a smaller branch around the corner on Queen Street, called the Philatelic Bureau (tel. 501/227-2201, ext. 35, same hours as above but closed for lunch); a third post office is at Queens Square in the Southside (tel. 501/227-1155).

Travel Agents

If you prefer to delegate the logistics of your trip, local travel agencies can book local and international transportation, tours, and accommodations across the country. **S & L Travel and Tours** (91 N. Front St., tel. 501/227-7514 or 227-7593, www.sltravel-belize.com) is easy to find, next door to the Image Factory. Belizean owners Sarita and Lascelle Tillet run a first-class and very personable operation; they've been in business for more than 25 years. They can get as creative as you like, whether you want a custom vacation, a photo safari, a bird-watching adventure, or anything else you can imagine.

Belize Global Travel Services (41 Albert St., tel. 501/227-7185 or 227-7363, www.belizeglobal.com) is one of the more established travel consultants in the city, offering a full range of Belizean tours, packages, and custom trips. A TACA Airlines counter and the country's only official American Express window are located in the same office. The Continental Airlines office is found at 80 Regent Street (tel. 501/227-8309 or U.S. tel. 800/266-3822, kimflyco@btl.net, 8 A.M.–5 P.M. Mon.–Fri., 8 A.M.–noon Sat.).

Laundry

G's Laundry (22 Dean St., between Albert and Canal, tel. 501/297-4461, 8 A.M.–8 P.M. Mon.–Sat., 8 A.M.–1 P.M. Sun.) charges US$4 to wash and dry.

Luggage Lockers

Check with the travel agencies in the main Caye Caulker Water Taxi Terminal; they may be able to rent a locker for your pack or arrange for longer storage (US$1/hr, US$5/day). Ask your guesthouse if you can leave a bag there as well.

Haircuts

How 'bout a little reggae with your haircut? Loud music blasts all day long at the **Ras Tash Barber Shop** on King Street (8:30 A.M.–8 P.M. Mon.–Sat., plus Sun. mornings, cut and shave US$5). Don't be surprised if your barber sings and bops while sculpting your 'do. If you're not into incredibly loud reggae music, choose from one of the (seemingly) thousands of other barbershops within a three-block radius.

GETTING THERE

By Air

From the international airport, it's a 20-minute drive to downtown Belize City, a trip that costs US$25 in a taxi (less in the opposite direction). The Municipal Airport (a.k.a. "Muni") is on the waterfront, practically in downtown Belize City. Belizean commuter planes provide steady service in and out of Belize City to outlying airports all over the country. It's cheaper to fly to local destinations out of Municipal.

By Bus

Domestic bus service is handled almost entirely out of **Novelo's Terminal,** located at the western terminus of King Street. If you arrive by bus and want to walk downtown, it's about 10 blocks to the Swing Bridge (from Novelo's, cross the canal and stay on King Street till you reach Albert Street, then make a left; continue for three blocks to the Swing Bridge and Water

Taxi Terminal). This walk should not be attempted at night but is usually safe during the day (remember, when in doubt, always take a cab). International bus service to Guatemala and Mexico is offered by a handful of companies with offices in the Caye Caulker Water Taxi Terminal.

By Boat

Arriving from San Pedro, Caye Caulker, or other islands, you'll most likely find yourself at the **Caye Caulker Water Taxi Terminal** on North Front Street, near the Swing Bridge (tel. 501/223-5752 or 226-0992, www.cayecaulkerwatertaxi.com). Here you'll find eager taxis and tour vans, ready to take you anywhere in the city—or the country, for that matter. The terminal is owned by the Belize Tourism Board (BTB), managed by the Belize Tourism Industry Association (BTIA), and serviced by 22 boats, the captains of which are all members of the Caye Caulker Water Taxi Association.

Boat transit to Caye Caulker takes about 45 minutes, then it's another half hour to Ambergris Caye. The trip to Caulker costs about US$7.50 one-way, US$12.50 round-trip; to San Pedro costs US$10 one-way. Most boats will stop at Caye Chapel or Long Caye on their way to Ambergris if you alert the captain as you board. The trip is pleasant on calm, sunny days, but be prepared for a cold and wet ride if the sky to the east is dark. A few of the boats are covered; others will pass out plastic tarps if it's really coming down.

The (roughly) hourly departures begin at 8 A.M., with the last boat leaving at 4 P.M. (the 5:30 P.M. express goes only to Caye Caulker). Two daily trips to St. George's Caye (US$15 one-way) leave at 10:30 A.M. and 4:30 P.M. The *Triple-J Shania* (tel. 501/207-7777) runs four daily boats to the cayes from its dock, just across Haulover Creek and 50 meters downstream from the C.C. Water Taxi Terminal. It's about the same price as the others.

GETTING AROUND

Most sights are relatively close together in Belize City, and you can walk from the

© JOSHUA BERMAN

Belize City boats

Southside's House of Culture to the National Museum near the old U.S. embassy in about twenty leisurely minutes. This route is generally safe during the day, especially if you are traveling in a group.

To hail a taxi, look for the green license plates, or ask your hotel to call you one. From the international airport to Belize City, the flat fare is US$25; from the municipal airstrip expect to pay US$5 or less. The fare for one passenger carried between any two points within Belize City (or any other district town) is US$3–5. If you plan to make several stops, tell the cabbie in advance and ask what the total will be; this eliminates lots of misunderstandings. Taxis can be hired by the hour (about US$25) for long trips out of town.

◖ GALES POINT

This tiny, unique Creole settlement occupies a thin, two-mile-long peninsula jutting north into the Southern Lagoon. Gales Point is 15 miles north of Dangriga or 25 miles southwest of Belize City, but getting there makes it feel farther. Depending on which accounts you read, the four hundred or so modern inhabitants are descended from either logwood cutters or escaped slaves known as "maroons" and settled here in the 1700s. Gales Point is a traditional Creole culture stronghold, renowned among international drummers who have come here seeking instruction from Emmeth Young, an expert in *sambaii,* Creole, and West African beats. If you're lucky, your visit to Gales Point will coincide with the full moon, when the entire village often participates in a roaming call-and-response drumming and dance circle. In the weeks before Christmas, the frequency of *sambaii* drumming events increases, reaching a crescendo on Christmas Day and Boxing Day with a unique village-wide celebration called *bram.* Gales Point is also known for its homemade cashew wine.

The Southern Lagoon (which surrounds Gales Point on three sides) is part of an extensive estuary bordered by thick mangroves. Their tangled roots provide the perfect breeding grounds for sport fish, crabs, shrimp, lobster, and a host

© JOSHUA BERMAN

Emmeth Young is an expert in *sambaii,* Creole, and West African beats, and gives lessons.

of other marine life. Rich beds of sea grass line the bottom of the lagoon and support a population of manatees. These gentle mammals are often seen basking on the surface of the water or coming up for air (which they must do about every four minutes). This is a popular spot to observe the manatees, often spotted close to a warm, spring-fed hole in the lagoon. A variety of tours to see manatees can be arranged through any of the Gales Point accommodations; trips are also available to see birds and caves in the region and to go fishing.

In July 2008 Gales Point experienced the most devastating floods in its history, as the entire lagoon rose and covered much of the peninsula, a phenomenon which did not even occur during Hurricane Hattie in 1961. It has since recovered, and remains just as remote and remarkable as ever.

Accommodations

There are some loose homestay programs and places to camp that are easily found upon arrival in the village; call the community phone at 501/209-8031 for the latest.

"Com gitchya Kriol Kultcha heeya" at **Metho's Coconut Campgrounds & Stone Bass Hideout** (tel. 501/603-6051, www.maroondrumschool.com), where you can camp for US$6 per person or stay in the stilted guest house with private bath, shared shower, and veranda for US$25: a double bed and bunk bed make it great for an adventurous family. All kinds of local culture tours are available. This facility is the home of the **Maroon Creole Drum School,** run by the widely traveled master drummer and drum maker Emmeth Young and friends. Many come for drumming lessons (US$10 per hour, lower rates for groups) and drum-making workshops (US$125 for a four-day drum-making class, price includes materials and you take your drum home with you). The on-site Sugar Shack features local painting and crafts; authentic Creole meals are also available for guests. **Gentle's Cool Spot** (tel. 501/609-4991) is another local service, providing traditional *fiyah haat* (fire hearth) cooking, plus a few stuffy clapboard rooms (US$15–20). Gentle's veranda is a favorite gathering place for locals and visitors alike, and Gentle provides tours.

The **Manatee Lodge** (tel. 501/220-8040, U.S. tel. 877/462-6283, www.manateelodge. com, US$85) is located at the very northern tip of the peninsula and caters to birders, sport fishermen, and independent nature-loving travelers and families. The eight rooms have nice wood furnishings, private bathrooms, 24-hour electricity, and a veranda with views of the surrounding lagoon and sunsets behind the Maya Mountains; rooms sleep up to four. The lodge offers access to a wildlife habitat completely different from the rest of Belize, living in the shallow brackish water and mangroves of the Southern Lagoon. The number of shorebirds and waterfowl is impressive, and to encourage guests to see local wildlife, the lodge provides each room with a canoe. Binoculars and bug repellent are a must. Children under six are free, ages 6–12 half price. Moderately priced and delicious home-cooked Creole (and continental) meals are available; so are transfers and multiday packages.

Getting There

To get to Gales Point by car, either choose the Manatee Highway (a.k.a. the Coastal Road) and expect rough muddy roads if it's raining, or take the Hummingbird Highway, which is about 25 miles longer, but smoother (for most of the way anyway). The most enjoyable—and expensive—way to reach Gales Point is the 90-minute boat ride from Belize City; you'll wind through bird-filled canals, rivers, and lagoons, and you may spot crocodiles, manatees, or dolphins. Manatee Lodge can arrange a boat transfer, but it costs more than US$300; it's worth it if you have a group. There used to be several weekly buses from Belize City, but they were not running regularly at last check; call the community phone (tel. 501/209-8031) or Manatee Lodge for current schedules or possible rides.

Along the Northern Highway

After escaping the city's traffic and passing the international airport, you'll cruise up the Northern Highway to either ruins or monkeys. Take your pick.

◖ ALTUN HA RUINS

Altun Ha (tel. 501/609-3540, 9 A.M.–5 P.M., US$5), a Maya trading center as well as a religious ceremonial site, is believed to have accommodated about 10,000 people. Archaeologists, working amidst a Maya community that has been living here for several centuries, have dated construction to about 1,500–2,000 years ago. It wasn't until the archaeologists came in 1964 that the old name "Rockstone Pond" was translated into the Maya words "Altun Ha." The site spans an area of about 25 square miles, most of which is covered by trees, vines, and jungle.

A team led by Dr. David Pendergast of the Royal Ontario Museum began work in 1965 on the central part of the ancient city, where upwards of 250 structures have been found in an area of about 1,000 square yards. So far, this is the most extensively excavated of all the Maya sites in Belize. For a trading center, Altun Ha was strategically located—a few miles from Little Rocky Point on the Caribbean and a few miles from Moho Caye at the mouth of the Belize River, both believed to have been major centers for the large trading canoes that worked up and down the coasts of Guatemala, Honduras, Belize, Mexico's Yucatán, and all the way to Panama.

Near Plaza B, the **Reservoir,** also known as **Rockstone Pond,** is fed by springs and rain runoff. It demonstrates the advanced knowledge of the Maya in just one of their many fields: engineering. Archaeologists say that an insignificant little stream ran through the jungle for centuries. No doubt it had been a source of fresh water for the Maya—but maybe not enough. The Maya diverted the creek and then began a major engineering project, digging and enlarging a deep, round hole that was

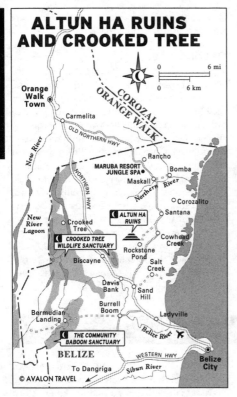

ALTUN HA RUINS AND CROOKED TREE

temples on top have typical small rooms built with the Maya trademark—the corbel arch.

Pendergast's team uncovered many valuable finds, such as unusual green obsidian blades, pearls, and more than 300 jade pieces—beads, earrings, and rings. Seven funeral chambers were discovered, including the **Temple of the Green Tomb,** rich with human remains and traditional funerary treasures. Maya scholars believe the first man buried was someone of great importance. He was draped with jade beads, pearls, and shells. And it was next to his right hand that the most exciting find was located—a solid jade head now referred to as **Kinich Ahau** ("The Sun God"). Kinich Ahau is, to date, the largest jade carving found in any Maya country. The head weighs nine pounds and measures nearly six inches from base to crown. It is reportedly now housed far away, in a museum in Canada. The two men who discovered the jade head some 40 years ago, Winston Herbert and William Leslie, still reside in Rockstone Pond and Lucky Strike villages. On November 29, 2006, they were honored by the National Institute of Culture and History for their discovery.

Altun Ha was rebuilt several times during the Pre-Classic, Classic, and Post-Classic Periods. The desecration of the structures leads scientists believe that the site may have been abandoned because of violence.

Tour Guides

A couple of local tour guides will be waiting for you at the entrance. They charge about US$10 per group per half hour and are well worth it, especially Ann-Marie Avona. If you're coming to Altun Ha as part of a package, consider insisting that your tour provider use a local guide. This is important to ensure that local communities receive something other than a crumbling road. To that end, you'll most likely also find tables of artisans with decent crafts for sale.

then plastered with limestone cement. Once the cement dried and hardened, the stream was rerouted to its original course and the newly built reservoir filled and overflowed at the east end, allowing the stream to continue on its age-old track. This made the area livable. Was all of this done before or after the temple structures were built? Is the completion of this reservoir what made the Maya elite choose to locate themselves in this area? We may never know for sure. Today Rockstone Pond is surrounded by thick brush, and the pond is alive with jungle creatures, including tarpon, small fish, and turtles and other reptiles.

The concentration of structures includes palaces and temples surrounding two main plazas. The tallest building (the **Sun God Temple**) is 59 feet above the plaza floor. At Altun Ha, the structure bases are oval and terraced. The small

Visiting the Ruins

From the Northern Highway, continue past the Burrell Boom turnoff (to the Baboon

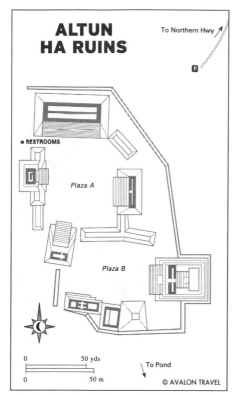

ALTUN HA RUINS

To Northern Hwy

P

■ RESTROOMS

Plaza A

Plaza B

0   50 yds

0   50 m

To Pond

© AVALON TRAVEL

avoid the crowds if you get there when the park first opens. You'll see more birds and wildlife that way as well.

Accommodations and Food

There are several budget-oriented lodgings in the area around Lucky Strike and Rockstone Pond villages, but few travelers choose to stay here, probably because there's not much offered in the area, apart from a short hike through the nearby ruins and the tranquil sounds of the jungle. The best option is only about a mile from the entrance to the ruins. There's a small casita at the **Mayan Wells Restaurant** (tel. 501/205-5641 or 225-5505, www.mayanwells. com); it has a kitchenette, a screened porch, and hammocks. You can also camp out for US$5 per person. Mayan Wells is set on a nice-size chunk of forest, walking distance from the Altun Ha ruins, and offers meals and tours.

MARUBA RESORT JUNGLE SPA

By any standard, Maruba Resort Jungle Spa (tel. 501/225-5555, U.S. tel. 800/627-8227, www.maruba-belize.com, US$130–700 per night) is an interesting sight in the middle of the forest, located at Mile 40½ on the Old Northern Highway, about a mile out of Maskall Village. Many visitors come just for the day—it's a popular stopover for Altun Ha explorers who decide to enjoy lunch and a mud mask before heading back to San Pedro, Belize City, or other nearby destinations.

The resort's verdant landscaping is enhanced by intriguing focal points spread around the grounds: a tiny, glass-decorated chapel, a palapa-covered stone chess table, a pool that seems to spring from the jungle, complete with waterfalls. The individually designed rooms are spread throughout the grounds for privacy and are addressed by name—Moon, Fertility, Mayan Loft, and Bondage, to name a few. All continue the eclectic motif—carved masks, mosaic-tile floors, standing candles, concrete fountains, tiled tubs, screened and shuttered windows, and fresh flowers on the massive feather beds and in the bathrooms.

Sanctuary) and continue to about Mile 19, where the road forks; the right fork is the Old Northern Highway and leads to Altun Ha and Maskall Village. Ten and a half miles from the intersection, you'll reach the Altun Ha entrance. The road is in horrible condition and is not getting any better with the increased traffic, mainly from long parades of buses carrying cruise ship passengers.

The ruins of Altun Ha have become one of the more popular day trips for groups and individuals venturing from Belize City, Ambergris Caye, and Caye Caulker. A gift shop and toilet facilities are at the entrance.

Note that Altun Ha is a popular destination for cruise ship passengers, so if you don't want to share your experience with 40 busloads of gawking cruisers, be sure to check with the park before coming. In general, it's easy to

© JOSHUA BERMAN

A tour of Altun Ha is a popular day trip from Belize City.

The restaurant often offers wild game in addition to standard fare, and at the bar you will find viper rum, with a warning label that reads "for real men only." Instructions on how to properly down a shot will be given by owner/bartender Nicky. Massages, mud wraps, manicures, and pedicures are available, as well as a free-weight gym. Packages are available with tours to the reefs, ruins, and inland destinations.

Getting to Altun Ha and Maruba

For those who want to bus it, ask at your hotel for current schedules and make sure there is a return bus the same day if you do not plan on staying in the area. Altun Ha is close enough to the city that a taxi is your best bet, or try a tour operator that specializes in these trips. Those going to Maruba should ask at the hotel about transfers when making reservations. There are a few community buses per week; ask about them at Novelo's Terminal in Belize City.

BURRELL BOOM

This is the gateway village to the Community Baboon Sanctuary and the destination of a popular day trip that involves taking a boat from Belize City up the Belize River and landing at the **Olde River Tavern,** where passengers find crafts, food, and beverages. Talk to the hustlers in Belize City's Tourism Village about this one, or to any tour operator in the city.

This is also the site of **El Chiclero Inn** (tel. 501/225-9005, www.elchicleroinn.com, US$65), a locally famous six-room hotel known mostly for its huge American-style menu, with everything from chili dogs to pizza to pastas, steaks, and Cajun pork chops—oh yeah, and they've allegedly got the only cashew pie in the country. The restaurant is open 7 A.M.–9 P.M. daily and there's a pool. The rooms are spacious and bright, with air conditioning, TVs, and private bathrooms. El Chiclero is often used by business travelers, as it is located a mere 11 miles from the international airport. Another Burrell Boom option (and an alternative for travelers who would otherwise stay in Belize City) is **Black Orchid Resort** (tel. 501/225-9158, www.blackorchidresort.com, US$120). Guests rave about this place, which is located right on the river, with spacious rooms (basic amenities plus private verandas) and all kinds of activities and services. There's a free airport shuttle. The owner is a native Belizean who lived in the United States for 36 years, so he knows what North Americans like. Besides trips to the nearby attractions, the resort offers a swimming pool, a volleyball net, shaded picnic tables, paddle boats, kayaks, and canoes.

⚫ THE COMMUNITY BABOON SANCTUARY (CBS)

The sanctuary (tel. 501/220-2181, www.howlermonkeys.org) is the result of the unique efforts of 220 members in nine local communities who have voluntarily agreed to manage their land in ways that will preserve their beloved baboon (the local term for the black howler monkey). Because of community-based efforts to preserve the creature, there are now 4,000 individuals waiting to be spotted and photographed by curious travelers. CBS feels remote, but in reality, it is only 26 miles from Belize City and 13 miles from the international airport, making it both a popular day trip *and* a common destination for tent-schlepping backpackers who'd rather wake up to the throaty roars of the Belizean baboon than the smelly bustle of Belize City.

History

One of the six species of howler monkeys in the world, the black howlers are the largest monkeys in the Americas. Robert Horwich, from the University of Wisconsin at Milwaukee, was the first zoologist to spend extended time in the howler's range, which covered southern Mexico, northeast Guatemala, and Belize.

The results of his study were disturbing. In Mexico, the monkeys were being hunted by the locals for food, and their habitat was fast being eliminated with the destruction of the rainforest. Conditions in Guatemala were only slightly better. Here, too, the monkeys were hunted by locals in the forests around Tikal, and as the forest habitat shrank in the country, so too did the number of howler monkeys.

In the Belizean village of Bermudian Landing, however, the communities of monkeys were strong and healthy, the forest was intact, and the locals seemed genuinely fond of the noisy creatures. This was definitely the place to start talking wildlife reserve.

Horwich, with the help of Jon Lyon, a botanist from the State University of New York, began a survey of the village in 1984. After many meetings with the town leaders, excitement grew about the idea of saving the "baboon." Homeowners agreed to leave the monkey's food trees—hogplums and sapodillas—and small strips of forest between cleared fields as aerial pathways for the primates, as well as 60 feet of forest along both sides of waterways.

An application was made to World Wildlife Fund USA in 1985 for funds to set up the reserve. Local landowners signed a voluntary management agreement set forth by Horwich and Lyon—and a sanctuary was born.

Continuing Results

According to sanctuary manager Fallett Young, there have been successful attempts to relocate some of the troops around the country, especially to southern areas like the Cockscomb Basin Wildlife Sanctuary, where howlers haven't been heard since they were decimated by yellow fever decades ago.

One of the outgrowths of this innovative plan in Belize is the knowledge that educating people about conservation and arousing in them a basic fondness for all of nature has been much more successful than enacting a stringent hunting law. The managers of the sanctuary are villagers who understand their neighbors; much of their time is spent with schoolchildren and adults in interested villages. Part of their education includes basic farming and sustained land use techniques that eliminate the constant need to cut forest for new *milpas* (cornfields); this might be the most important lesson for the forest inhabitants.

Another result is the unhindered growth of 100 species of trees, vines, and epiphytes. The animal life is thriving as well—anteaters, armadillos, iguanas, hicatee turtles, deer, coati,

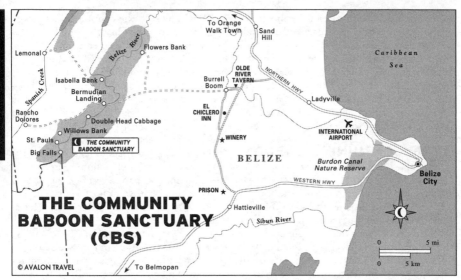

amphibians, reptiles, and about 200 species of birds all live here.

However, all is not perfect in this baboon paradise. Occasionally, people from urban areas still come to the sanctuary to kidnap baby monkeys to sell for pets. The only way anyone can kidnap a baby howler is by killing the mother, since she will never relinquish her young without a fight. A lively debate continues among traditional conservationists about allowing people to live within a wildlife preserve. However, Belize's grassroots conservation is proving that it can succeed. Other countries, such as Australia and Sierra Leone, are watching carefully to see how this concept can be adapted to the needs of their own endangered species without disturbing the people who have lived on the land for many generations.

Activities

There are enough trails, rivers, and guided tours to keep you busy here for a couple of days. It's always a thrill to watch a bright-eyed black monkey as it sits within five feet of you on a wild lime tree branch, happily munching the leaves. The monkeys seem to know they're protected here.

All activities are arranged through the CBS Visitor Center in Bermudian Landing (group trips and guides from local hotels are also available). The most basic is the 45-minute nature walk that is included with your US$5 entrance fee to the Natural History Museum. You are 100 percent guaranteed to see wild monkeys, as there is a troop of seven that lives in a tree right across the road.

There is also a three-hour canoe tour and a two-hour walking tour of some of the different sanctuary villages. Overnighters should absolutely take advantage of the nighttime trips, including a 3.5-hour crocodile canoe trip up Mussell Creek and a two-hour night hike into the surrounding forest.

Be aware that the trails are on private land, and visitors should not infringe on private property. A trail is maintained, and it's required that all visitors have a guide for orientation. The trails are marked with numbered signs that correspond with information provided in the book *Community Baboon Sanctuary,* which is available in most gift shops or at the sanctuary.

Accommodations and Food

A popular choice for adventurous travelers is

HATTIEVILLE CENTRAL PRISON GIFT SHOP

In 2002, management of Hattieville Central Prison was transferred from the government of Belize to the **Kolbe Foundation** (tel. 501/225-6190, www.kolbe.bz), a private, nonprofit Christian organization. The Hattieville facility had been in operation for less than a decade and was horribly constructed and disastrously overcrowded. The Kolbe Foundation's vision of a secure, humane facility based on meaningful rehabilitation and reintegration has had astonishing results in the short time they've been there.

A major part of the foundation's approach (in addition to piping Bible readings over the PA system) is education and skill building, including the creation and development of workshops and classroom courses. Inmates learn woodworking, jewelry making, tailoring, and welding. There is an agricultural program, which includes a large vegetable garden, a farm where chickens and pigs are raised, and a cement-block shop.

The **Prison Gift Shop and Tourist Center** features items made exclusively at the prison by the inmates in all the aforementioned workshops. You'll find beautiful furniture, jewelry, hammocks, delicate carvings, handicrafts, and many other items. The thatch-roof facility also has a snack shop, bathrooms, Internet access, and a mini-botanical garden and park.

The Prison Gift Shop is a step into the future for inmates, offering the means for their rehabilitation and for the prison itself to become economically self-sustainable. Your patronage will go a long way to assist in these goals.

To get to the gift shop (tel. 501/225-6218 or 225-6190, ext. 235), leave Belize City and follow the Western Highway until you reach the Hattieville roundabout at Mile 14. Turn right (north onto Boom Road) and travel for approximately two miles. The prison and gift shop are on the left side of the road. It's a perfect diversion for anyone headed either to the Community Baboon Sanctuary or to points west and south in Belize, as it's only two miles off your route.

---

the homestay program, where you'll stay with a local family in primitive conditions, bathing with a bucket and talking with your host family in the evening. The Women's Bed and Breakfast Group has established a network of accommodations throughout the seven sanctuary villages, offering visitors a traditional Creole-style stay. Arrange your stay in one of these "bed-and-breakfasts" (about US$13 pp, meals around US$4) at least 24 hours in advance through the Visitor Center at Bermudian Landing.

If you've got a tent, you can pitch it on the Visitor Center grounds or down by the river for US$5 per person. Eat at the on-site restaurant, or arrange a meal with a local family; both options are less than US$5 per meal. There are privies, but shower facilities are still in the making.

A couple notches up in comfort and price, and right next to the Visitor Center, is the **Nature Resort** (tel. 501/220-2121), with eight

cabanas, ranging from US$30 for a shared bath to US$55 for a full kitchenette and private bathroom. The cabins are new, well kept, and well equipped.

A few other simple lodges and cabanas are found in Bermudian Landing, Flower's Bank, and St. Paul's Bank villages; they offer private bathrooms, locally prepared meals, and cool showers right in the heart of the sanctuary.

Getting There and Away

Bermudian Landing is only 26 miles from Belize City; the bus ride takes about an hour. A few early-morning buses leave Bermudian Landing from 5 A.M.–6:45 A.M. and depart Belize City at noon, 4 P.M., 5 P.M., and 5:15 P.M. Catch the bus two blocks east of the main Novelo's Terminal at the corner of Euphrates and Amara Avenues. There are no buses in either direction on Sundays.

The sanctuary is close enough to the city or either airport that you can consider a taxi or an escorted tour for a day trip. Negotiate taxi prices ahead of time.

SPANISH CREEK WILDLIFE SANCTUARY

Spanish Creek Wildlife Sanctuary is located near Rancho Dolores, due west along the Burrell Boom Road, beyond the Community Baboon Sanctuary. This new protected area is rich in wildlife, but short on infrastructure so far. It's operated by the Rancho Dolores Environmental and Development Group, and is accessible by bus from Belize City (call Leonard Russell, tel. 510/610-5164 to arrange bus transport).

Crooked Tree

The island village and the wildlife sanctuary (which also encompasses the freshwater lagoon that surrounds the area) of Crooked Tree are only a 36-mile drive from Belize City and a primary destination for all serious bird-watchers who visit Belize. Others will enjoy paddling through the water, hiking various trails, or reveling at the annual cashew festival. Most visitors to the area also enjoy the simple pleasure of mingling with the islanders—most of whom grew up here—perhaps at one of the weekly cricket matches.

Crooked Tree is a network of inland lagoons, swamps, and waterways. **Crooked Tree Lagoon** is up to a mile wide and more than 20 miles long. Along its banks lies the town of Crooked Tree. An island surrounded by fresh water, accessible only by boats traveling up the Belize River and Black Creek, it was settled during the early days of the logwood era. The waterways were used to float the logs out to the sea.

◖ CROOKED TREE WILDLIFE SANCTUARY

The 16,400 acres of waterways, logwood swamps, and lagoon provide habitat for a diverse array of hundreds of resident and migratory birds—all year long. Explore the area by paddle power in a rented canoe or kayak, motor through on a guided tour, or hike the system of boardwalks through lowland savanna and logwood forests, with observation towers providing wide views across the lagoons.

The reserve was established by the Belize Audubon Society to protect its most famous habitant, the jabiru stork. It's the largest flying bird in the Western Hemisphere, with a wingspan of up to eight feet. Multitudes of other birds (285 species, at last count) find the sanctuary a safe resting spot during the dry season, with enormous food resources along the shorelines and in the trees. After a rain, thousands of minuscule frogs (no more than an inch long) seem to drop from the sky. They're fair game for the agami heron, snowy egret, and great egret—quick hunters with their long beaks. A fairly large bird, the snail kite uses its particular beak to hook meat out of the apple snails.

Two varieties of ducks, the black-bellied whistling duck and the Muscovy, nest in trees along the swamp. All five species of kingfishers live in the sanctuary, and you can see osprey and black-collared hawks diving for their morning catch.

On one trip, we watched from our dory (dugout canoe) as a peregrine falcon repeatedly tried but failed to nab one of a flock of floating American coots. Black Creek, with its forests of large trees, provides homes to monkeys, Morelet's crocodiles, coatimundi, turtles, and iguana. A profusion of wild ocher pokes up from the water, covered with millions of pale pink snail eggs. Grazing Brahma cattle wade into the shallows of the lagoon to munch on the tum tum (water lilies), a delicacy that keeps them fat and fit when the grasses turn brown in the dry season.

Hunting and fishing are not permitted.

Audubon Society

Although several organizations had a financial hand in founding the park, ongoing credit for supervision goes to the Belize Audubon Society (tel. 501/223-5004, www.belizeaudubon.org). The organization, with the continued help of devoted volunteers, maintains a small visitors center on the right just after you cross the causeway. Do sign in; this validates the sanctuary and gives the society a reason to sponsor it. It's also obligatory, as is the US$5 per person entrance fee; the office is open 8 A.M.– 4:30 P.M. 365 days a year. You will always find a knowledgeable curator willing to answer questions about the birds and flora encountered at the sanctuary.

THE VILLAGE

The village is divided into three neighborhoods: Crooked Tree, Pine Ridge, and Stain, with a total population under 1,000. Villagers operate farms, raise livestock, and have a small fishery. Visitors will find the village spread out on the island, with more cattle trails, halfroads, and fence line than actual public roads. There are a few well-grazed athletic fields, four churches, and scores of neat wooden houses (many on stilts) in the middle of large, wellkept plots of land, each with its own tank to catch rainwater. It's a tranquil community.

Crooked Tree mainly attracts nature lovers, but visitors will find barefoot boys going home for lunch with fishing poles over their shoulders as well as women with floppy hats gabbing over back fences. And if you indulge in conversation, you'll have a chance to hear the lovely soft Creole patois that is common throughout the country. While strolling through the village, you might see local children playing football, racing horses, or whacking a ball around the cricket pitch.

Chau Hiix Ruins

Archaeological site Chau Hiix is being studied nearby. Archaeologists have made some startling discoveries, including a ball court and ball-court marker, along with small artifacts. Preliminary studies indicate the site was occupied from 1200 B.C. to A.D. 1500. **Sapodilla Lagoon** is south of Crooked Tree on Spanish Creek.

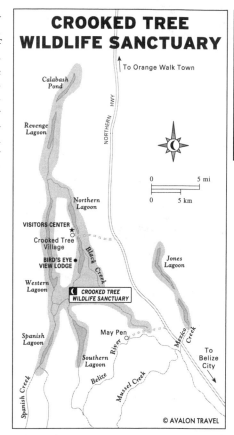

GUIDES AND TOURS

The recommended way to visit Crooked Tree is to hire a local guide who really knows his digs. Options include boat, horseback, and walking tours. The best way to really experience the lagoon is by boat, and there are all kinds available at each hotel. Belize Audubon Society will be happy to have a guide and boat waiting for you when you arrive at Crooked Tree.

ACCOMMODATIONS AND FOOD

This is a low-key tourist area with just a few locally run and owned accommodations and tiny cafés, usually an extension of someone's home.

CROOKED TREE CASHEW FESTIVAL

The namesake of this relaxed inland island village is the cashew tree, which grows prolifically throughout the area. The unique nut has always contributed to the community's economy, especially for its women, who have been able to secure additional income for their households by selling cashew products. The situation is even better today, as the products are more often sold directly to local consumers and tourists than to distributors in Belize City, as they were in the past.

To celebrate the bent branches and their heavy fruit, the people of Crooked Tree Village throw a big cashew harvest festival the first weekend in May. It's a lot of fun, a hometown fair with regional arts, music, folklore, dance, and crafts. And of course it's a chance to sample cashew wine, cashew jellies, stewed cashews . . . . you get the picture. Just make sure the "hometown fair" picture in your head includes *punta* music, fry jacks, and johnnycakes.

Seek out the demonstrations showing how the cashew nut is processed – interesting stuff. The fruit, or the cashew "apple," is either red or yellow, with the seed hanging from the bottom of the apple. The meat of the apple can be stewed or made into jam or wine, while the seedpod is roasted in an open fire on the ground. Roasting the cashew stabilizes the highly acidic oil and at the same time makes the pod brittle enough to crack. The nut is partially cooked during this step in the processing. The seeds are then raked so they cool evenly and quickly.

The cashews are then cracked by hand, one at a time. Those who handle the nuts wear gloves, as the shell contains a highly irritating poison that for most people causes blisters and inflammation. Processing removes all the poison.

All will allow you to camp on their grounds for US$5 per person.

As you approach the island on the causeway, on the shoreline off to your left, you'll see the buildings of the **Bird's Eye View Lodge** (tel. 501/225-7027 or 203-2040, www.birdseyeview-belize.com, US$70–90 for a couple). This hotel stands above the rest in modernity and dependable service, and this is reflected in its higher rates. The 18 rooms all have private bath and various comforts, including the option of air conditioning—something you may be happy for if visiting in April or May. Miss Verna will take good care of you. The rooftop bar and patio is a wonderful spot to take in the breeze and keep on bird-watching, even after your four-hour, daybreak bird-watching boat cruise on the lagoon. Meals are US$7 for breakfast and lunch; dinner is US$10. Boat rentals, tours, and airport pickups can be arranged.

Everyone is welcome to dine at **Triple J's,** and **Suzette's Burger Bar** is a fine little spot for burgers and hot dogs. Both are found by walking into Crooked Tree Village, and their hours vary depending on demand.

On the shore of the lagoon, to the north of the causeway, the region's newest venture, **Crooked Tree Lodge** (michaelcjwebb@hotmail.com) promises quiet rooms and tour services.

GETTING THERE

By car, drive north to Mile 33, turn left, and continue until the dirt road turns into the earthen causeway that will carry you into Crooked Tree. (Be prepared to give way to allow vehicles coming from the opposite direction to pass.) Or catch the **Jex Bus** to Crooked Tree in Belize City (at 34 Regent Street). From Crooked Tree to Belize City, buses depart only in the mornings; ask about times. This is fine for those who plan to spend the night; other options are to go by taxi or with a local tour operator. Check with the Audubon Society for further transportation information, rates, and an updated schedule.

THE NORTHERN CAYES

By the 17th century, pirates had discovered that the plentiful cayes (or islands, pronounced "keys") around the Belizean mainland were perfect for lying low, riding out a storm, drinking rum, and replenishing water and food supplies before setting sail for another round of pillaging and sacking. No doubt modern-day travelers to Belize's largest and most visited islands engage in at least a few of these activities. The more popular cayes are Caulker, Ambergris, St. George's, Chapel, Half-Moon, and Lighthouse. Caye Caulker and Ambergris Caye are surrounded by the same crystal blue waters and coral rainbows that attracted the original Maya inhabitants—followed by buccaneers and now you.

The Northern Cayes are considered the crown jewels of Belize's tourism industry. They have the most experience catering to visitors, have developed several different scenes between them, and continue to be the most popular destinations in the region. By one estimate, more than 70 percent of visitors to Belize come to at least one of these islands during their trip. It's not hard to imagine why—namely, immediate access to world-class diving, fishing, and snorkeling; hospitable Belizean islanders and fellow travelers from around the world; and an amazing selection of small, personable resorts and restaurants. Then, of course, there are palms, rum punches, boat rides, a clear blue ocean, and easy island time.

Enjoy and repeat after the locals: "Go slow!"

© JOSHUA BERMAN

HIGHLIGHTS

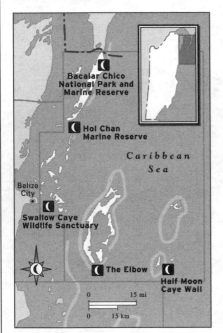

THE NORTHERN CAYES

LOOK FOR TO FIND RECOMMENDED SIGHTS, ACTIVITIES, DINING, AND LODGING.

(Hol Chan Marine Reserve: Belize's famous Barrier Reef, less than a mile offshore from both Caye Caulker and Ambergris Caye, is marked by this famous "cut," or break, in the reef, where the mixing water from the open ocean (and bait thrown in from tour boats) ensures plenty of wildlife (page 61).

(Bacalar Chico National Park and Marine Reserve: This UNESCO World Heritage Site occupies the northern tip of Ambergris Caye and boasts amazing snorkeling and diving; the area is rich with history and lore (page 61).

(Swallow Caye Wildlife Sanctuary: One of many ocean-bound excursions available from Belize's Northern Cayes, this protected area offers visitors manatees and shorebirds (page 83).

(The Elbow: The steep drop-off and clashing currents at Turneffe Island's southern tip make for a unique dive site because of the deep-water fish that frequent the area, as well as a thriving population of interesting sponges (page 93).

(Half Moon Caye Wall: The beautiful crescent-shaped island is at the southeast corner of Lighthouse Reef Atoll. The wall just offshore is one of Belize's most fascinating sites, with numerous tunnels and canyons in the reef crest, all swimming with wildlife (page 98).

PLANNING YOUR TIME

What to do? Dive? Snorkel? Kayak around the island? How about a sailing cruise at sunset? A day trip to the ruins on the mainland? Massage? Shopping? Deep-sea fishing? Or you can just lie back and read by the pool. Many visitors to Caulker, Ambergris, or the outlying atolls book their entire vacations on just one of these islands and are not disappointed—especially fishing and diving freaks on a mission. You can easily while away 7–10 days on any of these islands, no problem. Then there are the surf-and-turfers who do five days in the cayes and five days inland. Wanderers with wings on their backpacks often include only a couple of days in the North Cayes (or at least enough time to get scuba certified) before continuing on their Central American tours. If you focused your vacation elsewhere in the country and have only a day or two, it's still worth the trip to either Caulker or Ambergris, which are both less than an hour by boat from Belize City and worthy of the quickest of glimpses.

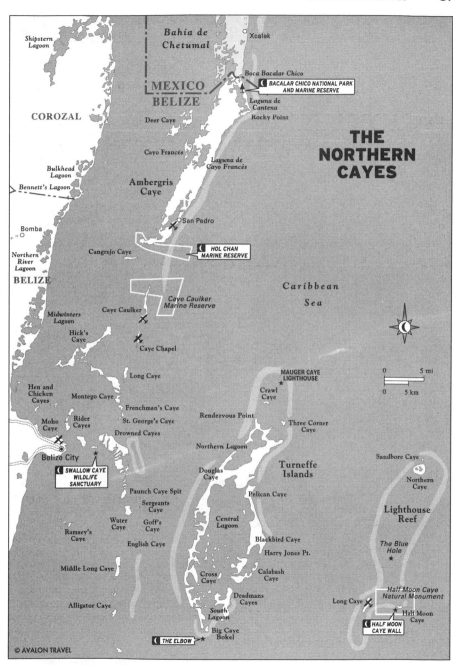

THE
NORTHERN
CAYES

San Pedro and Ambergris Caye

Ambergris Caye is Belize's largest island, just south of the Mexican Yucatán mainland, and stretching 24 miles into Belizean waters. Ambergris is a waxy substance originating in the intestines of the sperm whale. Don't laugh—this rare and valuable substance used to be a global commodity, used in the manufacture of perfume and going for top dollar. The island sits only 35 miles east of Belize City and about three-quarters of a mile west of the Barrier Reef. Ambergris's beach runs parallel to the reef, except at Rocky Point, where they briefly come together. Ambergris Caye was formed by an accumulation of coral fragments and silt from the Río Hondo as it emptied from what is now northern Belize. The caye is made up of mangrove swamps, a dozen lagoons, a plateau, and a series of low sand ridges. The largest lagoon, fed by 15 creeks, is 2.5-mile-long **Laguna de San Pedro** on the western side of the village.

San Pedro Town sits on a sand ridge at the southern end of the island, the only actual town on the island and the most-visited destination in Belize. It is chock-full of accommodations, restaurants, golf carts, and services; it's also the most expensive part of Belize, with prices for some basic goods and foods at double the mainland prices.

HISTORY
The Maya

As in the rest of Belize, the first people on the caye were the Maya. They managed to fight off invading Spaniards as early as 1508. A small Post-Classic site in the Basil Jones area and a few jade ornaments have been found along with obsidian flakes and fragments of pottery. Remnants indicate that Ambergris Caye was an important hub for trading. It is possible to visit these sites; transportation and guides are widely available. It is presumed that because of the location of Ambergris Caye (in the center of the sea-lane) it was a stopover for Maya traders traveling up and down the coast.

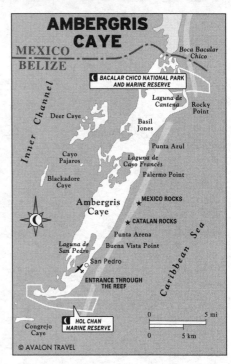

Four and a half miles north of Rocky Point, at Boca Bacalar Chico, a narrow channel separates Belize and Mexico. The Maya dug this strait by hand so that they could bring their canoes through rather than go all the way around the peninsula (which is now Ambergris Caye). In dry years, when the water receded it was impossible to get a boat through, so in 1899 the Mexican government expanded the channel.

The Blakes

Between 1848 and 1849, during the Caste War on the Yucatán Peninsula, Yucatecan mestizos migrated to Belize, and four families were the first permanent residents of present-day San Pedro. Before long, there was a population of about fifty self-sufficient fishermen, who were also growing corn and vegetables. Life was idyllic for these

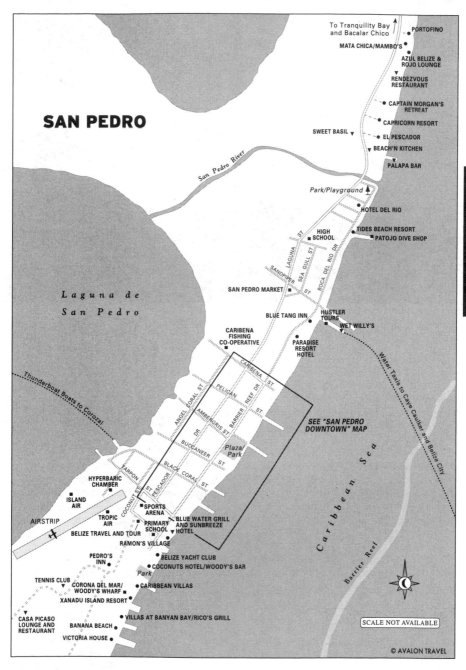

SAN PEDRO

To Tranquility Bay
and Bacalar Chico

PORTOFINO

MATA CHICA/MAMBO'S

AZUL BELIZE &
ROJO LOUNGE

RENDEZVOUS
RESTAURANT

CAPTAIN MORGAN'S
RETREAT

CAPRICORN RESORT

SWEET BASIL

EL PESCADOR

BEACH'N KITCHEN

PALAPA BAR

San Pedro River

Park/Playground

HOTEL DEL RIO

TIDES BEACH RESORT

HIGH
SCHOOL

PATOJO DIVE SHOP

LAGUNA ST

SEA GULL ST

BOCA DEL RIO DR

SANDPIPER ST

SAN PEDRO MARKET

Laguna de
San Pedro

BLUE TANG INN

HUSTLER
TOURS

WET WILLY'S

CARIBENA
FISHING
CO-OPERATIVE

PARADISE
RESORT
HOTEL

CARIBENA ST

PELICAN ST

REEF DR

ANGEL CORAL ST

AMBERGRIS ST

BARRIER ST

ST

Thunderbolt Boats to Corozal

BUCCANEER
DR

SEE "SAN PEDRO
DOWNTOWN" MAP

Plaza/
Park

BLACK CORAL ST

TARPON ST

HYPERBARIC
CHAMBER

COCONUT ST

PESCADOR ST

ISLAND
AIR

SPORTS
ARENA

AIRSTRIP

TROPIC
AIR

PRIMARY
SCHOOL

BLUE WATER GRILL
AND SUNBREEZE
HOTEL

BELIZE TRAVEL AND TOUR

RAMON'S VILLAGE

PEDRO'S
INN

BELIZE YACHT CLUB

COCONUTS HOTEL/WOODY'S BAR

Park

TENNIS CLUB

CORONA DEL MAR/
WOODY'S WHARF

CARIBBEAN VILLAS

XANADU ISLAND RESORT

CASA PICASO
LOUNGE AND
RESTAURANT

BANANA BEACH

VILLAS AT BANYAN BAY/RICO'S GRILL

VICTORIA HOUSE

Caribbean Sea

Water Taxis to Caye Caulker and Belize City

Barrier Reef

SCALE NOT AVAILABLE

© AVALON TRAVEL

THE NORTHERN CAYES

COURTESY OF THE BELIZE TOURISM BOARD

sea view from San Pedro

people—until 1874 and the coming of the Blake family, the first of many foreign real estate developers who would transform the island.

James Blake paid the Belize government BZE$650 for Ambergris Caye (taking over every parcel of land except one set aside for the Catholic church) and began collecting rent from people who had been there for many years. After this, the history of the island was tied up with the fortunes of the Blakes and their in-laws, the Parhams and Alamillas. Their story reads like a novel, including love affairs, illegitimate children, and unlikely marriages. The Blakes controlled everybody and everything on the island, including the coconut and fishing industries; after almost 100 years of this, the Belizean government stepped in and made a "forced purchase" of San Pedro. It redistributed the land, selling lots and parcels to the same islanders who had been living on the land for generations.

The Fishing Industry

The caye's main industry has shifted from logwood to *chicle* to coconuts, then to lobsters, fish, and conch. Before 1920, the spiny lobster was considered a nuisance, constantly getting caught in fishing nets, and thrown away. That all changed in 1921 when the lobster became a valuable export item. Though the fishermen were getting only a penny a pound, the business became lucrative when freezer vessels and freezer-equipped seaplanes began flying between the cayes and Florida.

Today's Ambergris

The establishment of a fishermen's co-op enabled the population to develop a middle-class economy over the years. The financial upswing allowed the town to improve the infrastructure of the island, which in turn has created a welcoming atmosphere for tourists. The earliest tourists came to Ambergris Caye aboard the boat *Pamelayne* in the 1920s. By 1965, the first hotel was established, and the industry has been growing ever since. The caye boasts 24-hour-a-day electricity (most of the time), modern communication to anywhere in the world, a few banks, and basic medical services. At last count, there were 108 hotels, 43 of which were foreign-owned.

TURTLE PENS TURNED SWIMMING POOLS

In the days when pirates roamed the high seas for months at a time, they had regular stopping places. Islands with abundant supplies of water were probably the most important. St. George's Caye was a favorite spot to pick up giant sea turtles. The seamen built large square pens (called *kraals*) at the end of wooden docks and would keep captured turtles there until leaving for the bounding main. Several turtles were taken on board and fed for a month or two, kept mostly on their backs and out of the way, until they were slaughtered for their meat. Often, turtle was the only meat the crews would eat for many months.

Over the years, the pirates dwindled, and St. George's Caye became the unofficial capital of Belize. Many more homes were built along the waterfront, and *kraals* became "crawls," swimming areas for people. Today, many of the bright-white wooden houses still have these small "pools" at the ends of their docks.

There is a steady, mellow buzz to San Pedro Town, which becomes a bit hectic and trendy at holiday times, especially El Día de San Pedro (June 26–29) and the Costa Maya Festival in August. There is no doubt that Ambergris is developing in an upscale direction, but don't be fooled—it's doing it Belizean style. You'll have to come down to find out for yourself what that means.

ORIENTATION

Whether arriving by air or sea, your trip to Ambergris begins in San Pedro Town. There are three roads running north-south and paralleling the beach on the island's east side. Most locals still refer to the streets by their historic names: **Front Street** (Barrier Reef Drive), **Middle Street** (Pescador Drive), and **Back Street** (Angel Coral Street). Another common landmark is at the north end of town, where the San Pedro River flows through a navigable cut. This spot is often referred to as **"the cut"** or "the split," or more recently, "the bridge," referring to the toll bridge that replaced the hand-drawn ferry. You'll often hear the term "south of town," referring to the continually developing area south of the airstrip, accessed by Coconut Drive.

SIGHTS
◖ Hol Chan Marine Reserve

Once a traditional fishing ground, back when San Pedro was a sleepy village of a few hundred people, Hol Chan is now the most popular dive and snorkel site in Belize, with tens of thousands of visitors each year. Once you visit, you'll quickly understand the popularity of the reserve—and why it is important to help preserve it. Established as a marine park in 1987, which banned fishing, the site boasts an amazing diversity of species. The reserve focuses its energy on creating a sustainable link between tourism and conservation, protecting the coral reef while allowing visitors to experience and learn about the marine life living there.

The Hol Chan Marine Reserve visitors center is on Caribena Street in the center of town and features an interactive display, information on the reserve, and details of the various zones of the reserve. Nearly all tour operators on Ambergris and Caye Caulker offer trips to the Hol Chan cut and Shark Ray Alley.

◖ Bacalar Chico National Park and Marine Reserve

Located on and around the northern tip of Ambergris Caye, Bacalar Chico National Park and Marine Reserve hosts an incredibly diverse array of wildlife, offers excellent snorkeling and diving, and is rich with history. The Bacalar Chico Canal is reputed to have been dug by Maya traders between A.D. 700 and 900, creating Ambergris Caye by separating it from the Yucatán Peninsula. The reserve has a wide range of wildlife habitat; 194 species of birds have been sighted there. The landscape consists in part of sinkholes and *cenotes* created by the

SNORKEL SITES NEAR AMBERGRIS CAYE

You don't need a license or a certification to snorkel; just put your face in the water and enjoy. Be sure to observe snorkel and reef etiquette, and consider leaving your fins at home, as they can be very destructive to the coral. Expect to pay about US$40 per person for a 2.5-hour snorkel tour, or US$70 per person for a full day (9 A.M.-3 P.M., lunch included). You'll save a few bucks if you have your own gear (rentals are about US$8/day).

For starters, grab your snorkel and mask for a swim around the dock at **Ramon's Village Resort.** With an artificial reef that is home to a wide variety of small reef fish, this spot is a favorite swimming hole for locals. For live coral, book a half-day trip to one or all of the following sites.

Mexico Rocks is on the reef north of town and is the place to go to see a huge diversity of coral formations. Only 12 feet at its deepest, it offers an abundance of coral, and the channel nearby brings in a lot of marine life, especially small reef fish. There aren't as many big fish here as in Hol Chan, but for some that's a plus. Near the northern tip of Ambergris Caye, **Bacalar Chico Marine Reserve** is another incredible site with a stunning diversity of wildlife and coral – it's home to at least 187 species of fish and several important spawning aggregation sites. There are also manatees and loggerhead, green, and hawksbill sea turtles living in Bacalar Chico. A little bit south of this area is **Tres Cocos,** a site gaining popularity because of the likelihood of seeing spotted eagle rays.

The crown jewel of San Pedro snorkeling is the **Hol Chan Marine Reserve,** located four miles southeast of San Pedro Town. Visitors are taken to the Hol Chan cut, a 30-foot-deep natural break in the Belize Barrier Reef. Snorkelers stay in the shallow inner reef area, but can swim through the cut. Because of the movement between the ocean and the inner reef lagoon through this area, it is high in nutrients and allows for marine animals of all types to thrive and increase in size. Be on the lookout for spiny lobsters, black groupers, nurse sharks, moray eels, and a plethora of reef fish showing off their bright colors. Rangers patrol the area during the day and help ensure the safety of visitors. Listen to your guide, though – the current at Hol Chan can be strong!

A mile south of the Hol Chan cut, **Shark Ray Alley** is also part of the reserve and offers visitors the rare opportunity to snorkel alongside southern stingrays and nurse sharks that frequent the area in search of food (which is kindly provided by your tour operator). Remember, only tour guides are allowed to feed these big fish, and please no touching! Large schools of horse-eyed jack and snapper also come here for the free handouts. There are spectacular coral formations on the back reef for snorkelers, and the fore reef gives scuba divers the chance to dive the *Amigos Del Mar* tugboat wreck.

When you step back onto dry land, stop in at the Hol Chan Marine Reserve office, on Caribena Street in the center of town. The interactive visitors center has information on the reserve, as well as displays detailing the various zones of the reserve and species. Not sure what you saw? Stop in and ask the staff – they're happy to answer questions and give more details on the reserve.

effects of weathering on the limestone bedrock of Ambergris Caye. On the eastern side of the Reserve is **Rocky Point,** the only location in the Belize Barrier Reef Reserve System where the reef touches the shore. Belize's most important and prolific sea turtle nesting sites are found in Bacalar Chico, and it is also home to at least 10 threatened species. In 1997, Bacalar Chico—along with the Belize Barrier Reef Reserve System—was designated a World Heritage Site by UNESCO.

Bacalar Chico contains at least nine archaeological sites: Maya trading, fishing, and agricultural settlements that were inhabited from at least A.D. 300–900. A 10th site just outside the reserve boundary is regarded as especially

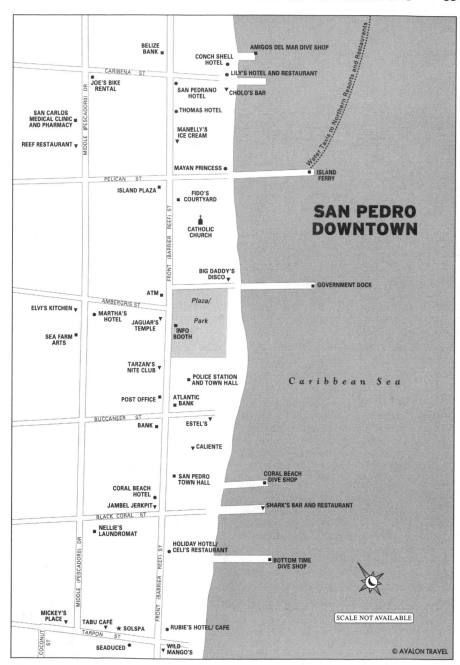

important for its remaining wall network throughout the settlement and its potential to provide missing information about the transition from the Classic Mayan period to modern times. The reserve also contains evidence of Spanish and English habitation during the colonial period, including several Spanish-period shipwrecks offshore.

The park office is at the northwest end of the park and offers a visitors center with displays of area history, including old glass bottles and Maya relics found within the reserve. There is a picnic area with a barbecue and grill. Most Ambergris dive shops will do dive/snorkel trips to Bacalar Chico if requested.

Beaches

Don't expect the wide-open clean beaches you've seen in other Caribbean destinations. A few hotels have good sand; most don't. Most of those that do had to dredge it from the lagoon side (an ecologically questionable activity). But the ocean is as beautiful as ever, and small docks are provided where swimming might otherwise be difficult. In some areas, you need to wade through sea grass to get to deep water, but it's usually worth it.

NIGHTLIFE

San Pedro boasts the best nightlife in the country, whether your idea of fun is dancing up a storm, drowning in alcohol, listening to live music, or watching chickens poop—it's all here. Wednesdays and Saturdays are the biggest nights out, and water taxis actually change their schedules to accommodate revelers. In general, the hot spots don't get going until 11 P.M. or midnight, with lots of warming up in various bars before the bumpin' and grindin' begins.

Bars

Diving by day and drinking by night is the standard Ambergris scene—although a number of proud underachievers substitute a full day of cocktails for diving. The bar at **BC's** (on the beach, back from the airstrip) is popular, open at 9 A.M. daily with barbecue lunch and

live music on Sundays. Standard tourist hangouts are found at **Fido's Courtyard,** which advertises live music every night in the high season and has an Italian restaurant and sushi bar. The **Sand Bar,** for folks on the south end of the island, is located on the beach a few hundred yards past Victoria House. The **Rehab Bar**, next to the Jaguar's Temple disco, is open daily and great for people watching.

Cholo's Sport Bar is one of the mellower local hangouts. **Casa Picasso** turns into a sensually lit martini lounge each evening, with half-price martinis to wash down scrumptious tapas.

Don't miss the Wednesday night **Chicken Drop,** at 6 P.M. at the **Pier Lounge** (in the Spindrift Hotel); a chicken is let loose on a numbered grid and revelers place bets on which numbered square the chicken will soil. Warm up at their two-for-one happy hour, 4 P.M.–6 P.M.

Crazy Canuck's Beach Bar has live *punta* music and dancing on Mondays, and all kinds of games (dice, cards, horseshoes, dominoes), including Saturday afternoon Scrabble competitions. Across Coconut Drive from Canuck's, look for the **Roadkill Bar**, where owner Casey sponsors a Monday night bluegrass jam.

Dancing

Wednesday is ladies' night at **Wet Willy's,** and Saturdays get going when Fido's closes at midnight and everyone wanders across the street to **Jaguar's Temple,** open at 9:30 P.M. Thursday, Friday, and Saturday. The night often ends at **Big Daddy's Disco** on the edge of the park and the ocean at Ambergris Street. Music and dancing can go until 3 A.M., sometimes later.

SHOPPING

Gift shops abound in San Pedro, especially on Front and Middle Streets: they've got your postcards, beach apparel, towels, hats, T-shirts, hot sauces, and the usual knickknacks. The sale sections at the **Toucan 1** and **Toucan 2** stores are treasured by local thrifters. Artisans sell their works on Front Street, mainly handmade zericote wood carvings and bowls.

A decent book selection is available at **Blue,** across from San Pedro Holiday Hotel, open daily at 8 A.M. **Barefoot Books,** at the south end of Pescador Drive (tel. 501/226-3563, www.barefootbooks-belize.com), boasts more than seven thousand new and used books. **Belizean Arts** in Fido's Courtyard sells art, jewelry, ceramics, and carvings by local and Belizean artists. The well-established shop has the largest selection of original paintings in Belize. Also in Fido's Courtyard is **Bambar,** offering handcrafted jewelry made with resin ambers, Maya jade, shells, and silver. **Mambo Chill** imports expensive women's clothing.

Ambergris Art Gallery is worth a look, with two stores: one on Middle Street near the men's clothing store Moonbreeze, the other in the Sunbreeze Hotel. **Orange,** just south of the airstrip, sells elegant home furnishings.

Get your rocks at **Ambergris Maya Jade and History Museum** (across from town hall, 9 A.M.–6 P.M. daily). Also a retail jade shop, it's designed "to give visitors an overview of 3,000 years of Mesoamerican jade and its importance to the cultures in the region." When you're finished, check out **The Emerald Mine,** a few doors down.

RECREATION
Diving

There are many dive shops on the island. Almost every hotel on Ambergris either employs local dive shops or has its own on-site shop and dive masters. They all offer pretty much the same thing: resort courses, PADI or NAUI certification classes, day trips, and snorkel trips. Some also offer things like night dives, and a few have Nitrox capabilities. What really makes the difference is the experience of the instructor or dive master, the quality of the equipment, the size of the boat, and the size of the groups. Prices are pretty standard around the island: local two-tank dive US$75, plus rental fee and tax; resort course US$150; open water certification US$450–470; advanced certification US$380; three-tank dive to the Blue Hole US$250, to Turneffe US$185. **Amigos del Mar** (tel. 501/226-2706, www.

DIVING TERMS

Don't know what the hard-core divers are talking about? Here are some definitions of some frequently used terms:

• **NAUI** – National Association of Underwater Instructors

• **Nitrox** – oxygen-enriched air (more than 21 percent oxygen) used as breathing gas for deep-water dives

• **PADI** – Professional Association of Diving Instructors

• **scuba** – self-contained underwater breathing apparatus

---

amigosdive.com), based on the pier near Cholo's Bar, is a bustling place with top-notch gear and a solid reputation as one of the best and safest operations on the island. Many clients return year after year to dive with the same long-term and friendly staff. Amigos specializes in trips to the Blue Hole in their 52-foot boat. **Patojo's** (tel. 501/226-2283, patojos@ btl.net), located on the pier off Boca del Rio Drive and part of the Tides Beach Resort, has an equally excellent reputation for professional service. **Ecologic Divers** (tel. 501/226-4118, www.ecologicdivers.com) provides a special touch, with hot minty towels when you exit the water, free digital pictures with every dive, and a 1:6 instructor-diver ratio. Ecologic is the only operation to carry automated external defibrillators on board.

Other professional operations to consider are **Belize Diving Adventures** (tel. 501/226-3082, www.belizedivingadventures.net) and **Bottom Time Dive Shop** (tel. 501/226-2014, holiday@btl.net), a full-service facility at the San Pedro Holiday Hotel.

Sailing Charters and Cruising

Explore the Caribbean the way it was meant to be traveled: by wind. You can book a variety of trips on the **Winnie Estelle** (tel. 501/226-2427, www.ambergriscaye.com/winnieestelle,

THE NORTHERN CAYES

US$55 per adult for day trips). Spend the day with the Rubio Brothers, snorkeling, fishing, drinking, and relaxing aboard *No Rush,* a 36-foot catamaran that can be booked through **Unity Tours** (tel. 501/226-4551, www.ambergriscaye.com/unitytours).

The *Katkandu* (www.belizecharters.com) is a 42-foot luxury cat that provides catered upscale cruises and multiday charters. Other cat cruises can be found at **Searious Adventures** (tel. 501/226-4202, www.seariousadventures.com) and **SEAduced by Belize** (tel. 501/226-3221, www.ambergriscaye.com/seaduced), both of which offer many different activities in addition to sailing.

Fishing

The area within the reef is a favorite for tarpon and bonefish. Outside the reef, the choice of big game is endless. Most hotels and dive shops will make arrangements for fishing, including boat and guide. Ask around the docks (and your hotel) for the best guides. Serious anglers should consider Abner Marin at **Go Fish Belize** (tel. 501/226-3121, www.gofishbelize.com), one of the most qualified and reputable guides around. Or try Richard French at **Belize Flats Fishing Expeditions** (tel. 501/226-2799, www.belizeflatsfishing.com). **Rubie's Hotel** has a shack on the beach, and the guys working there are rumored to be excellent guides. Another sure bet is **Fishing San Pedro** (tel. 501/226-2835, www.fishingsanpedro.com), where half- or full-day chartered fishing trips are relatively affordable (US$295 full day for two people includes tackle, bait, soda, and water); a fish/lobster barbecue adds a bit extra.

Fitness

The **San Pedro Fitness Center** (toward the south end of the airstrip, tel. 501/226-2682 or 226-2683) has an air-conditioned fully equipped (if small) workout room in an interesting, modern building. There are also two tennis courts; a 200,000-gallon pool designed to accommodate both lap swimmers and frolicking children; and Tae Bo, tai chi, and combat arts classes. Use of the facilities by tourists costs US$15/day, US$38/week, or US$110/month (locals get special rates). A small bar is open on weekends. From here you can watch the planes take off and land all day.

On the opposite end of town, almost at the split, you'll find the workingman's gym at **Oscar's Fitness Center** (tel. 501/206-2063; US$4/day, $9/week, $25/month). Oscar's is under new management with a new personal trainer, so expect changes and upgrades.

Massage and Bodywork

Yoga is a wandering affair in San Pedro, with individual instructors roaming from resort to resort. For those on the north side of the island, look into Judie Fisher's **Your Third Eye** (tel. 501/226-2922 or 620-3392, judie@blazinghammers.com, US$10 walk-in) for classes or private sessions at the location of your choice. Judie offers a gentle hatha/Iyengar style of practice.

Sol Spa (Vilma Linda Plaza, tel. 501/226-2410, www.belizesolspa.com) offers treatment for your "spirit, mind, and body"; ask about the special "Honeymoon Bliss" and "Solar Therapy" treatments. In addition to facials, nails, and waxing, they feature Maya Abdominal Massage and offer private yoga and Pilates classes.

Rosie Uejbe's **Ambergris Massage** (tel. 501/624-1024) is one of the oldest operations on the island; invite her to your hotel room for various types of massage, shiatsu, reflexology, facials, and wraps. The **Asian Garden Day Spa** (Coconut Drive, across from Ramon's Village, tel. 501/226-4072, www.asiangardendayspa.com) is a family-run affair in a lovely courtyard, specializing in Thai massage, hot stone therapy, reflexology, facials, scrubs, and specials like sunset or starlight couples massage. **Tropical Touch** (tel. 501/226-4666, www.tropicaltouchspaworks.com) is a full-service massage and day spa right on the water with all kinds of body treatments, including Maya Abdominal Massage. **The Art of Touch** (tel. 501/226-3357) is in the entrance to the Sunbreeze Hotel.

ACCOMMODATIONS

In addition to accommodations listed in these pages, there are many, many apartment and house rentals available across the island. Start by downloading the classifieds from the *San Pedro Sun* website (http://sanpedrosun.net).

Under US$25

"La Isla Bonita," as Ambergris Caye was once dubbed by Madonna, caters to those living in a material world when it comes to accommodations. There are only a few budget options, beginning with **Pedro's Inn** (tel. 501/226-3825, www.backpackersbelize.com, US$10 and up), where backpackers and British soldiers on leave usually choose to stay. There are 14 functional, simple rooms with single bed, locker, fan, and lamp; shared bathrooms are spotless and adequate. Deluxe rooms with two twin beds or one king go for US$35, and include air-conditioning, TV, private bath, and fan. There are weekly rates and discounts if you ask. It is a seven-minute walk to the town center. Pedro's has a small pool, a pizzeria and bar with a pool table, foosball, and Internet and Wii on a jumbo screen; ask about getting your name on the Jägermeister wall of fame (or "shame," take your pick). Work up a big enough bar tab and stay for free.

 Ruby's Hotel (tel. 501/226-2063, rubys@btl.net, US$18–40) boasts a central location and longstanding good reputation; sip coffee with local fishermen as the sun rises over Ruby's Café, then go back to your room's balcony and watch the beach traffic. Rooms have shared or private bath.

US$25-50

 Hotel San Pedrano (tel. 501/226-2054, sanpedrano@btl.net, US$33 with fan, US$43 with a/c) has six rooms that make up the island's self-proclaimed "top of the low end." From the breezy upstairs veranda, it's easy to eat a bite, read a book, or watch the street below. Each room has hot and cold water, private bath, and ceiling fan and air-conditioning—but if you use of the air conditioning you have to pay the higher rate.

 Thomas Hotel (tel. 501/226-2861,

THE NORTHERN CAYES

CHOOSING A HOTEL IN THE CAYES

Of Ambergris's 108 hotels, most are mid-range to upscale lodging. The couple of places geared toward backpackers and budget travelers are located either right in San Pedro Town or on the outskirts by the airstrip. Otherwise, here are a few things to keep in mind when deciding on a hotel:

First off, in downtown San Pedro, the word "beachside" refers to the very narrow strip of sand on the island's east side. It is used more as a pathway for pedestrians and boats than for lounging in the sand. As you move farther from town, either to the north or south along the island, the beaches fronting the resorts become wider, softer, and more exclusive.

Of course, what you give up in beach quality, you get back in location: "in town" means in the middle of cafés, bars, boutiques, dive shops, dancing, and dining. If you're more into privacy, all this action is easily accessible from any resort on the island by boat, taxi, or golf cart.

Keep in mind that rates across the board are subject to seasonal rate fluctuations, service charges, and government taxes. Always verify and ask about discounts before booking. Remember that rates reported in *Moon Belize* are for double occupancy during the high season.

US$30–35 plus tax) has seven cheap rooms, one short block from the beach. **Martha's Hotel** (Middle St., across from Elvi's, tel. 501/206-2053, julian@btl.net, from US$35) is two blocks from the waterfront. Rooms are upstairs and clean, with private baths, ceiling fans, and linoleum floors.

On the north end of town, toward the cut, **Hotel del Rio** (tel. 501/226-2286, www.ambergriscaye.com/hoteldelrio) is one of the best bargains on the island. Accommodations range from basic economy rooms with shared baths and cold water (US$30–45 a couple) to bigger casitas built of natural materials (US$65 for a king or two queen beds; sleep up to five people for US$145). Anglers, take note: The owner's husband, Fido, is a well-known fishing guide with his own 28-foot boat.

US$50-100

Tides Beach Resort (tel. 501/226-2283, patojos@btl.net, singles from US$85, doubles from US$100) is a friendly, family-run guesthouse located on the beach, away from the center of town. The eight light and airy units have tile floors and private bathrooms. This is also the home of the Jumping Frijoles beachside bar and Patojo's Scuba Center, one of the most respected outfits on the caye.

The **Coral Beach Hotel** (tel. 501/266-2013, www.coralbeachhotel.com, US$57 with fan, US$12 more for a/c) offers 19 clean, small rooms, each with private bath, hot and cold water, and air-conditioning or fan. There's a nice veranda overlooking the action on Front Street. Meal plans are available.

Lily's Hotel and Restaurant (tel. 501/206-2059, www.ambergriscaye.com/lilys, doubles US$65-75) has 10 good value rooms with private bath, air-conditioning, and very nice verandas on the beach. This simple hotel is run by Felipe Paz and family—friendly longtime residents of San Pedro. Lily's is located on the main reef-facing beach strip, near the dock where the *Triple J Shania* is tied up. Lily's has been known for years for offering excellent local food in plentiful family-style servings and offers complimentary coffee every morning.

The beachfront **Conch Shell Inn** (tel. 501/226-2062, belizeanmark@hotmail.com, US$49-99) is in the heart of San Pedro, beside Sunbreeze Suites. It was the third hotel to open in the early days of tourism. Renovated in 2008, the five upstairs single and double rooms have great views, and the cheaper downstairs rooms are steps from the sea. British owners Dr. Mark and wife Joan are well known for providing the free "Smiles" dental clinics to islanders.

Popular with birders and nature lovers, **Caribbean Villas** (tel. 501/226-2715, U.S. tel. 866/522-9960, www.caribbeanvillashotel.

com, from US$78) serves up "barefoot luxury" from its spot on the beach just south of town, offering a range of economy rooms and luxury suites (starting at US$180; a room for US$270 sleeps six). The property's small bird sanctuary is one of the few remaining areas of original littoral forest on the island. Water heating is supplemented by rooftop solar panels; irrigation is from rainwater catchment tanks. In addition, the rooms are designed to catch the cooling trade winds to reduce the need for air-conditioning. Another quaint and homey option south of town is **Changes in Latitudes Bed and Breakfast** (tel. 501/226-2986, U.S. tel. 800/631-9834, www.ambergriscaye.com/latitudes, US$95), with six cozy rooms with air-conditioning, ceiling fan, private bath, and pool privileges at Exotic Caye Beach Resort. They're serious about the breakfast, which is served daily in the common room.

US$100-150

The cheerful **San Pedro Holiday Hotel** (tel. 501/226-2014 or 226-2103, www.sanpedroholiday.com, from US$110 plus tax), the island's first hotel (still under the original family's management), keeps getting better. The 17 clean, spacious rooms have air-conditioning and fans, private baths, and beachfront verandas. Lots of water sports and boats are available.

Inside an elegant three-story building of tropical colonial design, on the corner of Sandpiper Street and the ocean, are the 14 suites comprising the ❿ **Blue Tang Inn** (tel. 501/226-2326, U.S. tel. 800/337-8203, www.bluetanginn.com, US$120-225). The tasteful rooms sport lots of warm, rich wood paneling and have kitchens, private baths, ceiling fans, and air-conditioning; third-floor rooms have whirlpool tubs. The grounds are well kept and the rooftop balcony is breezy and pleasant.

One of the island's biggest resorts, **Banana Beach Resort** (tel. 501/226-3890, www.bananabeach.com, from US$125) has a huge range of options among its 66 units, from smallish standard hotel rooms to deluxe four-bedroom suites. There's a pool, gift shop, bar, and steakhouse on site, and lots of packages are available.

© JOSHUA BERMAN

Mata Rocks Resort

Mata Rocks Resort (tel. 501/226-2336, U.S. tel. 888/628-2757, www.matarocks.com, US$135–180) has six beautifully designed suites and 11 rooms with wonderful ocean views around a pool; the design is pleasing and intimate, and the rooms, while not huge, have plenty of basic amenities, such as air-conditioning, cable, wireless Internet, bikes, transfers, and continental breakfast.

US$150-200

The ◖ **SunBreeze Beach Hotel** (tel. 501/226-2191, U.S. 800/688-0191, www. sunbreeze.net, from US$147 plus tax and service, deluxe rooms US$160) is a full-service oceanfront hotel with 42 rooms built around an open sand area and pool. Rooms have two queen beds, air-conditioning, tile floors, local artwork, private baths, and direct-dial phones; Front Street starts next door, and the entrance is yards from the airstrip. There's an on-site dive shop, a top-notch restaurant, and many other services. Located at the other end of Front Street, on the beach across from the Belize Bank, **SunBreeze Suites** (tel. 501/226-4675,

www.sunbreezesuites.com, US$150–200) are one-bedroom suites with full kitchens, guest queen sofa beds, and air-conditioning, and they can sleep up to four adults per room; families and children are welcome. They feel more like small condos than hotel rooms.

Occupy your own pleasure dome at **Xanadu Island Resort** (tel. 501/226-2814, www.xanaduresort-belize.com, from US$170). The resort features monolithic domes built to withstand winds of 300 miles per hour, with thatched overlay roofs nestled among natural lush landscaping. There is a beachfront pool, as well as a private nature walk and bird sanctuary. Nineteen suites are available with fully equipped kitchens, and there is a choice of studios and one-, two-, and three-bedrooms.

A full-service resort, **Ramon's Village** (tel. 501/226-2071, U.S. tel. 800/624-4215, www. ramons.com) has standard rooms from US$175 and a presidential suite for US$400; rooms are nice, but "kitchenettes" are not much more than a sink and microwave. The property's 500-foot beach is not far south of San Pedro Town; there is a decent restaurant and bar and a pool, as well as on-site dive shops, guides, and an inland tour operator. You can rent sailboards, aquacycles, speedboats, bicycles, and golf carts. Many packages are available.

Over US$200

SOUTH OF SAN PEDRO TOWN

Still one of the island's class acts, **((Victoria House** (tel. 501/226-2067, U.S. tel. 800/247-5159, www.victoria-house.com) has a luxurious selection of suites, from US$175 to US$1,650 a night for the largest of the multifamily mansion-like villas. Expect grand, colonial elegance on a well-manicured, tranquil piece of property about two miles south of town. The stucco and thatched casitas with tile floors are placed around several sleek infinity pools; you also get a full-service dive shop with private guides, the Admiral Nelson Bar, and one of the top-rated restaurants in the country.

Rent a plush villa at **Banyan Bay** (tel. 501/226-3739, U.S. tel. 866/466-2179, www.banyanbay.com, from US$300); this "luxury family resort" offers all the amenities in 70 suites, including a whirlpool tub in every room. Lots of activities and lessons for children are available; full dive/inland trips can be arranged. There's also a great on-site dock restaurant, Rico's.

NORTH OF SAN PEDRO TOWN

Amid the massive condominium construction projects north of the split, you'll find some of Belize's most well-respected, well-run, and well-known properties, all only a few hundred yards from Belize's famous barrier reef. **El Pescador** (tel. 501/226-2975, U.S. tel. 800/242-2017, www.elpescador.com, from US$200) was constructed in 1974 as one of the world's premier sportfishing lodges, and it has evolved into a modern resort for sportsmen and their families. Less than three miles north of San Pedro, the resort has 14 rooms in its colonial-style mahogany lodge and private one-, two-, and three-bedroom villa accommodations around stunning swimming pools and palms. Right next door, **Capricorn Resort** (tel. 501/226-2809, www.capricornresort.net, US$200) offers intimate

beachfront seclusion in one of three cabanas. Each cabana is decorated in tropical colors and has high Belizean wood ceilings, a private bathroom with showers made for two, and a balcony with hammock. Rates include a continental breakfast, bikes, and kayaks. Capricorn's restaurant is excellent.

A little more than four miles north of town, **Mata Chica Beach Resort** (tel. 501/220-5010, www.matachica.com, from US$256) has a dozen spacious casitas, suites, and luxury villas, exquisitely styled with local art and Oriental-tinged decor. It offers a full range of amenities, a spa, and a swanky lounge and the famous Mambo restaurant. The resort also specializes in "grand or intimate weddings, honeymoons, and secluded getaways." Rent the six-person beach mansion for a cool US$1,015 a night, plus taxes.

Or why not reserve one of two 3,000-square-foot villas at **Azul Belize** (tel. 501/226-4012, 501/226-4013, or 501/610-3555, www.azul-belize.com, US$1,995) and watch the horizon from your private rooftop Jacuzzi with one of Azul's famous frozen mojitos in hand. Your enormous three-floor crib boasts a full kitchen, exposed ladywood beams, wraparound balconies, plasma-screen TV, wireless Internet, and your own laptop and cell phone, should you wish to stay connected. Or unplug at the infinity pool or adjoining Rojo Lounge, where former punk record producer Jeff Spiegel prepares some of the island's best cuisine in his newfound incarnation as a world-class chef.

Guests at **Portofino** (tel. 501/220-5096, www.portofinobelize.com, from US$250) will find four duplex beachside units, two treetop suites, and a honeymoon/VIP villa with full amenities. Highly rated Le Bistro restaurant and bar is on site, and all kinds of activities featuring the nearby reef and mainland tours are available.

Tranquility Bay Resort (U.S. tel. 800/843-2293, www.tranquilitybayresort.com, from US$240) is nestled in the Bacalar Chico Marine Reserve, where the reef curves close to the shore, a relaxed 20-minute boat ride north from San Pedro. There are seven two-bedroom cabanas and four one-bedrooms, with lofts. Bedrooms are air-conditioned and each cabana is equipped with refrigerator and microwave. The resort offers Belizean hardwoods, Mexican tiles, and a white sandy beach at your doorstep, as well as spectacular ocean views from every cabana, free use of kayaks, and an on-site water-sports team ready to assist with fishing, snorkeling, scuba, or sailing trips. The Tackle Box Sea Bar hangs over the water and has been built in the colors and style of the San Pedro original.

FOOD
Bakeries and Cafés
Tabu (7 A.M.–3 P.M., closed Sun.) is a nice café offering specialty coffees, smoothies, breakfast, salads, sandwiches, and cakes. All wraps are US$7 and the most popular are the Thai wrap (grilled chicken and Thai peanut sauce) and the Tuscan (grilled chicken or vegetables with sun-dried tomato pesto and mozzarella). Tabu is located at the entrance to the purple Vilma Linda Plaza, a peaceful oasis in the bustle of downtown—the tiled courtyard is filled with lush plants and a small fishpond.

Go to **Manelly's** on Front Street for homemade ice cream—they are most proud of their "coconut creation." Grab a pastry or stuffed croissant at **La Popular Bakery,** in a big building near the cut, and also a small shop in the middle of town, around the corner from the post office.

Barbecue
Besides the informal street barbecues (which offer the best value food around), a rotating schedule ensures a beach barbecue nearly every night of the week, starting with **BC's** on the beach, 11 A.M.–3 P.M. Sunday. Your choice of chicken, ribs, or fish runs US$5–10. Also on Sunday, **Crazy Canuck's** throws in live music and a horseshoe tournament. The **Holiday Hotel** has live music to accompany its beach barbecue on Wednesday night; the **Lions Club** donates the money it makes from its Friday and Saturday night barbecues to those who need medical help and can't afford it; and **Ramon's** has Tuesday and Friday barbecues.

The island's only falafel joint, **Alibaba's** (across Coconut Dr. from the airport and Moncho's Golf Carts, tel. 501/226-4042), is best known for its takeout rotisserie chicken, served Lebanese style with hummus and tabouli.

Pizza
Pizza is available for delivery or dine-in at a number of places, and there is constant debate as to who's got the best 'za on the island. **Pepperoni's Pizza** (tel. 501/226-4515, 5 P.M.–10 P.M., closed Mon.) is popular for both quality and price—a large 16-inch specialty pie goes for US$20 and is served deep-dish style. **Papa Pedro's Pizzeria and Bistro** (at Pedro's Inn, tel. 501/226-3825) has a real Italian thin crust pie that is quickly making a name for itself (and also serves subs, salads, steaks, and seafood). Just north of the airstrip, **Pasta La Vista** (formerly Pauly's, tel. 501/226-2651, open 11 A.M.–10 P.M.) serves slices, whole pizzas (US$24 for a large cheese), and authentic Italian dishes, including an insanely popular lasagna. Northsiders can try **Pirate's Pizza** (behind Belizean Shores Resort, tel. 501/226-4663).

Belizean and Mexican
On the back side of the island, you'll find a plethora of fast-food and local eateries offering the cheapest burritos, rice and beans, and stew chicken dishes on the island.

Don Manuel's **Tropical Takeout,** across the street from the airport, has renowned homemade salsa, which is made fresh daily and invariably runs out around noon; supertasty *huevos rancheros* and other treats are offered—you know you're getting good value when all the cabbies hang out here. For inexpensive Mexican and seafood, try the **Reef Restaurant** on Pescador Drive.

A local favorite for all-day breakfast is **◖ Estel's** (located on the beach behind Atlantic Bank, 6 A.M.–5 P.M., closed Tuesday); the people are relaxed and the breakfast burrito (US$7) is delicious.

Ruby's has pastries and coffee early in the morning. Other reputable spots are **Ambergris**

Delights and **Celi's Deli,** near Ruby's. **Mickey's Place** on Tarpon Street is home of the huge Wednesday special burrito for US$6; Mickey's has an ample menu of local fare as well and offers a bit more ambience than the other Belizean places.

▐ **El Fogón** (basic meals for US$4–6) offers home-cooked Creole dishes in a very mellow outdoor atmosphere. Tucked toward the back side toward the back side of the island, just north of the airstrip, it won't let you down. A walk or ride to **Beach'n Kitchen** (past the toll bridge on the island's north side, next to the Palapa Bar dock, tel. 501/226-4456, 7 A.M.–3:30 P.M.) is well worth the trip. This cheery breakfast and lunch joint has Mexican, Belizean, and American food, all delectable and reasonably priced.

For Latin Caribbean cuisine, ▐ **Wild Mango's** (sandwiched between Ruby's Hotel and the library on the beach, noon–9 P.M.) features 140 items prepared by one of Belize's most distinguished chefs; you cannot go wrong here, from "Mango's Mongo Burrito" to various ceviches, *pabil,* or seafood specials. The cozy reggae-fueled kitchen of the **JamBel Jerk Pit** offers Jamaican dishes like coconut curry and jerk chicken dishes from US$8, or step up to the "Jamaican Me Crazy" sweet-and-sour shrimp (US$15). Open for lunch and dinner, it's located under the Coral Beach Hotel.

Caliente has waterfront Mexican and seafood. Open 11 A.M.–9:30 P.M. (but closed Mon.), it's famous for the lime soup at lunch and generous lobster dinners (US$22); other entrées start at US$12.

Celi's Restaurant, at Holiday Hotel, delivers icy piña coladas and some of the best conch ceviche on the island, plus a full menu, of course. It's been locally owned for many years.

Fine Island Cuisine

San Pedro is blessed with an ever-evolving selection of trendy restaurants offering international fare and flair; if you don't pay for such indulgence with an expanded waistline, you'll surely pay for it in cash. If you're *really* dining out—appetizer, a couple of drinks, entrée, and dessert—expect to pay as much as you would in New York City, from US$40–80 per person, more if you like your wine. Reservations are recommended at all of the following restaurants, especially in the high season. Each of the restaurants listed serves phenomenal food and is deserving of Top Pick status.

Some of the best dining ambience on the island is found at **Elvi's Kitchen** (on the corner of Middle St. and Ambergris St., tel. 501/226-2176, closed Sun., entrées US$10–40), open since 1974. The seafood specials, such as Maya fish, are especially good, and the frozen key lime pie is famous. There's live music on Thursday and a Maya buffet Friday (US$25 pp).

Of the finer restaurants, **Blue Water Grill** (on the beach behind the SunBreeze Hotel, tel. 501/226-3347) is known to offer some of the best values and biggest portions. The chef brings his experience in Hawaii and Southeast Asia to your table and prides himself on an awesome presentation; try the gourmet pizzas or Japanese spiced grouper with sizzling sesame vinaigrette. Sushi is offered on Tuesday and Thursday (entrées from US$19). **El Divino,** at Banana Beach Hotel, is a reputable steakhouse (entrées US$20–33, open for three meals), and **Rico's,** on the water behind Banyan Bay, is also highly rated.

Casa Picasso (tel. 501/226-4507 or 610-4056, from 5:30 P.M. Mon.–Sat.) fills a unique niche, with its tapas, pastas, desserts, and good tunes. You'll have to seek this place out, located out of the way near the south end of the airstrip, but you'll be glad you did—there are veggie options, fresh bread, and a huge drink and martini menu (tapas US$5–11 each, pasta bowls from US$10).

The chef at **Victoria House** (tel. 501/226-2067) was born in Mexico City, trained in the United States, and comes from a family of renowned chefs. His unique style is "Mayan Bistro," which combines the chili peppers of Mexico with fresh local produce, seafood, and meats. Start with crispy snapper cakes with chipotle beurre blanc, black bean, and roasted corn succotash; follow with black bean or chilapachole (corn) soup; then savor main dishes like cashew-crusted grouper, char-grilled beef tenderloin, or bacon-wrapped shrimp. Save room for the Molten Chocolate—a rich dessert that is so complex to prepare it needs to be ordered 20 minutes in advance.

A common Ambergris evening involves taking the water ferry to one of the posh restaurants on the island's north side. **Capricorn** (tel. 501/226-2809), three miles north of San Pedro, offers an intimate, beachfront dining experience. Reservations are a must; your table is yours for the night. Feast on fish, Italian or French cuisine, and daily specials like stuffed grouper, crab cakes, and seafood crepes. Capricorn's fisherman goes out each morning to catch that day's entrées. Save room for desserts such as creamy rum chocolate cake.

The **Rendezvous Restaurant** (tel. 501/226-3426) holds a stellar reputation for its blend of Thai and French cuisine. Start with escargot with lemon-garlic butter sauce for an appetizer (US$10); then have grilled shrimp (US$22) or chicken with coconut red-curry sauce (US$15). Rendezvous serves lunch and dinner; you'll need to take a water taxi here.

Up the coast a couple more miles, **Mambo's,** at the Mata Chica Resort, is pure indulgence, serving rich and artful heaps of seafood paella, glazed shrimp, lobster, and calamari (or a blue cheese–encrusted filet mignon); save room for the to-die-for chocolate mousse.

Rojo Lounge (at Azul Belize, tel. 501/226-4012 or 501/226-4013, entrées from US$27), has a succulently sophisticated menu that will leave you grasping for adjectives. Or maybe you'll just reach for your cocktail in stunned silence after each bite of cashew-crusted lobster, shrimp-stuffed grouper, or conch pizza; it's spendy but worth every savory cent. The self-made chef, Jeff Spiegel, is a former punk record producer from California.

Supermarkets and Specialty Foods

There are plentiful medium-sized supermarkets located throughout San Pedro Town; the cheapest is **Super Buy** on Back Street. The best selection is at **Island Supermarket** (on Coconut Dr., delivery tel. 501/226-2972).

The Greenhouse (tel. 501/226-2084) on Front Street is "the coolest place for the freshest produce." They have imported and local fruits, vegetables, seafood, meats, and tofu and soy products. **D & L Produce** is another option on Back Street.

Wine de Vine (tel. 501/226-3430, www.winedevine.com) has the finest selection of imported wines in all of Belize and a worldwide selection of cheeses and meats. They offer free wine tastings and also sell by the glass. The new location is on Coconut Drive before Island Supermarket. **Pinguino Wine Company** (tel. 501/226-2930, www.pinguinobelize.com) sells Napa Valley wine on their private Pinguino label, as well as gourmet olives and olive oil. **Premium Wines** (tel. 501/226-3700) on Front Street has a selection from seven countries and offers wholesale pricing: buy 12 bottles and get a 17 percent discount. Prices range from a US$12.50 California wine to US$130 for a French white table wine.

Kakow Chocolates (tel. 501/226-2327 or 600-9619, www.kakowchocolates.com) makes small batches of chocolate to order; the beans are grown organically on small family farms in southern Belize and the sugar comes from the north of the country. *Kakow* ("cacao" in Spanish) is the Maya word for the tree and fruit from which chocolate is produced. The chocolate is available at Wine de Vine, or visit the home production center.

For local breakfast items or gifts, pick up a bag of **Caye Coffee** (tel. 501/226-3568, www.cayecoffee.bz) or order some links at **The Sausage Factory** (tel. 501/226-2655).

INFORMATION

Things change quickly in San Pedro, especially prices. Before your trip, always take a good look at **www.ambergriscaye.com,** by far the best portal for all things Ambergris, including a lively message board filled with opinionated characters. You'll find links to hundreds of island businesses, as well as Ambergris's two weekly papers, the *San Pedro Sun* (tel.

SAN PEDRO HUMANE SOCIETY: A HEARTENING SAGA

Until recently, Belize's government-sanctioned animal control measures consisted of strychnine-laced meat tossed onto the streets at night. The **Saga Humane Society** was founded in March 1999, partly in response to this practice and to improve the poor conditions of Belize's stray animal scene. Saga Humane Society's mission is "preventing cruelty and promoting kindness to all animals, achieved through humane education, subsidized spay and neuter programs, and low cost veterinary services."

Saga started out in a little building across from Ramon's Resort, with a fenced-in yard that served as the only animal shelter in all of Belize. After much work and dedication, a proper shelter was built on land purchased by the Humane Society, and it was called "Fort Dog." Fort Dog houses lost, unwanted, and homeless animals who receive treatment and care until they are found adoptive families. The Humane Society headquarters on Sea Star Street houses the Saga cattery, where there are always plenty of kittens and cats looking for homes.

Fort Dog received a much-needed facelift in 2007 – including puppy and isolation areas and new storage and sanitation facilities. Saga can always use a helping hand and appreciates the generosity of visitors. It is a nonprofit organization funded solely by donations from the public and visitors to the island. Saga maintains an ongoing wish list of needed items for the clinic, so please check in before your trip and see what you can bring down: http://sagahumanesociety.org.

Not all Belizean dogs are as well cared for as this one.

© JOSHUA BERMAN

THE NORTHERN CAYES

501/226-2070, www.sanpedrosun.net) and *Ambergris Today* (tel. 501/226-3462), both important resources themselves.

Once you arrive, you'll want one of several free handy pocket guides to the island, packed with updated schedules, maps, and local ads. Another source of information is the **Ambergris Caye Chamber of Commerce** (tel. 501/226-3245, acchamber@hotmail.com).

SERVICES

The **post office** is on the corner of Front and Buccaneer Streets, open 8 A.M.–4 P.M. Monday–Thursday, 8 A.M.–3:30 P.M. on Fridays. It's fun to choose from Belize's beautiful, artistic, and often very large postage stamps; they make great gifts and are perfect for framing or for the traditional stamp collector.

Nellie's Laundromat (on Pescador Dr., tel. 501/226-2454, 7 A.M.–5 P.M. daily, US$1/lb) is a superb value and offers free pickup and delivery in town. A few blocks north, **Candice's** (tel. 501/226-2052) offers similar services.

Travel & Tour Belize (just north of the airstrip, tel. 501/226-2137 or 226-2031, www.traveltourbelize.com, 8 A.M.–5 P.M. Mon.–Fri., plus Sat. morning) is the oldest and only full-service travel agent in San Pedro; they'll handle all your bookings, both local and international, and can help with weddings and events too.

Money

There are four banks in town, though only the two most central (Atlantic and First Caribbean) have international ATMs. There's also an ATM in the big supermarket just south of Ramon's Village. If the banks are closed, change money at the **Casa de Cambio,** where you'll get the same rates for travelers checks (near Town Hall, 8 A.M.–5 P.M. Mon.–Sat.). **Milo's Money Exchange** is another option (on Middle St., tel. 501/226-2196). It exchanges Belizean, U.S., Guatemalan, Mexican, Canadian, and British currencies (and is also a Western Union branch).

Medical

Prescriptions and other medicines can be found at **R&L Pharmacy** (tel. 501/226-2890, open daily) by the airstrip. If you need medical attention, there's **Dr. L. Rodriguez Medical Services** (tel. 501/226-3197) and the **San Carlos Medical Center** (tel. 501/226-2918).

Internet Access

Many resorts and hotels have free computers and wireless Internet for guests; ask before checking in. As for cyber cafés, the huge differences in hourly Internet rates in San Pedro are baffling, making one expect competition to eventually even prices out across the board. In the meantime, **Caribbean Connection**, with its speedy DSL line, WiFi access, central location, coffee drinks, and air-conditioning, is a no-brainer, charging less than half as much as other providers (right across from the Caye Caulker Water Taxi Terminal, tel. 501/226-4664, www.sanpedrointernet.com, daily 7 A.M.–10 P.M., US$4/hour). Right across from the airport, **WiFi Island @ The Lime** (8 A.M.–8 P.M., US$10/hour) has counter space and a few laptops, plus a full bar, restaurant, and art gallery.

Island Internet (on the road south of town, daily 8 A.M.–10 P.M., though hours may vary, US$10/hour) has another strange drink/Internet pricing scheme: surf Island's speedy machines (DSL with satellite backup), and receive a complimentary beer, rum drink, espresso, or other beverage for every 20 minutes you're logged on—you do the math.

GETTING THERE
By Air

The 2,600-foot-long runway is located practically in downtown San Pedro (although there's been talk for years of moving the strip to a 550-acre spot south of town). Belize's two airlines (Maya Island Air and Tropic Air) fly a dozen daily flights between San Pedro, Caye Caulker, and Belize City—and another five to and from Corozal. Tropic Air has a computerized system and offers more reliable service. Maya Island Air sometimes gives 50 percent discounts on cash purchases; be sure to ask if a discount is available. The flight from Belize City's international airport to San Pedro takes about 15

DRIVE YOUR OWN GOLF CART

If you like to do your own driving, rent one of the hundreds of golf carts used on Ambergris Caye. They used to be all electric, but now most companies have gas-powered carts. It'll set you back as much as renting an automobile on the mainland, but if you're staying south of town and have multiple passengers (for example, a family), it's probably worth it. Expect to pay more than US$75 for 24 hours, and at least US$250 for a week.

You won't have trouble finding a cart, but if you're coming in the high season, you may wish to reserve a cart in advance. Most companies will deliver to your hotel. Or pick up a ride from **Moncho's** when you step off the plane; they're closest to the airstrip and boast one of the island's finest fleets (tel. 501/226-3262, www.monchosrentals.com). There's also **Cholo's** (on Jewfish St. in town, tel. 501/226-2406, www.choloscarts.com), **Island Adventures Golf Cart Rentals** (tel. 501/226-4343, islandadventure@btl.net), and one of the more reliable, newer companies, **Carts Belize** (tel. 501/226-4090, www.xanaduresort-belize.com).

When driving your cart, carry a valid driver's license and follow all normal traffic laws, in-

cruising San Pedro's Front Street in style

cluding one-way street rules! Be sure to pay attention to the map you are given. As the old *Green Guide* advised: "Don't count on the golf carts around you to have brakes. They're designed for lush fairways with a few sprinklers, not for high tides and potholes. When driving, please don't run over the children, or splash pedestrians, and note all the one-way streets on the town map."

Front Street closes to all but pedestrian traffic on Friday, Saturday, and Sunday evenings. Make sure you park on the correct side of the street (it alternates every few weeks; just do what the locals are doing).

---

minutes and costs US$120 round-trip. Flying in and out of Belize City's Municipal Airport is much cheaper.

By Boat

The **Caye Caulker Water Taxi Association** (tel. 501/226-2194 in San Pedro, 501/226-0992 in Caye Caulker, 501/223-5752 in Belize City, www.cayecaulkerwatertaxi.com) runs eight daily trips between Belize City and Ambergris Caye, a 75-minute ride that costs US$15 one-way, US$25 round-trip. In Belize City, the Caye Caulker Water Taxi Terminal is at the north end of the Swing Bridge, with boats leaving between 9 A.M. and 4:30 P.M. Boats depart San Pedro from Wet Willy's Pier from 7 A.M. to 3:30 P.M. Always check the schedule before making plans; usually there are extra boats on weekends and holidays.

Triple J. Express Water Taxi also offers service to Caye Caulker and Belize City, with four daily boats between 8 A.M. and 3 P.M. **Thunderbolt Travels** (tel. 501/226-2904 or 614-9074, thunderbolttravels@yahoo.com) runs two daily trips to Corozal (7 A.M. and 3 P.M., US$22.50 one-way, same schedule from Corozal).

No regularly scheduled trips are available between cayes other than Ambergris and Caye Caulker, but ask if you want to stop at St. George's Caye or Caye Chapel.

GETTING AROUND

Walking is feasible within the town of San Pedro itself; it's about a 20-minute stroll from the airstrip to the split. Once you start traveling between resorts to the south or north, however, you may wish to go by bike, golf cart, taxi, or boat. At one time, cars were a rarity, but together with golf carts they are taking over the town streets. Most of the electric golf carts have been replaced by gas-powered ones and hundreds ply San Pedro's rutted roads. New cobbled streets mean less dust and fewer potholes downtown.

By Taxi

Minivan taxis (green license plates) run north and south along the island at most hours; just wave one down and climb in. Expect to pay about US$6–7 to travel between town and points south. Within town, you'll pay around US$4. There are several drivers that you (or your accommodation's front desk) can call, as well, including **Island Taxi** (tel. 501/226-3125) and **Jesus Wiltshire** (tel. 501/614-8732). Taxis cannot take you anywhere north of the split.

By Bicycle

Many resorts have free bicycles for their guests, and others have them for rent, as do a handful of outside shops. Rentals are available by the hour

(about US$5), day (US$7.50), and week (US$25). **Joe's Bikes** (tel. 501/226-4371) has more than sixty bikes for rent, including kids' sizes.

By Boat

Usually the smoothest and quickest way to travel up and down the island, water taxis are available from the **Island Ferry** dock at Fido's Courtyard (tel. 501/226-3231 or 610-3411). Boats leave for points north on every two hours, from 7 A.M.–9 P.M., with special late-night schedules on big party nights (Wed.–Sat.). They return southward on even hours. The price depends on how far you are going but is roughly US$7–10 each way. Most restaurants will radio the ferry to arrange your ride back to San Pedro Town.

Crossing the Bridge

The new toll bridge connecting San Pedro Town with Ambergris's north side is free for pedestrians; between 6 A.M. and 10 P.M., bicycles pay a buck to cross and golf carts US$5 round-trip.

Caye Caulker

About 1,200 or so native Hicaqueños (hee-kaw-KEN-yos; or "Caulker Islanders") reside on this island 21 miles northeast of Belize City, just south of Ambergris Caye and less than a mile west of the reef. The island is four miles long from north to south. The developed and inhabited part is only a mile long, from the split to the airstrip.

Yes, there have been many changes and much development on the island as it has figured out its place in Belize's evolving tourism economy, but Caye Caulker remains less expensive than San Pedro and as *tranquilo* and friendly as everybody says.

HISTORY

Most historians agree that Caye Caulker was not permanently inhabited during the time of the pirates, but they did stop here—an anchor

dating from the 19th century was found in the channel on the southern end of the island, and a wreck equally old was discovered off the southern end of Caye Chapel. The island was known to be visited by Mexican fishermen during those centuries—for generations they handed down stories of putting ashore at Caye Caulker for fresh water from a "big hole" on the caye.

The island was uninhabited as late as the 1830s. It wasn't until the outbreak of the Yucatán Caste War in 1848, when refugees fled Mexico by the thousands, that people permanently settled on Ambergris Caye, a few finding their way south to Caye Caulker. Many of today's Hicaqueños can trace their family histories back to the Caste War and even know from which region in Mexico their ancestors originated.

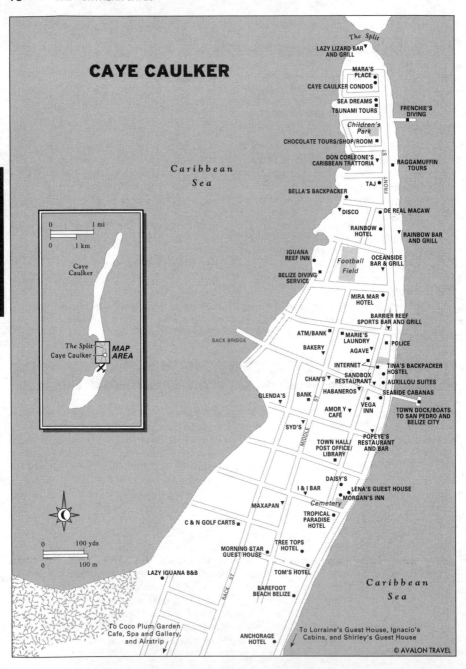

CAYE CAULKER

The Split

LAZY LIZARD BAR AND GRILL

MARA'S PLACE
CAYE CAULKER CONDOS

SEA DREAMS
TSUNAMI TOURS

FRENCHIE'S DIVING

Children's Park

CHOCOLATE TOURS/SHOP/ROOM

DON CORLEONE'S CARIBBEAN TRATTORIA
RAGGAMUFFIN TOURS

Caribbean Sea

TAJ

BELLA'S BACKPACKER

DISCO
DE REAL MACAW

RAINBOW HOTEL
RAINBOW BAR AND GRILL

IGUANA REEF INN
Football Field
OCEANSIDE BAR & GRILL

BELIZE DIVING SERVICE

MIRA MAR HOTEL

BARRIER REEF SPORTS BAR AND GRILL

ATM/BANK
MARIE'S LAUNDRY
POLICE

BACK BRIDGE
BAKERY
AGAVE

INTERNET
TINA'S BACKPACKER HOSTEL

SANDBOX RESTAURANT
CHAN'S
AUXILLOU SUITES

HABANEROS
SEASIDE CABANAS

GLENDA'S
BANK

AMOR Y CAFÉ
VEGA INN
TOWN DOCK/BOATS TO SAN PEDRO AND BELIZE CITY

SYD'S

POPEYE'S RESTAURANT AND BAR

TOWN HALL/POST OFFICE/LIBRARY

DAISY'S

I & I BAR
LENA'S GUEST HOUSE
MORGAN'S INN

MAXAPAN
Cemetery

C & N GOLF CARTS

TROPICAL PARADISE HOTEL

TREE TOPS HOTEL

MORNING STAR GUEST HOUSE

TOM'S HOTEL

LAZY IGUANA B&B

BAREFOOT BEACH BELIZE

Caribbean Sea

To Coco Plum Garden Cafe, Spa and Gallery, and Airstrip

ANCHORAGE HOTEL

To Lorraine's Guest House, Ignacio's Cabins, and Shirley's Guest House

© AVALON TRAVEL

0   1 mi
0   1 km

Caye Caulker

The Split
Caye Caulker
MAP AREA

0   100 yds
0   100 m

FRONT ST

BACK ST

THE NORTHERN CAYES

© JOSHUA BERMAN

Caye Caulker is smaller and slower than nearby San Pedro.

Exact dates of settlement on Caye Caulker are uncertain. The Reyes family tells of their great-grandfather, Luciano, who arrived in Mexico from Spain and worked as a logwood cutter along the coast. He fled with the rest and, after settling in San Pedro, eventually purchased Caye Caulker for BZE$300. Over the years, land was sold to various people; many descendants of the original landholders are still prominent families on Caye Caulker.

Early Economy

The town developed into a fishing village and *cocales* (coconut plantations) were established from one end of the caye to the other. Though no written records have been found, it is believed the original trees were planted in the 1880s and 1890s, at about the same time as those planted on Ambergris Caye. It took a lot of capital to plant a *cocal* and involved a great deal of time-consuming, laborious work. Reyes was one of the original planters. His workers would begin at the northern end of the island and stack the coconuts all along the shore, where they were picked up by boats. When

the workers finished their sweep of the island, it was time to begin again—the trees produced continually.

Slavery was never a part of the Caulker economy, which prevented the development of the plantation hierarchy based on race and class common in other parts of the Caribbean. Laborers earned a small cash wage, enabling them to use their incomes to buy the necessities to supplement their subsistence fishing. The people were very poor. Some of the older folks remember their grandparents and great-grandparents working long days and making only pennies.

Maybe because of the economic conditions, the families on the caye began helping each other early on. When one man got a large catch, his family and neighbors helped him with it and, in turn, always went home with some. When one man's fruit trees were bearing, he would share the fruit, knowing that he would benefit later. This created very strong ties, especially between families and extended families.

Independent fishermen liked being their own bosses. As a result, to this day Hicaqueños

WHERE THE STREETS HAVE TWO NAMES

In 2004, the growing village of Caye Caulker decided to name the island's tiny handful of streets after plants, animals, and historical events. Avenida Mangle (Mangrove Avenue), Crocodile Street, Luciana Reyes Street (named for an early settler of Caye Caulker), and Hattie Street (named after the 1961 hurricane that created the split) were among the names chosen. Old Front Street is now Hicaco Avenue (for the cocoplum fruit) and Middle Street is Avenida Langosta, honoring the role of lobster in the island's economic development.

Don't expect to hear too many of the new names in casual conversation though – people still commonly refer to Front, Middle, and Back Streets (or Way Back Street and "Back-a-bush," if you make it farther from town). There are no house numbers on Caye Caulker, so mail is addressed "General Post," and to receive parcels, residents look for their names scrawled on a poster outside the post office door.

(Contributed by Joni Miller, a resident of Caye Caulker who co-founded the first high school on the island, Caye Caulker Ocean Academy. She currently serves as both teacher and vice principal of the school.)

consider themselves independent thinkers. They take pride in their early roots on the island. Today, longtime fishing and lobstering families on Caulker continue to earn a living on the sea, whether by fishing, providing tourist services and tours, or a little of both.

The Future

Three words: fresh water supply. As the number of accommodations grows to serve the increasingly discerning stream of visitors, Caye Caulker's thin lens of groundwater (plus whatever rainwater gets collected) will be stretched ever thinner. At press time the streets were being dug up to lay pipes for a new water treatment system.

Several years ago, there was controversy when the old sewage treatment plant and the airport resulted in the destruction of seventeen acres of crocodile and bird-nesting land.

As for landownership, Caye Caulker islanders don't want to "lose" their island as they believe the San Pedranos have lost theirs on Ambergris Caye. But as more foreign-owned hotels and condos in the US$100-and-up category get built, we'll see what happens. (Caye Caulker's hotels are only 16 percent foreign owned, compared to more than 40 percent on Ambergris.) Some claim that everything south of the main dock remains "old Caye Caulker"

(that is, clapboard houses and little activity), while "new Caye Caulker" continues to overtake the north end, driving up prices and drawing more visitors.

ORIENTATION

Caye Caulker is cut into two pieces. The "split" or "cut" separates the southern inhabited part of the island from the northern mangrove swamps. This feature earned its name after Hurricane Hattie widened the channel in 1961. Travelers and locals come to the split to swim, snorkel, and sunbathe on the concrete blocks (there is no beach).

Moving south from the split on **Front Street,** the street that skirts the eastern shore (there are two more north-south streets: Middle and Back), you'll find seven sandy roads that cross three blocks to the other side of the island and Back Street.

On the western pier, there's a fuel pump. Sailors exploring nearby cayes anchor in the shallow protected waters offshore; the body of water here is open ocean but is still often referred to as a "lagoon."

Front Street's south terminus dead-ends by the **cemetery,** and you have two choices: follow the narrow beach path along the water, or turn right and then left, and you'll find another dusty avenue that leads to the airstrip.

Bordering the airstrip is a rapidly developing neighborhood called Bahia Puesta del Sol, which has a grocery store, a fruit stand, and a new high school. The land north of the split consists mostly of mangrove swamps, with a narrow strip of land along the east coast; this hasn't stopped people from building off-the-grid homes, though.

SPORTS AND RECREATION
Diving

The reef you see from Caulker's eastern shore provides fantastic diving right in your front yard. The most popular sites are Hol Chan Marine Park, Caye Chapel Canyons, and the reefs around St. George's Caye, Long Caye Wall, and Sergeant's Caye. Many visitors are willing to brave four hours (two each way) on a boat in mostly open ocean to dive the Blue Hole and Turneffe Island sites. There is no "best" dive site, as every diver is looking for something different—just be sure to discuss the options before booking the trip (and make sure you're comfortable with the boat, guides, and gear).

Caye Caulker's three dive shops offer similarly priced tours: Hol Chan (US$80 for two tanks); Blue Hole, Half Moon, and Lighthouse (US$190 for three tanks); Turneffe day trips (US$115 North and US$150 South); certification courses (US$300 for Open Water and Advanced, US$100 for a Discover Scuba single-tank dive); as well as a variety of snorkeling excursions and other trips.

Frenchie's (tel. 501/226-0234, frenchies@btl.net, www.frenchiesdivingbelize.com) has a rock-solid reputation for quality service and is owned by a native islander who has been diving these waters since he was a child. **Belize Diving Services** (located behind the soccer field, tel. 501/226-0143, www.belizedivingservice.com) is another excellent operation with discounts and gifts with purchase of multiple days of diving. **Big Fish Dive Center** (tel. 501/226-0450, www.bigfishdivebelize.com) is known for its big boats—the 45-footer is the island's only dive boat with onboard restroom and shower. It is ideal for farther destinations, such as the

© JOSHUA BERMAN

THE NORTHERN CAYES

another sunny day on the streets of Caye Caulker

Blue Hole. Albert Pacheco's **Extreme Tours** (tel. 501/226-0127) offers small private certification classes (three students with one instructor).

For US$40 **Anglers Abroad** will rent you an underwater digital camera and burn your photos onto a compact disc. **Tsunami Tours** also rents underwater cameras.

Snorkeling and Swimming

Masks and fins are available for US$5/day and can be used off almost any dock or at the island's most popular beach and snorkel spot: the split. You'll see flocks of sunbathers here on any given day, lounging like reptiles atop the various chunks of sand and cement, getting up only to splash on some more oil or order another Panty Ripper at the Lazy Lizard Bar, which provides mellow music for the scene. Be aware that swimming in the channel can be dangerous; this is a shallow and heavily trafficked area. The pull of the current can be enough to overpower children or weak swimmers. Also be aware of boat traffic, as serious accidents have occurred here. Around the bend, only a few yards out of the channel, the water is calm and safer. However, old construction materials have been dumped here for fill, so be careful where you step or dive.

Snorkel Tours

At least a dozen shops on the island rent gear and offer half-day snorkeling trips to the local reef and full-day trips to Hol Chan Marine Reserve (with snorkel stops at Shark and Sting Ray Alley and the Coral Gardens; lunch, not included, is in San Pedro). Many guides conclude their tours with a visit to the tiny Sea Horse Sanctuary behind the split. Other destinations include a number of local cayes.

The cheerful, capable guides at **⟨ Raggamuffin Tours** (tel. 501/226-0348, www.raggamuffintours.com) will take you out on *RaggaGal, RaggaQueen,* or *RaggaKing*—a trio of beautiful, Belizean-built boats designed especially to access shallow snorkeling spots. Raggamuffin regularly sails to Hol Chan (full-day trip for the same price as motorized trips and includes lunch on board) and offers sunset island cruises. The best adventure tour has to be the utterly unique overnight sailing trip south to Placencia (Tuesday and Friday departures), where you'll be dropped off to continue your travels; three days of sun and sea, and two nights camping out in style on idyllic cayes (US$300 pp includes all gear, food, snorkeling, and fishing).

If you agree that it's not right to touch wild marine animals, go with Belizean Carlos Miller, owner of **Red Mangrove** (tel. 501/226-0069, www.mangrovebelize.com), who runs eco-friendly and educational tours and specializes in trips to Turneffe, as well as local sites. **Carlos Tours** (tel. 501/226-0458 or 600-1654, carlosayala@hotmail.com) offers an uncommon level of personal attention and a focus on safety, and for this, Carlos has earned an excellent reputation. He guides with his own boat, *Gypsy,* and his office is on Front Street next to the Sand Box. A pair of local brothers run **Anwar Tours** (tel. 501/226-0327, www. anwartours.page.tl) and, with fifteen years

experience, they get good reviews for both snorkel trips and inland tours. **EZ Boy Tours** (tel. 501/226-0349, ezboytours-bze@yahoo. com) offers all the standard snorkel tours as well as overnight camping trips, and night snorkeling.

Tsunami Adventures (tel. 501/226-0462, www.tsunamiadventures.com) not only provides local snorkel excursions and a range of inland trips, but also serves as a local travel agent. The Tsunami office is located near the split, and the staff can book your dive trip.

Boating and Water Sports

For an ultra-irie time, join **Ras Creek** on his boat *Heritage Cruze,* docked at the Lazy Lizard Bar when not plying the reef with happy, reggae-crazy customers; this is one of the best ways to tour the Caye Caulker Marine Reserve (US$30). Ras Creek was the first to guide tourist to the Sea Horse Sanctuary behind the split.

Toucan Canoe and Kayaks (Stall #3 in Palapa Gardens on Front Street) has the most comprehensive canoe and kayak tours and rentals on the island ($5/hour for a single; $10/hour for a triple). Private and group lessons are offered by Canadian-Belizean owner Allie Ifield, who is a top-placing international canoe racer and licensed tour guide. All two-hour tours are US$25; ask Allie about Moonlight or Stargazing tours, Mangrove and Seahorses, and individual custom tours.

Rudolfo can teach you windsurfing and kiteboarding at **Kitexplorer,** located in Anglers Abroad's yard near the split (seasonal).

Fishing

Try to catch your dinner off one of the island's many piers. You can buy bait and rent fishing rods at the Badillo's house near the soccer field (look for a small porch sign). Or fish like a local and buy your hook, line, and weight at Chan's. Inquire at your hotel about making arrangements with a fisherman to take you on a hunt for the sweetest seafood in the Caribbean (tackle provided). Or take a walk to the back side of the island, where you'll find fishermen cleaning their fish, working on lobster traps, or mending their nets in the morning. Many will be willing to take you out for a reasonable fee. The main trophies are groupers, barracuda, snapper, and amberjack—all good eating. Small boats are available for rent by the hour.

For professional fishing tours, go to **Anglers Abroad** (tel. 501/226-0303, U.S. tel. 254/238-4149, www.anglersabroad.com) near the split. Owner Haywood Curry rents and sells a complete selection of fly and spin gear, and he is happy to give advice for the novice or expert fisherman. He offers lessons and DIY instruction by canoe or foot and sets up half-day, full-day, and overnight adventure trips. Group tours, as well as private lessons, are available. The shop works with well-known and experienced reefs and flats fishing guides, including Parnel Coc, Rafael Alamilla and Eloy Badillo.

Swallow Caye Wildlife Sanctuary

The protected area comprises nearly 9,000 acres of sea and mangrove near the Drowned Cayes, just a few miles east of Belize City. The sanctuary is co-managed by Friends of Swallow Caye and the Belize's Fisheries Department. Check out www.swallowcayemanatees.org for more information, including membership, tours, and manatee facts.

Many tour operators will take you to Swallow Caye, usually for US$60 per person, but **Chocolate's Manatee Tours** (tel. 501/226-0151, chocolateseashore@gmail.com) is the original. Chocolate is a local legend in the ecotourism trade; he was the first guide to take people on trips to Swallow Caye to see manatees, and he was instrumental in the creation of this sanctuary in July 2002. He has also earned environmental and tourism awards for providing quality trips to hundreds of tourists per season. The all-day excursion stops first in an open area where it is possible to approach manatees in their element—be careful not to disturb or harm the gentle creatures. After viewing the manatees for an hour or two,

Chocolate heads to the tiny white-sand island of Sergeant's Caye for snorkeling. If Chocolate is not going out, try other tour guides on the island—they offer similar trips.

Dorothy Beveridge of **Tropical Nature** (tel. 501/220-4079) offers educational nature walks that explore the mangrove and littoral forests. The walks start at sunrise, last about three hours, and cost US$20 per person. Biologist **Ellen McRae** (501/226-0178, sbf@btl.net) also does slide shows and nature excursions.

Fitness, Massage, and Bodywork

You'll feel like a new person after a session at Eva McFarlane's **Healing Touch Day Spa** (tel. 501/601-9731 or 226-0208, edenbelize@hotmail.com) on Front Street, upstairs from Caribbean Art Gallery. She does everything from deep tissue and Swedish massage to reiki, reflexology, aura cleansing, waxing, manicures, and facials. All treatments are US$30 for 30 minutes and US$50 for a full hour. **Coco Plum Garden Cafe, Spa & Gallery** (tel. 501/226-0226 or 622-2878, www.cocoplum.typepad.com) offers massage by Chris Roggema (US$60 for 90 minutes), tarot readings, and spa services. **Great Island Yoga** (www.greatislandyoga.com) offers classes from Christmas to Easter at a beautiful oceanfront location (Coco Plum can provide a schedule and map). Drop-in classes are US$6 and organized groups are also welcome. For those feeling more energetic, there is Louise's **step aerobics** Monday to Thursday (5–6 P.M.), upstairs from the Village Council Office. You can register or just drop in.

NIGHTLIFE

The biggest show in town is definitely the daily joining of sun and western horizon. **Lazy Lizard Bar,** at the split, has both the daytime sunbathing and sunset spot markets pretty well cornered. You can also find other, less crowded spots to watch the sunset by walking down the west side of the island and searching for an appropriate cocktail spot.

As for music and drumming, we'll see which way the tide flows as the island's "war on culture"

THE NORTHERN CAYES

WHERE THE MANATEES ROAM

THE GENTLE GIANTS OF BELIZE

Perhaps you already know that manatees are marine mammals that are warm-blooded, nurse their young with milk, breathe air, and have hair. Up close and personal, it is difficult to understand how these homely creatures could possibly be responsible for the mermaid legends of sailors' lore. But with a puppy-dog face, rotund body, flat and rounded tail, and dexterous paddle-shaped forelimbs, the elusive manatee makes up for lack of beauty with charismatic curiosity.

Commonly referred to as the "gentle giants of the sea," manatees are large and bulky – weighing 300–500 kilograms (600–1,200 pounds). Along with their Indo-Pacific cousin, the dugong *(Dugong dugon)*, manatees belong to the taxonomic order Sirenia, a group of four species that represents the only herbivorous marine mammals living today. There are three species of manatees: the Amazonian manatee *(Trichechus inunguis)*, the West African manatee *(Trichechus senegalensis)*, and the West Indian manatee *(Trichechus manatus)*. The two subspecies of the West Indian manatee are the Florida manatee *(T. m. latirostris)* and the Antillean manatee *(T. m. manatus)*.

Belize has long been considered the last stronghold for West Indian manatees in Central America and the Caribbean. West Indian manatees are found year-round in Florida, are sparsely distributed throughout Central America and the Caribbean, and occur as far south as Brazil. The Antillean subspecies (which excludes the Florida animals) are red-listed by the World Conservation Union (IUCN) as vulnerable, in continuing decline, with severely fragmented populations. The U.N. Caribbean Environmental Program considers Antillean manatees an endangered and protected species of regional concern.

With a relatively short coastline extending from the Gulf of Honduras in the south to Chetumal Bay in the north, Belize reports the greatest density of Antillean manatees in the Caribbean region, perhaps because of the extensive sea grass, mangrove, coastal, and riverine habitat within the Belize Barrier Reef Lagoon system or perhaps because manatees have been protected by local laws since the 1930s and are currently listed as endangered under the Wildlife Protection Act of 1981. But, more likely, it's because the people of Belize exhibit a strong conservation ethic and care deeply about their wildlife and other natural resources.

MANATEE CONSERVATION

The governmental agency charged with manatee issues in Belize is the Conservation Division of the Forestry Department. Belize has designated several wildlife sanctuaries and protected areas for the benefit of manatees and other marine life, including Swallow Caye Wildlife Sanctuary, Southern Lagoon Wildlife Sanctuary, Corozal Bay Wildlife Sanctuary, Bacalar Chico National Park and Marine Reserve, South Water Caye Marine Reserve, Burden Canal (part of the Belize River system), and Port Honduras Marine Reserve. Belize was also one of the first Caribbean countries to establish a National Manatee Working Group and a National Stranding Network and to adopt a Manatee Recovery Plan. Many Belizeans, including manatee researcher Nicole Auil (Wildlife Trust Belize), have dedicated years of work to a countrywide research program, aerial surveys, and the stranding network through Coastal Zone Management Institute (www.coastalzonebelize.org).

With the help of both local and international NGOs, the Coastal Zone Management Institute and the Belize Marine Mammal Stranding Network have successfully rescued and rehabilitated four orphaned manatees: Hercules, Woody, Tiny, and Buttons. Hercules, Woody, and Tiny have been released back into the wild in Southern Lagoon Wildlife Sanctuary and Buttons in the Corozal Bay Wildlife Sanctuary. Orphaned manatees in Belize are cared for by Wildtracks in Sarteneja, where volunteer positions are often available.

CONTINUED THREATS

Despite extensive local and national efforts, manatees in Belize are still increasingly threatened by anthropogenic impacts, including

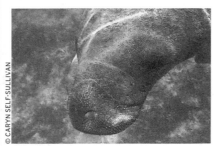
© CARYN SELF-SULLIVAN

the gentle giant "sea cow"

Caye Wildlife Sanctuary (SCWS), an 8,970-acre protected manatee area and the premier location for manatee tours. The SCWS lobbying efforts began in the early 1990s and were spearheaded by Chocolate Heredia, of Caye Caulker. Another long-term project is based in the Southern Lagoon Wildlife Sanctuary.

THE FUTURE

But designating protected areas is just the beginning; much work is still in progress as diverse stakeholders attempt to come to a consensus on setting and enforcing rules and regulations for the sanctuary. The reserve is co-managed by Friends of Swallow Caye (an NGO founded by Chocolate in 1998) and the Department of Natural Resources.

Other local NGOs involved in manatee conservation and education include the Hugh Parkey Foundation for Marine Awareness and Education in Belize City, SWEET in Sarteneja, Green Reef in San Pedro, Friends of Nature (SEA Belize) in Placencia, and the Toledo Institute for Development and the Environment (TIDE) in Punta Gorda.

(Contributed by Caryn Self-Sullivan, PhD, president of Sirenian International and a marine scientist who has been studying manatee ecology and behavior in Belize since 1998. For more information about manatees around the world, visit www.sirenian.org.)

poaching, boat strikes, entanglement in fishing gear, and habitat degradation. The most significant threats appear to be boat strikes and destruction of habitat. Because manatees are elusive and endangered and have slow reproductive rates, long-term studies in Belize are necessary to evaluate and monitor their relatively healthy status and develop practical conservation plans to ensure continued survival of the population, and ultimately, the subspecies.

One such study, in the Drowned Cayes area near Belize City, focuses on manatee ecology and behavior. The Drowned Cayes area has long been designated as an important manatee habitat, but it is being impacted by rising tourist numbers. Data provided by the Earthwatch project were influential in including a portion of the Drowned Cayes in Swallow

THE NORTHERN CAYES

(as some call it) is resulting in stricter noise statutes. Still, you'll find live music at **Oceanside** on Friday nights ("Gringo Night" with Dennis Wolfe), which is also the happening hot spot on Saturday, with dancing till 3 A.M. (since they soundproofed the place). Tuesday is ladies night, Wednesday is reggae, and Thursday and Saturday undiscovered stars flock to karaoke; at midnight the *punta* dancing begins. There is occasionally a late-night dancehall scene at a ramshackle disco near the back side of town.

Team Trivia Night at the **Barrier Reef Sports Bar and Grill** (Sunday, Wednesday, and Friday at 7:30 P.M.) can get competitive,

with the top teams winning money off their bar tabs, not to mention bragging rights. In case of a tie, the judge will either ask a final question, or teams must select their top drinker (rather than thinker) for a beer chug race to victory. Of course, Barrier Reef also has large-screen TVs with lots of sports.

Do not leave the island without enjoying a beverage in **The I & I Bar,** a three-story tower of reggae located in the middle of the island. We could try to explain the swing-seats and Monkey Walk, but you're better off just going yourself. **Herbal Tribe,** up Front Street, is developing quite the rootsy nighttime scene as well.

SHOPPING

You'll find **Toucan** and a sprinkling of small gift shops on and around Front Street selling T-shirts, hot sauce, hammocks, sarongs, beach wear, postcards, photo albums, and other typical Belizean souvenirs. Caye Caulker's sandy streets are starting to attract several skilled artisan vendors. On Front Street are a collection of numbered stalls called **Palapa Gardens.** Here you can find hand-carved zericote and rosewood, hand-painted T-shirts, Guatemalan textiles and handicrafts, beautiful model sailboats complete with rigging, jewelry, and music CDs.

Jewelry is a popular craft on the island and often sold from tables set up in the street. Calvin sells cool island necklaces at his table set up on the corner of Habaneros and Sandbox, and Carlos's high-end jewelry, featuring silver and semiprecious stones, is for sale at his street table in front of Sports Bar. **Celi's Music** is where Mr. August can be found at a small table beside the shop, cutting and polishing conch shell pieces.

Cooper's Art Gallery (tel. 501/226-0330, www.debbiecooperart.com) on Front Street sells colorful Caribbean primitive art and posters, many in funky frames hand-painted by her husband in the shop. Lee Vanderwalker-Alamina's **Caribbean Colors Art Gallery** (www.caribbean-colors.com) is now located in a small storefront near the split. The **Go Slow Art Gallery,** in Palapa Gardens stalls #6 and #7, encourages the Belizean art community and sells paintings of different styles, including acrylic on canvas, realism, and primitive. Seek out pieces by well-known local artists Nelson Young and Marcos Manzanero. Hair braiders create "head art" with their lightning-fast fingers, braiding intricate designs and adding colorful beads and extensions. Anita Baker and her daughter are very popular and set up their outdoor salon across the street from Palapa Gardens.

For clothing, **Chocolate's Gift Shop,** run by Annie Seashore, sells high-quality Balinese sarongs, bags, and Guatemalan textiles. A selection of skirts, sandals, jewelry, and bags is for sale at Caye Cyber Connection. Several small shops sell a limited selection of imported women's clothing.

ACCOMMODATIONS

Prices below are for high-season doubles, but you can often get discounts, especially if staying for five or more days. Note that in Caye Caulker the "beach" is little more than a sandy sidewalk for foot traffic and golf carts. At last count, there were 72 licensed hotels on the island. During high season (late December, mid-February, and Easter week), rooms are quickly filled as water taxis arrive from Belize City; throughout the rest of the year, reservations are rarely necessary. When you step off your boat or plane, ignore any pushy taxi driver who grabs your bag and yells out a hotel name; the driver is getting a commission from a lazy hotel owner, and playing their game only encourages pushier behavior. If you're packing a tent, the only place to camp is on the beach at **Vega Inn and Gardens** (www.vegabelize. com, US$11 pp); the site provides communal hot/cold showers, flush toilets, luggage storage, and security.

Under US$25

This is the price range where Caye Caulker excels—if the following places are full, don't worry, there are many plain-Jane budget rooms along Front Street that are easy to find.

 Tina's Backpacker's Hostel (tel. 501/206-0019, tinasbackpackershostel@ yahoo.com) is a converted private home, located to your right as you walk off the town dock. Tina, a well-traveled islander, offers dorm-style rooms (US$10), plus a few private rooms (US$20–30) with shared bathroom and kitchen and a relaxed community atmosphere. Hang out on her funky little dock or garden benches and hammocks. The rooms are small, clean, and colorful.

Blue Wave Guest House (tel. 501/669-0114, bluewave@btl.net, US$20) has rooms with shared bath, an outdoor communal kitchen, and a private dock. They've also got private rooms for US$75; look for the log cabin–style building. Toward the south end of town you'll find a handful of old-school family-run guesthouses: **Edith's Hotel** (tel. 501/206-0069, US$20–25), with small and tidy rooms, is a landmark on the center street of the island. Rooms come with hot/cold water, ceiling fans, and shared or private bath. **Daisy's Hotel** (tel. 501/226-0150, US$20) is another oldie and goodie, on Front Street, just inland from Lena's. Eleven simple wooden rooms have fans and hot water in shared baths.

A bit farther south along the beach, you'll find **Tom's Hotel** (tel. 501/226-0102, toms@btl.net, US$18–30), popular with backpackers. There are many options—32 rooms, plus a few simple bungalows. Tom's is very well kept and clean, with hot/cold water, fans, louvered windows, tile floors, and a sea view.

Continuing south on the beach, past the Anchorage, look for **(Lorraine's Guesthouse** (tel. 501/206-0162, US$20), with seven simple yellow casitas, three of them on stilts. A nice dock is available for sunbathing, and chairs and hammocks are on the beach.

Each casita has a private bath, hot/cold water, and two beds.

US$25-50

For a relaxed dose of "old Caye Caulker," check into one of the funky beachfront cabins at **Morgan's Inn** (tucked away in a cluster of palms near the cemetery, tel. 501/226-0178, sbf@btl.net, US$28–40); cabins are spacious and rustic, with outside toilet and inside showers. Kayaks and windsurfing are available.

The colorful building on your right as you get off of the water taxi is **Trends Beachfront Hotel** (tel. 501/226-0094 or 226-0307, www.trendsbze.com, US$35–40) with seven rooms, comfortable queen-sized beds, refrigerator, fans, and private baths. Trends also has a building a block and a half away with simpler rooms for US$20 (with private bath), an excellent value.

Very popular with low-maintenance travelers, the brightly colored **(Rainbow Hotel** (tel. 501/226-0123, www.rainbowhotel-cayecaulker.com, US$35–52) has 17 clean,

© JOSHUA BERMAN

Tranquil accommodations are found at Morgan's Inn.

THE NORTHERN CAYES

stucco rooms with hot/cold water, private baths, TV, and tile floors; there are also two suites: La Casita and Cielo Azul. The popular Rainbow Bar and Grill is across the street on a dock over the water. Up the street, **Costa Maya Beach Cabanas** (tel. 501/226-0432, costamaya@tsunamiadventures.com, US$50–65) offers nine beach cabanas with fridge, private bath, wireless Internet, TV, fan and air-conditioning, hot water, and complimentary bicycles and canoes. The six wood cabins at **Mara's Place** (by the split, tel. 501/206-0056, from US$37.50) are a great value, with private hot-water baths and small porches with hammocks. The property has a private dock with lounge chairs for guests to use and an outdoor communal kitchen.

US$50-100

De Real Macaw (tel. 501/226-0459, www.derealmacaw.biz, US$50–70 rooms or US$130 for condo-apartment and beach house) is a small pet-friendly place whose eight units have private baths, mini-kitchens, TV, and quality beds. There are nice views of the ocean from the various verandas.

Sea Dreams Hotel and Guest Houses (tel. 501/226-0388 or 226-0303, U.S. tel. 254/238-4149, www.seadreamsbelize.com, starting at US$55) is in a great location beside the split. There are five rooms, two apartments, and three guesthouses. The rooms include air-conditioning, wireless Internet, TV, and coffeemakers; the larger accommodations include fully equipped kitchens. There's also a fully equipped "Family Home" for $165, which sleeps up to six. Complimentary bikes, use of a canoe, and access to a rooftop deck and sunset pier make this an excellent deal.

Popeye's Beach Resort (tel. 501/226-0032, www.popeyesbeachresort.com, US$55–75) is quiet and family friendly and has four cabanas and three family rooms (with two double beds), right on the beach near the dock; all rooms have private bath, hot/cold water, and air-conditioning. There is a small beach bar with hammocks (8 A.M.–6 P.M.). Popeye's has an on-site travel agent for Tropic Air and bus tickets.

The **Jaguar Morning Star Guest House**

(tel. 501/226-0347, www.jaguarmorningstar.com, US$53) is a big white building with a jungle mural, located across from the Catholic church and primary school. It is an excellent bargain, with two modern top-floor rooms each with private bath, fridge, coffeemaker, and TV. There is a shared deck with a great ocean view and breeze. The owners planted many tropical trees and flowers to create a lovely garden.

The southernmost beachfront option is a good one; the five cabins at **Shirley's Guest House** (tel. 501/226-0145 or 600-0069, www.shirleysguesthouse.com, US$50–90, adults only) are built with beautiful tropical woods and are clean, quiet, and comfortable. The nicely appointed cabins offer a range of amenities.

You'll find six bright, newly upgraded accommodations at the front and seven at the back of **Barefoot Beach Resort Belize** (tel. 501/226-0161, www.barefootcariberesort.com, US$69–89), all clustered together and right on the beach; a few bigger suites go for US$129–145. The quaint and cozy rooms have comfortable queen or king beds, ceiling fans, sitting areas, small refrigerators, private baths with hot showers, and air-conditioning, plus their own deck or patio with seating and access to the sunning dock.

The **Tree Tops Hotel** (tel. 501/226-0240, www.treetopsbelize.com, US$50–100) is tucked back from the water near Tom's, and is a luxurious little gem in a tall white building. The owner has created a nice ambience with colorful ceramics and thematically decorated rooms—including two suites (the Sunrise and Sunset) that have private balconies, TV, fridge, and hot/cold water bathrooms. Two cheaper rooms share a bath and all have TV, fan, and fridge; there's also "Room #4" and "Luxury Suite," all within the price range above.

Oasi (tel. 501/226-0384, www.holidaybelize.com, US$70–80) is located outside the main buzz of town, toward the airstrip, so if you're looking for homey and quiet, try one of these three self-contained apartments with air-conditioning and ceiling fan, hot/cold

GIVING BACK ON CAYE CAULKER

If you find yourself inspired to leave something other than footprints behind in Caye Caulker, here are a few island projects that accept donations (materials and cash) and sometimes volunteers.

Until recently, Caye Caulker's only school stopped at Grade 7. Only a few privileged families could finance the daily commute to mainland schools for their children. In September 2008, thanks to a concerted community effort and a handful of committed, generous individuals, **Ocean Academy** (located near the airstrip, tel. 501/226-0321, www.cayecaulkerschool.com) opened its doors to 38 students. In addition to core academics, Ocean Academy gives courses on marine biology, water-based tourism sports (kayaking, scuba diving, windsurfing, and boat repair), and craftwork (carpentry, guitar, sewing, baking, jewelry making). Computer literacy is integrated into the curriculum and laptop donations are at the top

of Ocean Academy's wish list (see the website for an updated wish list). Student-run businesses teach entrepreneurial skills and the profits are used to fund field trips.

Ocean Academy has accepted donations of books, used laptops, school supplies, soccer uniforms, and the like. To donate materials, contact Vice Principal Joni Miller at miller_joni@hotmail.com. Groups (school, church, or university) looking for a 10-14 day service-learning experience are welcome to work and interact with local students on school projects. Couples or individual travelers who are staying a few days to a week and want to share a skill like boat repair, computer literacy, or dance are also welcome to contact the school.

There is a youth environmental club based out of the **Caye Caulker Community Library** (located beside the post office); they've had volunteers teach sign language and ecology classes before. The library needs computers and printers as well.

---

rainwater shower, equipped kitchen, and DSL. The entrance is a lovely tropical garden with fountain. Your hosts, Luciana Essenziale and Michael Joseph, will help you plan your days; complimentary bikes make the five-minute ride to town go quickly. There are a few other similarly priced and equipped apartments and rooms for rent in this area, including **Picololo** (tel. 501/226-0371, US$75) and **Maxapan Cabañas** (tel. 501/226-0118, US$60).

US$100-150

This price range is still new to the island and continues to grow with each edition of this book. There are also many apartment rentals in this range—check **Caye Caulker Rentals** (www.cayecaulkerrentals.com) or the online classifieds at the San Pedro Sun (http://sanpedrosun.net).

Located at the foot of the town dock, **Seaside Cabanas** (tel. 501/226-0498, www.seasidecabanas.com, US$105–130) is a brightly painted 16-room mini-resort. The

smart rooms and cabanas are equipped with air-conditioning, cable TV, and cheerful decor, surrounding the island's first swimming pool and sporting lots of rooftop hang space.

The Lazy Iguana B&B (tel. 501/226-0350, www.lazyiguana.net, US$105) is a three-story secluded home. The four spacious rooms have private baths, hot water, air-conditioning, and WiFi. The top floor is a deck for lounging with a 360-degree view of the island. Rates include a massive breakfast in the owners' kitchen. It's a short walk from the village center, toward the back side of the island. There are rainwater showers; bikes are available.

Just up from the main dock, you'll see some colorful, upscale beachfront suites with full amenities. These are **Dianne's Beach House and Sailwinds Beach Suites** (tel. 501/226-0286, www.staycayecaulker.com, US$129) and **Auxillou Suites** (tel. 501/226-0370, www.auxilloubeachsuites.com, US$129).

The **Iguana Reef Inn** (tel. 501/226-0213, www.iguanareefinn.com, US$139–164) continues to raise the bar with its 13 large, up-scale rooms built around a well-kept complex on the west side of the island, behind the soccer field. Its rooms are spacious and colorful, some with vaulted ceilings and all with comfortable touches like mini-fridge, porch, bathtub, hot/cold water, and other modern conveniences. Continental breakfast is included. The bar, swimming pool, and clean beach area face the sunset and are more private and quiet than those on the island's windward side.

Apartment-style accommodations are found at **Caye Caulker Condos** (tel. 501/226-0072, www.cayecaulkercondos.com, US$110–130), near the north end of the village; "relax in style" in one of seven fully furnished suites with all the amenities. The balconies and roof-top hangout are stunning.

FOOD

Caye Caulker is finally shedding its reputation for mediocre food; style and service are creeping in, and you'll enjoy exploring the various options.

Bakeries and Belizean

You'll want to sample the treats from some of Caye Caulker's famous walking bakeries, beginning with Lloyd, a.k.a. **"The Cake Man,"** balancing his basket of homemade chocolate macaroon and cheesecake brownies, banana bread, key lime pie, and sometimes cookies; he begins his daily rounds at 4:30 P.M. at the split and works south through the village. **Toni** rides her bike down Front Street at lunch time with tasty jalapeño bread, ham and cheese rollups, hummus and pita, chicken pilaf, and carrot cake. **Errol** will sell you meat pies and banana bread from his rolling cart. And don't forget to buy a bag of popcorn after school from young Marconi, Kenya, Stephanie, and Jasmine (US$1), and support other local kids who are selling their mothers' johnnycakes, fudge, and buns.

Affectionately known as "Auntie's," **Chan's Fast Food** is a small window-service establishment selling cheap Belizean favorites like stew chicken and fry chicken, rice and beans,

beef stew, and the like. One of the few places where you truly are inside someone's home, **Glenda's** on Back Street, on the west side of the island, is as good as ever, with delicious buns. She serves inexpensive food and cheap lobster burritos in a very homey atmosphere. In the morning, try her homemade cinnamon rolls and fresh-squeezed orange juice—by the glass or in a recycled bottle—the best two bucks you'll spend on the island. A little farther south on Back Street is **Little Kitchen,** where you can get excellent *salbutes* (US$0.50), *garnaches* and *panades* (3 for US$1), burritos (US$1.50), and home-cooked seafood and main dishes as well. Seating is casual at outdoor picnic tables and the kitchen, while indeed little, is in the front room, and the cook is the friendly owner, Ms. Elba. For a cheap early-morning nosh, seek out the **"taco lady"** in front of Habaneros—you'll have to queue up behind the hungry construction workers. **Marin's Upstairs Diner,** down the street from the Tropical Paradise, has a nice menu and always-fresh fish. Across the street is **Tortilleria Asunción,** for fresh tortillas and chips.

The Pastry Shop, at Jan's Place on Front Street, has incredible European pastries prepared by a German chef; chocolate croissants, raisin brioche, baguettes, fruit flan, cakes, and the like are delish.

Barbecues

Belizeans love their barbecues. They often set up grills right on the beach and serve chicken, lobster, fish, or shrimp for a few bucks; the sides are tortillas, white rice and beans, stew beans, mashed potato, macaroni, or coleslaw. **Jolly Roger's Grill,** in Palapa Gardens on Front Street, is a real favorite, grilling up whole lobster (in season; US$12.50), chicken, fish, and shrimp (US$10). Roger is proud of his 2007 silver medal for "Best Food in All Central America." Private beach barbecues with entertainment can be arranged for your group. **Rose's Grill and Bar,** on Front Street behind Habaneros, is always filled with satisfied customers; it's very popular for the dinner barbecue grilled right in front of you and specializes in fresh seafood; chips and ceviche are free. **Fran's**, on Front Street opposite Oceanside, is always packed with tourists seated at outside picnic benches.

Cafés

Two blocks south of the dock, **◖ Amor y Cafe** (6–11:30 A.M.) specializes in breakfast: eggs, yogurt, granola, grilled sandwiches, and coffee and juices. It's a friendly place to have breakfast and people-watch on the street below the porch. **Coco Plum Garden Cafe, Spa & Gallery** (8 A.M.–4 P.M., www.cocoplum.typepad.com) is well worth the walk south of the village and toward the airstrip; you'll find all kinds of organic, whole, gourmet food, including a lobster pizza and great salads. Exquisite omelets are US$12 and "pancrepes" US$6. There's a Belizean craft and art store as well as massage and healing work in the lovely new spa.

Femi's Café and Lounge (8 A.M.–10 P.M.) serves smoothies and coffees, as well as meals from a small kitchen. The deck is right beside the sea and bar swings and hammocks add a nice ambience.

Casual Dining

At the **Sand Box** (7 A.M.–10 P.M.), right at the end of the water taxi dock, you'll find an indoor sand floor and a relaxed atmosphere. There are great breakfast offerings and lots of seafood: fish with curry rice, conch ceviche, and seafood salad, plus stuffed eggplant and mushrooms (meals US$3–10).

◖ Syd's, on Middle Street, makes good burritos and has a tasty Saturday night barbecue; prices are very reasonable, and the place is popular with locals. The seating has been expanded to include a lovely garden patio in the back. **Island View Restaurant**, on Front Street, also gives good value for the dollar.

The **Barrier Reef Sports Bar and Grill** (open 9 A.M.–midnight), on Front Street, opens onto the beach and serves breakfast, lunch, and dinner. The food here is surprisingly good, with steaks, seafood, and pasta entrées going for US$12–25. And, oh yeah, lots of televisions and sports, via HD satellite. Barrier Reef has opened

up **Los Cocos Cantina and Giftshop** next door, for Mexican snack foods and breakfasts.

Happy Lobster (6 A.M.–5 P.M.) on Front Street is a popular choice for breakfast and people-watching. **Sobre Las Olas** (7 A.M.–10 P.M.) is opposite Barefoot Caribe on Front Street. The most popular meal is the US$23 combo special—crab claw, shrimp, and lobster (in season).

WishWilly's Bar and Grill is located in a ramshackle yard with extremely laid-back dinner service, happy hours, and seafood prepared by Chicago-Belizean chef Maurice. His sign on Front Street, two blocks from the split, points the way.

If you have a hankering for curry, grab a bite at the **Taj Hotel** (tel. 501/226-0034) for authentic east Indian dishes.

Fine Island Dining

◖ Don Corleone's Caribbean Trattoria (tel. 501/226-0025, 5 P.M.–9 P.M. Mon.–Sat.) has an elegant oceanview ambience and friendly, attentive staff. Entrées start from US$10–15 and choices include homemade fettuccine, lasagna, and seafood (US$12–13), along with an impressive wine list. It's located on Front Street, across from Raggamuffin Tours.

◖ Habanero's (tel. 501/226-0487, 6–9 P.M.) offers an "eclectic international" menu and swanky lounge bar. Meals are lavishly presented with an international flair.

The **◖ Rainbow Bar and Grill** offers diners great seaside ambience—the deck stretches over the water—and consistently excellent food. Lunch is very popular with day-trippers to the island.

Groceries, Fruit, and Fish

Chan's Mini Mart on Middle Street is pretty much the heart of "downtown" Caulker—check the bulletin board for ads and events or go inside for canned goods, meats, cereals, beverages, and snacks. **Chinatown Grocery,** on Middle Street near Edith's, also has a good selection. There are a few fruit, vegetable, and juice stalls around town (look near the bakery and Atlantic Bank). **Julia's Juice,** on southern Front Street, sells watermelon, orange, lime, soursop, and mixed-fruit juice in recycled plastic bottles (US$2.50). If you want fresh fish or lobster, go to the **Lobstermen's Co-op Dock** on the back side of the island and ask what time the fishermen come in with their catch. This is always a good place to buy fresh fish.

INFORMATION

There is plenty of online research you can do while planning your trip. The official site of the Caye Caulker Belize Tourism Industry Association (CCBTIA) is **www.gocayecaulker. com**. The most well-run and active site is probably **www.ambergriscaye.com**. The forum has a section for Caye Caulker where you'll find a large community of knowledgeable folks. There is no general information booth on the island; just walk off the dock and ask around.

SERVICES

Alliance Bank and Atlantic Bank are both located on Middle Street (9 A.M.–4:30 P.M. Mon.–Fri., 9 A.M.–noon Sat.). Atlantic's ATM accepts international cards. A Western Union office is next door.

There are a couple of reliable laundry places in town. The best are Marie (across from Atlantic Bank, US$5 for 8 lbs.) and Ruby's Wash and Fold, near Rose's.

At the south end of Front Street is the Village Council office (community center upstairs) and community library, health clinic, and post office (9 A.M.–noon and 1–5 P.M. Mon.–Thurs., closes a bit earlier on Fri.). The mail goes out three times a week (Monday, Wednesday, and Friday). **Fed Ex** services are available at the **Tropic Air** cargo office at the airstrip.

The health clinic will help you with meds *if* they have the supplies; it is staffed by a Cuban doctor and Belizean nurse. For any serious emergency, your best bet is an emergency flight to the mainland.

Internet Access

Many hotels offer wireless Internet to guests and wireless is also available at the split's **Lazy Lizard Bar** and Front Street's **Barrier Reef Sports Bar and Grill**. There are two Internet cafés on Front Street: **Caye Caulker Cyber Café** (7 A.M.–10 P.M. daily, US$6/hour) has the most computers, air-conditioning, a wet bar, and a jewelry gift shop. They offer the island's photocopier services. **Cayeboard Connection** is both an Internet café and a used bookstore (8 A.M.–9 P.M. daily) and will burn CDs and print photos.

Travel Agencies

Treasured Travels (Front St., tel. 501/226-0286, www.staycayecaulker.com) acts as a full-service travel agent. **Tsunami Adventures** (tel. 501/226-0462, www.tsunamiadventures.com), located up toward the split, acts as a local travel agency and can book your dive trip as well. Seaside and Popeye's hotels also have reliable travel agents. The town's Internet cafés can arrange bus tickets to Guatemala or Mexico and boat trips to Honduras.

GETTING THERE
By Air

Maya Island Air and Tropic Air make daily flights to Caye Caulker, flying to and from Belize City's municipal and international airports as part of their San Pedro run. The airstrip on Caulker is simple—you wait under a tree or on the veranda of the small building that serves all flights. Fares are US$25 one-way to the municipal airport (about 10 minutes) and about US$43 one-way to the international airport (12 minutes).

By Boat

The short cruise between Caulker and either Belize City or San Pedro is the most common way to get to the island. In Belize City, you'll find the Caye Caulker Water Taxi Terminal (tel. 501/226-2194 in San Pedro, 501/226-0992 in Caye Caulker, 501/223-5752 in Belize City, www.cayecaulkerwatertaxi.com) at the north end of the Swing Bridge, with boats leaving between 8 A.M. and 5:30 P.M.

Boats depart Caye Caulker from the municipal dock on the east side of the island; buy tickets at the office right on the dock before boarding the boat. Departures to Belize City run 6:30 A.M.–4 P.M., with a 5 P.M. run on weekends and holidays; to San Pedro 7 A.M.–3:50 P.M. The trip to or from Belize City costs US$10 one-way, US$15 round-trip; US$10 to San Pedro.

No regularly scheduled trips are available between cayes other than Ambergris and Caye Caulker, but you can request a stop at St. George's Caye or Caye Chapel. Many boats are partially open-air; a light wrap or rain jacket is handy for windy trips. The boats are often packed to the point of being overloaded. They are supposed to have a passenger limit, but it isn't always observed.

GETTING AROUND

The navigable part of town—from the airstrip north to the split—is a mile long and easily traversed on foot. Still, a bicycle will make things easier, especially if you're staying in one of the more southern accommodations. Ask if your hotel provides one, or rent at **Friendship Center** on Front Street, beside the bakery on Middle Street. **Island Boy Rental** near the soccer field also has bikes (US$2/hour or US$40/week).

If you're staying south of the village, you might consider renting a golf cart from **C&N, Island Boy,** or **CC Golf Cart Rentals**—about US$12.50/hour or US$62.50/day.

A golf cart taxi could be very helpful when moving around the island with luggage. Taxi guy **George Delcid** (tel. 501/601-4330) is responsive, friendly, and accommodating, and taxis operate from the Rainbow Hotel front desk (tel. 501/226-0123).

Turneffe Islands Atoll

This is a renowned diving and fishing destination about 30 miles east of Belize City. Most of the Turneffe islands are small dots of sand, mangrove clusters, and swamp, home only to seabirds and wading birds, ospreys, manatees, and crocodiles; a few support small colonies of fishermen and shellfish divers. Only **Blackbird Caye** and **Douglas Caye** are of habitable size.

If you're looking to hook a bonefish or permit, miles of crystal flats are alive with the hard-fighting fish. Tarpon are abundant late March–June within the protected creeks and channels throughout the islands. Those who seek larger trophies will find a grand choice of marlin, sailfish, wahoo, groupers, blackfin tuna, and many more.

Most visitors to Turneffe are day-tripping divers based in Ambergris Caye or Caye Caulker; a select few choose to book an island vacation package. There are a couple of upscale resorts and one research facility where ocean-loving visitors can stay.

DIVING
Rendezvous Point

This is a popular first dive for overnighters out of Ambergris Caye. It provides a great opportunity for divers who haven't been under in a while to get their feet wet again. The depth is about 40–50 feet and affords sufficient bottom time for you to get a good look at a wide variety of reef life. Angelfish, butterfly fish, parrot fish, yellowtails, and morays are represented well. This will whet appetites for the outstanding diving to come.

(The Elbow

Most divers have heard of the Elbow (just 10 minutes from Turneffe Island Lodge), a point of coral that juts out into the ocean. This now-famous dive site offers a steep, sloping drop-off covered with tube sponges and deep-water gorgonians, along with shoals of snappers (sometimes numbering in the hundreds) and other pelagic creatures. Predators such as bar jacks,

THE NORTHERN CAYES

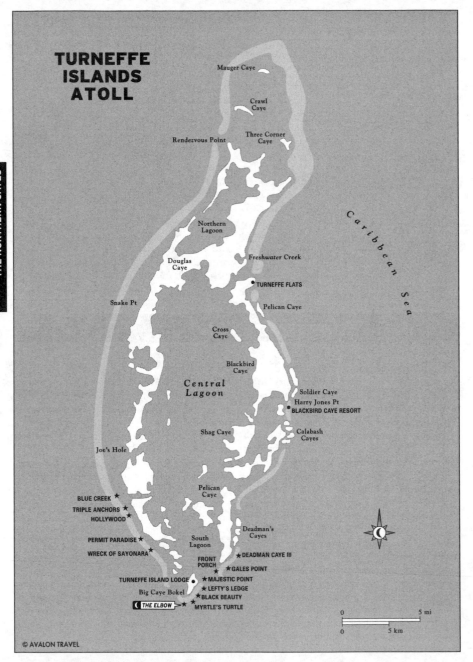

TURNEFFE
ISLANDS
ATOLL

Mauger Caye

Crawl
Caye

Three Corner
Caye

Rendezvous Point

Caribbean Sea

Northern
Lagoon

Douglas
Caye

Freshwater Creek

● TURNEFFE FLATS

Snake Pt

Pelican Caye

Cross
Caye

Blackbird
Caye

**Central
Lagoon**

Soldier Caye
Harry Jones Pt
● **BLACKBIRD CAYE RESORT**

Shag Caye

Calabash
Cayes

Joe's Hole

Pelican
Caye

BLUE CREEK ★
TRIPLE ANCHORS ★
HOLLYWOOD ★

Deadman's
Cayes

PERMIT PARADISE ★
WRECK OF SAYONARA ★

South
Lagoon

FRONT
PORCH

★ DEADMAN CAYE III

★ GALES POINT

TURNEFFE ISLAND LODGE ● ★ MAJESTIC POINT
Big Caye Bokel   ★ LEFTY'S LEDGE
★ BLACK BEAUTY
❰ **THE ELBOW** ★ MYRTLE'S TURTLE

0 _____ 5 mi
0 _____ 5 km

© AVALON TRAVEL

wahoo, and permits cruise the reef, and the drop-off is impressive. Currents sweep the face of the wall most of the time, and they typically run from the north. However, occasionally they reverse or cease all together.

Lefty's Ledge

A short distance farther up the eastern side of the atoll is another dive to excite even those with a lot of bottom time under their weight belts. Lefty's Ledge features dramatic spur-and-groove formations that create a wealth of habitats. Correspondingly, divers will see a head-turning display of undersea life, both reef and pelagic species. Jacks, mackerels, permits, and groupers are present in impressive numbers. Wrasses, rays, parrot fish, and butterfly fish are evident around the sandy canyons. Cleaning stations are also evident, where you'll see large predators allowing themselves to be groomed by small cleaner shrimp or fish. The dive begins at about 50 feet and the bottom slopes to about 100 feet before dropping off into the blue.

Gales Point

Another "don't-miss" dive, Gales Point is a short distance farther up the eastern side of the atoll. Here the reef juts out into the current at a depth of about 45 feet, sloping to about 100 feet before the drop-off. Along the wall and the slope just above it are numerous ledges and cavelike formations. Rays and groupers are especially common here—some say this may be a grouper breeding area. Corals and sponges are everywhere in numerous varieties.

Sayonara

On the leeward, or eastern, side of the atoll, the wreck of the *Sayonara,* a tender sunk by Dave Bennett of Turneffe Island Lodge, lies in about 30 feet of water. Close by is a sloping ledge with interesting tunnels and spur-and-groove formations. Healthy numbers of reef fish play among the coral, and some barracudas tag along. Large schools of permit are often drawn down by divers' bubbles. They give a marvelous three-dimensional quality to the

dive as you see them spiraling down from the surface like a squadron of fighter planes.

Hollywood

A bit farther up the atoll, Hollywood offers divers a relatively shallow dive (30–40 feet) with moderate visibility, unless the currents have reversed. Here you'll find lots of basket and tube sponges and lush coral growth. Many angelfish, parrot fish, grunts, and snappers swim here. Although not as dramatic as an eastern side dive, Hollywood has plenty to see.

ACCOMMODATIONS

Turneffe Island Lodge (tel. 501/220-4011 or 220-4142, U.S. tel. 800/874-0118, www.turneffelodge.com) is on Little Caye Bokel, 12 acres of beautiful palm-lined beachfront and mangroves. It has eight ground-floor deluxe rooms, four second-floor superior rooms, and eight stand-alone cabanas. It's a popular location for divers, anglers, and those who just want a hammock under the palms. At the southern tip of the atoll, the lodge is a short distance north of its larger relative, Big Caye Bokel. This strategic location offers enthusiasts a wide range of underwater experiences—it's within minutes of nearly 200 dive sites. Shallow areas are perfect for photography or snorkeling; you can see nurse sharks, rays, reef fish, and dolphins in the flats a few hundred yards from the dock. All the dives mentioned earlier and many more lie within 15 minutes by boat. The dive operation is first rate, and advanced instruction and equipment rentals are available. Anglers have a choice of fishing for snappers, permit, jacks, mackerel, and billfish from the drop-offs. They can stalk the near-record numbers of snook, bonefish, and tarpon in the flats and mangroves. The lodge's fishing guide has an uncanny way of knowing where the fish will be.

On the eastern side of the Turneffe islands, **Blackbird Caye Resort** (tel. 501/223-2772, U.S. tel. 888/271-3483, www.blackbirdresort. com) encompasses 166 acres of beach and jungle. It can accommodate 36 guests (double occupancy) with hot-water showers, private baths, and double and queen beds, as well as a duplex and triplex featuring private rooms and air-conditioning. A variety of snorkeling, fishing, and diving packages are offered for about $2,000–3,000 per week (depending on activities and accommodations) and include three dives a day, all meals, lodging, and airport transfers.

Turneffe Flats (tel. 501/220-4046, U.S. tel. 800/512-8812, www.tflats.com) is famous among international saltwater fly fishers who know the value of being able to sight fish in wadable flats for permit, bonefish, and tarpon. Or go for barracuda, snapper, jacks, or snook, and eat it up at night. Guided fishing is in the lodge's 16-foot Super Skiff flats boats. Divers are welcome and will enjoy daily forays to scores of sites throughout Turneffe Atoll and Lighthouse Reef. Varied beach accommodations are comfortable and well-appointed and meals are eaten family-style.

Lighthouse Reef Atoll

The most easterly of Belize's three atolls, Lighthouse Reef lies 50 miles southeast of Belize City. The 30-mile-long, 8-mile-wide lagoon is the location of the Blue Hole, a dive spot that was made famous by Jacques Cousteau and that is a favorite destination of dive boats from Belize City, Ambergris Caye, and Caye Caulker. The best dive spots, however, are along the walls of Half Moon Caye and Long Caye, where the diving rivals that of any in the world.

Think of the atoll as a large spatula with a short handle and a long blade. At the northern tip of the spatula blade, **Sandbore Caye** is home to a rusty lighthouse and a few fishing shacks. It is also the favorite anchorage of several of the dive boats that do overnight stops, including *Reef Roamer II.*

Big Northern Caye, across a narrow strait, is the location of Lighthouse Reef Resort. A landing strip just behind the resort is a convenient means of entry for resort guests and divers who wish to make only a day trip without the long water-crossing going and coming, which eats up most of the day. Here are long stretches of beach to walk, beautiful vistas, and large areas of mangroves and lagoons, home to snowy egrets and crocodiles.

Halfway down the spatula-shaped atoll, about where the blade meets the handle, lies the magnificent Blue Hole, a formation best appreciated from the air, but also impressive from the bridge of a boat.

At the elbow of the handle is **Half Moon Caye,** a historical natural monument and protected area with its lighthouse, bird sanctuary, shipwrecks, and incredible diving offshore. Finally, on the handle, we come upon **Long Caye,** a lonely outpost with a small dock, large palms, and glassy water.

DIVING
Blue Hole
This circular underwater formation, with its magnificent blue-to-black hues surrounded by neon water, is emblematic of Belize itself; this submerged shaft is a karst-eroded sinkhole with depths exceeding 400 feet. In the early 1970s, Jacques Cousteau and his crew explored the tunnels, caverns, and stalactites that were angled by past earthquakes.

Most dive groups descend to a depth of about 135 feet. Technically, this is not a dive for novices or even intermediate divers, though thousands have done it. It requires a rapid descent, a very short period at depth, and a careful ascent. For a group of 10 or more, at least three dive masters should be present. Critics write the Blue Hole off as a "hyped-up macho dive," but my personal experience there—descending with an entourage of circling reef sharks and turtles—was extraordinary. The lip of the crater down to about 60–80 feet has the most life: fat midnight parrot fish, stingrays, angelfish, butterfly fish, and other small reef fish cluster around coral heads and outcroppings.

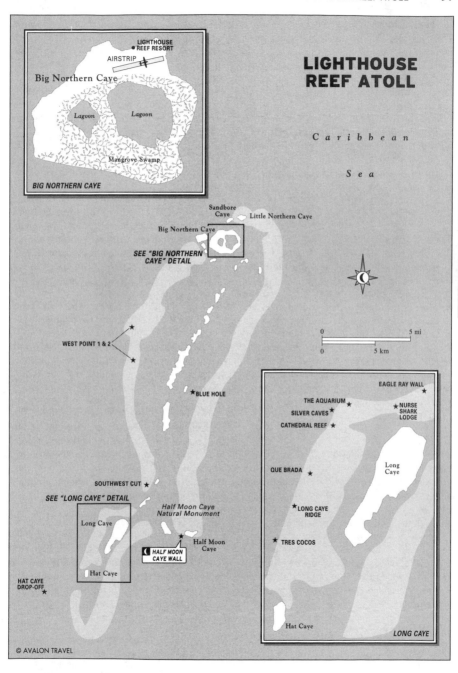

LIGHTHOUSE REEF RESORT

AIRSTRIP

Big Northern Caye

Lagoon

Lagoon

Mangrove Swamp

BIG NORTHERN CAYE

LIGHTHOUSE REEF ATOLL

C a r i b b e a n

S e a

Sandbore Caye

Little Northern Caye

Big Northern Caye

SEE "BIG NORTHERN CAYE" DETAIL

WEST POINT 1 & 2

0   5 mi
0   5 km

★BLUE HOLE

EAGLE RAY WALL ★

THE AQUARIUM ★
★ NURSE SHARK LODGE
SILVER CAVES ★
CATHEDRAL REEF ★

QUE BRADA ★

Long Caye

SOUTHWEST CUT ★

SEE "LONG CAYE" DETAIL

Long Caye

Half Moon Caye Natural Monument

★ LONG CAYE RIDGE

★ TRES COCOS

HALF MOON CAYE WALL

Half Moon Caye

Hat Caye

HAT CAYE DROP-OFF ★

Hat Caye

LONG CAYE

© AVALON TRAVEL

◖ Half Moon Caye Wall

They just don't come much better than this. Here on the eastern side of the atoll, the reef has a shallow shelf in about 15 feet of water where garden eels are plentiful. The sandy area broken with corals extends downward till you run into the reef wall, which rises some 20 feet toward the surface. Most boats anchor in the sandy area above the reef wall. Numerous fissures in the reef crest form canyons or tunnels leading out to the vertical face. In this area, sandy shelves and valleys frequently harbor nurse sharks and gigantic stingrays. Divers here are sure to return with a wealth of wonderful pictures.

Tres Cocos

On the western wall, "Three Coconuts" refers to trees on nearby Long Caye. The sandy bottom slopes from about 30 feet to about 40 feet deep before it plunges downward. Overhangs here are common features, and sponges and soft corals adorn the walls. Another fish lover's paradise, Tres Cocos does not have the outstanding coral formations you'll see at several other dives in the area, but who cares? There's a rainbow of marine life all about. Turtles, morays, jacks, coral, shrimp, cowfish, rays, and angelfish are among the actors on this colorful stage.

Silver Caves

The shoals of silversides (small gleaming minnows) that gave this western atoll site its name are gone. But Silver Caves is still impressive and enjoyable. The coral formations are riddled with large crevices and caves that cut clear through the reef. As you enter the water above the sandy slope where most boats anchor, you'll be in about 30 feet of water and surrounded by friendly yellowtail snappers. Once again you'll see the downwardly sloping bottom, the rising reef crest, and the stomach-flipping drop into the blue.

West Point

Farther north and about even with the Blue Hole, West Point is well worth a dive. Visibility may be a bit more limited than down south, but it's still very acceptable. The reef face here is stepped. The first drop plunges from about 30 feet to well over 100 feet deep. Another coral and sand slope at that depth extends a short distance before dropping vertically into very deep water. The first and shallow wall has pronounced overhangs and lush coral and sponge growth.

HALF MOON CAYE

Dedicated as a monument in 1982, this crescent-shaped island was the first protected area in Belize. Half Moon Caye, at the southeast corner of Lighthouse Reef, measures 45 square acres, half of which is a thriving (but endangered) littoral forest; the other half is a stunning palm-dotted beach. This is also the only red-footed booby sanctuary in the Western Hemisphere besides the Galápagos. The US$40 per person admission fee is sometimes included in your dive boat fee, but sometimes you'll pay it directly to the park ranger when you disembark.

As you approach Half Moon Caye, you'll believe you have arrived at some South Sea paradise. Offshore, boaters use the rusted hull of a wreck, the *Elksund*, as a landmark in these waters. Its dark hulk looms over the surreal blue and black of the reef world. The caye, eight feet above sea level, was formed by the accretion of coral bits, shells, and calcareous algae. It's divided into two ecosystems: The section on the western side has dense vegetation with rich fertile soil, while the eastern section primarily supports coconut palms and little other vegetation.

Besides offshore waters that are among the clearest in Belize, the caye's beaches are wonderful. You must climb the eight-foot-high central ridge that divides the island and gaze south before you see the striking half-moon beach with its unrelenting surf erupting against limestone rocks. Half Moon Caye's first lighthouse, built in 1820, sits on the eastern side of the caye. Another was built in 1848 and modernized and enlarged in 1931; today the lighthouse runs on solar power.

The Tower

Everyone should go to the observation tower, built by the Audubon Society in the zericote forest; climb above the forest canopy for an unbelievable view. Every tree is covered with perched booby birds in some stage of growth or mating. In the right season, you'll have a close-up view of nests where feathered parents tend their hatchlings. The air is filled with boobies coming and going, attempting to make their usually clumsy landings (those webbed feet weren't designed for landing in trees). Visitors also have a wonderful opportunity to see the other myriad inhabitants of the caye. Magnificent thieving frigates (the symbol of the Belize Audubon Society) swoop in to steal eggs, and iguanas crawl around in the branches, also looking for a snack.

Getting There

Only chartered or privately owned boats and seaplanes travel to Half Moon Caye Monument; no regular public transportation is available, although many resort guests fly. An option would be to take an inexpensive water taxi from Belize City to Ambergris or Caye Caulker and take one of the *Reef Seekers* out to Half Moon Caye (US$40 one-way, US$80 round-trip) the next day. Or check with the Belize Audubon Society in Belize City for other suggestions.

Other Northern Cayes

CAYE CHAPEL

Just one-by-three miles, Caye Chapel is about 15 miles and 25 minutes by boat from Belize City. The caye is owned by a wealthy Kentuckian who is trying to attract corporate America to his 18-hole golf course and retreat.

Some people have criticized the development and management of the caye, citing environmental damage from dredging and fertilizer runoff. The resort claims otherwise, presenting a list of environmental accomplishments. If you've got the cash and want to see for yourself, contact Caye Chapel Island Resort (tel. 800/901-8938 or 501/226-8250, www.belizegolf.cc). For nonguest golfers looking for some links, a US$220 per person day package includes round-trip air service from San Pedro or Belize City, unlimited rounds of golf (9 A.M.–4 P.M.), golf cart, clubs, and use of the resort's swimming pool complex, hot tub, and beach area. Or stay the night at one of the luxury villas or cabanas (US$300–1,000).

ST. GEORGE'S CAYE

This small caye, nine miles from Belize City, is shaped something like a boomerang, with its open ends facing the mainland. The caye is steeped in history and was the first capital of the British settlement (1650–1784). It was also the scene of the great sea battle between the Spaniards and the British settlers. Today, the small cemetery gives evidence of St. George's heroic past.

St. George's Caye is far from commercialized—on the contrary, it's very quiet, with mostly residential homes and their docks. There are several upscale accommodations with full-service dive shops here, plus the vacation homes of quite a few of Belize's elite. Check **St. George's Caye Lodge** (tel. 877/517-9365 or 501/220-4444, www.gooddiving.com, from US$168).

THE BLUEFIELD RANGE

Scattered along the coast is a constellation of small cayes, some accessible by tourists, others only by drug traffickers. Seeking out accommodations on any of these islands is guaranteed to get you a unique Belize experience, as you'll be well away from the crowds of the more standard island destinations.

The Bluefield Range is a group of cayes a short distance south of Belize City. On one of the islands, 21 miles south of the city, is **Ricardo's Beach Huts and Lobster Camp**

THE GRAY LADY

In all good myths and legends, the details are often sketchy, but facts are usually delicious. In the legend of the Gray Lady, it is said that famed buccaneer Henry Morgan often roamed the waters of the Caribbean, frequently off the coast of Belize City. In his wanderings, Henry brought his fair lady with him, a very independent miss. It's easy to imagine that lovers occasionally get testy living in such close quarters aboard a caravel. And though Henry and his lady usually kissed and made up, one lightning-slashed night, just off the coast of St. George's Caye, they were unable to settle a nasty argument – something to do with the seaman standing watch the night before? Morgan was the captain after all; his word was law! The lady ended up walking the plank into the stormy sea, gray gossamer gown whipping around her legs in the angry wind. Since that fateful night, the lady in gray has been roaming the small caye of St. George, trying to find her blackguard lover. Don't scoff; some islanders will speak no ill of the Gray Lady, and on stormy nights they stay safely behind closed doors.

(tel. 501/227-8469 or 203-4970), the ultimate in funky. At last check, the accommodations were quite rustic and reasonably priced. Expect campout conditions: outhouse, bucket shower, bugs. Bring mosquito coils, repellent, and a mosquito net bed/tent. On the upside, this is one of the few chances to experience outer island living just as it has been for the people who spend their lives fishing these waters.

ENGLISH CAYE

Though this is just a small collection of palm trees, sand, and coral, an important lighthouse sits here at the entrance to the Belize City harbor from the Caribbean Sea. Large ships stop at English Caye to pick up one of the two pilots who navigate the 10 miles in and out of the busy harbor. Overnights are not allowed here, but it's a pleasant day trip location.

GOFF'S CAYE

Near English Caye, Goff's Caye is a favorite little island stop for picnics and day trips out of Caye Caulker and Belize City, thanks to a beautiful sandy beach and promising snorkeling areas. Sailboats often stop overnight; camping can be arranged from Caye Caulker by talking with any reputable guide. Bring your own tent and supplies. Goff's is a protected caye, so note the rules posted by the pier. Goff's has seen a major impact by the cruise ship industry, which sometimes sends thousands of people per week to snorkel around and party on the tiny piece of sand, and a few reports have said this is destroying the coral.

SPANISH LOOKOUT CAYE

This is a 187-acre mangrove island, located at the southern tip of the Drowned Cayes, only 10 miles east of Belize City. There are many day trip possibilities to Spanish Lookout Caye, including the country's first and only "dolphin encounter" program, a beach, kayaks, and snorkeling.

If you're not researching manatees or mangroves with Earthwatch Institute, you're most likely coming to meet the dolphins or stay at **Belize Adventure Lodge** (tel. 501/223-4526, U.S. reservations 888/223-5403, www.belizeadventurelodge.com), a full-service island facility offering 12 quasi-colonial cabanas over the water, two student dormitories, classrooms, a restaurant, a bar, a gift shop, and a dive center. Five colorful cabanas with 10 rooms, hot showers, and private baths are connected to the island by a dock. The resort offers popular three-night packages that include all meals and transfers to the island.

Diving is one of the favorite activities here. So are educational and research programs. Manatees and dolphins are regularly seen foraging near the island. Juvenile reef fish, seahorses, lobster, and mollusks live among the red mangrove roots and sea grass beds. Tarpon and barracuda often come into the bay to feed on the abundant silversides. The resort is only one mile west of the main Barrier Reef and about eight miles west of central Turneffe Island.

BELMOPAN AND THE HUMMINGBIRD HIGHWAY

Central Belize comprises Belmopan, the unpretentious capital of the country, as well as one of the region's most stunning roads, the Hummingbird Highway. Driving west from Belize City, you'll pass from wetlands to pine savanna, with the Maya Mountains beyond—and a massive cave system beneath. Most of this region is drained by the Sibun and Caves Branch Rivers, which empty out into a large, lowland marshy region before arriving at the sea.

PLANNING YOUR TIME

Some people spend their entire vacations (or at least the inland portion of them) in one of the adventure lodges of the region. The city of Belmopan certainly doesn't require much of your time, but the rest of the region may warrant a day or two. As you drive the Western Highway out of Belize City, save at least an hour to visit the Belize Zoo, and another half hour for the hike in Guanacaste National Park.

© JOSHUA BERMAN

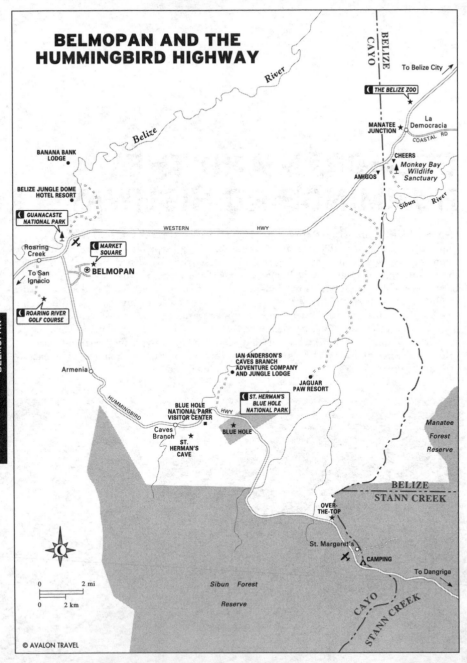

BELMOPAN AND THE HUMMINGBIRD HIGHWAY

BELIZE
CAYO

To Belize City

☾ THE BELIZE ZOO
★

MANATEE
JUNCTION ★

La
Democracia

COASTAL RD

River

Belize

BANANA BANK
LODGE

CHEERS
☂ *Monkey Bay
Wildlife
Sanctuary*

AMIGOS ▾

BELIZE JUNGLE DOME
HOTEL RESORT

☾ GUANACASTE
NATIONAL PARK

Sibun River

Roaring
Creek ✗

☾ MARKET
SQUARE ★

WESTERN HWY

To San
Ignacio

✺ **BELMOPAN**

☾ ROARING RIVER
GOLF COURSE ★

Armenia

IAN ANDERSON'S
CAVES BRANCH
ADVENTURE COMPANY
AND JUNGLE LODGE

JAGUAR
PAW RESORT

HUMMINGBIRD

BLUE HOLE
NATIONAL PARK
VISITOR CENTER

☾ ST. HERMAN'S
BLUE HOLE
NATIONAL PARK

HWY ★
BLUE HOLE

Caves
Branch ★
ST.
HERMAN'S
CAVE

Manatee

Forest

Reserve

BELIZE
STANN CREEK

OVER-
THE-TOP ★

St. Margaret's ○
✈ ☨ CAMPING

To Dangriga

Sibun Forest

Reserve

CAYO

STANN CREEK

0   2 mi
0   2 km

© AVALON TRAVEL

BELMOPAN

HIGHLIGHTS

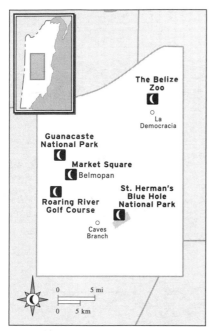

Guanacaste National Park

(Market Square

(Roaring River Golf Course

Belmopan

(St. Herman's Blue Hole National Park

The Belize Zoo
(

○ La Democracia

○ Caves Branch

0   5 mi

0   5 km

(Market Square: Take a stroll through Belmopan's small, bustling outdoor commercial section, then walk over to the plaza by the government buildings (page 104).

(Guanacaste National Park: An easy stop along the Western Highway, this 50-acre patch of forest has flat, well-maintained hiking trails through massive trees and ferns that the whole family will enjoy (page 107).

(Roaring River Golf Course: Shoot a leisurely nine holes at this relaxed set of links, just west of Belmopan (page 108).

(The Belize Zoo: This famous, lush home for animal ex-movie stars and more is an easy stopover as you travel between Belize City and points south and west. It is also home of the Belize Tropical Education Center, where educational and study opportunities abound (page 109).

(St. Herman's Blue Hole National Park: Get out the hiking boots, binoculars, and a bathing suit for a visit to this park and St. Herman's Cave, halfway down the Hummingbird Highway (page 112).

LOOK FOR **(** TO FIND RECOMMENDED SIGHTS, ACTIVITIES, DINING, AND LODGING.

Belmopan

After Hurricane Hattie destroyed government buildings (and records) in Belize City in 1961, Belmopan was built far away from the coast to keep it safe from storm damage, with the expectation that large numbers of the population of Belize City would move with the government center. They didn't. Industry stayed behind, and so did most jobs. Today, though there is some growth in Belmopan, the masses are still in Belize City, which remains the cultural and commercial hub of the country. Some capital employees live in Belize City and commute 50 miles back and forth each day.

However, Belmopan was designed for growth and continues to expand, with the population approaching 10,000 souls. Today, the feel inside the city grid (within Ring Road) has been compared to a lower-middle-class Los Angeles suburb, with rows of small cement homes and chain-link fencing.

Some students and scientists come to Belmopan to do research in the **Belize Archives Department** (tel. 501/822-2097, archives@btl.net), a closed-stacks library popular with both local students and foreign researchers.

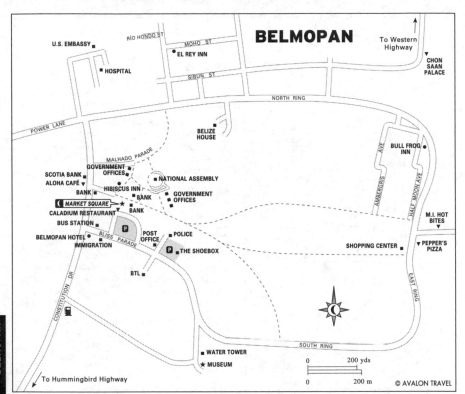

The majority of travelers, however, see only Belmopan's bus terminal and, if they have time, the small open-air market right next door. Some jog across the market to take a peek at the government buildings (only a couple hundred yards away)—an incredibly gray, squat, post-apocalyptic bit of architecture. Their intentionally Maya-influenced arrangement—built around a central plaza—gives the scene just enough strange irony to make it worth the visit.

ORIENTATION

Belmopan is just east of the Hummingbird Highway (and just south of the Western Highway) and is usually accessed by Constitution Drive, which leads straight into the center from a roundabout. Banks, buses, the market, and government buildings are tightly clustered within easy walking distance of one another. Turning right on Bliss Parade from Constitution Drive, you'll find the dilapidated Belmopan Hotel on your right, and the Novelo's bus station and the market on your left. Bliss Parade joins Ring Road, which loops around the central town district. Ring Road passes various government buildings and embassies on the left before meeting back up with Constitution Drive.

◖ MARKET SQUARE

This is where the action is for the locals, the lines of stalls alive with the commerce and gossip of the area. Hang out here for a little while and you are sure to see a parade of local farmers, government workers, and colorful characters going about their business. Try a tasty tamale or a plate of *garnaches* (crispy tortillas topped with tomato, cabbage, cheese, and hot sauce) for next to nothing. Bananas, oranges, mangoes, tomatoes, chilies, and carrots are cheap, too; stock up before heading deeper into Belize.

ENTERTAINMENT AND NIGHTLIFE

Despite Belmopan's reputation for being a "dead" town, weekends can be quite alive in the capital city. Thursdays start with karaoke at the **Bull Frog,** but turn into a rockin' dance party around 11 P.M., when the place gets packed. The rest of the weekend is ruled by **Tropical Delites** (better known by its old name, **Roundabout**), located on the northeast corner of the traffic circle on the Hummingbird Highway. For a mellow, unpretentious bar, be sure to hit **La Cabaña,** in the western part of town by Las Flores, with cheap bar food and a friendly vibe.

SHOPPING

Besides the market, you'll find a few handy stores in Belmopan. **Angelus Press** has a good office supply and bookstore right by the bus station. **The Art Box** is on the Hummingbird Highway and has a unique selection of woodworking, watercolors, and picture frames, in addition to the standard gift shop fare (as well as Christian books and CDs).

ACCOMMODATIONS

It's slim pickings for decent accommodations in Belmopan, especially for budget travelers; then again, if you're staying in Belmopan, you're either a businessperson, a diplomat, or a development worker—or just lost. The least offensive of the offerings, and the most reasonably priced, is **El Rey Inn** (23 Moho St., tel. 501/822-3438, hibiscus@btl.net, US$27 plus key deposit), with 11 tidy, white, austere rooms with private bath, hot/cold water, and fans. The same owners run the **Hibiscus Hotel** (tel. 501/822-1418, hibiscus@btl.net, US$45–65), located near the bus station; rooms there have air-conditioning and television and are a good bet if you want something central, safe, and simple.

SANDALISTAS REJOICE!

Belmopan is home to the only Birkenstock dealer in Belize. **The Shoe Box** (tel. 501/822-0727, theshoebox@btl.net) resides in a tiny shipping container in the Civic Center parking lot, across from the big BTL antenna. Browse the latest sandal styles direct from Germany, or have your old Birks rebuilt more cheaply than in the United States or Canada.

© JOSHUA BERMAN

Get your kicks recorked in Belmopan.

The **Bull Frog Inn** (25 Half Moon Ave., tel. 501/822-2111, www.bullfroginn.com, US$85 plus tax) has 28 rooms that could be mistaken for those of any basic roadside hotel in the States. The inn reports that 80 percent of the guests are businesspeople doing work for the government or private businesses. The on-site restaurant serves good food, and the bar turns into an all-night disco on Thursdays.

Convenient to Market Square, government buildings, and the bus station, the **Belmopan Hotel** (tel. 501/822-2130, gsosa@btl.net, US$60) has seen better days. The 20 worn rooms have private bath, air-conditioning, fans, and cable TV, but peeling paint and dark hallways make it a last-resort choice.

FOOD

There are so few decent places to eat in Belmopan that you'll have no problem finding one. Starting at the bus station, you'll find the

BELMOPAN

cheapest meals at the rows of market stalls and small restaurants that surround the terminal; if you have the time before your connection, walk across Constitution Drive to the 🍦 **Aloha Cafe** (located to the right of the Scotia Bank) for a meal, or at least a milkshake; the owners have done a great job creating a unique and comfortable atmosphere here. **Pepper's Pizza** (tel. 501/822-0666) delivers free anywhere in town. Or try **Pasquale's Pizzeria** (corner of Forest Dr. and Slim La., delivery tel. 501/822-4663); a large hand-tossed "New York–style" pizza is US$24.

The open-air restaurant and bar at the **Bull Frog Inn** have a solid reputation among even the elite of Belmopan, and this is one of the most popular spots in town to dine. The fish fillet, chicken, and burgers are all good here and moderately priced (entrées from US$10, much cheaper lunches and appetizers). The inn serves fresh orange, lime, and grapefruit juice. **M.I. Hot Bites** (tel. 501/822-3281, open daily 10 A.M.–10 P.M.), beyond the eastern edge of Belmopan's loop road, is an authentic Indian restaurant with a big air-conditioned dining room and a savory menu of central Indian and Rajasthani fare; entrés are US$11–19.

The Oasis is a new place across the Hummingbird Highway, on the river, that has gotten excellent reviews. Among the many Chinese restaurants in town, **Chon Saan Palace** (7069 George Price Blvd., tel. 501/822-3388), which boasts its longevity ("since 1974!"), is rated the best.

GETTING THERE

If you are traveling Belize by bus, it's near impossible *not* to visit Belmopan, as every bus traveling between Belize City and points west and south—even expresses—pulls into the main Belmopan terminal for 5–30 minutes as they rustle up new passengers (and the driver takes a lunch and smoke break).

JUNGLE LODGES ACROSS THE RIVER

When they first arrived in Belize 30 years ago, Montana cowboy John Carr and his wife, Carolyn, ran **Banana Bank Lodge and Jungle Equestrian Adventure** (tel. 501/820-2020, www.bananabank.com, US$77–175) as a working cattle ranch. Today, most of the pastures have been converted to fields for growing corn and beans (or allowed to turn back to jungle), and the ranch now hosts their lodge. Half of the 4,000-acre ranch is covered in jungle, and within its borders guests will discover not only a wide variety of wildlife but a Maya ruin. Scattered around the property are many more small archaeological "house mounds." Rooms, suites, cabanas, and chalets are fanciful—no two are alike—and most have beautifully funky bathtubs. The food is served family style. Five cabanas each sleep up to six people, and there are five rooms in the main house, three with shared bathroom, to accommodate guests. Breakfast is included in the room rate. Lunch is US$10, dinner US$15.

With more than a hundred saddle horses in its stables, Banana Bank features horseback riding but is also a place to bird-watch, fish, hike, or take a boat trip down the Belize River, with plenty of time left for a cooling swim—in the river or the on-site swimming pool. A lazy ride via horse-drawn buggy into the surrounding countryside is another treat, as is nighttime stargazing through a massive 14-inch telescope. There is also a zoo of sorts, which includes an aviary, a resident jaguar, and a couple of monkeys; most of the animals were given to the Carrs to care for.

The Carrs actively involve the local communities of Belizeans in their operation, and they even host a soccer team. Carolyn is considered one of the country's premier artists, and if you admire her on-site studio and gallery, be sure to seek out her paintings in the House of Culture in Belize City.

Banana Bank is located across the Belize River, a mile or so north of the Western Highway as it passes Belmopan at Mile 47. Park your vehicle to the right under the trees, ring the gong, and wait at the dock—shortly, someone will pull a boat along the rope stretched from bank to bank to fetch you.

Next door to Banana Bank Lodge, the

Belize Jungle Dome Hotel Resort (tel. 501/822-2124, www.greendragonbelize.com, US$105–200) has five rooms in a totally unique geodesic dome setting, just across the Belize River from Belmopan. The rooms are fully equipped with queen bed, air-conditioning, private bath, and wireless Internet. The Jungle Dome serves three meals and caters to all dietary requirements. The resort is also a licensed tour operator and runs a full range of tours, as well as airport transfers. The website and blog (http://belizevacation.blogspot.com) are particularly informative and fun, with many videos.

GUANACASTE NATIONAL PARK

Located at the T junction on the Western Highway where the Hummingbird Highway begins, the 50-acre Guanacaste National Park packs a lot within its small area. Managed by the Belize Audubon Society and the government, the park gets its name from the massive guanacaste, or *tubroos,* tree near the southwestern edge of the property. Ceiba, cohune palms, mammee apple, mahogany, quamwood, and other trees also populate the forest. Agouti, armadillo, coati, deer, iguana, jaguarundi, and kinkajou have all been observed in the park, along with

more than 100 species of birds. Among the rarer finds are resident blue-crowned motmots.

There are about two miles of very easy trail to explore; feel free to bring a swimsuit and take a dip at the quiet spot where the Belize River and Roaring Creek meet. Picnic tables, benches, restrooms, and trash cans have slowly been added to the site, mostly with the help of Peace Corps volunteers.

The park was originally the home of the British city planner who was commissioned to relocate the capital to Belmopan after Hurricane Hattie heavily damaged Belize City in 1961. It's said that he chose the spot because of the proximity to the spectacular old guanacaste tree. The official decided almost immediately that the meadow should be set aside as a government reserve for future generations to enjoy. The huge tree, well over 100 years old, is more than 25 feet in diameter and host to more than 35 species of exotic flora, including orchids, bromeliads, ferns, philodendrons, and cacti, along with a large termite nest and myriad birds twittering and fluttering in the branches—a tree of life! When rivers were the main method of transport, travelers stopped here to spend the night under the protection of the tree's wide-spreading branches. The only thing that saved the tree from loggers was its crooked trunk.

As you enter the park, walk across the grassy field; go left to get to the trail that brings you to the guanacaste. Beyond the tree, there's a looter's trench—someone long ago thought there was treasure buried here. The trench graphically demonstrates how a looter excavates and works a would-be treasure site (including, for example, at a Maya structure). Farther on, the path meets the shore of Roaring Creek, the westernmost boundary of the park. This is a wonderful and easy trail; you may or may not see another hiker, but you'll certainly see birds, delicate ferns, flowers, and long parades of wee-wee ants.

Another option from the park entrance is to cross the meadow and veer to the right. Here you'll find the steps that lead down to the Belize River. Along the shore, nature quietly continues its pattern of creation and subsistence. The *amate* fig grows profusely on the

water's edge and provides an important part of the howler monkey's diet. In the center of this scheme is the tuba fish, which eats the figs that fall into the water, dispersing the seeds up and down the river—starting more *amate* fig trees. And so it goes—on and on. At dusk on a quiet evening, howler monkeys roar the news that they're having dinner—keep your distance, world! Park hours are 8 A.M.–4:30 P.M.; entrance is US$2.50 per person, naturalist guides are free. Telephone through the Belize Audubon Society at 501/223-4987.

ROARING RIVER GOLF COURSE

An unpretentious, executive-type nine-holer (2,022 yards, par 32), the Roaring River Golf Course (Mile 50¼ Western Highway, tel. 501/664-5441 or 820-2031, www.belizegolf.net), located a short drive from Belmopan, is one of the only golf courses in Belize. The feel of the course, clubhouse, and equipment is perfectly Belizean—a bit rough around the edges but in a natural, comfortable way. A nine-hole round is only US$17.50 per person, plus US$5 to rent clubs and pull carts; new tee boxes make it possible to play a varied 18 holes (US$25; see scorecard on website). The course is well maintained with a level layout, but with interesting landscaping dividing the fairways; greens boast Bermuda grass, grown from seed, and Paul, the South African owner, notes that his course uses chemicals very sparingly—"just a bit of spraying for the ants." In 2008, the course added the "Meating Place" restaurant and four villas with air-conditioning, Internet, TV, queen beds, fridge, coffeemaker, work counter, lounge suite, and a stunning view of the river outside. It's a perfect option for someone who really wants to get some early rounds in.

There are in excess of 120 bird species on and around the course, as well as other wildlife. After sweating out a round, dip in one of the cool, shady pools of the river that runs through the course; the water is fresh from the Thousand Foot Falls just upstream. Plant your nongolfing family members in the river for the day while you hit those links and confront the crocodiles in the water hazards.

Along the Western Highway

FROM BELIZE CITY TO BELMOPAN

As you head west along the Western Highway, savanna and scraggly pines border the road. The milepost markers between Belize City and San Ignacio will help you find your way around the countryside. If you're driving, you can match the markers as you go by setting your odometer to zero as you turn onto Cemetery Road at the western edge of Belize City. You'll pass two service stations between the Western Highway and the turnoff for Belmopan.

Freetown Sibun

Three miles south of Hattieville, you'll find a small village (community tel. 501/209-6006) with a population of less than 100. The village was founded by runaway slaves back in the day, and its population used to peak around 2,000 during big logging runs. Today, you'll find campsites, canoe rentals, and hiking trails. Taxis are plentiful from the roundabout in Hattieville.

Manatee Junction

Driving west, note the junction with **Manatee Road** on your left at about Mile 29. (Look for the **Midway Resting Place,** a service station and motel of sorts on the southeast corner of the junction; its tall Texaco sign makes an especially good landmark at night, when the sign glows with bright colors.) This improved dirt road is the shortcut to Gales Point, Dangriga, and the Southern Highway. It's always a good idea to top off your tank, stock up on cold drinks, and ask for current road conditions here. Heavy rains can cause washouts on a lot of these "highways." This is a drive best done in daylight because of the picturesque views of jungle, Maya villages, and the Maya Mountains in the distance.

❰ THE BELIZE ZOO

Established in 1983, the Belize Zoo (tel. 501/220-8004, www.belizezoo.org, 8:30 A.M.–4 P.M. daily, US$10) is settled on 29 acres of tropical savanna and exhibits more than 125 animals, all native to Belize. The zoo

BELMOPAN

© JOSHUA BERMAN

ocelot at the "best little zoo" in Belize

keeps only orphaned animals, those injured and rehabilitated, those born in the zoo, and those received as gifts from other zoos. The environment is as natural as possible, with thick native vegetation, and each animal lives in its own wild-looking compound. New displays include the rare harpy eagle; ask about the zoo's restoration program to put these raptors back into forested areas in Belize.

The zoo is located at Mile 29 on the Western Highway. It is included in many day tours from Belize City and often as a stop during your airport transfer to or from your lodge in the western or southern parts of Belize. Independent travelers can jump off the bus from Belize City or Cayo (bus fare from Belize City is only US$1–2).

History

Zoo director Sharon Matola's accidental career began when, as a former lion tamer, she agreed to manage a backyard collection of local animals for a nature film company next door. However, after she had worked only five months on the project, funds were severely reduced, and it became evident that the group of animal "film stars" would have to be disbanded.

Sharon says that not only had these wild cats, birds, anteaters, and snakes become her friends and companions, but semitame animals, dependent on people for care, could not just be released back into the wild. As an alternative, she thought, "This country has never had a zoo. Perhaps if I offered the chance for Belizeans to see these unique animals, their existence here could be permanently established."

And so a zoo was born. From the very beginning, the amount of local interest in the zoo was incredible. The majority of the people in Belize live in urban areas, and their knowledge of the local fauna is minimal. The Belize Zoo offers Belizeans and tourists alike the opportunity to see the native animals of Belize. Today, the Belize Zoo receives over 10,000 Belizean schoolchildren every year as part of its progressive education programs.

Jaguar Restoration

In collaborations with the organization Panthera, the government of Belize, and the U.S. Fish and Wildlife Service, the Belize Zoo runs the only problem jaguar rehabilitation program and in situ jaguar research program in the world. Problem jaguars (which prey on livestock and domestic animals) are trapped and brought to the zoo for behavior modification training—instead of a bullet. In difficult cases, the animals are transferred to zoos in the United States (the Milwaukee and Philadelphia zoos have received problem cats from Belize).

The Belize Tropical Education Center

Across the street from the zoo, the Tropical Education Center (tel. 501/220-8003, tec@belizezoo.org) was created to promote environmental education and scientific research. Meetings are held here for zoological news, reports, and educational seminars attended and given by people involved in zoology from around the world. The Center is equipped with a classroom, a library, a kitchen and dining area, and dormitories that can accommodate as many as 30 people (rates from US$15 pp). Great nature trails weave through the 84-acre site, and birdwatchers can avail themselves of a bird-viewing deck. Also available are canoe trips, nocturnal zoo tours, and natural history lectures.

MONKEY BAY WILDLIFE SANCTUARY

Monkey Bay Wildlife Sanctuary consists of tropical forest and riparian and savanna habitats, stretching from the Western Highway down to the Sibun River, which flows from the Maya Mountains through the coastal savanna on its path to the Caribbean Sea. Located at Mile 31 on the Western Highway, the 3,300-acre wildlands of Monkey Bay (tel. 501/820-3032, www.monkeybaybelize.org) include the natural habitat of nearly all the animals represented at the Belize Zoo, which lies just a mile east on the Western Highway.

This is a fantastic retreat—for student groups, families, naturalists, and paddlers alike (though most of the sanctuary's business is with

© DANIELLE VAUGHN

the lodge at Monkey Bay: hostel, library, and sanctuary headquarters

BELMOPAN

study-abroad and service groups). The sanctuary maintains field stations in the Mountain Pine Ridge and Tobacco Caye. The main campus is home to exotic mammal species, including tapir, puma, jaguar, and Morelet's crocodile. More than 250 species of birds have been recorded. The sanctuary borders the Sibun River biological corridor and contains documented remains of ancient Maya settlements and ceremonial caves. A newly built trail system carries you through it all; you can hike, rent a canoe, or hire a caving guide—this is serious spelunking country as well. One option is a three-night camping expedition, where you'll hike to Five Blues Lake National Park.

You'll find two miles of trails, a 20-acre arboretum, and good swimming at nearby Sibun River. With the government's 1992 declaration of the 2,250-acre **Monkey Bay Nature Reserve** across the river, there now exists a wildlands corridor between the **Manatee Forest Reserve** to the south and the sanctuary.

Accommodations

Some travelers find themselves so intrigued by the goings-on at this environmental education center and tropical watershed research station that they opt to stay in one of Monkey Bay's primitively rustic rooms longer than they had planned. The accommodations share the grounds with a screened-in dining area, a shared barnlike library and study space (more than 500 titles are available for reference, with lots of local information), and an iguana breeding center (eggs are collected from the Sibun River area and raised in a safe environment; the iguanas are set free after two years). For sleeping, there's a campground in a grove of pine trees with sturdy wooden tent platforms (US$7 pp). There are dormitories (US$15 pp) as well. All share common composting toilets and solar showers. You can also stay in one of the primitive wooden field station rooms in the central building (US$20). Including all the bunks in the dormitory, there are 52 beds here. Fresh-prepared meals are available, plus a range of learning and adventure activities throughout Belize.

Monkey Bay offers various cultural learning programs that include homestays with Maya, Creole, and Garinagu communities; it also has a curriculum of tropical watershed ecology field courses. Groups and individuals are welcome for internships and volunteer programs as well. Homestays have a community service component.

PIT STOPS AND FOOD

There are a few notable restaurants clustered around Mile 31, right around where you first see the sleeping Maya giant in hills to the south.

You'll first come to **Cheers** (tel. 501/614-9311, 6 A.M.–8:30 P.M. daily), with its interesting collection of orchids, license plates, and T-shirts. A bit farther, just past the turnoff for Monkey Bay, is **Amigos** (tel. 501/802-8000, open 8 A.M.–9 P.M. daily), another friendly, screened-in bar and restaurant with excellent Belizean and continental food, from US$5–9 per plate.

Along the Hummingbird Highway

This famous stretch of road was paved only a few years ago and boasts some of the most scenic driving in Central America (in my humble opinion). The drive from Belmopan southeast toward Dangriga is an awesome reminder of just how green and wild Belize really is. The highway passes through towering karst hills and long views of broadleaf jungle as you cross the Caves Branch Bridge and enter the Valley of Caves. After another twenty miles, you'll climb into the Maya Mountains, then descend toward the sea. The junction with the Southern Highway is 20 miles east of Over the Top pass—Dangriga is 25. You'll pass through citrus groves, tiny workers' villages perched on the banks of rocky streams, craggy cliffs crusted with beards of vegetation, and thick tracts of cohune palm forest.

◖ ST. HERMAN'S BLUE HOLE NATIONAL PARK

Covering 575 acres, St. Herman's Blue Hole National Park encompasses this water-filled sink, St. Herman's Cave, and the surrounding jungle. (Belize's other Blue Hole lies in the ocean at Lighthouse Reef.) Rich in wildlife, St. Herman's Blue Hole National Park harbors the jaguar, ocelot, tapir, peccary, tamandua, boa constrictor, fer-de-lance, toucan, crested guan, blue-crowned motmot, and red-legged honeycreeper. At about Mile 12½ past Belmopan is a sign for St. Herman's Cave; ignore it and continue to the main park entrance about a mile down the road. You'll find a parking area and a changing room for a dip in the deep blue waters of the Blue Hole.

The pool of the **Blue Hole** is an oblong collapsed karst sinkhole, 300 feet across in some places and about 100 feet deep. Water destined for the nearby Sibun River surfaces briefly here only to disappear once more beneath the ground. Steps lead down to the swimming area, a pool 25 feet deep or so.

St. Herman's Cave is not as convenient to access. As you face the Blue Hole, the trail to St. Herman's Cave lies to the right and requires a hike of a little more than a mile and a half over rugged ground. The trail begins by the changing room. A flashlight and rugged shoes are necessities, and a light windbreaker or sweater is a wise choice for extended stays if you visit in the winter. The nearest of the three entrances to the cave is a huge sinkhole measuring nearly 200 feet across, funneling down to about 65 feet at the cave's lip. Concrete steps laid over the Maya originals aid explorers who wish to descend. The cave doesn't offer the advanced spelunker a real challenge, but neophytes will safely explore it to a distance of about a mile. Pottery, spears, and the remains of torches have been found in many caves in the area. The pottery was used to collect the clear water of cave drippings, called *Zuh uy Ha* by the Maya.

The entire area is a labyrinth of caves where the ancient Maya once lived and roamed; some of the chambers still show signs of rituals long past. A variety of caves lie in the hilly limestone nearby and include **Mountain Cow** and **Petroglyph Caves.** The caves include cathedral-like ceilings hundreds of feet high as well

driving the Hummingbird Highway

© JOSHUA BERMAN

as narrow, cramped passageways. Some have crystal-coated stalactites and stalagmites; others have underground streams that at times seem to speak in murmured voices. And while you won't likely find any Maya living in the caves, you will find a number of harmless bats. Remember: Bring a flashlight, extra batteries, and sturdy walking shoes. The surrounding lush jungle is thick with tropical plants, delicate ferns, bromeliads, and orchids.

It's best to visit most caves with a guide, and at the least, don't visit the park unless the wardens are there (8:30 A.M.–4:30 P.M.). The entrance fee is US$5 per person. Make sure to lock your car, and don't leave valuables in view.

FIVE BLUES LAKE NATIONAL PARK

Located on the Hummingbird Highway at Mile 32, the park can be reached by taking a local bus from the terminal in Belmopan to St. Margaret's Village. Within the village, the park office is on the way to the park, but when I stopped there last it was closed up and surrounded by weeds. When you can find them,

local rangers are both knowledgeable and willing to help with questions that you may have. From the park office, a rutted, four-kilometer road leads to the park. This road can be hiked, or the rangers will be more than willing to provide transportation.

Within Five Blues Lake National Park, several Maya sites are accessible to visitors. Within the Duende Caves, ceremonial pottery can still be found. While some of the more significant sites are heavily regulated by the Belizean Institute of Archaeology, Five Blues Lake provides ample opportunity for visitors to witness Maya writings and pottery. In 2006, a mysterious draining of some of the lakes occurred as the earth sucked some of the famous blue water back into the limestone. There are still many birds and wildlife here, including coatamundi, collared peccary, and agoutis.

Entrance fees (US$5 pp) go toward supporting the park and can be paid to the ranger on duty. At the park's entrance, a visitors center with maps of the trails is available, along with picnic tables. In addition, bathroom facilities are available behind the visitors center. From

BELMOPAN

the visitors center, you can take any of the park's trails or go directly to the lake. Be sure to explore St. Margaret's Village and ask about camping and homestay accommodations.

BILLY BARQUEDIER NATIONAL PARK

This 1,500-acre parcel of crucial watershed was declared a protected area in 2001 and is co-managed by the Forestry Department and a unique village-based cooperative effort, in the form of an NGO, called the Steadfast Tourism and Conservation Association (STACA; tel. 501/603-9936, hya172003@ yahoo.com). This green chunk of the Upper Mullins River Basin holds stunning waterfalls, trails, wildlife, and swimming holes. The entrance is at Mile 17; campgrounds are available. Entrance to the park is US$8 per person, and to camp it's US$10 per person per night. Guides can be found in Dangriga, including **C & G Tours and Charters** (29 Oak St., Dangriga, tel. 501/522-3641 or 610-2277, www.cgtourscharters.com).

ADVENTURE TRAVEL

Neither a "sightseeing" business nor a "resort," **Ian Anderson's Caves Branch Adventure Company and Jungle Lodge** (Mile 41½ Hummingbird Hwy., tel. 501/822-2800, www.cavesbranch.com) offers expeditions that can be strenuous and exciting. This is a hub for social, active trippers; as Ian said a few years ago, "We're certainly not for everyone—thank God!"

The lodge is located on the bank of the Caves Branch River, under a 100-foot jungle canopy. All the guests come together in the open dining room for family-style meals (breakfast and lunch US$12, dinner US$18). Lodging rates are US$5 for the beautiful riverside tent sites (bring your own gear); US$15 for the fine-screened thatched co-ed dormitory with eight bunk beds, linen provided; and US$98–195 for a range of beautifully simple jungle cabanas and suites. The screened accommodations are open to the sights and sounds of the surrounding wildness. Many are shared

bath, and privacy can be limited; ask about jungle and treehouse suites. The main building has electricity, but accommodation lighting is by the glow of kerosene lamps—flush toilets and hot and cold water are available throughout (actually, the warm "jungle shower" is the highlight of many a guest's stay).

On the 58,000 acres of this private estate are 68 known caves, and Ian has discovered and explored them all, developing a variety of trips around many of them. The longest and deepest of these Maya ceremonial caves extends seven miles. Pristine dry caves glisten with crystal formations. Some caves still have pottery shards, skeletal remains, and footprints coated with an icing of rock crystals. Ian offers 1–7 day expeditions, including tubing trips through river caves. Ask about all the different packages and about joining one of the "Bad-Ass" scouting expeditions, when the Caves Branch guides take off in search of new trips to offer their guests, usually in the low season. All expedition guides have received intensive training in cave and wilderness rescue/evacuation and first aid.

Access to Ian Anderson's Caves Branch is located on the Hummingbird Highway between the St. Herman's Blue Hole National Park visitors center and the parking lot for the Blue Hole itself; turn left (if headed south) and continue to the end of the mile-long dirt road. If traveling by bus, you'll have to hike in from here if you haven't arranged to be picked up by lodge staff.

Owned and operated by Upclose Wildlife Tours, the **Green Acres Ranch and Horseback Adventures** (Mile 36 Hummingbird Hwy., tel. 501/670-0091, www.upclosebelize.com) offers a variety of riding and nonriding opportunities. There are accommodations next door at the **Yamwits'** (six rooms with private bath, hot/cold water, and fans are US$50 per night). It's located 17 miles south of Belmopan; turn off the highway after the Sibun Bridge. A quick drive through the orange orchard, across the brook, and up the hill, and you'll find well-built, healthy quarter horses waiting to take you into the countryside. Green Acres welcomes inexperienced riders (including children) and offers a high level of personalized attention from their guides. Rides vary from one to two hours depending on rider experience. Hourly rides, day rides, and even overnight camping rides are available. A US$85 per person fee includes round-trip transfer from Belize City (or equal distance), two to three hours of on-site riding, and a farm-fresh lunch served under the thatched *palapa,* including grilled meats, homemade tortillas, salads, and drinks.

ACCOMMODATIONS

"Bed-and-breakfast" homestay options are sometimes available in several villages up and down the Hummingbird Highway, notably Armenia. This is a quiet settlement, eight miles south of Belmopan, with a Maya and Latino population offering **Hummingbird Homestays** (community tel. 501/809-2036, hummingbirdhomestays@gmail.com). There are 18 participating families, with a wide range of accommodations, though all are simple, rustic, and usually within the home of your hosts (US$22.50 for a night's lodging and three meals). Ask for a tour of the area by the members of the village Youth and Environment Group.

St. Margaret's, at Mile 32, is the entrance to Five Blues Lake National Park and may have some of the same services as Armenia, including accommodations. A much surer bet is to continue to Mile 29½, where you'll find **Alma and Albert's** (or just "A&A's," tel. 501/606-2765), offering a tent site (US$5 pp with your own gear, or US$10 more to rent) and a two-room cabin (US$40) at a gorgeous bend in the river. Alma and Albert are very friendly people with a lovely property, and they'll cook you typical Belizean food in their little roadside eatery and bar.

BELMOPAN

CAYO AND THE MOUNTAIN PINE RIDGE

Between the Caribbean coast "and the inhabited part of Central America is a wilderness, unbroken even by an Indian path. There is no communication with the interior except by the Golfo Dolce or the Balize River; and, from the want of roads, a residence there is more confining than living on an island."

Thus wrote John Lloyd Stephens of Belize's western highlands in the 19th century, well before the construction of the Western Highway that now zips travelers from Belize City to the Guatemalan border in under two hours. Still, there remains a remote feeling to the largest and most temperate of Belize's six districts. And, as you move away from the highway, Stephens's words are as true as ever—it really is a jungle out there. So put away your mask and snorkel and make your way west, mon!

Cayo District's broad eastern edge is guarded by Belmopan, Belize's tiny capital; its western side runs the length of the border with Guatemala and comprises some of Belize's steepest, most remote interior. This area is serviced by San Ignacio, a cool town with low-key international restaurants and a great Saturday outdoor market. Cayo's tourism scene is based on a long and varied menu of tours—and its unique selection of accommodations, from remote river resorts and upscale jungle lodges to the burgeoning budget scene in San Ignacio. There are also a few favorite backpacker digs in the area. Activities include caving, biking, and paddling expeditions.

Cayo boasts a rich mixture of people, places, and creatures. Mayans, Mennonites, mestizos, gringos, Lebanese, Creoles, Guatemalans, and

© JOSHUA BERMAN

HIGHLIGHTS

Medicinal Jungle Trail and Iguana Exhibit: A pleasant and informative guided walk, it's less than an hour long and a short walk from downtown San Ignacio (page 124).

Cahal Pech Archaeological Site: The site is unique for both its archaeological intrigue and its location within the city limits of San Ignacio, and the walk up the hill is well worth it (page 124).

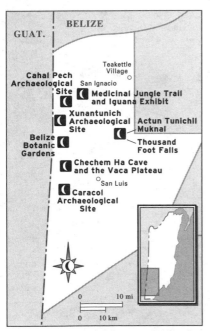

Actun Tunichil Muknal: Spelunk it in any of Cayo's fascinating caves, especially this one. The "Cave of the Crystal Maiden" is the wettest, dirtiest, most adventurous underground trip available. More caving action is available at **Barton Creek, Río Frio,** and **Chechem Ha Caves** (page 132).

Thousand Foot Falls: The trip to Central America's highest waterfall is well worth enduring the rough access road. You can't swim here, but the vista of the falls from the lookout on the canyon's edge is stunning (page 139).

Caracol Archaeological Site: One of the more difficult major ruins to access in Belize (you'll endure a bumpy, multihour ride along the Mountain Pine Ridge), Caracol is rife with discovery, beauty, and long, peaceful views of the wild countryside from atop its newly excavated temples (page 142).

Belize Botanic Gardens: This unique, low-key attraction features hiking trails through a variety of habitats; the operation is totally organic (zero chemicals) and the orchid house is magical (page 145).

Xunantunich Archaeological Site: It's definitely worth crossing the river to spend a long morning or a lazy afternoon in this ancient Maya city (page 148).

Chechem Ha Cave and the Vaca Plateau: The only thing more inspiring than the pottery and mystery found inside Chechem Ha Cave is the waterfall by the same name and the views across the Macal River from this incredible perch on the plateau (page 151).

LOOK FOR **(** TO FIND RECOMMENDED SIGHTS, ACTIVITIES, DINING, AND LODGING.

MOUNTAIN PINE RIDGE

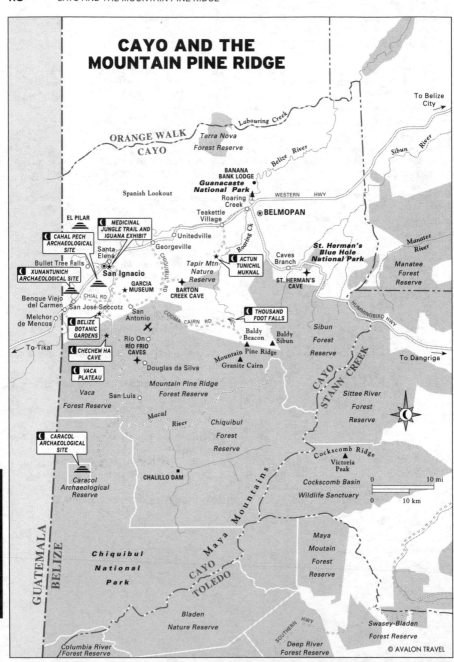

CAYO AND THE MOUNTAIN PINE RIDGE

© AVALON TRAVEL

Chinese all commingle in government, commerce, agriculture, and tourism. The Maya Mountains, Vaca Plateau, and Mountain Pine Ridge are important geological features, and several major rivers drain these highlands, including the Branch, Macal, Mopan, and Sibun Rivers. Savanna, broadleaf jungle, and pinelands form a patchwork of habitats for a wide diversity of flora and fauna.

At one time, the majority of the people in Cayo were mestizos from Guatemala. In those days, this bustling area depended mostly on the forests, especially at the port of San Ignacio, where logs and *chicle* were sent down the river to the sea, then shipped across the world's oceans. Access to the area around San Ignacio, bordered on two sides by rivers, was limited to river traffic. Thus rose the name *Cayo,* or "island" in Spanish. (San Ignacio used to be named "Cayo," and many locals still call it that.) Cayo District still relies on its natural resources, producing some lumber, and also dealing in new agricultural ventures (citrus, peanuts, and cattle), oil, and tourism.

Cayo

PLANNING YOUR TIME

Budget travelers are always pleased to see that their dollar goes farther in Cayo than in other parts of Belize, often enticing them to stick around longer than they'd planned. Days go by differently here than they do at the beach—maybe because of how busy most Cayo visitors find themselves, signing up for a new activity every day or just lazing by the river. But there's no rush, and you can easily bop around the area for weeks without getting weary (unless you're the kind of person who gets bored by too many trees, ruins, and spectacular waterfalls).

But alas, most travelers are on tight schedules, and must be efficient with their allotted Cayo days. In that case, begin in San Ignacio or base yourself in Bullet Tree Falls—strike up a friendship with fellow guests at your hotel, enjoy the narrow streets and cafés, then set off early in the morning for a local tour with a packed lunch and plenty of water. Save one day for caving, one for canoeing, one for Maya ruins, and one for a hike—how many's that? Add one or two more days to rest and recuperate before heading back to the Caribbean. If you can't spare a week, Cayo offers several time-saving combinations of the aforementioned activities—Actun Tunichil Muknal, for instance, is a hiking, swimming, caving, and archaeology adventure all wrapped in one. And even if you've only got a day or two, San Ignacio is close enough to the coast and worth a trip; the forest runs right up to the city limits, where you'll find several trails and a decent archaeological site.

Another option is to light out for the bush after a night or two of orientation in San Ignacio. Staying farther afield—along the Mountain Pine Ridge, or at Martz Farm, or at one of the campgrounds west or south of town—gets you even closer to nature.

SPORTS AND RECREATION

Cayo District is home to a beautiful lattice of trails, from short **nature walks** and **medicine trails** to a range of **hiking trips** through the surrounding hills. **Mountain biking** the Cayo District is fun, beautiful, and a great way to burn off a few Belikins. Routes abound—take the dirt roads around San Ignacio and Bullet Tree, or head up into the Mountain Pine Ridge area; swimming holes and waterfalls beckon as destinations.

Equestrians will find **horseback riding** at a growing number of resorts and tour operators in and outside San Ignacio.

The archaeological sites of Cahal Pech, El Pilar, and Xunantunich are within easy driving (or walking, horseback riding, or biking) distance of San Ignacio. Countless mounds and ruins are scattered throughout the surrounding jungle—and of course, Caracol, the granddaddy of Belizean archaeological sites, is a two-hour drive into the jungle, well worth the trip.

Many Cayo resorts offer excellent guided **cave trips** of varying levels of difficulty, for everyone from the beginning spelunker to the professional speleologist; day and overnight trips are available. Ask about the varied experiences to be had in Handprint Cave, Yaxsahau (Cave of the Ceiba Tree Lord), Actun Tunichil Muknal, Barton Creek Cave, Chechem Ha Cave, or any of the most recently discovered ones that are as yet unnamed.

A wise man once said, "The only way to float is downstream." **Canoeing, kayaking,** and **tubing** are all popular ways to enjoy the Macal and Mopan Rivers. Actually, one popular trip is to paddle *up* the Macal River from downtown San Ignacio, making your way to the Ix Chel Medicine Trail or Belize Botanic Garden.

SHOPPING

Much Belizean craftwork originates here in Cayo, and it is available for sale at a few roadside gift shops, galleries, and workshops. There are many shops along Burns Avenue in San Ignacio, but there are a few notable spots outside of town as well. The most extensive is **Orange Gifts** (formerly Caesar's), a friendly shop at Mile 60 on the Western Highway. Orange Gifts has probably the best selection going of laminated maps of Belize, sarongs, books, and Gallon Jug Coffee packages, and a great little restaurant to boot. Nearby **Hot Mama's Belize** (tel. 501/824-0444 or 610-1624, www.hotmamasfoods.biz) makes some of the finest and spiciest condiments in the country. Gift packages and other sundries, as well as tours, are available.

Some of the country's most famous **slate carvers** are in the area, as is Octavio Sixto in Benque Viejo, with his detailed miniature replicas of Belizean shacks and landmark buildings. There is always a row of Belizean and Guatemalan craft stalls by the Xunantunich Ferry (San José Succotz) and a number of cramped and brimming gift shops in downtown San Ignacio. The Magana family has two shops, **Magana Zactunich Art Gallery,**

south of Cristo Rey Village, and **Magana's Art Center,** at the east edge of San José Succotz. Both sell small ceramics, slate carvings, and other crafts. On the north edge of San Antonio, the Garcia sisters run their **Tanah Mayan Art Museum** and store. In Benque Viejo, **Galeria del Arte de Gucumaz** has a choice of Belizean and Guatemalan crafts at reasonable prices.

GUIDES AND TOUR OPERATORS

At last count, there were 150 licensed tour guides in the Cayo District, Belize's largest chapter of the Tour Guide Association, and the number was growing. Most guides work either directly for one of the area jungle lodges or for one of the tour operators listed below, and a few are independently famous and run their own trips. Signing up for a tour is as easy as walking into the office of one of Cayo's tour operators (most are on Burns Avenue or among the row of shacks on the road toward the Wooden Bridge). Booking through your guesthouse's front desk, which sometimes is both cheaper and more convenient. Eva's (tel. 501/804-2267, www.evasonline.com) is also a great source for respected, independent guides and can set up just about anything for you while you drink a tall papaya smoothie.

In addition to the Actun Tunichil Muknal cave trip, **Pacz Tours** (tel. 501/824-2477 or 600-7419, www.pacztours.net) offers a number of expeditions, including overnight camping options involving some combination of river running, waterfall quests, ruins, caves, and rappelling. As for their professionalism and gear, well, put it this way: when National Geographic staff come to Belize, they call Pacz. Equally reputable, **Hun Chi'ik Tours** (tel. 501/600-9192, hunchiik@belizemail.net) has very experienced guides and is "your path to ancient secrets" on all the best tours.

Mayawalk Adventures (tel. 501/824-3070, www.mayawalk.com) maintains an open-air shop at 19 Burns Avenue, right across from Eva's, and will take you to Actun Tunichil Muknal and beyond; Mayawalk has an impressive fleet of vans and canoes. **River Rat** (tel.

501/625-4636, www.riverratbelize.com) specializes in Actun Tunichil Muknal, kayak expeditions, and overnight float trips; ask around town for "Gonzo," the amiable chief guide. You could also contact **Cayo Gial Tours** through the San Ignacio Resort Hotel.

Be sure to walk the row of tour operator shacks near the open market—they are all small, Belizean-owned operations and may be cheaper if you are booking yourself independently. Among these, **David's Tours** (tel. 501/824-3674) is one of the old standbys, offering volumes of local knowledge and the full range of tours. Also check **Maya Mystic** (tel. 501/804-0055), open seven days; ask about the "Monkey Tail" overnight camping trip. **Green Valley** (tel. 501/601-4740) also has an overnight trip, plus the basic menu.

Tony's Guided Tours (tel. 501/824-3292) is probably the most economical independent trip on the river at US$17.50 per person. For the more adventurous, Tony also offers a five-day canoe/camp trip to Belize City (US$65 pp per day, all-inclusive). He provides everything except your personal effects.

Amigos Belize (tel. 501/603-9436, www.amigosbelize.com), located on the Santa Elena side of the Hawksworth Bridge, specializes in day and overnight canoe trips on the Macal River, as well as overnights to their private paradise on Turneffe Island, with camping and a couple of cabanas.

For unique caving expeditions in the upper Macal River Valley (sometimes involving hiking, rapelling, and camping), call **Belizean Sun** (tel. 501/601-2630, www.belizean-sun.com), based in San José de Succotz at **OnDWay Café.**

San Ignacio

There is something indescribably alluring about the capital of Belize's western district. Maybe it's some remnant Maya magic, trickling downhill from the ruins of Cahal Pech, or maybe it's the soft mist itself, quieting the village on rainy-season mornings and blanketing the floodplains to the east. Maybe it's the raw vitality of the surrounding wilderness that bumps right up against the town and breathes so much healthy energy through San Ignacio's streets—or maybe it's what happens when all of these factors combine with a kind, good-hearted, diverse community of people. Belizeans of all creeds and colors happily reside in San Ignacio, as do an increasing number of both transient and transplanted foreigners. Roots, culture, and music are in the air, and there is as much Rasta flavor in Cayo as there is Creole, Guatemalan, Garinagu, and gringo.

There is budget lodging galore in San Ignacio, as well as a broad range of food—from rice and beans to curried lamb, from veggie burgers to pork ribs. And, of course, there is more to do than anyone—even permanent residents—has time for, with all manner of active expeditions leaving from Burns Avenue each and every morning.

ORIENTATION

Visitors to San Ignacio from the east first pass through its sister city of Santa Elena, turning right at the Social Security building and continuing across the **Wooden Bridge,** a low-resting affair that places you on the San Ignacio side of the Macal River, close to the open market grounds. From there, turning left will take you directly into "downtown" San Ignacio, marked by a five-pronged intersection that is nearly always abuzz with activity. **Burns Avenue** crosses here and is the main drag for locals and tourists alike. The Novelo's bus station is located about three blocks up Burns Avenue from the big intersection. Within two or three blocks in any direction of that intersection, you'll find most of San Ignacio's budget accommodations, restaurants, Internet cafés, and tour operators.

The town's three banks are on the block of Burns Avenue that stems east (toward the river)

MOUNTAIN PINE RIDGE

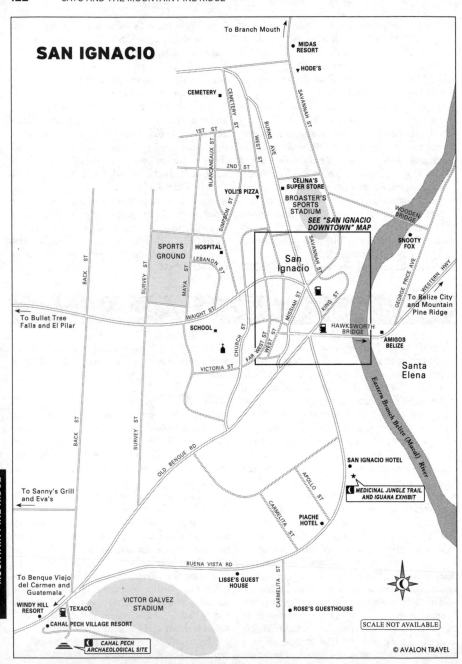

SAN IGNACIO

To Branch Mouth

MIDAS RESORT

HODE'S

CEMETERY

CEMETERY ST

SAVANNAH ST

BURNS AVE

1ST ST

BLANCANEAUX ST

WEST ST

2ND ST

CELINA'S SUPER STORE

YOLI'S PIZZA

BROASTER'S SPORTS STADIUM

SIMPSON ST

SEE "SAN IGNACIO DOWNTOWN" MAP

WOODEN BRIDGE

SNOOTY FOX

SPORTS GROUND

HOSPITAL

LEBANON ST

MAYA ST

San Ignacio

SAVANNAH ST

GEORGE PRICE AVE

WESTERN HWY

BACK ST

SURVEY ST

MISSIAH ST

KING ST

To Belize City and Mountain Pine Ridge

To Bullet Tree Falls and El Pilar

WAIGHT ST

SCHOOL

CHURCH ST

FAR WEST ST

WEST ST

HAWKSWORTH BRIDGE

AMIGOS BELIZE

VICTORIA ST

Santa Elena

Eastern Branch Belize (Macal) River

BACK ST

SURVEY ST

OLD BENQUE RD

SAN IGNACIO HOTEL

APOLLO ST

MEDICINAL JUNGLE TRAIL AND IGUANA EXHIBIT

To Sanny's Grill and Eva's

CARMELITA ST

PIACHE HOTEL

BUENA VISTA RD

To Benque Viejo del Carmen and Guatemala

LISSE'S GUEST HOUSE

CARMELITA ST

WINDY HILL RESORT

TEXACO

VICTOR GALVEZ STADIUM

ROSE'S GUESTHOUSE

CAHAL PECH VILLAGE RESORT

SCALE NOT AVAILABLE

CAHAL PECH ARCHAEOLOGICAL SITE

© AVALON TRAVEL

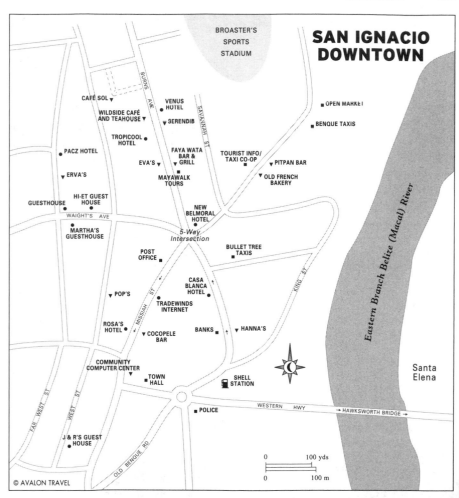

SAN IGNACIO DOWNTOWN

BROASTER'S SPORTS STADIUM

CAFÉ SOL

VENUS HOTEL

WILDSIDE CAFÉ AND TEAHOUSE

SERENDIB

OPEN MARKET

BENQUE TAXIS

TROPICOOL HOTEL

PACZ HOTEL

FAYA WATA BAR & GRILL

EVA'S

TOURIST INFO/ TAXI CO-OP

PITPAN BAR

ERVA'S

MAYAWALK TOURS

OLD FRENCH BAKERY

HI-ET GUEST HOUSE

GUESTHOUSE

WAIGHT'S AVE

NEW BELMORAL HOTEL

MARTHA'S GUESTHOUSE

5-Way Intersection

POST OFFICE

BULLET TREE TAXIS

POP'S

CASA BLANCA HOTEL

TRADEWINDS INTERNET

ROSA'S HOTEL

COCOPELE BAR

BANKS

HANNA'S

COMMUNITY COMPUTER CENTER

TOWN HALL

SHELL STATION

Santa Elena

POLICE

WESTERN HWY

HAWKSWORTH BRIDGE

J & R'S GUEST HOUSE

OLD BENQUE RD.

FAR WEST ST.

WEST ST.

MISSIAH ST.

KING ST.

SAVANNAH ST.

BURNS AVE

Eastern Branch Belize (Macal) River

0   100 yds
0   100 m

© AVALON TRAVEL

MOUNTAIN PINE RIDGE

from the big intersection, and at the end of that block you'll find a tiny traffic circle in front of the police station, which guards the western abutment of the **Hawksworth Bridge.** Normally, only eastbound traffic is allowed on the one-lane bridge from Santa Elena to San Ignacio (except when the lower bridge floods and traffic is diverted, as it was several times in 2008 during the highest recorded river levels since 1961). Built in 1949, the Hawksworth is the only suspension bridge in Belize; it is also the starting line of the big canoe race in March. During the bridge's two-way past, whoever reached the center first had the right of way, and the other vehicle had to back off; occasionally the local gendarme had to come along and measure car distances to settle drivers' arguments. Any of the roads that lead uphill from downtown San Ignacio will eventually place you back on the Western Highway heading toward Benque.

SIGHTS

Even if you arrive late in the afternoon, there is still time to enjoy a tour of the Cahal Pech ruins or a short nature hike on the banks of the Macal River (only three blocks from the city center).

Medicinal Jungle Trail and Iguana Exhibit

This interpretive herb trail and iguana breeding project (the full name is the Green Iguana Conservation Project), on 14 lush riverside acres, is accessed through the San Ignacio Resort Hotel (tel. 501/824-2034, 501/824-2125, or 800/822-3274 www.sanignaciobelize.com). Tours of the herb trail or the iguana project are available for less than US$6 a person; plan on 45 minutes for either talk. With the money earned from curious tourists, the hotel owners are able to keep the trail maintained and the iguana project going—and to prevent the heavily vegetated riverbank from being developed (crucial to the cleanliness of the local water supply). To date, 175 species of birds have been observed here (including a rare family pair of black hawk eagles), plus a number of mammals.

When the iguana population was on a noticeable downward cycle, the folks at the San Ignacio Resort Hotel created this successful breeding and release project. Groups go on hunts, capture the females, and hijack the eggs, which they raise in a predator-free, food-rich environment before releasing the iguanas back into the wild. The program has also trained former iguana hunters to become iguana guides, a far more profitable and sustainable endeavor, and hosts many school groups, featuring the Iguana Kids Club and Adopt an Iguana Program.

Cahal Pech Archaeological Site

The ruins of Cahal Pech ("Place of the Ticks") still have a decent number of trees throughout the excavated series of plazas and royal residences. A steep 10-minute walk from downtown San Ignacio, Cahal Pech is a great, tree-shaded destination, where your imagination can run wild with all that once occurred here. Cahal Pech was discovered in the early 1950s, but scientific research did not begin until 1988, when a team from San Diego State University's anthropology department began work with local

The ruins at Cahal Pech are peaceful and shady at any time of day.

archaeology guru Dr. Jaime Awe. Thirty-four structures were compacted into a three-acre area. Excavation is ongoing and visitors are welcome. It is well worth your trip and admission fee (US$5 at Cahal Pech Visitor Center, tel. 501/824-4236, 6 A.M.–6 P.M. daily). The visitors center also houses a small museum of artifacts found at the site (and a skeleton from Xunantunich). Nearby **Tipu** was a Christian Maya town during the early years of colonization. Tipu was as far as the Spanish were able to penetrate in the 16th century.

RECREATION
Horseback Riding

Book your horseback riding trip at **Easy Rider** (tel. 501/824-3310), an independent operator who charges reasonable rates and gives good service, based out of an office in San Ignacio next door to Eva's; novices welcome. Also recommended is **Nabitunich Horseback Riding** (ask at Eva's). Expect to pay about US$20 for two hours, maybe US$30 for a trip to Xunantunich.

Mountain Rider is a small, no-frills, family-run operation just past the village of San Antonio as you drive toward the Mountain Pine Ridge; look for the sign and stop in to find out more details. Also check with **Mountain**

© JOSHUA BERMAN

MOUNTAIN PINE RIDGE

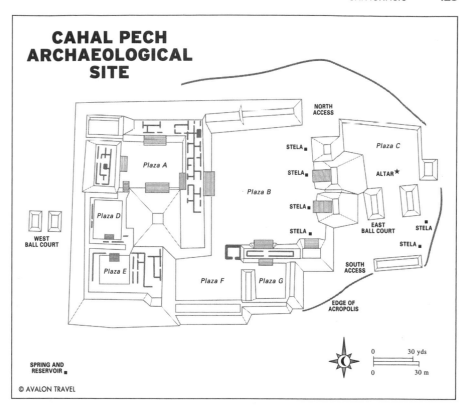

CAHAL PECH ARCHAEOLOGICAL SITE

NORTH ACCESS

STELA

Plaza C

Plaza A

STELA

ALTAR ★

Plaza B

STELA

Plaza D

STELA

EAST BALL COURT

STELA

WEST BALL COURT

STELA

STELA

SOUTH ACCESS

Plaza E

Plaza F

Plaza G

EDGE OF ACROPOLIS

0   30 yds
0   30 m

SPRING AND RESERVOIR

© AVALON TRAVEL

Equestrian Trails, which has one of the biggest trail systems in the Pine Ridge.

Bicycling
Rental bicycles can be found at the Tropicool Hotel in San Ignacio, plus a few other places. Top-notch mountain bike tours are offered at Chaa Creek; very skilled and experienced guides take riders on some reportedly kickass single track.

Boating
Canoe five miles up the Macal River to visit Chaa Creek and the Botanic Gardens at duPlooy's; rent a boat and guide from **Tony's Guided Tours** (tel. 501/824-3292), **Amigos Belize** (tel. 501/603-9436, www.amigosbelize.com), or **Cayo Gial Tours** (tel. 501/824-

2034, 501/824-2125, or 800/822-3274, www.sanignaciobelize.com, about US$25–30 pp). If you're here in March, you won't miss the excitement of La Ruta Maya Belize River Challenge, a long-distance paddle race to the ocean.

Massage, Bodywork, and Healing
Eva's Massage Therapy (4 Blue Bird St., tel. 501/824-3423, ebuhler@btl.net) is located just down from the Texaco station on the Western Highway, exiting town toward Benque. For US$30, get an hour-long full body massage or a 30–40 minute "back and neck therapy session."

Therapeutic Massage Studio (tel. 501/604-0314, sharane@pacific.net, about US$40/hour) is located in town, between Tropicool and Café Sol, and offers a wonderful range of massage, energy work, reflexology, and more.

MOUNTAIN PINE RIDGE

CANOES ON LA RUTA MAYA

One of the world's longest canoe races, **La Ruta Maya Belize River Challenge** (www.larutamayabelize.com) features several hundred canoes racing over five days down the 180-mile length of the Belize River, from San Ignacio to the Caribbean Sea. The race is held during the first week of March, timed to coincide with Baron Bliss Day celebrations. Increasingly popular since its inception in 1998, La Ruta Maya has a number of different divisions and offers more than US$15,000 in prize money. The race features special divisions, such as "Master's" (over 40), women's, mixed gender, and amateur. They are part athletic event, part tourism draw, and part fiesta. The competitive feeling among the tiny Belizean population makes it a lot of fun. The **Belize Extreme Canoe Adventure Race** is held in September, when participants paddle nonstop for 19-24 hours.

There are some options for visiting yogis, but class schedules are loose and ever-changing. Classes are sometimes given at the Therapeutic Massage Studio or at the San Ignacio Resort Hotel (tel. 501/824-2034, 501/824-2125, or 800/822-3274, www.sanignaciobelize.com). To find out the latest, contact Kate Devine at **Cayo Yoga** (tel. 510/665-1972, cayoyoga@hotmail.com) or look for posters.

NIGHTLIFE

If you have the energy after a day out on the river or hiking the jungles, you have several good choices. Just follow the masses as they trek between bars and discos. Many start the night at **Cocopele** (open daily at 5 P.M.), where expats and locals mingle over pool tables, dart boards, and the hardwood bar—or else down by the river at the **Pitpan,** where you'll find a great collection of Belikin beer on tap—then head up to the dancing at **Legends 2000** or the **Roomba Room.** It's a small town, so finding the party is not difficult.

For live music, **Lisse's Guest House,** located on the hill leading up out of town (toward Benque), is known for hosting some of the area's finest local musicians. Occasionally, the **Riverside River Lodge** in Bullet Tree hosts concerts and festivals.

Got no dancing skills? Check with the San Ignacio Resort Hotel to see if they're still offering **Latin dance lessons.** It's only US$5 for basic bachata, merengue, and salsa steps.

ACCOMMODATIONS

Choices abound for such a small town, many of them cheap, clean, converted family homes, and most of them are densely clustered within a few blocks of each other. There are more quality guesthouses than there is room in this book, so feel free to poke around on your own. Cayo can get hot at times, but remember that it's generally cooler than the rest of the country, so air-conditioning may not be a big priority, especially between June and December. Also, note that most accommodations in Cayo (but not all) quote prices with tax and service charges inclusive; most also offer respectable discounts in low season and for multiple nights. As always, I've reported high-season double-occupancy rates throughout this chapter.

Camping

Smith's Family Farm (tel. 501/604-2227) is a peaceful 25-acre retreat up Branch Mouth Road with a lovely shaded campground (US$5 pp) and collection of cabins (US$20–30), all with private bath, hot/cold water, and simple furniture. Weekly rates are also available.

Cosmos Camping (15 Branch Mouth Rd., tel. 501/824-2116, cosmoscamping@btl.net, US$5 pp) is a 15-minute walk from town, just past Midas Tropical Resort, and has pretty grounds, lots of big trees, and mowed lawns where you can pitch a tent. It's on the Mopan River and has shared bath and showers, but is kind of isolated, as the office is back up the road toward town. Campers are also welcome at **Midas Tropical Resort** (tel. 501/824-3845, US$7).

Inglewood (tel. 501/824-3555, www.ingle-woodcampinggrounds.com) offers full hookups for RVs on the side of the highway a couple miles west of San Ignacio. Following the same road, you'll find campgrounds at the **Clarissa Falls Resort** (tel. 501/824-3916, www.clarissafalls.com) and the **Trek Stop** (tel. 501/823-2265, www.thetrekstop.com)inSan José de Succotz.

Under US$25

The **Hi-Et Guest House** (tel. 501/824-2828, thehiet@yahoo.com, US$10–12.50 for shared bath, US$20–25 for private bath) is an excellent budget option on West Street, built right into the owner's large home. The five rooms with shared baths and cold water are clean and comfortable with hardwood floors. The five rooms with private bath in the next building are a big step up in quality and not much in price—they're well kept, with tiled floors and balconies. Around the corner, the **Tropicool Hotel** (30A Burns Ave., tel. 501/804-3052) has 10 simple, clean rooms with shared bath (US$14) and very nicely kept and furnished cabins with private bath, TV, and fan (US$28).

Very reasonable, friendly lodging can be found at **J & R's Guest House** (20 Far West St., tel. 501/824-2502, jrguesthouse@yahoo.com, from US$10); there are only three rooms, one with private bath (US$17.50), breakfast is included, and there's a lovely porch. In the center of town on Far West Street, **Pacz Guest House** (tel. 501/824-4538, pacz@btl.net, US$12.50/20 s/d for shared bath, a bit more for private bath) is a small hostelry with five clean, simple rooms. Free tea or coffee is available in the morning, and there's a nice common space around a television. Lots of exciting tours are offered.

A longtime standard is **Venus Hotel** (tel. 501/824-3203, www.venushotelbelize.com) on Burns Avenue, with 32 rooms starting at US$16 for shared bath (they're a bit run-down, with no windows). The rooms with private bath (US$25–43) are in better condition, and you can take your pick of those overlooking the park or the street.

US$25-50

One of the best value midrange hotels has to be the **Casa Blanca Guest House** (tel. 501/824-2080, www.casablancaguesthouse.com, US$20–50, US$50 for a/c), winner of the 2004 Best Small Hotel in Belize award, with eight immaculate, cozy rooms with private bath, hot/cold water, TV; access to beautiful common living room, kitchen, balcony, and rooftop deck. It's located on Burns Avenue near the banks. **Rosa's Hotel** (tel. 501/804-2265, rosashotel@yahoo.com, from US$28) has a selection of rooms with private bath and fan or air-conditioning (US$38); rooms range from small and stuffy to high and airy—check out a few before deciding.

US$50-100

Martha's Guesthouse (10 West St., tel. 501/824-3647, www.marthasbelize.com, US$40–80) continues to offer a truly charming, tasteful atmosphere in a homey setting, with an abundance of common lounging areas for guests to mingle in if they so desire. It's located one block off the five-way intersection; the rooms are classy, with hardwood floors and furniture, private bath, fans, hot water, and cable television. Laundry services are available. There's an excellent restaurant downstairs, as well as a front desk to arrange tours. Martha's just expanded into a six-room annex, about a three-minute walk up Burns Avenue, with beautiful apartment-style options, several with kitchenettes and porches (US$50–65, weekly rates available).

About a quarter mile out of town, at Branch Mouth Road, check out **Midas Tropical Resort** (tel. 501/824-3172, www.midasbelize.com, from US$54), a small, family-run lodging. You'll find seven cool and airy cottages with private bath (air-conditioning available), situated on seven acres along the banks of the Macal River (down a 300-yard path from the cottages). Campers are welcome. A restaurant serves breakfast and lunch, and a small gift shop in the reception area has a few knickknacks.

Talk about a vista! **Cahal Pech Village** (tel. 501/824-3740, www.cahalpech.com, US$79–119) offers a variety of rooms and cabanas spread out on a spacious hillside with stunning views of San Ignacio and the valley below. The 15 rooms have private bath and air-conditioning, or choose a thatch-and-wood

MOUNTAIN PINE RIDGE

cabana with private bath, hot/cold water, and porch. Family suites and cabanas are available too. A restaurant, bar, and creative swimming pool round out the resort, in addition to its quick access to the Cahal Pech ruins right next door.

Over US$100

Fit for royalty, **San Ignacio Resort Hotel** (tel. 501/824-2034, 501/824-2125, or 800/822-3274, www.sanignaciobelize.com, US$170–200) is rightly proud of having hosted Her Majesty Queen Elizabeth II in 1994 and, as of 2006, has a new grand marble lobby and reception hall to prove it. The hotel is perched above the lush Macal River Valley and a short downhill walk from the center of town, offering incredible views of forest and wildlife from each of its 24 deluxe air-conditioned rooms, some with their own secluded balconies; the rooms have private tiled baths, TV, comfy furniture, and telephones. There is also a honeymoon suite on the second floor, above the beautiful marble lobby. The hotel also hosts the Stork Club Bar & Grill, Running W Steakhouse & Restaurant, a jungle-view patio deck and swimming pool, a basketball court, tennis, a disco, sightseeing tours, and convention and wedding facilities. As "the only jungle in town," it has 14 acres of forest along the river with marked trails and a swimming beach. Bird-watching tours are available with the on-site guide, who will also show you the **Green Iguana Conservation Project** and the **Medicinal Jungle Trail,** located on the hotel's grounds.

FOOD
Fast and Cheap

San Ignacio has a higher than average number of cheap Mexican fast-food places, and a few *pupuserias* (serving an El Salvadorean dish: fried tortillas stuffed with beans, cheese, and meat) for good measure. Check out the stalls in the basement of the Burns Avenue Mall or across from the Belize Bank. Saturday morning, super early, is the best bet for cheap eats, as organic farmers, local cooks, and produce vendors congregate at the outdoor market. Dim sum snacks, barbecue, and other treats run out fast. This is the best place to chow down before catching a bus to other areas.

The **Old French Bakery** (7 A.M.–9 P.M. Mon.–Sat.) is over by the Pitpan bar and serves delicious breads and pastries. The tiny **coffee shop** connected to the Serendib Restaurant sells ice cream as well as meat pies and generous vegetable patties: a perfect meal on the go. Almost directly across the street, **Lucy's** is a fantastic little taco and burrito stand.

The best **barbecue** chefs set up in Santa Elena, just over the Hawksworth Bridge, and they cater especially to weekend party crowds, offering greasy mounds of meat, rice, and beans used by many customers to soak up all that beer sloshing around in their stomachs.

Low-Key Belizean

Some have called **Erva's** (4 Far West St.) the best Belizean food in Belize—a bold statement, indeed; try for yourself. It is a cozy, quality, family-run restaurant that often caters to groups. **(Pop's** may be the closest Belize comes to a small-town, cramped American diner, with booths, bottomless cups of coffee, and customers watching CNN and talking religion and politics—except Pop's is owned by a 100 percent Belizean Hemingway look-alike (6:30 A.M.–2:30 P.M. daily). It's located just to the south, around the corner from the five-way intersection; ask anyone nearby for directions. **Elvira's Diner** (7 A.M.–8 P.M. daily) also has a down-home feel and is located under the guesthouse of the same name.

Eva's Restaurant and Bar (22 Burns Ave., tel. 501/804-2267, evas@btl.net) is not only a tourist and activity center, it's also the place for basic dishes like stew chicken, burgers, pork chops, burritos, and a lot more (meals around US$5). Box lunches are available, as is fresh-squeezed OJ. Check out the patio through the back door; there's Internet access and art for sale and you can book your tour while you wait. Right across the street, **Faya Wata Sports Bar and Grill** features a porch barbecue, free Internet, darts, live music, and sports on TV.

For ambience, you'll want to try **Sanny's Grill,** which is a bit out of the way (located toward the western exit to Benque, just down from the Texaco station), but well worth it for the fine menu and nice lighting and music. The **Eagle Landing** restaurant, tucked down a side street off of Burns Avenue, across from Belize Bank, caters to late-night revelers and taxi drivers. The menu is varied and an excellent burger platter can be had for US$5.

International

(Hanna's** offers all the basic Belizean food, but it's also got a huge, cosmopolitan menu that includes Asian, Indian, and vegetarian dishes (and an ample wine list), all prepared with organic ingredients and meat raised by the owner himself, a transplanted Zimbabwean; it's open for all three meals and very popular with tourists. The same goes for **(** Café Sol**, a comfortable, colorful place about halfway up Burns Avenue—you can't go wrong with anything on the menu here, which includes wraps, soy burgers, pastas, and salads (also Internet and fresh bagels!). It's open 7 A.M.–9 P.M., closed Monday. Entrées at both places are in the US$5–12 range.

Near the Venus Hotel, you'll find the **Serendib Restaurant,** owned by a Sri Lankan and which, along with good hamburgers and chow mein, serves excellent curries and dal. It's reasonably priced; a broiled lobster dinner or San Ignacio Giant Steak will set you back only about US$12. **Greedy's Pizza** understands the importance of a super-hot oven in the production of succulent crust. Find these great pies right across from the Venus Hotel. Greedy's also does a kick-ass breakfast and burger platter.

Maxim's Chinese Restaurant (23 Far West St.) has a good reputation among the locals; a family-run café, it serves mainly lunch and dinner. Prices are moderate; you won't pay much over US$10 for the best meal in the house and a beer.

Martha's Kitchen has some of the best pizza in Cayo, plus a full menu including stir-fried vegetables (about US$6), T-bone steak with gravy and fries (US$8), and a simple club sandwich (US$4). There's a wood-fire pizza oven at **Firenza Cafe,** with 10-inch pies only US$5 (and a full Italian menu to boot; located within

a block of the five-way intersection). Visitors also give high praise to **Yoli's Pizza.**

In addition to steaks, pork chops, and seafood entrées from US$10, the **Running W Steakhouse & Restaurant** (in the San Ignacio Resort Hotel, tel. 501/824-2125) also serves up an open-air dining patio above the Macal River. Belizean classic plates start at US$4 and feature meat from the restaurant's own ranch.

INFORMATION

There is an official tourist information post at the Cahal Pech Visitor Center (tel. 501/824-4236), and the Belize Tourism Industry Association, offering brochures for local resorts, taxi charters, and a town map, has a stand near the Savannah Taxi Co-op downtown. However, you'll find out much more by reading the posters and advertisements at Eva's Restaurant—it's like reading a four-walled catalog for the area's activities and accommodations. Many travelers make Eva's their first stop in town, as it's a gathering spot not only for knowledgeable wanderers but also for the folks who run the cottages and tours. New owner Jana Hill and her staff are very helpful in terms of hooking up travelers with the more remote lodges. Former owner Bob Jones is a walking database of information and operates Pacz Tours, farther down the street. Information and tour booking is available in many other restaurants, at hotel front desks, and at Internet places in San Ignacio as well, notably at the Green Dragon.

SERVICES

Atlantic Bank, Scotia Bank, and **Belize Bank** are all on Burns Avenue, just past the Hawksworth Bridge as you come into town. Martha's Guesthouse offers daily **laundry** service (7 A.M.–8 P.M.), as does a launderette tucked into a DVD rental place across from the main bus/taxi stand (US$5 for wash, dry, and fold). Across from BTL., **Celina's Super Store** (43 Burns Ave., tel. 501/824-2247) is the largest, best-equipped supermarket in town, but there are many other Chinese shops scattered around as well. **Angelus Press,** on the top floor of the Burns Avenue Mall, also has some books, in addition to copy machines and office supplies. **Belicolor,** next to the post office, develops film, sells many camera batteries, and has some camera equipment.

For travel arrangements, **Exodus International** (tel. 501/824-4400, exodus@ btl.net) is located at the beginning of Burns Avenue (near the bridge).

Internet Access

Many hotels have a computer you can use for free. **Tradewinds** (7 A.M.–11 P.M., closed Sun.) has big, comfy chairs and fast machines. Just up the block, the **Community Computer Center** is cheapest by far and has the most machines. **Cafe Cayo** (located on Burns Ave. next to the Belize Bank, 8 A.M.–midnight, closed Tues., about US$3/hour) has monitors arranged beneath desks to offer privacy. You'll also find a pleasant lounge and a food and beverage menu.

GETTING THERE

All the resorts can arrange for a transfer from the international airport in Belize City, from US$125. A shared shuttle to the Caye Caulker Water Taxi Terminal can be arranged at a number of tour operators, for not much more than an express bus ticket if you have enough people.

GETTING AROUND

Downtown San Ignacio is tiny and entirely walkable. The hill to Cahal Pech isn't long, but it's still quite a workout. Taxis there or anywhere else within the city limits cost US$3–4 per person. Cheap *colectivo* taxis run from San Ignacio in all directions throughout the day, making it easy to get to towns and destinations in the immediate vicinity (including Bullet Tree, Succotz, and Benque). In addition to the main buses running back and forth on the Western Highway, village buses come into Market Square from most surrounding towns, returning to the hills in the afternoons. To the south, buses only run as far as the village of San Antonio—perhaps someone will think to start public transportation to Caracol once the road is improved.

Car Rentals

Anyone wishing to travel independently to the Mountain Pine Ridge, Caracol, the Hydro Road, or El Pilar might consider renting a car—either in Belize City or at one of the few places in San Ignacio and Santa Elena. Renting in Cayo is cheaper than in Belize (as low as US$60/day) and a good way to go if you really want to explore this area.

At the top of the Old Benque Road at the western edge of San Ignacio, you'll find **Cayo Rentals** (tel. 501/824-2153, abscomputer@btl. net), with a handful of newish vehicles for rent in the Texaco station parking lot; US$75 per 24 hours *includes* taxes and insurance (which is cheaper than any place in Belize City). Across the bridge in Santa Elena, **Safe Tours Belize** (tel. 501/824-4262 or 614-4476, www.safe-toursbelize.com) has a small fleet of Isuzu Troopers and 15-passenger vans. There's also **Matus Car Rentals** (tel. 501/663-4702 or 824-2089, matuscarrental@yahoo.com), on the hill up from the town center, which offers decent weekly rates.

By Bus

Westbound buses from Belize City and Belmopan run through the middle of town, stopping at the park as part of the daily runs to Benque. Expect only limited service on Sunday. Expresses take about two hours between Belize City and San Ignacio, including the quick stop in Belmopan. Regular buses leave every hour, and there are a handful of daily expresses between 7 A.M. and 7 P.M. Check on the express departure times the day before your journey, as the schedule changes from time to time. Bus schedules are constantly changing as companies battle it out over routes and turf. Ask the locals, who will know what is best.

Airport Shuttles

All of the main tour operators offer airport shuttles, usually dependent on how many people sign up; they often don't run with fewer than four passengers. Individual resorts offer airport transfers as well, but they charge an arm and a leg. The cheapest option is to get to and from the airport by bus.

To Guatemala or Mexico

The Mexican bus lines Linea Dorada and San Juan both travel through Belize between Guatemala and Chetumal, with a stop at Amigos Belize Tour Company (tel. 501/603-9436, www.amigosbelize.com). The stop is located at the Santa Elena end of the Hawksworth Bridge, where you can buy bus tickets to anywhere in Mexico.

East of San Ignacio

The stretch of Western Highway between Guanacaste National Park (where the Hummingbird Highway heads south) and Santa Elena has a number of notable destinations and lodgings.

ALONG THE WESTERN HIGHWAY

As you drive toward Cayo from Belize City and Belmopan, after passing the Hummingbird Highway junction, the roadside village of Teakettle greets you with a jarring series of speed bumps. Turning left at the Pook's Hill sign carries you past cornfields grown atop ancient Maya residential mounds, all the while skirting a massive chunk of seriously beautiful bush that comprises the following areas.

Covering 6,741 acres, the **Tapir Mountain Nature Reserve** is one of the newest jewels in the country's crown of natural treasures. The deep, steamy jungle is ripe with an abundance of plant life. Every wild thing native to the region roams its forests, from toucans to tapirs, coatis to kinkajous. At present, the reserve is off-limits to all but scientific expeditions. However, you can see a piece of it by going on an Actun Tunichil Muknal trip.

Pook's Hill Lodge

Once you arrive at the remote clearing that is Pook's Hill Lodge (tel. 501/820-2017, pookshill@btl.net, www.pookshillbelize.com, US$148), you'll have a hard time believing that you are only 12 miles from Belmopan and 21 miles from San Ignacio, so dense and peaceful is the forest around you. Towering hardwoods, flowering bromeliads, and exotic birds hem in the accommodations, which are built around a small Maya residential ruin. Pook's Hill is a 300-acre private nature reserve, bordered by the Tapir Mountain Nature Reserve and the Roaring River and offering active travelers 10 thatch-roof, mid-scale cabanas from which to base their Cayo explorations. The cottages have private baths, electricity, and comfortable furnishings. The lounge/bar area overlooks a grassy knoll that gently slopes toward the creek; be sure to take advantage of one of the many natural history books in the bookcase. The dining room is downstairs from the lounge, and good, filling meals are served family style. Vegetarian or other preferences can be accommodated with advance notice.

To get there, call for a free transfer from Belmopan; if driving, look for the hand-painted sign at Teakettle Village (around Mile 52½), turn left onto the road, and follow the signs that lead the way. After four miles, turn right—the property begins less than a mile down the road. The road can be rough; another three-quarters of a mile through a tunnel of broadleaf will take you to the lodge.

Accommodations and Food

Continuing west toward San Ignacio, you'll come across the best and most complete gift shop in the country, **Orange Gifts** (formerly Caesar's Place, tel. 501/824-2341, www.orangegifts.com), which is also a restaurant, bar, and lodging (although that may be soon phased out). Located at Mile 60, about 10 miles west of San Ignacio, the shop (8 A.M.–5:30 P.M. daily) is a borderline museum, with

MOUNTAIN PINE RIDGE

all conceivable Belizean crafts in addition to Indonesian wood carvings, Dominican paintings, Guatemalan masks, Nicaraguan soapstone statues, and Haitian woodworking (plus amazing carvings and sculptures from the on-site woodshop). Check your e-mail, browse the shop, and then enjoy a glass of wine or a meal in the shaded café. The food is fantastic (US$7 breakfast and lunch, more for dinner, from 6:30 A.M. daily). Orange Gifts's six clean garden rooms, each with private bath, hot/cold water, tile floors, and ceiling fans, go for US$75. Camping is US$10 per person; full RV hookups can be negotiated, too. This is also the home office of the **Black Rock River Lodge.**

At Mile 62½ on the Western Highway, near Central Farm, **Garden of Eve Resort** (tel. 501/824-3688, www.gardenofeveresort.com, US$80–100) has a huge swimming pool and spacious, air-conditioned, wired villas. Even if you don't spend the night, the place offers a welcome respite—lunch, swim, and a drink anyone? Sundays are busy, but not rowdy, when family groups show up to use the pool, playground, and other facilities. Guests wanting to stay for more than two weeks can take advantage of deeper discounts. Camping and RV camping is available year-round.

Spanish Lookout

Turn off the highway at the Spanish Lookout sign and watch the landscape change from ragged forest to neat barns and rolling green countryside, like a tropical Switzerland. This is one of the Mennonite communities, whose founders brought a small bit of Europe with them (via Canada and Mexico) and, over the years, developed an industry that supplies a large part of the milk, cheese, and chicken for the country. Many Mennonites here have embraced organic living, and if you drive around you'll find produce and items that cannot be found anywhere else in Belize. The recent discovery of oil in the area has added a modern twist to this unique scene.

Spanish Lookout has no tourist accommodations but boasts some great food, as well as shopping and services (Scotia Bank has an ATM here and there are three gas stations). Folks from all over Belize come to shop at places like Farmer's Trading Centre, Reimer's Feeds, the Computer Ranch, and Westrac (the best place for car parts, period). Eat at **The Golden Corral,** but get there just before noon if you want a seat and first selection. It's about US$7.50 for all-you-can-eat and all-you-can-drink homemade iced tea!

Do not look for smokes or beer; this is pious country. There are three ways into Spanish Lookout, some involving a ferry crossing. It's about a 30-minute drive from San Ignacio.

◖ ACTUN TUNICHIL MUKNAL

This is the acclaimed "Cave of the Crystal Maiden," featured in *National Geographic* magazine and quickly becoming Belize's most popular underground experience. This cave is for fit and active people who do not mind getting wet and muddy—and who are able to tread lightly. After the initial 45-minute hike to the entrance (with three river fords) and a swim into the cave's innards, you will be asked to remove your shoes upon climbing up the limestone into the main cathedral-like chambers. The rooms are littered with delicate Maya pottery and the crystallized remains of 14 humans. There are no pathways, fences, glass, or other partitions separating the visitor from the artifacts. Nor are there any installed lights. The only infrastructure is a rickety ladder leading up to the chamber of the Crystal Maiden herself, a full female skeleton that sparkles with calcite under your headlamp's glare, more so during the drier months.

Please be careful—the fact that tourists are allowed to walk here at all is as astonishing as the sights themselves (at the time of this writing, somebody had already trod on and broken one of the skulls). Only two tour companies are licensed to take guests here: **Pacz Tours** and **Mayawalk,** both based in downtown San Ignacio. The Actun Tunichil Muknal cave is not for the weak at heart nor recommended for children or claustrophobics.

North of San Ignacio

BULLET TREE FALLS

This old, lazy village lies less than three miles out of San Ignacio on the road to El Pilar. Bullet Tree's ultramellow riverbank mood, combined with cheap and easy access to the relative bustle of San Ignacio, make it a pleasant midrange alternative to the usual Cayo fare of jungle lodges and backpacker camps. There are now five clusters of riverside cabins, each on its own hammock-equipped compound of *palapa* shades and broadleaf riparian jungle. There are also a few famed healers in town and a nearby medicine trail, which you can walk to with a guide. Then float back down the Mopan River (just don't miss your hotel's dock or you'll end up in Belize City). Of course, Bullet Tree overnighters still have access to the full range of Cayo area activities, right down the road and easily reached by *colectivo* taxi (US$1 pp) or private cab (US$5).

Some come to Bullet Tree specifically for the services of local Maya healer **Miss Beatrice,** who offers very reasonably priced consults for various health and spirit problems. Excellent horseback tours to El Pilar or other sites start at **Bullet Tree Rides** (next to Parrot Nest; ask at the office next to the Savannah Taxi stand or at Cohune Palms).

EL PILAR ARCHAEOLOGICAL SITE

Seven miles north of Bullet Tree Falls, these jungle-choked Maya ruins are only visited by a handful of curious tourists each day; the rough approach road plus the lack of attention paid to the site by most tour operators helps make El Pilar the excellent, uncrowded day trip that it is. Two groupings of temple mounds, courtyards, and ball courts overlook a forested valley. Aqueducts and a causeway lead toward Guatemala, just 500 meters away. There have been some minor excavations here, including those of illegal looters, but the site is very overgrown, so the ruins retain an intriguing air of mystery. Many trees shade the site: allspice,

gumbo-limbo, ramon, cohune palm, and locust. It's a beautiful hiking area and wildlife experience as well.

Even if you book your El Pilar trip in San Ignacio, be sure to start your quest with a visit to the **Amigos de El Pilar** visitors center (9 A.M.–5 P.M. daily) and **Be Pukte Cultural Center** in Bullet Tree Falls. Here you'll find a scale model of the ruins, some helpful booklets and maps, and guide and taxi arrangements (it's about US$25 for a taxi to drive a group out and wait a few hours before taking them back). Or you can rent a mountain bike at Cohune Palms and make a workout of it—the road's so bad, you'll probably beat the cab anyway. There's also a surprisingly wide selection of booklets and information available at the gift shop in the San Ignacio Resort Hotel.

Accommodations

Rolling into town, you'll pass the soccer field on your right, then come to a fork in the road; this is the bus stop. Fork left to cross the bridge and reach the turnoff for El Pilar, right to check in at one of three accommodations.

At the end of the short road, **Cohune Palms** (tel. 501/824-0166 or 669-2738, www.cohunepalms.com, US$65) offers four thatch, bamboo, and wooden structures around a common area with hammocks and a kitchen, all enveloped in a truly wild environment and perched atop a steep bank of the Mopan. The recently renovated rooms (loft bedrooms, colorful paint and tiles, private bath) offer some of the best values in Cayo—no joke. Owners Bevin and Mike are a wealth of Bullet Tree knowledge, and they'll help you plan your time and get to and from San Ignacio and rent you tubes and bicycles with which to explore their backyard. Contact them at the number above or at their Cohune Palms Guest House in San Ignacio. Yummy meals are available, as is plenty of common space in the kitchen or on the new yoga deck next to the river.

A stone's throw upstream, the **Parrot's**

MOUNTAIN PINE RIDGE

Nest (tel. 501/820-4058 or 602-6817, www. parrot-nest.com, US$40–100) has fantastic on-site bird-watching in the trees and on the lawn that surround six simple, cozy cabins, including two "tree houses" on stilts under the limbs of a gigantic guanacaste tree. Each cabin has 24-hour electricity, a linoleum floor, and a simple single or double bed, with the breeze providing "natural" air-conditioning with the help of fans.

The first place you see after turning at the bus stop, **Iguana Junction** (tel. 501/820-4021, US$30 s/d shared bath, US$40 s/d private bath and hot water) has eight straightforward rooms and cabins. Meals are available. The **Riverside River Lodge** (tel. 501/820-4007, US$65), across the bridge, is the only place in town to party it up to loud music, and sometimes live shows. Of course, if there's a party, you probably shouldn't plan on getting much sleep.

Cristo Rey and the Mountain Pine Ridge

You'll encounter many of Cayo's natural treasures within this vast crinkle of mountains, as well as some of the region's most charming accommodations. Despite bark beetle damage to vast tracts of pine trees in the Mountain Pine Ridge Forest Reserve, its waterfalls, swimming holes, and vistas are still worth enduring the rutted-out roads, and you'll see the pine forests regenerating. Points of interest, parks, and accommodations are presented in the order they are found as one travels south from San Ignacio (along the two roads that access the Pine Ridge). Many resorts are destinations in their own right—travelers come to enjoy the waterfalls at Five Sisters and the restaurant at Blancaneaux, for exampl e, just as they seek out the area's Maya ruins and caves.

THE CRISTO REY ROAD

Heading south from Santa Elena, this road winds through the villages of Cristo Rey and San Antonio before joining the Chiquibul Road and the Mountain Pine Ridge. It is usually better maintained than the alternative route along the Chiquibul Road, and there are a handful of interesting stops along the way. Village buses that travel the road leave the center of San Ignacio daily, and shared taxis should be available for reasonable rates as well. Most tour operators who travel this road will stop at any of the following places, depending on group size and desires.

Maya Mountain Lodge and Tours

Only one mile south of the Western Highway, Maya Mountain Lodge (tel. 501/824-2164, www.mayamountain.com, US$59–119) feels remote enough to warrant a listing outside of town. This is a moderately priced jungle hideaway, operated for the last 22 years by Suzi and Bart Mickler. The lodge is only a short distance off the Western Highway, yet miles from the rest of the world. A meandering trail through the gardens has signs identifying a variety of plants, trees, and birds. Accommodations range from six primitive rooms to quaint cottages with extra bunks and wood furniture. The Micklers take pride in the friendliness and efficiency of their staff—and in their restaurant. They claim to serve "gourmet in the jungle," featuring homemade breads and buckets of fresh-squeezed orange juice (their Baha'i faith prevents them from selling liquor for profit, but you are welcome to bring your own). Breakfast and lunch cost US$8, and dinner is US$16. Ask about workshops on biodiversity and multiculturalism. This is a great place for families, with discounted (or free) rooms and tours for children.

Crystal Paradise Resort

Owned and operated by the Tut family, Crystal Paradise (tel. 501/824-2772, www.crystalparadise.com, US$85–125) is a wonderful retreat overlooking the Macal River. Before the advent of tourism, the Tut family (Victor and Teresa

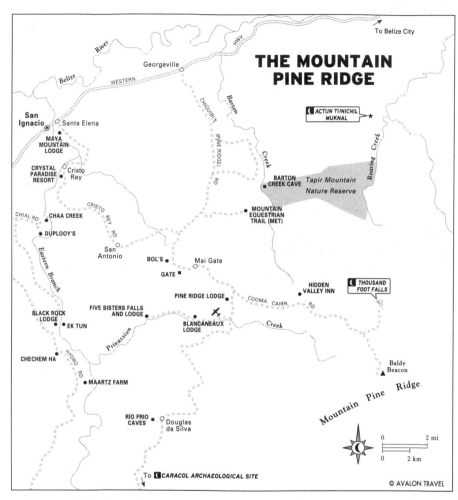

and their 10 children) grew fruits and vegetables and then transported them by canoe to the town market in San Ignacio. These days, Victor still grows fruits and vegetables and is working on a future addition to Crystal Paradise Resort, a jungle campground facility. The sons, who are avid bird-watchers and nature lovers, maintain the beautiful grounds and serve as your guides on a variety of tours, including hiking, biking, horseback riding, kayaking, and bird-watching. Teresa and daughters keep the guest rooms clean and comfortable and also cook up the best in traditional Belizean and international cuisine. Accommodations come in several styles on the property. If you're lucky, you may get one of the simple thatched cabanas near the wide, open dining *palapa* that overlooks the river. These have compelling views of the Macal Valley and have cement walls, tiled floors, hot/cold showers, and shaded verandas for relaxing. Others are clean and comfortable but more of a clapboard style; all offer ceiling fans and electricity. The Tuts also offer bird-watching, nature walks, and tours. Rates include breakfast and dinner.

Table Rock Jungle Lodge

Located at Mile 5 on Cristo Rey Road, Table Rock Jungle Lodge (tel. 501/670-4910, www.tablerockbelize.com, from US$150) is a self-contained, ecofriendly touch of class on a 100-acre preserve. Two gorgeous cabanas are designed to stay cool the natural way, using adobe construction. There is a beautiful trail leading down a series of stone steps to the Macal River, where guests can go canoeing or tubing. The dining room has a very Balinese feel and the food is fantastic, in an elegant setting but without the high prices.

Slate Carving Art Galleries

About six miles south, look for the **Sak Tunich Art Gallery,** home of the Magana brothers, Jose and Javier. This indoor-outdoor display is built into the hillside on your left and is worth a look for anyone interested in Maya crafts. They've got a couple of new cabanas they're calling **Next to the Jungle Stay** (tel. 501/661-8166, US$25), which sleep up to four, but don't have electricity. Lots of cultural activities are available, including copal cleansing, herbal baths, and music.

A couple miles farther, you'll find more art at **The Garcia Sisters'** (tel. 501/820-4023, artistmai1981@btl.net, open varying hours and days). These six siblings made a nationwide name for themselves when, in 1981, they turned to their Maya heritage and began recreating slate carvings reminiscent of those done by their ancestors at Caracol. Their Maya art gallery, shop, and museum are called the **Tanah Mayan Art Museum,** located on the Cristo Rey Road, just outside of San Antonio. The Tanah Museum is a one-room affair, built in the old Maya way with limestone and clay walls; the floor is a parquet of logs and limestone and the roof is typical thatch of bay and palm leaves, picked and placed on the nights of the full moon to give them a longer life. The sisters, nieces of the famed healer Don Eligio Panti, are charming and determined ambassadors of San Antonio village. They're also clever artists who make Belizean dolls, native jewelry, and hand-drawn art cards. Ask about the

Itzamna Society, a community-based NGO, of which Maria is the chairperson, that works to protect the forest and community.

Village of San Antonio

With a population of 2,350 Maya descendants, mostly milpa farmers and, increasingly, employees of nearby lodges, San Antonio has the potential to serve as a low-key gateway to the surrounding wilderness. There are horse and hiking trails nearby, as well as several caves, waterfalls, and ruins. Ask at the small **Eligio Panti Museum** about available guesthouse lodging, camping, and guided tours in the area. Continuing beyond San Antonio, you'll find **Mountain Rider,** a small horseback riding operation.

Accommodations are offered by a women's group bed-and-breakfast and by **Chichan Kaa Lodge** (tel. 501/091-2023, www.epnp.org), positioned atop a hill above the village.

Noj Kaax Meen Elijio Panti National Park

This new 13,000-acre reserve of mountains surrounding the village of San Antonio is a community-based effort to preserve the forest and honor the wildlife and spirits that reside there. The visitors center is located three miles outside of town, but the contact is María Garcia (tel. 501/820-4023, artistmai1981@btl.net). Ask around town regarding guides to take you to the trails, waterfalls, and peaks. The park is also reportedly an experiment in people power and agroforestry, augmenting the unreliable tourism dollar with cooperative production of cacao, *xate,* and hardwood. Learn more at www.epnp.org.

THE CHIQUIBUL/ PINE RIDGE ROAD

The Chiquibul Road begins at Mile 63 on the Western Highway (at Georgeville) and heads south over the Mountain Pine Ridge to end, 30-something miles after it began, at Caracol. You'll pass through tropical foothills, citrus farms, and cattle ranches before the terrain rises, gradually changing to sand, rocky soil, red clay, then, finally, groves of sweet-smelling pines. Creases of land within narrow river valleys are rich with stands of hardwood trees, many covered with orchids and bromeliads. Here and there small clearings have been carved out of the jungle by *milperos* (slash-and-burn farmers), and picturesque clusters of thatch huts surrounded by banana and cohune palms suggest the daily struggles of the campesino. The road is notorious for becoming a slushy mud bed after long rains; recent improvements for dam workers (at the Chalillo site) and a grant to improve the final stretch to Caracol should make things better.

Slate Creek Preserve

A group of local landowners and lodge operators have set aside 3,000 acres as a private preserve. The purpose of the preserve is to protect the watershed, plants, and animals of a valley called the Vega, one of several valleys in the area. The unique ecosystem of limestone karst, which borders the Mountain Pine Ridge Forest Reserve, teems with life. Mahogany, Santa Maria, ceiba, cedar, and cohune palms tower above. Orchids, ferns, and bromeliads are common. Birds such as the aracari, emerald toucanet, keel-billed toucan, keel-billed motmot, king vulture, and various parrots and hummingbirds are to be found here. Puma, ocelot, coati, paca, and anteater roam the forests.

Mountain Equestrian Trails (MET)

There is no better way to explore the Slate Creek Preserve than on one of the Bevis family's regal steeds, returning each afternoon to rest up in one of their lovely jungle cabanas (tel. 501/820-4041 or 620-4978, U.S. tel. 800/838-3918, www.metbelize.com, from US$132). Visitors have a choice of gentle or spirited horses to carry them over the 60 miles of trails that wander through the surrounding forest. Trips are designed to suit every taste, with mountain trails that wander past magnificent waterfalls, swimming holes, pine forests, Maya caves, exotic butterflies, and more than 150 species of orchids. The equestrian trails are only a few miles from Río Frio Caves and Thousand Foot Falls, where the water drops 1,600 feet into the jungle below. Programs are designed for both beginners and experienced riders—children aged at least 10 with previous riding experience are welcome. Guests will find 10 lovely, spacious cabanas of thatch and stucco with exotic wood interiors and private bathrooms with hot/cold water (no electricity—yet). Meals are served in the cozy cantina/restaurant, which offers a variety of excellent food (breakfast US$7, lunch US$10, dinner US$18, plus tax). No matter that the small cantina is a 20-minute drive from San Ignacio; it still attracts visitors and locals from all around for drinks, dinner, and good conversation. All-inclusive, multiday packages are available, riding fees extra. Riders are required to carry personal liability insurance to cover themselves while touring. **Chiclero Trails Campsite** offers safari-style tents located under the rainforest canopy, with beds, mattresses, linens, a private covered deck, and close access to restrooms and showers, for US$20 per person per night. Meals for groups are served in an insulated tent in the camp.

Green Hills Butterfly Ranch and Botanical Collections

Located at Mile 8, this outstanding butterfly breeding, education, and interpretive center is run by Jan Meerman and Tineke Boomsma (meerman@btl.net). Displays include all stages of the life cycle of a butterfly (egg-caterpillar-pupa-butterfly), and visitors can watch them all. Between 25 and 30 different species are raised at the center, including the tiny glasswing, the banana owl (the largest butterfly in Belize), and of course the magnificent blue morpho. Arrive early enough in the morning and watch a butterfly emerge from a pupa right before your eyes—a grand experience. Jan's newest guidebook on butterflies, *Lepidoptera of Belize,* should be available soon. Tours of the center take about an hour and give you a chance to see and learn about these beautiful fluttering creatures. The tour through the flight rooms (2,700 sq. ft.) brings you up close to hundreds of flitting butterflies of all colors.

Open 8 A.M.–4 P.M. daily. The last tour begins at 3:30 P.M. The entrance fee for a guided tour is US$4 per person, minimum of two people. Group rates are available.

Barton Creek Cave and Outpost

This is a cathedral-like wet cave, once used for ceremonial purposes and human sacrifices by the Maya, now ragingly popular among Cayo visitors who fancy floating through the tall, quiet cavern. The experience is impressive and available to anybody physically able enough to step into a canoe. Contemplate the quiet as your guide slowly paddles you deeper into the earth, the watery sound of his paddle echoing on the limestone. The cave was rediscovered in 1970 by a pair of Peace Corps volunteers who found that the cave had already been extensively looted. Archaeologists didn't study the cave until 1998; they found large ceramics on high ledges, plus evidence of 20 human remains, including a necklace made of finger bones. The cave is at least seven miles deep, but tours only go in about a mile or so before turning around.

Barton Creek is protected and managed by government archaeologists and is accessed by turning off the Chiquibul Road around Mile 4, then driving 20–30 minutes on a bumpy road through orange groves and a small Mennonite settlement (you'll need to have someone who knows the way with you, as there are many roads and no signs). The visitors center charges US$5 per person, then you'll have to rent canoes (US$7.50 per boat), lights, and a guide, all available at **Mike's Place,** right there at the cave's entrance. Most visitors, however, arrive as part of a prepaid tour and won't need to worry about such details.

Stay at **Barton Creek Outpost** (tel. 501/662-4797, www.bartoncreekoutpost.com, from US$10 per person), run by the intrepid Jacquelyn and Jim Brit (and their knowledgeable children). Jackie is one fantastic cook and does vegan on request. Jim loves to take campers out on all-day hikes to Big Rock Falls and other places. If you bring your own camping gear, you can stay for free, or they can rent tents and mattresses. Sleep up on the deck and pass out to the sounds of the wildlife and creek. A recent photo shoot by the Eddie Bauer crew was staged here. Horse rides can be arranged, as well as rentals of canoes, lights, and guides for the cave tour. Meal plans and work-to-stay programs are available.

THE MOUNTAIN PINE RIDGE FOREST RESERVE

After you steadily ascend along the Chiquibul (Pine Ridge) Road for 21 miles, a gate across the road marks your entrance to Belize's largest and oldest protected area, established in 1944. The 300-square-mile area (126,825 acres) features Caribbean pine and bracken ferns instead of the typical tropical vegetation found in the rest of Belize. It also features a massive granite uplifting; the exposed rocks are some of the oldest formations in the Americas (they also make for incredible swimming holes and waterfalls). In fact, some geologists think that the Mountain Pine Ridge (whose highest point is 3,336 feet above sea level at Baldy Beacon) was one of the only exposed islands when the rest of Central America was underwater.

Cycles of Disaster

Shortly after its creation, the Pine Ridge experienced a huge forest fire which, combined with the cycles of logging, left an unnaturally uniform population of trees, making the forest further susceptible to disease and insects. Most recently, a three-year drought helped establish a disastrous infestation of the southern pine bark beetle *(Dendroctonus frontalis),* a destructive bug that has devastated many other forests in Central and North America.

The beetle establishes itself under the bark, where it eats, mates, and lays eggs. It spreads by jumping from tree to tree; the only way to stop it is by clear-cutting massive buffer zones—as large as 240 feet wide—around the affected areas (similar to how forest fires are fought). This was how the battle was played out when government foresters and the two local timber concessions went to war against the beetle in 2000—cutting, burning, cleaning, and cutting some more. Their efforts were too little too late, and only a small section of the forest was saved (look across the creek from either Blancaneaux or Five Sisters to see some of the surviving forest patches). The beetles spread faster than the pine cones could mature, effectively interrupting the trees' reproductive cycle.

Today, the forest is coming back wonderfully—thanks to both naturally rich seed sets and a massive replanting campaign (24 million seedlings are required for reforestation of 70,000 acres over four years). It will be another 15–20 years before the new generation of pines fully matures, however. Check out www.reforestbelize.com for an update and to find out how you can help.

Visiting the Reserve

Most tour operators offer day trips to the Pine Ridge's attractions, listed in this section, often combined with a trip to Caracol Ruins. There are way more sights than can fit into a day, but there are a number of lodges that can put you right in the thick of it all.

The forestry station at Douglas De Silva Reserve (formerly called Augustine) used to be a small village of loggers and forestry workers before the pine beetle and massive layoffs. You can now camp on the mowed grounds of the old school, but the blackflies can be pretty horrendous here. Those interested in camping must get permission from the forest guard at the entrance.

Hidden Valley Inn

Situated on 7,200 acres of private property in the heart of the Mountain Pine Ridge Forest Reserve, Hidden Valley Inn (tel. 501/822-3320, www.hiddenvalleyinn.com, about US$185 plus meals and taxes) is a quiet paradise for hikers and bird-watchers, who will have a blast exploring the resort's 90-plus miles of walking trails and old logging roads—and then cozying up in front of their cottage's fireplace, listening to the birdsong outside (especially nice during the cool, misty rainy season). The property encompasses lush broadleaf forest and pine tree habitat, and the two diverse ecosystems

are divided by a geological fault line, which marks the edge of a towering 1,000-foot escarpment. Numerous watercourses spring from the mountain and then cascade down the steep slopes, often into deep, inviting pools; Hidden Valley's trail system runs through it all. The active trekker can spend days exploring, and the staff at the inn can assist with vehicle shuttles. Bird-watchers, be prepared to check off orange-breasted falcons, king vultures, stygian owls, azure-crowned hummingbirds, green jays, and golden-hooded tanagers. Picnic lunches are provided for the myriad day trips available.

The inn itself comprises a main house built of local hardwoods that feels more like a comfy ski lodge than a tropical resort, with several spacious common rooms, including a fireside lounge, a card room, a TV room, a library, and the restaurant, where creative dinners are served in candlelit splendor. The 12 cottages have saltillo tile floors, vaulted ceilings, cypress-paneled walls, fireplaces, ceiling fans, screened louvered windows, comfy beds, and private baths with hot/cold water. Ask about special packages. Hidden Valley Inn is located three miles in from the Mile 14 turnoff onto Cooma Cairn Road—just follow the signs.

⟨ Thousand Foot Falls

Occasionally referred to as "Hidden Valley Falls," this torrent of Roaring Creek is probably a good deal taller than a thousand feet and is considered the highest waterfall in all of Central America. The turnoff to the falls is located only a couple of miles beyond the Forest Reserve gate and is well signed. From the turnoff, the road continues down for about four miles and brings you to the falls and a picnic area. View the falls from across the gorge and through breaks in the mist (US$2 pp). A small store and picnic tables can be found at the viewpoint, open 7 A.M.–5 P.M. daily.

Pine Ridge Lodge

Five miles beyond the Forest Reserve gate, you'll find yet another unique hillside lodging with its own primitively comfortable personality. On the banks of the Little Vaqueros

© JOSHUA BERMAN

Thousand Foot Falls is actually 1,660 feet tall.

Creek, the Pine Ridge Lodge (local radio tel. 501/606-4557, U.S. tel. 800/316-0706, www.pineridgelodge.com, US$99) offers six rooms in "forestview, mayan, and riverview cottages," all with private bathroom, hot water, porch, and appealing decor and furnishings. There's no electricity, just quaint kerosene lanterns for reading at night. True, the beetle blight left the place with a collection of pine stumps, but owners Vicki and Gary Seewald have done a superhuman job of restoring the grounds—they've planted bright and beautiful gardens that feature a growing collection of orchids and other epiphytes, all surrounded by scores of pine tree seedlings that are getting along just fine. Screened-in creekside lounge areas offer shade and a babbling brook, which is great after that bumpy, 32-mile trip back from Caracol—and before your walk down to the Pine Ridge Lodge's 85-foot waterfall. Room rate includes continental breakfast (freshly baked rolls, local honey, coffee, and fresh fruit); lunch is US$7, dinner US$21.50. Catering to vegetarians is a specialty. The

lodge is only seven miles north of Río On Pools; ask about tours and transfers.

Blancaneaux Lodge

Francis Ford Coppola first came to Belize just after the country gained independence in 1981; he tried and failed to persuade the new government to apply for a satellite license in order to become a hub of world communications. He did, however, succeed in finding an abandoned lodge on a pine-carpeted bluff overlooking the rocks and falls of Privassion Creek. Blancaneaux served as a private retreat for the film producer until 1993 when he "tricked it open" by flying a group of family and friends down for his 54th birthday.

Blancaneaux Lodge (tel. 501/824-4912, www.blancaneaux.com, from US$250) remains one of Central America's premier resorts, featuring the design and decor of the Coppolas and Mexican architect Manolo Mestre. Tropical splashes of color, dark hardwoods, Central American lines, and soaring thatch ceilings mark Blancaneaux's 10 cabanas and seven luxurious villas. New additions include a U-shaped hot pool above the river and a spa built in an Indonesian rice house with Thai massage therapists. Blancaneaux's **Ristorante Montagna** offers an exquisite Italian-centric menu, with a range of salads, pastas (US$14), sandwiches, delicious pizzas from one of the country's only wood-burning pizza ovens (US$18), and, of course, a selection of wines from Coppola's Napa Valley vineyards—smooth, but costly. The restaurant is often lively at night, with live music, roaming mariachis, and candlelit splendor under the stars. Two honeymoon cabanas with their own private infinity pools and choice of two views (from US$290–390) are a stunning new addition to Blancaneaux. The Enchanted Cottage is pure luxury, set aside from the main resort for those seeking solitude. A golf cart is available and whatever the guests need can be brought right to them. The Enchanted Cottage is also available for a small group of friends looking to celebrate a special event—and who can afford US$1600 per night.

© JOSHUA BERMAN

Blancaneaux Lodge rests on the banks of Privassion Creek.

An on-site hydroelectric dam powers the entire operation, and a 3.5-acre organic herb and vegetable garden supplies many of the restaurant's needs (and those of Turtle Inn). The lodge is located at Mile 14½ and has its own airstrip, which many guests prefer to the 2.5-hour drive from Belize City.

Five Sisters Lodge

The Five Sisters Lodge (tel. 501/820-4005, www.fivesisterslodge.com, US$85–105), high above the inviting Privassion Creek, has been a destination since 1991. Inspired by the natural beauty of his property, Belizean Carlos Popper set off to design his lodge with one clear objective: to provide sustainable architecture in harmony with the natural world around it. Considering the location above the famous falls (from which the lodge gets its name), prices are very reasonable, and value for your buck is excellent. All rooms and suites are perched on the top of the steep canyon; accommodations range from beautifully thatched cabanas overlooking the river to an exclusive riverside villa—19 units in all. The honeymoon suite

has brightly colored bedspreads, mosquito netting, and complete privacy, and a new gazebo is popular for weddings. Restaurant prices are also relatively low, and packages for longer stays are offered. Even if you don't stay here, come by, have a beer on the outdoor deck, and enjoy the commanding view above the river. The hearty can walk the 300 steps down to the river; if you're too tired after splashing around, not to worry—the motorized funicular will carry you back up the hill, at least between 8 A.M. and 4 P.M.

Río On Pools and Río Frio Cave

Most Caracol packages try to squeeze in an afternoon stopover at these lovely sites. Continuing south toward Augustine, you will cross the Río On. It's well worth the climb over an assortment of worn boulders and rocks to a delightful site with waterfalls and several warm-water pools; don't forget your camera. There's a parking area just off the road. Turn right at Douglas De Silva Ranger Station (the western division of the Forestry Department) and continue for about five miles to reach Río

MOUNTAIN PINE RIDGE

Frio Cave. Follow the signs to the parking lot. From here, visitors have a choice of exploring nature trails (note the purple ground orchids growing along the paths) and two small caves on the road or continuing to the largest and most well-known river cave in Belize, the Río Frio, with an enormous arched entryway into the half-mile-long cave. Filtered light highlights ferns, mosses, stalactites, and geometric patterns of striations on rocks. Each step stirs up the musty smells of the damp rocky cave. Watch where you walk; sinkholes are scattered here and there, and a narrow stream flows along the gravel riverbed.

⬛ CARACOL ARCHAEOLOGICAL SITE

Archaeologists Diane and Arlen Chase believe that Caracol, one of the largest sites in Belize, is the Maya city-state that toppled mighty Tikal, just to the northwest, effectively shutting it down for 130 years. Located within the **Chiquibul Forest Reserve,** Caracol is *out there,* offering both natural wonders and Maya

mystery. To date, only a small percentage of the 177 square kilometers that make up the site has even been mapped, identifying only 5,000 of the estimated 36,000 structures lying beneath the forest canopy.

The centerpiece is no doubt the pyramid of **Canaa,** which, at 136 feet above the plaza floor (roughly two meters higher than El Castillo at Xunantunich), is one of the tallest structures—modern or ancient—in Belize. Canaa was only completely unveiled of vegetation in 2005, by the Tourism Development Project (TDP), whose work is responsible for most of the structures you see. The vistas from the top of Canaa are extensive and memorable.

In addition to the aforementioned superlatives, Caracol, a Classic Period site, is noted for its large masks and giant date glyphs on circular stone altars. There is also a fine display of the Maya's engineering skills, with extensive reservoirs, agricultural terraces, and several mysterious ramps. Caracol has been studied for more than 20 years by the Chases and their assistants, student interns from Tulane

COURTESY OF THE BELIZE TOURISM BOARD/ALEX NUNEZ

viewing the ruins at the Caracol Archaeological Site

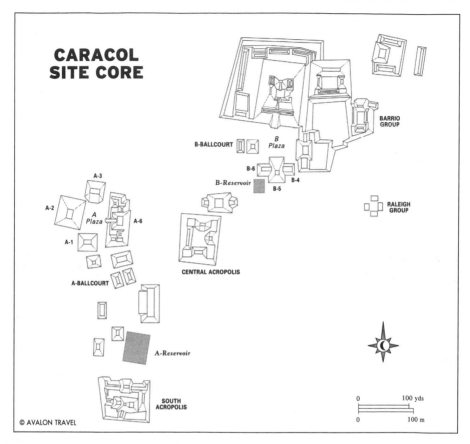

CARACOL
SITE CORE

BARRIO
GROUP

B-BALLCOURT   *B
                Plaza*

B-6

A-3
B-Reservoir   B-4
                 B-5

A-2   RALEIGH
      A   A-6   GROUP
      Plaza

A-1

A-BALLCOURT

CENTRAL ACROPOLIS

A-Reservoir

SOUTH
ACROPOLIS

0   100 yds

0   100 m

© AVALON TRAVEL

University and the University of Central Florida. According to John Morris, an archaeologist with Belize's Institute of Archaeology, a lifetime of exploration remains to be done for six to nine miles in every direction of the excavated part of Caracol. It's proving to have been a powerful site that controlled a very large area, with possibly over 100,000 inhabitants. The jungle you see now would have been totally absent in those days, the wood cleared to provide fuel and agricultural lands to support so many people.

Many carvings are dated A.D. 500–800, and ceramic evidence indicates that Caracol was settled around A.D. 300 and continued to flourish when other Maya sites were in decline.

Carvings on the site also indicate that Caracol and Tikal engaged in ongoing conflicts, each defeating the other on various occasions. After the war in A.D. 562, Caracol flourished for more than a century in the mountains and valleys surrounding the site. A former archaeological commissioner named the site "Caracol" ("snail" in Spanish) because of the winding logging road to reach it, although some contend it was because of all the snail shells found during initial excavations.

Visiting the Site

The small visitors center presents a scale model and interesting information based mostly on the work of the Chases over the last two decades. A new **Monument Museum** will allow tourists to view a range of artifacts and stelae from the site and will be based on the work of the TDP. There are no official guides on-site, as most groups arrive with their own. However, the caretakers know Caracol well and will be glad to walk you through and explain the site for a few dollars. Most tours start with the Raleigh Group, move by the enormous ceiba trees, then circle through the archaeologists' camp and end with a bang by climbing Canaa. To prepare yourself—and to check on the latest discoveries and trail maps—click over to www.caracol.org.

Most tour operators offer Caracol day trips, often involving stops at various caves and swimming holes on the way back through the Mountain Pine Ridge. A few, like **Everald's Caracol Shuttle** (tel. 501/804-0090 or 603-5705, caracolshuttle@hotmail.com), specialize in it. The ride should take anywhere from two to three hours, depending on both the weather and the progress made by road improvement crews, who hopefully will not run out of money before you read this. If driving, four-wheel drive vehicles are a must; gas is not available along the 50-mile road, so carry ample fuel. Camping is not allowed in the area without permission from the Institute of Archaeology in Belmopan. The closest accommodations are those along the Pine Ridge Road.

West of San Ignacio

It is only about 11 miles to the border with Guatemala, but, in true Belizean fashion, the short distance—and the hills around it—is jam-packed with attractions and accommodations for all budgets and active tastes.

ALONG THE WESTERN HIGHWAY

Although the chief attraction on this stretch of road between San Ignacio and the Guatemalan border is the Xunantunich Archaeological Site, there are also a handful of resorts, budget lodgings, and campgrounds where many travelers stay and explore in between their Guatemalan and Caribbean adventures. Most of these places are close enough to San Ignacio that guests can easily pop into town for dinner and then back out to their tent or cabin in a bus or cheap taxi.

Only a two-minute drive from the edge of San Ignacio proper, **Windy Hill Resort** (tel. 501/824-2017, www.windyhillresort.com, US$95–119) sits on its own lovely rise. You'll find well-appointed, clean thatch-roof cottages, green grass, private baths, hot/cold water, ceiling fans, a swimming pool, and a recreation hut complete with TV, hammocks, bar, table tennis, and billiards. Windy Hill specializes in all kinds of tours and multiday packages with meal plans. Guests enjoy the friendly efficiency with which the place is run and the variety of activities: canoeing, caving, horseback riding, nature tours, and hiking trails. Ask about escorted tours to Guatemala and archaeological sites in the area. Meals are served in the casual, thatch-roof **Black Orchid Restaurant.** Across the way, a simpler, budget option is found in **Log Cab-Inn** (Mile 68, tel. 501/824-3367, www.logcabinns-belize.com, US$65), whose nine basic units are private and simple; ask about meal plans.

Ka'ana Boutique Hotel & Spa (tel. 501/824-3350, www.kaanabelize.com, US$250 and up), which opened in 2007 at Mile 69, offers an upscale restaurant, a bar, spa treatments, a pool, and resort services. Memory foam mattresses make it easy to forget the trials of travel when you sink into a very comfy bed. Ka'ana is gaining a reputation with the local business elite as the place to dine and enjoy drinks. Each evening there are tastings held at 7 P.M. in the well-stocked, climate-controlled wine cellar; the restaurant menu, under the guidance of award-winning chef Manolo, is exciting and bold.

the upper Macal River, in western Cayo

© JOSHUA BERMAN

and any special needs. This Belizean family-owned and operated resort offers clean, comfortable accommodations for 1–3 persons for US$100. Set on 70 acres abutting the Mopan River, Maya Vista's friendly and knowledgeable owners, the Shish family, can arrange just about any activity and for reasonable prices. Orchid aficionados and those seeking peace and quiet will enjoy staying here, as it is well off the busy Western Highway.

DOWN THE CHIAL ROAD

About five miles west of San Ignacio, look for a turnoff to the left onto a well-maintained dirt road (you will see the hacienda of Belize's "Toilet Paper King" lording over the valley from a hilltop on your left); the Chial Road will carry you to several worthwhile sites, as well as some of Belize's most acclaimed accommodations on the banks of the Macal River.

◖ Belize Botanic Gardens

Visiting the country's only Botanic Gardens (tel. 501/824-3101, www.belizebotanic.org, entrance US$5, guided walk US$10) makes a wonderful half-day activity, no matter where in the area you are staying. Walk through fruit trees, broadleaf palms, and hardwoods as you learn about the medicinal and ritual "Plants of the Maya" and experience the lush orchid house with more than 100 species. Botanists' work here has resulted in 20 new orchid records for Belize and one species new to science: *Pleurothallis duplooyii* (named after Ken duPlooy), which has a bloom about the size of a flea! There is also a rainforest trail, a pine forest habitat complete with 30-foot fire tower, a puzzle trail for children, education programs for local schoolchildren and visitors, and a rustic visitors center for meetings, yoga, and other activities. The Belize Botanic Garden sponsors a volunteer program where specialists pay US$500 for room and board while working on various garden projects. Call to find out about a shuttle from San Ignacio, or hire your own cab for US$15–25. The garden office is above the reception area of duPlooy's Cottage Resort.

Clarissa Falls Resort (tel. 501/824-3916, www.clarissafalls.com) is located at the end of a mile-long dirt road, accessed on the right at Mile 70½ of the Western Highway. This is a laid-back, riverside affair where guests either camp in their own tents (US$7.50 pp), bunk up in the bamboo and thatch dormitory (US$15 pp), or stay in an overpriced cottage with private bath (US$65). The shared toilet and shower building has hot and cold water and is cement-basic. The Mopan River is the main attraction here; don't miss the nature trails and a hike (or horseback ride) to Xunantunich, the highest pyramid visible from the cottages. The dining room serves good food, including a few specialties such as black mole soup and great, cheap Mexican-style tacos; it will be around US$6 for a meal like stuffed squash. Continuing down the Western Highway towards Succotz, about two miles past the Clarissa Falls turnoff, take a right at the sign for **Maya Vista Resort** (tel. 609/828-1163, www.mayavistabelize.com); they'll arrange for pickups from Belize City

MOUNTAIN PINE RIDGE

Rainforest Medicine Trail

There are a number of attractions available to nonguests at The Lodge at Chaa Creek (tel. 501/824-2037, entrance US$10 pp), including this short riverside hike, highlighting the medicinal plants of the Maya and their uses. The site also boasts the **Blue Morpho Butterfly Breeding Center,** the **Chaa Creek Natural History Museum** (with exhibit areas that examine ecosystems, geology, and Maya culture in the Cayo area), and a gift shop. Touring all of these can take a half day; the office is at The Lodge at Chaa Creek.

Accommodations

Set on 90 lush acres of rolling countryside on the banks of the Macal River is ❰ **duPlooy's Cottage Resort** (tel. 501/824-3101, www. duplooys.com). The duPlooys have planted thousands of trees, a fruit orchard, and the **Belize Botanic Garden.** Guests have a number of choices of where to stay, including Jungle Lodge Rooms (US$145 for up to four people) and comfy bungalows (US$185 for up to four), accessed by a wooden catwalk and offering their own canopy tour on the steep riverbank, plus king bed, refrigerator, bathtub, and hammocks on the deck. Other available options are great for families and groups, including La Casita, which sleeps eight for US$275 a night. Meal plans, packed lunches, and the dining room provide top-notch, cow-free sustenance—vegetarians are welcome. In addition, duPlooy's offers a sandy river beach with swimming, walks in the garden, horse trails, hiking, orchids, and bird-watching tours. Of course, the full retinue of local trips is available, including nearby caves, waterfalls, ruins, and even Tikal in nearby Guatemala. Or you can float in a tube or canoe downstream to other jungle resorts where you'll radio back to duPlooy's for a pickup. It's worth noting that duPlooy's is one of the few resorts in Belize that *really* walks the walk when it comes to environmentally friendly and sustainable practices. In addition to composting, waste reduction, recycling, and the avoidance of the nonsustainable practice of palm frond roof thatching, they

also have zero chemical use on the vast landscaping—which, considering the 10-foot-deep wee-wee ant complexes that have to be dug up and destroyed by hand, is no small feat in the rainforest.

As you continue upstream on the Macal, **Ek' Tun** (tel. 501/820-3002, www.ektunbelize.com, US$190, plus US$28 for breakfast and dinner) is one of the most remote, romantic accommodations in Belize, consisting of two quaint, tastefully appointed cottages in the middle of a vast, green chunk of the upper Macal River Valley. The cascade-fed, mineral water swimming pool surrounded by beautiful landscaping and meditation platforms is unique in all of Central America. Excellent meals include Mexican specialties, fresh fruit, spicy local dishes, and desserts; accommodations are rustically elegant and comfortable (there is no electricity). Ek' Tun's intimate atmosphere makes this a favorite for honeymooners (no children, couples only, three-night minimum).

Another couple of river bends brings you to **Black Rock Belize Jungle River Lodge** (tel. 501/824-2341, www.blackrocklodge.com, US$110–145 plus meals and taxes), which has 14 cabins, including a few deluxe options. Excellent food is served in an open-air dining pavilion. Though in a primitive setting of 250 jungle acres, Black Rock uses solar and hydro technology. Lots of activities and packages are available.

Just downstream of duPlooy's, **The Lodge at Chaa Creek** (tel. 501/824-2037, www.chaacreek.com, from US$230, breakfast included) is more than just one of the top-rated jungle lodges in Central America; this was the first cottage resort of its kind in the Cayo District. Chaa Creek's 365 acres on the Macal River host the ever-evolving vision of owners Mick and Lucy Fleming, an American wife/British husband team who came to Belize in the late 1970s, fell in love with the land, and never left. The 23 *palapa*-roof cottages have electricity and private verandas for viewing wildlife and are furnished with fine fabrics and works of art from around the world; two "treetop" Jacuzzi suites perch on the riverbank, their

© JOSHUA BERMAN

the fire hearth of the romantic, rustic Ek' Tun resort

wide porches boasting views of massive igua-nas basking in the branches. All have access to a new pool with gorgeous views. The Belizean chef prepares wonderful meals, with many of the ingredients coming from a local Maya farm (which guests can visit); a packed lunch is US$10, dinner US$32. The spa is set on a beautiful bluff above the lodge, with views of the hills across the river; one feels relaxed just walking into the open-air lounge area and lis-tening to the music over a cup of tea. Full and modern treatments are available to guests and walk-ins alike. Contact the Chaa Creek front desk or their office in San Ignacio.

In addition to the standard menu of day trips, Chaa Creek guests can choose from a number of on-site activities for no extra charge: daily early morning bird-watching walks, swimming in the Macal, hiking the trails, or venturing out in a canoe—San Ignacio is a two-hour paddle downstream, or you can work your way upstream to duPlooy's to tour the Botanic Garden (strong paddlers only). The lodge has a fleet of high-end Specialized moun-tain bikes also available to guests. Chaa Creek

guides are available for all trips, including ca-noeing, hiking, and biking, and they undergo an impressive training program—including U.S. National Park Service ranger and res-cue training, plus bike training in the Grand Canyon and Utah slickrock country.

Chaa Creek's **Macal River Camp** is a group of 10 canvas-roofed, stilted cabin-tents, in their own clearing near the river, about a 10-minute walk along the medicine trail from the activity of the main lodge. Just US$55 per person gets you a lantern-lit cabin with an almost-private porch, dinner and breakfast, and use of the shared bathroom and shower house. Meals are eaten communally under a thatch roof, with a bar available as well. And, of course, camp guests have access to all the main Chaa Creek facilities and activities.

On the same road, about a half-mile off of the highway, is the Belizean owned **Mystic Jungle Resort** (tel. 501/823-3002 or 668-3479, www.aguallos.com/mysticjungle, from US$35). It is being renovated but has great promise if one is looking for less expensive accommodations. It features a funky bar,

MOUNTAIN PINE RIDGE

pool, and cabanas. The owner is affable, accommodating, and entertaining. This place caters to the families of San Ignacio on the weekends and holidays, so expect some raucous good fun.

SAN JOSÉ DE SUCCOTZ AND XUNANTUNICH

About 6.5 miles from San Ignacio, you'll find this hillside village on your left, above the Mopan River, right where the ferry to Xunantunich is located. In Succotz, the first language is Spanish, and the most colorful time to visit is during one of their fiestas: March 19 (feast day of St. Joseph) and May 3 (feast day of the Holy Cross).

A stroll through the rough village streets is enjoyable if you're into observing village life. **Magana's Art Center** is the workshop of David Magana, who works with the youth of the area, encouraging them to continue the arts and crafts of their ancestors. You'll find the results inside in the form of local wood carvings, baskets, jewelry, and stone (slate) carvings unique to Belize. There are a few taco stands in town, including the popular local eatery **Benny's Kitchen,** where one can get a substantial breakfast and other tasty items for low prices. Cold draft Belikin is served in frosty mugs, a nice touch.

Accommodations

Just before entering the roadside village of San José de Succotz, look on your left for the ⟨ **Trek Stop** (tel. 501/823-2265, www.the-trekstop.com), a backpacker classic offering 10 cabins set in lush gardens on 22 acres of second-growth tropical forest; or, as they put it, "eco-lodging for savvy travelers." You can hear the highway, but you can also hear howler monkeys, birds, and the inspired conversation of your hosts and fellow travelers. There are camping facilities (access to composting toilets and solar showers), a patio restaurant with inexpensive Belizean dishes, and walking access to the Xunantunich ruins. Rates are US$10 per person for the simple wood cabins with twin or double beds, electricity, porches, and

shared bath; a larger, more private cabin with private bath costs US$35. Tent sites are available for US$5 per person. Inner tubes, inflatable kayaks, and mountain bikes are available for rent. Even if you're not spending the night here, come visit the **Tropical Wings Nature Center,** one of the best and most diverse butterfly ranches in the country. Be sure to leave time for a round on Belize's only **Disk Golf Course,** a nine-basket Frisbee golf game through the jungle, disks available (US$2.50 per person). The course is a par 31 with narrow and challenging fairways that leave little room for error (wear long pants and closed footwear to retrieve those errant drives). There is a nice view (and sometimes breeze) from the Maya ruins atop Hole 6.

The all-inclusive **Mopan River Resort** (tel. 501/823-2047, www.mopanriverresort. com, Nov.–June only) is set on 10 beautiful acres across from the village of Benque del Viejo and is a fine option for travelers looking for comfort and easy access to Tikal and all the Cayo attractions. Packages (three-day minimum) run around US$200 per day and are truly all-inclusive: lodging, meals, alcohol, tours, and airport transfers; the daily rate drops the longer you stay. The nicely furnished cabanas are also equipped with TV/VCRs, and a selection of movies is available in the gift shop. Buffet and family-style dinners are themed, and breakfasts are cooked to your liking. Swimming in the river is not advised, but a lovely pool is provided for guests. Small weddings are welcome. Pam, one of the owners, is a minister and can tie the knot for you in the riverside chapel.

⟨ Xunantunich Archaeological Site

One of Belize's most impressive Maya ceremonial centers, Xunantunich rests atop a natural limestone ridge with a grand view of the entire Cayo District and Guatemala countryside. The local name for the site, Xunantunich (shoo-NAHN-ta-nich), or "stone lady," continues to be used, even after the ancients' own name for the site, Ka-at Witz, or "Supernatural

COURTESY OF THE BELIZE TOURISM BOARD/TONY RATH

Xunantunich

Mountain," was recently discovered, carved into a chunk of stone.

Xunantunich is believed to have been built sometime around 400 B.C. and deserted around A.D. 1000; at its peak, some 7,000–10,000 Maya lived here. Though certainly not the biggest of Maya structures, at 135 feet high, **El Castillo** is the second tallest pyramid in Belize (missing first place by one foot!). The eastern side of the structure displays an unusual stucco frieze (a reproduction), and you can see three carved stelae in the plaza. Xunantunich contains three ceremonial plazas surrounded by house mounds. It was rediscovered in 1894, but not studied until 1938, by archaeologist Sir J. Eric Thompson. As the first Maya ruin to be opened in the country, it has attracted the attention and exploration of many other archaeologists over the years.

In 1950, the University of Pennsylvania (noted for its years of outstanding work across the Guatemala border in Tikal) built a facility in Xunantunich for more study. In 1954, visitors were invited to explore the site after a road was opened and a small ferry built. In 1959,

archaeologist Evan Mackie made news in the Maya world when he discovered evidence that part of Xunantunich had been destroyed by an earthquake in the Late Classic Period. Some believe it was then that the people began to lose faith in their leaders—they saw the earthquake as an unearthly sign from the gods. But for whatever reason, Xunantunich ceased to be a religious center long before the end of the Classic Period.

Located eight miles west of San Ignacio, the site is accessed by crossing the Mopan River on the Succotz Ferry, easily found at the end of a line of crafts vendors. The hand-cranked ferry shuttles you (and your vehicle, if you have one) across the river, after which you'll have about a mile's hike (or drive) up a hill to the site. The ferry, which operates 8 A.M.–3 P.M. daily, is free, but tipping the operator is a kind and much-appreciated gesture. Don't miss the 4 P.M. return ferry with the park rangers, or you'll be swimming. Be forewarned that during rainy season the Mopan River can rise, run fast, and flood, thus ceasing this service until conditions improve.

MOUNTAIN PINE RIDGE

MOUNTAIN PINE RIDGE

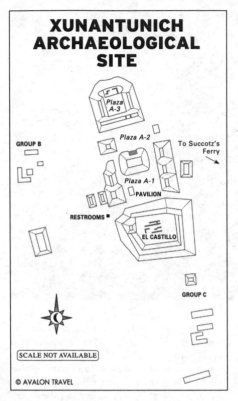

XUNANTUNICH ARCHAEOLOGICAL SITE

Plaza A-3

GROUP B

Plaza A-2

To Succotz's Ferry

Plaza A-1

PAVILION

RESTROOMS

EL CASTILLO

GROUP C

SCALE NOT AVAILABLE

© AVALON TRAVEL

Entrance to the site is US$2.50 per person; guides are available for US$20 per group and are recommended—both to learn about what you're seeing and to support sustainable tourism, as all guides are local and very knowledgeable.

BENQUE VIEJO DEL CARMEN

After the ferry, the village of Succotz creeps over the hill and becomes Benque Viejo, the last town in Belize (the border is about one mile farther). This is a quiet little town with a peaceful atmosphere. Benque Viejo has been greatly influenced by the Spanish, both from its historical past when Spain ruled Guatemala and later when Spanish-speaking *chicleros* and loggers worked the forest. At one time, Benque Viejo ("Old Bank"; riverside logging camps were referred to as

"banks") was a logging camp. This was the gathering place for *chicle* workers, and logs were floated down the river from here for shipment to England.

The Latin influence persists with today's influx of Guatemalans. A group of foreign doctors who donate free medical assistance visit the Good Shepherd Clinic in Benque Viejo every year. People come from all over the district for this needed service; families even come from across the Guatemala border. Tourists generally do not choose to stay in the town of Benque, as so many options are available right up the road. There are a couple of dismal hotels however, and some decent Chinese restaurants, notably Allan's. You might find some Guatemalan crafts for sale if you walk around.

Getting There and Away

Buses between Belize City, Benque, and the Guatemala border run daily, starting at ungodly hours on both ends. Most bus service to and from San Ignacio also services Benque and the border. The most efficient way to travel to the border (or to any of the sites along the Western Highway mentioned earlier in this chapter) from San Ignacio is by *colectivo* taxis, which run in a constant and steady flow roughly 6 A.M.–7 P.M.; the ride should cost approximately US$2, but you take the chance of sharing your cab with as many people as your driver can fit. By private taxi, expect to pay about US$10 per cab for the same trip.

SOUTH ON THE HYDRO ROAD

You'll find the turnoff in the middle of Benque Viejo. It leads south to a small selection of attractions and accommodations, all well off the beaten path.

Poustinia Land Art Park

This is a reclaimed cattle ranch, now devoted to the nurturing of art and nature, where foreign and Belizean artists can stay and contribute to the ongoing project, and visitors can come take a look and soak it all in. The lush grounds are part of a 270-acre second-growth forest. Visiting the unique **Poustinia Land Art Park** (www.poustiniaonline.org) is by appointment only and can be arranged at the **Benque Viejo House of Culture** (tel. 501/823-2697). Adjacent to the park are the **El Dorado Cabins** (contact Luis Alberto and Deborah Ruiz in Belmopan, tel. 501/822-3532, US$40). The two wooden cabins are equipped with a kitchenette, a private bathroom with running water, a small dining area, and a deck; limited electricity is available.

◖ Chechem Ha Cave and the Vaca Plateau

Just before reaching the border station in Benque, a well-graded and maintained dirt road splits off to the left and heads south 11 miles, where it dead-ends at the Mollejon Dam. The country is sparsely populated broadleaf forest with a scattering of small farms, steep hills, waterfalls, caves, and two primitive accommodations from which to explore it all. Both are located on the Vaca Plateau, with accessible views of the ancient Macal River Valley. Both are also remote and very close to nature—if you can't go without modern amenities for a day or two, you'd better stay in town.

The road is equipped with mile markers on small white posts. A couple miles in, a right turn leads to the border village of Arenal. Nothing there but a few hundred tight-knit *milperos* scraping a life from the soils of the Mopan River Valley.

At Mile 8, you'll find a turnoff to the left for **Chechem Ha Farm** (tel. 501/820-4063), located a mile or so down a rutted road and belonging to the Morales family. The place is designed to give nature-loving tourists the chance to enjoy the Chechem Ha Spring, Chechem Ha Falls (a spectacular 175-foot cascade with a treacherous trail down to its misty bottom), and the increasingly popular Chechem Ha Cave, a dry cave—except for the dripping water that has created all the formations over the years. Loaded with Maya pottery, the ceremonial Chechem Ha Cave is protected by the government, which allows only guided tours, and (of course) nothing can be removed. The pottery inside is estimated to be as much as 2,000 years old. You can climb and explore various ledges and passageways, but the highlight is a deep ceremonial chamber in the heart of the hill. In some places, you need a rope to help you get around. While those of average physical abilities can enjoy Chechem Ha Cave, take care when moving amid the pottery.

Stay at the farm in one of several simple cabins made of clay, rock, wood, and thatch; they are well constructed and comfy looking. There is also a new bar, restaurant, and gift shop. For US$41 per person, you get a night's stay and three meals (no electricity; outhouses). Camping is US$5 per person, bring your own tent. Individual meals are available (US$5–10), as is an inexpensive transfer from Benque. Fireflies will light up the night, and all manner of jungle birds will call from the trees. You'll eat under a thatch *palapa* and bathe in the nearby stream or under the waterfall below the lip of the plateau.

Martz Farm

Less than a mile beyond the Chechem Ha road, another left turn will carry you to ◖ **Martz Farm** (tel. 501/614-6462, www.martzfarm. com, US$20–28), a wonderfully unique and relaxed homestead on the Toucan Trail, built and maintained by the hardworking Martinez family—and featuring the burly, good-natured Joe and Lazaro, who hacked this place out of raw bush. They've constructed a handful of tree houses and natural cabins, each apparently sprung from wild childhood fantasies. All are open to the forest air (mosquito nets provided), and one is even built over a private dip pool in the passing creek. Family-style meals are cooked over a traditional fire hearth in a quaint kitchen by Joe's German wife, Miriam, and farm animals wander the grounds with the guests. Home-cooked meal plans and free transfers from San Ignacio or Benque are available. The facilities are slowly improving, with a few new flush toilets and hot water and showers.

MOUNTAIN PINE RIDGE

Into Guatemala: Tikal National Park

Tikal National Park is a wildlife preserve covering 25 square miles. The Tikal ruins are among the more outstanding in the Maya world. They have been excavated and restored extensively, but what you'll see is only a small part of what is still buried and unexplored in the rainforest.

As at most Maya ceremonial centers, archaeologists are learning more and more about life in Tikal and its 3,000 structures (with 10,000 more foundations). They have mapped 250 stelae that the Maya left behind. In recent years, they have learned to decipher the Maya hieroglyphs, and about 80 percent of the Maya's written record has been translated.

Tikal National Park has been protected from loggers and *milperos* for more than three decades, so in addition to the cultural attraction, Tikal is a phenomenal nature and wildlife experience. You'll hear and, with luck (if you're up very early in the morning), see the howler monkeys that live in the treetops on the site. Hundreds of parrots will squawk at you as you wander through **Twin Complex Q and R**—this is their domain. And while wandering the **Great Plaza** and the **Lost City,** you'll see colorful toucans fly between ancient stone structures and tall vine-covered trees.

Throughout the site, you'll see several twin complexes with identical pyramids facing each other across a central plaza. No one knows why they were built this way. At Twin Complex Q and R, one pyramid has been excavated and restored, while its opposite is just as it was found—covered with vines and jungle growth. You'll see this sort of juxtaposition frequently throughout Tikal.

Tikal is huge, and a full explanation of the site is beyond the scope of this book; check out *Moon Guatemala* or pick up a map and booklet at the visitors center and enjoy. I also recommend archaeologist William Coe's *Tikal: A Handbook of the Ancient Maya Ruins,* which has the best map of the site.

HISTORY
The Maya

The first Tikal Maya were farmers who, as far back as 750 B.C., chose the high ground that rose above the vast, steamy swamps of Petén for their settlement. The earliest evidence of their presence is some of the trash they left behind. Living on a major route between the lowlands and the cooler highlands, the Tikal villagers began a healthy trade in flint. The stone was plentiful here and was prized for tools and weapons.

By 600 B.C., the Maya had begun their construction of Tikal ("The Place of Voices"). Over the next 1,500 years, they built their platformed city in layers, razing structures to gather material to build more.

By about 200 B.C., the Maya were building ceremonial structures. By 100 B.C., the great Acropolis was in place, and the Great Plaza was already as large as it would be hundreds of years later, when the population of Tikal reached its peak of about 55,000 people. From 50 B.C. to A.D. 250, the Maya created even more elaborate architecture on these early foundations. They also carved monuments, though they did not yet use hieroglyphics.

With the beginning of the Early Classic Period in about A.D. 250, the Maya's monuments grew larger and became more formal and less ornate, but the plans for their temples changed little. They built the causeways to connect the parts of their city and carried on a thriving trade. Carvings on monuments and burial practices show a close relationship with Teotihuacán in Mexico. The monuments also describe Great-Jaguar-Paw and Smoking-Frog's conquest of nearby Uaxactún in A.D. 378. In 562, Lord Water of Caracol defeated Tikal in a great "ax war," and Tikal produced no monuments for 135 years. But in 682, Ah-Cacau took the throne and began to restore Tikal to its former glory. The great king was buried in the Temple of the Giant Jaguar.

SAFETY CONCERNS IN GUATEMALA

Guatemala has experienced considerably more political instability and domestic strife than its neighbor, Belize, in the last few decades; consequently, the country has, at times, been prone to bouts of desperation-fueled robberies and assaults. Stories occasionally surface regarding Guatemalan thugs targeting tourists in the Tikal area and occasionally crossing over into Belize's Cayo District. Although things are always apt to change and the odd incident can happen any time, traveler security has never been better in Guatemala, thanks in large part to a new force of tourist police, called **Politur,** trained and assigned specifically to protect,

inform, and aid visitors to the country's top destinations, including Tikal. There are about 425 officers in the country, with roughly 60 individuals assigned to Tikal National Park and its approach road. Politur is made up of trained police officers, armed with pistols but still lacking in basic supplies, transportation, and English skills.

Check with the **State Department Travel Advisory Office** in Washington, D.C. (tel. 202/647-5225), or for more detailed information, contact the **Guatemalan Embassy** in Washington, D.C. (tel. 202/745-4952). Your lodge hosts should have a good local idea of the security situation, as well.

Most of the construction at Tikal was in the Late Classic Period, which began in A.D. 550 (shortly before Tikal's defeat by Caracol) and ended in A.D. 900 (when the entire society collapsed). In and around the ceremonial parts of the city lie 200 stone monuments in the form of stelae and altars. Archaeologists have pieced together Tikal's history from the carvings. The burials at Tikal also hold a clue to the structure of the society.

In the six square miles of Tikal that have been excavated, archaeologists have found hundreds of little buildings that they believe were domestic. Usually they're found in small clusters on elevated sites suitable for housing an extended family. Most people were buried beneath the floors of their houses. Their bones were smaller and weaker than the bones of the folks buried in the great tombs. The range of the housing construction, in size and quality, also suggests great variety in people's status and wealth.

But in A.D. 900, the entire society fell apart, not only at Tikal but throughout the Maya world. Post-Classic Maya continued to use the site for several centuries, and even moved several of the stelae around in an attempt to restore the city for their own purposes, but the jungle eventually reclaimed Tikal.

The Archaeologists

Hidden Tikal was mentioned in 18th-century Guatemalan archives, but not until 1848 did the government mount an official expedition. The governor and commissioner of the Petén visited Tikal, and their report, along with an artist's drawings of the stelae and lintels, attracted attention in Europe, where the report was published. A Swiss doctor, Gustav Bernoulli, visited in 1877. He had some of the lintels removed (from Temples I and IV).

The first maps of Tikal were drawn by Alfred Percival Maudslay, who visited in 1881 and 1882 and whose workmen liberated the temples from the forest. He published his accounts along with the first photographs of the site. Teobert Maler continued in this vein; he visited in 1895 and 1904, mapping and photographing for the Peabody Museum of Harvard University. He wouldn't relinquish his site map, though, and the museum hired Mayanists Alfred Marston Tozzer and R. E. Merwin to finish the job.

Sylvanus G. Morley, for whom the Tikal museum is named and former head of the Carnegie Institution's archaeology department, used Maudslay's and the Peabody Museum's reports as a base and devoted himself to recording the writing of the Maya. In 1956, the

MOUNTAIN PINE RIDGE

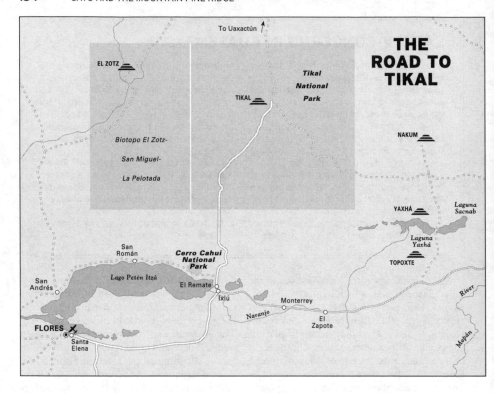

THE ROAD TO TIKAL

To Uaxactún

EL ZOTZ

Tikal National Park

TIKAL

NAKUM

Biotopo El Zotz-

San Miguel-

La Pelotada

YAXHÁ   Laguna Sacnab

Laguna Yaxhá

San Román

Cerro Cahui National Park

TOPOXTE

San Andrés

Lago Petén Itzá   El Remate

Ixlú

Monterrey

Naranjo   El Zapote

FLORES

Santa Elena

River

Mopán

MOUNTAIN PINE RIDGE

University of Pennsylvania launched the project to excavate Tikal and appointed Carnegie archaeologist Edwin Shook to lead the project. Since then, only part of the immense site has been excavated and restored.

VISITING THE RUINS
Entrance Fees and Hours

Entrance fees are now paid in the park itself, after entering through the main gate, where, if you are in a private vehicle, your license plates will be noted and you will be asked to respect the speed limits. The entrance fees (Q150, about US$25) are now collected at what used to be the kiosk for the tour guides. This sharp spike in admission from the long-standing Q50 rate has caught many travelers off guard, so make sure you have extra money in case it goes up again. Do not lose your ticket! There is a visitors center complex on your left; there's a

museum, a few gift shops, a tour guide stand, an overpriced restaurant, and the famous white plaster scale model of the Tikal ruins. Beyond these buildings, on the right, is a large parking lot (and former airstrip), where you'll find the park's three hotels and one campground.

The ruins proper—and the gorgeous trail network that runs through and around them—are officially open 6 A.M.–6 P.M. Depending on the time of year, these hours may interfere with visitors' plans to watch the sun rise or set from the top of Temple IV (because of dangerously slick limestone and degradation of the ruins, climbing to the top of the other structures that rise above the tree canopy is often prohibited). Some say you can talk with the ticket control officers to get special permission to enter early or stay late, but this could not be verified. A ticket purchased after 3 P.M. is valid for the next day; you'll need to show it

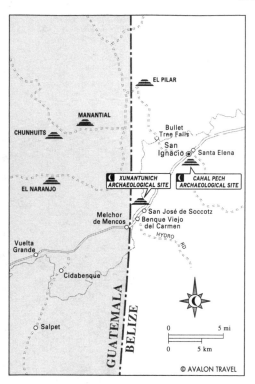

The ruins of Tikal encompass six square miles

climbing the pyramids themselves. Prepare as you would for a nature hike rather than a museum visit—comfortable walking shoes, a snack, more water than you think you'll need, and a rain jacket during the wet season (and also for the monkeys who take great pleasure in urinating on hikers—seriously). There are a number of shelters in case it really starts coming down, and a few beverage stands, but no food is available.

Wandering the ruins on your own is an unforgettable and perfectly enjoyable experience. As long as you stay on the trails among the ruins and within earshot of other visitors and park guards, you shouldn't need to worry about getting lost, but be advised: Tikal is surrounded by a vast and wild jungle and there are no fences or markers to denote the boundary. It is not unheard of for distracted visitors to find some old trail leading away from the ruins (be especially careful around Complex P, as one can easily end up on the road to Uaxactún).

Tour Guides

If you plan on spending a few days exploring the ruins (most agree that you need at least two full days to take it all in), hiring one of Tikal's 50 or so guides on your first foray will prepare you for further solo trips into the park. Guides are readily available at the visitors center, speak many different languages, and cost about US$10 per person for a 3.5-hour tour (this is the *colectivo* rate, personal guides are a bit more).

The Great Plaza

One mile from the museum, this plaza, considered the heart of ancient Tikal, is highly complex in design. The Great Plaza covers three acres; its plastered floor, now covered with grass, is made of four layers, the earliest laid in 150 B.C. and the latest in A.D. 700. Two great temples, I and II, face each other across the plaza, around which are scattered palaces, altars, a ball court, and 70 stelae—the memorial stones carved of limestone that tell of Maya life and conquest. Terraces and stairways lead up and down into a plethora of architecturally

to ticket control when you enter the following morning. If you overnighted in the park and need a new ticket, you can purchase it right there at ticket control.

If ziplining is your thing, this is a great spot to try it at. As well, INGUAT, the Guatemalan tourist authority, has been very active with new signage along the route from Melchor to Flores. INGUAT has a new complex on the right side of the road before reaching Flores, and it is worth a stop here to gather free travel information, maps, and such if continuing farther into Guatemala.

Walking the Site

The ruins of Tikal encompass six square miles and are connected by a fantastic, although sometimes confusing, trail system. This means you'll be doing quite a bit of walking, nearly all of it on flat ground—except, of course, when

MOUNTAIN PINE RIDGE

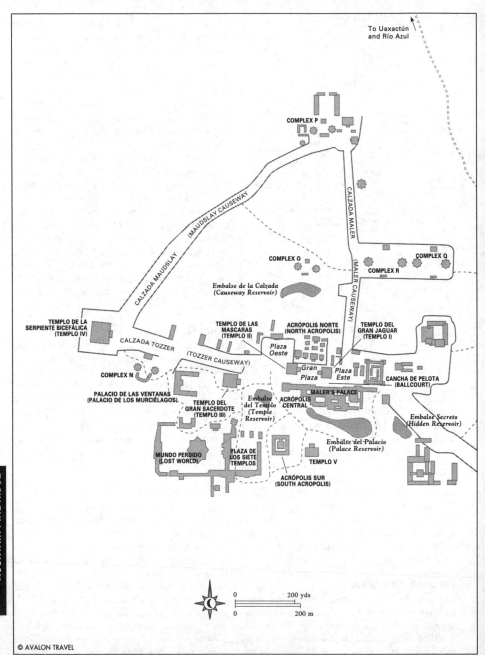

To Uaxactún
and Río Azul

COMPLEX P

CALZADA MALER

CALZADA MAUDSLAY

(MAUDSLAY CAUSEWAY)

COMPLEX O

COMPLEX Q

COMPLEX R

(MALER CAUSEWAY)

Embalse de la Calzada
(Causeway Reservoir)

TEMPLO DE LA
SERPIENTE BICEFÁLICA
(TEMPLO IV)

CALZADA TOZZER

(TOZZER CAUSEWAY)

TEMPLO DE LAS
MASCARAS
(TEMPLO II)

ACRÓPOLIS NORTE
(NORTH ACROPOLIS)

TEMPLO DEL
GRAN JAGUAR
(TEMPLO I)

Plaza
Oeste

COMPLEX N

Gran
Plaza

Plaza
Este

CANCHA DE PELOTA
(BALLCOURT)

PALACIO DE LAS VENTANAS
(PALACIO DE LOS MURCIÉLAGOS)

MALER'S PALACE

TEMPLO DEL
GRAN SACERDOTE
(TEMPLO III)

Embalse
del Templo
(Temple
Reservoir)

ACRÓPOLIS
CENTRAL

Embalse Secreto
(Hidden Reservoir)

Embalse del Palacio
(Palace Reservoir)

MUNDO PERDIDO
(LOST WORLD)

PLAZA DE
LOS SIETE
TEMPLOS

TEMPLO V

ACRÓPOLIS SUR
(SOUTH ACROPOLIS)

0   200 yds

0   200 m

MOUNTAIN PINE RIDGE

© AVALON TRAVEL

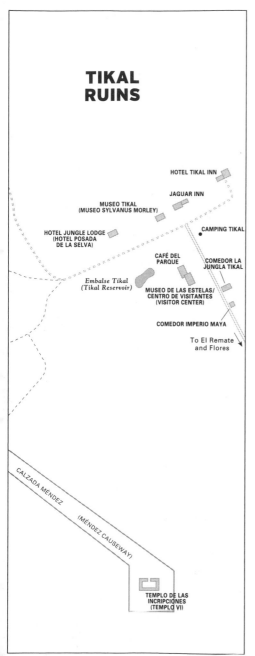

TIKAL RUINS

HOTEL TIKAL INN

JAGUAR INN

MUSEO TIKAL
(MUSEO SYLVANUS MORLEY)

HOTEL JUNGLE LODGE
(HOTEL POSADA
DE LA SELVA)

CAMPING TIKAL

CAFÉ DEL
PARQUE

COMEDOR LA
JUNGLA TIKAL

*Embalse Tikal
(Tikal Reservoir)*

MUSEO DE LAS ESTELAS/
CENTRO DE VISITANTES
(VISITOR CENTER)

COMEDOR IMPERIO MAYA

To El Remate
and Flores

CALZADA MÉNDEZ

(MÉNDEZ CAUSEWAY)

TEMPLO DE LAS
INCRIPCIONES
(TEMPLO VI)

intense buildings. Most of these palaces were ceremonial centers, but a few are believed to have been apartments. If you climbed and poked around into every structure at the Great Plaza, it would take you at least an entire day.

Temple I

Because of its grace, form, and balance, this is probably the most photographed temple at Tikal. Also known as the **Temple of the Giant Jaguar** (named for a carving on one of its lintels), it rises 172 feet above the East Plaza behind it. Nine sloping terraces mark its sides, and its roof comb sits 145 feet above the Great Plaza floor. Atop the building platform is a three-room temple. Its central stair was used by workmen to haul building materials to the top of the temple. It's believed to have been built in about A.D. 700 for King Ah-Cacau, who brought Tikal out of its dark ages after its defeat by Caracol. His tomb was found inside during the restoration, and some of the grave goods, including 180 jade ornaments, pearls, and bone carvings, are on display in the museum/visitors center.

Temple II

Called the **Temple of the Masks** for the carvings on its lintel, this smaller structure faces Temple I across the Great Plaza. One of the few Maya temples ever dedicated to a woman, it was built for Ah-Cacau's queen and is smaller and less steep than his. It stands about 125 feet above the Great Plaza, though if its roof comb were intact, the temple would have stood close to 140 feet high. Like its counterpart across the way, it also has three rooms at the crest. In front of Temple II lies a large block that archaeologists speculate served as a reviewing stand—priests standing on it could see the crowds in the plaza below and in turn they could be seen by all.

East Plaza

This immense plaza, east of the Great Plaza and backing up to the Temple of the Giant Jaguar, was once a formal plastered area covering 5.5 acres. Two of the city's causeways, **Mendez** and **Maler,** lead from here. This plaza is the site of the only known sweathouse at Tikal, and it's also the site of a ball court and what appears to be the marketplace. Trash and other evidence show that the Maya continued to use the ball court after the collapse of Tikal in A.D. 900.

Temple IV

It's another long walk, but follow your map and visit challenging Temple IV, the **Temple of the Double-Headed Serpent.** Facing east, it's a popular spot from which to watch the sunrise. The platform itself has not been excavated, and only those in good physical condition will want to climb the six ladders (sometimes all you can cling to are roots and branches) to the top. Yaxkin Caan Chac, the son and successor of Ah-Cacau, built Temple IV about 40 years after Temple I was built for his father. Today, Temple IV is the tallest surviving Maya structure from pre-Columbian history—212 feet from the base of its platform to the top. Not until the 1900s, when elevators became commonplace, were taller buildings constructed in this hemisphere. Temple IV also houses a three-room temple, with walls up to 40 feet thick. From the summit of Temple IV, the view of the entire area is breathtaking. The jungle canopy itself rises 100 feet into the air, and the tops of the other white temples of Tikal rise above the tops of the trees.

Temple V

Though the climb to the top of Temple IV is strenuous, it pales in comparison with the ascent to the north-facing Temple V. Like Temple I, it was built about A.D. 700; it rises about 190 feet. After clambering through underbrush to reach the top of the former stairway, hardy climbers have the option of hoisting themselves up through a hole in the roof comb that appears to have been dug sometime before archaeologists discovered Tikal. Some travelers have reported that the dark, forbidding interior of the roof comb contains ropes and ladders to gain access to the very top of Temple V, from which there is a remarkably focused view of the other temples of Tikal.

Hieroglyphs and Stelae

The earliest stela at Tikal, number 29, was probably carved in A.D. 292. The latest is number 11, carved in 869. In between, the stelae record the births and deaths of kings, the cycle of festivals and seasons, and sagas of war. Even a long pause in the production of stelae, beginning in 557 and ending in 692, has a story to tell. Mayanists have deduced (now that they have discovered how to read as much as 80 percent of Maya writing here and at other Maya sites) that Tikal lost a great battle with Caracol, and the hiatus coincides with Caracol's dominance of the region. The inscriptions of Tikal also show that a single dynasty ruled the kingdom from the Early Classic Period until the society collapsed in A.D. 900. Yax-Moch-Xoc founded the line and ruled for about 219–238. Though he was not the first leader to be memorialized at Tikal, he apparently was so magnificent that he was recognized as the founder of a dynasty—the inscriptions are the first in which the Maya recorded the concept of a founding ancestor. His descendants made up the royalty of Tikal. Among them were kings with nicknames like Great-Jaguar-Paw, Moon-Zero Bird (who took the throne in A.D. 320), and Curl-Snout (A.D. 379), all of whom followed the founder of the Tikal royal line, Yax-Moch-Xoc.

ACCOMMODATIONS AND FOOD

Accommodations within Tikal National Park obviously put you closest to the ruins, great for travelers who really want to focus on the pyramids and catch a sunrise or two. The majority of overnight Tikal visitors, however, book themselves in the island city of Flores or its sister town of Santa Elena, about an hour's drive southwest of the park; that's where you'll find the greatest quantity and widest range of lodging and restaurant options. Additionally, as security issues continue to improve and the number of visitors increase, the village of El Remate is an increasingly popular base camp; it is only 30 kilometers south of Tikal, boasts plentiful budget lodging and camping, and is a relaxed, lakeside destination in its own right.

At the Ruins

Hotel development in the park has been kept wonderfully *tranquilo,* with only three hotels and one campground. This translates into a limited supply for a sometimes high demand, especially around Christmas, New Year's, and Easter, when reservations are recommended. Accommodations are simple; most do not have 24-hour electricity or telephones (This also means that credit cards may not work). Each hotel has its own low-key dining room and shuttle services to Flores and the Belize border. Phone numbers listed here usually connect to a Santa Elena office. There is also a campground run from an office in the visitors center (about US$4 a person), with bathroom and shower.

Hotel Jaguar Inn (tel. 502/7783-3647, solis@quetzal.net, US$60) has 13 bungalows and a small camping area (US$3.50); mosquito-netted hammocks (US$6.50) also available. Electricity (private generator) is on until about 10 P.M.; candles are provided for later in the evening.

The **Jungle Lodge,** also called **Hotel Posada de la Selva** (tel. 502/476-8775 in Guatemala City, reservaciones@junglelodge.guate.com), under renovation at press time, offers rooms from US$31–72. The 50 rooms have hot showers, ceiling fans, and porches. A bit more upscale, the **Tikal Inn** (tel. 502/926-0065, US$81) has 17 bungalows and 11 rooms surrounding a pleasant swimming pool. Rates include breakfast and dinner.

In addition to the hotel restaurants, there are three reasonably priced *comedores* near the visitors center. As for services, there is a post office in the visitors center. Internet is available at a few of the hotels.

El Remate

A picturesque village of about 300 families strung along the road to Tikal, El Remate is located on the east end of Lake Petén-Itza, 30 kilometers from both Flores and the park. Camping and budget accommodations are plentiful, as is transportation both north and south. Although El Remate serves most travelers as a convenient, relaxed base camp for their Tikal experience, this is also the gateway to the

Biotopo Cerro Cahuí, a 650-hectare broadleaf forest preserve located a short walk along the road that breaks off to follow the north shore of the lake. The Biotopo boasts an excellent six-kilometer trail with the chance to see a few of the 300 bird species, 40 mammal species, 20 reptile and amphibian species, and 20 species of fish that have been identified here. There are also great views of the lake.

El Remate is located just a few minutes' drive north of the junction at Ixlu. There are basic services here, plus a nice row of craft huts along the west side of the road, selling Guatemalan textiles, wood carvings, jade pieces, and more. Stop in for a cold Gallo at **La Canoa de San Pablo**—great coffee, too, to drink by candlelight as you strain your eyes to look at the crafts for sale.

There are plenty of new accommodations going up in El Remate, so be sure to poke around before making a decision. There are several campgrounds near the south end of town, including the longstanding backpacker-friendly **Camping y Hospedaje Sal Itzá,** set back from the road on the right, with thatched structures and mosquito-netted mattresses or campsites for less than US$3 per person. There are a few funky places built into the hillside on the right as you continue into town, including the **Mirador del Duende** (Dwarf's Lookout), with open bungalows for under US$5 per person. Camping is available, and there are great sunset lake views and a reasonable vegetarian restaurant. A bit farther north, on the left, the **Hotel Sun Breeze** is an excellent choice, with simple rooms with shared bath (US$5/7 s/d) and a very friendly staff.

Just after the Hotel Sun Breeze, the road to Cerro Cahuí splits to the left to follow the lakeshore, while the main highway continues north; the Centro de Salud (Health Clinic) and police station are here on your right. At the road junction, you'll find the **Casa de Don David**—El Remate's longstanding meeting place, homestyle restaurant, and midrange hotel. Friendly, family-run Don David (tel. 502/306-2190, info@lacasadedondavid.com, US$38–52) offers some excellent, fully equipped room options. Lots of tourist information and day trips available.

Upscale hotels on the shores of the lake include the **Westin Camino Real Tikal** (tel. 502/926-0204, U.S. tel. 800/937-8461, www.caminoreal.com.gt) and Francis Ford Coppola's **La Lancha Resort** (tel. 502/7928-8331, U.S. tel. 800/746-3743, www.blancaneaux.com). If traveling from Belize and planning to stay at La Lancha, transport can be arranged in advanced through Blancaneaux Lodge, the sister hotel in the Mountain Pine Ridge of Belize. Pickup service from Flores Airport can be prearranged.

GETTING THERE AND AWAY
By Air
Many visitors opt to come by plane, and flights are available from Belize City, Guatemala City, and Mexico City. Flights from Belize's Philip Goldson International Airport are scheduled on Tropic Air (US$186 round-trip). The airport in Flores (tel. 502/926-0348) is newish and modern, much more so than the town it services.

By Ground
Most Belize tourists who sign up for a trip to Tikal will have all their transportation taken care of, either in a private shuttle from Belize City or San Ignacio or directly from their resort or lodge. Independent (i.e., patient and tolerant) travelers should also have no problem piecing together their own route to the ruins or to any of the nearby towns.

The road in Guatemala is terrible, and it will take about 1.5 hours to reach the entrance to Tikal National Park, after which the road is excellent for the final 30 kilometers to the site itself. There is no direct public transportation from the Belize border to Tikal (except in chartered taxis and minibuses, a good option for groups). The only bus that runs from the border is a Guatemalan public bus that goes to Flores. You can spend the night there and take the morning bus to Tikal (board in front of the San Juan Hotel). The border-to-Flores bus is usually very crowded with chickens and the works. Or get off at the crossroads in Ixlu, where another northbound bus can whisk you to El Remate or all the way to Tikal.

From Belize City
You can always go to Novelo's, catch a local bus to the border, then walk across and go it alone from there, making all your own connections. If, however, you are less confident in your Spanish and would rather go direct for a few dollars more, there are at least four small, private tour companies, all based at various kiosks in the Water Taxi Terminal by the Swing Bridge in Belize City, that offer direct bus service to Chetumal, Mexico, and Flores and Tikal, Guatemala. They are: **S & L Travel and Tours** (tel. 501/227-7593 or 227-5145, sltravel@btl.net, www.sltravelbelize.com), **Mundo Maya Deli, Gifts, Travel & Tours** (tel. 501/223-1235, mundomayatravel@btl.net), **Kaisa International,** and **San Juan Tours.** Daily, direct service is available to both Flores (US$15) and Tikal (US$20). It takes about 4.5 hours to either one, although border hassles can increase that time significantly. From Flores, it's another 8 hours or so to Guatemala City, 12 to Antigua.

From Cayo
Mexican bus lines Linea Dorada and San Juan both stop at **Amigos Belize** (tel. 501/603-9436, www.amigosbelize.com), a tour operator located at the Santa Elena end of the Hawksworth Bridge, where you can buy bus tickets to anywhere in Mexico.

FLORES AND SANTA ELENA
This is a truly unique destination, and it's not far from the Belizean border at Melchor. In the first edition of *Moon Guatemala,* Wayne Bernhardson extolled the island city of Flores for having "greater intrinsic charm than almost any other Guatemalan town—its irregular street pattern and narrow, circuitous alleyways give it a medieval feeling, and the many gingerbread porches and balconies add a touch of vernacular architectural distinction." Flores, about an hour by road from Tikal, is a popular overnight spot for Tikal tourists, especially since the area's main airstrip was relocated from the park to Santa Elena, right outside Flores.

Flores and Santa Elena have most services, transportation, and accommodations, from roachy dives to the lap of luxury. It is worth it to stay here if only to enjoy a relaxing evening walk around the island town. There is no shortage of coffee bars and cheap eateries.

YAXHA RUINS

Despite recent fame on the television program *Survivor: Guatemala,* Yaxha is still ignored by travelers, even though it is a scant 7 miles off of the main road before Ixlu. Admission to the park is Q80 (US$11). Nearby is an inexpensive, rustic, and absolutely quiet hotel, **El Sombrero** (tel. 502/7783-3923, gabriella_moretti@hotmail.com, www.ecosombrero.com). Located on the shores of Laguna Yaxha, it has clean cabana rooms for reasonable prices. The owner speaks fluent Italian and Spanish and a little English. On site is a restaurant and lounging area serving up basic fare and cold Gallo beer. Observe the size of the crocodile heads on display and you will know why this lake is not crowded with resorts.

THE BORDER AT MELCHOR

The western *frontera* into Guatemala is a quick 11 miles from San Ignacio, a trip made for around US$3 per person in a *colectivo* taxi, less in a passing bus bound for Benque Viejo. A private taxi from San Ignacio should cost about US$15 total. Be prepared to pay your US$19 exit fee on the Belizean side, which includes the PACT fee (they will ask for exact change); the rest of the money goes to the private "Border Management" company, a point of contention for local tour providers and would-be Guatemala day-trippers. Expect the usual throng of money-changers to greet you on both sides of the border—they're fine to use, as long as you know what rate you should be getting—or you can use the official Casas de Cambio on either side.

If you're driving your own car, make sure you have all the necessary papers of ownership and attendant photocopies of all your documents, including license and passport, which they *will* want to see. You are required by law to have your tires fumigated when entering/exiting Belize and Guatemala, for which the cost is a few Belizean dollars. If driving a private or rental vehicle into Guatemala you will have to pay a "toll" to cross the bridge going over the Mopan into Melchor. If your car has Belize tags, the fee can be as low as Q5. Speaking good Spanish helps. If your tags are from far away, like Canada or the United States, be prepared to pay Q50 and not one penny more, as some tourists have had to do. Save the receipt if you are returning to Belize, as it is good for a two-way crossing. As well, based on some reports, travelers have to ensure that they have received a proper exit stamp leaving Belize for themselves and for their vehicle. Double check your passport before continuing on to Guatemala.

After clearing Guatemalan immigration and shaking off the sometimes aggressive *taxistas,* you'll find yourself on the edge of the Mopan River, across which begins the town of **Melchor de Mencos.** Before crossing the bridge, you'll find the **Río Mopan Lodge** (tel. 502/926-5126, info@tikaltravel.com) on your left, a nice riverside hotel and restaurant, whose proprietors (a Swiss-Spanish couple) are a wealth of information on remote ruins in the area; riverside rooms go for US$15 with private bath. There are a number of other places in Melchor if you get stranded in town for some reason or are embarking on your own jungle expedition to unexplored ruins.

Once across the border, it's pretty easy sailing, but keep a couple of things in mind. When passing military camps (and you will pass several on the way to Tikal), do not take *any* photos. If you're aiming your lens at the lovely river and the water happens to flow in front of the guard station, you can get into difficulties, no matter how innocent it seems to you. Don't be surprised if you're stopped by the military and asked for your papers; keep your passport and visitor's permit handy, smile, and answer all questions, and you'll soon be on your way.

For the first 20 kilometers west out of Melchor the road is not paved, but it is usually well-maintained. Ironically, it is when one hits the tarmac that the fun begins. You or your driver will be dodging some large potholes, but thankfully the road improves vastly by the time you reach the Ixlu turnoff for El Remate and Tikal.

MOUNTAIN PINE RIDGE

SOUTHERN COAST: DANGRIGA TO PLACENCIA

Stann Creek District is made up of a wide range of habitats. To the east: underwater worlds surrounding scores of Caribbean cayes, or islets. To the west: wildlife, birds galore, rivers, and ruins in the shadow of Belize's highest peaks. Between them: miles of beaches, swamps, citrus plantations, shrimp farms, and—in a few areas—condominium developments aimed at rich foreigners.

Dangriga is home to a third of Stann Creek District's 36,000 inhabitants. Stann Creek's economy is as varied as its culture and geography, with tourism being as important as the orange, banana, and shrimp industries. In Dangriga town and the surrounding villages, the Garinagu (or Garifuna) survive and thrive as they confront the challenges of maintaining their unique culture. Spanish-speaking fishermen paddle through the cayes, diving for lobster and conch for days on end.

There are plenty of things to do and places to stay throughout this region, from full-on tourist destinations like Placencia with its pleasant village and handful of upscale resorts to low-key, slack-paced settlements like Hopkins and Sittee River. All of these areas serve the traveler as bases from which to explore nearby cayes, coral, and the Cockscomb Basin.

PLANNING YOUR TIME

There's not much to see in 'Griga, as Dangriga is affectionately known, except a typically multiethnic array of Belizeans going about their daily lives. Still, many travelers are glad they chose to spend a night here on their way to or from **Tobacco Caye, Southwater Caye,** or **Glover's Reef.**

© JOSHUA BERMAN

HIGHLIGHTS

《 Gulisi Garinagu Museum: The long-awaited cultural attraction is located on the outskirts of Dangriga and offers an interactive history lesson on the proud Garinagu (Garifuna) people (page 167).

《 Tobacco Caye: Sitting right atop Belize's Barrier Reef, Tobacco Caye can be as much a social gathering of world travelers as it can an isolated island experience, depending on the time of year (page 173).

《 Hopkins: This village is on an ultra-tranquil stretch of beach and can serve as a mellow base for canoeing, diving, sailing, windsurfing, fishing, and other trips – or for just doing nothing on the beach (page 176).

《 Cockscomb Basin Wildlife Sanctuary: Go for a nature hike and river float in this extensive reserve, famous for its multitude of birds, jaguar tracks, and other jungle critters. Stay overnight or do it as a day trip from anywhere in the area (page 183).

《 The Sidewalk Strip: In Belize's low-key tourist hangout, Placencia, check out the world's narrowest street – it's 4,071 feet long and four feet wide. Walking its length offers ample opportunities for shopping, eating, and getting a sense of village life (page 191).

《 Laughing Bird Caye: Palms, sand, snorkeling, and sun are found at this national park, part of a 10,000-acre protected marine area (page 202).

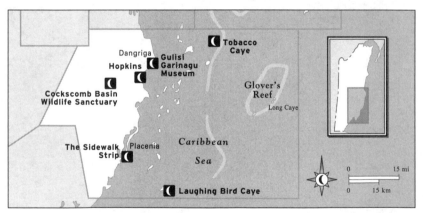

LOOK FOR **《** TO FIND RECOMMENDED SIGHTS, ACTIVITIES, DINING, AND LODGING.

Want to plant yourself in the sand and have drinks brought to you for a week? Pick a resort, any resort—there are plenty of respected properties throughout the region, covering all budgets. Camp primitively in the jungle or recline in the lap of luxury. There is enough in this one district of Belize to entertain a curious traveler for weeks. Here's an ultimate Stann Creek tour for someone with an open mind and vacation time to burn: Spend a week in Dangriga, Hopkins, and Sittee River, getting a feel for the Garinagu way of living; take a drumming lesson and sample some home-brewed bitters. Then turn into the hills, trekking to a waterfall in Mayflower Bocawina National Park before bouncing down the road to spend a night in Maya Center. Here you can shop for local crafts, converse with herbal healers, and arrange a Maya Mountain expedition within the Cockscomb Basin Wildlife

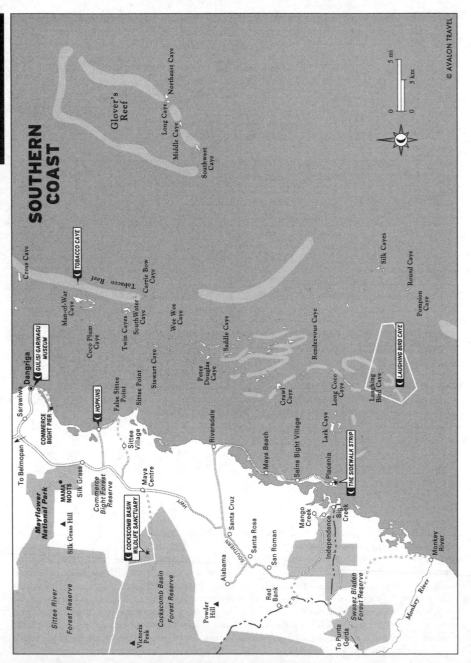

SOUTHERN COAST

Glover's Reef

Northeast Caye
Long Caye
Middle Caye
Southwest Caye

5 mi
5 km

© AVALON TRAVEL

Cross Caye

TOBACCO CAYE

Tobacco Reef

Silk Cayes
Round Caye

Man-of-War Caye

Carrie Bow Caye

Pompion Caye

Coco Plum Caye

Twin Caves
SouthWater Caye

Wee Wee Caye

Saddle Caye

Rendezvous Caye

Dangriga

Sarawiwa

GULISI GARINAGU MUSEUM

Stewart Caye

Peter Douglas Caye

Crawl Caye

Laughing Bird Caye

LAUGHING BIRD CAYE

To Belmopan

COMMERCE BIGHT PIER

HOPKINS

False Sittee Point

Sittee Point

Long Coco Caye

Sittee Village

Riversdale

Maya Beach

Lark Caye

Placencia

THE SIDEWALK STRIP

Mayflower National Park

MAMA NOOTS

Silk Grass

Commerce Bight Forest Reserve

Maya Centre

Seine Bight Village

Silk Grass Hill

COCKSCOMB BASIN WILDLIFE SANCTUARY

Santa Cruz

Santa Rosa

Mango Creek

Big Creek

Independence

Sittee River Forest Reserve

Cockscomb Basin Forest Reserve

San Roman

SOUTHERN HWY

Alabama

Swasey Bladen Forest Reserve

Victoria Peak

Powder Hill

Red Bank

Monkey River

To Punta Gorda

Monkey River

Sanctuary with a local guide whose last gig was leading a National Geographic team in the same area.

Then pop over to the shoreline and charter a sailboat to play pirate in the cayes; strand yourself for a week in Glover's Atoll and attempt to photograph a whale shark or manta ray. Finally, run your boat aground on the Placencia Peninsula and rent a cheap cabana in which to recuperate.

Of course, if you've only got a week, simply pick and choose from the above list and plan according to your needs.

THE LAND AND PEOPLE

The indigenous population of southern Belize dates back 3,600 years, and the Mopan Maya are still well represented, especially in towns like Maya Center and other villages in these hills. The earliest white settlers were Puritans from the island of New Providence in the Bahamas. These simple-living people began a trading post (also known as a "stand," which over time deteriorated to "Stann") and spread south into the Placencia area. The town's destiny was drastically altered when the first boats of Garinagu people reached the shore from Roatan.

Over the millennia, rivers and streams gushing from the Maya Mountains have deposited a rich layer of fertile soil, making the coastal and valley regions ideal farming areas. The banana industry, once vital in the area, was wiped out by a disease called "Panama Rot" many years back. However, with new technology, a strain of bananas has been developed that appears to be surviving and promises to grow into a profitable operation. Stann Creek's citrus industry produces Valencia oranges and grapefruits, which are then processed (on site) into juice—one of Belize's most important exports.

Dangriga

"Mabuiga!" shouts the sign in Garifuna, welcoming you to this cultural hub and district capital. Built on the Caribbean shoreline and straddling North Stann Creek (or Gumagarugu River), Dangriga's primary boast is its status as the Garinagu people's original port of entry into Belize—and their modern-day ethnic center. But although the majority of Dangriga's 11,000 or so inhabitants are Garinagu descendants of that much-celebrated 1823 landing, the rest are a typically rich mix of Chinese, Creoles, mestizos, and Maya, all of whom can be seen interacting on the town's main drag.

Aside from Dangriga's ideal location for accessing the surrounding mountains and seas—and the limited, barely adequate tourist services available to do so—its chief attraction may just be its total lack of pretense. Dangriga (formerly known as Stann Creek Town) does not outwardly cater to its foreign visitors as does Placencia or San Pedro—there is simply too much else going on in this commercial center, including fishing, farming, and serving the influx of Stann Creek villagers who come weekly to stock up on supplies. Consequently, this area is still relatively undeveloped for tourism, which is either a shortcoming or an attraction, depending on what kind of traveler you are.

If poking around the casually bustling vibe of Dangriga (which, by the way, means something like "sweet, still waters" in Garifuna) sounds intriguing, you'd do well to stay a couple nights as you pass between surf and turf. And if it's culture you're looking for, just listen for the drumming.

ORIENTATION

As you pull into town, three massive ceremonial *dugu* drums of iron will greet you. This is the "Drums of Our Fathers Monument," erected in 2003 as a symbol of Garinagu pride—and as a call to war against the ills of society. Turn right to reach the deep dock at Commerce Bight, left (north) to enter Dangriga Town. Heading north from the drums on St. Vincent Street,

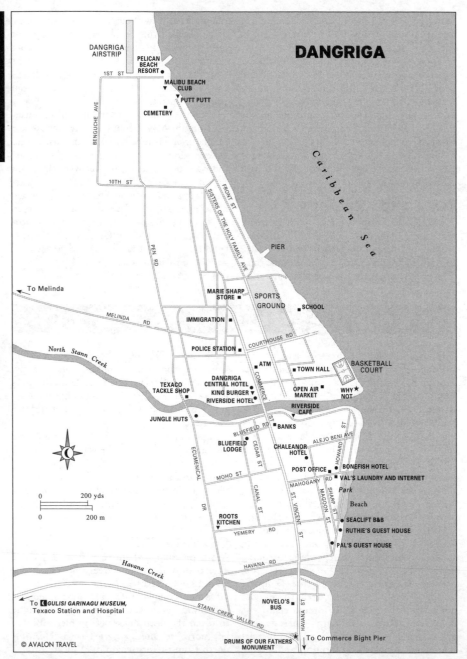

DANGRIGA

DANGRIGA AIRSTRIP

PELICAN BEACH RESORT

1ST ST

MALIBU BEACH CLUB

PUTT PUTT

CEMETERY

BENGUCHE AVE

10TH ST

FRONT ST

SISTERS OF THE HOLY FAMILY AVE

PEN RD

PIER

Caribbean Sea

To Melinda

MELINDA RD

MARIE SHARP STORE

SPORTS GROUND

SCHOOL

IMMIGRATION

North Stann Creek

POLICE STATION

COURTHOUSE RD

ATM

TOWN HALL

BASKETBALL COURT

COMMERCE

TEXACO TACKLE SHOP

DANGRIGA CENTRAL HOTEL

KING BURGER

RIVERSIDE HOTEL

OPEN AIR MARKET

WHY NOT ★

RIVERSIDE CAFÉ

JUNGLE HUTS

BANKS

BLUEFIELD RD

BLUEFIELD LODGE

CEDAR ST

CHALEANOR HOTEL

ALEJO BENI AVE

HOWARD ST

POST OFFICE

BONEFISH HOTEL

VAL'S LAUNDRY AND INTERNET

ECUMENICAL

MOHO ST

MAHOGANY RD

Park

CANAL ST

ST. VINCENT ST

MAGOON ST

SHARP ST

Beach

0   200 yds

0   200 m

ROOTS KITCHEN

YEMERY RD

SEACLIFT B&B

RUTHIE'S GUEST HOUSE

PAL'S GUEST HOUSE

DR

Havana Creek

HAVANA RD

To **G** *GULISI GARINAGU MUSEUM,*
Texaco Station and Hospital

STANN CREEK VALLEY RD

NOVELO'S BUS

HAVANA ST

DRUMS OF OUR FATHERS MONUMENT

To Commerce Bight Pier

© AVALON TRAVEL

the old bus terminal is on your left before the first bridge. Continuing, you'll find more shops and eateries, culminating in the center of town on either side of the North Stann Creek Bridge; crossing the bridge, St. Vincent Street turns into Commerce Street and offers an informal market often set up along the north bank of the river. Catch a boat to the cayes from one of several places here. The airstrip is located a mile or so north of Stann Creek, where you'll also find Pelican Beach Resort, Dangriga's fanciest digs.

SIGHTS

Dangriga does not offer many traditional "sights," per se, but there is plenty going on, and the town makes a good base for excursions around the region. You can browse the few crafts and music stores on St. Vincent Street, and ask around for the drum-making workshops, one of which is sometimes set up at the **Why Not** compound by the beach at Stann Creek. Drums are often heard throughout the town to mark celebrations and funerals; sometimes it's simply a few people practicing the rhythms of their history. Seeking out the town's workshops can be a fun activity, and if you've got the cash, expect to walk away with an instrument of your own. Austin Rodriquez is known for his authentic Garinagu drums. Other local artists of national prominence include painter Benjamin Nicholas and Mercy Sabal, who makes colorful dolls that are sold all over the country.

◖ Gulisi Garinagu Museum

The long-awaited Garinagu Museum (tel. 501/669-0639, ngcbelize@gmail.com, 10 A.M.–5 P.M. Mon.–Fri., 8 A.M.–noon Sat., US$5) is located a mile or so west of town, on the south side of the highway; you'll see it on your right when driving into Dangriga, right next to the thrusting Chuluhadiwa Garinagu Monument (taxi from downtown US$2–3). The small, four-room museum is packed with a wealth of information and an interesting collection of artifacts; feel free to talk history with the curator, Peter Ciego. The museum

The Gulisi Garinagu Museum, just outside Dangriga, is worth the visit.

© JOSHUA BERMAN

is named after the person thought to be the first Garinagu woman to arrive and settle in Dangriga. She had thirteen sons and many of Dangriga's modern residents believe they are descended from her.

Marie Sharp's Store and Factory

Be sure to save time to stop by the **Marie Sharp Store** (in Dangriga, a few blocks north of Stann Creek Bridge, tel. 501/522-2370, 8 A.M.–5 P.M. Mon.–Fri.) to stock up on the area's famous hot sauce and other products; purchase hot sauce for a tiny fraction of the normal retail price. Better yet, make the trip to the **Marie Sharp Factory** (tel. 501/520-2087, www.mariesharps-bz.com), where you'll be offered a free tour of the farm and factory. This is a true Belizean success story: the factory sits on a 400-acre estate. To find it, drive west on the Hummingbird Highway from Dangriga about eight miles and turn right after you cross a bridge and see the White Swan on your left.

GARINAGU SETTLEMENT DAY

The hour before dawn, we make our way through the darkness along the edge of the sea, heading toward the persistent beat of distant drums. Orange streaks begin to widen across the horizon as we climb over a half-fallen wooden bridge spanning a creek, cutting a muddy path to the Caribbean. We are on our way to Dangriga on Garinagu Settlement Day, one of Belize's lively national holidays, celebrated each year on November 19 to commemorate the arrival of the Garinagu people to Belize.

Rains that had been pouring down for a week subsided only a few hours ago, and by the time we reach the center of town and the river shoreline, crowds of revelers are beginning to gather in the breaking dawn. This is a day of reflection and good times in Belize, a severe contrast to the Garinagu beginnings that for decades were filled with misery and tragedy.

Settlement Day is a happy celebration. Everyone dresses in colorful new clothes, and while waiting for the "landing," family, friends, and strangers from all over Belize catch up on local gossip, make new acquaintances, and enjoy the party. Sounds of beating drums emanate from small circles of people on both sides of the river, from the backs of pickup trucks, and from rooftops. In lieu of drums, young men push through the crowds shouldering giant boomboxes that broadcast the beat. Excitement (and umbrellas) hangs in the air as the assemblage waits for the canoes and the beginning of the pageant.

Now, in the early dawn, the crowd cheers. It spots two dugout canoes paddling from the open sea into the river. Years ago, the first refugees from Roatan crowded into just such boats, along with a few meager necessities, to start a new life in a new land. Today's reenactment is orchestrated according to verbal history handed down through generations. Leaves and vines are wrapped around the arrivals' heads and waists. Drums, baskets that carry simple cooking utensils, young banana trees, and cassava roots are all among the precious cargo the Garinagu originally brought to start their new lives in Dangriga.

© JOSHUA BERMAN

The reenactment is performed up and down Belize's coast on Settlement Day.

The canoes paddle past cheering crowds. Each November is a reminder of the past, and even outsiders are swept along in the excitement and thoughts of what this day represents to the Garinagu citizens of Belize.

The canoes travel up the river and under the bridge and back again so that everyone lining the bank and bridge can see them. When the actors come ashore, they're joined by hundreds of onlookers. The colorful procession then winds through the narrow streets, with young and old dancing and singing to the drumbeats; they proudly lead the parade to the Catholic church, where a special service takes place. Dignitaries from all over Belize attend and tell of the past and, more important, of the hopes of the future.

The Catholic church plays a unique part in the life of the Garinagu. Some years back, the church reached an unspoken working agreement with the Garinagu. It's nothing formal, just a look-the-other-way attitude while the

SOUTHERN COAST

Garinagu parishioners mix Catholic dogma with ancient ritual. It wasn't always this way. For generations, the people were forced to keep their religion alive in clandestine meetings or suffer severe punishment and persecution.

Rain, much like time, has not stopped the Garinagu celebrations nor the dancing that is an integral part of the festivities. Street dances (traditionally held along village streets for many nights leading up to Settlement Day) continue and are moved indoors to escape the flooded streets. Small bars and open *palapa* (thatch) structures are crowded with fun-lovers and reverberate with the pounding of exotic triple drums (always three). Drums bring their magic, and parties continue with both modern *punta* rock and traditional dances into the early hours of the morning. The Garinagu are a people filled with music. The songs sung in the Garifuna language tell stories — some happy, some sad — and many melodies go hand-in-hand with daily tasks.

At an open *palapa* hut, three talented drummers begin the beat. The old Garinagu women, honoring their African beginnings, insist on marshaling the dances the old way. The first tempo is the *paranda*, a dance just for women. A circle is created in the dirt-floored room and the elderly women begin a low-key, heavy-footed, repetitive shuffle with subtle hand movements accompanied by timeworn words that we don't understand but are told tell a tale of survival.

Every few minutes a reveler filled with too much rum pushes through the circle of people and joins the dancing women. He's quickly chased out of the ring by an umbrella-wielding elder who aims her prods at the more vulnerable parts of his body. If that doesn't work, she resorts to pulling the intoxicated dancer off the floor by his ear — a little comic relief that adds to the down-home entertainment.

The *paranda* continues, and little kids energetically join in the dances on the outside of the circle or watch wide-eyed from the rafters near the top of the *palapa* roof, entranced by the beat, dim light, and music — the magic of the holiday. The recurring rain adds an extra beat to the exotic cadence of the drums; dance after dance continues.

The *huguhugn* dance is open to everyone, but the sexy *punta* is the popular favorite, with one couple at a time in the ring. Handsome men and beautiful women slowly undulate their bodies with flamboyant grace and sexual suggestion. This is the courtship dance born from African roots. If you miss Settlement Day parties, stop by a bar or nightclub anywhere in Belize and you'll see locals doing a modern version called "*punta* rock."

During Settlement Day, a walk down the narrow streets takes you past small parties and family gatherings under stilted houses where dancing and singing is the rule; others enjoy holiday foods (including cassava bread) and drinks. You may very well be invited to share a rum-spiked cup of coffee dipped from an old porcelain kettle. If so, enjoy!

(Contributed by Chicki Mallan, who wrote the first edition of Moon Belize *in 1991)*

Gra Gra Lagoon National Park

This 1,197-acre wetland and forest reserve includes a 300-acre lagoon that is wonderful to paddle in a canoe or kayak. Inquire at the Friends of Gra Gra Lagoon office (tel. 501/502-0043 or 600-6222, gglagoon@yahoo.com), diagonally across from the old bus station.

Tour Operators

A few operators run trips to nearby trails, waterfalls, caves, and other attractions up the Hummingbird Highway, including those at Five Blues Lake and Billy Barquedier National Parks. For ideas of what to do and a wealth of local wisdom, award-winning **C & G Tours and Charters** (29 Oak St., tel. 501/522-3641 or 610-2277, www.cgtourscharters.com) will take care of all your needs. C & G is a locally owned and highly recommended tour operator who speaks many languages and is experienced at taking everyone from single travelers to groups around the area.

ENTERTAINMENT AND EVENTS

Dangriga is home to the Warribaggabagga Dancers, the Punta Rebels, the Turtle Shell Band, and the Griga Boyz, among other nationally known party bands. The music and dancing, including syncopated African rhythms, is an enchanting mixture of the various cultures of southern Belize. There is often live music on weekends at **Griga 2000,** right near the main bridge, and sometimes at the **Malibu Beach Club** on the north end of town. Be advised that karaoke, especially to American country music, is very popular 'round these parts.

The biggest celebrations of the year are Settlement Day (November 19), Boxing Day (December 26), and New Year's Day, when you'll find plenty of drumming, dancing, and drinking in the streets. Local hotels are often booked up to a year in advance for dates in November, because of Garinagu families visiting from the United States. At other times of the year, many hotels can arrange a special cultural event for you.

ACCOMMODATIONS
Under US$25

Dangriga's main drag has a handful of low-budget options, including the **Riverside Hotel** (north end of bridge on Commerce St., tel. 501/660-1041, US$12.50 pp). Pick one of the front rooms for a chance of a breeze; all have shared bath, wood floor, and fans. A better budget bet is **Val's** (tel. 501/522-3687, valsbelize@yahoo.com, US$8 pp). Val is a cheerful and friendly host who loves meeting her guests from around the world and putting them up in one of her cement bunk rooms, where you'll find a bed and hopefully a breeze flowing through. There is wireless Internet and bikes, and it's all very close to a pleasant park overlooking the ocean. There's also a nice private room with couch, chairs, TV, and private bath for US$33.

◖ Bluefield Lodge (6 Bluefield Rd., tel. 501/522-2742, bluefield@btl.net, US$15–35) is an excellent choice. The owner, Miss Louise, has six attractively furnished rooms with fans

and hot/cold water. Everything about the place bespeaks the pride and care she takes in her lodge; she also offers great local maps and an information board.

Pal's Guest House (868 Magoon St., tel. 501/522-2095 or 522-2365, palbz@btl.net), around the corner from the bus station, has 19 clean, modest cement rooms at the corner of North Havana Road and Magoon Street. Rooms with shared bath in the back building cost US$17.50 for a double, but are really basic. Seaside rooms (US$35) are better, with linoleum floors, ceiling fans, hot/cold private showers, TV, and balconies at the ocean's edge; louvered windows on both ends of the rooms create good cross-ventilation.

US$25-50

At the towering **◖ Chaleanor Hotel** (35 Magoon St., tel. 501/522-2587, chaleanor@btl.net, US$50), friendly and tirelessly accommodating owners Chad and Eleanor offer a homey atmosphere in a residential neighborhood. Ten well-used rooms have private baths and hot water, and some have TV and air-conditioning. Laundry service is available. There's a gift counter in the lobby, and you can help yourself to coffee and bananas all day long. Numerous tour operators book their guests in the Chaleanor, sometimes arranging a drumming or dance session on the roof.

If you'd rather hear the waves lapping below your window, try one of the three stilted wooden cabanas at **Ruthie's** (tel. 501/522-3184, ruthies@btl.net, US$28), a good value if you snag one of the newer cabins.

US$50-100

Next door to Ruthie's, the **Seaclift Bed and Breakfast** (tel. 501/502-2350, www.seaclift.com, US$50–100) has three nicely furnished rooms in the upstairs of a family home with old, creaky wood floors. The cheaper rooms share a bath. They also just constructed four new rooms in an annex, a stone's throw away. The place has a very nice, homey feel and is right on the ocean. The **Bonefish Hotel** (15 Mahogany St., tel. 501/522-2243, www.

bluemarlinlodge.com, US$95) is near the water with seven rooms and a second-floor lobby and bar. It caters to active travelers who want to tour the area, fish, or dive—most guests continue on to Blue Marlin Lodge on South Water Caye, which is allied with the Bonefish. Rooms are clean and carpeted with private hot/cold water bathrooms, cable TV, wireless Internet, and air-conditioning.

Over US$100

'Griga's high end is found at the north end of town at the end of Ecumenical Drive, right next to the airstrip: The **Pelican Beach Resort** (tel. 501/522-2044, www.pelicanbeachbelize.com, from US$134 plus taxes, includes breakfast) rests comfortably on the Caribbean and just enjoyed a massive renovation. There are 17 rooms, all open and well lit with wood and tile floors, bathtubs, and porches facing the ocean. Various packages are available that include meal plans, excursions, and time spent at the Pelican's sister resort on South Water Caye. This is a full-service accommodation with many amenities.

FOOD

Most of Dangriga's eateries are open only during meal times, so expect some closed doors in the middle of the afternoon and on Sundays when only the Chinese restaurants are open. Your best value is probably ◀ **King Burger,** located on the left as you cross the North Stann Creek bridge from the south (7 A.M.–3 P.M. and 6 P.M.–10 P.M. Mon.–Sat.). It offers excellent ice cream, breakfast, fresh juices, sandwiches, shakes, and simple comfort dinners.

Another standby is the **Riverside Café** (7 A.M.–9 P.M. six or seven days a week). It's popular with travelers (boats to the cayes leave from right outside) and a gathering spot for local fishermen. If you want to witness a real slice of Dangriga, set up camp at the Riverside bar, order a Guinness with your eggs and beans, and watch the deals go down; it's US$4 for stew chicken, US$6 and up for fish and shrimp. For cheaper food, walk back to the main drag and grab a fistful of street tacos for pennies. Street barbecues are another common sight, offering a plate of grilled chicken with flour tortillas, beans, and coleslaw for about US$2.50. There are a few local shacks with great dishes for US$3 and under; start with **Roots Kitchen** back on Ecumenical Drive, just a wooden shack with real Belizean food, open from 6 A.M. all day.

Tired of rice and beans? There are many Chinese restaurants, the top two of which are **Starlight** (8 A.M.–11 P.M., closed afternoons), on the north end of Commerce Street, and the good food and crappy service at **Sunlight,** on the south end of Commerce Street. There is "fry chicken to take" at any number of Chinese shops.

Dangriga's only proper restaurant is found at the **Pelican Beach Resort,** where delicious food is prepared by Creole cooks and served in the dining room or in an open beachside eating area. The happy hour on Thursday and Friday is 5–9 P.M. and is very popular, especially on the 15th and 30th of each month (pay day).

SERVICES

Belize Bank (8 A.M.–1 P.M. Mon.–Thurs., 8 A.M.–4:30 P.M. Fri.) and **Scotia Bank** (similar hours, but also open 9 A.M.–noon Sat.) are on St. Vincent Street near the bridge, and First Caribbean is across the bridge; all have ATMs. Mail your postcards at the **post office** on Mahogany Road.

Val's Laundry and Internet (tel. 501/502-3324, www.valsbelize.com, 7:30 A.M.–7 P.M. Mon.–Sat., plus Sun. mornings) is near the post office on Sharp Street. Fast and friendly satellite Internet is available for US$2.50 an hour, as well as FedEx service, local information, and organic, fresh-squeezed juices.

Health and Emergencies

Southern Regional Hospital is located just out of town and services the entire population of Stann Creek District (tel. 501/522-2078 or 522-2225, dannhis@btl.net).

GETTING THERE AND AWAY

Dangriga is on the coast, only 36 miles south of Belize City as the crow (or local airline) flies.

However, the land trip is much longer, roughly 75 miles along the Manatee Road or 100 miles via the Hummingbird Highway.

By Air

Maya Island Air (tel. 501/223-1140, U.S. tel. 800/225-6732, mayair@btl.net, www.mayaislandair.com) and Tropic Air (tel. 501/226-2012, U.S. tel. 800/422-3435, reservations@tropicair.com, www.tropicair.com) have a number of daily 20-minute flights between Belize City and Dangriga. It's also possible to fly between Dangriga, Placencia, and Punta Gorda.

By Boat

Boat service from Belize City is entirely custom arranged—they tried running a regularly scheduled shuttle, but it didn't make money. Ask around the docks by the Texaco station, at your hotel, or at the Belize Tourism Board. Expect to pay a decent sum for this trip (probably US$100 each way). Service to and from local cayes or other coastal villages is also dependent on how many people want to go. Only two passengers are required to make the trip to Tobacco Caye (US$15 each); ask around the Riverside Café or Texaco Station Tackle Stop.

By Bus

Bus service between Belize City and Dangriga takes close to three hours, including a stop in Belmopan, and costs US$6 each way; buses run between 4:30 A.M. and about 5:30 P.M. There are a few expresses during the day, but the schedule is changing all the time.

There are eight daily buses to Punta Gorda, from 8 A.M. to the day's only express at 5:30 P.M.—a three-hour trip. As of press time, there are four daily buses to Placencia: 10:30 A.M. through 5:15 P.M., 2.5 hours to reach Placencia town. These buses used to always stop in Hopkins and Sittee River, but that schedule is in question, so ask around the station.

By Car

From Belize City, take the Western Highway to either the Coastal (Manatee) Road or Hummingbird Highway, which you'll follow till it ends. Taking the Coastal Road may shave 20 minutes off the Hummingbird Highway route—but the rutted, red-dirt surface may also destroy your suspension and jar your fillings loose. The unpaved Coastal Road is flat and relatively straight and is occasionally graded into a passable highway, but you better have a sturdy ride. Be prepared for lots of dust in the dry season and boggy mud after a rain. Numerous tiny bridges with no railings cross creeks flowing out of the west, and the landscape of pine savanna and forested limestone bluffs has nary a sign of humans (except for the crappy road, of course). About halfway to the junction with the Hummingbird Highway, you'll find a pleasant place to stop and take a dip at Soldier Creek; just look for the biggest bridge of your trip and pull over. Watch out for snakes in the bush and, once you reach your destination, try not to spend those hard-earned extra 20 minutes all in one place.

Islands near Dangriga

TOBACCO CAYE

If your tropical island dream includes sharing said island with a few dozen fellow travelers, snorkelers, divers, rum drinkers, and hammock sitters from around the world, then Tobacco Caye is your place, especially if you don't mind the close quarters and smoldering trash piles. This tiny island perched practically on top of the Belize Barrier Reef has long been a popular backpacker and Belizean tourist destination, especially for divers. Tobacco Caye is just north of Tobacco Cut (a "cut" is a break in the reef through which boats navigate). Guesthouse owners have boats to whisk you each day to snorkeling and fishing trips or to Man-O-War Caye and Tobacco Range to look for manatees. Glover's Atoll trips are also available.

Tobacco Caye's five "resorts" offer similar packages but for a range of budgets. All six places are Belizean-run family affairs, each a bit different according to the owner's vision, and are comfortably crowded together on the five acres of sand. Apart from some basic differences in room quality, the more you pay, the better food you'll be eating—a pretty important thing when checking into a room that also locks you into a meal plan. The following prices are all per person per night and include three meals!

Gaviota's Reef Resort welcomes you to "the Lifestyle of a Chosen Few" in one of four rooms or five cabanas (tel. 501/509-5032, US$45, shared bath); there are three boats that can be used for visiting the reef and cayes. An on-site marine station often hosts visiting scientists, and you can ask to check out their reference materials on the area's habitats and species. **Paradise Lodge** occupies the northern tip of the island with rooms from US$12.50–17.50; **Lana's on the Reef** (tel. 501/520-5036 or 522-2571) has four basic rooms for US$40.

Stepping things up a notch, find **Reef's End Lodge** on the southern shore (tel. 501/570-0558, www.reefsendlodge.com, US$65); rooms and cabanas have air-conditioning and hot/cold water with private baths. Reef's End has one of the caye's dive shops, which can be utilized by anyone on the island. **Tobacco Caye Lodge** (tel. 501/520-5033 or 227-6247, www.tclodgebelize.com, US$45 US pp Jul–Nov., US$55 pp Dec.–June) occupies a middle strip of the island and offers three units.

Water taxis to Tobacco Caye leave when the captain says there are enough passengers; usually around mid-afternoon from the Riverside Café or the Tackle Stop farther upstream. Captains Buck and Compa are spoken of as the most reliable; just ask around. The trip costs US$35 round-trip, with a return trip usually made midmorning. By calling ahead to Gaviota, Reef's End, or Tobacco Caye Lodge you can arrange a pickup any time from Dangriga and ensure a boat will still be there if you are arriving after midday. Captain Fermin has the newest, largest, and most comfortable boats (tel. 501/509-5032). Be advised, if you need a boat after 3 P.M., you'll pay a lot more—seas get rough and a private charter is necessary; plan accordingly.

SOUTH WATER CAYE

South Water Caye is another postcard-perfect, privately owned island 14 miles offshore from Dangriga and 35 miles southeast of Belize City. The reef crests just a stone's throw offshore, sitting atop a 1,000-foot coral wall awash in wildlife. The island stretches 0.75 miles from north to south and 0.25 miles at its widest point.

The **Pelican Beach Resort** (tel. 501/522-2044, www.southwatercaye.com, US$258–292, includes three meals) occupies the entire southern end of the island, with five second-story rooms, three duplex cottages, and two single-unit cabanas. The beach is available to other island guests and offers some of Belize's best walk-in snorkeling sites. Power is from the sun, and composting toilets help protect the fragile island ecology. The owners also have a strip of island toward the north end that is home to **Pelican's University,** which hosts student research groups throughout the year. Plenty of day trips are available with Pelican's guides or with one of the island dive shops; they charge US$62 per person for the boat transfer to the island.

Lesley Cottages is the common name for **International Zoological Expeditions** (IZE; tel. 501/523-7076, U.S. tel. 800/548-5843, www.ize2belize.com, US$175 pp). Named for an old local fisherman, Dan Lesley, the compound here specializes primarily in student groups and "educational tourism" but also has some nice, exclusive cabins in addition to their own dive shop, dormitory, classroom, and the like. Beautiful rooms are nestled on the shoreline; included are three meals and transport. It's a great spot for couples (but check to see if you'll be sharing with student groups).

Blue Marlin Lodge (tel. 501/520-5104, U.S. tel. 800/798-1558, www.bluemarlinlodge.com), sister resort of the Bonefish Hotel in Dangriga, offers a variety of rooms, air-conditioned igloos (I swear), and cabanas just steps away from the sea. The bar/dining room over the sea serves meals, snacks (included), and drinks (three meals roughly US$60). The Blue Marlin specializes in fishing trips, plus has a full dive shop, cable TV, and Internet. Many packages are available with a three-night minimum stay.

CARRIE BOW CAYE

This dot of sand and palms, close to both the reef and mangrove systems, is home to the Smithsonian Museum of Natural History's **Caribbean Coral Reef Ecosystems Program** which, since 1972, has produced over 800 published papers. The caye houses up to six international scientists at a time, as well as a real-time weather station, accessible online at www.nmnh.si.edu/biodiversity/ccre.htm. The public is welcome to check things out, but only if you arrange something first through your host on South Water Caye or elsewhere.

GLOVER'S REEF ATOLL

The southernmost of Belize's unique atolls, Glover's (named for a pirate, of course) is an 80-square-mile nearly continuous ring of brilliant coral, flanked on its southeastern curve by five tiny islands. The atoll is 18 miles long and 6 miles across at its widest point; to the east, the ocean bottom drops sharply and keeps on dropping, eventually to depths of 15,000 feet at the western end of the Caiman Trench, one of the deepest in the world.

The southern section of the atoll around the cayes serves as a protected marine reserve; however, someone should remind the government Fishery Department rangers on Middle Caye of this fact, as they reportedly regularly skip patrols and ignore illegal fishing activity (although they're very efficient at collecting tourist fees).

Divers and snorkelers will find a fabulous wall surrounding the atoll, plus more than 700 shallow coral patches within the rainbow-colored lagoon. There are wreck dives and an abundance of marine life, especially turtles, manta rays, and all types of sharks, including reefs, hammerheads, and whale sharks. The names of the dive sites speak for themselves: Shark Point, Grouper Flats, Emerald Forest Reef, Octopus Alley, Manta Reef, Dolphin Dance, and Turtle Tavern.

Anglers will have a chance at bonefish and permit, as well as the big trophies, including sailfish, marlin, wahoo, snapper, and grouper. There is also fantastic paddling, sailing, and anything else you can dream up. Glover's is a special place indeed.

Southwest Cayes

The first bit of land you'll reach from the mainland is owned by the Usher clan, which runs the high-end, full-service **Isla Marisol Resort** (tel. 501/520-2056, toll-free 866/990-9904, www.islamarisolresort.com) for serious divers and sport fishermen. There are comfortable, equipped cabanas, or stay in the reef house. Many all-inclusive packages are available, three-night minimum.

Island Expeditions (U.S. tel. 800/667-1630, www.islandexpeditions.com) is an adventure travel outfitter with a tent camp on the north tip of Southwest Caye; it's a well-run, professional operation and a great option if you like meeting other travelers and bonding with them on a group trip.

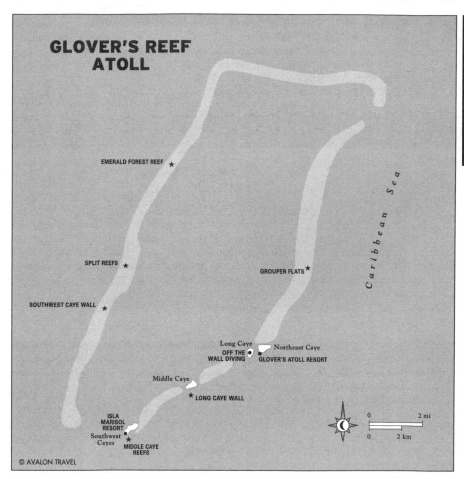

Middle Caye

No accommodations here, unless you're a Belize Fisheries Department ranger or a marine biologist with the Wildlife Conservation Society. If staying on one of the surrounding cayes, ask your host about arranging a trip to see what's going on here.

Long Caye

The 13 acres here form the gorgeous backdrop to **Slickrock Adventures'** thatch-roof base camp (U.S. tel. 800/390-5715, www.slickrock. com); check out the website for a range of active

Belize adventures. Slickrock has a veritable armada of kayaks, sailboards, and other water toys; conditions and equipment will cover beginners and experts alike. Guests stay in very private rustic beach cabins overlooking the reef and equipped with kerosene lamps, foam-pad mattresses, and great views. Outhouse toilets are of the *plein air* variety, surrounded by palm leaf "walls"—offering possibly the best views from a WC in the entire country. Book a trip to the island, or link the trip with wild inland adventures as well (call for a catalog).

Long Caye is also home to **Off the Wall Dive**

Center (tel. 501/614-6348, offthewall@btl.net, www.offthewallbelize.com), Jim and Kendra Schofield's dive shop and resort. Dive packages are available with Off the Wall, whose facilities consist of a top-notch dive shop, bar, and gift shop, plus a couple of rustic cabanas, which can accommodate six people on week-long charter trips—package prices include seven days' lodging, transport, all meals, and 12 dives. Diving, snorkeling, and fishing are available as well, and yachties are welcome to come ashore and browse the gift shop.

Northeast Caye

This island is owned and run as **Glover's Atoll Resort and Island Lodge,** a primitive island camp run by the Lomont family, who also has **Glover's Guest House** in Sittee River (tel. 501/520-5016 or 614-7177, www.glovers.com. bz). They've got a 68-foot catamaran to whisk you out to Glover's most remote caye, where you will camp or shack up for the cheapest weekly rates on the atoll: US$149 for a week of camping, US$199 to stay in the dorm, US$249–299 for rustic thatch cabins. These per-person prices include transport, a week's worth of primitive lodging, use of the kitchen, and nothing more. Show up at the guesthouse in Sittee River at 7 A.M. Saturday, and be prepared for the week. You're welcome to bring all your own food (a kitchen is available) and drinking water, or pay about US$30/day to be served. A dive shop and kayak rentals are also available.

According to reader mail I receive—and to the copious and varied online reviews and trip reports about Glover's Atoll Resort—guests either love or hate this experience. The most concerning reviews report safety concerns and personality clashes with Glover's Atoll Resort staff. Be sure to ask plenty of questions so you know *exactly* what is available and what will cost you extra once you're out there.

OTHER NEARBY CAYES

Man-O-War Caye (Bird Isle) is a bird-choked, raucously chirping clump of protected mangroves that is a crucial nesting site for frigates and boobies. **Coco Plum Caye** (tel. 501/520-2041, www.cocoplumislandresort.com) hosts a cluster of bright cabins that is part of the Jaguar Reef Lodge in Sittee, but the public is welcome to dock up and enjoy the gorgeous sandbar—and the wet bar perched above it. The island was dredged and mangroves cut to form the development, so sand flies may be bad, and the cottages appear to be sinking into the imported sand.

Wee Wee Caye, affiliated with the Possum Point Biological Station, on the mainland near Sittee River, hosts a tropic field station, marine lab, and educational center, featuring a neat system of raised catwalks through the mangroves (beautiful, but lots of bugs). The caye also hosts a population of boa constrictors; contact Paul and Mary Shave (tel. 501/523-7021, www.marineecology.com).

South of Dangriga

◖ HOPKINS

Hopkins was built in 1942 after a hurricane washed away Newtown just up the coast; it is a loose coastal fishing village steering more and more toward tourism. Ignore the monstrous condos going up on either end of the Hopkins coast road—nearly everything in between remains chill, spread out, and reasonably priced. Hopkins's thousand or so inhabitants are mostly Garinagu, making this one of the more

exciting places to be for Garifuna Settlement Day (November 19).

With the advent of new resorts and time-share condos in Sittee, and the continual trickle of backpackers that still show up in Hopkins village proper, there are a few decent makeshift art galleries and craft shops along the main drag. Other than that, there really aren't any sights beyond those that make up everyday village life. On a Saturday night,

SOUTHERN COAST

© JOSHUA BERMAN

the beach at Hopkins

this means drinking beer and bitters, playing drums and dominoes, and laughing away another hot, breezy day. Of course, things pick up considerably on festival days, Christmas, and Easter Week (expect rooms to be in high demand during these times).

Orientation

The road that carries you into town from Dangriga also splits Hopkins into Northside (or "Baila") and Southside (or "False Sittee"). Northside is a bit more dense with local flavor and Southside hosts most of the places to stay and eat.

Recreation and Diving

For diving, you'll have to make plans at Hamanasi Resort's dive shop. For snorkeling or fly-fishing, Noel Nuñez (tel. 510/523-7219 or 609-1991) is your man, located in his tour shack at the Watering Hole. Most guesthouses in Hopkins rent kayaks and other small craft. **Oliver Guthoff** (www.windsurfing-belize.com) has a nice selection of windsurfing boards of various sizes for rent and offers lessons for all levels.

Entertainment

King Cassava's (tel. 501/608-6188 or 503-7305, 7 A.M.–midnight, with a two-hour afternoon break, daily) is located at the intersection where the road from Dangriga meets the sea. Here you'll find a bar, restaurant, taxi service, pool hall, and bus stop (when the buses are running, anyway). Lobster dinners go for US$10, shots of bitters are a buck, and they also serve finger-lickin' barbecue. It's a great place to meet the parade of local characters.

The **Lebeha Drumming Center** (tel. 501/608-3143), way up on the northside (*lebeha* means "the end" in Garifuna), is a notable drumming school, where Garinagu drum master Jabbar Lambey offers both private (US$15 per hour) and group lessons (US$12.50 for two hours).

Save time for a walk or bike ride just south of the village to pay a visit to **Sew Much Hemp,** where Barbara, a dreadlocked Oregonian, will teach you anything you need to know about the plant that can save the world—she's got excellent hemp products for sale as well. If sand flies are out, this is a great place to pick up some natural repellent!

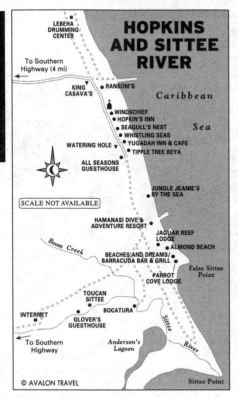

Accommodations

Starting on the northside of Hopkins, budget travelers love the couple of rooms and mellow tent sites at **Lebeha Drumming Center** (www.lebeha.com), which has campsites (US$5) and a couple of shared-bath stilted wooden rooms, very simple, for US$15. Lebeha also has three furnished cabanas on the beach—very nice houses with kitchens, wireless Internet, and screened porches (http://hopkinscabanas.com, US$49–65 plus tax). Ask about dive package opportunities they are forming with local providers.

From the main junction, head south on the road (or beach), and you'll find several decent clusters of beachside cabins, including **Seagull's Nest** (tel. 501/523-7243, jcseagulls@yahoo.com, from US$15) with shared-bath doubles and nice common space,

though the yard outside is kind of junky. **Whistling Seas Vacation Inn** (tel. 501/669-2548, marcello@whistlingseas.com, US$46), offers five private cement rooms with fridge and fan. Whistling Seas is classy for the neighborhood, with a new restaurant.

Probably the most attractive budget option is **Tipple Tree Beya** (tel. 501/520-7006 or 603-7613, www.tippletree.com). It's a long-time favorite, a well-maintained spot right on the beach, with rooms from US$30 with shared bath (US$40 rooms have private bath, en suite two-bedroom options US$75, camping US$5). There are lovely hammock-adorned porches and *palapas*.

Walking south from King Cassava's, you'll come across the eccentric, garden-choked **Ransom's Cabana** (cabanabelize@hotmail.com, US$30). A bit farther, there are two very pleasant stilted cabanas at █ **Windschief** (tel. 501/523-7249, www.windschief.com, US$25–40), right next to owner Oliver's Internet bar and windsurfing school.

The top of the line for midrange prices is █ **Hopkins Inn Bed & Breakfast** (tel. 501/523-7283, www.hopkinsinn.com, US$59), with four fully furnished cabanas and a nice breakfast of fruits and local pastries. They're a bargain for what you get. You'll also find good value at the **All Seasons Guesthouse** (tel. 501/523-7209, www.allseasonsbelize.com, US$45–75 includes tax and coffee, US$7 more per night if you turn on the air-conditioning). It's not on the beach, but it's not far from it, and the rooms are comfortable and nicely decorated. There's a barbecue pit to cook your own fish at the end of the day.

A short distance after the pavement of Hopkins village runs out, look for the left turn to **Jungle Jeanie's by the Sea** (tel. 501/523-7047, www.junglejeaniebythesea.com, US$50–120). This is a wonderful stretch of beach for guests staying in Jeanie's six spacious cabanas (some on the beach, some engulfed in lush, natural vegetation), plus a tree house, all with private bathrooms, living areas, and porches. There is an on-site restaurant and bar, campgrounds (US$10 pp), and a raised, roofed "jungle plaza" for yoga, torchlight drumming ceremonies, or anything else you feel like doing.

Food

There are four Chinese groceries in Hopkins these days, making it easier to stock up on nibbles and booze without breaking the bank. There are only a few eateries in Hopkins, most very low-key. Most obvious is **King Cassava's,** located right at the main junction and providing a central, laid-back atmosphere. A bit south of there, **The Watering Hole,** across from Tipple Tree, is very delicious. Down on Southside, you'll find good but slow food at **Innie's;** also check out the **Yugadah Café** and **Iris's**—all have similarly relaxed menus and atmospheres. There's a nice East Indian place next to Hopkins Inn Bed & Breakfast. For anything fancier, you'll have to head a couple miles south to the resorts.

There are always a few fun and funky options on Northside as well, especially the **Swinging Armadillo** (daily from 10:30 A.M.), where you can eat and drink (and sleep; they have rooms now!) directly above the lapping waves. There's also the **Larumi Hati Beybu Diner** (from 10 A.M.), with nice Belizean and Mexican dishes for US$4–6, right on the beach under a cool thatch roof. Get your Chinese fix at **Rainbow Restaurant.**

Services

The **Windschief Internet** café and cocktail bar is where it's at, though many midrange hotels in Hopkins also offer computers and wireless service. At press time, an ATM had been purchased for the community, but they were still figuring out where to put it.

Getting There and Around

If you have your own transportation, getting to Hopkins is easy: just follow the Southern Highway until you see the well-signed turnoff on your left; from there it's a four-mile straight stretch of dirt road (which can be under water during intense rains). Figure 30–40 minutes' total drive from Dangriga. Only a couple of buses each day make the detour from the highway into Hopkins and Sittee, and the situation changes daily; inquire at the bus stations in Dangriga (or Placencia or Punta Gorda). Otherwise it's an expensive hotel shuttle or local taxi—which can cost up to US$50. Once you're there, rent a scooter at All Seasons Guesthouse for US$38–50 a day; some people do this to get to the Mayflower Reserve or other nearby hiking spots. Bikes are also easy to find and good for exploring the village.

FALSE SITTEE POINT

A few minutes' bicycle ride south from Hopkins Village will bring you to an oceanside strip of upscale resorts and condos. The water off the beach resorts at False Sittee can be muddy at times because of the proximity of emptying rivers and streams, and depending on the time of year, sand flies and mosquitoes can get fierce. Still, this is a popular spot to stay because of its direct access to so many inland and offshore attractions and activities.

Accommodations

The most low-key option in this stretch of resorts along False Sittee Point is **❮ Beaches and Dreams Seafront Inn and Restaurant** (tel. 501/523-7259, www.beachesanddreams. com, US$120), whose four ample rooms have tiled floors, porches, and private bathrooms; ask about the new tree house, great for families. The on-site restaurant, the **❮ Barracuda Bar and Grill** (open for happy hour and dinner, closed Tuesdays, bocce tournaments on Fridays) features Chef "Alaska" Tony Marisco's amazing menu, including smoked prime rib, lots of seafood, and some of the best pizza this side of the Sittee River (from US$20–25 per person for a full dinner, US$25 for a large cheese pizza). Another pleasant midrange option is next door at **Parrot Cove Lodge** (tel. 501/523-7225, U.S. tel. 800/207-7139, http:// parrotcovelodge.com, US$130–250), with a handful of standard rooms and suites plus a few homes and villas for rent. All the standard sea and land tours are available.

Jaguar Reef Resort (tel. 501/520-7040,

SOUTHERN COAST

U.S. tel. 800/289-5756, www.jaguarreef.com, US$190–275) is a full-service accommodation with an ever-improving variety of spacious, comfortably furnished rooms and cottages. If you can afford it, there is a new selection of ridiculously large luxury suites next door at **Almond Beach** (U.S. tel. 866/624-1516, www.almondbeachbelize.com, US$160–295), a sister boutique resort associated with Jaguar Reef. There's a large open dining space shared by the two properties; several pools and bars, plus bikes, kayaks, and sand volleyball; and a large menu of activity-based packages. Almond Beach rooms and suites go for US$180–325, or take the ultra-luxe "beachfront vista suite" for a cool US$820 a night (includes private chef). This is a popular spot for fancy weddings, especially with the addition of the Butterflies Spa, offering a full range of treatments at about the same rates as back home.

A hundred yards north of Jaguar Reef, **Hamanasi Resort** (tel. 501/520-7073, U.S. tel. 877/522-3483, www.hamanasi.com, US$275–350, includes breakfast and taxes) is the area's premier diving operation. Sitting on 17 acres, including 400 feet of beachfront, Hamanasi offers eight rooms and four suites (including a honeymoon option), all with a view and tiled bathrooms, air-conditioning, fans, porches, and colorful Guatemalan bedspreads. Meals include good pasta and, of course, fresh seafood.

SITTEE RIVER

Continuing on the road from Hopkins, you'll pass through False Sittee, followed by the village of Sittee River, occupying a few bends of the slow, flat river of the same name. The road turns upstream, looping westward, about six miles back to the Southern Highway. Sittee River qualifies as a village only in the loosest sense, with a few houses, Reynold's Store, some jungly places to stay, a few dive shops and upscale resorts, and more often than not, a few bugs. There are a few fully screened accommodations from which to soak up the thick,

the beach near False Sittee Point

© JOSHUA BERMAN

tropical tranquility around you. There are dive shops and boats to whisk you out to the cayes, excellent fishing (snook, tarpon, peacock bass, sheepshead, and barracuda), and, only 12 miles to the west, the entrance to the Cockscomb Basin Wildlife Sanctuary.

Near the soccer field, you'll find high-speed, air-conditioned Internet—and coffee, juice, beer, and gifts—at **Sittee River Internet** (www.sitteeriver.net).

Sports and Recreation

Sittee River Internet is also where you'll find famed local guide **Horace Andrews** (tel. 501/603-8358, www.belizebyhorace.com), right across from his dock. Horace does river tours on the Sittee River, snorkel trips to the cayes, fishing trips to the cayes or lagoons, and inland tours such as Cockscomb, Mayflower, and Red Bank to see the scarlet macaws in season.

Bocatura Banks (tel. 501/606-4590 or 668-4590, U.S. tel. 207/288-3400, bocaturabank@yahoo.com), whose owner, Alan

Stewart, a marine biologist, photographer, sailor, and dive master who first came to Belize in the mid-1980s, runs sailing charters on a 40-foot catamaran named *Toucan Play.* The boat can carry up to 20 people; an all-day snorkeling trip is US$75 per person, with park fees, food, and drinks all included. He also maintains four riverside cottages on his property in Sittee River, where he docks the boat. A restaurant provides meals in a nice setting and many activities are available.

On the road to Bocatura, you'll also find **Second Nature Divers** and the **Diversity Cafe** (contact Martin or Jeanette at 501/523-7038, www.secondnaturedivers.com). Their dive shop may be moving across from Jaguar Reef soon.

Accommodations and Food

The new owners of **Sir Thomas' at Toucan Sittee** (tel. 501/523-7039 or 670-4892, www.sir-thomas-at-toucan-sittee.com, from $95 plus tax) have added extensive upgrades to

© JOSHUA BARMAN

stilted accommodations on Sittee River

these six unique wood bungalows, including private bathrooms and hot water, comfy mattresses, and nice semi-outdoor jungle showers. The 18-acre property on the bank of the Sittee River is popular with birders, nature lovers, and families. You can camp on the grounds for US$20; bring your own gear. Accommodations are set amid hundreds of fruit and other trees planted by the previous hosts. Ask about guided river and lagoon canoe trips—for fishing or just nature viewing. A major highlight is the spooky night canoe paddle up Boom Creek; this canopied waterway is filled with wildlife and jaw-dropping vegetation (and insects, be prepared).

Glover's Guest House (tel. 501/509-7099, www.glovers.com.bz) provides cheap, spartan lodging for both passersby and guests of the Glover's Atoll Resort. Stay in a cozy bunkhouse on stilts for US$9 per person, or in one of the private stilted, screened-in riverside cabins for US$29; meals and cooking area available. Camping is US$5, tents provided. You can use the guesthouse's canoes and kayaks to explore the river.

Getting There

This area is about a ten-minute drive east of the Southern Highway through mostly orange fields and riverside lots. There are *usually* two daily buses that drive through Sittee River and False Sittee Point, but this schedule is always up in the air; most accommodations will provide some sort of transfer from Dangriga.

MAYFLOWER BOCAWINA NATIONAL PARK

More than 7,100 acres of Maya Mountain wilderness make up this stretch of jungle, waterfalls, and green-fringed ancient ruins. There's great hiking on excellent trails. A walk in Mayflower can be combined with a day trip to Cockscomb (just to the south) or can easily fill a whole day or more. This area is new to tourism; caves, ruins, and waterfalls are being discovered all the time.

The biggest challenge to enjoying Mayflower is simply getting to the trailhead, which lies 4.5 miles west of the Southern Highway with no public transport of any kind making the trip. The turnoff is just north of Silk Grass Village. The park office and interpretive center, where you'll register and pay US$5 per person, greet you when you arrive. The office is open 8 A.M.–4 P.M.

For information, go to Silk Grass Village and seek out Ramon and Doreen Guzman (tel. 501/503-7309). Ramon is a long-time park warden and Doreen is an officer in the **Friends of Mayflower Bocawina National Park,** an organization that co-manages the park with the government. Another contact is Genovivo "Gino" Peck, found in his Tsimin Chac thatch-roof restaurant on the Southern Highway in Silk Grass. Gino (tel. 501/668-7202) is a warden at Mayflower. If he can't take you into the park, he'll find someone who can. In Dangriga, **C & G Tours and Charters** (29 Oak St., 501/522-3641 or 610-2277, www.cgtourscharters.com) can arrange a trip to Mayflower; in Sittee River, Horace Andrews is the best guide around (tel. 501/603-8358, belizebyhorace.com).

Accommodations

There is a campground at the park entrance (US$10 pp); bring your own gear. Your other option is **Mama Noots Backabush Jungle Resort** (tel. 501/670-8019, www.mamanoots.com, US$90–150), a 50-acre spread in the middle of thousands of acres of protected forest and parklands. The gorgeous natural surroundings combine with the Noots' daughters' Belizean-Hollywood flair in the property's landscaping and design. Everything is newly renovated, from the duplex family cabana to the simpler jungle-chic units with thatch roof, tile floor, and comfy living areas; a few smallish lodge rooms with private baths are also available. The resort uses solar, wind, and hydro power; there's wireless Internet in the restaurant and bar; and they even hold occasional "Howl at the Moon" parties. On-site guides will help you explore the immense wilderness in your new backyard.

The Cockscomb Basin

The land rises gradually from the coastal plains to the Maya Mountains; driving south on the Southern Highway, you'll see the highlands a way to the west and flatlands to the left, mostly covered by orange and banana groves. The highway passes through a few villages and soon delivers you to the area's prime attraction: Maya Center village and Cockscomb Basin Wildlife Sanctuary. Heavy rain along the peaks of the Maya range (as much as 160 inches a year) runs off into lush rainforest thick with trees, orchids, palms, ferns, abundant birds, and exotic animals, including peccaries, anteaters, armadillos, tapirs, and jaguars.

◖ COCKSCOMB BASIN WILDLIFE SANCTUARY

Also commonly called CBWS or simply the "Jaguar Preserve," this is one of the best undisturbed natural centers in the country, and easily one of the most beautiful. A large tract of approximately 155 square miles of forest was declared a forest reserve in 1984, and in 1986 the government of Belize set the region aside as a preserve for the largest cat in the Americas, the jaguar. The area is alive with wildlife, including the margay, ocelot, puma, jaguarundi, tapir, deer, paca, iguana, kinkajou, and armadillo (to name just a few), hundreds of bird species, and some unusual reptiles, including the red-eyed tree frog. And though you probably won't spot large cats roaming during the day (they hunt at night), it's exciting to see their prints and other signs—and to know that even if you don't see one, you'll probably *be seen* by one.

Just past the entrance gate into the park is a gift shop and office where you'll be asked to sign in. Visitor facilities include a small museum, picnic area, and outhouse. You'll also find an "office" of the World Wildlife Fund, an important sponsor of the park, along with the Belize Audubon Society (www.belizeaudubon.org) and the government, who manage the protected area. Entrance is US$5 for non-Belizeans (pay back at the highway, at the Maya

A jaguar stops for a drink in the Cockscomb Basin Wildlife Sanctuary.

COURTESY OF THE BELIZE TOURISM BOARD/ TONY RATH

Center Women's Group craft shop located at the head of the access road, immediately off the Southern Highway), and the park is open 7:30 A.M.–4:30 P.M.

Hiking the Trails

From the visitors center, many trails go off in different directions into the park. There are more than 20 miles of maintained hiking trails, which range from an easy hour-long stroll along the river to a four-day Victoria Peak expedition. Check out the front of the visitors center building for a detailed map. There may be guides at the center; if not, there are several renowned wilderness guides who grew up in these forests and who can be found up the road in Maya Center. Bring your swimsuit; you'll find cool natural pools for a refreshing plunge, especially along Stann Creek. All visitors are also encouraged to bring sturdy shoes, a long-sleeved shirt, long pants, insect repellent, sunscreen, and plenty of water.

LOOKING FORWARD: THE JAGUAR'S FUTURE

The first scientist to research the jaguar population in Belize, Dr. Alan Rabinowitz, thought it would take several generations to see any ecological or cultural benefits of the Cockscomb Basin Wildlife Sanctuary's creation – but they occurred much more quickly. This was, he admits, partly due to luck: The formation of a protected area based on the jaguar's natural habitat (which was the first of its kind in the world) happened at a fortuitous time in Belize's history, basically at the very beginning of the country's efforts to attract more tourists. Cockscomb helped set the stage for the local preservation movement, giving a crucial boost to the country's fledgling ecotourism efforts.

Jaguar research continues in the Cockscomb Basin, only now the animals are tracked using infrared-triggered camera traps. Current data supports original density estimates that were based on radiotelemetry, which necessi-

tated the invasive, sometimes harmful practice of physically capturing and collaring the cats and then tracking them from dangerous, low-flying airplanes. "The jaguar's prey are back," reports Rabinowitz, from behind a tiny, cluttered desk in his cramped office at New York's Bronx Zoo, where he is now Director of Science and Exploration for the Wildlife Conservation Society (WCS). "There are peccary all over the place and the jaguars are eating a lot, but their population density has stayed level – it's maxed out – even after 20 years. Also, we've found that the more protected area you give the jaguar, the less complaints there are of jaguars coming out after dogs and cattle – the opposite of what you'd expect."

Rabinowitz also notes that the Maya of the Cockscomb area now show natural curiosity about the big cats, instead of fear. Whereas before locals never entered the bush without a rifle, today they carry binoculars, pointing

If you climb **Ben's Bluff,** you're not just looking out over a park where jaguars live—you're at the entrance of a forest that goes all the way into the Guatemalan Petén, part of the largest contiguous block of protected forest in Central America. It's an easy one-day hike, and the park managers are planning to build a lookout tower.

Victoria Peak

The second highest point in the country is the top of Victoria Peak (3,675 feet). Geologists believe the mountain is four million years old, the oldest geologic formation in Central America. Reportedly, area Maya populations thought the peak was surrounded by a lake, unapproachable to man, and occupied by a powerful spirit. The first people (a party led by Roger T. Goldsworth, governor of then–British Honduras) reached the summit in 1888. Today, it is a protected natural monument, managed by the Belize Audubon Society. You can arrange a summit trip in the dry season only (February to May), and only with a permit

and guide. This 30-mile round-trip trek takes three or four days and is for burly hikers only. See the Belize Audubon Society website (www.belizeaudubon.org) for trail and campsite details; entrance is US$5 per person.

Accommodations

Bring your own tent to stay at one of three well-maintained campgrounds (US$10 pp). The park's overnight accommodations range from bare clapboard buildings with about a dozen bunks and metal roofs (US$20 for a bed in a shared "rustic cabin" or a bunk in the main dormitory; clean sheets with shared bathrooms). There are a few private cabins as well; US$54 gets you six beds and a kitchen. Finally, the "White House," up the road (US$81), features a screened veranda in an isolated jungle setting, a unique experience for a nature-loving family.

Be prepared with food and supplies if you plan to stay a few days; the only food for sale in the visitors center is chips, cookies, candy bars, and soft drinks. There are a couple of bigger stores in Maya Center, so feel free to stock up

out jaguar tracks and exotic birds to groups of tourists. "Now I go back to Cockscomb and I see these young adults – sons of people I worked with – working as tour guides. They've known Cockscomb as a protected area since they were children and they realize how important it is, both economically and ecologically. Plus, the women are empowered, with the money from their crafts sales, and you don't see children walking around with parasites and swollen bellies."

Rabinowitz tracked the area's cat population while living in a small clearing of jungle (now the site of the park's visitors center) for nearly two years in the early 1980s and recounted his story in his fascinating "eco-memoir" *Jaguar: One Man's Struggle to Establish the World's First Jaguar Preserve* (reprinted by Island Press in 2000). He has traveled extensively since then, studying jaguars, clouded leopards, tigers, and other large mammal species in Borneo, Taiwan, Thailand, Laos, and Myanmar (Burma).

And while he has moved on from Cockscomb, the restless biologist does not see the Belizean park as a mere thing of the past. Quite the contrary. His ambitious goal now is to save jaguars throughout their entire range – from Mexico to Argentina – by creating and securing a natural, unbroken corridor of wildland on both public and private lands where jaguars can thrive into the future. "We've already made tremendous strides toward that objective," he says, "with jaguar surveys and rancher outreach programs."

The **Save the Jaguar** project is dependent on private and corporate donations (Jaguar Cars has been extremely supportive). You can learn more about current studies and projects – and about how to help – by visiting www.savethejaguar.com and also by checking out WCS's **Adopt-a-Jaguar Project** at www.wcs.org.

there before catching your cab into the park. You may also be able to arrange for meals to be cooked in Maya Center and brought in. Otherwise, there is a communal kitchen with stoves and crockery and cooking utensils for rent. Again, visitors are required to bring their own food and water. A walled-off washing area has buckets, and a separate cooking area has a gas stove and a few pots and such.

Getting There

CBWS is about six miles west of the Southern Highway and the village of Maya Center (from Dangriga, it's a total of 20 miles). Driving into Cockscomb is best done with a four-wheel drive vehicle, especially after a rain. By public transport, hop off any bus traveling between Dangriga and points south at Maya Center. From there, it's a long walk or a US$15–20 taxi ride from Maya Center.

MAYA CENTER

This small village is at the turnoff to the famous Cockscomb Basin Wildlife Sanctuary. Many of the 400 or so Mopan Maya who live here were relocated when their original home within the Cockscomb reserve was given protected status. Since then, they have had to change their lifestyles; instead of continuing to clear patches of rainforest for short-term agriculture, many men now work as guides and taxi drivers, while the women create and sell artwork. Still, the people of Maya Center are struggling to support their town with tourism. Ever since they were prohibited from using the now-protected jungle for subsistence farming and hunting, tourism has been their only hope, aside from working for slave wages at the nearby banana and citrus farms. The village has a few places to stay, eat, and experience village life, literally right down the road from the famous reserve.

At the very least, make sure that you—or the driver of your tour bus—stop at one of the three Maya crafts stores, all on the road into the park. At the turnoff from the Southern Highway, you'll find the **Village Women's Cooperative Craft Store and Visitor's**

Center (7:30 A.M.–4:30 P.M.); a quarter mile farther toward the park is the **Nu'uk Che'il Gift Shop**. Both offer fine jewelry, slate carvings, baskets, herbs, and other crafts. Another small shop is in between.

Right across the road from the women's co-op, look for the sign and trail across the creek to William Sho's **Butterfly Farm** (7 A.M.–5 P.M. daily, US$2.50, possible fee to take photos), boasting several dozen species.

Julio Saqui runs the store next to the women's co-op and offers satellite Internet access (US$4/hour) and taxi service. Julio is also a great guide and offers many services; information is available on his website (www.cockscombmayatours.com).

Accommodations

There are two guesthouses in Maya Center, each owned by a different family who offers transport in and out of the preserve, guides, meals, and other services.

Nu'uk Che'il Cottages and Hmen Herbal Center (tel. 501/520-3033 or 615-2091, nuukcheil@btl.net) offers tranquil accommodations, which are more removed from the highway than the village's other guesthouse. Bunks with shared bath are US$10 per person, and private rooms are US$30 (hot showers available, tax not included). Camping is US$4 per person. There are also a few shared-bath units for US$23. The place is very well kept, with beautifully planted grounds; the guesthouse has experience hosting student groups and can arrange seminars on herbal medicine, cultural performances, and the like. Proprietress Aurora Garcia Saqui's husband, Ernesto, was

director of the Cockscomb Basin Wildlife Sanctuary until 2005 and is extremely knowledgeable about the area. Her late uncle, Don Eligio Panti, was a famous healer; she took over his work when he died in 1996. Aurora offers Mayan spiritual blessings, prayer healings, acupuncture, and massage (each for under US$15). Aurora also has a four-acre botanical garden and medicine trail (US$2.50 entrance), offers herbs for sale, and can arrange homestays in the village (US$30 includes a one-night stay with a local family, one dinner and one breakfast per person).

Another decent option is located right on the highway, about 100 meters north of the entrance to Cockscomb: **Tutzil Nah Cottages** (tel. 501/520-3044, www.mayacenter.com, US$14–22) is owned and operated by the Chun family (they helped Dr. Alan Rabinowitz in his original jaguar studies and appear in his book, *Jaguar*). There are four screened wooden rooms, two with private bath, two with shared bath and shower; all have queen beds, fans, ample space, nice furniture, and a raised deck. Meals are US$6–12, as is camping on the grounds or in a separate campground about a quarter mile into the bush. Inventive trips are available as an alternative to the standard fare, including kayak floats and night hikes.

Getting There

Maya Center is accessed by hopping off any bus passing between Placencia or Punta Gorda and points north. Taxis will take you from the village to the Cockscomb Basin Wildlife Sanctuary for about US$15–20 (per cab, not per person).

The Placencia Peninsula

This ribbon of barrier beach and mangroves winds 16 miles southward from the coastal wetlands and shrimp farms near Riverside village all the way to Placencia Village proper, away on the tip of the peninsula. The area used to be a forgotten cul-de-sac on the tourist trail, but no more. Traveling to nearby cayes and inland attractions like the Cockscomb Basin Wildlife Sanctuary, Maya villages, and ruins of Toledo District is possible from anywhere on the peninsula. The area offers the full range of accommodations—whether you prefer to mingle with backpackers in Placencia Village or rub elbows with fellow guests at any of a number of beach resorts, each with its own personality. This is also the site of several enormous, ambitious, and controversial development projects, more of which are springing up all over the area every year.

MAYA BEACH

About halfway down the peninsula, you'll enter Maya Beach, which is nothing more than a loose strip of simple, small accommodations. Actually, they're quite nice, in a relaxed, isolated way, offering more value for your money than nearly anything else in the area. The beach here is also more pleasant than many places in Belize. You just have to be content with the relative lack of services in Maya Beach, since getting to and from Placencia Village can be a dusty, expensive endeavor, even though it's only seven miles away.

Accommodations

Maya Beach hotels are of the beach cabana variety, with a few furnished apartments, too, many with kitchenettes for cooking on your own. Most of these hotels also manage full houses and a few condos in the area—ask about weekly and monthly rates.

The first place you'll come to from the north is (**Maya Beach Hotel** (tel. 501/520-8040, U.S. tel. 800/503-5124, www.mayabeachhotel.com, US$90–125), with five well-kept, immaculate rooms, a few with gorgeous waterfront

© JOS-HUA BERMAN

The Placencia Peninsula stretches 16 miles along Belize's southern coast.

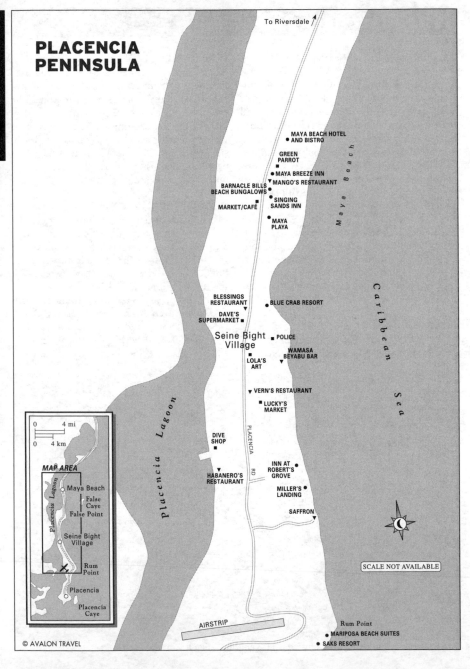

PLACENCIA PENINSULA

To Riversdale

MAYA BEACH HOTEL
AND BISTRO

GREEN
PARROT

MAYA BREEZE INN

MANGO'S RESTAURANT

BARNACLE BILLS
BEACH BUNGALOWS

SINGING
SANDS INN

MARKET/CAFÉ

MAYA
PLAYA

Maya Beach

BLESSINGS
RESTAURANT

BLUE CRAB RESORT

DAVE'S
SUPERMARKET

Seine Bight
Village

POLICE

WAMASA
BEYABU BAR

LOLA'S
ART

VERN'S RESTAURANT

LUCKY'S
MARKET

Placencia Lagoon

DIVE
SHOP

PLACENCIA RD

HABANERO'S
RESTAURANT

INN AT
ROBERT'S
GROVE

MILLER'S
LANDING

SAFFRON

Caribbean Sea

SCALE NOT AVAILABLE

AIRSTRIP

Rum Point

MARIPOSA BEACH SUITES

SAKS RESORT

0   4 mi
0   4 km

MAP AREA

Placencia Lagoon

Maya Beach

False
Caye

False Point

Seine Bight
Village

Rum
Point

Placencia

Placencia
Caye

© AVALON TRAVEL

decks, all with wireless Internet, private bath, hot showers, and a great stretch of sand—oh, and one of the best restaurants in Placencia (the Maya Beach Hotel Bistro).

The Green Parrot Beach Houses (tel. 501/523-2488, www.greenparrot-belize.com, US$130–180 plus tax) features eight thatch-roof A-frame cabanas with decks and loft bedrooms facing the ocean. Each sleeps four people and includes multiple beds, couches, a kitchen, and hammocks. There's a restaurant and beach bar, but some readers have complained of feeling pressured into using *only* Green Parrot's services.

The **Maya Breeze Inn** (tel. 501/523-8012, U.S. tel. 888/458-8581, www.mayabreezeinn.com, from US$100) offers three cabins on stilts with kitchenettes, two suites with full kitchens, and four deluxe hotel rooms with small fridge, cable TV, and air-conditioning. All are close to the beach and are great options for families and multiple couples. The inn offers free kayaks for nearby lagoon and ocean paddling.

Catering to relaxed couples and honeymooners, **(** Barnacle Bill's Beach Bungalows** (tel. 501/523-8010, www.gotobelize.com/barnacle, US$110) consists of two secluded bungalows on the beach, with full kitchen, fans, and hot/cold water. Each sleeps three adults (children under 12 not permitted). Tours and free kayaks are available, and the staff will stock the fridge prior to your arrival.

Plant and orchid lovers will enjoy **Singing Sands Inn** (tel. 501/520-8022, U.S. tel. 888/201-6425, www.singingsands.com, US$100–125 plus tax). The six thatch-roof oceanfront cabanas have front porches, and the four standard rooms offer ocean and garden views. All units provide private bath, ceiling fan, and constant ocean breezes. Portable air-conditioning is available if desired. Breakfast is served in the open-air restaurant next to the pool; fresh lunches and dinners are served as well. Drinks and light fare can be enjoyed on the pier bar 200 feet out into the Caribbean. Bikes, canoes, sail boats, and snorkel gear are available, as are snorkeling classes, tours, and transportation. Families, groups, and weddings are welcome.

The most economical—and the most primitive—option is **Maya Playa** (tel. 501/523-8121, mayaplaya@btl.net, US$75) with three two-story cabanas on the beach offering loft, private outdoor bath/garden, and hot water. There's no restaurant, but a bare bones kitchen area is provided overlooking the ocean, and owner Chuck offers complimentary fruit and coffee, as he has been doing for many years.

Food

When you get tired of cooking in your cabana's kitchenette, visit the **Hungry Gecko** (6:30 A.M.–9 P.M.), which serves a cheap and delicious menu of Honduran and local goodies, fresh seafood, and smoothies. The one store in town, the **Maya Point Market,** is open mornings and afternoons (closed Sun.). **Mango's Bar** has a nice menu and a breezy view to enjoy with your beer. It's popular with the handful of locals, offering darts and poker some nights; Cuban cigars are available.

The **(** Maya Beach Hotel Bistro** (dinner reservations tel. 501/520-8040, open from 7 A.M., closed Mon.) is a breath of fresh, garlic-roasted air on the Belize culinary scene. Just reading the appetizer and meal choices will make your mouth water—few restaurants in the country have a menu this savory and creative. Australian chef John prepares dinner entrées like Sassy Shrimp Pot, Cocoa Pork, and Boathouse Pie (a half-pound fish fillet smothered in truffle and Jim Beam cream sauce, baked into a pie; entrées US$16–32), not to mention fresh bread, an inspired bar food menu ("Honey-Coconut Ribs" and "Bacon-wrapped Shrimp"), and a lovely assortment of breakfasts (US$5–9), including homemade bagels and imported lox.

SEINE BIGHT

Continuing south, a couple more miles of dirt road will put you in the Garinagu village of Seine Bight. In this tiny, unkempt town, most of the men are fishermen and the women tend family gardens. Some are attempting to clean up the town, with hopes it will become a low-key tourist destination, but they've still got a ways to go, as foreign-owned resorts sprout like mushrooms up and down the coast around them. Supposedly, men and women lead split lives here; the women even claim to have their own language that the men don't understand (sound familiar?).

Shopping

Lola's Art Gallery is a must-stop (it's located behind the soccer field; follow the well-marked signs). Lola sells handmade dolls, as well as a selection of bright, inspired artwork, including cards and paintings on canvas; there are lots of cheerful primary colors and village life scenes. Lola's is open 8 A.M.–8 P.M.

Accommodations

On a clean, shallow beach on the very northern end of Seine Bight is **Blue Crab Resort** (tel. 501/523-3544, www.bluecrabbeach.com, US$90–100). American-Belizean–owned, this humble hotel has four rooms with air-conditioning, fridge, coffeemaker, fans, and cable TV; plus two cabanas with high thatch roof, louvered windows, private bath, and three fans. Blue Crab is on the primitive side, made of mostly wood and thatch. The popular restaurant (call for reservations) is run by the hotel's proprietress and cook, Linn, who brings her Taiwanese ancestry to your Belizean table; specials include Lobster Formosan and Thai Shrimp Soup. They also run a tiny chocolate factory in the house across the road.

Awarded "Hotel of the Year 2008" by the Belize Tourist Board, **The Inn at Robert's Grove** (tel. 501/523-3565, U.S. tel. 800/565-9757, www.robertsgrove.com, from US$215) is a grand affair. Its various structures are situated close together along a short stretch of decent beach, and even though this is one of the most upscale operations in the country, it maintains a very relaxed feel. The inn is owned and operated by New Yorkers Robert and Risa Frackman, who go out of their way to accommodate guests; this includes hiring some of the most professional staff in Belize. The various guest rooms and suites are spacious, with high ceilings, king-size beds, and many amenities. There are two pools, a tennis court, a trio of rooftop hot tubs, and an excellent open-air restaurant. Robert's Grove has its own dive shop on the lagoon side (next to its Mexican restaurant, Habanero's) and offers all kinds of underwater, offshore, and inland trips and packages. The inn is popular with couples, families, and groups.

Food

Get a cheery, cheap, home-cooked Honduran meal at an unnamed little **thatch shack** with no sign, about a quarter mile north of Seine Bight, on the west side of the road (open 6 A.M.–7 P.M.). Fresh, hot tortillas come with your dish. Grab a couple of "dark and lovelies" (bottles of Guinness) or a glass of locally brewed bitters at the reggae-colored **Wamasa Beyabu Bar,** which greets you as you enter town from the north. Wamasa just opened a bigger operation on the beach as well, which can be pretty happening on weekends.

Habanero's (3–9 P.M., closed Aug.–Oct., US$9–15) is an excellent lagoon-side Mexican restaurant across the road from the Inn at Robert's Grove, just south of Seine Bight village.

Placencia Village

A fishing village since the time of the Maya and periodically flattened by hurricanes (the last was Iris in 2001), Placencia continues rebuilding and redefining itself, in large part to accommodate the influx of foreigners who are arriving in increasing numbers each year. Placencia Village is still worlds away from the condo-dominated landscape of San Pedro on Ambergris Caye, and most locals claim it will never go that way, but time will tell. On my last trip to Placencia, I saw plenty of bulldozers, swaths of cut mangroves, and golf carts for rent . . .

Despite area development, this town will remain the *tranquilo,* ramshackle village it is today for years to come. Find a room, book some day tours, pencil in a massage before happy hour, and relax. Oh yeah, feel free to drink the tap water as you explore: Placencia's *agua* is piped in from an artesian well across the lagoon in Independence, reportedly the result of an unsuccessful attempt to drill for oil, and is clean and pure.

ORIENTATION

The north-south Placencia Road runs the length of the peninsula, doglegs around the airstrip, continues along the lagoon, then parallels the famous central sidewalk as it enters town. You'll see the soccer field on your right before the road curves slightly to the left, terminating at the Shell station and main docks. If there is a "downtown" Placencia, it's probably here, in front of the gas station and dock: This is where buses come and go, taxis hang out, and most dive shops are based.

◖ THE SIDEWALK STRIP

Aside from the beach, the main attraction in Placencia is the world-renowned main-street sidewalk, cited in the *Guinness Book of World Records* as "the world's most narrow street." It's 24 inches wide in spots and runs north-south through the sand for over a mile. Homes, hotels, Guatemalan goods shops, and tour guide offices line both sides.

© JOSHUA BERMAN

Placencia's record-breaking "sidewalk street"

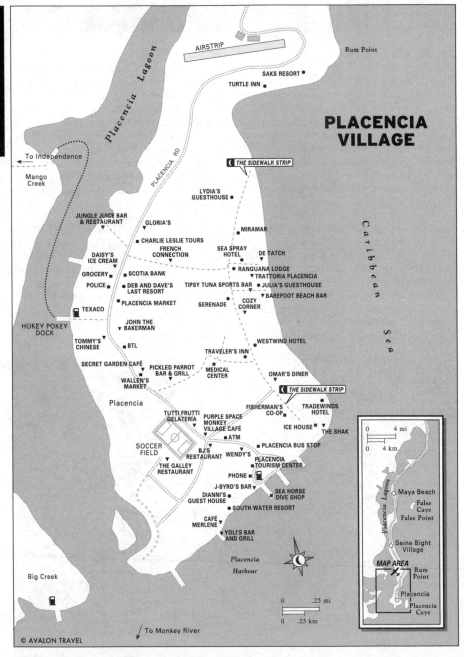

PLACENCIA VILLAGE

Placencia Lagoon

AIRSTRIP

Rum Point

SAKS RESORT

TURTLE INN

To Independence

Mango Creek

PLACENCIA RD

THE SIDEWALK STRIP

LYDIA'S GUESTHOUSE

JUNGLE JUICE BAR & RESTAURANT

GLORIA'S

MIRAMAR

CHARLIE LESLIE TOURS

DAISY'S ICE CREAM

FRENCH CONNECTION

SEA SPRAY HOTEL

DE TATCH

Caribbean Sea

GROCERY

SCOTIA BANK

RANGUANA LODGE

TRATTORIA PLACENCIA

POLICE

DEB AND DAVE'S LAST RESORT

TIPSY TUNA SPORTS BAR

JULIA'S GUESTHOUSE

BAREFOOT BEACH BAR

PLACENCIA MARKET

SERENADE

COZY CORNER

TEXACO

JOHN THE BAKERMAN

HOKEY POKEY DOCK

TOMMY'S CHINESE

BTL

WESTWIND HOTEL

SECRET GARDEN CAFÉ

TRAVELER'S INN

Placencia

PICKLED PARROT BAR & GRILL

MEDICAL CENTER

OMAR'S DINER

WALLEN'S MARKET

THE SIDEWALK STRIP

TUTTI FRUTTI GELATERIA

FISHERMAN'S CO-OP

TRADEWINDS HOTEL

PURPLE SPACE MONKEY VILLAGE CAFÉ

ICE HOUSE

THE SHAK

SOCCER FIELD

ATM

PLACENCIA BUS STOP

BJ'S RESTAURANT

WENDY'S

PLACENCIA TOURISM CENTER

THE GALLEY RESTAURANT

PHONE

J-BYRD'S BAR

DIANNI'S GUEST HOUSE

SEA HORSE DIVE SHOP

SOUTH WATER RESORT

CAFÉ MERLENE

YOLI'S BAR AND GRILL

Placencia Harbour

Big Creek

To Monkey River

0   .25 mi

0   .25 km

0   4 mi

0   4 km

Placencia Lagoon

Maya Beach

False Caye

False Point

Seine Bight Village

MAP AREA

Rum Point

Placencia

Placencia Caye

© AVALON TRAVEL

BRING A BOOK TO PLACENCIA

Placencia's school and library are stocked almost entirely by donated books, giving visitors from up north an easy way to contribute something to the children and community. Bring a single book or a whole box and drop them off at the Placencia Tourism office, at Deb 'n Dave's Last Resort, or with Principal Rodney Griffith (find contact information at www.placencia.com or www.placenciabreeze.com). The school also rarely turns away volunteers who'd like to spend time in a Belizean classroom, especially art teachers.

RECREATION
Snorkeling and Diving

Although the beach is usually fine for swimming and lounging, you won't see much with a mask and snorkel except sand, sea grass, a few fish, and other bathers. A short boat ride, however, will bring you to the barrier reef and the kind of underwater viewing you can write home about. Snorkel gear is available for rent everywhere (US$5 per day), as are trips to the cayes and reefs (around US$50 per half-day, depending on distance).

Belize's famous Barrier Reef extends past Placencia and is accessible by boat. There are six dive shops, with more sure to come (and go). Prices are comparable, and you can either let your hotel arrange everything or do it yourself. **Seahorse**, located on its own dock by the Shell station (tel. 501/523-3166, seahorse@btl.net), is a good bet, too, as is **Splash Dive Shop** (tel. 501/523-3345, http://splashbelize.com). To the north, you'll find a handful of serious dive operations linked to their respective resorts, with professional shops at both The Inn at Robert's Grove and Turtle Inn.

Sea Kayaking

An unforgettable, underrated way to explore the near-shore cayes, mangroves, creeks, and rivers is by paddle. Open plastic kayaks are available to guests at most resorts, and many tour operators and dive shops have some for rent as well. Boats are also available for rent at the **Sugar Reef Bar** and are perfect for putting in and paddling up the lagoon in search of birds, manatees, and dolphins. If you're into extended sea kayaking expeditions, see Dave Vernon at **Toadal Adventure** (tel. 501/523-3207 or 606-1399, debanddave@btl.net). Dave is one of Belize's premier naturalists and tour guides, and the opportunity to take a personal paddle trip with him is well worth the trip. He'll take you on any of a number of overnight paddling trips, such as a three-night Monkey River tour or a week-long caye exploration. He also rents boats for US$25 a day, with which you can paddle out to any number of cayes and make your own adventure.

Fishing

Placencia has always been a fishing town for sustenance, but with the advent of tourism, it has gained a worldwide reputation for sportfishing. Deep-water possibilities include wahoo, sailfish, marlin, kingfish, and dolphin fish; fly-fishing can hook you a grand slam: bonefish, tarpon, permit, and snook (all catch-and-release). Fortunately, serious angling means serious local guides, several of whom (like the Godfrey brothers, Earl and Kurt) have been featured on ESPN and in multiple fishing magazines. Hire Earl at **Trip'N Travel Southern Guides Fly Fishing and Saltwater Adventures** (located in the Placencia Office Supply building, tel. 501/523-3433, lgodfrey@direcway.com). Most tour operators listed throughout this chapter offer fishing trips, and a few specialize in them, like **Kingfisher's Tarpon Caye Lodge,** boasting 30 years of experience (tel. 501/523-3323, cell 501/600-6071, kingfisher@btl.net, www.tarponcayelodge.com). Charlie Leslie Sr., owner and head guide, has a stellar reputation and will take you to a variety of spots, from inshore

© JOSHUA BERMAN

Placencia beach

places that include nearby flats to Tarpon Caye and the remote Ycacos area. Also ask about their island cabanas for rent. Check www.placencia.com for more options.

Sailing

Opportunities abound for day trips, sunset cruises, snorkel voyages, and sail charters. Climb aboard **Jap's** 25-foot vessel for day trips (US$50 pp) or even overnight camping expeditions to Caye Caulker (about US$100 pp). Check www.sailingbelize.com (tel. 501/523-3138 or 600-2508). Expensive, high-end **The Moorings** (U.S. tel. 800/535-7289, www.moorings.com) has a base in Placencia for multiple catamaran adventures.

Massage and Bodywork

Sign up for a massage or other treatment at **The Secret Garden** (behind Wallen's, tel. 501/523-3617, www.secretgardenplacencia.com), where an hour massage costs US$50 and a special four-hands treatment a bit more. Secret Garden masseuse Lee Nyhus is also popular at **The Inn at Robert's Grove Spa** (tel. 501/523-3565),

north of town, where you can also get a full range of treatments—for more premium prices, of course. **The Turtle Inn** also has pampering services, as does a Thai massage place right in Placencia Village Square, run by experienced Thais who offer seaweed treatments and papaya body polish (massage US$75 per hour). Also check into **Z-Touch Beauty Salon and Massage** (tel. 501/523-3513, massage US$50 per hour).

Tour Guides

There's no shortage of guide services in Placencia, where most tour operators offer service to *all* nearby destinations: Cockscomb Basin Wildlife Sanctuary, Monkey River, snorkeling and fishing trips with lunch on a beautiful caye, Maya ruins of Lubaantun and Nim Li Punit, and a variety of paddling tours. For any of these trips, please also refer to the dive shops and fishing guides listed in this chapter.

Many tour operators have their offices/shacks clustered by the main dock in town, just past the gas station; most are subcontracted by the hotels that offer tours to their guests. If you're going it on your own, ask around and know that prices often rely on a minimum number of passengers. Prices vary little, but it's definitely worth comparing. Monkey River day trips, for example, range US$40–50 per person, depending on whether lunch is included and the size of the boat. Half-day snorkel trips are about US$35–45 per person.

Right by the main dock, **Nite Wind** (tel. 501/523-3487 or 523-3176, renidrag_99@yahoo.com) is very reliable; just up the sidewalk you'll find **Ocean Motion** (tel. 501/523-3363 or 523-3162, oceanmotion@btl.net). Hubert and Karen Young's **Joy Tours** (tel. 501/523-3325, www.belizewithjoy.com) is located next to the Western Horizon Chinese restaurant. There are also some individual guide gurus lurking around town, notably the famed **David Westby,** who, according to one local, knows more than any living man "bout everyt'ing out dere" (pointing to the ocean). Ask around your hotel or at restaurants.

Caribbean Tours and Travel (tel. 501/523 3481, www.caribbeantoursbelize.com) has two offices in town and is one of the more professionally run travel agencies and guide services. The Belizean owner, Lance McKenzie, worked as a travel agent in the United States for 30 years.

ENTERTAINMENT AND EVENTS

Placencia's bars, restaurants, and resorts do a decent job of coordination, so special events like beach barbecues, horseshoe tournaments, karaoke, and live music are offered throughout the entire week—especially during the high season. Your best bet is to check the *Placencia Breeze* newspaper and look for current schedules.

The **Barefoot Beach Bar** (11:30 A.M.–10 P.M., closed Mon.) is wildly popular, especially in the high season. Sandy-toed revelers choose from literally hundreds of froofy cocktails and a lip-smackin' bar food menu; Friday night is Ladies' Night, Saturday Jam Night, and Sunday live music, with happy hour daily from 5–6 P.M. Another happening bar is **J-Byrd's** (10 A.M.–midnight daily), right

on the water behind the gas station, with live bands most Fridays and Sundays. A bit farther, **Loly's** also has its own dock bar and restaurant, and around the corner, **Sugar Reef** is a mellow lagoon-side hangout with weekly horseshoe tourneys. The town's main disco was washed away by Hurricane Iris, and the loud music at the **Tipsy Tuna Sports Bar** is a poor substitute, although the white monstrosity of a building is right on the beach.

The biggest party of the year happens the third week of June, during **Lobsterfest.** The whole south end of town closes down for lobster-catching tournaments, costumes, dances, and food booths everywhere. **Easter weekend** is insanely popular as well, as Placencia is a destination for many Belizeans as well as foreign visitors; they typically book their rooms months in advance, so be prepared for the crowds. Look for a Halloween celebration, complete with parade and trick-or-treating (for kids and adults alike). Another annual gig, the **Mistletoe Ball,** wanders to a different hotel before Christmas every year and doubles as a fundraiser for the local Belize Tourism Industry Association chapter. The town humane society organizes various fundraising events as well; keep an eye out.

SHOPPING

Most gift stores feature Guatemalan crafts and clothes, plus local jewelry and sea-inspired artwork. In addition to the numerous shops, stalls, and tables along the sidewalk, **Myrna's** by the gas station has a huge, colorful selection. Happy huntin'.

ACCOMMODATIONS

All of Placencia's budget lodgings are found on (or within shouting distance of) the sidewalk, and most of the high-end resorts are strung along the beach north of town. Remember, these are high-season double occupancy prices only! Expect significant discounts and negotiable rates between May and November.

Under US$25

There is one campground on the northern tip of Placencia Village, where you can pitch your tent and use the bathrooms, showers, and grill for US$5 per person; rent gear for another US$5. It's run by a couple from Oregon. Miss Lucille's **Travellers Inn** (tel. 501/523-3190, joytour@btl.net), right in the middle of the village, is a no-frills, bottom-of-the-barrel place to rest, only one lot away from the beach where most guests spend their days; rooms with shared bath are US$15, doubles with private bath US$20. The wood rooms are hot, the bathrooms grungy. Right on the sidewalk, **Omar's** is another wooden flophouse ($9 pp in the dorm to $15 for a double with private bath); there's great home-cooked food at this family-run business.

A much better budget bet is (**Lydia's Guesthouse** (tel. 501/523-3117, lydias@btl. net, US$25), located toward the north end of the sidewalk. Lydia's is a longtime favorite among weary backpackers. The eight clean rooms with shared tile-floor bath also share a sociable two-story porch, communal kitchen, fans, hammocks, and a 30-second walk to the beach. Miss Lydia will make you breakfast if you make arrangements the day before; she also makes fresh Creole bread and guava jam.

US$25-50

On the left side of the road as you enter Placencia, (**Deb'n' Dave's Last Resort** (tel. 501/523-3207 or 606-1399, www.toadaladventure.com, US$25) consists of four small, clean rooms surrounding a gorgeous sand courtyard and garden favored by a small, cute army of neighborhood cats; the common screened-in porch space is excellent for meeting your neighbors and telling war stories from the day's paddling and snorkeling trips; there are shared bathrooms for all. Owner Dave is head guide for **Toadal Adventures** and is renowned for his local knowledge and trip-leading skills.

Claiming to be the "first established hotel on the Placencia Peninsula" (since 1964), the (**Sea Spray Hotel** (tel. 501/523-3148, www.seasprayhotel.com, US$25–65) is a great choice—30 feet from the ocean, 20 rooms with private bath, refrigerators, hot/cold water, and coffeepots. There are economy rooms and nicer

ones closer to the water, where guests can relax in hammocks and chairs under palm trees. De Tatch restaurant on the premises serves breakfast, lunch, dinner, and Internet.

The **Cozy Corner Hotel** (tel. 501/523-3280 or 523-3540, cozycorner@btl.net, US$39–65) has 10 decent rooms with private bath and basic amenities, located right behind their bar/restaurant on the beach, with a nice breezy second-story porch; some rooms have air-conditioning. Suites are US$75.

US$50-100

At the extreme southern end of Placencia Village, look for the brightly painted **Tradewinds Hotel** (tel. 501/523-3122 or 523-3412, trdewndpla@btl.net, from US$75–95) on five acres near the sea, offering nine cabanas with spacious rooms, fans, refrigerators, coffeepots, and private yards just feet away from the ocean; there are two new deluxe rooms. **Dianni's Guest House** (located back by The Moorings dock, tel. 501/523-3159, dianni@btl.net, US$59) is a simple, clean, quiet affair, with six rooms with private bath, fan, and coffeemaker, plus wireless Internet, tour service, bikes, and a book exchange.

(**Westwind Hotel** (tel. 501/523-3255, www.westwindhotel.com, US$65–150) has ten rooms with views, light tile floor, sunny decks, private baths, and fans (air-conditioning is optional, costs a little extra if you turn it on); there's wireless Internet too. The family unit goes for US$150 a night. The hotel has a great, friendly vibe and a nice beach to relax on. The **Ranguana Lodge** (tel. 501/523-3112, www.ranguanabelize.com, US$84) has five private cabanas, three of them on the beach. All are spacious with beautiful wood floors, walls, and ceilings; optional kitchen and air-conditioning.

US$100-150

Rent one of four fully furnished, air-conditioned units at **Easy Living Apartments** (tel. 501/227-6464 or 523-3524, www.easyliving.bz, from US$125). You should book two to four weeks in advance; various houses are

YOUR OWN ISLAND

Who's never dreamed of starring in his or her own episode of *Castaway* or *Lost*? If you've got the money, you've got access to a handful of Belize's cayes all to yourself (actually, most properties come with at least one caretaker). Though there are a few budget island options, including the Raggamuffin Tours sailing/camping trip from Caye Caulker to Placencia, most cost a pretty penny. If you can't afford the US$12,000 a night to rent Cayo Espanto (www.aprivateisland.com, includes personal butler service but *not* wine), then try one of the following.

Most options seem to be based in Placencia, where a few island rentals are available. **Ranguana Caye** (tel. 501/503-8452) is two acres in size and 18 miles (90 minutes by boat) from the mainland. It's managed by the Inn at Robert's Grove (www.robertsgrove.com), as is **Robert's Caye,** a one-acre island 10 miles from the coast, with four well-appointed thatch-roof cabanas and access to a small bar and restaurant; it's all yours for US$400 per person per night. Robert's and Ranguana are only semiprivate.

French Louie Caye (www.frenchlouiecayebelize.com) has its own beach, coral reef, and fishing dock, and a couple of cabanas among the mangroves overlooking the water. The caye is about 12 miles off the coast and the simple wooden cabin has a stocked kitchen and stove. It is very private and the honeymoon experience of a lifetime (I know from experience). You do have to share the island with the caretaker – who is a great cook. It's US$380 per couple for the first night.

Tarpon Caye Lodge (tel. 501/523-3323, www.tarponcayelodge.com) offers fly fishing, spin fishing and deep sea fishing from a private island lodge. It also caters to people looking to simply relax on a private Caribbean island.

Reef Conservation International (tel. 501/702-2117, on Frank's Caye 501/509-5015, www.reefci.com) offers weekly and monthly dive packages based on four-and-a-half-acre **Frank's Caye,** 28 miles off the coast from Punta Gorda. This is one of the best places to view whale sharks, dolphins, and grouper spawning events – and you will most likely be the **only** dive boat in the water. Nondivers are also welcome, and Reef Conservation International offers various packages and degrees of marine conservation work; or just camp on the beach and snorkel the days away. The boat leaves Punta Gorda Monday morning and returns on Friday afternoon.

There are many other islands in the **Sapodilla Cayes** at the southern end of Belize's Barrier Reef. Ask tour operators in Punta Gorda about exploring **Seal Caye** and others. You may be able to camp on some of them.

---

available. One of the only true upscale options in Placencia Village, the **Sunset Pointe Apartments** (U.S. tel. 904/471-3599, www.sunsetpointebelize.com) offers luxury condos for short- or long-term rental. They're back on the lagoon side, so there's potential for it to be a bit buggy, but they all have raised roof decks to help you escape in the breezes. It's only a five-minute walk to the beach from here, and there are many accessible restaurants and shops.

Turtle Inn (tel. 501/523-3244 or 523-3150, www.turtleinn.com) is one of the nation's premier luxe destinations, located about a mile north of Placencia Village. Prices start at US$315 a night for the Garden View Cottages, and go up to US$1,600 a night for the master two-bedroom pavilion. Even if you're not staying there, swing by to treat yourself to a fine meal with beautifully framed views of the ocean. This is one of U.S. film producer Francis Ford Coppola's two Belizean properties. Turtle Inn has seven luxury villas and 18 cottages on offer, as well as two swimming pools, an über-mellow beach bar, and one of the peninsula's premier restaurants (Mare Restaurant). The rooms are designed along Indonesian and Belizean lines, with lots of natural materials and airy space. The high thatch ceilings absorb the heat, so there are fans only, no air-conditioning (but there are music players for your iPod and fancy shell phones). There is also an on-site Belizean eatery and a new grill.

FOOD

Placencia has a small restaurant offering but enough variety to keep you stuffed during your visit: seafood cooked in coconut milk and local herbs, Creole stews and "fry chicken," sandwiches, burritos, burgers, chow mein, French, and Italian (and adequate vegetarian options nearly everywhere you go).

Cafés, Bakeries, and Ice Cream

Check near the Shell station for **Norman's Bakery** (6 A.M.–9 P.M. daily), where you can get cheap breakfasts (including a US$2.50 "Backpacker Special") and dinners for US$7.50, not to mention coffee and baked goods. In the new little Placencia Village Square, **Tutti Frutti Gelatería** (9 A.M.–9 P.M. daily) serves up some of the best homemade Italian ice cream you've ever had in your life (a bold statement, and I stand by it); it's made fresh daily with local fruits and traditional flavors. **John the Bakerman** makes great breads; look for his sign on the sidewalk. **Daisy's** (7 A.M.–10:30 P.M.), on the main road, makes its own ice cream and offers cakes, pies, and other goodies, like seaweed shakes and fruit smoothies (about US$4 for a meal).

Restaurant, Diners, and Bar Food

Omar's Diner (7 A.M.–11 P.M., closed Fri. night–Sat. sunset, no alcohol served) will take care of you all day, with a lobster omelet and handmade corn tortillas to start the day off (US$8), then a burrito for lunch (US$4), and a fish plate (from US$8) for dinner (or pork chops, conch steak, or lobster). Come for the food, and stay for the conversation with the vivacious Omar and family; buy his children's impressive artwork. Also look for Omar's little food shack on the main road as it enters town.

The Secret Garden Restaurant and Coffee House (tel. 501/523-3617, www.secretgardenplacencia.com, 7 A.M.–9 P.M., closed Mon.) has a pleasant shady area and a homey lounge where you can enjoy coffee drinks, free

wireless Internet, and yummy burritos, burgers, and Thai curries. There is also an on-site day spa. Up the road (past the town dock), look for **The Shak** (7 A.M.–7 P.M.), a smoothie bar with a healthy vegetarian menu, a view of the water, and good breakfasts.

BJ's (on the corner of the soccer field, 7 A.M.–10 P.M., closes at 4 P.M. on Sun.), "where good food and God's people meet," has an outdoor porch and cheap fare: sandwiches from US$2.50, seafood and stir-fry dinners from US$9. Next door, ❨ **Wendy's** (tel. 501/523-3335, 7 A.M.–9 P.M.) offers a varied menu at reasonable prices, plus a glassed-in, air-conditioned eating area and a full bar. This is a great, cool place to come to for Creole cooking, burgers (US$3), burritos (US$4.50), and fancier seafood items (US$13–23). **The Cozy Corner** is one of the nicer beach bars, with a lobster burger for US$7, fish dinners from US$9, and good bar food (open 11 A.M.–10 P.M. daily).

The Pickled Parrot (between the sidewalk and main road, just off from the soccer field, 11:30 A.M.–9:30 P.M.) is good for seafood specials (US$11 fish plate, US$15 lobster), burgers, and blender drinks (including a three-rum "Parrot Piss" cocktail, US$6). The owner, Wendy, also rents a couple of nice hardwood cabanas out back.

The **Purple Space Monkey Village** (6 A.M.–midnight) has some of the best pizza, panini sandwiches, and comfort food (Belizean dishes, bagels, pizza, etc.) in town; there's also an espresso bar, free wireless Internet, and laptops for your use.

International

Start with the ❨ **French Connection** (reservations strongly recommended, tel. 501/523-3656, 6 P.M.–11 P.M. Wed.–Sat., plus brunch on the weekends). Placencia Village's sole Italian restaurant is **La Dolce Vita,** with decent fare above Wallen's Market.

Most of the resorts north of town have fine restaurants to brag about. Grab a fistful of dollars and a taxi and *bon appétit*. At The Turtle Inn's **Mare Restaurant,** the chef prepares meals with greens from his own on-site organic herb

HELP THE PLACENCIA HUMANE SOCIETY

The **Placencia Humane Society** (PHS) was formed in 1999, primarily to respond to the need for regular veterinary care on the peninsula. Today it is one of the country's most successful animal welfare organizations – and it's an entirely volunteer-run organization. In addition to basic veterinary services, the PHS also offers temporary emergency shelter for stray and injured pets, no-interest loans to area residents who need help caring for their pets, and spaying and neutering clinics for feral cats. It is in the process of raising funds to build a permanent clinic facility on land leased from the Placencia Village Council.

Clinics are held the third weekend of each month at the Placencia Community Center, for surgeries and general appointments. If visitors (especially visiting veterinary surgeons and technicians) are interested in visiting or helping the clinic during their visits to Belize, they should contact the PHS president (tel. 501/520-4057, info@placencia-pets.org, www.placencia-pets.org). PHS accepts donations of medical supplies in addition to monetary contributions through memberships or donations (or items sold on the website). All monies raised are used for the welfare of animals in the area. The website offers additional descriptions of PHS services, information for volunteers, and a list of PHS-sponsored local events.

---

garden, as well as those grown in their upland sister resort's extensive organic vegetable garden. In fact, this is the best place to come for a fresh green salad in Placencia—as well as seafood, pasta, and oven-baked gourmet pizza.

Chef Frank de Silva at the **Seaside Restaurant** at The Inn at Robert's Grove serves mouthwatering seafood and imported U.S. steaks (reservations tel. 501/523-3565, entrées from US$12, surf-and-turf tenderloin US$28). Don't forget **Habanero's** for excellent Mexican food, just south of Seine Bight. A few miles farther north, **Maya Beach Hotel Bistro** (dinner reservations tel. 501/520-8040, open from 7 A.M., closed Mon.) has Placencians raving—and unanimously declaring that the food and experience is well worth the US$15 taxi trip from town (or US$1 on the afternoon bus).

INFORMATION

The Placencia Tourism Center is one of the most organized and useful in the country. Before leaving for your trip, check the website for updates and events: www.placencia. com. Upon arriving in town, head straight to the **Tourism Office** (tel. 501/523-4045, placencia@btl.net, 9 A.M.–5 P.M. Mon.–Fri., closed 1.5 hours at lunchtime) in Placencia Village Square; after reading the various fiesta postings on the wall, pick up a copy of the latest *Placencia Breeze* (www.placenciabreeze. com), a monthly rag with many helpful schedules and listings, including house rentals. The tourism office also sells books, maps, music CDs, and postcards and has a mail drop; the office will *not*, however, recommend one business over another.

SERVICES

The Shell station, located at the southern terminus of the road, is open 6 A.M.–7 P.M. Atlantic Bank is open 9 A.M.–2 P.M. and has an ATM in town, toward the Shell station. The new Scotia Bank branch also has an ATM, just north of the BTL office, and Belize Bank is on the way.

Communications and Internet

The **BTL office,** located at the bottom of the big red-and-white antenna, is open 8 A.M.–5 P.M. Monday–Friday but closes for lunch.

Placencia Office Supply, tucked off the main road in the town center (tel. 501/523-3433, fax 501/523-3205, 8:30 A.M.–7 P.M. Mon.–Sat., closed at lunchtime), has a copy machine, Internet service, fax, and more—they'll let you plug into their Ethernet line or use their WiFi as well, US$4/hour. Free wireless broadband is available at the **Secret Garden, Purple Space Monkey Internet Café,** and an ever-growing number of resorts and accommodations.

Groceries

At **Tommy's Market** and **Wallen's Market,** both on the main road, you can fill almost all of your needs, including groceries, dry goods, and sundries. **Everyday Supermarket,** in the center of town, is open 7 A.M.–9 P.M. There is a pharmacy above Wallen's Market (tel. 501/523-3346).

For wine, liquor, deli items, and gourmet groceries, visit **Peckish** (tel. 501/523-3636, www.peckishbelize.com, open 8 A.M.–5 P.M.) at Live Oak Plaza, just south of the airstrip; Peckish also offers custom provisioning for boats and condos.

Laundry

Cheaper places usually have someone available to wash clothes by hand. Otherwise, take your load to Omar's Diner and drop it off with Cara (US$10). Nearby, Julia (of Julia and Lawrence Guesthouse) also does laundry (US$5–12). At Live Oak Plaza (near the airstrip), **Cyberwash** is a clean, air-conditioned Laundromat with cable TV and wireless Internet service.

GETTING THERE

There are a number of ways to travel the 100-plus miles between Placencia Village and Belize City. The tip of the long peninsula is not as isolated as it used to be, and various options exist for continuing on to points south and west, including Guatemala and Honduras.

By Air

At last check, there were more than 20 daily flights in and out of Placencia's precarious little airstrip, to and from various destinations throughout Belize. Planes generally hop from either of Belize City's two airports to Dangriga, Placencia, and Punta Gorda (in that order, usually landing at all three), then turn around for the reverse trip north. For current schedules and fares, check directly with the two airlines: **Maya Island Air** (tel. 501/223-1140, U.S. tel. 800/225-6732, www.mayaislandair.com) or **Tropic Air** (tel. 501/226-2012, U.S. tel. 800/422-3435, www.tropicair.com). There is new air service between Savannah Airport (near Independence Village) and San Pedro Sula in Honduras; three flights a week run about US$160.

By Car

Placencia's 21-mile road from the town to where the peninsula hits the mainland has been a rutted, dusty nightmare for decades; however, in July 2008 the highest officials in the land gathered at the Inn at Robert's Grove and signed the papers to begin the paving project that many thought would never happen. Hopefully it will be paved by the time you read this, but I've written those same words in previous editions with no luck<!p>.<!p>.<!p>. In any case, it's about a three- or four-hour drive from Belize City. Most people go by the Hummingbird and Southern Highways. About a half hour after turning south near Dangriga, look for a left turn to Riverside, where you'll begin the peninsula road. If it's been raining, four-wheel drive is necessary.

By Bus

Placencia Village is serviced by four daily bus departures and arrivals (in high season, anyway; spotty service the rest of the year). Buses come and go from the Shell station, usually two in the morning and two in the afternoon, and current schedules are posted on the Placencia Tourism Office door. You'll need to change in Dangriga to reach Belize City. You can change again in Belmopan for a westbound Cayo bus. Cost is about US$5 or less for each leg of the journey. The more common—and quickest—bus route is via the boat to Mango Creek and Independence Village.

By Boat to Mango Creek

For those traveling to points south, like Punta Gorda or Guatemala, or for those who wish to avoid the Placencia Road, a boat/bus combo will get you back to the mainland and on your way. **Hokey Pokey Water Taxi** (tel. 501/523-2376 or 601-0271) provides regular service between the Texaco station dock and the dilapidated landing at Mango Creek, charging US$5 one-way for the 15-minute trip through bird-filled mangrove lagoons. Boats leave Placencia at 6:45 A.M., 10 A.M., 12:30 P.M., 2:30 P.M., 4 P.M., and 5 P.M.; the same boat turns around for the reverse trip.

Bus connections to all points are coordinated with the 10 A.M. and 4 P.M. boats from Placencia, so the traveler needs only to worry about stepping onto the correct bus as soon as her boat lands in Independence (after the quick taxi shuttle to the bus depot by Sherl's Restaurant, US$0.50). Hokey Pokey is a reliable family-run operation, proudly steered by Captains Pole, Lito, and Caral.

By Boat to Honduras and Guatemala

The ship to Puerto Cortés leaves every Friday at 9:30 A.M., returning Monday afternoon at 2 P.M. (tel. 501/202-4506 or 603-7787, Hon. tel. 504/665-1200). The trip costs US$50 and takes roughly four hours, stopping in Big Creek, Belize, for immigration purposes, and carrying a maximum of 50 passengers. Buy tickets at the Placencia Tourism Office. Every now and then (sometimes as often as a couple times a week), a boatload of passengers arrives in Placencia from Livingston, Guatemala, and seeks passengers to take with them back to Livingston (with an immigration stop in Punta Gorda). Inquire at Caribbean Tours and Travels.

GETTING AROUND

Placencia Village itself is small enough to walk, and if you're commuting on the sidewalk, walking is your only option (riding a bike on the sidewalk can earn you a US$50 fine). Speaking of two-wheeled options, there are plenty of bicycle rentals in town; I advise against biking north on the Placencia Road, with all the dust and construction trucks, but if you go, know that Seine Bight is 5 miles from

© JOSHUA BERMAN

boats to the mainland on the Hokey Pokey Water Taxi

Placencia and Maya Beach another 2.5. The cheapest way (besides walking) to get up and down the peninsula is to hop on a bus as it travels to or from Dangriga.

Taxis

There used to be a free shuttle service up and down the peninsula; perhaps it'll be reinstated when the road is paved. In the meantime, there are at least a dozen green-plated taxis hanging around the Shell station and airstrip. Rides from town to the airstrip cost US$6 for one or two people, to the Seine Bight area one-way US$12, to Maya Beach US$15. Ask around the gas station and tourist office and look for posted rate lists to know what you should be paying. The more trusted and long-standing taxi services are listed in the *Placencia Breeze* and include **Sam Burgess** (tel. 501/523-3310 or 603-2819), **Cornell** (tel. 501/609-1077), **Percy Neal** (tel. 501/523-3202 or 614-7831), **Radiance Ritchie** (tel. 501/600-6050 or 523-3321), and **Traveling Gecko** (tel. 501/603-0553 or 523-4078).

Car Rental

Rent a car for do-it-yourself land tours to the Jaguar or Mayflower nature reserves, or for trips to the ruins near Punta Gorda. Otherwise you'll pay $50–100 per person to join a tour group. **Barefoot Rentals** (tel. 501/523-3438, http://barefootrentalsbelize. com) has a selection of cars and golf carts (US$25–130 per day for cars; US$65–95 a day for golf carts).

Near Placencia

MONKEY RIVER

An easy 35-minute boat ride from Placencia brings you to the mouth of the Monkey River and the village of the same name. Founded in 1891, Monkey River Village was once a thriving town of several thousand loggers, *chicleros,* banana farmers, and fishermen; that was then. Now, the super-sleepy village of 30 families (about 150 people) makes its way with fishing and, you guessed it, tourism. Many villagers are trained and licensed tour guides who work with hotels in Placencia to provide a truly unique wildlife-viewing experience.

Ninety percent of the structures you see have been rebuilt since Hurricane Iris destroyed the town in 2001. The village is accessible by boat—most often through the mangroves from Placencia, but there is also an 11-mile road from the Southern Highway that ends across the river from the village.

If you're on a tour from Placencia, after negotiating the mangrove maze, your guide will take you into the river's mouth and dock up in town for a bathroom break and a chance to place your lunch order for later in the day. Then you'll be off upstream, all eyes peeled for animals. You'll beach up at the trailhead to explore a piece of **Payne's Creek National Park,** a 31,000-acre reserve that is surrounded by even more protected area. You'll hike through the dense brush, now a regenerating broadleaf forest, which will take decades to reach its pre-Iris glory. Then it's back down the river for lunch and a stroll through the village. Most head back to their rooms in Placencia, but you may wish to consider staying a night or two, either to experience the village life or to get some serious fishing time in.

Accommodations

The options in Monkey River are casual inns, best appreciated by those who enjoy isolation and primitive surroundings. Most offer a set menu (a different entrée served each day). Reservations are required for meals, though all of these small cafés will serve drop-ins something, such as a burger or a beer.

Near the breezy part of town by the mini-basketball court, **Alice's Restaurant** (tel. 501/720-2033) offers meals for about US$6, served in a large dining room with a view of the sea; renting one of her airy wood rooms in a neighboring building costs US$23, with fan and shared bath with hot/cold water. A room with private bath is planned. **Sunset Inn** (tel. 501/720-2028, www.monkeyriverfishing.com, US$50) is a two-story structure with eight musty rooms with private bath, fan, and hot/cold water. Decent meals can be had for about US$8. The **Black Coral Gift Shop, Bar, and Restaurant** offers simple fare, local crafts, and Internet. The family that runs this hotel has an acclaimed guide service too, especially for sportfishing trips.

All hotels and resorts offer sea and land tours and trips. Local guides and fishermen are experts. Sorry, no dive shop yet, but bring your snorkeling gear. Overnight caye trips are available, as are river camping trips (you're dropped off at the Bladen bridge and canoe down the river, stopping at night to camp).

◖ LAUGHING BIRD CAYE

Managed by the nonprofit Southern Environmental Association, a.k.a. SEA Belize, a.k.a. Friends of Nature (office near Placencia Town dock, tel. 501/523-3377, www.

friendsofnaturebelize.org), **Laughing Bird Caye National Park** is an important protected area encompassing over 10,000 acres of sea; it's a popular day trip destination from Placencia. Swaying palms, small beautiful beaches, an absence of biting bugs, shallow sandy swimming areas, and interesting snorkeling and diving all make this an easy must-see.

This particular kind of caye is referred to as a *faro,* and the arms on each end make a kind of enclosure around a lagoon area on the leeward side. In this way, the island acts much like a mini-atoll. That's good news for those wishing to dive the eastern side of the island. You'll find a lot of elkhorn coral and fish life. Grunts, damselfish, parrot fish, houndfish, bonefish, and even rays and nurse sharks are to be found here.

This site was designated in December 1991. The reserve is visited regularly, mostly by researchers and tourists carried out by tour operators from Placencia for picnics, snorkeling, and diving. Previously, the reserve was used for overnight camping, but no longer, because of the lack of toilet or other waste disposal facilities. Some mooring buoys have been installed to prevent anchor damage to the surrounding reef. Private yachts and sea kayaks also use the site regularly. There is one trail through the center of the caye.

Friends of Nature also manages **Gladden Spit and Silk Cayes Marine Reserve,** a famous whale shark site, where they plan to build a resource center for fishermen and tour guides.

MANGO CREEK (INDEPENDENCE VILLAGE)

This coastal population and transport hub began as Mango Creek and later expanded into Independence Village; it is referred to alternately by both names. This is a dispersed community with a sweltering climate and no attractions aimed at tourism, except as a transportation stop. There is also a deep water port, where Belize's oil is being exported. The only reason a traveler will find himself here for any length of time is if he is waiting for a boat or bus or perhaps volunteering in one of the medical facilities. Independence has the nearest 24-hour clinic to Placencia, and if a medevac to Belize City is not possible, this is where a patient will be taken in an emergency. The private clinic (tel. 501/601-2769) is located on Water Side Street; there is also a public hospital providing health care to the poor. Independence is also the site of the area's secondary school, and a boatload of students from Placencia make the daily trip to conduct their studies, as there is no high school on the peninsula.

Practicalities

There are a few places to stay in Independence if you miss your boat and are stuck here, including thirteen rooms at **Ursella's Guest House** (up the street behind the basketball court, tel. 501/503-2062, US$20 shared bath) and **Hotel Hello** (near the bus "station," tel. 501/523-2428, US$25/40 s/d), which has a restaurant. The nicest option, **Hotel Cardie's** (tel. 501/523-2421, US$50), is on the main road to the highway. Rooms have air-conditioning, private bath, and TV, and there's also a decent on-site restaurant.

Eat at **Sheri's** (6:30 A.M.–9 P.M.), behind the gas station where you'll board or get off your bus. There are cheap plates of food and a bathroom, or try the Chinese restaurant by the park. There is an **Alliance Bank** branch by the park (tel. 501/523-2588, 8 A.M.–2 P.M. Tues.–Fri.).

Bus service through Independence is provided on a perplexing timetable. You probably won't have to worry about bus times, though, since your boat will hook you right onto your bus. The best we could make out, the last bus to Punta Gorda leaves at 8 P.M. and the last ride to Dangriga and Belize City is at 5:30 P.M.

PUNTA GORDA AND THE TOLEDO VILLAGES

There's a lot going on in southern Belize—wild, remote attractions serviced by a new crop of creative accommodations. Improvements to the Southern Highway and daily air service to and from Punta Gorda is helping to put Toledo on the map as the "Unforgettable" corner of Belize, rather than its traditional reputation as the "Forgotten" corner. The majority of Toledo District's attraction gems are found in the form of remote villages, caves, waterfalls, and offshore cayes. It seems natural that the area's tourism scene will keep growing. For now, though, Toledo is still about as off the beaten track as you can get in Belize.

Toledo District is a blend of many cultures—Q'eqchi' and Mopan Maya, mestizo, Mennonite, Garinagu, Creole, Caucasian, Chinese, Palestinian, and East Indian, to name a few of the local communities. More than 10,000 Q'eqchi' and Mopan Maya are subsistence farmers in the Toledo countryside.

Toledo is the district in Belize with the lowest per capita income, and it is also the most expensive in which to live. Money earmarked for development and tourism rarely finds its way south, although the first signs of growth and real estate—swapping around Punta Gorda are showing themselves, and there are finally a few upscale lodges in the area, in addition to the cheap flophouses and backpacker digs that have been around a lot longer. Up till now, tourism has been coming to the district in small, interesting doses: Student groups, researchers, and independent travelers have shown a great interest in the network of Maya villages and the world-famous ecotourism

© JOSHUA BERMAN

HIGHLIGHTS

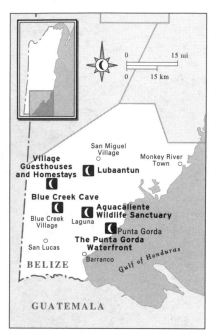

The Punta Gorda Waterfront: It's neither developed nor pristine, but don't miss a casual walk along the Caribbean – then wander to Central Park for ice cream (page 209).

Lubaantun: The ancestors of today's Maya used this ceremonial center which – along with nearby Nim Li Punit and Uxbenka – boasts stunning views, thick forests, and several longstanding legends (page 220).

Aguacaliente Wildlife Sanctuary: Swing through the relaxing village of Laguna to access the boardwalks of this premier birding destination (page 222).

Blue Creek Cave: Near the village of Blue Creek, the cave of the same name is the source of the Río Blanco – you can swim 600 yards inside it. Also check out nearby **Río Blanco National Park** and **Ho Keb Ha Caves** (page 225).

Village Guesthouses and Homestays: Head upcountry to experience a cultural immersion program in one of a dozen simple country villages. In addition to the cultural adventure, expect guided hiking, swimming, caving, and river trips (page 226).

LOOK FOR **(** TO FIND RECOMMENDED SIGHTS, ACTIVITIES, DINING, AND LODGING.

THE TOLEDO VILLAGES

programs hosted here. Of course there are also Garinagu, Mennonites, and your typical assortment of foreigners, including the biggest concentration of Peace Corps volunteers in the country.

PLANNING YOUR TIME

If you are coming to the area by bus, plan on nearly a full day of travel on either end of your trip south (at least five to six hours from Belize City); consider taking the quick flight between Belize City (or Placencia or Dangriga) and Punta Gorda (PG). If you plan on heading into the upcountry Toledo villages, you'll have to come to Punta Gorda first to set up the trip, usually necessitating at least one night in

town, maybe more, depending on the limited village bus schedules. Basically, if you really want to explore Toledo District, one or two days ain't gonna cut it. You'll need to set aside at least four or five days, more if you'd like to get out to the cayes or down to Livingston, Guatemala.

HISTORY

Originally, this area served as a coastal trading center for the Mayans, who sent trading parties out to sea and guided them back home with hilltop bonfires. In the 1860s, British settlers encouraged Americans to come and begin new lives in Belize. During the American Civil War, arms dealers became familiar with the southern

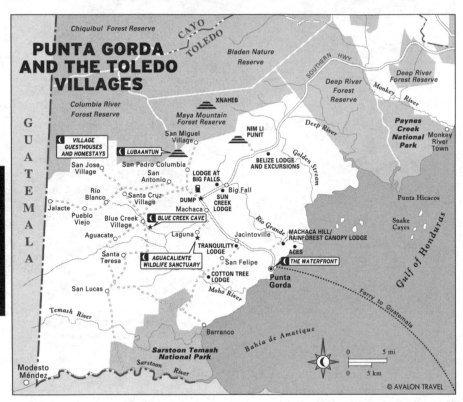

Belizean coast and hundreds of ex-Confederate soldiers arrived and cleared land after the war. Most of the American settlers returned to the United States, though one group of Methodists from Mississippi stayed in Toledo District long enough to develop a dozen sugar plantations. By 1910, most of the Mississippians were gone, but their sugar became popular during U.S. Prohibition; boats decked out as fishing crafts reportedly ran rum from Belize to Florida.

Big changes may be afoot for sleepy Toledo. The controversial Plan Puebla Panamá (PPP), a massive, multibillion-dollar infrastructure project between Mexico and Colombia, may use the area as part of an isthmus-long superhighway, opening up Belize's Southern Highway for international trade across the new Guatemalan border crossing at Jalacte. For travelers, this would mean additional options to loop into Guatemala. For the local Maya, who have always been the most marginalized people in Belize, however, it could be disastrous. Many Maya families who came to Belize as unofficial homesteaders have never needed to accept traditional Western ideas of landownership; efforts to secure them titles to their land are now underway before their plots get snatched away from under their feet. Having won their case before the Organization of American States and the Belize Supreme Court, Maya groups are still battling to uphold their land rights.

Punta Gorda

Toledo District's county seat and biggest town, "PG" is simultaneously the lazy end of the road and an exciting jumping-off point for forays to upland villages, offshore cayes, Guatemala, and Honduras. Punta Gorda's 5,000 or so inhabitants live their daily lives, getting by from hurricane to hurricane.

Punta Gorda is a simple port, not superclean, with no real beach, and its crooked streets are framed by mostly old, dilapidated wooden buildings. The majority of inhabitants in town are of Garinagu and East Indian descent, though there are representatives of most of the groups mentioned above. Fishing was the main support of the local people for centuries; today many fishermen work for a nearby high-tech shrimp farm. Local farmers grow rice, mangoes, bananas, sugarcane, and beans—mainly for themselves and the local market. Fair trade–certified and organic cacao beans are an important export as well, used to make chocolate by the Green & Black's company in England.

ORIENTATION

Punta Gorda is a casual village with few street names. Arriving from the north, you'll cross a bridge over Joe Taylor Creek, then be greeted by the towering Sea Front Inn, with the Caribbean on your left. After the road splits at a Texaco station, it forms North Park Street (a diagonal street a block long) on the right and Front Street on the left. Following Front Street will take you through town, past the boat taxi pier, the immigration office, the market, and several eating establishments; continue south to Nature's Way Guest House at the bottom of Church Street, followed by Blue Belize. The municipal dock and town plaza, just a couple blocks in from the sea, form the town center.

If arriving by bus, or at the town dock from Guatemala, prepare to be greeted by a few local

© JOSHUA BERMAN

Everything at the Punta Gorda Market is grown in Toledo.

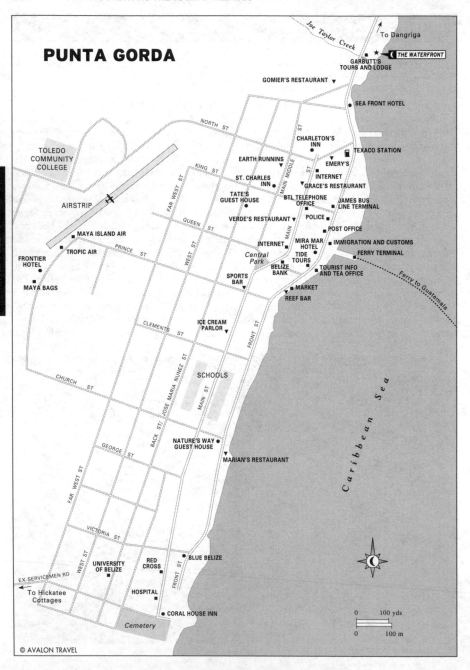

PUNTA GORDA

To Dangriga

THE WATERFRONT

GARBUTT'S TOURS AND LODGE

Joe Taylor Creek

GOMIER'S RESTAURANT ▼

SEA FRONT HOTEL

NORTH ST

CHARLETON'S INN

TOLEDO COMMUNITY COLLEGE

EARTH RUNNINS ▼

KING ST

TEXACO STATION

EMERY'S

ST. CHARLES INN

INTERNET

GRACE'S RESTAURANT ▼

AIRSTRIP

TATE'S GUEST HOUSE

BTL TELEPHONE OFFICE

JAMES BUS LINE TERMINAL

FAR WEST ST

QUEEN ST

VERDE'S RESTAURANT ▼

POLICE

MAYA ISLAND AIR

PRINCE ST

INTERNET

MIRA MAR HOTEL

POST OFFICE

IMMIGRATION AND CUSTOMS

TROPIC AIR

WEST ST

Central Park

TIDE TOURS

FERRY TERMINAL

FRONTIER HOTEL

BELIZE BANK

TOURIST INFO AND TEA OFFICE

MAYA BAGS

SPORTS BAR ▼

MARKET

Ferry to Guatemala

REEF BAR

CLEMENTS ST

FRONT ST

ICE CREAM PARLOR ▼

CHURCH ST

JOSE MARIA NUNEZ ST

SCHOOLS

MAIN ST

Caribbean Sea

BACK ST

GEORGE ST

NATURE'S WAY GUEST HOUSE

MARIAN'S RESTAURANT ▼

FAR WEST ST

VICTORIA ST

BLUE BELIZE

WEST ST

UNIVERSITY OF BELIZE

RED CROSS

FRONT ST

EX-SERVICEMEN RD

← To Hickatee Cottages

HOSPITAL

CORAL HOUSE INN

Cemetery

0   100 yds

0   100 m

© AVALON TRAVEL

hustlers; feel free to shake them off by firmly refusing their services.

SIGHTS
◖ The Waterfront
Even though there is no real lounging beach or developed waterfront, people go swimming off (and sunbathing on) the dock just north of Joe Taylor Creek. The waterfront is rocky, but quiet and tranquil, with small waves lapping the shoreline, and a walk along its length, especially at sunrise, should be a top priority of your visit.

Central Park
The town park, on a small triangle of soil roughly in the center of town, has an appropriately sleepy air to it. At the north end is a raised stage dedicated to the "Pioneers of Belizean Independence." In the center of the park is a dry fountain, and here and there are some green cement benches. A clock tower on the south end of the park has hands everlastingly stuck, as if holding time at bay. On market days, this is an especially pleasant spot to take a break, enjoy the blue sky, and watch the activities of the villagers who have come in to sell their produce.

Market Days
Although there are four weekly market days, Wednesdays and Saturdays are the biggest. Monday and Friday are smaller, but still interesting. Many Maya vendors sell wild coriander, yellow or white corn, chili peppers of various hues, cassava, tamales wrapped in banana leaves, star fruit, mangoes, and much more. Many of the women and children bring handmade crafts as well. Laughing children help their parents. If you're inclined to snap a photo, ask permission first—it wouldn't hurt to buy something, as well. If refused, smile and put your lens cap in place.

RECREATION
Diving, Snorkeling, and Water Sports
The Sapodilla Cayes make up the hooked southern end of the Belize Barrier Reef and the continental shelf, and they offer incredible wall dives and very few dive boats. There are also a number of more gradual walls. In general, most sites offer either beautiful coral formations or lots of fish, but rarely both.

For fishing, the waterways and sea around Punta Gorda offer anglers the rare chance to bag a grand slam (permit, tarpon, bonefish, and snook). Fly-fishing is generally possible between November and May, in shallow areas around the cayes, mangroves, and river mouths. Reel fishing is available throughout the year, up the rivers or in the ocean; cast for snapper, grouper, jacks, barracuda, mackerel, or king fish. Most guides help you bring your fish back and find someone to cook it up for you. Fishing trips can run upward of US$400–500 for four people.

Tours
Garbutt's Fishing Lodge, next to Joe Taylor Creek, at the entrance to Punta Gorda, is run by the Garbutt brothers, a local duo who grew up exploring these waters. They offer one of the most reliable ways to get out to the cayes and go sport fishing, diving, or snorkeling; they also maintain a few cabins on Lime Caye, and you can paddle up the creek in a kayak. Another diving option is **Wild Encounters** (tel. 501/722-2716 or 722-2300), operating out of the Seafront Hotel.

Reef Conservation International (tel. 501/626 1429, www.reefci.com) offers weekly and monthly dive packages, including certification courses and survey diving to help with research projects, always in small groups. It's worth stressing that not only will you be diving in the Sapodilla Cayes—the famous fishhook terminus of the Belize Barrier Reef, internationally renowned for its whale sharks, dolphins, and grouper spawning events—but you will also most likely be the *only* dive boat in the water, an extraordinary opportunity. Nondivers are also welcome. ReefCI offers various packages; there's often a discount for walk-in travelers and last-minute bookings (up to 50 percent). It's also possible to camp on the beach and snorkel the days away. The boat leaves Punta Gorda

THE BIGGEST FISH: WHALE SHARKS OF BELIZE

An opportunity to share the water with a creature larger than a school bus does not come often in life – and is not soon forgotten. If you're diving in southern Belizean waters between March and June, you may be lucky enough to encounter a whale shark. The whale shark (*Rhincodon typus*) is a real shark, with a cartilaginous skeleton and gills, that feeds on plankton like a whale. Most places in which whale sharks can be encountered (Belize, Mexico, Honduras, Madagascar, Australia, Mozambique, the Galápagos Islands, and Djibouti, to name a few whale shark aggregation sites) offer some form of protection to the species, in part by promoting responsible ecotourism.

Biologist Rachel Graham, PhD, has been studying whale sharks since 1998, in the waters of Belize, Cuba, Mexico, the Seychelles, and Madagascar, and is now working with the Wildlife Conservation Society on a global Ocean Giants program. She has spent over 2,000 hours in the water with whale sharks and has had over 1,000 encounters with these famous gentle giants.

I asked Dr. Graham to provide some basic facts about whale sharks, and also talk about her personal experiences sharing the water with them.

What is a whale shark?
Aside from being the largest fish in the sea (up to 20 meters in length and over 15 tons), the whale shark evolved over 90 million years ago to feed on plankton and small fish. Whale sharks bear live young and are believed to be long-lived – living more than 60 years – and may require up to 30 years to mature.

Whale sharks are iconic creatures that put our relatively small lives and aspirations into perspective. They fly the banner for many less charismatic species and

© POLLY WOOD

the largest fish in the world

their movements weave a pattern across our tropical ocean landscapes, linking sites and making them true ambassadors of the seas. I truly believe that the world would be a poorer place without whale sharks, which is why we must protect them.

How is Belize unique in the world in regard to whale shark populations? Belize hosts the only known aggregation of whale sharks that feeds on the eggs of large schools of reproducing snappers. Although this must occur elsewhere in the world, to date, Belize is the only known site where this takes place.

What are some important things to remember when snorkeling or diving with whale sharks? The key rule is not to touch, chase, ride, or harm whale sharks in any way. Stay at least three meters away from the shark unless it comes up to you, in which case do nothing and enjoy the unforced close encounter. I ask boat drivers to not cut off the path of a whale shark when it's moving and to drop guests off 15 meters away from the shark (as opposed to right on top of the animal). We also strongly recommend not using flash photography or underwater motorized vehicles.

What current research has been done with the Belize whale shark population? Much of the work on whale sharks in Belize was undertaken between 1998 and 2004. Their movements, site fidelity, feeding behavior, tourism value, and population size and structure were researched. I found at least 106 individuals identified from over 580 encounters. The majority of sharks encountered were immature males with an average length of six meters. The whale sharks visiting Gladden Spit are capable of arriving exactly when the snappers spawn and leave when spawning ceases to provide enough food. After this, they move

to other feeding sites along the Mesoamerican Barrier Reef, such as Holbox/Isla Contoy and into the Gulf of Mexico to the north; to the south and southeast, they travel to Utila (Honduras) and beyond. Since these studies, the Belizean NGO Friends of Nature (in Placencia) is noting the number of whale sharks encountered and the number of tourists visiting Gladden Spit.

What is the most amazing experience you've ever had swimming with whale sharks? Probably with a whale shark named "Mr. Facey," whose name comes from a Creole word for someone with an attitude. Mr. Facey is a young male (about six meters) who reveled in surprising divers, doing "peekaboo" moves behind them, and swimming up to them and placing his snout in their midriffs. In my case, Mr. Facey swam up to me at 25 meters depth and parked his snout at the level of my stomach. We sat there for a while not really knowing what to do as this was a bit facey for a first date. Since I could not move sideways or downwards, I eventually crawled on top of his head and pushed away against his dorsal fin. He came back several more times, always gently, always hanging in the water. In the end I almost ran out of air and had to surface.

Any scary moments? Never a scary moment. Whale sharks are gentle giants and even though I have encountered many in my nine years of diving with them, I remain in awe of their grace, docility, and curiosity.

To learn more about whale sharks, visit www.wcs.org, www.marinemeganet.org, www. sharktrust.org, or www.shepherdproject.org. To plan your whale-watching trip, contact **ReefCI** in Punta Gorda or **Friends of Nature** in Placencia. Dive shops in either of these areas can help, as well as can the resorts and shops on Glover's Reef Atoll.

TOLEDO'S CHOCOLATE TRAIL

The cacao tree (*Theobroma cacao* or "food of the gods") has gained renewed importance in the culture and economy of Mayans in southern Belize. Thousands of years ago, Maya kings and priests worshipped the cacao bean, using it as currency and drinking it in a sacred, spicy beverage. Today, farmers sell their cacao crop to the **Toledo Cacao Growers Association (TCGA),** a nonprofit coalition of about a thousand small farms which, in turn, sells the beans to acclaimed chocolatier Green & Black's, a UK-based company specializing in fair trade and organic-certified chocolate bars. Some beans remain in Belize, used by a few Maya families and small-batch chocolate makers to produce chocolate for the domestic market. Stop by the **TCGA office** (one block north of the town park on Main Street in Punta Gorda, tel. 501/722-2992, tcga@btl.net) to see if they are offering any tours or products.

Sustainable Harvest International (tel. 501/722 2010, U.S. tel. 919/967-3662, www.sustainableharvest.org), a nonprofit organization working to alleviate poverty and deforestation throughout Central America, is active in Belize's Toledo District. The organization works with more than 100 cacao-growing families, helping them develop multistory forest plots that mimic the natural forest; this provides a diversity of food and marketable produce for the families, plus a home for threatened plants and animals. Coffee, plantains, and other shade-loving crops are planted alongside the cacao trees, under a hardwood canopy – sometimes along with spices like turmeric, black pepper, ginger, and vanilla. Sustainable Harvest Belize estimates that for every acre converted to multistory cacao forest, five acres are saved from destructive slash-and-burn practices. The organization offers sustainable chocolate tours and other voluntourism opportunities at work sites in southern Belize. Accommodations range from rustic homestays to the stilted cabins of Cotton Tree Lodge, where SHI maintains a demo garden.

This revival of southern Belize's cacao industry has also led to choco-tourism. A few area lodges and families have found ways to connect ancient cacao farming with the modern craze for high-quality fair-trade food and products. **Cyrila Cho** and her family, in the village of San Felipe (tel. 501/666-3444 or 501/664-3132, chocolatescirila@gmail.com), are one example, offering a five-hour chocolate tour beginning with a visit to an organic cacao farm and continuing with lunch in Cyrila's home, where she and her daughter then lead a chocolate-making session. Sustainable Harvest Belize also offers half-day cacao trips; contact the organization through the website above.

Ask your hotel hosts about other cacao day trips and tours. In addition to tours, **Cotton Tree Lodge** offers special week-long chocolate packages and produces its own small-batch chocolate bars (call 501/621-8776 to visit the mini-chocolate factory in PG). There's also the Annual **Cacao Fest,** held in late May, celebrating all things chocolate by offering a host of local products – from cupcakes and kisses to cacao wine and martinis – as well as numerous cultural events. For information, visit www.toledochocolate.com.

Cacao is king in Toledo.

© JOSHUA BERMAN

Monday morning and returns on Friday afternoon; check the website for rates.

In addition to diving for fun, ReefCI customers have the opportunity to get involved in a number of projects, such as helping the Belizean Department of Fisheries enforce fish spawning, lobster breeding, and other special preservation zones in the Sapodilla Cayes Marine Reserve (SCMR). The main focus is to understand the complex ecosystem of the SCMR in order to maximize conservation efforts and to monitor the long-term general health of the coral reef. ReefCI customers have the unique opportunity to get involved with the survey work, learn about the environment, and identify fish, coral, and invertebrates—and to combine this with recreational dives and other activities.

BlueBelize Tours (tel. 501/722 0063 or 722-2678, www.bluebelize.com) is owned and run by Dan Castellanos, a local fisherman, guide, and PADI dive master (and operator of BlueBelize Guest House) who specializes in fishing and snorkeling tours. You'll have to catch him when he's not staffing biological research or filming expeditions (last year he worked with National Geographic and BBC film crews and provided support for Matt Lauer's "End of the Earth" segment on the *Today Show*).

Your best bet for caving, hiking, waterfalls, ruins, and culture tours, **Sun Creek Lodge and IBTM Tours** (tel. 501/614-2080, ibtm@btl.net, www.suncreeklodge.com) now has a travel office in Punta Gorda. In addition to all the standard land tours, your German guide, Bruno, can take you to some of Belize's burliest backcountry—including the Maya Divide Trail and Jungle Survival Expedition to Doyle's Delight, Belize's highest peak.

TIDE Tours (tel. 501/722-2129, www.tidetours.org) offers numerous inland and ocean trips, including kayaking, biking, island hopping, fishing, exploring villages, and more. This is the customer service branch of the Toledo Institute for Development and Environment (TIDE; www.tidebelize.org), Belize's only "ridges to reef" NGO. TIDE does

much of the guide training in the area, helping to teach people sustainable, often tourism-related, skills. TIDE staff promote tours to protected areas and give presentations on their work in the Port Honduras Marine Reserve, in Paynes Creek National Park, and on the Private Lands Initiative. They also do tours to archaeological sites, caves, and other inland attractions. Revenue generated from TIDE Tours is used for education and outreach efforts. Half-day kayak/bird-watching trips run less than US$30; a full-day trip to the cayes, US$50 a person. Ask about evening Río Grande float trips in a dugout canoe for US$20 per person. Also ask about multiday tour packages.

NIGHTLIFE

There are a handful of small bars scattered around town, some with pool tables, all with lots of booze. **Waluco's** (it means "son of the soil" in Garifuna) is right across from the ocean, a short walk north of town, and is usually a happening spot, especially during festival times and after soccer games at Union Field.

SHOPPING

Start next door to the airstrip, at the **Maya Bags** craft workshop (www.mayabags.org). About 50 area women participate in this craft and export venture; pick up a hand-embroidered heirloom, a 100 percent linen gift, or a travel bag and support a good cause. If you have time, you can order a custom embroidered design.

Tienda La Indita Maya (24 Main Middle St.) lies just north of Central Park (at the end opposite the clock tower). Also check the **Fajina Craft Center of Belize** on Front Street near the ferry pier. It's a small co-op for quality Maya crafts run by the Q'eqchi' and Mopan women. You'll find baskets, slate carvings, textiles, and embroidered clothes—when they're open, that is. If the door is closed, ask around to get it opened up.

ACCOMMODATIONS
Under US$25

Punta Gorda's seedier options occupy the block of Front Street near the main dock; a good rule of thumb is *not* to book a room that is accessed via a smoky bar and pool hall (e.g., the Mira Mar Hotel). Quieter options are only a few blocks off the waterfront.

St. Charles Inn (tel. 501/722-2149, stcharlespg@btl.net, US$25, US$33 with a/c) is centrally located, with a dozen comfortable rooms and a shady veranda that allows you to observe village life below. Well-kept rooms include private bath, fan, and a small TV.

You're apt to run into all sorts of interesting travelers from around the world at **Nature's Way Guest House** (tel. 501/702-2119, natureswayguesthouse@hotmail.com, US$19 d). Six small wooden rooms are basic and fan-cooled in pleasant surroundings; all share bathroom. Nature's Way serves a good breakfast, and you'll have access to all the activities in the area. The place is run by Chet Schmidt and his Belizean wife. Chet is an American expat and Vietnam veteran who has been here for over three decades; he also spent 13 years teaching in the surrounding villages. He can help arrange kayak trips, jungle treks, camping, exploration of uninhabited cayes, visits to archaeology sites, and Maya and Garinagu guesthouse stays.

A mile and a half outside Punta Gorda, in Cattle Landing, you'll find a uniquely relaxed experience at **Irie Belize** (tel. 501/625-5485, milanusher@yahoo.com, US$18), which offers a few simple rooms by the sea: thatched roof, sand floor and friendly folks. There's a chill bar and grill, and the owner Marlon Usher has a boat for tours, and provides shuttle service from the airport or town. He also can set you up in a backabush campground on the Barranco Road, in a cabin or your own tent. To get to Irie Belize, take the last left as you depart PG, before you hit the curve (look for the sign). Then follow the road until you see the bar on your right.

US$25-50

As you step off the tarmac at the airport, you'll see the **Frontier Inn** (3 Airport St., tel. 501/722-2450, US$33), a two-story white cement building. Good value, tile-floored rooms

have TV, private bath, and hot water; the place is owned by a local airplane pilot. **Charleton's Inn** (tel. 501/722-2197, US$35) is close to everything in town, and James buses stop across the street. The 26 rooms are well kept with hot/cold water, private baths, TV, and either air-conditioning or fans; prices depend on room size and are lower without air-conditioning.

Tate's Guest House (30 Jose Maria Nunez St., tel. 501/722-0147, tatesguesthouse@yahoo.com, US$23–35) is a comfortable, friendly lodging with five double rooms in a quiet neighborhood setting. Rooms without air-conditioning are considerably cheaper. Ask for room 4 or 5; they are spacious with ceiling fans, TV, sunrooms, louvered windows, and tile floors, and each has an additional entrance through the backyard. Internet and breakfast are available.

US$50-100

Occupying a breezy, ocean-looking rise next to the cemetery, **Coral House Inn** (151 Main St., tel. 501/722-2878, www.coralhouseinn.net, US$83–100) is an excellent oceanfront bed-and-breakfast with a small pool and bar and a quiet yard next to the cemetery. It was opened after the owners drove to Belize from Idaho in their VW Microbus (which you'll recognize zipping around town on errands). The four rooms are pleasantly decorated with soft colors, local artwork, and comfortable beds; bicycles and wireless Internet are free for guests. This is where the last prime minister used to stay when in Punta Gorda. Ask about the Seaglass Cottage, a little one-bedroom, one-bathroom, small-kitchen option, pitched on a bluff above the ocean, with a very pleasant rooftop (US$125).

One mile outside Punta Gorda, up Ex-Servicemen Road, **Hickatee Cottages** (tel. 501/662-4475, www.hickatee.com, US$75) is a wonderful option on the edge of the jungle. After you've settled into your well-appointed wooden cottage (with private bathroom, hardwood furniture, ceiling fans, and veranda), take a walk through the beautiful grounds and nature trail, followed by a dip in the delicious plunge pool. Ask about visiting the farm, fruit trees, nursery, orchid tunnel, and butterflies. Your expatriate British hosts are knowledgeable about local flora and fauna, are passionate about their "lifestyle business," and strive to run a green hotel and involve the local community as much as possible. This spot is very popular with birders and naturalists; there are free bicycles to get to and from town. On-site **Charlie's Bar** offers home-cooked, healthy meals (about US$8 for breakfast and lunch, US$17.50 for dinner).

BlueBelize Guest House (tel. 501/722-0063 or 722-2678, www.bluebelize.com, US$70 plus tax) is owned by marine biologist Rachel Graham and grew out of her husband Dan Castellanos's well-respected guiding service. The four furnished apartments are large and tastefully decorated, with one or two bedrooms, en suite bathrooms, kitchenettes or full kitchens, hot and cold water, ceiling fans, and wireless Internet. The rooms open onto verandas or patios—literally a stone's throw from the water's edge. BlueBelize is very popular with visiting doctors, scientists, and volunteers, as well as folks wanting to escape dark cold winters up north.

The **Sea Front Inn** (4 Front St., tel. 501/722-2300, www.seafrontinn.com, US$60–75) consists of the two towering stone buildings that greet you as you drive into the north end of town. The 13 rooms and apartments are also available for monthly rentals. Guests find comfortable, spacious rooms, no two alike, with TV, fans, air-conditioning, private bath, and handmade furniture built with hardwoods. The third floor is the kitchen/dining room/common area that overlooks the ocean.

Also on the waterfront, **Beya Suites** looks like a giant pink-and-white wedding cake (tel. 501/722-2188, www.beyasuites.com, US$75). Inside you'll find bright and cheery staff to show you to one of the comfortable, air-conditioned, tile-floored rooms with large bathrooms and a sinus-clearing floral scent. There's a great rooftop, a restaurant, a bar, a conference area, and fast Internet. Ask about apartments and weekly rates.

Over US$100

Wildlife-loving, adventurous travelers can stay in one of two luxury cottages that fund ongoing crocodilian scientific research and conservation work at **ACES/American Crocodile Education Sanctuary** (by reservation only, tel. 501/665-2762, www.americancrocodilesanctuary.org, US$170). Located downstream from Laughing Falcon Reserve on the Río Grande River, the private wildlife sanctuary is less than a mile from the Caribbean by boat and only a 15-minute drive from Punta Gorda. Solar-operated accommodations, built of Belizean hardwoods and bamboo, have hot and cold water, private bathrooms, and full kitchens equipped with butane stoves and fridges; stays include unlimited crocodile viewing. A four-wheel drive vehicle is available for rent.

Cotton Tree Lodge (tel. 510/670-0557, U.S. tel. 866/480-4534, www.cottontreelodge.com, about US$200 pp all-inclusive) is located 12 miles up the Moho River from Punta Gorda, accessed by boat or via the road to Barranco. Its eleven stilted thatch-roof cabins along the river's edge are connected by a raised plank walkway; ask about the deep-jungle tree house. The lodge is one of several in the area trying to take "green" to new levels; Cotton Tree conducts agroforestry projects with Sustainable Harvest International, has developed a unique septic system using banana plants, and raises 50 percent of the food it serves in its own organic garden. Available activities include the cacao trail, treks to Blue Creek and Hokeb Ha Caves, mountain hikes, river and village trips, visits to ruins, and the like, plus hands-on classes in subjects like chocolate making and Garifuna drumming. Sportfishing and fly-fishing trips are available as well. There is one honeymoon suite with a Jacuzzi and one cabin with wheelchair access.

The area's premier upscale property is **Machaca Hill Rainforest Canopy Lodge** (tel. 501/722-0050, www.machacahill.com, US$725 all-inclusive), located on a forested perch high above the Río Grande and a gorgeous expanse of mature rainforest, 5 miles north of Punta Gorda. Machaca Hill (formerly El Pescador) encompasses 12,000 acres of rainforest and organic citrus, coffee, and cacao farms, including 4.5 miles of riverfront. The property also includes Nicholas Caye, a pristine island in the Sapodilla Cayes. The ocean is a 20-minute boat ride down the river, where you'll head for your sportfishing and snorkeling tours. In-house professional guides will keep guests busy with forays into the surrounding forest—unless you'd rather lounge by the pool, in the restaurant, in the break-away sitting room and veranda, at the spa, or on the screened rainforest veranda of the plush tree house.

FOOD

Punta Gorda offers mainly cheap, local eats, with the added benefit of fresh seafood and a few excellent vegetarian options. Many restaurants are closed on Sundays or for a few hours between meals. The town has several good bakeries, and fruit and veggies are cheap and abundant on market days (Monday, Wednesday, Friday, and Saturday). Some of the best breakfast and lunch joints in the market building—the most delicious of which is **Marril's**—are also only open these days. Ask at any corner store for a sampling of the local Mennonite yogurt and bread. Also be sure to try a seaweed shake, which you can buy fresh and cold at Johnson's Hardware Store, across from the market. The tortilla factory, located just south of the bank, makes fresh tortillas every day; they also make tacos, *panades,* and the like. The shack next to the immigration dock has excellent tacos and sometimes coconut fudge—convenient for that early morning boat trip. The best johnnycakes are baked across the street from the fire station. There are some great fast-food places surrounding Central Park, too, including **Jamal's.**

The **Reef Bar** (tel. 501/626-1429, 11 A.M. to midnight) is a convivial rooftop affair on the water's edge, above the market, with nice views and frequent drum sessions. Lunch and dinner are offered, with a nice selection of fish specials, including conch and lobster in season. There's Garifuna drumming and dancing on Friday nights. Another popular spot for good reason

is the **Snack Shack** (7 A.M.–4 P.M. Mon.–Sat.), with breakfast, US$3 burritos, fruit shakes, French toast, and sometimes bagels.

For Jamaican I-tal food, veggie burritos on whole-wheat tortillas, homemade hummus, fish dishes, and a mellow Rasta-flavored bar/lounge scene, stop by ❰ **Earth Runnins Cafe and Bukut Bar** (7 A.M.–2 P.M. and 5 P.M.–11 P.M., closed Tues.). There's a barbecue on Sunday and occasionally live music. Earth Runnins has some of the best cocktails in town and offers a few computers for Internet (as well as wireless access). Very *tranquilo* atmosphere.

Gomier's Restaurant, located at the north entrance to town, right across from the Punta Gorda welcome sign, offers a delicious veggie menu oozing with whole grains, homemade tofu, and good karma. The restaurant is tiny and has tasty and creative daily specials, such as barbecued tofu served with baked beans, bread, and coleslaw, plus a veggie grain casserole, served with a salad (about US$5), a bulging soysage burger (only US$3), and tofu pizza. There are also fresh fruit juices, soy milk, and soy ice cream. Gomier opens around 8 A.M. and closes around 7 P.M. (though he often closes up shop at random times). It's closed on Sundays.

Look for the **Cotton Tree Chocolate Shop** (No. 2 on Front Street, just south of the Texaco Station, tel. 501/621-8776, www.cottontreechocolate.com). In addition to free tours and chocolate samples, you'll find espresso and pastries. Covered outdoor seating area faces the ocean.

Keep an eye out for **Mr. Buns,** who pedals around on his bike with homemade cinnamon rolls and cheese buns.

Emery's (11:30 A.M.–10 P.M., with a few breaks between meals) is one of the most reliable places in town for a solid lunch or dinner; slow service makes it easy to meet people over daily seafood specials. Another easy place to recommend is ❰ **Marian's Bayview Restaurant** (open daily for lunch and dinner), located on a rooftop over the water, on the south edge of Punta Gorda (across from Nature's Way). Marian's serves East Indian cuisine, seafood, or a good ole plate of rice 'n' beans for US$4—all with a view of Guatemala and Honduras across the water. **Nature's Way Guest House** and the **Sea Front Inn** both serve filling breakfasts, although the Sea Front may make you wait a while for it. Another option is **El Café**, around the corner from Charlton's Inn, with cheap, diner-style Belizean food all day long.

Merenco's, next to the **Ice Cream Parlor** (1.5 blocks south of the park), has super-cheap burritos, famous fishbowl-size natural fruit juices, and a selection of dinners, as well as sandwiches and snacks. **Grace's Restaurant** is a longstanding joint with typical Belizean fare like stew chicken (US$4), tasty conch soup (US$5), and great fry jacks; it's slow service with a frown.

A few Chinese restaurants offer reliable chop suey, especially **Tai Song** and **Fei Wang,** although the latter is sometimes frequented by sloppy drunks. Some expats call **Hang Cheon,** on Main Street next to Marenco's, the best Chinese in town.

As you follow the highway north out of Punta Gorda, look for a driveway and sign on your left just as the road is about to turn away from the sea, and you'll find ▓ **Mangrove Inn and Restaurant** (tel. 501/722-2270 or 622-1645, open from 5 P.M. every day). This is a family affair—literally! You have to walk through your hosts' living room to get to the dining balcony. Your cook, Iconie, has worked in fancy resorts across Belize but prefers working at home these days. Expect savory fish dishes, pot pies, lasagna, fresh salads, and rolls; it runs roughly US$6–10 per plate.

Outside town: **Charlie's Bar,** at Hickatee Cottages, is open to the public on weekends; there are three entrée choices, home-cooked from local, healthy ingredients (about US$16 per person).

INFORMATION

Look for the **Toledo Visitors' Information Center** on Front Street, not far from the Town Dock (8:30 A.M.–4:30 P.M., Sat. till noon). This is a concerted effort by local businesses to provide excellent and organized information to tourists; they'll recommend accommodations, tour companies, transport, and so on.

The **Toledo Ecotourism Association** (TEA; tel. 501/722-2531, teabelize@yahoo. com, www.plenty.org/mayan-ecotours), whose office is currently based in the Toledo Visitors' Information Center, is where you sign up to stay in one of the eight village guesthouses. Also, contact the Toledo branch of the **Belize Tourism Industry Association** (tel. 501/722-2119) and look for a copy of *Total Toledo* magazine. You can also call the **Belize Tourism Board** at tel. 501/722-2531.

SERVICES

Near the municipal dock, you'll find the **immigration** office (tel. 501/722-2247). Opposite that are a couple of government buildings, including the **post office. PG Laundry,** across from the Belize Bank, is open 8 A.M.–5 P.M. (closed Sundays) and charges by the pound. Fill your gas tank at the **Texaco** station at the north end of Front Street, right across from the ocean; they accept travelers checks and credit cards.

Health and Emergencies

Contact the police at 501/722-2247, the fire department at 501/722-2032, and the hospital at 501/722-2026.

Money

The **Belize Bank** (tel. 501/722-2326, 8 A.M.–1 P.M. Mon.–Thurs., 8 A.M.–1 P.M. and 3–6 P.M. Fri.) is right across from the town square; it is still the only bank in town and has a new ATM. Grace's Restaurant is also a licensed **Casa de Cambio** and can change dollars, *quetzales,* or travelers checks. You may also find a freelance moneychanger hanging around the dock at boat time.

Internet Access

There are two Internet places just north of the park, both with freezing air-conditioning and decent machines. Of these, **Dreamlight** is open 8 A.M.–8 P.M.

Groceries

Check at Mel's Mart or one of the two Supaul's stores for local yogurt. Sophia Supaul's store on Alejandro Vernon Street (known locally as "Green Supaul's") carries lots of foreigner-friendly food treats, including imported cheeses (French brie in PG!), local jams and honey, a decent wine selection, couscous, white chocolate, vegetables, and fruits.

GETTING THERE
By Air

Daily southbound flights from Belize City to Dangriga continue to Placencia and then to Punta Gorda. This is the quickest and most comfortable way to get to Punta Gorda. For the return trip, **Tropic Air** (tel. 501/226-2012, U.S. tel. 800/422-3435, www.tropicair.com) and **Maya Island Air** (tel. 501/223-1140, U.S. tel. 800/225-6732, www.mayaislandair.com) each offer five daily flights to Placencia, Dangriga, and Belize City, between 6:45 A.M. and 4 P.M. Tropic is usually more reliable and frequent in southern Belize.

By Land

Punta Gorda is just under 200 miles from Belize City, a long haul by bus, even with the newly surfaced Southern Highway speeding things up. Count on three to four hours by car, five to six hours by express bus, or seven hours in a non-express. **James Bus Lines** (tel. 501/702-2049) has a centrally located terminal in Punta Gorda, across from the police station, and runs up to nine daily buses between Punta Gorda and Belize City, departing 4 A.M.–3 P.M., with one express at 6 A.M. The first departure from Belize City is a 5:30 A.M. express, then service continues until 3:30 P.M. (the only other express is this last bus of the day); the fare is US$11 one-way. A few other bus lines make the trip, but much less regularly.

Remember you can get off in Independence and take a boat to Placencia, or you can get off at any other point, like Cockscomb Jaguar Preserve or Dangriga.

To the Maya Villages

Every day has a different schedule, but buses go to the Maya villages on Monday, Wednesday,

the James bus to Punta Gorda

© JOSHUA BERMAN

Friday, and Saturday, generally around noon, and depart from Central Park. From here it's possible to get to the villages of **Golden Stream, Silver Creek, San Pedro, San Miguel, Aguacate, Blue Creek, San Antonio,** and others. Some buses drop you off at the entrance road, leaving a walk of a mile or two. Check at the TEA office or the Toledo Visitors' Information Center for updated village bus schedules.

GETTING AROUND
Punta Gorda's taxis will take you anywhere within city limits for about US$3–4; look for their green license plates. It's US$10 to drive the six miles to Machaca Hill and US$12.50 to Jacintoville and the Tranquility Lodge. Or call on **Pablo Bouchub's Taxi and Tour**

Service; Don Pablo is also a natural healer and can get you all manner of medicinal herbs and roots (tel. 501/722-2834 or 608-2879). Also try **Castro's Taxi** (tel. 501/602-3632) or **Galvez's Taxi Tours** (tel. 501/722-2402). Ask your hotel if they provide a free bicycle, or rent one at **Abaisehi** ("One Love") bike rental, on North Street, for US$12.50 per day (less for a few hours). Abaisehi also offers a bike tour of Punta Gorda.

Car Rental
The folks at Sun Creek Lodge will deliver a rental car anywhere in Punta Gorda (if you're not staying with them); it's US$70/day or US$420/week for their 4x4 vehicles (tel. 501/614-2080, suncreek@hughes.net).

Upcountry

The wild, unique, and stunning southwestern chunk of Belize is referred to as "upcountry" or simply "the villages." There are dozens more waterfalls, caves, trails, and hills to climb than appear in these pages. Punta Gorda is also the gateway to the southern hook of the Belize Barrier Reef, a swoosh of tiny cayes and coral that are the least visited of any of Belize's Caribbean jewels.

THE CAYES
There are some 138 islands off the coast, although only a handful are actually made of sand and palm trees. This is where you'll find the **Port of Honduras Marine Reserve (PHMR),** the largest protected area in the country, spanning 160 square miles of ocean. The southernmost reach of Belize's Barrier Reef lies just offshore, as do the **Snake Cayes** and a few other accessible island paradises. There is a week-long raging party on **Hunting Caye** at Easter time, and you'll find camping and simple accommodations on **Lime Caye.**

You've also got the **Sapodilla Cayes Marine Reserve,** declared a World Heritage Site in 1996 as part of the Belize Barrier Reef Reserve

System. The reserve covers about 80 square miles and is co-managed by the Fisheries Department and the **Toledo Association for Sustainable Tourism and Empowerment** (TASTE; 53 Main St., Punta Gorda Town, tel. 501/672-0191), an NGO that focuses on using the reserve to educate local youths about their environment. Contact the office to find out about volunteering or possible tourism-related projects centered around these stunning islands.

MAYA ARCHAEOLOGICAL SITES
Nim Li Punit
At about Mile 75 on the Southern Highway, near the village of Indian Creek, 25 miles north of Punta Gorda Town, Nim Li Punit is located atop a hill with expansive views of the surrounding forests and mountains (it's about a half mile west of the highway, along a narrow road marked by a small sign). The site saw preliminary excavations in 1970 that documented a 30-foot-tall carved stela, the tallest ever found in Belize—and among the tallest in all the Maya world. A total of about

© JOSHUA BERMAN

stela at the Nim Li Punit ruins

25 stelae have been found on the site, most dated A.D. 700–800. Although looters damaged the site, excavations by archaeologist Richard Leventhal in 1986 and by the Belize Institute of Archaeology (IOA) in the late'90s and early 2000s uncovered several new stelae and some notable tombs. The stelae and artifacts are displayed in the very nice visitors center built by the IOA. The ruins are open from 7 A.M.–5 P.M. daily; entrance is US$5. The small office can be reached at 501/665-5126.

Lubaantun

On a ridge between two creeks, Lubaantun ("Place of the Fallen Stones") consists of five layers of construction, unique from other sites because of the absence of engraved stelae. The site was first reported in 1875, by American Civil War refugees from the southern United States, and first studied in 1915. It is believed that as many as 20,000 people lived in this trading center.

Lubaantun was built and occupied during the Late Classic Period (A.D. 730–890). Eleven major structures are grouped around five main plazas—in total the site has 18 plazas and three ball courts. The tallest structure rises 50 feet above the plaza, and from it you can see the Caribbean Sea, 20 miles distant. Lubaantun's disparate architecture is completely different from Maya construction in other parts of Latin America.

Most of the structures are terraced, and you'll notice that some corners are rounded—an uncommon feature throughout the Mundo Maya. Lubaantun has been studied and surveyed several times by Thomas Gann and, more recently, in 1970, by Norman Hammond. Distinctive clay whistle figurines (similar to those found in Mexico's Isla Jaina) illustrate lifestyles and occupations of the era. Other artifacts include the mysterious crystal skull, obsidian blades, grinding stones (much like those still used today to grind corn), beads, shells, turquoise, and shards of pottery. From all of this, archaeologists have determined that the city flourished until the 8th century A.D. It was a farming community that traded with the highland areas of today's Guatemala, and the people worked the sea and maybe the cayes just offshore.

To get to Lubaantun from Punta Gorda,

MAYA MYSTERIES: THE CRYSTAL SKULL

Allegedly found in 1924 at the Lubaantun archaeological site, by the daughter of explorer F. A. Mitchell-Hedges on her 17th birthday, this perfectly formed quartz skull has been the subject of much mystery and controversy over the years. Was it made by the Mayans? Aliens? Atlanteans? Did Mitchell-Hedges plant it for the pleasure of his daughter? Or is the whole story a hoax, as some suggest? The questions persist. The skull currently resides in Canada.

go 1.5 miles west past the gas station to the Southern Highway, then take a right. Two miles farther, you'll come to the village of San Pedro. From here, go left around the church to the concrete bridge. Cross and go almost a mile—the road is passable during the dry season.

Uxbenka

Difficult to access and largely unexcavated (actually, some recent excavations were covered back up to protect them), Uxbenka was discovered in 1984 and has more than 20 stelae. The site is perched on a ridge overlooking the traditional Maya village of Santa Cruz and provides a grand view of the foothills and valleys of the Maya Mountains. Here you'll see hillsides lined with cut stones. This construction method is unique to the Toledo District. Uxbenka ("Old Place") was named by the people of nearby Santa Cruz. It's located just outside Santa Cruz, about three miles west of San Antonio village. The most convenient way to see the site is with a rental car. Ask around the village for a guide; you may find someone, or you may not.

RÍO BLANCO NATIONAL PARK

Established in 1994 and co-managed by the Rio Blanco Mayan Association (composed of seven executives from Santa Elena and Santa Cruz who volunteer their time as the park wardens) and by the government, the park provides amazing scenery and natural beauty for the tourist and an alternative income for members of neighboring villages. Río Blanco National Park is 105 acres and encompasses a spectacular waterfall that is 20 feet high and ranges from a raging 100 feet wide during the rainy season to about 10 feet during the dry season. The pool that the waterfall empties into has been deemed bottomless by the locals (one claims to have dived 60 feet and never touched bottom). If you are adventurous, you can jump off of the surrounding rocks and fall 20 feet into the crystal-clear water. There are also two miles of nature trails, which include the cave where the Río Blanco river enters the mountain and a suspended cable bridge over the river.

Surrounding the falls is a beautiful forest with thriving flora and fauna populations and a possibility of jaguar sightings. Because the park is a community-based effort, 10 percent of all entrance fees collected at the park go back to the villages.

The surrounding villages are made up of indigenous Maya, and a trip to the park allows visitors to drive through Santa Cruz, a very typical village with thatch huts and no electricity, where women wear traditional dresses.

Accommodations and Services

Camping and furnished dorms are available at Río Blanco National Park. Visit the **Craft & Snack Shop,** run by the Río Blanco Women's Association. They have everything from baskets to jewelry to embroidery, plus the only cold refreshing beverages you'll find out there! A picnic area is under the visitors center.

Getting There

The park is located about 30 miles west of Punta Gorda, between the villages of Santa Cruz and Santa Elena on the road to Jalacte. Buses to the village of Jalacte run on Monday, Wednesday, Friday, and Saturday, leaving from the square in Punta Gorda at 11:00 A.M., 11:30 A.M., and noon; they return from the village on the same mornings before 5 A.M. Also, local tour guides in Punta Gorda can be hired to take you to Río Blanco National Park; ask around Carysha's or at one of the Punta Gorda tour operators listed above.

◖ AGUACALIENTE WILDLIFE SANCTUARY

The Aguacaliente Wildlife Sanctuary comprises a myriad of ecosystems, including rainforests, lagoons, and grasslands found nowhere else in Belize and hosting an incredible variety of flora and fauna. The diversity of its native and migratory bird species makes it one of the premier birding destinations in the entire Mesoamerican Biological Corridor. During the dry season, hike through lush seasonal grasslands to see the great jabiru stork, the roseate spoonbill, or any of the other 150 bird species that call Aguacaliente home. During the rainy season, take a canoe through the lagoons to see four-foot tarpon and flowering orchids.

From Punta Gorda, take the Southern Highway north until the turnoff to Laguna Village (approximately 10 miles, to just before the Toledo Forest Department Machaca Station), then turn left and travel about three

---

SPEAKING Q'EQCHI': IS THERE HAPPINESS IN YOUR HEART?

Most of southern Belize's people of indigenous descent speak Q'eqchi' Maya – though some communities speak the Mopan language instead, which is more closely related to Yukatek or Itzá Maya.

In Belize, you may see the word Q'eqchi' spelled different ways. "Kekchi" is how Protestant missionaries labeled the Maya of southern Belize, and British colonial officials wrote "Ketchi." Today, in neighboring Guatemala, the indigenous leaders of the Guatemalan Academy of Maya Languages (ALMG) have developed a standard Maya alphabet that the Q'eqchi' leaders in Belize have begun to use as well.

Making even a small attempt to speak and learn the language of your Maya hosts will deepen your experience. Never mind the laughs your funny accent will attract – your noble attempts are an amusing novelty, and no one means any harm. Persist, and you will be rewarded in ways you would never have expected – indeed, learning another language in such an immersing setting is one of the most humbling and empowering experiences a traveler can have.

Should you want to learn more than the few words presented here, track down the grammar book and cassette tapes by Q'eqchi' linguist Rigoberto Baq, available in Guatemala

City at the Academia de Lenguas Mayas (www. almg.org.gt) or at their regional offices in Coban, Alta Verapaz (in the municipal palace), or Poptán, Petén.

BASIC PHRASES

All Q'eqchi' words have an accent on the last syllable. One of the first things you will probably be asked is, "B'ar xat chalk chaq?" (bar shaht chalk chok), to which you can respond, "Xin chalk chaq sa' New York" (sheen chalk chok sah New York, or wherever you are from).

In Q'eqchi', there are no words for "good morning," "good afternoon," or "good evening." You simply use the standard greeting, "Ma sa sa' laa ch'ool" (mah sah sah laa ch'ohl), literally, "Is there happiness in your heart?" (In Q'eqchi', however, you wouldn't use a question mark because the "Ma" indicates a question.) A proper response would be "Sa in ch'ool" (sah een ch'ohl), "Yes, my heart is happy."

Although it is falling out of custom with the younger generation, if you are speaking with an older woman or man, she or he would be delighted to be greeted with the terms of respect for the elderly: "Nachin" (nah cheen) for an elder woman, and "Wachin" (kwah cheen) for an elder man.

miles into Laguna; bear right and look for the Aguacaliente Wildlife Sanctuary.

The suggested donation is US$5 per person, payable in neighboring Laguna Village. Complimentary use of dories is included.

UPCOUNTRY VILLAGES

This is a loose term used to describe the Toledo District settlements to the west of Punta Gorda. Most villagers are Q'eqchi' or Mopan Maya, whose descendants fled to Belize to escape oppression and forced labor in their native Guatemala. Anthropologists now believe that the Mopan were probably the original inhabitants of Belize, but that they were forcibly removed by the Spanish in the late 17th century. The Q'eqchi' were close neighbors with the Mopan and the Manche Ch'ol, a Maya group completely exterminated by the Spanish. The older folks continue to maintain longtime traditional farming methods, culture, and dress. Modern machinery is sparse—they use simple digging sticks and machetes to till the soil, and water is hand-carried to the fields during dry spells. It's not an easy life.

On the outskirts of each town, the dwellings are relatively primitive; they often have open doorways covered by a hanging cloth,

THE TOLEDO VILLAGES

If you decide to go swimming in one of Toledo's beautiful rivers, you might want to ask first, "Ma wan li ahin sa' li nima'" (mah kwan lee aheen sa li neemah), which means "Are there crocodiles in the river?"

"Ani laa kab'a?" (anee lah kabah) means "What's your name?" You can respond: "Ix (eesh) WOMAN'S NAME in kab'a (een kabah)" or "Laj MAN'S NAME in kab'a (een kabah)."

MORE PHRASES AND VOCABULARY

Chan xaawil? (chan shaa kwil) – What's up?
Jo xaqa'in (hoe shakaeen) – Not much, just fine.
B'an usilal (ban ooseelal) – Please.
B'antiox (ban teeosh) or T'ho-kre (ta-HOH cree) – Thank you.
Us (oos) – Good.
Yib' i ru (yeeb ee rue) – Bad, ugly.
Hehc (eheh) – Yes.
Ink'a (eenk'ah) – No.
K'aru? (kaieeroo) – What?
B'ar? (bar) – Where?
Joq'e? (hoekay) – When?
Jarub'? (hahrueb) – How many?
Jonimal tzaq? (hoeneemahl ssahq) – How much does it cost?
Chaawil aawib (chah kwil aakweeb) – Take care of yourself (a good way to say goodbye).

Jowan chik (hoekwan cheek) – See you later.
Wi chik (kwee cheek) – Again.
wa (kwah) – tortilla
kenq (kenk) – beans
molb' (mohlb') – eggs
kaxlan wa (kashlan kwah) – bread
tib' (cheeb) – meat
tzilan (sseeelan) – chicken
kuy (kue-ee) – pork/pig
kar (car) – fish
chin (cheen) – orange
kakaw (cacao) – chocolate
ha' (hah) – water
woqxinb'il ha' (kwohk sheen bill hah) – boiled water
cape (kahpay) – coffee
sulul (suelul) – mud
ab' (ahb) – hammock
chaat (chaht) – bed
nima' (neemah) – river
kokal (kohkahl) – children
chaab'il (chahbill) – good
kaw (kauw) – hard
najt (nahjt) – far
nach (nahch) – close

(Special thanks to Clark University anthropologist Liza Grandia, PhD, who spent four years among the Maya.)

hammocks, and dirt floors. Chickens and sometimes dogs wander through the houses in search of scraps. People use the most primitive of latrines or just take a walk into the jungle. They bathe in the nearest creek or river, a routine that becomes a source of fun as much as cleanliness.

As you walk into town, past the thatched homes on each side of the road, it becomes apparent that the effects of modern conveniences are only beginning to arrive. When a family can finally afford electricity, the first things that appear are a couple of lights and a refrigerator—the latter allows the family to earn a few dollars by selling chilled soft drinks and such. After that, it's a television set; you can see folks sitting in open doorways, their faces lit by the light inside.

Laguna

Laguna is a small Q'eqchi' Maya village of around 250 people, living against a backdrop of limestone karst hills. The scenery is also home to howler monkeys and many types of parrots, which can be seen flying over the village daily. The village's namesake lagoon is now a protected area called **Aguacaliente Wildlife Sanctuary** and is one of the best spots in Toledo to go birding. With the new mile-long boardwalk, it is easily accessible (except for the first five minutes of the walk, which can get a bit muddy). Laguna is also home to a loosely organized women's crafts group that produces *cuxtales* (traditional woven Maya bags, pronounced "CUSH-tal-les"), table mats, beading, baskets, embroidery, beaded necklaces, and earrings.

There is also a long muddy farmers' road that leads to the confluence of Blue Creek and the Moho River; this 2–3 hour flat hike is very beautiful but only recommended in the dry season (March–May). There's also a super-cool cave about a 20-minute hike away; ask your guide. To get to the village, take the Laguna bus directly to the village, or take any bus that can drop you at the Laguna junction (10 miles from Punta Gorda). It is only about two miles to the village from the highway. Laguna

is part of the TEA, and there is a guesthouse with a nice veranda with hammocks; beds are equipped with mosquito nets. A TEA guesthouse stay includes all meals and the opportunity to interact and cook or farm with local Q'eqchi' indigenous people.

San Pedro Columbia

To get there, take the main road in Punta Gorda, which goes inland about 10 miles toward San Antonio. Just before you get to San Antonio, a dirt track to the right breaks off to the village of San Pedro. If you're without a vehicle, take the bus, which makes this trip about three times a week. Or you can hire a cab by the day—a bit pricey, but the most convenient way to come and go according to your personal schedule. The owner of the Shell station you pass once in the general area has also been known to take people into the villages for a fee.

San Pedro is one of the biggest of the villages. A small Catholic church in town has an equally small cemetery. It sits on a hilltop surrounded by a few thatched dwellings. Not far away is a prefab-looking school that was erected, we were told, with the assistance of National Guardsmen from the United States who were getting jungle training.

Local guides take visitors out of their village past a towering ceiba tree and into what appears to be secondary forest. If there's been rain, the going is muddy. We slogged up and down hilly trails, over little streamlets, and through glens. It's worth it. Everywhere is a stunning parade of life. Hummingbirds, toucans, parrots, and other birds flit about the canopy. Our guide pointed out a jaguar's track, plainly imprinted in the mud of the trail. We were able to follow it for a spell before it led off into the bush. We were impressed by the coolness of the jungle interior and more impressed with the guide's knowledge. He could point out and name every variety of flora and fauna along the path. He plucked wild coriander for us to savor and led us to a farmer's *milpa,* where corn was drying under a *palapa.* What a difference between the oppressive heat in the open

© JOSHUA BERMAN

THE TOLEDO VILLAGES

a typical, tranquil Upcountry village

cornfields and the cooling relief in the dark shadows of the jungle.

San Antonio

After leaving San Pedro and returning to the main road, make a right turn and you'll soon be in San Antonio, just down the road. The village of San Antonio is famous for its exquisite traditional Q'eqchi' embroidery. However, the younger generation is being whisked right along into 21st-century Belizean society, so who knows how much longer it will survive.

There should be a local tourism representative in San Antonio who can give helpful advice about the area and direct you to local guides in town willing to take you to **Ho Keb Ha Caves** and **Blue Creek** (bring your swimsuit). This is great bird-watching country.

From here the road is passable as far as Aguacate (another Q'eqchi' village). But if you intend to visit the ruins at **Pusilha,** near the Guatemala border, you must travel either on foot or horseback. Another ruin, **Uxbenka** (described earlier in this chapter), is west of San

Antonio near the village of Santa Cruz and is easy to get to via the trucks that haul supplies a couple of times a week. Not known by anyone but locals until 1984, Uxbenka is where seven carved stelae were found, including one dating from the Early Classic Period.

◖ Blue Creek Cave

This village of some 275 Q'eqchi' and Mopan Maya was first settled in 1925 and is also called Ho Keb Ha, "the place where the water comes out," describing this spot where the Río Blanco emerges from the side of a mountain, becoming Blue Creek and home to an extensive cave system. You'll need a guide who's familiar with these caves; ask at Punta Gorda or at one of the nearby Maya villages. Many of these folks know the nearby caves well. Go prepared with flashlights. You can swim up to 600 yards into the cave; it's pretty stunning.

San Miguel

This friendly Q'eqchi' Maya village has a village guesthouse, a nearby river, thatched houses, traditional dress, and children carrying dishes and clothes in buckets on their heads from the swiftly flowing river. San Miguel is also experiencing intense change with recent access to electricity, water, better roads, and increased educational opportunities.

During times when the villagers are harvesting coffee, you can witness the process of picking, shelling, drying, and grinding organic coffee. Tours of the village, cave, and *milpa* are also available. All activities are US$3.50 per hour. The Mayan site of Lubaantun, famous for the discovery of the Crystal Skull and unique architectural features, is about three miles from San Miguel. You can either walk to the site or charter a vehicle (US$7.50). The village does not have a restaurant, but meals are cooked and served at local homes (US$3.25 breakfast or supper, US$4 for lunch).

San Miguel is home to one guesthouse, run by Maria Ack and her family, who live across the street from the accommodations. The guesthouse is a traditional thatch structure comprised of a bedroom, which may be shared among multiple travelers (although it is likely you will be the only one there); a main living area with a desk, chair, and hammock; and a covered outdoor veranda with hammocks. They also provide electricity, linens, and mosquito nets, and a shower and toilet are on the premises. Rates are under US$10 for a dorm bed. The family offers cooking lessons where you can learn to make corn tortillas (*Xoroc li cua* in Q'eqchi'), along with *caldo* and other traditional dishes. They also offer handicraft lessons on calabash carving and traditional embroidery.

San Miguel buses leave from Punta Gorda two times a day, Monday–Saturday. You can catch the village bus at the park in the center of town. The first bus leaves at 11:30 A.M. and is marked "Silver Creek." The bus has a 30-minute layover in Silver Creek before heading on to San Miguel. The second is marked "San Miguel" and leaves the park at 4:30 P.M. The bus ride is about an hour and 15 minutes (the 11:30 bus is half an hour longer due to the layover). Buses leave San Miguel for Punta Gorda at 5:15 A.M. and 12:45 P.M.

Barranco

Barranco is an isolated Garinagu village, where activities include fishing along the river as well as traveling by dugout canoe up the river into the Sarstoon-Temash Forest Reserve to see howler monkeys, hickatees, and iguana. Return for a refreshing glass of *hiu* (a spicy drink made of cassava and sweet potato) and an evening of drumming. Get there by bus from the park in Punta Gorda, or by boat from the Punta Gorda dock. Ask for times, as transportation is scarce; charter boats can be arranged.

Numerous individuals of Barranco's 600 inhabitants have traveled far from their village to become some of Belize's most renowned musicians, painters, and researchers; many have earned advanced degrees in their fields, giving Barranco one of the highest per capita PhD percentages in Central America.

(VILLAGE GUESTHOUSES AND HOMESTAYS

For the culturally curious traveler who doesn't mind using an outhouse, the unique experiential accommodation programs in the Toledo District offer a three-fold attraction: 1) firsthand observation of daily rural life in southern Belize, 2) a chance to interact with one of several proud, distinct cultures while participating in a world-renowned model of ecotourism, and 3) a unique way to go deep into the lush, natural world of the forests, rivers, caves, and waterfalls of southwestern Belize.

Simple guesthouse and family home networks in participating villages offer a range of conditions and privacy, but most are simple, primitive, and appreciated most by those with an open mind. Activities include tours of the villages and surrounding natural attractions. For nighttime entertainment, traditional dancing, singing, and music can usually be arranged; otherwise it's just stargazing and conversation.

These are poor villages, and the local brand of ecotourism provides an alternative to subsistence farming that entails slashing and burning the rainforest. Additionally, the community-controlled infrastructure helps ensure a more equitable distribution of tourism dollars than most tour operations (members rotate duties of guiding, preparing meals, and organizing activities).

Dem Dats Doin' (office in Punta Gorda located next to Scotia Bank, demdatsdoin@ btl.net) has maintained the Maya Village Homestay Network since 1991, offering traditional village accommodations, in which you stay in a Maya home, maybe in a hammock (not much privacy, but plenty of cultural exchange). The office in Punta Gorda is open only on Wednesday and Friday mornings. It's less than US$20 per person per night for homestays and all meals; families are in the villages of Aguacate, Na Luum Ca, and San Jose. The same folks run the Toledo Botanical Arboretum (US$5 pp).

Prices and Practicalities

For the Toledo Ecotourism Association (TEA) program, a registration fee, one night's lodging, and three meals run about US$25 per person per night; this includes two guided tours. Other activities, like storytelling, crafts lessons, paddling trips, and music/dance sessions may be extra, but will be extremely reasonable—especially with a group. TEA is currently based in the main BTIA tourist office in Punta Gorda (tel. 501/722-2096, teabelize@yahoo.com, www. plenty.org/mayan-ecotours). TEA is the umbrella organization for the guesthouse program, which is cooperatively managed and includes village representatives in their respective towns (at last count there were 6 participating villages, down from 12 a few years ago). Participants must arrange their visits from the central TEA office in Punta Gorda, where you will be briefed about the program and told how to get out to the village or villages of your choice.

Bring comfortable walking shoes, bug repellent, a poncho, a swimsuit, a flashlight with extra batteries, and lightweight slacks and a long-sleeved shirt. Photos of your own family and home—or postcards of your hometown—are appreciated and good icebreakers. Be sure to fill out the evaluation form afterwards to help TEA improve the program.

2009 update: TEA is doing the best it can in the face of relatively low interest in the program. Though TEA still successfully hosts travelers from all over the world, the overall low number of visitors makes it difficult to properly maintain some facilities—not to mention villagers' interest. In addition, TEA doesn't have funding for a person to work at the Punta Gorda office full-time (it's too much of a commitment for farmers and housewives); the temporary solution has been to staff the office with volunteers from the local BTIA, with whom TEA shares an office. Despite these problems, TEA is an engaging community-based tourism project that is well worth supporting and experiencing; if you sign up, please let us know how it goes!

Meals

You'll usually pay about US$13 for three meals. Breakfast in Maya villages is generally eggs, homemade tortillas, and coffee or a cacao drink. All meals are ethnic and lunch is the largest meal of the day; it is often chicken *caldo* (a stew cooked with Maya herbs) or occasionally a local meat dish like iguana ("bush chicken") or gibnut (paca, a large rodent). Fresh tortillas round out the meal. Supper is the lightest meal of the day and generally includes "ground" food (a root food such as potatoes) that the guide and visitors might "harvest" along the jungle trail. The *comal* (tortilla grill) is always hot, and if you're invited to try your hand at making tortillas, go ahead—this is a wonderful way to break the ice with the usually shy Maya women. In a Garinagu village, be prepared for simple but traditional cooking. It can be tasty, but it's guaranteed to be different. We especially like the *sere,* or fish in coconut milk.

OUTLYING ACCOMMODATIONS

For those who choose not to participate in the guesthouse or homestay programs, there is an eclectic selection of unique resorts and bush camps from which you can base your southern wanderings. Discover the villages by day and then kick back and soak in the surroundings by night, in a hammock or over a candlelit dinner, to the sound of birds and crickets.

Near Jacintoville

Tucked away on the San Felipe Road, about eight miles outside Punta Gorda, **Tranquility Lodge** (no phone, www.tranquility-lodge.com, US$60–75) offers four well-appointed rooms popular with avid bird-watchers and orchid lovers; both have plenty to explore right here on Tranquility's 20 lush acres (only five of which are developed at the lodge area). There were 75 species of orchids at last count—both planted and volunteers—and more than 200 identified species of birds. Rates include breakfast; rooms have clean tile floors, private bath, air-conditioning, and fan. When there are no other guests, it's like having your own private lodge. Upstairs from the rooms is a beautiful, screened-in (but very open) dining room, where you'll enjoy gourmet dinners for US$15. All rates are negotiable in the off-season. There's direct access to an excellent swimming hole on the Jacinto River, as well as a number of walking trails.

Near Big Falls

Hugging a lush bend of the Río Grande as it sweeps past the roadside village, **The Lodge at Big Falls** (tel. 501/614-2888, www.thelodgeatbigfalls.com, US$155) is a classy, quiet, riverside retreat in a peaceful, well-manicured, and vividly green clearing. The six cabanas are ideal for the nature-loving couple looking for a comfortable base from which to explore the surrounding country or just to laze in the pool and listen to the forest sounds. Special rates are offered for multiple nights and families.

Sun Creek Lodge (tel. 501/614-2080, www.suncreeklodge.de, US$40–60) is the backabush dream of a German-Belizean couple who have worked very hard to construct the four octagonal cabanas with center post and thatch roof. Some have shared jungle showers and toilets, a few have private bath, and there is the spacious Sun Creek Suite for families or groups. Sun Creek is popular with European backpackers in that comfy-yet-primitive way. The on-site tour company will take you wherever you want to go in the area, with active hikes being their forte—including trips and expeditions unavailable anywhere else. Car rental is available. Sun Creek Lodge is located at Mile 14 on the Southern Highway, about two miles from "Dump." If you haven't arranged for a pickup in Punta Gorda, look for the broken cement sign with "Sun Creek" painted on it as you drive south on the Southern Highway—get off the bus there.

If you're driving through the area, make time for lunch (or any other meal) at **Coleman's Cafe** (tel. 501/720-2017, 7 A.M.–7 P.M., afternoon break from 3–6 P.M.), located just off the highway, on the entrance road to Rice Mill. This is home-cooked Belizean food at its finest, and the restaurant is run by a friendly and accommodating family. Creole dishes, cohune cabbage, and East Indian curries are among the offerings.

Near San Pedro Columbia

Two miles upriver from the village of San Pedro Columbia, situated on 70 acres, you'll find **Maya Mountain Research Farm (MMRF)** (www.mmrfbz.org), a registered NGO and working demonstration farm that promotes sustainable agriculture, renewable energy, appropriate technology, and food security using permaculture principles and applied biodiversity. The farm also lives on solar power and offers a number of courses. The property has over 500 species of plants (including lots of cacao), and the staff are working to establish an ethnobotanical garden of useful plants with their Q'eqchi' Maya names and uses. The farm suffered a devastating fire in 2008 but quickly recovered. Accommodations are simple rustic affairs, with solar lighting and Internet access.

Near Blue Creek

The same outfit that has a resort and research center on South Water Caye also has one in Toledo. **International Zoological Expeditions** (IZE; U.S. tel. 800/548-5843, ize2belize@aol.com, www.ize2belize.com) has a lodge at the Blue Creek Rainforest Station, which can host cottage guests at the rustic site. Guests must hike one-third of a mile up into the rainforest along a trail that borders Blue Creek to reach the group of simple cabins with bunk beds, screens, lights, and electric fans. One cabin has a queen-size bed. Bathrooms are in the main lodge, where meals are served. Your rate of US$115 per person per night covers lodging, three meals, and two daily activities of your choice (for example, guided hikes into the rainforest and cave).

Belize Lodge and Excursions

This one-of-a-kind operation features a circuit of remote, all-inclusive, upscale safari-style lodges on a vast swath of protected lowland tropical jungle stretching from the Maya Mountain foothills to the sea. (The property was pieced together out of land that otherwise would have gone to shrimp and cattle farms.) Belize Lodge and Excursions (tel. 501/223-6324, U.S. tel. 888/292-2462, www.belizelodge.com, from US$285–400 per day per person) offers a unique three-lodge circuit in an all-inclusive package, modeled after similar circuits in the African safari scene. Guests can land at BLE's private airstrip and begin their eco-adventures at either Indian Creek Lodge, located across the road from the Nim Li Punit archaeological site, or Ballum Na (House of the Jaguar), where guests stay in a unique jaguar enclosure and see big cats out their bedroom windows. They continue their journey by floating down the pristine Golden Stream, to accommodations at Jungle Camp, and then on to Moho Caye Lodge, located in the Port Honduras Marine Reserve. Rooms and amenities are quite luxurious, considering how remote they are, yet they are in tune with the surrounding natural landscape.

GETTING UPCOUNTRY

To get to Maya country from Punta Gorda, you have several choices. If you plan an overnight with the homestay or guesthouse programs, TEA will assist you. They may simply direct you to the appropriate village bus from Punta Gorda.

The **Chun Bus** (tel. 501/722-2666) makes the run to San Antonio Monday, Wednesday, and Friday, returning to Punta Gorda Tuesday, Thursday, and Saturday (about US$4 roundtrip). This bus doesn't stop in San Pedro; instead you will have to leave the bus at the road and trek in several miles. You can also catch a bus as far as Pueblo Viejo, "the edge of the known world." Catch the Chun Bus at Central Park to ensure getting a seat. Remember: No buses run on Sunday.

If traveling by car, you have the option of exploring every little road you see (four-wheel drive recommended). From the turnoff for Punta Gorda at Mile 86 on the Southern Highway, take the road north. At about Mile 1½, there will be a turnoff on the right that heads for San Pedro and other villages.

Across the Border

One of the many Central American backpacker routes involves entering Belize after a visit to Tikal, then re-entering Guatemala via boat from southern Belize. From there, one can travel up the Río Dulce, take a bus to Guatemala City, or take a series of hired cars to the Honduran border. Conversely, some backpackers do a loop from Punta Gorda that includes Livingston, Río Dulce, and Tikal, then heads into Belize again.

Before leaving Punta Gorda, you'll get your passport stamped at the customs office at the municipal dock; you'll also be charged a US$4 PACT fee to help support Belize's protected areas—or maybe you won't. If traveling directly to Livingston, be sure to walk up the hill from the dock to check in at the **Migracion Office,** where you'll get stamped and pay a tiny fee (less than US$2); if you fail to do this, you'll have problems leaving Guatemala. In Puerto Barrios,

Migracion is located 1.5 blocks east of the dock and is open 24 hours. If leaving for Belize, you'll need to pay a US$10 exit fee here when you get your passport *ponchada* (stamped). Be sure to do this *before* buying your boat ticket to Punta Gorda. There is no fee to enter Belize.

INTO GUATEMALA
Livingston

A day trip or overnight to the coastal vacation town of Livingston can be an exciting breath of activity after sleepy Punta Gorda. Livingston is situated on the Caribbean shore and the wide mouth of the Río Dulce, making it an ideal base for upriver jungle explorations. Highly recommended is a trip to the **Siete Altares** waterfalls, which one reader described as "perhaps the most beautiful place I've ever been to in Guatemala." Local Garinagu men offer walking tours.

Livingston boasts numerous restaurants, open-air street cafés, and a rich Garinagu presence (most readily experienced at the Rasta-colored **Abafu Bar,** where you'll find live drumming, potent bitters, and lots of reggae).

There is an ATM in Livingston, but it is unreliable. Keep a stash of cash.

ACCOMMODATIONS AND FOOD

Livingston is a popular destination for vacationing Guatemalans and foreign tourists alike. Mid-priced accommodations are abundant and close to the pier; expect to pay US$15 for a double with private bath. In fact, prices of everything from beer to hotel rooms are less than half of what they are in Belize, and many budget accommodations are available as well. **The African Place** is a real bargain; it's a 10-minute walk out of "downtown," and US$7.50 gets you a double room in a fantastically decorated mosaicked castle-like structure. Highly recommended by one friend is **Casa Rosada** (US$20): "Good food, great coffee, shared bath, very clean."

You can also catch a boat up the river to **El Hotelito Perdido** (www.hotelitoperdido.com, dorm US$6, bungalows US$18–24), in the middle of the rainforest on Río Lampara, a small river connected to Río Dulce. It is popular with

Check in at the Punta Gorda immigration office when leaving or arriving in the country.

© JOSHUA BERMAN

backpackers, run by a Polish couple, and located in the deep bush. There's no beach on the river, just a dock. Another option up the Río Dulce is **Texan Bay Marina** (www.texanbaymarina.com), which is always a good time, serving Texas-sized burgers in the middle of the jungle.

GETTING THERE AND AWAY

A triangular boat run between the municipal docks of Punta Gorda, Puerto Barrios, and Livingston shuttles travelers across this section of Central American coastline. The trip is done in rather small boats with minimal shelter, so prepare for cold, wet, and rough seas during the rainy season. The direct leg between Livingston and Punta Gorda runs only Tuesdays and Fridays, leaving at 7 A.M. from Livingston, then shoving off from Punta Gorda at 10 A.M. If you miss that boat, you'll have to travel first to Puerto Barrios (the hour-long trip costs US$25), then catch a regular *colectivo* water taxi to Livingston (leaves about every hour, 40 minute trip, under US$4). There are two trips every day between Punta Gorda and

Puerto Barrios, one based in Belize (**Requena's Charter Service,** tel. 501/722-2070, water-taxi@btl.net) and the other based in Guatemala (**El Chato,** tel. 502/948-5525, pichilingo2000@ yahoo.com). Boats leave Punta Gorda around 9:30 A.M. and 4 P.M. daily and depart from Puerto Barrios at 10 A.M. and 2 P.M. Another boat man is **Memo's,** with daily departures to Puerto Barrios and Livingston and also Río Dulce tours (tel. 501/625-0464).

Puerto Barrios

This trash-strewn, rough-and-tumble port town is primarily a deep-water banana-loading dock and not much more. Puerto Barrios has a reputation for hard drugs, prostitution, and bar fights. Many travelers stop only as long as necessary to make their boat connections and get the hell out of Dodge. Express buses to Guatemala City leave the **Terminal de Autobuses Litegua** (eight blocks from the dock in Puerto Barrios, a 10-minute walk or US$1.50 cab ride); the 5.5-hour ride costs about US$5.

INTO HONDURAS

There is no legal direct boat service to Puerto Cortés, Honduras, from the Punta Gorda docks, but there is service from Placencia and Dangriga, and those boats stop in Punta Gorda for immigration purposes. Otherwise, to get to Honduras from Punta Gorda, first take a daily boat shuttle from Punta Gorda to Puerto Barrios. Buses and taxis in Puerto Barrios can whisk you to the Honduran border. Look for one of the many minivans trolling for passengers around the docks and market; it's about an hour to the border at Corinto, then another 1.5 hours to the coastal backpacker hideout of Omoa, Honduras. From there, it is under an hour to Puerto Cortés and San Pedro Sula, where you'll find connecting buses and flights to Copan, the Bay Islands, and points farther south. There is a new air service between Savannah airstrip near Independence (about two hours north of Punta Gorda) and San Pedro Sula; inquire at Maya Island Air (www.mayaairways.com).

THE TOLEDO VILLAGES

NORTHERN BELIZE

The Orange Walk and Corozal Districts are overlooked by most tourists, even though the area's protected areas have some of the highest densities of jaguars and rare birds on the continent. In addition, the extensive coastal lagoons of Shipstern and Sarteneja are largely undeveloped, home to manatee, dolphin, and flocks of native and migratory birds.

The second-largest district of Belize, Orange Walk encompasses vast tracts of wilderness, peaceful waterways, and Maya ruins; Orange Walk Town is the area's hub, a small commercial and farming center on the Northern Highway.

New River Lagoon, which you must navigate to reach the Lamanai ruins, is Belize's largest body of fresh water—28 miles long, its dark waters are smooth, changing with every cloud

that passes. Morelet's crocodiles and hickatee turtles inhabit these waters, along with abundant fish, wading birds, and waterfowl.

The north's largest town is the bayside city of Corozal, just nine miles from the Río Hondo and Mexican border, 96 miles north of Belize City. There, you'll enjoy a peaceful stroll along the seawall as you plot where to go next: North to Mexico? East to Sarteneja? Or southeast by boat to San Pedro?

PLANNING YOUR TIME

Few travelers choose to stay in Orange Walk or Corozal Town, even though both have some decent budget and midrange options. Both towns are small enough to be explored in a couple hours each. There are day trips from either town, to Chetumal, Mexico, and the Lamanai

© JOSHUA BERMAN

HIGHLIGHTS

(Banquitas House of Culture: Located in Orange Walk Town and featuring exhibits on history, industry, and culture, this is one of the country's premier museums (page 236).

(New River and New River Lagoon: A fabulous wildlife-viewing float trip can also take you to Lamanai(page 236).

(Indian Church Village Artisans Center: Much of the craftwork you'll find at this community-based initiative is inspired by the ancient designs of the nearby archaeological site of Lamanai (page 241).

(Río Bravo Conservation Area: Go deep into the northwest to explore this area before continuing to the ruins and lodge at Chan Chich; you'll participate in a variety of research projects at Programme for Belize's field stations. Getting there necessitates a long boat ride, a sturdy truck, or a chartered flight (page 243).

(Sarteneja: This remote village of fishermen and boat builders is the perfect off-the-beaten-path destination for curious travelers (page 253).

LOOK FOR **(** TO FIND RECOMMENDED SIGHTS, ACTIVITIES, DINING, AND LODGING.

and Cerros archaeological sites. To really dig into the north, plan on at least a night or two at the Lamanai Outpost Lodge or in Indian Church village; by being situated so close to the ruins and not having to travel hours to reach them, this is the best, fullest way to experience Lamanai and the jungle around it. Lamanai is also offered as a day trip from Belize City, the North Cayes, Orange Walk, and Corozal. Add an extra couple of days if you attempt to venture to the Río Bravo Conservation Area or Gallon Jug Estates. Some travelers link Corozal into a loop that includes Ambergris Caye, using the boat service between Corozal and San Pedro, with a chance to stop off at Sarteneja, a remote fishing village.

HISTORY

Belize's northern region was settled in the 19th century, by refugees from southern Mexico during the Caste War, and you'll still hear more Spanish than English here. What's left of two forts, Mundy and Cairns, in Orange Walk Town reminds one that this was the scene of violent battles between Belizean settlers and war-minded Maya trying to rid the area of outsiders. The last battle took place in 1872.

For centuries, before settlement by farming-inclined mestizo refugees from Yucatán (Mexico) in 1849, this was timber country. Logs from the north and middle districts of Belize were floated down the New River to Corozal Bay, and then to Belize City; from

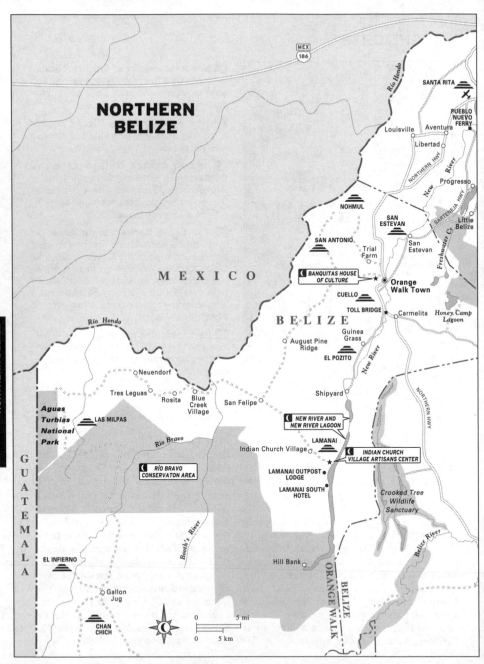

NORTHERN BELIZE

MEX 186

SANTA RITA

PUEBLO NUEVO FERRY

Louisville Aventura

Libertad

NORTHERN HWY

New River

Progresso

SARTENEJA HWY

Little Belize

NOHMUL

SAN ESTEVAN

SAN ANTONIO

San Estevan

Trial Farm

MEXICO

BANQUITAS HOUSE OF CULTURE

Orange Walk Town

CUELLO

Freshwater Ck.

TOLL BRIDGE Carmelita

Honey Camp Lagoon

BELIZE

Guinea Grass

August Pine Ridge

EL POZITO

New River

Río Hondo

Neuendorf

Tres Leguas Rosita

Blue Creek Village

San Felipe

Shipyard

NORTHERN HWY

Aguas Turbias National Park

LAS MILPAS

Río Bravo

NEW RIVER AND NEW RIVER LAGOON

LAMANAI

Indian Church Village

INDIAN CHURCH VILLAGE ARTISANS CENTER

GUATEMALA

RÍO BRAVO CONSERVATON AREA

LAMANAI OUTPOST LODGE

LAMANAI SOUTH HOTEL

Crooked Tree Wildlife Sanctuary

Booth's River

EL INFIERNO

Gallon Jug

Hill Bank

ORANGE WALK

BELIZE

Belize River

CHAN CHICH

0   5 mi

0   5 km

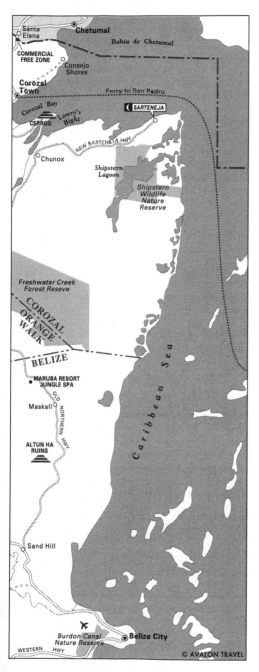

there they were shipped all over the world. If you travel about two miles south past Orange Walk Town, you'll find a toll bridge over the New River. Tree harvesting is still going on, and you'll encounter large logging trucks crossing the toll bridge.

At one time, sugarcane was the most important Belizean crop. Now farmers grow more and more citrus, and beef producers supply not only the local market but are tapping into the export market. Caribbean rum (a product of sugarcane) is still big business in this area. During the cane harvest, the one-lane highway is a parade of trucks stacked high with sugarcane and waiting in long lines at the side of the road to get into the Tower Hill sugar mill. Night drivers beware: The trucks aren't new and often have no lights.

Orange Walk Town

Located 66 miles north of Belize City and 30 miles south of Corozal, Orange Walk is one of the larger communities in Belize. Its 15,000 inhabitants work in local industry and agriculture. If passing through, stop and look around. The town has two banks, a few hotels, and a choice of small, casual eateries. Roads stemming from Orange Walk access 20 villages and a handful of small, lesser known archaeological sites. Elsewhere in Orange Walk District, you'll find historic sites including **Indian Church Village;** a 16th-century Spanish mission; and the ruins of Belize's original sugar mill, a 19th-century structure built by British colonialists. Heading west and then southwest, you'll find **Blue Creek,** a Mennonite development where Belize's first hydroelectric plant was built. This is also your gateway to New River Lagoon and the Lamanai ruins.

SIGHTS AND RECREATION
【 Banquitas House of Culture

Banquitas Plaza (tel. 501/322-0517, 10 A.M.–6 P.M. Tues.–Fri., 8 A.M.–1 P.M. Sat.) is an exhibition hall that presents a broad exhibit about Orange Walk–area history, culture, and industry, and the work of local artisans. The hall also hosts special traveling exhibits on Maya and African archaeology and the modern culture of Central America. This is the place for a slow evening watching the light die on the New River and the landscaped grounds of the Banquitas Plaza. The plaza comes alive on Friday and Saturday nights, when young Orange Walk couples stroll the river walk enjoying the cool evening together. The nearby amphitheater hosts monthly cultural activities.

【 New River and
New River Lagoon

Trips up and down the New River and around the New River Lagoon are adventures for the entire family, with a chance to see Morelet's crocodiles and iguanas sunning on the bank. By day you'll see the sights of verdant jungle

and wildlife along the river. Most people combine a river trip with a visit to the ruins of Lamanai. It is the most impressive way to approach the site, and a time-saver, as well, compared to going by land. Contact your Orange Walk hotel or any of the local guide companies. Night safaris can be equally exciting. It's a chance to see the habits of animals that come out to play only after the sun sets; you'll need the help of a good guide and a spotlight.

Honey Camp Lagoon

About 20 minutes south of Orange Walk Town, on the old Northern Highway, you can join the locals to indulge in white sandy beaches and shady coconut trees as nice as any on the cayes. It's mostly a locals' picnic spot, and you'll find some basic food services and tons of people during Semana Santa (Easter week).

Nohmul

This major Maya ceremonial center means "Great Mound," and the top of the pyramid is the highest point in the Orange Walk and Corozal Districts. Twin ceremonial groups are connected by a *sacbe* (raised causeway). The center catered to a thriving population in the Late Pre-Classic and Late Classic Periods (350 B.C.–A.D. 250 and A.D. 600–900, respectively) and controlled an area of about 12 square miles. Nohmul ("Big Hill") was named by the people living in the vicinity of the site.

Not much has been consolidated for tourists here. The entrance to the site is about 10 miles north of Orange Walk Town, in the sugarcane fields west of the village of San Pablo; it is one mile from the center of the village. Public transportation from Belize City, Orange Walk Town, and Corozal passes through the village of San Pablo several times daily.

ACCOMMODATIONS

There has been an interesting sprouting of several new, well-equipped, business-oriented hotels in Orange Walk, plus a few old budget standards.

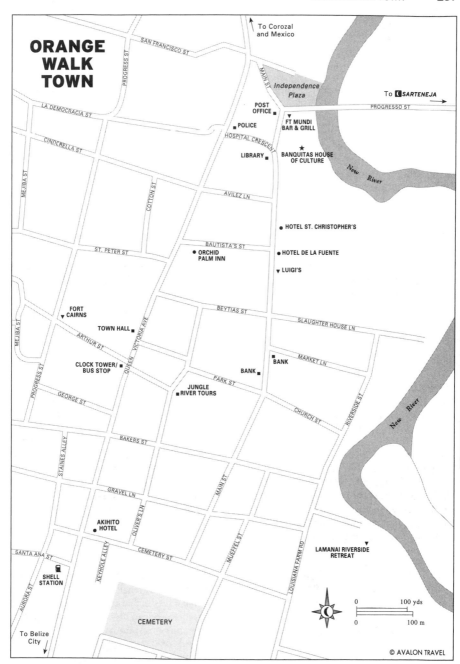

ORANGE
WALK
TOWN

To Corozal
and Mexico

Independence
Plaza

To ⊂SARTENEJA

NORTHERN BELIZE

New River

© AVALON TRAVEL

Under US$25

Akihito Hotel (tel. 501/302-0185 or 302-3018, akihitolee@yahoo.com) charges US$15 for singles and doubles, more for air-conditioning; all rooms have shared bath. Soon, they'll offer dorm beds for US$9. Run by the Lees, this is a good sleep for the dollar. It's clean, with cool tiled interiors and a downstairs shop serving beverages and a few necessities, and offers just about every basic amenity the traveler needs: laundry service, credit-card phone calls, high-speed Internet, cable television, and a whirlpool tub. The Lees are an excellent source of information about the Orange Walk area, which restaurants are good, and which bars to avoid. By press time they may have completed the rooftop dormitories and terrace. Did we mention the whirlpool tub?

Lucia's Guesthouse (68 San Antonio Rd., tel. 501/322-2244, US$11) is a basic traveler's rest house; most rooms have private baths. Air-conditioning is available. Coming from Belize City, hang a left at the fire station downtown, and then it's about a half mile down on the left.

US$25-50

Run by four sisters who take good care of things, **Hotel St. Christopher's** (tel. 501/302-1064, www.stchristophershotelbze.com) is an ideal stop for drivers; it has colorful, traditional Spanish-feeling rooms with tiled floors and private bath for US$27 with fan, US$46 with air-conditioning. A few of the rooms have shared balconies with a view of the river. Right next door, you'll find great value at **Hotel de la Fuente** (tel. 501/322-2290, www.hoteldelafuente.com, US$35–60), where 12 varied rooms offer a range of amenities, including fully equipped apartments and free wireless Internet; it's great for business travelers. Around the corner, **(Orchid Palm Inn** (22 Queen Victoria Ave., tel. 501/322-3947, www.orchidpalminn.com, US$40–60) offers similar amenities, including a nice lobby and wireless Internet. All these places are centrally located.

FOOD

Orange Walk may actually have the highest per capita number of Chinese restaurants in all of Central America, but **Aki Hito** or **Tan's Delight** are probably your best bets. Or maybe **Lee's Chinese Restaurant,** near the fire station, with passable versions of chicken chow mein (US$3.25), sweet and sour fish (US$7.50), or black soybean lobster (US$12).

(Central Park Restaurant (New Market near the bus terminal, a.k.a. "Fort Cairns") is actually a collection of six restaurants styled after the old-school open market located next door. They serve everything a hungry traveler could want: burgers, tacos, empanadas, pizza, hot dogs, bacon and eggs breakfasts, sweet cakes, waffles, and the usual assortment of beverages, all for a couple of bucks. The **Ft. Mundi Bar & Grill,** located at Banquitas Plaza, is better for drinks than meals, as are the handful of music-blasting bars by the park.

Another traveler's standard for a basic Belizean meal is **Luigi's,** next door to Hotel de la Fuente. For pizza delivery, call 501/322-2669.

There are many other cafés in town, offering cuisines of many nationalities. Check any of them out, but you might first make sure the restaurant meets your hygiene standards.

Entering town on the Belize/Corozal Road, you will see a **service station/convenience store** on the left. This store has light snacks, cold drinks, and a few staples. If you are headed by car to Río Bravo or Chan Chich, this is a good place to top off the gas tank.

Orange Walk's fanciest meals are found outside of town at **El Establo.** Ask any taxi driver to take you there.

SERVICES

This is the commercial center of the district, so there are many small shops selling all kinds of merchandise, including agricultural supplies and used American clothing. There are two major banks on Main Street, a few Internet cafés, and basic traveler services, like laundry and cheap food.

GETTING THERE AND AWAY
By Bus

There is no main station, but the buses traveling between Corozal and Belize City all stop to idle next to the Town Hall (across from the park) for a few minutes before lumbering on—they pass about every hour until 6 P.M. Some of the buses are express, but it's hard to tell which ones. Sunday service is about every two hours. Buses to Indian Church village (near Lamanai) leave only on Friday, returning Monday. There are hourly buses to San Felipe to the west and Sarteneja to the east.

By Boat

Going by boat is a pleasant way to get anywhere, especially up the New River to Lamanai. Enjoy nature's best along the shore of the river and the labyrinthine passageways through the wetlands. You never know what you'll see next—long-legged birds, orchids in tall trees, hummingbirds, crocs—it's like a treasure hunt. Bring your binocs. Ask anywhere for directions to the boat dock.

Tours and Transport

All regional tour operators in Orange Walk, Corozal, and Belize City offer tours to Lamanai. Ask about night safaris, bird-watching tours, and sunrise trips up and down the New River. Most hotels employ their own licensed guides, or know how to find one. Tour providers throughout San Pedro and Caye Caulker also transfer guests into the interior, where they often subcontract local boats and guides for the trip to the ruins. Most tours include entrance fee, drinks, and a catered lunch as part of the deal; prices range US$40–60 per person. Freddy Gomez, owner of **Transport Services** (21 St. Peters St., tel. 501/322-2037 or 609-9641), has a 15-passenger van and a Crown Vic and is a highly knowledgeable guide who can arrange insightful tours anywhere in Orange Walk District. **Elvis Usher** (tel. 501/669-6686, elvisusher31@hotmail.com) is another notable guide and is available for group or private tours.

Jungle River Tours (20 Lovers La., tel. 501/302-2293 or 615-1712) is the oldest operating guide service, with a reputation for giving the best tours of Lamanai. Jungle River boats leave from docks near Banquitas Plaza in Orange Walk. **Errol Cadle Eco Tours** (errolcadle1@yahoo.com) is a top-notch guide and will cater to travelers who wish for a less frenetic pace when it comes to their boat trips; meals and drinks are provided. **Lamanai EcoAdventures** (tel. 501/322-3653 or 610-1753) also has a dock just south of the Tower Hill Toll Bridge, as does **New River Cruises.**

Lamanai Archaeological Zone

Set on the edge of a forested broad lagoon are the temples of Lamanai. One of the largest and longest-inhabited ceremonial centers in Belize, Lamanai is believed to have served as an imperial port city encompassing ball courts, pyramids, and several more exotic Maya features. Hundreds of buildings have been identified in the two-square-mile area. Archaeologist David Pendergast headed a team from the Royal Ontario Museum that, after finding a number of children's bones buried under a stela, presumed that human sacrifice was a part of the residents' religion. Large masks that depict a ruler wearing a crocodile headdress were found in several locations, hence the name Lamanai ("Submerged Crocodile").

The ruins of Lamanai huddle to one side of New River Lagoon and sprawl westward through the forest and under the village of Indian Church (which was relocated by the government from one part of the site to another in 1992). It is reachable by boat from Orange Walk or by road from San Felipe. The Institute of Archaeology has done a great deal of work at this site, and the main temples are impressive even to the uneducated eye. The High Temple can be climbed to yield a 360-degree view of the surrounding jungle and lagoon.

With the advent of midday cruise ship tours, the site boasts a new dock, visitors center, craft shops, and museum. Lamanai is also a popular site for day-trippers from Ambergris Caye and can be quite crowded in the middle of the day, especially during the week. If you want a more solitary experience, go early in the morning or late in the afternoon, as cruise ship crowds arrive at noon and disappear in less than two hours. The reserve is open to the public 8 A.M.–5 P.M.

THE RUINS

Today, visitors can see four large temples, a residential complex, and a reproduction stela of a Maya elite, Lord Smoking Shell. Excavations reveal continuous occupation and a high standard of living into the Post-Classic Period, unlike in other colonies in the region. Lamanai is believed to have been occupied from 1500 B.C. to the 19th century—Spanish occupation is also apparent, with the remains of two Christian churches and a sugar mill that was built by British colonialists.

The landscape at most of the site is overgrown, and trees and thick vines grow from the tops of buildings. The only sounds are birdcalls and howler monkey voices echoing off the stone temples. These are some of the notable sites:

- **The Mask Temple N9-56:** Here two significant tombs were found, as well as two Early Classic stone masks. It was built around 450 A.D.

- **The High Temple N10-43:** At 33 meters (100 feet) high, this is the tallest securely dated Pre-Classic structure in the Maya area. Among many findings were a dish containing the skeleton of a bird and Pre-Classic vessels dating to 100 B.C. The view above the canopy is marvelous, and on a clear day you can see the hills of Quintana Roo, Mexico.

- **The Ball Court:** The game played in this area held great ritual significance for the Maya, though because of the small size of

There are surprises around every corner at Lamanai.

© ROSEY GOODMAN

Lamanai's court, some think it was just symbolic. In 1980, archaeologists raised the huge stone disc marking the center of the court and found lidded vessels on top of a mercury puddle. Miniature vessels inside contained small jade and shell objects.

- **Royal Complex:** Excavated in 2005, this was the residence of up to two dozen elite Lamanai citizens; you can see their beds, doorways, and the like.

- **Jaguar Temple N10-9:** Dated to the 6th century A.D., this temple had structural modifications in the 8th and 13th centuries. Jade jewelry and a jade mask were discovered here, as was an animal motif dish. Based on the animal remains and other evidence, archaeologists now believe that this was the site of an enormous party and feast to celebrate the end of a drought in 950 A.D.

Wildlife

The trip to the site is great; it's located in Orange Walk District on the high banks of

New River Lagoon, about 50 miles north-west of Belize City. Most people travel by boat through tropical flora and fauna, and on the way you might see such exotics as black orchids, old tree trunks covered with sprays of tiny golden orchids, and a multitude of bird life, possibly even the jabiru stork (the largest flying bird in the New World).

This area is a reserve, so look for some wildlife you might not see in other, more inhabited areas. On the paths, you'll see numbered trees that correspond to an informational pamphlet available from the caretakers at the entrance of Lamanai Reserve.

Birders, look around the Mask Temple and High Temple for **black oropendola** and their drooping nests. The **black vulture** is often spotted slowly gliding over the entire area. A woodpecker with a distinct double-tap rhythm and a red cap is the male **Guatemalan ivorybill**. Near the High Temple, the **collared aracari**, a variety of toucan, sits on the highest trees and chirps like an insect. The **citreoline trogon** is covered with color: a yellow chest, a black-and-white tail, and a back of blue and green. Though it looks as if the **northern jacana** is walking on water, it's the delicate floating vegetation that holds the long-toed bird above the water as it searches along the water's edge for edible delicacies.

Other fauna spotted by those who live there are jaguarundi, agouti, armadillo, hickatee turtle, and the roaring howler monkey. Up in the village, pay a visit to the **Xochil Ku Butterfly Farm,** an effort by Don Guillermo Melchor Ramos.

◀ Indian Church Village Artisans Center

Contribute directly to the local economy by shopping at this community-based organization, founded in 2000 with the assistance of professional archaeologists, artisans, and architects working at the nearby Lamanai site. The center provides workspace, tools, material, craft training, English classes, and a computer center to interested villagers. The center has a small shop at the Lamanai site, or you can check out the artisans' wares at their workshop in the village. Artisans produce silver and bronze jewelry, hand-sewn purses, bags, embroidered pillowcases, and fired clay statues. Most of the artwork emulates artifacts found at the Lamanai site, including silver pendants of the Lord Smoking Shell stela. Stop by the village workshop yourself or ask your guide to take you by the shop at the Lamanai site. Also ask about the **"Carretas Culturales"** tour, which will take you through the forest and village in a quaint Mennonite cart to visit the Artisan Center and Butterfly Farm and lunch at **Las Orquídias Restaurant** (US$25 per adult, tel. 501/603-1068 or 663-7797).

Getting There

Most visitors use one of the tour companies listed above or the transfer services of their lodge, but it is possible to do it yourself as well. A two-person boat transfer from Orange Walk should cost about US$125, less if you can get in with a bigger group. You can drive the San Felipe road in about 1.5 hours, depending on road conditions. Or you can take the village bus to Indian Church, leaving Orange Walk at 4 p.m. on Fridays and Mondays. The same buses depart Indian Church at 5:15 a.m. on the same days, so you'll have to make a weekend out of it—or more. On the opposite end of the time, comfort, and price spectrum, you can charter a 15-minute flight from Belize City to Lamanai Outpost Lodge's airstrip with one of Belize's private charter services.

ACCOMMODATIONS

The Indian Church villagers have been hosting groups of foreign archaeologists, anthropologists, and biologists (and the odd gringo volunteer) for decades. In addition to the places listed below, there are a few informal homestay options available. Find out the latest developments in the village's foray into tourism by calling the community phone at 501/309-1015, or just wander into town and see what you find. Note that Indian Church is off the electricity and telephone grid, and power is provided by solar panels and gasoline generators. All budget options provide meals and cultural activities and can hook you up with local guides for the ruins and wildlife tours.

US$25-50

Olivia and David Gonzalez (tel. 510/603-1068, 660-3826, or 309-1015, from US$20–30 per person) have moved up from rustic wooden rooms connected to their home to a row of modern cement rooms with private bath and basic amenities, including a few hours of electricity each evening. **Doña Blanca Hotel** (tel. 501/603-7243 or 309-1015, US$25 s/d, more for new cabanas) has 15 rooms with private bath, solar power, and hot/cold showers.

Jungle Lodges

About a half mile up the bank of the lagoon from the Lamanai archaeological site, **Lamanai Outpost Lodge** (tel. 501/223-3578, U.S. tel. 888/733-7864, www.lamanai.com, from US$195–340) is one of Belize's premier jungle retreats. From the moment the staff greets you at the dock, you know you're in capable, welcoming hands. The lodge boasts 16 elegantly rustic thatch-roof, rough-hewn wood cabanas detailed with converted brass oil lamps and other amenities that contribute to an old-fashioned feel (although a couple of rooms add plasma-screen TV, air-conditioning, and wireless Internet access to the old-timey mix). Outside, lush, landscaped grounds of orchids, ceiba trees, and palmettos provide cooling shade as you walk the gravel paths. Below the resort's lodge and dining room (which are the only parts of the complex visible from the river) lies the shore of the lagoon, where you'll find a dock, a swimming area, canoes, boats of various types, and an assortment of beach chairs. The dock is particularly peaceful at sunset. Activities keep you busy from pre-dawn hikes and canoe trips to nighttime "spotlight cruises." There are many all-inclusive packages that include meals and transit to and from Belize City and allow guests to take advantage of all the guided tours.

The owners of Lamanai Outpost are involved in several scientific research projects that also allow nature-study opportunities for guests. Study topics include local bats, archaeology, howler monkeys, Morelet's crocodiles, and ornithology. Guests with some group programs can participate in the work.

Another option is **Lamanai South** (www.lamanaisouth.com), just a bit farther up the lagoon from Lamanai Outpost Lodge. It is a simpler affair than its neighbor, and a bit cheaper at US$150.

Both lodges are low-key, escape-to-nature kind of settings, perfect for the bird-watcher, Mayaphile, naturalist, or traveler who wants to get away from the tourist trail for a while. The area is rich in animal life, including more than 300 species of birds, as well as crocodiles, margays, jaguarundis, anteaters, arboreal porcupines, and the fishing bulldog bat.

FOOD

In Indian Church village, you'll find cheap local food (about US$5 a meal) at the **Grupo de Mujeres Las Orquidias Restaurant**. This is a communal effort of nine women from nine families who are adept at dealing with both groups and individuals. **Doña Blanca** also serves food at her hotel.

West of Orange Walk Town

CUELLO RUINS

Four miles west of Orange Walk on Yo Creek, on the property of a Caribbean rum warehouse, are the minor ruins of **Cuello**. Check in at the gate office (tel. 501/322-2141, 8:30 A.M.– 4:30 P.M.), then investigate these relatively undisturbed ruins, consisting of a large plaza with seven structures in a long horizontal mound. There are three temples; see if you can find the uncovered ones. These structures (as in Cahal Pech) have a different look than most Maya sites. They are covered with a layer of white stucco, as they were in the days of the Maya.

The ruins of Cuello were studied in the 1970s by a Cambridge University archaeology team led by Norman Hammond. A small ceremonial center, a proto-Classic temple, has been excavated. Lying directly in front is a large excavation trench, partially backfilled, where the archaeologists gathered the historical information that revolutionized previous concepts of the antiquity of the ancient Maya. Artifacts indicate that the Maya traded with people hundreds of miles away. Among the archaeologists' out-of-the-ordinary findings were bits of wood that proved, after carbon testing, that Cuello had been occupied as early as 2600 B.C., much earlier than ever believed. Archaeologists now find, however, that these tests may have been incorrect, and the age is in dispute.

Also found was an unusual style of pottery— apparently in some burials, clay urns were placed over the heads of the deceased. It's also speculated that it was here, over a long period, that the primitive strain of corn seen in early years was refined and developed into the higher-producing plant of the Classic Period. Continuous occupation for approximately 4,000 years was surmised, with repeated layers of structures all the way into the Classic Period.

Continuing West

As the road meanders west from there, numerous small villages dot the border region. Occasionally you see a soft drink sign attached to a building, but there's not much in the way of facilities between Orange Walk and Blue Creek. Heading west from San Felipe, you soon find flat, open farmland, with Mennonite accoutrements, dominating the landscape. Low, open rice paddies provide great bird-watching opportunities as well as placid scenery.

Soon, however, you hit the foothills of the Maya highlands near **Blue Creek** village. Climbing up into the foothills you can see the flatlands of the Río Hondo and New River drainages to the east. The small village to the right is **La Union**, on the other side of the Mexico border. This part of Orange Walk District is much hillier and has an increasingly wild feel to it. In the village of Blue Creek, you'll find **The Hillside Bed & Breakfast** (tel. 501/323-0155, US$40) on the left coming up the hill. At the top of the hill is the **Linda Vista Credit Union** and a gas station/ general store. Fill the tank if you're driving on to Río Bravo or Chan Chich, as this is the last gas station until you come back this way.

As you continue farther west, the area becomes progressively more forested until you reach the dramatic boundary of the Programme for Belize Río Bravo Conservation Area. Here, the cleared pastureland runs smack dab into a wall of jungle, and there is a gate at the border. If you aren't expected, the guard won't let you pass. Once inside the gate, you've entered the Río Bravo Conservation Area.

◖ RÍO BRAVO CONSERVATION AREA

Programme for Belize is a Belizean nonprofit organization, established in 1988, to promote the conservation of the natural heritage of Belize and wise use of its natural resources, centering on the Río Bravo Conservation and Management Area (RBCMA), a 260,000- acre chunk of Belize where Programme for Belize demonstrates the practical application of its principles (the land was originally slated for clearing). The RBCMA represents

NORTHERN BELIZE

approximately 4 percent of Belize's total land area and is home to a rich sample of biodiversity, which includes 392 species of birds, 200 species of trees, 70 species of mammals, 30 species of freshwater fish, and 27 species of conservation concern.

Within the conservation area, the research station is housed in a cluster of small thatch-roof buildings. Programme for Belize is dedicated to scientific research, agricultural experimentation, and the protection of indigenous wildlife and the area's Maya archaeological locations—all this while creating self-sufficiency through development of ecotourism and sustainable rainforest agriculture such as *chicle* production. A scientific study continues to determine the best management plan for the reserve and its forests.

Ongoing projects include archaeological research at the La Milpa Maya Site and other sites on the RBCMA in conjunction with Boston University and the University of Texas; timber and pine savanna research programs aimed at identifying the most optimal approach to sustainable timber extraction on the RBCMA; a carbon sequestration pilot program, the first of seven globally approved projects to start on-the-ground research on how forest conservation could combat global warming; ecological research and monitoring of migratory and resident avifauna such as the yellow-headed parrot; a freshwater management program, which looks at the New River Lagoon, its tributaries, and the New River; and the biological connectivity program, which looks at the RBCMA and the critical links it forms with other protected areas in Northern Belize.

Scientists, research volunteers, donors, and interested travelers are encouraged to contact **Programme for Belize** (in Belize City, 1 Eyre St., tel. 501/207-5616 or 227-1020, U.S. tel. 617/259-9500, www.pfbelize.org).

La Milpa Field Station

Programme for Belize's La Milpa Field Station lies nestled deep in the forests of northwestern Belize. This field station is located only three miles from the third-largest archaeological site

in Belize. The La Milpa Archaeological Site is only one of at least 60 archaeological sites found on the Río Bravo. Hiking nature trails, jungle trekking, and birding are the order of the day at La Milpa. Spend a day in the nearby mestizo and Mennonite villages for a taste of Belizean culture. Tour breathtaking and majestic ancient Maya sites. Birders can compile a list of more than 150 species during a three-day trip to La Milpa.

For accommodations, guests can choose between charmingly rustic thatch-roof cabanas with private baths or a comfortable and tastefully decorated dormitory featuring state-of-the-art "green" technology with shared baths. The La Milpa venue has meeting facilities, telephones, and dining facilities and is family oriented, with 24-hour electricity and hot/cold water. Room rates are about US$135 per person per night and include your room, three meals, and two guided tours on the property.

Hill Bank Field Station

Located on the banks of the New River Lagoon, the Hill Bank Field Station serves as a research base for sustainable forest management and specialized tourism, which incorporates research activities into the visitors' forest experience. Hill Bank, an important site in Belize's colonial history, served as a center of intensive timber extraction for more than 150 years, commencing in the 17th century. The Hill Bank experience brings to life the architecture and artifacts of colonial land use, such as the quaint wooden buildings of logging camps, antique steam engines, and railroad tracks.

Explore the wilds of Hill Bank by canoeing, crocodile spotting, hiking nature trails, birding, and jungle trekking. The scenic boat ride, replete with wildlife sightings along the New River Lagoon, is a great experience in itself. For accommodations, guests stay in Hill Bank's Caza Balanza, which features 100 percent solar power, no-flush composting toilets, and a rainwater collection system with shared baths. Or choose a charming double cabana with private baths with verandas overlooking the New River Lagoon. Rates are the same as at La Milpa.

FIRE ON THE (MAYA) MOUNTAIN

Driving through the village of San Felipe during the dry season, you may see distant plumes of smoke rising into an otherwise cloudless blue sky. The smoke may be from agricultural fires, set by descendants of the Maya – or it may be the result of controlled blazes, set and monitored by professional firefighters (a.k.a. "fire managers") working in the Río Bravo Conservation Area.

San Felipe and many villages in the upland regions of Belize reside in an ecosystem known as upland pine savanna, consisting of gangly Caribbean pines and open grassland. Fire plays an instrumental role in this ecosystem, causing both destruction and renewal for vegetation and wildlife. Grasses, palmettos, and pine trees adapt quite successfully to both nature- and human-caused fires, but some species, like the endangered yellow-headed parrot, are not faring as well (although their declines are as much due to habitat destruction as predation by locals for the exotic pet trade).

Fire is not only used to clean fields of brush before planting; it has also been used by rural folk for thousands of years to encourage grazing for such game species as peccary, deer, and gibnut (or paca, a large rodent). Locals also burn the upland savanna in order to provide access to the riverine lowland forests, which yield highly profitable timber harvests. Also, sugarcane farmers have come to rely on fire to dry their fields and prepare them for harvest.

For many years, the professionals of the Río Bravo Conservation Area suppressed all fires when they were capable, because the general cultural belief was that all wildfire was bad for wildlife as well as a risk to human settlements.

However, recent studies have revealed the interdependency between the yellow-headed parrot nest trees and low-intensity, high-frequency fires. In response, the Río Bravo Conservation Area managers have begun a program of controlled burns that will restore the savanna to a state that is beneficial for the nesting trees. This burning is implemented in a controlled manner on allotted acres in order to rejuvenate the grasslands, prevent invasion of broadleaf trees, and prevent damage to the nest trees.

The foresters of the Hill Bank Field Station have conducted successful burns for several years with the help of the Nature Conservancy and the U.S. Forest Service. The Caribbean pine savanna is extensive throughout Belize and many Central American countries, and the Río Bravo fire program serves as a model for potential future savanna management throughout the region.

So not only is the preservation of the yellow-headed parrot served by the smoke you see in the sky, but entire ecosystems and additional rare species are served by this scientific management as well. The prescribed fire program is an integral tool in habitat management, serving to reduce fire-suppression costs, recycle nutrients, and prevent invasion by non-native vegetative species. As you eye the tops of the rough-barked pine trees, looking for yellow-headed parrots, give a moment of thanks for the hard, dirty work of the Río Bravo firefighters – maybe you'll be blessed with a sighting.

(Contributed by James Savage, a firefighter for the U.S. National Park Service)

NORTHERN BELIZE

CHAN CHICH
Chan Chich Ruins

As recently as 1986, the only way in to the Maya site of Chan Chich (Kaxil Uinich) was with machete in hand and a canoe to cross the swiftly flowing rivers. Most people making the trip were either loggers, pot farmers, or grave robbers. Then, in the northwestern corner of Belize in Orange Walk District, near the Guatemala border, an old overgrown logging road, originally blazed by the Belize Estate and Produce Company (logging operators), was reopened, and consequently, the site of Chan Chich was rediscovered.

When found, three of the temples showed obvious signs of looting with vertical slit trenches—just as the looters had left them. No one will ever know what valuable artifacts were removed and sold to private collectors all over the world. The large main temple on the upper plaza had been violated to the heart of what appears to be one or more burial chambers. A painted frieze runs around the low ceiling. Today, the only temple inhabitants greeting outsiders are armies of small bats and spider monkeys.

The ruins provide opportunity for discovery and exploration, and the population and diversity of wildlife here is probably greater than anywhere else in Belize. The nine miles of hiking trails wind through the verdant jungle and give ample chance to sight wildlife, including big cats.

Gallon Jug Estate

Originally the hub of the British Belize Estate and Produce Company's mahogany logging operation, Gallon Jug village and estate is now an incredibly diverse working farm, ranch, and community, with an airstrip, post office, coffee-roasting facility, and school. It's all part of Belizean-born Barry Bowen's empire.

Chan Chich Lodge

The ruins' new steward is Barry Bowen, owner of the property, who has built a dozen upscale thatch-roof cabanas in one of the open plazas of the Maya site. Though deplored by some archaeologists, the lodge is popular with bird-watchers and Mayaphiles, who agree with Bowen that the presence of Chan Chich Lodge is a deterrent to temple looters and marijuana traffickers.

The lodge is an elegant and luxurious retreat set among the plazas of the Chan Chich Maya ruins and surrounded on all sides by unexcavated pyramids and the largest contiguous forest north of the Amazon basin. The family of staff running the lodge offer top-notch service in everything that they do. The landscaped grounds, subtly lit pool and Jacuzzi, and sunset view from the tops of the mounds surround spacious cabanas with modern amenities, including water cooler, refrigerator, huge tiled bathrooms, and natural insulation and ventilation that keep them cool all day long. There is also a fully equipped luxury jungle villa with furnished living spaces and Jacuzzi. The rooms

© JOSHUA BERMAN

The Chan Chich Lodge is built among unexcavated ruins.

are great to come back to after a full day explor-ing the ruins and hiking trails, canoeing at the nearby Laguna Verde, or horseback riding from the Gallon Jug stables. Birding opportunities in-clude seeing trogons, ocellated turkeys, toucans, and hundreds of other birds. All five species of Belizean cat live in the surrounding forest. Tours of the coffee plantation and experimental farm at Gallon Jug provide the opportunity to learn all the steps in the coffee-making process as well as about other sustainable agricultural initiatives taking place here. And the day doesn't end at the peaceful dining veranda. If you're not signed up for the night safari, then you can finish off at the Looter's Trench Bar.

The Chan Chich office in Belize City is located near the water at 1 King Street (tel. 501/223-4419, U.S. tel. 800/343-8009, www.chanchich.com). The remarkable experience at Chan Chich Lodge does not come cheap, but considering the logistics of running a lodge so far out in the forest, it's not such a bad deal: US$250 for a double room, plus $70 per day for meals, plus tours, guides, and taxes. Ask about inclusive packages to bring the cost and complications down.

Chan Chich is 130 miles from Belize City, an all-day drive on all-weather roads from the international airport or (much easier) a 30-min-ute charter flight to Gallon Jug. Call or write for more information; the lodge can make all your travel arrangements.

Corozal

Corozal Town's nine thousand or so inhabit-ants casually get by while the bay washes against the seawall running the length of town. While English is the official language, Spanish is just as common, since many residents are descendants of early-day Maya and mestizo refugees from neigh-boring Mexico. Historically, Corozal was the scene of attacks by the Mayans during the Caste War. What remains of the old fort can be found in the center of town (west of Central Park).

The town was almost entirely wiped out dur-ing Hurricane Janet in 1955 and has since been rebuilt. As you stroll through the quiet streets, you'll find a library, a museum, town hall, government administrative offices, a Catholic church, two secondary schools, five elementary schools, three gas stations, a government hospi-tal, a clinic, a few small hotels, a couple of bars, and several restaurants. There's not a whole lot of activity here, unless you happen to be in town during the Mexican-style "Spanish" fiestas of Christmas, Carnaval, and Columbus Day; there are also a few local events in mid-September.

ORIENTATION
Visitors enter Corozal from the north (from Mexico), from the south on the Northern Highway, or from Ambergris Caye to the east by boat or plane. Getting oriented to Corozal is easy, since it's laid out on a grid system with avenues running north and south (parallel to the seawall) and streets running east and west. Corozal's two primary avenues, 4th and 5th, run the length of town. The majority of restau-rants and stores of interest to travelers lie on, or adjacent to, these streets.

SIGHTS AND RECREATION
There are no tourist attractions, per se, in Corozal, but it's an unassuming base for fishing trips, nature watching, and tours of a few nearby ruins and waterways. Wander through the town square, stroll down the waterfront, and strike up a conversation with the locals or expats who've come to love the laid-back lifestyle.

In the town hall, you'll find a dramatic his-torical **mural** painted by Manuel Villamour. The bright painting depicts the history of Corozal, including the drama of the downtrod-den Maya, the explosive revolt called the Caste War, and the inequities of colonial rule.

Some trips include day trips to the Shipstern Wildlife Nature Reserve, Sarteneja Village, and the Maya sites of Cerros and Santa Rita.

NORTHERN BELIZE

NORTHERN BELIZE

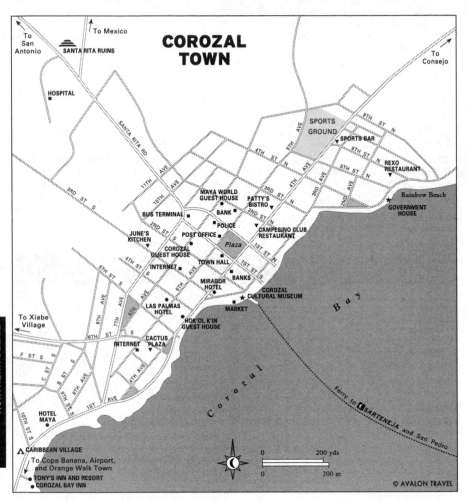

Local Guides and Tour Companies

One of the best independent guides around is **Vitalino Reyes** (tel. 501/602-8975, www. cavetubing.bz), whose years of experience qualify him to teach and certify many of Corozal's other guides. Vital will take you to local ruins, to the caves at Jaguar Paw, to the Belize Zoo, on night safaris, or anywhere else you want to go. **Belize VIP Transfer Services** (tel. 501/422-2725, www.belizetransfers.com) is your best bet for charter transportation, using brand-new vehicles that are great for groups. Belize VIP specializes in local tours (including a day tour of Corozal and Cerros), Lamanai trips, Chetumal transfers (and other Mexican attractions), and Tikal/Flores trips to Guatemala. **Hok'ol K'in Guest House** handles all such trips as well, especially to local villages. For travel agencies or flight bookings, go to the **Hotel Maya.**

ARCHAEOLOGICAL SITES NEAR COROZAL

The nearby ruins of **Cerros** and **Santa Rita** are not as immediately awe-inspiring as, say, Lamanai or Caracol, but they are still interesting and easy to visit.

CERROS

Cerros looms over both sea and jungle on a peninsula across from Corozal called Lawry's Bite. Cerros was an important coastal trading center during the Late Pre-Classic Period (350 B.C.-A.D. 250) and was occupied as late as 1300 A.D. Magnificent frescoes and stone heads were uncovered by archaeologist David Friedel, signifying that elite rule was firmly fixed by the end of the Pre-Classic Period. The tallest of Cerros's temples rises to 70 feet, and because of the rise in the sea level, the one-time stone residences of the elite Maya are partially flooded.

It would appear that Cerros not only provisioned oceangoing canoes, but also was in an ideal location to control ancient trade routes that traced the Río Hondo and New River from the Yucatán to Petén and the Usumacinta basin. A plaster-lined canal for the sturdy, oversized ocean canoes was constructed around Cerros. Archaeologists have determined that extensive fishing and farming on raised fields took place, probably to outfit the traders. But always the question remains: Why did progress suddenly stop?

Be prepared for vicious mosquitoes at Cerros, especially if there's no breeze. You can reach the site by boat in minutes – hire one at **Tony's Inn** in Corozal or check with a travel agent. If you travel during the dry season (Jan.-Apr.), you can get to Cerros by car; it takes up to 45 minutes, and you'll have to employ the hand-cranked Pueblo Nuevo Ferry. Admission to the ruins is US$5 per person.

SANTA RITA

This site, one mile northeast of Corozal, was still a populated community of Maya when the Spanish arrived. The largest Santa Rita structure was explored at the turn of the 20th century by Thomas Gann. Sculptured friezes and stucco murals were found along with a burial site that indicates flourishing occupation in the Early Classic Period (about A.D. 300), as well as during the Late Post-Classic Period (A.D. 1350-1530). Two significant burials were found from distant periods in the history of Santa Rita: one from A.D. 300 was a female and the other was a king from a period 200 years later.

In 1985, archaeologists Diane and Arlen Chase discovered a tomb with a skeleton covered in jade and mica ornaments. It has been excavated and somewhat reconstructed under the Chases' jurisdiction; only one structure is accessible to the public. Post-Classic murals, mostly destroyed over the years, combined Maya and Mexican styles that depict the ecumenical flavor of the period. Some believe that Santa Rita was part of a series of coastal lookouts. Santa Rita is probably more appealing to serious archaeology buffs than to the average tourist.

NORTHERN BELIZE

ACCOMMODATIONS
Under US$25

Maya World Guest House (tel. 501/624-4790, byronchuster@gmail.com) has clean rooms that start at US$22.50 and surround a well-kept, cheery garden. **Caribbean Village RV Park and Campground** (tel. 501/422-2725, menziestours@btl.net) offers full RV hookups for US$20 a night (camping US$5) and an apartment with kitchen for US$25, a bargain if you have a family or a group of friends. Recently renovated by a Welsh expat, the **Sea Breeze Hotel** (tel. 501/422-3051 or 605-9341, www.theseabreezehotel.com, US$18–30) offers the best budget accommodations in Corozal. Rooms have balconies overlooking the bay. Call ahead or email as this place gets busy. The second-floor bar is a great place to meet other travelers and is quick walk from the main thoroughfares.

US$25-50

Just two blocks south of the town center, and right across from the water, the **Hok'ol K'in**

© JOSHUA BERMAN

sunrise in Corozal

Guest House (tel. 501/422-3329, maya@btl. net, www.corozal.net, US$21–65) was begun by an ex–Peace Corps volunteer with the intention of supporting local Maya community endeavors. In Yucateca Mayan, "Hok'ol K'in" means "Coming of the Rising Sun," a sight you'll see from your window if you're up early enough—follow your sun salutations with an excellent breakfast (and real coffee!) on the patio downstairs. Hok'ol K'in's 10 immaculate rooms have private baths, veranda, and fan; free wireless Internet is available. Ask about available trips and homestays (or visits) with local families; the staff are very helpful in arranging things to do. This is one of the few lodgings in Belize that's equipped to handle a wheelchair (one room only, so be sure to specify if it's needed). The restaurant serves a variety of good meals.

The Mark Anthony Hotel, Butchies Bar (2nd Ave. North at 4th St. North, tel. 501/422-3141 or 600-1899), overlooking Corozal Bay, has nine rooms with cable, hot and cold water, queen beds and air-conditioning starting at US$35. A wide selection of souvenirs is available and the restaurant has some of the best food to be had in town. **The Oasis** (2nd St., off

Northern Highway, tel. 501/402-0391, darlenebartlett@gmail.com) is an affordable option geared toward both long- and short-term stays. Rooms are about US$30; apartments start at US$300 a month. A communal kitchen is on site as well as a lovely swimming pool and tranquil garden area.

Hotel Mirador (tel. 501/422-0189, www. mirador.bz, US$35–75) is a 24-room lodging across from the main dock and seawall, whose rooftop boasts the best views in town. The rooms are sparkling and spotless, with private bath and air-conditioning, and the hallways cavernous. There's wireless Internet, plus you'll get lots of friendly help from your hosts, Jose and Lydia Gongora.

On the road leading into town from the south, the **Hotel Maya** (tel. 501/422-2082 or 422-2874, www.hotelmaya.net) offers 16 rooms with air-conditioning, TV, and private bath for US$50 for two double beds; the restaurant serves breakfast only. There is also a gift shop and travel agency that can arrange trips to local destinations, as well as transport across the borders to Tikal, Chetumal, or even Cancún.

Las Palmas Hotel (formerly Nestor's, but completely rebuilt, tel. 501/422-0196, www. laspalmashotelbelize.com, US$45 and up) is in a brand-new building in the heart of town, with 25 full-service rooms that include air-conditioning, private baths, hot/cold water, DSL lines in rooms, parking, 24-hour security, and a backup generator.

US$50-100

Three seaside options reside on the south end of town, clustered together on what is locally known as "Gringo Lane." At **Tony's Inn and Beach Resort** (tel. 501/422-2055 or 422-3555, tonys@btl.net, US$45–75), "beach" may be stretching it a bit, and the 24 rooms are set up more like a Motel 6 than a resort. Still, the large rooms have air-conditioning, private baths, and hot/cold water. The Y-Not Bar and Grill is in a nice setting on the water, and the hotel has its own marina and runs a variety of local trips.

Right next door, you'll find the **Corozal Bay Inn** (tel. 501/422-2691, www.corozalbayinn.com, from US$55), a couples-oriented cluster of 10 cute thatch-roof cabanas set around 396 truckloads of sand imported from Belize's Pine Mountain Ridge; the inn offers a swimming pool, a lively bar, and rooms with air-conditioning, big-screen TV, private bath, and fridge. A bit more to the south, in a very quiet, out-of-the-way spot, the **Copa Banana** (tel. 501/422-0284, www.copabanana.bz, US$55) has lovely, tropical-decor rooms and suites open to the sea breeze (but also air-conditioned), with a shared living room and kitchen area and lots of space, plus free bikes, coffee, tea, and juices.

Corozal's newest offering is **Serenity Sands Bed and Breakfast** (three miles north of Corozal and one mile off of Consejo Road, www.serenitysands.com, tel. 501/669-2394, Can. tel. 250/992-6583), whose four tastefully decorated upper-level rooms have queen or twin beds, air-conditioning, and private balcony over Corozal Bay. The hotel is off-the-grid and uses organic products as often as possible. There's complimentary Internet access and a well-stocked library.

FOOD

For solid, super-cheap Mexican snacks and meals, **Cactus Plaza** has a very popular streetside café; drinks, beers, and juices are served all night (till the club inside closes, anyway). This is also the center of the nightlife on weekends. There are plenty of Chinese options, but **Chon King,** near the park, is said to be the best. The Japanese seaweed salad and homemade dim sum make this a stand-out option. A close runner-up is the **Romantic Bar and Restaurant,** located on the ground floor of the Mirador Hotel.

Patty's Bistro (tel. 510/402-0174, 10 A.M.–10 P.M., dine in or take out) is a wonderful option for authentic Belizean lunches and dinners, where the conch soup has a unique hint of coconut, as does the curry shrimp entrée (US$7.50). Fajitas and chicken dishes cost less. Be sure to sign your name on the wall with all the other satisfied customers. Just as good are the home-cooked daily specials in **June's Kitchen** (tel. 510/422-2559), where rice 'n' beans with stew chicken will set you back only US$4; breakfasts are huge and famous. You're basically eating in Miss June's living room or on her porch. The town market has a selection of cheap eats and is your best bet early in the morning if you have to eat and run to catch a bus just up the street. The **Purple Toucan Restaurant Bar and Grill,** beside Atlantic Bank on 4th Avenue, features *cochinita pibil, poc chuc,* and other Yucatecan specialties. If hamburgers are your fancy, head to **Butchies** (Mark Anthony Hotel, 2nd Ave. North at 4th St. North).

For bars, try Machie's (2nd St. North near 4th Ave. North) for billiards and dominoes tournaments.

INFORMATION AND SERVICES

Corozal has lots of little shops, grocery stores, bookstores, and a few gift shops. You'll find locally made jewelry, pottery, wood carvings, clothing, textiles, and a host of other mementos here and there, but the place is not overrun with gift shops yet. **U Sav Supermarket** is near the Hok'ol K'in Guest House. Gifts, books, postcards, and other supplies can be obtained at **A&R,** on 4th Avenue near Patty's Bistro.

Nearly all of the businesses mentioned in

this chapter have websites found on Corozal's main portals: **www.corozal.bz** is more tourist- and business-related, while **www.corozal.com** offers many local resources.

If you need to change money, go to the **Casa de Cambio** (tel. 501/422-2516, 8 A.M.–5 P.M. Mon.–Fri., 8 A.M.–noon Sat.), a block south of the park, where you're guaranteed a better exchange rate than at the banks, even for travelers checks. For other needs, Corozal has several ATMs and branches of **Belize Bank, Nova Scotia Bank,** and **Atlantic Bank** (all open 8 A.M.–2 P.M. Mon.–Thurs., 8:30 A.M.–4:30 P.M. Fri.).

Emergency numbers are fire, 501/422-2105; police, 501/422-2022; and hospital, 501/422-2076.

The main places to get online are the Hotel Mirador and **M.E. Computer Systems** (3rd St. South, 9 A.M.–9 P.M., closed Sun.).

GETTING THERE

By Air

There are five inexpensive daily flights on each airline between Corozal and San Pedro only. Call Tropic Air (tel. 501/226-2012, U.S. tel. 800/422-3435, www.tropicair.com) or Maya Island Air (tel. 501/223-1140, U.S. tel. 800/225-6732, mayair@btl.net, www.mayaislandair.com) for schedules.

By Bus

Buses are in disarray, so check the schedule at Corozal's **Northern Transport Bus Station** before departure. Northbound buses from Belize City alternate final destinations between Corozal and Chetumal, taking three hours to Corozal and leaving Belize City frequently from 5:30 A.M.–7:30 P.M. (US$6). Southbound buses from Corozal leave regularly between 3:30 A.M. and 7:15 P.M., all of them originating an hour or so earlier in Chetumal. Ask about bus service to the Guatemalan border at Benque; it runs intermittently and was last seen operating Friday–Monday at 4 P.M. If you have connections to make in Chetumal, be aware that, unlike Belize, Mexico practices daylight saving time.

By Boat

The Thunderbolt (tel. 501/422-0026 or 610-4475, crivero@btl.net) has daily 7 A.M. and 3 P.M. runs to San Pedro for US$23 per person. Special promotions are often run during peak holiday times, so call ahead. The same boats leave San Pedro's Westside dock at the same times. Stops in Sarteneja are possible going either way.

GETTING AROUND

There are a few taxi stands in town: one at the bus station (tel. 501/422-3626) and another closer to the water (tel. 501/422-2035). You can get around town for US$2.50, to the border for US$10, or to Chetumal and Cerros for US$30, all convenient ways to go if you have a few people to split the costs. Or check with the tour companies listed above.

Near Corozal

CONSEJO VILLAGE

Nine miles north of Corozal, the tiny fishing village of Consejo is home to a beach hideaway, an upscale hotel, a nine-hole golf course, and a retirement community of some 400 North Americans called **Consejo Shores** (www.consejoshores.com).

Rent one of three bayside units at **Smuggler's Den** (two miles northwest of Consejo, tel. 501/600-9723, www.smugglersdenbelize.tripod.com, US$40–65), nicely furnished and with hot/cold water—quite a bargain if you're looking for isolation. Two have private bath and kitchenette; the unit without a kitchen is cheaper. Discounts can be had if requested. Smuggler's is locally famous for their Sunday afternoon roast beef dinners; reserve in advance.

Right in Consejo, **Casablanca by the Sea** (tel. 501/423-1018, U.S. tel. 781/235-1024, www.casablanca-bythesea.com, from US$65) is an intimate hotel with lovely grounds and views of the Bay of Consejo. Casablanca has eight stately rooms with queen-size beds, private bathrooms, air-conditioning, hot/cold water, and TV. The bar and dining room offer excel lent seafood dishes and other meals, eaten while watching the lights of Chetumal, just across the bay. There's rooftop stargazing, volleyball, and top-notch conference/group facilities.

The **New Millennium Restaurant,** in the heart of Consejo Village, is a friendly watering hole and eatery serving up daily specials at great prices. (Closed Tues.) **Derricks Cozy Bar** is a popular hangout in the afternoons, and you can meet other expats. Challenge Mr. Derrick to a game of dominoes, as he is a wily player.

SHIPSTERN WILDLIFE NATURE RESERVE

In Corozal District, Shipstern is in the northeastern corner of the Belize coast. Thirty-two square miles of moist forest, savanna, and wetlands have been set aside to preserve as-yet-unspoiled habitats of well-known insect, bird, and mammal species associated with the tropics. The reserve encompasses the shallow **Shipstern Lagoon,** which, although hardly navigable, creates a wonderful habitat for a huge selection of wading and fish-eating birds. The reserve is home to about 200 species of birds, 60 species of reptiles and amphibians, and nearly 200 species of butterflies (they began the production of live butterfly pupae through intensive breeding).

The Audubon Society and International Tropical Conservation Foundation have been extremely generous in their support. As at most reserves, the objective is to manage and protect habitats and wildlife, as well as to develop an education program that entails teaching the local community and introducing children to the concept of wildlife conservation in their area. Shipstern, however, goes a step further by conducting an investigation of how tropical countries such as Belize can develop self-

supporting conservation areas through the controlled, intensive production of natural commodities found within such wildlife settlements. Developing facilities for the scientific study of the reserve area and its wildlife is part of this important program. For information about a few cabins at the reserve for US$10, email the Belize Audubon Society at basc@btl.net.

It's essential that visitors go first to the visitors center. A guided tour costs US$5 per person. Admission is US$7.50. The forest is alive with nature's critters and fascinating flora, and the guides' discerning eyes spot things that most city folk often miss, even though they are right in front of them. Hours for touring are 9 A.M.–noon and 1–3 P.M. daily except for Christmas, New Year's Day, and Easter.

Botanical Trail

This lovely trail starts at the parking lot by the visitors center and meanders through the forest. You will have the opportunity to see three types of hardwood forests with 100 species of hardwood. Many of the trees are labeled with their Latin and Yucatec Maya names. Before starting your 20- to 30-minute walk, pick up a book with detailed descriptions of the trail and the trees at the park's visitors center, about 3 miles outside of Sarteneja.

Getting There

It is easiest to take a boat from Corozal or to hire a local tour guide to arrange travel. From Corozal and Orange Walk, figure a little more than an hour to drive there. The road takes you through **San Estevan** and then to **Progreso.** Turn right just before entering Progreso, to **Little Belize** (a Mennonite community). Continue on to **Chunox. Sarteneja** is three miles beyond Shipstern. Don't forget a long-sleeved shirt, pants, mosquito repellent, binoculars, and a camera for your exploration of the reserve.

◖ SARTENEJA

From the Maya "Tzaten-a-ha" or "give me the water," Sarteneja was named after the 13 Maya

NORTHERN BELIZE

© ZOE WALKER

Sarteneja is known for its boat builders and fishermen.

Sanctuary). It is also known for the annual regatta that takes place each Easter, with newly painted sailboats of the artisan fishing fleet, crewed by local fishermen, racing against each other in a tradition that has continued since 1950. During fishing season, these boats dock in Belize City, by the Swing Bridge.

With access to nearby Maya sites and ties to the Barrier Reef at Bacalar Chico, Sarteneja has a lot to offer the adventurous tourist in search of the real Belize. The community is aware of its resources, and community groups have joined forces to form the Sarteneja Alliance for Conservation and Development. Local fishermen, now trained as tour guides, offer a number of guided tours—both marine and inland. Sarteneja is also the location of the Manatee Rehabilitation Centre, run by Wildtracks, a local NGO, which takes in and rehabilitates orphan manatee calves as part of a national program to protect this threatened species. The center isn't open to visitors unless by special agreement—check with the Sarteneja Tour Guide Association for details. The region can get pretty buggy, so take precautions.

wells found in the area, carved into limestone bedrock and providing potable water. This picturesque fishing village in the northeast corner of Belize was first established by the Maya as an important trading area. It is thought to have been occupied from 600 B.C. to 1200 A.D., and gold, copper, and shells continue to turn up in the area. Mexican refugees from the Yucatán Caste Wars settled here in the mid-19th century, again attracted by the availability of drinking water. The village took a pounding from Hurricane Janet in 1955 but rebounded and became known for its boat builders and free-diving lobster and conch fishermen.

Today, 80 percent of Sarteneja's households remain reliant on the resources of the Belize Reef. Tourism is just barely creeping in, and Sarteneja offers one of the more off-the-beaten-path experiences in the country. Located on Corozal Bay, it is a well-kept secret in Belize, and few tourists have heard about its breathtaking sunsets, sportfishing, and importance as a protected area for manatees and bird nesting colonies (in the Corozal Bay Wildlife

Accommodations

Most accommodations, eateries, and bars can be found along Front Street, abutting the sea and dock. A homestay program is being started by the Sarteneja Tour Guide Association; the office is located on the seafront. They can help visitors find licensed local tour guides.

Backpackers Paradise (http://bluegreenbelize.org) is located right outside Sarteneja; it's a funky, laid-back, rustic, and friendly hangout where accommodations range from campgrounds (US$3.50 pp) to a few private cabanas (US$10–17.50). The on-site restaurant serves up wonderful and cheap dishes, including crepes made by the Vietnamese/French proprietress. Wireless Internet access is available for a fee; bicycles, horses, and guided day trips are available as well.

◖ Fernando's Seaside Guesthouse (tel. 501/423-2085, www.cybercayecaulker.com/sarteneja.html, US$35 plus tax) has rooms with private bath (and optional air-conditioning); a larger cabana is also available. Like most folks in Sarteneja, the owner, Fernando Alamilla, was once a full-time fisherman who used to sail and fish for up to 10 days at a time. You can also stay at **Candelie's Sunset Cabanas** (tel. 501/423-2005 or 660-8795, candeliescabanas@yahoo.com, US$60–80), with three well-appointed cabins with air-conditioning, double beds, cots, and beer fridge. The neighboring **Krisamis Hotel** is managed by the same family.

Food

Ritchie's Place (Front Street, tel. 501/423-2031) has a good selection of fresh dishes, prepared by his wife, featuring fish empanadas. Owner Ritchie Cruz will also arrange fishing trips. **Liz's Fast Food,** two streets back from the seafront, serves tasty, traditional food in a friendly, snack-stall setting: tacos, empanadas, and *garnaches,* as well as rice and beans. The homemade *horchata* (rice-based drink) is well worth trying.

Getting There and Away

Sarteneja has been linked to the rest of Belize by land for less than 40 years—roads are rugged and dusty, and during rainy season often flooded and rutted. Most visitors get to Sarteneja **by boat** from Corozal or San Pedro. Thunderbolt water taxis (www.ambergriscaye.com/thunderbolt) will stop in Sarteneja on their twice-daily Corozal–San Pedro run. They depart Corozal at 7 A.M. and 3 P.M., arriving in Sarteneja 40 minutes later (7:40 A.M. and 3:40 P.M.), before heading on to San Pedro. The San Pedro–Corozal boat also departs at 7:00 A.M. and 3:00 P.M. from San Pedro, stopping at Sarteneja at approximately 8:15 A.M. and 4:15 P.M. Sarteneja is a request stop, so purchase a ticket from Tino at Tiny's Internet Café on Front Street in advance if you want to be sure of leaving Sarteneja by boat (US$12.50 to Corozal, US$22.50 to San Pedro).

By air, Tropic Air has two flights a day that will stop at Sarteneja's tiny airstrip on request. Flights leave San Pedro at 7:00 A.M. and 4:45 P.M., arriving in Sarteneja 10 minutes

© JOSH-UA BERMAN

typical transportation in Corozal

NORTHERN BELIZE

later, as part of the San Pedro–Corozal schedule. Flights will stop later in the day if there is more than one passenger requesting to be dropped off or picked up in Sarteneja.

The bus from Belize City is often full of returning fishermen and is the most exciting way to get here. The distinctive light-blue Sarteneja buses leave Belize City daily except Sunday, from a riverside lot on Albert Street in Belize City, next to the Swing Bridge. Four buses make the three-hour ride each day (US$5 one-way), the first at 11:30 A.M. and the last at 5:00 P.M. All stop outside St. Christopher's Hotel in Orange Walk to pick up more passengers. Buses depart Sarteneja for Belize City (via Orange Walk) between 4:00 and 6:30 A.M. There is a direct bus from Chetumal, via Corozal and Orange Walk, which runs every day (including Sundays), leaving Chetumal at midday or 1:00 P.M. (depending on whether or not Mexico is on daylight saving time). It departs for Corozal and Chetumal at 6 A.M. every morning. Buses from Corozal are intermittent, so it's best to check with the Corozal bus station first. There is also local traffic going to Sarteneja from Orange Walk via San Estevan.

By car from Corozal, head south and turn left at the sign for Tony's Inn. Follow this road, veering right until you come to a stone wall; then go left. Follow this road until you reach the first ferry across the New River, an experience in itself and free. Sometimes there are lineups on Fridays and Mondays, so anticipate a bit of a wait. After crossing, continue on the unsurfaced road until you reach a T junction. Turn left toward Copper Bank, Cerros, and the ferry to Chunox. Upon entering Copper Bank, keep driving until you see the signs for Donna's Place (an excellent eatery) and the Cerros ruins. If you're not stopping to eat or visit the ruins, turn left at the ruins sign and proceed until you see the sign for the ferry crossing. After crossing, continue until you reach another T junction. Turn left for Sarteneja, or right for Chunox and the grinding drive through Little Belize back to Orange Walk.

Chetumal, Mexico

An exciting dose of culture shock is an easy 15 miles from Corozal. Chetumal, capital of the Mexican state of Quintana Roo, is a relatively modern, midsize city of about 200,000—nearly as many people as in the entire country of Belize! If you don't come for the culture (wonderful museums, a few parks, a zoo, and a delicious seafront), then you must be here to shop in the new American-style mall or see a first-run film in Chet's brand-new airconditioned Cineplex, located in the **Plaza de las Americas** mall.

Chetumal can be seen as a day trip from Corozal or used as a base from which to visit the many Yucatecan archaeological sights, like Tulum, just up the coast. It's also a gateway to Mexico's well-known Caribbean resorts: Cancún, Cozumel, Playa del Carmen, and Akumal. Chetumal presents the businesslike atmosphere of a growing metropolis, without the bikini-clad, touristy crowds of the north. A 10-minute walk takes you to the waterfront from the marketplace and most of the hotels. Modern, sculpted monuments stand along a breezy promenade that skirts the broad crescent of the bay. Also explore the back streets, where worn, wooden buildings still have a Central American/Caribbean look. The largest building in town—white, three stories, close to the waterfront—houses most of the government offices. Wide, tree-lined avenues and sidewalks front dozens of small variety shops.

SIGHTS

Do not miss the **Museo de la Cultura Maya** (9 A.M.–7 P.M. Sun. and Tues.–Thurs., 9 A.M.–8 P.M. Fri. and Sat., US$5), located at the new market; it is an impressive and creative

© JOSHUA BERMAN

Corozal is only a short ride from the Mexican border.

experience by any standards. The **Museo Municipal** is excellent as well, with a great deal of contemporary Mexican art.

On Avenida Heroes, five miles north of the city, is **Calderitas Bay,** a breezy area for picnicking, dining, camping, and RVing. Tiny **Isla Tamalcas,** 1.5 miles off the shore of Calderitas, is the home of the primitive capybara, the largest of all rodents.

Twenty-one miles north of Chetumal (on Highway 307) is **Cenote Azul,** a circular *cenote* 61.5 meters deep and 185 meters across and filled with brilliant blue water. This is a spectacular place to stop for a swim, lunch at the outdoor restaurant, or just to have a cold drink.

ACCOMMODATIONS AND FOOD

Chetumal has quite a few hotels in all price categories (including a Holiday Inn near the new market), as well as many fine cafés specializing in fresh seafood. Check out *Moon Yucatán Peninsula* for details.

The cheapest hotels in Chetumal are **Hotel Brasilia** (US$18, limited on-street parking

only) and our favorite, the vibrantly decorated **Hotel Ucum** (US$20; parking, pool, and hot showers included). Both are visible from Avenida Heroes, the main street which is home to most of the city's other hotels and the Museo Mundo Maya.

GETTING THERE

Buses between Belize City, Corozal, and Chetumal travel throughout the day, taking you all the way through the border (you'll need to get off twice to pass through Immigration and pay a US$19 exit fee) to the Mercado Viejo in Chetumal. A local Chetumal bus from Corozal costs US$1.50, a taxi to the border US$10. The express trip to Chetumal from Belize City takes about four hours and costs US$11. Also check with the various kiosks in the Water Taxi Terminal by the Swing Bridge in Belize City for direct bus service to Chetumal with **S & L Travel and Tours** (tel. 501/227-7593 or 227-5145, sltravel@btl.net, www.sltravelbelize.com); **Mundo Maya Deli, Gifts, Travel & Tours** (tel. 501/223-1235, mundomayatravel@ btl.net); **Kaisa International;** and **San Juan**

Tours. Most of these companies offer one or two daily buses, leaving between 9 A.M. and noon. Mundo Maya will go one step further and book you to points beyond on the main Mexican bus line (Autobuses del Oriente), all the way to Brownsville, Texas, if you so desire. The trip to Mexico City, by the way, takes roughly 20–22 hours from Chetumal.

Also, Corozal-based **Belize VIP Transfer Services** (tel. 501/422-2725, www.belizetransfers.com) will arrange Chetumal transfers (and other Mexican attractions) and trips to local ruins. Also check other Corozal travel folks at the **Hok'ol K'in Guest House** or with **Herman Pollard** (tel. 501/422-3329). For travel agencies, stop by the **Hotel Maya** or **Jal's Travel Agency** (tel. 501/422-2163, ligializama@hotmail.com).

Continuing North from Chetumal

Chetumal is a midsize Mexican city, just over the border from Belize. A good paved road connects Chetumal with Mérida, Campeche, Villahermosa, and Francisco Escarcega; Highway 307 links all of the Quintana Roo coastal cities. Expect little traffic, and you'll find that gas stations are well spaced if you top off at each one. Car rentals are scarce in Chetumal; go to the Hotel Los Cocos for Avis. Chetumal is an economical place to rent your car (if one is available), since the tax is only 6 percent. If you're driving, watch out for No Left Turn signs in Chetumal.

GETTING AROUND

Taxis are available from the old market into town for US$1.50; if going to the mall, ask to be let off at the Plaza de las Americas before arriving at the station. Bus travel is a versatile and inexpensive way to travel the Quintana Roo coast—there are frequent trips to Playa del Carmen and Cancún, and a new fleet of luxury express buses are a treat after Belize's school bus system. Chetumal is part of the loop between Campeche, Cancún, and Mérida. Fares and schedules change regularly; currently the fare to Cancún is about US$30.

BACKGROUND

The Land

GEOGRAPHY

Belize lies on the northeast coast of Central America, above the corner where the Honduran coast takes off to the east. Belize's 8,866 square miles of territory are bordered on the north by Mexico, on the west and south by Guatemala, and on the east by the Caribbean Sea and the Belize Barrier Reef. From the northern Río Hondo border with Mexico to the southern border with Guatemala, Belize's mainland measures 180 miles long, and it is 68 miles across at its widest point. Offshore, Belize has more than 200 cayes, or islands. Both the coastal region and the northern half of the mainland are flat, but the land rises in the south and west to over 3,000 feet above sea level. The Maya Mountains and Cockscomb range form the country's backbone, and include **Victoria Peak** (3,675 feet). Mangrove swamps cover much of the humid coastal plain.

In the west, the Cayo District contains the **Mountain Pine Ridge Reserve.** At one time a magnificent pine forest, it has, over the decades, been reduced by lumber removal, fires, and the pine bark beetle. Despite vast beetle damage, the upper regions of Mountain Pine Ridge still provide spectacular scenery, with sections of thick forest surrounding the **Macal River** as it tumbles over huge granite boulders (except where the river was dammed at Chalillo).

© JOSHUA BERMAN

BELIZE: WHAT'S IN A NAME?

No one knows for sure where the name Belize originated or what it means. The country was called Belize long before the British took the country over and renamed it British Honduras. In 1973, the locals changed it back to the original Belize as a first step on the road to independence. There are several well-known theories about its meaning. Some say it's a corruption of the name Wallis (wahl-EEZ), from the pirate (Peter Wallace) who roamed the high seas centuries ago and visited Belize. Others suggest that it's a distortion of the Maya word *belix*, which means "muddy river." Still others say it could be a further distortion of the Maya word *belikin* (which is also the name of the local beer). And of course it could be another of those mysterious Maya secrets we may never learn.

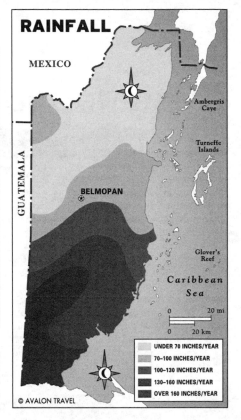

Hidden Valley Falls plunges 1,600 feet to the valley below and is the highest waterfall in all of Central America. The **Río Frio** cave system offers massive stalactites and stalagmites to the avid spelunker. The diverse landscape includes limestone-fringed granite boulders.

Over thousands of years, what was once a sea in the northern half of Belize has become a combination of scrub vegetation and rich tropical hardwood forest. Near the Mexican border, much of the land has been cleared, and it's here that the majority of sugar crops are raised, along with family plots of corn and beans. Most of the northern coast is swampy, with a variety of grasses and mangroves that attract hundreds of species of waterfowl. Rainfall in the north averages 60 inches annually, though it's generally dry November–May.

CLIMATE

The climate in Belize is subtropical, with a mean annual temperature of 79°F, so you can expect a variance between 50 and 95°F. The dry season generally lasts from Decemberish through May and the wet season June through November, although it has been known to rain sporadically all the way into February.

Rainfall varies widely between the north and south of Belize. Corozal in the north receives 40–60 inches a year, while Punta Gorda averages 160–190 inches, with an average humidity of 85 percent. Occasionally during the winter, "northers" (a.k.a. cold fronts) sweep down from North America across the Gulf of Mexico, bringing rainfall, strong winds, and cooling temperatures. Usually lasting only a couple of days, they often interrupt fishing and influence the activity of lobster and other fish. Fishermen invariably report increases in their catches several days before a norther.

CAVES AND THE MAYA

MYTHOLOGY

Large populations of Maya were concentrated in the limestone foothills, where water supplies and clay deposits were plentiful. Caves were a source of fresh water, especially during dry periods. Clay pots of grain were safely stored for long periods of time in the cool air and, thousands of years later, can be seen today. Looting of caves has been a problem for decades, and as a result, all caves in Belize are considered archaeological sites.

The Maya used caves for utilitarian as well as religious and ceremonial purposes. The ancient Maya believed that upon entering a cave, one entered the underworld, or Xibalba, the place of beginnings and of fright. The Maya believed there were nine layers of the underworld, and as much as death and disease and rot were represented by the underworld, so was the beginning of life. Caves were a source of water − a source of life − for the Maya. Water that dripped from stalactites was used as holy water for ceremonial purposes. The underworld was also an area where souls had hopes of defeating death and becoming ancestors. As a result, rituals, ceremonies, and even sacrifices were performed in caves, evidenced today by many pots, shards, implements, and burial sites.

Caves were important burial chambers for the ancient Maya, and more than 200 skeletons have been found in more than 20 caves. One chamber in Caves Branch was the final earthly resting spot for 25 individuals. Many of these burial chambers are found deep in the caves, leading to speculation that death came by sacrificing the living, as opposed to carrying in the dead. Some burial sites show possible evidence of commoners being sacrificed to accompany the journey with an elite who had died − but who really knows?

SPELIO-ARCHAEOLOGY

The first written accounts related to cave archaeology began in the late 1800s. A British medical officer by the name of Thomas Gann wrote of his extensive exploration of caves throughout the country. In the late 1920s, he was also part of the first formal study of some ruins and caves in the Toledo District, and his papers provide insight no one else can give to modern-day archaeologists.

Little else was done until 1955, when the Institute of Archaeology was created by the government of Belize. Starting in 1957, excavations were organized throughout the years under various archaeologists. Excavations in the 1970s led to many important archaeological discoveries, including pots, vessels, and altars. In the 1980s, a series of expeditions was undertaken to survey the Chiquibul cave system. Other finds during this time period include a burial chamber and one cave with over 60 complete vessels and other ceremonial implements.

Today, projects are underway in many caves around the country. The Institute of Archaeology does not have a museum − yet. They've been talking about one for years. In the meantime, you may have to get a little wet and dirty to go visit some of these artifacts yourself.

The *"mauger"* season, when the air is still and the sea is calm, generally comes in August; it can last for a week or more. All activity halts while locals stay indoors as much as possible to avoid the onslaught of mosquitoes and other insects.

Hurricanes

Since record keeping began in 1787, scores of hurricanes have made landfall in Belize. In an unnamed storm in 1931, 2,000 people were killed and almost all of Belize City was destroyed. The water rose nine feet in some areas, even onto Belize City's Swing Bridge. Though forewarned by Pan American Airlines that the hurricane was heading their way, most of the townsfolk were unconcerned, believing that their protective reef would keep massive waves away from their shores. They were wrong.

The next devastation came with Hurricane Hattie in 1961. Winds reached a velocity of 150 mph, with gusts of 200 mph; 262 people

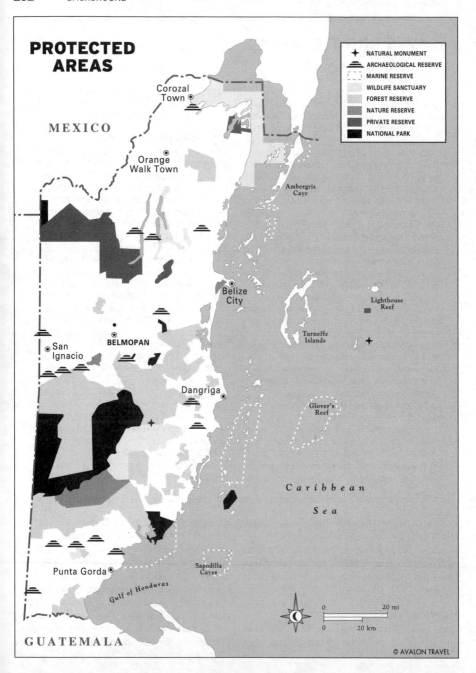

PROTECTED AREAS

NATURAL MONUMENT
ARCHAEOLOGICAL RESERVE
MARINE RESERVE
WILDLIFE SANCTUARY
FOREST RESERVE
NATURE RESERVE
PRIVATE RESERVE
NATIONAL PARK

MEXICO

Corozal Town

Orange Walk Town

Ambergris Caye

Lighthouse Reef

Belize City

Turneffe Islands

San Ignacio

BELMOPAN

Dangriga

Glover's Reef

Caribbean Sea

Punta Gorda

Sapodilla Cayes

Gulf of Honduras

GUATEMALA

0   20 mi
0   20 km

© AVALON TRAVEL

drowned. It was after Hurricane Hattie that the capital of the country was moved from Belize City (just 18 inches above sea level) to Belmopan. Then, in 1978, Hurricane Greta took a heavy toll in dollar damage, though no lives were lost. More recent serious hurricanes affecting Belize include Mitch in 1998, Keith in 2000, Iris in 2001, and Arthur in 2008. There have also been a number of less serious "northers." In the summer of 2008 when several Belizean communities suffered severe flooding and major bridges were washed out.

ENVIRONMENTAL ISSUES

Because of the country's impressive network of protected areas and relatively low population density, the widespread deforestation that occurs in other parts of Central America is not nearly as big a problem in Belize. However, Belize faces its own set of challenges. Perhaps the biggest problem is improper disposal of solid and liquid wastes, both municipal and industrial, particularly agro-wastes from the shrimp and citrus industries.

Mining of aggregates from rivers and streams has negative impacts on local watersheds and the coastal zones into which they empty, where sedimentation can be destructive to reef and other marine systems. Unchecked, unplanned development, especially in sensitive areas like barrier beaches, mangroves, islands, and riverbanks, where changes to the landscape often have wide and unanticipated effects, is another problem.

Energy—or lack thereof—is also a major issue for Belize, which has historically had to buy expensive power from neighboring Mexico. The controversial construction of the Chalillo Dam on the upper Macal River brought all of Belize's energy and environmental issues to the forefront; the saga of Chalillo is brilliantly narrated in *Last Flight of the Scarlet Macaw* by Bruce Barcott.

The Sea

CAYES AND ATOLLS

More than 200 cayes (pronounced "keys" and derived from the Spanish *cayo* for "key" or "islet") dot the blue waters off Belize's eastern coast. They range in size from barren patches that are submerged at high tide to the largest, Ambergris Caye—25 miles long and nearly 4.5 miles across at its widest point. Some cayes are inhabited by people, others only by wildlife. The majority are lush patches of mangrove that challenge the geographer's definition of what makes an island (that's why you'll never see a precise figure of how many there are).

Most of the cayes lie within the protection of the Belize Barrier Reef (almost 200 miles long), which parallels the mainland. Without the protection of the reef—in essence a breakwater—the islands would be washed away. Within the reef, the sea is relatively calm and shallow.

Beyond the reef lie three of the Caribbean's four atolls: **Glover's Reef, Turneffe Islands,** and **Lighthouse Reef.** An atoll is a ring-shaped coral island surrounding a lagoon, always beautiful, and almost exclusively found in the South Pacific. The three types of cayes are **wet cayes,** which are submerged part of the time and can support only mangrove swamps; **bare coral outcroppings** that are equally uninhabitable; and **sandy islands** with palm trees, jungle shrubbery, and their own set of animals. The more inhabited cayes lie in the northern part of the reef and include Caye Caulker, Ambergris Caye, St. George's Caye, and Caye Chapel.

REEFS

Reefs are divided into three types: atoll, fringing, and barrier. An **atoll** can be formed around the crater of a submerged volcano. The polyps begin building their colonies on the round edge of the crater, forming a circular coral island with a lagoon in the center. Thousands of atolls occupy the world's tropical waters. Only four are in the Caribbean Sea; three of those are in Belize's waters.

SWIM LIGHTLY: REEF ETIQUETTE

Divers and other coral reef visitors are becoming some of the strongest and most effective advocates for coral reef conservation. Good divers know the best way to enjoy a reef is to slow down, relax, and watch as reef creatures go about their daily lives undisturbed. Learn all you can about coral reefs – they are fascinating and fragile environments. Follow these simple guidelines to be a "coral-friendly" diver. You should also learn about local laws and regulations, as they may differ from these general guidelines. And speak up; make sure your dive buddies understand these simple but important conservation practices.

PREPARING FOR YOUR DIVE TRIP

Support coral reef conservation by choosing your resort with care and being a "green consumer" with your vacation dollars. Opt for environmentally conscious places to stay. Look for coral parks and other marine conservation areas, and pay user fees that support marine conservation. Keep your diving skills finely tuned, and be sure to practice them away from the reef. And choose coral-friendly dive operations that practice reef conservation by

- giving diver orientations and briefings.

- holding buoyancy control workshops.

- actively supporting local coral parks.

- using available moorings – anchors and chains destroy fragile corals.

- using available wastewater pump-out facilities.

- making sure garbage is well stowed, especially light plastic items.

- taking away everything brought on board, such as packaging and used batteries.

IN THE WATER

- Never touch corals; even a slight contact can harm them and some corals can sting or cut you.

- Carefully select points of entry and exit to avoid walking on corals.

- Make sure all of your equipment is well secured.

- Make sure you are neutrally buoyant at all times.

- Maintain a comfortable distance from the reef, so that you're certain you can avoid contact.

- Learn to swim without using your arms.

- Move slowly and deliberately in the water – relax and take your time.

- Practice good finning and body control to avoid accidental contact with the reef or stirring up the sediment.

- Know where your fins are at all times and don't kick up sand.

- Stay off the bottom and never stand or rest on corals.

- Avoid using gloves and kneepads in coral environments.

- Take nothing living or dead out of the water, except recent garbage.

- Do not chase, harass, or try to ride marine life.

- Do not touch or handle marine life except under expert guidance and following established guidelines. Never feed marine life.

- Use photographic and video equipment only if you are an advanced diver; cameras are cumbersome and affects a diver's buoyancy and mobility; It is all too easy to touch and damage marine life when concentrating on "the shot."

- Remember, look but don't touch.

(These guidelines were developed by the Coral Reef Alliance (CORAL, www.coral.org), © CORAL.)

A **fringing reef** is coral living on a shallow shelf that extends outward from shore into the sea. A **barrier reef** runs parallel to the coast, with water separating it from the land. Sometimes it's actually a series of reefs with channels of water in between. This is the case with some of the larger barrier reefs in the Pacific and Indian Oceans.

The Belize Barrier Reef is part of the greater Mesoamerican Reef, which extends from Mexico's Isla Mujeres to the Bay Islands of Honduras. The Belizean portion of the reef begins at Bacalar Chico in the north and ends with the Sapodilla Cayes in the south. This 180-mile-long reef is the longest reef in the Western and Northern Hemispheres.

Coral

Coral is a unique limestone formation that grows in innumerable shapes, such as delicate lace, trees with reaching branches, pleated mushrooms, stovepipes, petaled flowers, fans, domes, heads of cabbage, and stalks of broccoli. Corals are formed by millions of tiny carnivorous polyps that feed on minute organisms and live in large colonies of individual species. These small creatures are generally less than half an inch long. Related to the jellyfish and sea anemone, polyps need sunlight and clear saltwater not colder than 70°F to survive. Coral polyps have cylinder-shaped bodies. One end is attached to a hard surface (the bottom of the ocean, the rim of a submerged volcano, or the reef itself). The mouth at the other end is encircled with tiny tentacles that capture the polyp's minute prey with a deadly sting.

How a Reef Grows

As these small creatures continue to reproduce and die, their sturdy skeletons accumulate. Over eons, broken bits of coral, animal waste, and granules of soil contribute to the strong foundation for a reef that will slowly rise toward the surface. In a healthy environment, it can grow one to two inches a year. One small piece of coral represents millions of polyps and many years of construction.

© RICH WILSON

mooring buoys are installed to protect the reefs

Protecting the Reefs

Belize's reefs are being impacted by overfishing, coastal development, sewage and sedimentation, coral bleaching, and inappropriate and uninformed marine tourism practices, according to Rich Wilson, Mesoamerica Program Manager of the Coral Reef Alliance, a nonprofit organization dedicated to protecting coral reefs around the world. It has been proven that the most effective way to protect reefs is through well-managed protected areas marine areas. In this sense, says Wilson, "Belize is ahead of the curve. They also have a well-established national tour guide training program, which you don't find in many places around the world."

When I asked top Belizean naturalist Dave Vernon about the number one way people can be responsible tourists, his immediate response was, "Leave the fins at home!" Beginning snorkelers, he explained, panic when they come up to clear their masks, automatically standing on the coral or kicking it with their fins. "Coral grows one to one-and-a-half inches a year," he says, and when somebody starts kicking his fins, "you see hundreds of years of coral growth wiped out in seconds."

Do your part by following the guidelines listed in the sidebar on reef etiquette in this chapter.

ESTUARIES

The marshy areas and bays at the mouths of rivers where saltwater and fresh water mix are called estuaries. Here, nutrients from inland are carried out to sea by currents and tides to nourish reefs, sea grass beds, and the open ocean. Many plants and animals feed, live, or mate in these waters. Conch, crabs, shrimp, and other shellfish thrive here, and several types of jellyfish and other invertebrates call this home. Seabirds, shorebirds, and waterfowl of all types frequent estuaries to feed, nest, and mate. Crocodiles, dolphins, and manatees are regular visitors. Rays, sharks, and tarpon hunt and mate here. During the wet season, the estuaries of Belize pump a tremendous amount of nutrients into the sea.

THE FUTURE OF THE REEF

Rich Wilson is the Mesoamerica Program Manager for the Coral Reef Alliance (CORAL). Here, he answers some questions about the work that CORAL does, and his hopes for the future.

What is your background? How and when did you first come to Belize? I began my work in conservation nearly fifteen years ago as a marine naturalist aboard charter boats in Maui. After witnessing firsthand the damage that tour boat anchors inflict on coral reefs, I left the charter industry to coordinate Hawaii's Day-Use Mooring Program. As a volunteer project leader, I built coalitions among state government, private industry, and the conservation community, spearheading several projects that placed boat moorings at popular snorkel and dive sites throughout south Maui. I also worked as a park ranger at Maui's Haleakala National Park, educating the public with interpretive programs about Hawaiian ecology, geology, and park service history, and leading a variety of backcountry resource management projects. Prior to joining CORAL in 2003, I was a chief scientist and team leader with the National Marine Fisheries Service Marine Debris program in Honolulu.

How long has the Coral Reef Alliance been working in Belize? CORAL first started working in Belize in 2004 as the lead organization implementing the sustainable tourism component of the International Coral Reef Action Network (ICRAN) Mesoamerican Reef Alliance (MAR) project. The primary focus of the ICRAN MAR project was to develop regional voluntary environmental performance standards for the marine tourism sector throughout the MAR region, build alliances and capacity for local conservation, and create incentives for sustainable business practices. Prior to that, CORAL supported mooring buoy projects off the coast of Ambergris Caye and worked with the Hol Chan Marine Reserve in a global marine protected area needs assessment survey that we did in 2003.

What projects are you working on in Belize? In which parts of Belize have you worked? Our two main project sites in Belize are the town of San Pedro on the island of Ambergris Caye, and Placencia in Southern Belize. However, because our conservation model allows for the organic growth of our programs to neighboring communities, we also include Belize City and Caye Caulker in the mix.

Since publishing the Voluntary Standards for Marine Recreation in the Mesoamerican Reef System in 2007, CORAL has been implementing the standards through a program we developed called **Environmental Walk-Through (EWT).** CORAL staff meets with marine tour operators on a voluntary basis to evaluate their business practices and make recommendations for improvements. We also continue to conduct our Sustainable Marine Recreation and Conservation in Action workshops with members of multiple tour guide associations,

MANGROVES

Mangroves live on the edge between land and sea, forming dense thickets that act as a protective border against the forces of wind and waves. Four species grow along many low-lying coastal areas on the mainland and along island lagoons and fringes. Of these, the red mangrove and the black mangrove are most prolific. Red mangrove in excess of 30 feet high is found in tidal areas, inland lagoons, and river mouths, but always close to the sea. Its signature is its arching prop roots. Black mangrove grows to almost double that height. Its roots are slender, upright projectiles that grow to about 12 inches, protruding all around the mother tree. Both types of roots provide air to the tree.

Mangrove Succession

Red mangroves *(Rhizophora mangle)* specialize in creating land—the seedpods fall into the water and take root on the sandy bottom of a shallow shoal. The roots, which can survive in seawater, then collect particles from the water and the tree's own dropping leaves to create

marine protected area managers, and representatives of government agencies.

A core part of our **Conservation in Action workshops** is an interactive exercise where the workshop participants identify the most pressing local threats to their reefs and then brainstorm local conservation initiatives that will help reduce or eliminate those threats. CORAL facilitates the process of developing these local action plans, then invites the community to apply for CORAL-funded microgrants to support the work. In Belize, two very successful programs that have grown from this process include a robust national mooring buoy program that has resulted in the installation of 60+ mooring buoys, and an educational program called **Kids in Action,** where elementary school kids and teachers participate in eco-field trips.

Through our **Coral Reef Leadership Network program,** we recently trained nine local leaders – marine recreation business owners, operations managers, and protected area staff – to train their peers in our Sustainable Marine Recreation workshops. By training a local group of leaders, we are able to educate more people more quickly than if we conducted the trainings on our own. The Leadership Network program has recently been adopted as a specialty component of Belize's National Tour Guide Training Program, so all tour guides in Belize will eventually be trained in Sustainable Marine Recreation.

How do Belize's reefs compare to other reefs in the world, as far as their condition/deterioration and also historic/current conservation efforts? This is really a better question for some of my biologist colleagues, but I can say that, like most reefs in the world, Belize's reef is suffering from a variety of impacts, including overfishing, coastal development, sewage and sedimentation, coral bleaching, and inappropriate and uninformed marine tourism practices. Science tells us that well-managed marine protected areas are the best chance we have to save coral reefs. So Belize is ahead of the curve compared to many places in that they have an established network of functioning marine protected areas. They also have a well-established national tour guide training program, which you don't find in many places around the world.

Is bleaching a problem in Belize's reefs? Yes, a biologist who is training in our Coral Reef Leadership Network program this week told me that a lot of new bleaching has been observed across Belize's reef this year.

What is the top priority right now for protecting Belize's reefs? The priorities are continuing to strengthen the management of Belize's network of marine protected areas, securing widespread adoption of the voluntary marine recreation standards, providing regular training opportunities in sustainable business practices, and building capacity for locally led conservation initiatives and wise use of coral reef resources.

MANGROVES AND HUMANS

The doctor on Christopher Columbus's ship reported in 1494 that mangroves in the Caribbean were "so thick that a rabbit could scarcely walk through." The mangroves are just as dense today, a wall of bright green along the shore, but their location is probably not the same. Over a period of several hundred years, depending on hurricanes and other localized natural events, the red mangroves may have extended the edge of a coastline a mile or more in their determined march into the sea.

Mangroves are vital to coastal ecosystems, for building islands, and protecting the mainland.

Mangrove islands and coastal forests play an essential role in protecting Belize's coastline from destruction during natural events such as hurricanes and tropical storms. Along with the sea grass beds, they also protect the Belize Barrier Reef by filtering sediment from river runoff before it reaches and smothers the delicate coral polyps. However, dense mangrove forests are also home to mosquitoes and biting flies. The mud and peat beneath mangrove thickets is often malodorous with decaying plant matter and hydrogen sulfide–producing bacteria. Many developers would like nothing better than to eliminate mangroves and replace them with sandy beaches surrounded by seawalls. But such modification to the coastline causes accelerated erosion and destruction of seaside properties, especially during severe storms.

IMPORTANCE TO WILDLIFE

Birds of many species use the mangrove branches for roosting and nesting sites, including swallows, redstarts, warblers, grackles, herons, egrets, osprey, kingfishers, pelicans, and roseate spoonbills. Along the seaside edge of red mangrove forests, prop roots extend into the water, creating tangled thickets unparalleled as nurseries of the sea. Juveniles of commercial fisheries, such as snapper, hogfish, and lobster, find a safe haven here. The flats around mangrove islands are famous for recreational fisheries such as bonefish and tarpon. Prop roots that extend below the low tide mark provide important substrate (a platform to which organisms settle or attach) for sessile (immobile) marine invertebrates such as sponges, hydroids, corals, tube worms, mollusks, anemones, and tunicates. In many areas, snorkeling along a mangrove is often more colorful and exciting than along a reef.

The three-dimensional labyrinth created by expanding red mangroves, sea grass beds, and bogues (small channels of seawater flowing through the mangroves) provides the home and nursery habitat for nurse sharks, American crocodiles, dolphins, and manatees.

PROTECTION

Fortunately, the Belize government enforces laws that make it difficult to disturb these natural wonders. Destruction of mangroves is illegal in most areas; cutting and removal of mangroves requires a special permit and mitigation. Despite some illegal cutting, you can still see miles and miles of red mangrove forests edging the coast and islands of Belize, in some places as extensive as they were hundreds of years ago when the *Hispaniola* sailed through these waters.

(Contributed by Caryn Self-Sullivan, PhD, president of Sirenian International and a marine scientist who has been studying manatee ecology and behavior in Belize since 1998. For more information about manatees around the world, visit www.sirenian.org.)

FISHING REGULATIONS

BONE FISH *(ALBULBA VULPES)*
Also known locally as macabi. No person shall buy or sell any bone fish.

CONCH *(STROMBUS GIGAS)*
Shell length should exceed seven inches, and market clean weight should exceed three ounces, no diced or fillet. The season is closed July 1–September 30.

CORAL
It is illegal for any person to take, buy, sell, or have in his possession any type of coral. An exception is made in the case of black coral (order *Antipatharia*), which may only be bought, sold, or exported with a license from the Fisheries Administrator.

HICKATEE *(DERMATEMY MAWII)*
No person shall have in his possession more than three, or transport on any vehicle more than five such turtles, or fish for female hickatee that are greater than 43 centimeters (17.2 inches) or smaller than 38 centimeters (15.2 inches). The season is closed May 1–31.

LOBSTER *(PANULIRUS ARGUS)*
Minimum cape length is three inches, minimum tail weight is four ounces; no diced or fillet. The season is closed February 15–June 14.

MARINE TURTLES
No person should interfere with any turtle nest. No person may take any turtle unless with a license from the Fisheries Administrator (traditional use only). No person shall buy, sell, or have in his possession any articles made of turtle shell.

**NASSAU GROUPER
*(EPINEPHELUS STRIATUS)***
No person shall take in the waters of Belize, or buy, sell, or have in his possession, any Nassau grouper between December 1 and March 31, except from Maugre Caye at Turneffe Islands and Northern Two Caye at Lighthouse Reef. At these two places a special license is granted to traditional fishers.

SHRIMP
Trawling: the season is closed April 15–August 14. No one should fish using scuba gear except under license from the Fisheries Administrator. Contact the Fisheries Department for further information: P.O. Box 148, Belize City, tel. 501/223-2623, 224-4552, or 223-2187, species@btl.net.

---

soil. Once the red mangrove forest has created land, it makes way for the next mangrove in the succession process. The black mangrove *(Avicennia germinans)* can actually out-compete the red mangrove at this stage, because of its ability to live in anoxic soil (without oxygen). In this way, the red mangrove appears to do itself in by creating an anoxic environment. But while the black mangrove is taking over the upland of the community, the red mangrove continues to dominate the perimeter, as it continuously creates more land from the sea. One way to identify a black mangrove forest is by the thousands of dense pneumataphores (tiny air roots) covering the ground under the trees.

Soon, burrowing organisms such as insects and crabs begin to inhabit the floor of the black mangrove forest, and the first ground covers, *Salicornia* and salt wart *(Batis maritima)* take hold—thereby aerating the soil and enabling the third and fourth mangrove species in succession to move in: the white mangrove *(Laguncularia racemosa)* and the gray mangrove *(Conocarpus erectus)*, also known locally as buttonwood.

Desalinizers

Each of the three primary mangrove species lives in a very salty environment and each has its own special way of eliminating salt. The red mangrove concentrates the salt taken up with seawater into individual leaves, which turn bright yellow and fall into the prop roots, thereby adding organic matter to the system. The black mangrove eliminates salt from the underside of each leaf. If you pick a black mangrove leaf and lick the back, it will taste very salty. The white mangrove eliminates salt through two tiny salt pores located on the petiole (the stem that connects the leaf to the branch). If you sleep in a hammock under a white mangrove tree, you will feel drops of salty water as the tree "cries" upon you! The buttonwood also has tiny salt pores on each petiole.

SEA GRASS BEDS

Standing on Ambergris Caye and looking seaward, many tourists are surprised to see something dark in the shallow water just offshore. They expect the sandy bottom typical of many Caribbean islands. However, it is this "dark stuff" that eventually will make their day's snorkeling, fishing, or dining experience more enjoyable. What they are noticing is sea grass, another of the ocean's great nurseries.

Sea grasses are plants with elongated, ribbon-like leaves. Just like the land plants they evolved from, sea grasses flower and have extensive root systems. They live in sandy areas around estuaries, mangroves, reefs, and open coastal waters. Turtle grass has broader, tapelike leaves and is common down to about 60 feet. Manatee grass, found to depths of around 40 feet, has thinner, more cylindrical leaves. Both cover large areas of seafloor and intermix in some areas, harboring an amazing variety of marine plants and animals. Barnacles, conch, crabs, and many other shellfish proliferate in the fields of sea grass. Anemones, seahorses, sponges, and starfish live here. Grunts, filefish, flounder, jacks, rays, and wrasses feed here. Sea turtles and manatees often graze in these lush marine pastures.

These beds and flats are being threatened in some areas by unscrupulous developers who are dredging sand for cement and landfill material (especially on Ambergris Caye).

Flora and Fauna

Belize's position at the biological crossroads between North and South America has blessed it with an astonishingly broad assortment of wildlife. Belize's wide-ranging geography and habitat have also been a primary factor in the diversity and complexity of its ecosystems and their denizens.

FLORA

Belize is a Garden of Eden. Four thousand species of native flowering plants include 250 species of orchids and approximately 700 species of trees. Most of the country's forests have been logged off and on for more than 300 years (2,000 years, if you count the widespread deforestation during the time of the ancient Maya). The areas closest to the rivers and coast were the hardest hit, because boats could be docked and logs easily loaded to be taken farther out to sea to the large ships used to haul the precious timber.

Forests

Flying over the countryside gives you a view of the patchwork landscape of cleared areas and secondary growth. Belize consists of four distinct forest communities: pine-oak, mixed broadleaf, cohune palm, and riverine forests. Pine-oak forests are found in sandy, dry soils. In the same areas, large numbers of mango, cashew, and coconut palm are grown near homes and villages. The mixed broadleaf forest is a transition area between the sandy pine soils and the clay soils found along the river. Often the mixed broadleaf forest is broken up here and there and doesn't reach great height; it's species-rich but not as diverse as the cohune forest. The cohune forest area is characterized by the cohune palm, which is found in fertile clay soil where a moderate amount of rain falls throughout the year. The cohune nut was an important part of the Maya diet. Archaeologists say that where they see a cohune forest, they know they'll find evidence of the Maya.

The cohune forest gives way to the riverine forest along river shorelines, where vast amounts of water are found year-round from excessive rain and from the flooding rivers. About 50–60 tree varieties and hundreds of species of vines, epiphytes, and shrubs grow here. Logwood, mahogany, cedar, and pine are difficult to find along the easily accessible rivers because of extensive logging. The forest is in different stages of growth and age. To find virgin forest, it's necessary to go high into the mountains that divide Belize. Because of the rugged terrain and distance from the rivers, these areas were left almost untouched. Even today, few roads exist. If left undisturbed for many, many years, the forest will eventually regenerate itself.

Among the plant life of Belize, look for mangroves, bamboo, and swamp cypresses, as well as ferns, vines, and flowers creeping from tree to tree, creating a dense growth. On topmost limbs, orchids and air ferns reach for the sun. As you go farther south, you'll find the classic tropical rainforest, including tall mahoganies, *campeche, sapote,* and ceiba, thick with vines.

Orchids

In remote areas of Belize, one of the more exotic blooms, the orchid, is often found on the highest limbs of tall trees. Of all the orchid species reported in Belize, 20 percent are terrestrial (growing in the ground) and 80 percent are epiphytic (attached to a host plant—in this case trees—and deriving moisture and nutrients from the air and rain). Both types grow in many sizes and shapes: tiny buttons, spanning the length of a long branch; large-petaled blossoms with ruffled edges; or intense, tiger-striped miniatures. The lovely flowers come in a wide variety of colors, some subtle, some brilliant. The black orchid is Belize's national flower. All orchids are protected by strict laws, so look but don't pick.

FAUNA

A walk through the jungle brings you close to myriad animal and bird species, many of which are almost extinct in other Central American countries—and the world. Bring your binoculars and some fast film, and be vewy, vewy quiet.

Following is a short introduction to a few of the creatures you are likely to see in the wild if you spend any amount of time outside your room. This is an incomplete, quite random selection; for more detailed information, find yourself one of the abundant field guides to the various flora and fauna of Belize.

Birds

If you're a serious bird-watcher, you know all about Belize. Scores of species can be seen while sitting on the deck of your jungle lodge: big and small, rare and common, and with local guides aplenty to help find them in all the vegetation. The **keel-billed toucan** is the national bird of Belize and is often seen perched high on a bare limb in the early morning.

Bats

Bats cling to the ceilings of caves, often attracted to warm pockets of air. Bats are harmless to humans (although confused vampire bats, which carry a risk of rabies, may bite, but only if you are sleeping outside); most that live in the caves are insect-eating bats. Their eyesight is excellent, as is their use of echolocation; fly-bys occur only if they go after the bugs attracted to your headlamp. Some scientists warn about a pulmonary disease that can be carried in the dry dust of bat droppings. If you are concerned, ask your doctor and perhaps wear a breathing mask of some sort.

Cats

Seven species of cats are found in North America, five of them in Belize. For years, rich adventurers came to Belize on safari to hunt the jaguar for its beautiful skin. Likewise, hunting margay, puma, ocelots, and jaguarundis was a popular sport in the rainforest. All of that has changed. Hunting any endangered species in Belize is not allowed, and there is much protected area in which they freely wander.

© CHERIE ROSE

American Crocodile and Little Blue Heron near Punta Gorda

The **jaguar** is heavy-chested with sturdy, muscled forelegs; a relatively short tail; and small, rounded ears. Its tawny coat is uniformly spotted and the spots form rosettes: large circles with smaller spots in the center. The jaguar's belly is white with black spots. The male can weigh 145–255 pounds, females 125–165 pounds. Largest of the cats in Central America and third-largest cat in the world, the jaguar is about the same size as a leopard. It is nocturnal, spending most daylight hours snoozing in the sun. The male marks an area of about 65 square miles and spends its nights stalking deer, peccaries, agoutis, tapirs, monkeys, and birds. If hunting is poor and times are tough, the jaguar will go into rivers and scoop fish with its large paws. The river is also a favorite spot for the jaguar to hunt the large tapir when it comes to drink. Females begin breeding at about three years old and generally produce twin cubs.

The smallest of the Belizean cats is the **margay,** weighing in at about 11 pounds and marked by a velvety coat with exotic designs in yellow and black and a tail that's half the length of its body. The bright eye shine indicates it has exceptional night vision. A shy animal, it is seldom seen in open country, preferring the protection of the dense forest. The "tiger cat," as it is called by locals, hunts mainly in the trees, satisfied with birds, monkeys, and insects as well as lizards and figs.

Larger and not nearly as catlike as the margay, the black or brown **jaguarundi** has a small flattened head, rounded ears, short legs, and a long tail. It hunts by day for birds and small mammals in the rainforests of Central America. The **ocelot** has a striped and spotted coat and an average weight of about 35 pounds. A good climber, the cat hunts in trees as well as on the ground. Its prey include birds, monkeys, snakes, rabbits, young deer, and fish. Ocelots usually have litters of two kittens but can have as many as four. The **puma** is also known as the cougar or mountain lion. The adult male measures about six feet in length and weighs up to 198 pounds. It thrives in any environment that supports deer, porcupine, or rabbit. The puma hunts day or night.

Primates

In Creole, the **black howler monkey** is referred to as a "baboon" (in Spanish, *saraguate*), though it has no close connection to its African relatives. Because the howler prefers low-lying tropical rainforests (under 1,000 feet of elevation), Belize is a perfect habitat. The monkeys are more commonly found near the riverine forests, especially on the Belize River and its major branches. The adult howler monkey is entirely black and weighs 15–25 pounds. Its most distinctive trait is a roar that can be heard up to a mile distant. A bone in the throat acts as an amplifier; the cry sounds much like that of a jaguar. The howler's unforgettable bark is said by some to be used to warn other monkey troops away from its territory. Locals, on the other hand, say the howlers roar when it's about to rain, to greet the sun, to say good night, or when they're feeding.

To protect the howler monkey, the **Community Baboon Sanctuary** was organized in Bermudian Landing to help conserve the lands where it lives. Thanks to an all-out effort involving local property owners, the Belize Ministry of Natural Resources, the U.S. World Wildlife Fund, the Belize Audubon Society, and the Peace Corps, the land that provides for the howler will be saved. The sanctuary is an ideal place for researchers to study the howler's habits and perhaps discover the key to its survival among encroaching humans (and for tourists to get close to these creatures in their natural habitat). In fact, natural breeding was so successful there that troops of howlers have been relocated to Cockscomb and other regions where the monkey was decimated by yellow fever decades ago.

Spider monkeys are smaller than black howlers and live in troops of a dozen or more, feeding on leaves, fruits, and flowers high in the jungle canopy. Slender limbs and elongated prehensile tails assist them as they climb and swing from tree to tree. With a border of white around their faces, adults look like little old people. Baby spider monkeys are winsome in appearance too, and often are captured for pets. So curious and mischievous are they,

SHHH! I'M LOOKING FOR WILDLIFE!

It takes many years of practice to fine tune your wildlife-viewing skills, hours upon hours of patient sitting and walking sessions to learn some of Mother Nature's more subtle communication skills. Growing up and living off the forest helps — that's why hiring a native guide will guarantee you more sightings than going it on your own. Spending years in the Belizean bush studying jaguars and other cats is a good method as well, the one employed by biologist Alan Rabinowitz in his landmark studies of the Cockscomb Basin. He shares some of his hard-won knowledge in the following passage from his book *Jaguar*:

> The forest is teeming with wildlife, but you see and hear very little just by walking through it. It often seems simply a quiet, green darkness, but that appearance is deceiving. When you learn to read the signs of an animal's passing, it's like watching the wildlife. A nibbled twig tells you a red brocket deer has been feeding; a muddy wallow says a tapir has been by; chewed nuts from the cohune palm tree indicate that a paca has fed the night before; and a musky smell warns you that a group of peccaries may be closer than you'd like.

however, that frustrated owners frequently cage them or even release them back into the wild. Without the skills to survive or the support of a troop, such freed orphans are doomed to perish. Unlike howler monkeys, which may allow human proximity during their midday siesta, spider monkeys rarely approve. They usually dissolve into the forest canopy. On occasion, they have been known to aim small sticks,

baby sea turtles

© JOSHUA BERMAN

urine, and worse at intruders. Though not as numerous in Belize as howler monkeys because of disease and habitat loss, they remain an important part of the country's natural legacy.

Rodents of Unusual Size

A relative of the rabbit, the **agouti** or "Indian rabbit" has coarse gray-brown fur and a hopping gait. It is most often encountered scampering along a forest trail or clearing. Not the brightest of creatures, it makes up for this lack of wit with typical rodent libido and fecundity. Though it inhabits the same areas as the paca, these two seldom meet, as the agouti minds its business during the day and the paca prefers nighttime pursuits. The agouti is less delectable than the paca. Nonetheless, it is taken by animal and human hunters and is a staple food of jaguars.

The **paca**, or **gibnut,** is a quick, brownish rodent about the size of a small dog, with white spots along its back. Nocturnal by habit and highly prized as a food item by many Belizeans, the gibnut is more apt to be seen by the visitor on an occasional restaurant menu than in the wild.

A member of the raccoon family, the **coatimundi**—or **quash**—has a long, ringed tail, a masked face, and a lengthy snout. Sharp claws aid the coati in climbing trees and digging up insects and other small prey. Omnivorous, the quash also relishes jungle fruits. A sensitive, agile nose helps it sniff out trees bearing these favored goodies. Usually seen in small troops of females and young, coatis have an amusing, jaunty appearance as they cross a jungle path, tails at attention.

Next to deer, **peccaries** are the most widely hunted game in Central America. Other names for this piglike creature are "musk hog" and "javelina." Some compare these nocturnal mammals to the wild pigs found in Europe, though in fact they are native to America. Two species found in Belize are the collared and the white-lipped peccaries. The feisty collared peccary stands one foot at the shoulder and can be three feet long, weighing as much as 65 pounds. It is black and white with a narrow semicircular collar of white hair on the shoulders. In Spanish, *javalina* means "spear," descriptive of the two spearlike tusks that protrude from its mouth. Also with tusks, the white-lipped peccary, or "warrie," is reddish-brown to black and has an area of white around the mouth. This larger animal, which can grow to four feet long, dwells deep in tropical rainforests and at one time lived in herds of 100 or more. White-lipped peccaries are more dangerous than their smaller cousins and should be given a wide berth.

Tapir

The national animal of Belize, the South American **tapir** is found from the southern part of Mexico to southern Brazil. It is stout-bodied (200–300 kg or 91–136 lbs.), with short legs, a short tail, small eyes, and rounded ears. Its nose and upper lip extend into a short but very mobile proboscis. Totally herbivorous, tapirs usually live near streams or rivers in the forest. They bathe daily and also use the water as an escape when hunted either by humans or by their prime predator, the jaguar. Shy, unaggressive animals, they are nocturnal with a definite home range, wearing a path between the jungle and their feeding area.

Reptiles

Found all over Central America, lizards of the family *Iguanidae* include various large plant-eaters, in many sizes and typically dark in color with slight variations. The young **iguana** is bright emerald green. The common lizard grows to three feet long and has a blunt head and long flat tail. Bands of black and gray circle its body, and a serrated column reaches down the middle of its back, almost to its tail. During mating season, it's common to see brilliant orange males on a sunny branch hoping to attract girlfriends.

Very large and shy, the iguana uses its forelimbs to hold the front half of its body up off the ground while the two back limbs remain relaxed and splayed alongside its hindquarters. However, when the iguana is frightened, its hind legs do everything they're supposed to, and the iguana crashes quickly (though clumsily) into the brush searching for its burrow and safety. This reptile is not aggressive, but if cornered it will bite and use its tail in self-defense.

The iguana mostly enjoys basking in the bright sunshine along the Caribbean.

Though hawks prey on young iguanas and their eggs, the human still remains its most dangerous predator. It is not unusual to see locals along dirt paths carrying sturdy specimens by the tail to put in the cook pot. From centuries past, recorded references attest to the medicinal value of this lizard, partly explaining the active trade in live iguanas in marketplaces in some parts of Belize. Iguana stew is believed to cure or relieve various human ailments, such as impotence. The unlaid eggs of iguanas caught before the nesting season are considered a delicacy. Another reason for their popularity at the market is their delicate white flesh, which tastes much like chicken. If people say they're having "bamboo chicken" for dinner, they are dining on iguana.

Though often referred to as alligators, Belize has only **crocodiles,** the American (up to 20 feet) and the Morelet's (up to 8 feet). Crocodiles have a well-earned bad reputation in Africa, Australia, and New Guinea as man-eaters, especially the larger saltwater varieties. Their American cousins are fussier about their cuisine, preferring fish, dogs, and other small mammals to people. The territories of both species overlap in estuaries and brackish coastal waters. Able to filter excess salt from its system, only the American crocodile ventures to the more distant cayes. Endangered throughout their ranges, both crocs are protected by international law and should be left undisturbed. Often seen floating near the edge of lagoons or canals during midday, they are best observed at night with the help of a powerful flashlight. When caught in the beam, their eyes glow an eerie red. Crocodiles are most abundant in the rivers, swamps, and lagoons of the Belize City, Orange Walk, and Toledo Districts, as well as areas around the Turneffe Islands. Don't miss the Crocodile Reserve at Monkey Bay.

Of the 59 species of **snakes** that have been identified in Belize, at least nine are venomous, most notably the infamous fer-de-lance (locally called a "Tommygoff") and the coral snake.

History

Early recorded comments following Columbus's fourth voyage to the New World led the Spaniards to hastily conclude that the swampy shoreline of what is now Belize was unfit for human habitation. Someone should have told that to the Maya, who had been enjoying the area for quite some time already.

ANCIENT CIVILIZATION
Earliest Humans
During the Pleistocene epoch (about 50,000 B.C.), when the level of the sea fell, people and animals from Asia crossed the Bering land bridge into the American continent. For nearly 50,000 years, humans continued the epic trek southward.

As early as 10,000 B.C., Ice Age man hunted woolly mammoth and other large animals roaming the cool, moist landscape of Central America. Between 7000 and 2000 B.C., society evolved from hunters and gatherers to farmers. Such crops as corn, squash, and beans were independently domesticated in widely separated areas of Mesoamerica after about 6000 B.C. The remains of clay figurines from the Pre-Classic Period, presumed to be fertility symbols, marked the rise of religion in Mesoamerica, beginning about 2000 B.C.

Around 1000 B.C., the Olmec culture, believed to be the earliest in the area and the predecessors to the Maya, began to spread throughout Mesoamerica. Large-scale ceremonial centers grew along Gulf Coast lands, and much of Mesoamerica was influenced by the Olmecs' religion of worshipping jaguar-like gods. The Olmecs also developed the New World's first calendar and an early system of writing.

Classic Period
The Classic Period, beginning about A.D. 300, is now hailed as the peak of cultural development among the Maya. Until A.D. 900, they made phenomenal progress in the development of artistic, architectural, and astronomical

skills. They constructed impressive buildings during this period and wrote codices (folded bark books) filled with hieroglyphic symbols that detailed complicated mathematical calculations of days, months, and years. Only the priests and the privileged held this knowledge and continued to learn and develop it until, for some unexplained reason, the growth suddenly halted. A new militaristic society was born, built around a blend of ceremonialism, civic and social organization, and conquest.

A Society Collapses
Priests and noblemen, the guardians of religion, science, and the arts, conducted their ritual ceremonies and studies in the large stone pyramids and platforms found today in ruins throughout the jungle. Consequently, more specific questions arise: What happened to the priests and noblemen? Why were the centers abandoned? What happened to the knowledge of the intelligentsia? They studied the skies, wrote the books, and designed the pyramids. Theories abound. Some speculate about a revolution—the people were tired of subservience and were no longer willing to farm the land to provide food, clothing, and support for the priests and nobles. Another theory is that there just wasn't enough land to farm and provide food and necessities for the large population.

All signs point to an abrupt work stoppage. After about A.D. 900, no buildings were constructed and no stelae, which carefully detailed names and dates to inform future generations of their roots, were erected.

Whatever happened, it's clear that the special knowledge concerning astronomy, hieroglyphics, and architecture was not passed on to Maya descendants. Sociologists who have lived with the indigenous people in isolated villages are convinced that this privileged information is not known by today's Maya. Why did the masses disperse, leaving once-sacred stone cities unused and ignored? It's possible

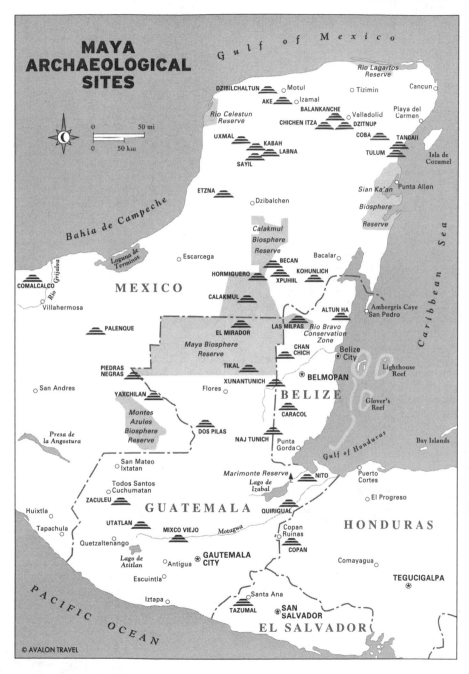

MAYA ARCHAEOLOGICAL SITES

Gulf of Mexico

Rio Lagartos Reserve

DZIBILCHALTUN   Motul
AKE   Izamal   Tizimin   Cancun
Rio Celestun Reserve   BALANKANCHE   Valladolid   Playa del Carmen
CHICHEN ITZA   DZITNUP
UXMAL   COBA   TANCAII
KABAH   LABNA   TULUM   Isla de Cozumel
SAYIL

ETZNA   Dzibalchen   Sian Ka'an   Punta Allen
Biosphere

Calakmul Biosphere Reserve   Reserve

Bahia de Campeche   BECAN   Bacalar
Escarcega   HORMIGUERO   KOHUNLICH
Laguna de Terminos   XPUHIIL

COMALCALCO   CALAKMUL   ALTUN HA   Ambergris Caye
MEXICO   San Pedro
Villahermosa   LAS MILPAS   Rio Bravo Conservation Zone
PALENQUE   EL MIRADOR   CHAN CHICH   Belize City
Maya Biosphere Reserve
PIEDRAS NEGRAS   TIKAL   Lighthouse Reef
San Andres   XUNANTUNICH   ⊛ BELMOPAN
YAXCHILAN   Flores   **BELIZE**
Montes Azules Biosphere Reserve   CARACOL   Glover's Reef
Presa de la Angostura   DOS PILAS   NAJ TUNICH   Punta Gorda   Bay Islands
Gulf of Honduras
San Mateo Ixtatan   Marimonte Reserve   NITO   Puerto Cortes
Todos Santos Cuchumatan   Lago de Izabal   El Progreso
ZACULEU   QUIRIGUAL
Huixtla   **GUATEMALA**   **HONDURAS**
UTATLAN   MIXCO VIEJO   *Motagua*
Tapachula   Copan Ruinas
Quetzaltenango   ⊛ GAUTEMALA CITY   COPAN   Comayagua
Lago de Atitlan   Antigua   TEGUCIGALPA ⊛
Escuintla   Santa Ana
Iztapa   TAZUMAL   ⊛ SAN SALVADOR
PACIFIC OCEAN   **EL SALVADOR**

Caribbean Sea

0   50 mi
0   50 km

© AVALON TRAVEL

that lengthy periods of drought, famine, and epidemic caused the people to leave their once-glorious sacred centers. No longer important in day-to-day life, these structures were ignored for a thousand years and faced the whimsy of nature and its corroding elements.

Anthropologists and historians do know that perhaps as many as 500,000 Maya were killed by diseases such as smallpox after the arrival of the Spaniards into the New World. But no one really knows for sure what halted the progress of the Maya culture.

Secrets of the Ruins
With today's technology, astronauts have seen many wonders from outer space, spotting over-grown structures within the thick uninhabited jungle of La Ruta Maya. These large treasures of knowledge are just waiting to be reopened. But until the funds and plans are in hand, these mounds are left unsung and untouched in hopes that looters will not find them be-fore archaeologists are able to open them up. Looters generally are not interested in the knowledge gained from an artifact, just money. Not only has much been lost in these criminal actions, but their heavy-handed methods have also destroyed countless artifacts. As new finds are made, the history of the Maya develops new depth and breadth. Archaeologists, ethnolo-gists, art historians, and linguists continue to unravel the ongoing mystery with constant new discoveries of temples and artifacts, each with a story to tell.

COLONIALISM
The pre-Columbian history of Belize is closely associated with that of its nearby neighbors: Mexico, Guatemala, and Honduras. The Maya were the first people to inhabit the land re-ferred to as La Ruta Maya. They planted *milpas* (cornfields), built ceremonial centers, and es-tablished villages with large numbers of people throughout the region. Hernán Cortés passed through the southern part of the country on his trek northward searching for treasure. In 1530, the conquistador Montejo attacked the Nachankan and Belize Maya, but his attempt

---

BELIZE HISTORY IN A NUTSHELL

The peaceful country of Belize is a sover-eign democratic state of Central America located on the Caribbean. The govern-ment is patterned on the system of par-liamentary democracy and experiences no more political turmoil than any other similar government, such as Great Britain or the United States.

IMPORTANT DATES
1862: Became a British colony
1954: Attained universal adult suffrage
1964: Began self-government
1981: Attained full independence

---

to conquer them failed. This introduction of Spanish influence did not have the impact on Belize that it did in the northern part of the Caribbean coast until the Caste War.

Hernán Cortés and Other Explorers
After Columbus's arrival in the New World, other adventurers traveling the same seas soon found the Yucatán Peninsula. In 1519, 34-year-old Cortés sailed from Cuba against the will of the Spanish governor. With 11 ships, 120 sail-ors, and 550 soldiers, he set out to search for slaves, a lucrative business with or without the blessings of the government. His search began on the Yucatán coast and eventually encom-passed most of Mexico. However, he hadn't counted on the ferocious resistance and cun-ning of the Maya. The fighting was destined to continue for many years—a time of bloodshed and death for many of his men. This "war" didn't *really* end on the peninsula until the Chan Santa Cruz people finally made peace with the Mexican federal government in 1935, more than 400 years later.

Although the Maya in Mérida, in Yucatán, Mexico, were a long distance from Belize and not directly bothered by the intrusion of the Spanish, the actions of the Spanish Franciscan priests toward the Mérida Maya would have a great influence on Belize in the years that followed. The Catholic priests were wiping out ceremonies and all other traces of the Maya, further setting the stage for the bloodshed to come. The ripple effect that followed eventually exploded into the Caste War, which, in turn, brought both Maya and mestizos across the borders of Belize.

Diego de Landa was the Franciscan priest who, while trying to gather the Maya into the fold of Christianity, leaned on them and their beliefs with a heavy hand, destroying thousands of Maya idols, many of their temples, and all but four of their books. Because his methods were often cruel, in 1563 he was called back to Spain after colonial civil and religious leaders accused him of "despotic mismanagement." He spent a year in prison, and while his fate was being decided, he wrote a book, *Relaciones de las Cosas de Yucatán,* defending himself against the charges.

Ironically, this book gave extensive information about the Maya, their beliefs, the growth and preparation of their food, the structure of their society, the priesthood, and the sciences—essentially a broad insight into the culture that otherwise would have been lost forever. Fortunately, he included in his book a one-line formula that, when used as a mathematical and chronological key, opened up the science of Maya calculations and their great knowledge of astronomy. De Landa then returned to the Yucatán Peninsula and lived out his remaining years, continuing his previous methods of proselytizing until his death in 1579.

Catholicism

Over the years, the majority of Maya were baptized into the Catholic faith. Most priests did their best to educate the people, teach them to read and write, and protect them from the growing number of Spanish settlers who used them as slaves. The Maya practiced Catholicism in their own manner, combining their ancient beliefs, handed down throughout the centuries, with Christian doctrine. These mystic yet Christian ceremonies are still performed in baptism, courtship, marriage, illness, farming, house building, and fiestas.

Pirates and the Baymen

While all of Mesoamerica dealt with the problems of economic colonialism, the Yucatán Peninsula had an additional problem: harassment by vicious pirates who made life in the coastal areas unstable. In other parts of the Yucatán Peninsula, the passive people were ground down, their lands taken away, and their numbers greatly reduced by the European settlers' epidemics and mistreatment.

British buccaneers sailed the coast, attacking the Spanish fleet at every opportunity. These ships were known to carry unimaginable riches of gold and silver from the New World back to the king of Spain. The Belizean coast became a convenient place for pirates to hole up during bad weather or for a good drinking bout. And, though no one planned it as a permanent layover, by 1650 the coast had the beginnings of a British pirate lair/settlement. As pirating slacked off on the high seas, British buccaneers discovered they could use their ships to carry logwood back to a ready market in England. These early settlers were nicknamed the Baymen.

In the meantime, the Spanish desperately tried to maintain control of this vast New World they had grasped from across the ocean. But it was a difficult task, and brutal conflicts continually flared between the Spanish and either the British inhabitants or the Maya. The British Baymen were continually run out but always returned. Treaties were signed and then rescinded. However, the British relentlessly made inroads into the country, importing slaves from Africa, beginning in the 1720s, to laboriously thrash through the jungles and cut the timber—work that the fiercely independent Maya resisted with their lives.

In 1763, Spain "officially" agreed to let the British cut logwood. The decree allowed roads (along the then-designated frontiers) to be built in the future, though definite boundaries were to be agreed upon later. For nearly 150 years, the only "roads" built were narrow tracks to the rivers; the rivers became Belize's major highways. Boats were common transport along the coast, and somehow road building was postponed, leaving boundaries vaguely defined and countrymen on both sides of the border unsure. This was the important bit of history that later encouraged the Spanish-influenced Guatemalans to believe that Belize had failed to carry out the 1763 agreement by building roads, so it was their turf. Even after Spain vacated Guatemala, Guatemalans tried for generations to assume ownership across the existing Belize borders. Since 1988, however, the boundary disagreement *appears* to have blown over with the Guatemalan threat of a takeover stopping on their side of the frontier. But because no official agreements have been made, most believe this conflict is still unresolved.

Treaty of Paris

Politically, Belize (or, more to the point, its timber) was up for grabs, and a series of treaties did little to calm the ping-pong effect between the British and the Spanish over the years. One such agreement, the Treaty of Paris, did little to control the Baymen—or the Spanish. With license, British plantation owners continued to divest the forests of logs, leaving Belize with nothing more than a legacy of brutality and tyrannical control over the slaves (who worked under cruel conditions while making rich men of their masters). The Spanish continued to claim sovereignty over the land but never settled in Belize. They continued their efforts to take over by sporadically harassing and attacking the Baymen—only to fail each time when the British returned and held on to their settlement.

The Baymen held on with only limited rights to the area until the final skirmish in 1798 on St. George, a small caye just off Belize City. The Baymen, with the help of an armed sloop and three companies of a West Indian regiment, won the battle of St. George's Caye on September 10, ending the Spanish claim to Belize once and for all. After that battle, Belize was ruled by the British Crown until gaining its independence in 1981.

During the first 400 years after Europeans arrived, nothing much was done to develop the country, not even building (as mentioned) roads or railroads, and you can count on one hand how many historic buildings are standing (because few were ever built).

Land Rights

In 1807, slavery was *officially* abolished in Belize by England. This was not agreeable to the powerful British landowners, and in many quarters it continued to flourish. Changes were then made to accommodate the will of the powerful. The local government no longer "gave" land to settlers as it had for years (the British law now permitted former slaves and other "coloureds" to hold title). The easiest way to keep them from possessing the land was to charge for it—essentially barring the majority in the country from landownership. So, in essence, slavery continued.

Caste War

It was inevitable that the Maya would eventually erupt in a furious attack. This bloody uprising in the Yucatán Peninsula in the 1840s was called the Caste War. Though the Maya were farmers and for the most part not soldiers, in this savage war they took revenge on every white man, woman, and child by rape and murder. When the winds of war reversed themselves and the Maya were on the losing side, vengeance on them was merciless. Some settlers immediately killed any Maya on sight, regardless of his beliefs. Some Maya were taken prisoner and sold to Cuba as slaves; others left their villages and hid in the jungles, in some cases for decades. Between 1846 and 1850, the population of the Yucatán Peninsula was reduced from 500,000 to 300,000. Guerrilla warfare ensued, with the escaped Maya making repeated sneak attacks upon the white settlers. Quintana Roo, adjacent to Belize along the Caribbean coast, was considered a dangerous no-man's-land for more than a hundred years until, in 1974, with the promise of tourism, the territory was admitted to the Federation of States of Mexico.

19TH-CENTURY TOURISTS

The next day we had to make preparations for our journey into the interior, besides which we had an opportunity of seeing a little of Balize. The Honduras Almanac, which assumes to be the chronicler of this settlement, throws a romance around its early history by ascribing its origin to a Scotch bucanier named Wallace. The fame of the wealth of the New World, and the return of the Spanish galleons laden with the riches of Mexico and Peru, brought upon the coast of America hordes of adventurers – to call them by no harsher name – from England and France, of whom Wallace, one of the most noted and daring, found refuge and security behind the keys and reefs which protect the harbour of Balize. The place where he built his log huts and fortalice is still pointed out; but their site is now occupied by warehouses. Strengthened by a close

alliance with the Indians of the Moscheto shore, and by the adhesion of numerous British adventurers, who descended upon the coast of Honduras for the purpose of cutting mahogany, he set the Spaniards at defiance. Ever since, the territory of Balize has been the subject of negotiation and contest, and to this day the people of Central America claim it as their own. It has grown by the exportation of mahogany; but, as the trees in the neighbourhood have been almost all cut down, and Central America is so impoverished by wars that it offers but a poor market for British goods, the place is languishing, and will probably continue to dwindle away until the enterprise of her merchants discovers other channels of trade.

John L. Stephens, *Incidents of Travel in Central America, Chiapas and Yucatán*, 1841

Restored Maya Pride

Many of the Maya who escaped slaughter during the Caste War fled to the isolated jungles of Quintana Roo and Belize. The Maya revived the religion of the "talking cross," a pre-Columbian oracle representing gods of the four cardinal directions. This was a religious/political marriage. Three determined survivors of the Caste War—a priest, a master spy, and a ventriloquist—all wise leaders, knew their people's desperate need for divine leadership. As a result of their leadership and advice from the talking cross, the shattered people came together in large numbers and began to organize. The community guarded the location of the cross, and its advice made the Maya strong once again.

They called themselves Chan Santa Cruz ("People of the Little Holy Cross"). As their confidence developed, so did the growth and power of their communities. Living very close

to the Belize (then British Honduras) border, they found they had something their neighbors wanted. The Chan Santa Cruz Maya began selling timber to the British and in return received arms, giving the Maya even more power. Between 1847 and 1850, in the years of strife during the Caste War in neighboring Yucatán, thousands of Maya, mestizo, and Mexican refugees who were fleeing the Spaniards entered Belize. The Yucatecans introduced the Latin culture, the Catholic religion, and agriculture. This was the beginning of the Mexican tradition in northern Belize, locally referred to as "Spanish tradition." The food is typically Mexican, with tortillas, black beans, tamales, squash, and plantain (a type of banana that can be cooked). For many years, these mestizos kept to themselves and were independent of Belize City. The colonial administration kept its distance, and a community-appointed headman made and kept the laws. Both Hispanic and non-Hispanic Belizeans who live in the northern area speak Spanish. Today, however, all the towns and cities of Belize come under the jurisdiction of the central Belizean government.

The Sugar Industry

Though most of the refugees ultimately returned to their homes in Mexico, the ones who stayed and began farming the land were making the first real attempt at much-needed agriculture. Large tracts that had been cleared of trees were empty, and rich landowners were willing to rent acreage (cheaply) to the refugees for farming. Until then, almost all foodstuffs had been imported from other countries (and to this day, it's not unusual to see many tinned foods from Australia, England, and the United States on market shelves).

The mestizos settled mostly in the northern sections of the country, which is apparent by the Spanish names of the cities: Corozal, San Estevan, San Pedro, and Punta Consejo. By 1857, the immigrants were growing enough

sugar to supply Belize, with enough left over to export the surplus (along with rum) to Britain. After their success proved to the tree barons that sugarcane could be lucrative, the big landowners became involved. Even in today's world of low-priced sugar, the industry is still important to Belize's economy.

Timber

For 300 years, Belize was plundered and neglected—and not just by hard-living buccaneers. Its forests were denuded of valuable logwood (which provided rich dyes for Europe's growing textile industry until man-made dyes were developed). When the demand for logwood ceased, plantation owners found a viable substitute for their logging interests—removing mahogany trees from thick virgin forests. For three centuries, the local economy depended on exported logs and imported food.

In a 1984 Audubon Society report, it was noted that despite the widespread use of slash-and-burn farming by the Maya a millennium ago, and the more recent selective logging of

Sugar is one of a handful of Belizean exports.

© JOSHUA BERMAN

THE BELIZE NATIONAL ANTHEM

LAND OF THE FREE

O, Land of the Free by the Carib Sea,
Our manhood we pledge to thy liberty!
No tyrants here linger, despots must flee
This tranquil haven of democracy.
The blood of our sires which hallows the sod,
Brought freedom from slavery oppression's rod,
By the might of truth and the grace of God.
No longer shall we be hewers of wood.

Arise! ye sons of the Baymen's clan,
Put on your armours, clear the land!
Drive back the tyrants, let despots flee –
Land of the Free by the Carib Sea!

Nature has blessed thee with wealth untold,
O'er mountains and valleys where prairies roll;
Our fathers, the Baymen, valiant and bold
Drove back the invader; this heritage bold
From proud Río Hondo to old Sarstoon,
Through coral isle, over blue lagoon;
Keep watch with the angels, the stars and moon;
For freedom comes tomorrow's noon.

"climax" status. The removal of logwood had little effect on the forest structure. It's in today's economy that logging can cause serious damage to the forest, with the indiscriminate removal of large tracts of trees, no matter the variety, because of modern methods and high-tech equipment.

INDEPENDENCE

In 1862, Belize officially became British Honduras, though it had been ruled by the British Crown since 1798. The average Belizean had few rights and a very low living standard. Political unrest grew in a stifled atmosphere. Even when a contingent of Belizean soldiers traveled to Europe to fight for the British in World War I, the black men were scorned. But when these men returned from abroad, the pot of change began to boil. Over the next 50 years, the country struggled through power plays, another world war, and economic crises. But always the seed was there—a growing desire to be independent. The colonial system had been falling apart around the world, and when India gained its freedom in 1947, the pattern was set. Many small undeveloped countries soon began to gain independence and started to rely on their own ingenuity to build an economy that would benefit the people.

Even though Belize was self-governing by 1964, it was still dominated by outside influences until September 1981, when it gained its independence from the British Crown. In September 1981, the Belizean flag was raised for the first time—the birth of a new country. Belize joined the United Nations, the Commonwealth of Nations, and the Non-Aligned Movement. The infant country's first parliamentary elections were held in 1984.

logwood and mahogany since the 16th century, Belize still has extensive forests. The large-scale abandonment of farms with the decline of the Maya civilization about A.D. 900 permitted forest regeneration that has attained what plant ecologists consider to be

Government and Economy

GOVERNMENT

The Government of Belize, or "GOB," as you'll see it referred to in the newspapers, is directed by an elected prime minister. The bicameral legislature, or National Assembly, comprises an appointed senate and elected house of representatives. Belize has two main political parties, PUP (People's United Party) and UDP (United Democratic Party). As in most democracies, the political rhetoric can get very animated, but political-based violence is unheard of.

The current prime minister, Dean Barrow of the UDP, took the post from long-time PUP frontman Said Musa, who led the country for a decade before losing his seat in 2008. Barrow's party had been gaining ground in recent years, especially as PUP rulers became increasingly implicated in various corruption scandals.

The official GOB website is www.governmentofbelize.gov.bz. The country's constitution, judicial code, and other legal documents are explained and can be downloaded at the Ministry of the Attorney General's homepage, www.belizelaw.org.

ECONOMY

The economy of Belize was traditionally based on the export of logwood, mahogany, and *chicle*

CRUISE SHIPS

The image of four or five hulking cruise ships on the watery eastern horizon, as seen from Belize City, can be ominous, especially on a gray morning. It is difficult not to imagine them as preparing to invade. The sheer scale of these ships so dwarfs anything that exists in Belize that the effect cannot but be impressive.

The arrival of the cruise industry to Belize's shores in the 1990s was a much-hailed – and highly contentious – event. Belize soon recorded the highest growth in cruise ship arrivals in the entire Caribbean region (according to the Caribbean Tourism Organization). The Belize Tourism Board (BTB) reports that annual cruise arrivals grew from 14,183 in 1998 to a peak of more than 851,000 in 2004.

There is no doubt that Belize desperately needs the cash cruise passengers are expected to bring. Some argue however, that passengers don't spend much, if anything, onshore, and that few dollars trickle very far from the pockets of those who own Tourism Village and the cruise concessions. This includes a scant handful of well-off invested stakeholders. Cruise ship arrivals are also boom days for taxi drivers, ragtag tour operators, generic Viagra salesmen, and sex workers. Cruise ship passengers on cheap Texas- and Florida-based circuits often arrive in Belize City having been given the impression that "the only thing worth buying in Belize City is cheap prescription drugs," as one red-faced couple told me on their way out of the Tourism Village cruise dock and mini-mall. Their cruise director had told them to "wait until Cozumel to really shop."

Another question is how to balance cruise ship dollars against the impact to Belize's tiny infrastructure. This has included damage to roads by bus traffic, stopped-up septic systems, trash on the trails and in the caves, and the like. At least one cruise line offloads trash onto a small Belizean barge, which then presumably dumps it into Belize City's miserable, leaking landfill (I have video).

The number of cruise arrivals in Belize has declined (to about 600,000 in 2007), but bringing this subject up at a Belizean cocktail party is still bound to open a big can of worms. Despite the recent dip in numbers, there continue to be several massive cruise ship-targeted projects up for review, including deep docking facilities and an ambitious (some would say "absurd") causeway system between the mainland and the cayes.

(the base for chewing gum, from the *chicle* tree). Today, tourism, agriculture, fisheries, aquaculture (shrimp farming), and small manufactured goods give the country an important economic boost, but it is still dependent on imported goods to get by. The main exports are sugar, citrus, bananas, lobster, and timber. Overall, domestic industry is severely constrained by relatively high labor and energy costs, a very small domestic market, and the "brain drain" of Belize's most qualified managers, health professionals, and academics to the United States and Europe.

In general, and despite books by PUP economists declaring that all is well, Belize's economy is a mess, and the GOB has been on the verge of bankruptcy for several years. In 2004, the government was rocked by a scandal over the use of millions of dollars of pension funds to pay the foreign debts of bankrupt companies controlled by government insiders. This led to the collapse of the overextended Development Finance Corporation (DFC), the effects of which are still being felt and evaluated today.

Thanks to tax concessions given to foreign investors, Belize has attracted new manufacturing industries, including plywood, veneer, matches, beer, rum, soft drinks, furniture, boat building, and battery assembly.

TOURISM

No longer the unknown backwater it once was, Belize is now a common destination for North American and European travelers, about two hundred thousand of whom arrive each year. The **Belize Tourism Board** (BTB; www.travelbelize.org) has gotten the word "Belize" buzzing on the lips of millions of potential visitors who, only a few years ago, had never even heard of the tiny country. Tourism is one of the top moneymakers in the country, responsible for about 15 percent of all jobs. It has encouraged the preservation of vast tracts of forests and reefs. Tourism has also helped the Institute of Archaeology to enhance and develop Belize's archaeological sites as destinations, making possible astounding excavations and discoveries at the Caracol, Xunantunich, Lamanai, Altun Ha, and Cahal Pech ruins.

Of course, tourism is not all mangoes and cream; Belize's founding father, George Price, warned against it, saying it would make Belizeans indentured servants to rich foreigners. Decades later, tourism remains more complex than it first appears, with a host of unintended and unseen effects.

People and Culture

The extraordinary diversity of Belize's tiny population (an estimated 300,000 in 2008) allows Belizeans to be doubly proud of their heritage—once for their family's background (Maya, Creole, Garinagu, Mennonite, etc.) and again for their country. The mestizo (mixed Spanish and indigenous descent) population has risen to about 50 percent of the country's total, with Creoles making up about 25 percent, Maya 10–12 percent, Garinagu 6 percent, and others 9 percent (2000 census).

Here's a bit of background about Belize's diverse demography, but keep in mind that every one of these groups continues to mingle with the others, at least to some extent, ensuring continuing creolization.

CREOLES

Creoles share two distinctive traits: some degree of African-European ancestry and the use of the local English-Creole dialect. Skin color runs from very dark to very light, but some old trace of English logger or buccaneer is back there. Many Creoles are also descended from other groups of immigrants.

The center of Creole territory is Belize City. Half of Belize's ethnic Creoles live here, and they make up more than three-fourths of the city's population. Rural Creoles live along the highway between Belmopan and San Ignacio, in isolated clusters in northern Belize District, and in a few coastal spots to the south—Gales Point, Mullins River, Mango Creek, Placencia, and Monkey River Town.

Cheap labor was needed to do the grueling timber work in thick, tall jungles. The British failed to force it on the maverick Maya, so they brought slaves from Africa, indentured laborers from India, and Caribs from distant Caribbean islands, as was common in the early 16th and 17th centuries. "Creolization" started when the first waves of British and Scottish began to intermingle with these imported slaves and servants.

MESTIZOS

Also referred to as "Ladinos" or just "Spanish," mestizos make up the quickest-growing demographic group in Belize and encompass all Spanish-speaking Belizeans, descended from some mix of Maya and Europeans. These immigrants to Belize hail from the nearby countries of Guatemala, El Salvador, Honduras, and Mexico. Once the predominant population (after immigration from the Yucatecan Caste War), mestizos are now the second most-populous ethnic group of Belize. They occupy the old "Mexican-Mestizo corridor" that runs along New River between Corozal and Orange Walk. In west-central Belize—Benque Viejo and San Ignacio—indigenous people from Guatemala have recently joined the earlier Spanish-speaking immigrants from Yucatán.

THE MAYA

Small villages of Maya—Mopan, Yucatec, and Q'eqchi'—still practicing some form of their ancient culture dot the landscape and comprise roughly 10–12 percent of Belize's population. Records show that after the Europeans arrived and settled in Belize, many of the Maya moved away from the coast to escape hostile Spanish and British intruders who arrived by ship to search for slaves. The independent Maya refused to be subjugated, so traders brought boatloads of African slaves into the Caribbean. Both the Maya and the Africans had religious beliefs that were inconsistent with the lifestyles of European settlers, who considered them sub-human. As a result, the Maya and the Garinagu for years kept to themselves.

Many Maya communities continue to live much as their ancestors did and are still the most politically marginalized people in Belize, although certain villages are becoming increasingly empowered and developed, thanks in part to tourism (although some would argue at a cultural cost).

Most modern Maya practice some form of Christian religion integrated with ancient beliefs—in southern Belize, the Q'eqchi' have their own Mennonite church. But ancient Maya ceremonies are still quietly practiced in secluded pockets of the country, especially in southern Belize.

GARINAGU

The Garinagu, as a group, are relative newcomers to the world. They are also commonly called "Garifuna," which technically only refers to their language, a fascinating blend of African tribal, Arawak, Spanish, and other tongues. (Another name for the Garinagu, the "Black Carib," has fallen out of favor.) The Garinagu came to exist on the Lesser Antillean island of San Vicente, which in the 1700s had become a refuge for escaped slaves from the sugar plantations of the Caribbean and Jamaica. These displaced Africans were accepted by the native Carib islanders, with whom they freely intermingled. The new island community members vehemently denied their African origins and proclaimed themselves Native Americans. As the French and English began to settle the island, the Garinagu (as they had become known) established a worldwide reputation as expert canoe navigators and fierce warriors, resisting European control. The English finally got the upper hand in the conflict after tricking and killing the Garinagu leader, and in 1797, they forcefully evacuated the population from San Vicente to the Honduran Bay Island of Roatan. From there, a large part of the Garinagu migrated to mainland Central America, all along the Mosquito Coast.

© JOSHUA BERMAN

Garinagu rhythm in a turtle-shell band

On November 19, 1823, so the story goes, the first Garinagu boats landed on the beaches of what is now Dangriga, one of the chief cultural capitals of the people. They landed in Belize under the leadership of Alejo Beni, and a small Garinagu settlement grew in Stann Creek, where they fished and farmed. They began bringing fresh produce to Belize City, but were not welcome to stay for more than 48 hours without getting a special permit—the Baymen wanted the produce but feared that these free blacks would help slaves escape, causing a loss of the Baymen's tight control.

Garifuna language is a mixture of Amerindian, African, Arawak, and Carib, dating from the 1700s. The Garinagu continued to practice what was still familiar from their ancient African traditions—cooking, dancing, and especially music, which consisted of complex rhythms with a call-and-response pattern that was an important part of their social and religious celebrations. An eminent person in the village is still the drum maker, who continues the old traditions, along with making other instruments used in these singing and dancing ceremonies that often last all night.

One of the most enduring customs, the practice of black magic known as *obeah,* was regarded with great suspicion and concern by the colonialists in Belize City, even after laws were enacted that made it illegal "for any man or woman to take money or other effects in return for fetishes or amulets, ritual formulas, or other magical mischief that could immunize slaves from the wrath of their masters." The practice continues—mostly in private. The *obeah* works through dances, drumbeats, trances, and trancelike contact with the dead.

There are a number of old dances and drum rhythms still used for a variety of occasions, especially around Christmas and New Year's. If you are visiting Dangriga, Hopkins, Seine Bight, Punta Gorda, or Barranco during these times (or on Settlement Day, November 19), expect to see (and possibly partake in) some drumming. Feel free to taste the typical foods and drinks. If you consume too much "local dynamite" (rum and coconut milk) or bitters, have a cup of strong chicory coffee, said by the Garinagu "to make we not have goma" (a hangover).

RASTAFARIANS

Belizean Rastafarians are part of a religion that believes in the eventual redemption of blacks and their return to Africa. They wear dreadlocks as a sacrament. Their beliefs, according to the biblical laws of the Nazarites, forbid the cutting of their hair. Rastafarians use ganja (marijuana) in their rituals and venerate Haile Selassie I, late emperor of Ethiopia, as their god. Selassie's precoronation name was Ras Tafari Makonnen, hence the name (Ras is simply an honorific title). He allegedly descended from King Solomon and the Queen of Sheba.

Belizean Rastas are difficult to quantify, as the religion and customs are found throughout the country's sundry cultures, including Bob Marley–worshipping Latinos, Creoles, and Maya alike. Many Rastas are strict vegetarians and cook wonderful "I-tal" dishes, as they refer to their diet (from the English *vital*). Particularly tasty I-tal joints are found at a few places in Cayo and in PG at Gomier's.

EAST INDIANS

From 1844 to 1917, under British colonialism, 41,600 East Indians were brought to British colonies in the Caribbean as indentured workers. They agreed to work for a given length of time for one "master." Then they could either return to India or stay on and work freely. Unfortunately, the time spent in Belize was not as lucrative as they were led to believe it would be. In some cases, they owed so much money to the company store (where they received half their wages in trade and not nearly enough to live on) that they were forced to "re-enlist" for a longer period. Most of them worked on sugar plantations in the Toledo and Corozal Districts, and many of the East Indian men were assigned to work as local police in Belize City. In a town aptly named Calcutta, south of Corozal Town, many of the population today are descendants of the original indentured East Indians. Forest Home near Punta Gorda also has a large settlement. About 47 percent of the ethnic group live in these two locations. The East Indians usually have large families and live on small farms with orchards adjacent to their homes. A few trade in pigs and dry goods in mom-and-pop businesses. Descendants of earlier East Indian immigrants speak Creole and Spanish. A few communities of Hindi-speaking East Indian merchants live in Belize City, Belmopan, and Orange Walk.

MENNONITES

German-speaking Mennonites are the most recent group to enter Belize on a large scale. This group of Protestant settlers from the Swiss Alps wandered over the years to northern Germany, southern Russia, Pennsylvania, and Canada in the early 1800s, and to northern Mexico after World War I. For some reason, the quiet, staid Mennonites disturbed local governments in these other countries, and restrictions on their isolated agrarian lifestyle led to a more nomadic existence. Most of Belize's Mennonites first migrated from Mexico between 1958 and 1962. A few came from Peace River in Canada. In contrast to other areas where they lived, the Mennonites bought large blocks of land (about 148,000 acres) and began to farm. Shipyard (in Orange Walk District) was settled by a conservative wing; Spanish Lookout (in Cayo District) and Blue Creek (in Orange Walk District) were settled by more progressive members. In hopes of averting future problems with the government, Mennonites made agreements with Belize officials that guarantee them freedom to practice their religion, use their language in locally controlled schools, organize their own financial institutions, and be exempt from military service. Over the 30-plus years that Mennonites have been in Belize, they have slowly merged into Belizean activities. Although they practice complete separation of church and state (and do not vote), their innovations in agricultural production and marketing have advanced the entire country. Mennonite farmers are probably the most productive in Belize; they commonly pool their resources to make large purchases such as equipment, machinery (in those communities that use machinery), and supplies. Their fine dairy industry is the best in the country, and they supply the domestic market with eggs, poultry, fresh milk, cheese, and vegetables.

BELIZEANS ABROAD

By some estimates, there are more Belizeans living in the United States than there are in Belize. They are concentrated mostly in New York City, Chicago, Los Angeles, and New Orleans. Of these, many young Belizeans have served in the U.S. armed forces. The money these emigrants send home is an important source of income for their Belizean families. Some Belizean expats stay in the States, but many return with new skills. On the flip side are those who have been deported back to Belize because of illegal activities in the United States, bringing the negative impacts of U.S. gang culture with them, a problem plaguing Belize City.

CONCEPT OF TIME

As in many other Central American and Caribbean cultures, the Belizean clock is not as rigidly precise as it is in other parts of the world. "Nine o'clock A.M." is not necessarily a moment in time that occurs once a morning, as it is a general guideline that could extend an hour or two in either direction (usually later). Creoles say "Time longa den da roop, mon" ("time is longer than the rope"), which means the same as the Spanish *"Hay mas tiempo que vida"* ("there is more time than there is life")—both of which boil down to the unofficial motto of Caye Caulker: "Go slow!"

A great deal of patience is required of the traveler who wishes to adapt to this looser concept of time. Buses generally leave when they are scheduled, but may stop for frustratingly long breaks during the journey. Don't use Belize Time as an excuse to be late for your tour bus pickup, and don't get angry when your taxi driver stops to briefly chat and laugh with a friend.

© JOSHUA BERMAN

Currently living in Germany, musician Pen Cayetano is one of Belize's cultural ambassadors.

THE ARTS

The turn of the millennium has brought a series of happy events in the small Belizean art community. In February 2002 the **Museum of Belize** opened in a colonial brick building and former prison. In May 2002 the **Belize Centre for Art Education** opened, offering courses in painting, drawing, ceramics, printmaking, and graphic design. In November 2003 the renovated Governor's colonial mansion was transformed into the **House of Culture,** providing more space for exhibits, concerts, and exchanges. In March 2004 a modern 600-seat theater, the **Bliss Centre for the Performing Arts,** opened and has since hosted hundreds of performances in music, dance, and drama.

Most importantly, in 2003, the Government of Belize created the **National Institute for Culture and History** (NICH; www.nichbelize. org) to bring together diverse government departments which had historically worked to preserve and promote different aspects of Belizean culture, from painting and music to archaeology. NICH encompasses the **Institute for the Creative Arts (ICA),** which is responsible for the promotion of the performing, visual, and plastic arts. The ICA is headquartered at the newly renovated Bliss Centre for the Performing Arts. The other three branches that make up NICH are the Institute of Archaeology (IOA), the Museum of Belize, and the Institute of Cultural and Social Research (ISCR).

CRAFTS

You'll have a selection of Belizean and Guatemalan crafts to choose from when visiting any archaeological site, as vendors typically set up rows of stalls with similar gifts, crafts, textiles, and basketwork. You'll also see slate carvings, a recently resurrected skill of the Maya. Among the leading slate carvers are **the Garcia Sisters, Lesley Glaspie,** and the **Magana family.** Their work can be found in several Cayo shops as well as elsewhere in the country (especially Aurora's shop near the entrance to Cockscomb). The Garcia sisters helped revive the slate craze, and their quality has always been high. **Mennonite furniture,** like hardwood chairs and small tables, make possible take-home items.

MUSIC

The music of Belize is heavily influenced by the syncopated beats of Africa as they combine with modern sounds from throughout Latin America, the Caribbean, and North America.

The most popular Belizean music is **punta,** a fusion of traditional Garifuna rhythms and modern electric instruments. The "Ambassador of Punta Rock" was Andy Palacio, a prolific musician from the southern village of Barranco, who died in 2008 and was honored as a national hero. The newer form of *punta* is characterized by driving, repetitive dance rhythms and has its acoustic roots in a type of music called *"paranda."* A recent PBS special described *paranda* as "nostalgic ballads coupling acoustic guitar with Latin melodies and raw, gritty vocals…which can feature traditional Garifuna percussion like wood blocks, turtle shells, forks, bottles, and nails." A few of the original *paranda* masters, like Paul Nabor in PG, can still be found in their hometowns throughout Belize. Several excellent compilation albums of Belizean and Honduran *punta* and *paranda* music are available from Stonetree Records.

Brukdown (or "Bruckdong") began in the timber camps of the 1800s, when the workers, isolated from civilization for months at a time, would let off steam by drinking a full bottle of rum and then beating on the empty bottle— or the jawbone of an ass, a coconut shell, or a wooden block—anything that made a sound. Add to that a harmonica, guitar, and banjo, and you've got the unique sound of *brukdown.* This is a traditional Creole rhythm kept alive by the legendary Mr. Peters and his **Boom and Chime** band.

Over the last five years, dub-poetry has emerged as an important format for musical expression in Belize. The most popular artist of this is **Leroy "The Grandmaster" Young,** whose album "Just Like That" is a wonderful listening experience and has been acclaimed by numerous international reviewers.

In the southern part of Belize, you'll likely hear the strains of ancient Maya melodies played on homemade wooden instruments including Q'eqchi' harps, violins, and guitars. In Cayo District in the west, listen for the resonant sounds of marimbas and wooden xylophones—from the Latin influence across the Guatemala border. In the Corozal and Orange Walk Districts in the north, Mexican *ranchera* and *romantica* music is extremely popular. Of course reggae is popular throughout the country, especially on the islands (Bob Marley is king in Belize).

Stonetree Records (www.stonetreerecords. com) has the most complete catalogue of truly Belizean music, covering a wide range of musical genres and styles. This author's favorite is **"Belize City Boil-Up,"** an incredibly funky collection of re-mastered vintage Belizean soul tracks from the '50s, '60s, and '70s, featuring The Lord Rhaburn Combo, Jesus Acosta and the Professionals, The Web, Harmonettes, Nadia Cattouse, and Soul Creations. From the record's description, "In a Belizean musical landscape that is currently dominated by *punta,* rap, and reggae, it's easy to forget that there was actually a time when the Belizean scene was alive with cool jazz, smooth rhythm and blues, and even psychedelic funk."

In addition to recording and marketing dozens of albums, Stonetree, based in Benque Viejo in western Belize, is also very active in encouraging new Belizean musicians to experiment and develop their individual sounds. Buy albums online, or pick up a couple of CDs at any gift shop during your visit.

LANGUAGE

English is the official language, although Belize Creole English (or Kriol) serves as the main spoken tongue among and between groups. There is an increasing number of Spanish speakers in Belize, as Central American immigrants continue to arrive. Spanish is the primary language of many native Belizean families as well—descendants of Yucatecan immigrants who inhabit the Northern Cayes, as well as Orange Walk and Corozal Districts.

SPEAKING BELIZEAN KRIOL

If you think Belize Kriol refers to nothing more than the exotic Caribbean accent of your Belizean hosts, think again. Better yet, *listen* as they talk casually with each other; you'll hear an entirely different language than the Rasta-tinted English Belizeans reserve for foreigners.

Belize Kriol, or "Creole" in its English spelling (not to be confused with the French Creole of New Orleans, which is completely different), is a Belize-ified version of the greater Caribbean pidgin conglomerations heard elsewhere in the region. It's a rare and dedicated foreigner who learns to speak fluent Belize Kriol, but trying out a few local phrases, proverbs, and dirty words can go a long way to getting laughs and making friends.

The National Kriol Council of Belize (www.kriol.org.bz) created the Belize Kriol Project to help you do just that – and to promote the unique culture and language of the Kriol people of Belize. In their Belize City office (next to the House of Culture), pick up one of several publications in written Kriol, including dictionaries, phrase books, poetry, and prose (my favorite is the *Chravl Buk eena Kriol ahn Inglish,* or "Travel Book in Kriol and English"). For an introduction to Belize Kriol before your trip, subscribe to a mailing list or online forum, where you can see the language as it is used in active conversation (do an online search to find these).

To speak Kriol, listen to the spoken language. If you are comfortable doing so, ask the speaker to slow it down and explain the words and phrases to you. Writing these down phonetically and practicing saying them, over and over, is the best, most humbling way to learn any language. Here are a few facts and phrases to get you started.

For one thing, there is no past tense in Belize Kriol, which explains menu items like "fry chicken" and "stew fish." You should also be aware of a few Kriolized English phrases. For example, "Right now" means "Just a moment," or "Coming right up," and despite its promise of promptness, actually refers to a time period between the present moment and three to four lazy hours into the future. Also, money

(continues on next page)

© JOSHUA BERMAN

Most Belizeans communicate in Kriol.

SPEAKING BELIZEAN KRIOL (continued)

and numbers are expressed as "Wan dollah, two dollah, chree dollah, etc." A "five dollah" bill, by the way, is also known as a "red bwai" (red boy). Another expression is "Life without a wife, is like kitchen without a knife." Happy yappin'!

GREETINGS

Weh yu nayhn? – What is your name?
Ah nayhn (or) **Mee naym** – My name is
Weh di go aan? – What's up? Hello.
Gud maanin – Good morning.
Da how yu di du? – How are you?
Aarait – Fine, thank you.
Weh taim yu gat? – What time is it?

EXCLAMATIONS

Choh! – Exasperated expression; "I don't want to hear it!"
Haul your rass! – Get the hell out of here!
Dat da lone rass! – That's bullshit!
Belly full, boti glad! – Declaration after a good meal.
Stap u rass! – Shut your mouth; stop your foolishness.
Kohn ya! – Come here!

Madda Fiyah! – Gosh darnit!

OTHER USEFUL PHRASES

Gud-gud! – Good, fine.
Ah sari. – I am sorry.
Dat okay. – It's okay.
Fa tru? – For true? Really?
Dis meet ya haaf raa. – This meat isn't done.
Yu da lamp up. – You are lazy.
Mek ah tel yu sumting. – Let me tell you something.
We gwan bash tonight. – We're gonna party tonight.
How much pikni yu got? – How many children do you have?
Jook. – To have sex.
Shuck your corn. – Have sex with, as in "I wan shuck your corn." Synonym: "Flip your gizzard."
Hamahingi – A well-endowed male member. Synonym: "anaconda."
Mutha fry chicken. – Idiot.

This random, irreverent selection of Belize Kriol was contributed, in part, by a few Belizean and gringo friends: you know who you are. Thank you!

As a tourist, there are only a few areas of Belize, mainly rural outposts in Northern and Western Belize, where knowing Spanish is essential to communicate. The Garinagu people speak Garifuna, and the various Mennonite communities speak different dialects of Old German. Then there are Mopan, Yucateca, and Q'eqchi' Mayan tongues.

FESTIVALS AND EVENTS

When a public holiday falls on Sunday, it is celebrated on the following Monday. If you plan to visit during holiday time, make advance hotel reservations—especially if you plan to spend time in Dangriga during Settlement Day on November 19 (the area has limited accommodations).

Note: On Sundays and a few holidays (Easter and Christmas), most businesses close for the day, and some close the day after Christmas (Boxing Day); on Good Friday most buses do not run. Check ahead of time.

Garinagu (Garifuna) Settlement Day

On November 19, Belize recognizes the 1823 arrival and settlement of the first Garinagu (also called Garifuna) in the southern districts of Belize. Belizeans from all over the country gather in Dangriga, Hopkins, Punta Gorda, and Belize City to celebrate with the Garinagu. The day begins with the **reenactment** of the arrival of the settlers and continues with all-night dancing to the local Garinagu drums and live *punta* bands. Traditional food—and copious amounts of rum, beer, and bitters—is available at street stands and local cafés.

© JOSHUA BERMAN

Settlement Day revelers

St. George's Caye Day

On September 10, 1798, at St. George's Caye off the coast of Belize, British buccaneers fought and defeated the Spaniards over the territory of Belize. The tradition of celebrating this victory is still carried on each year, followed by a weeklong calendar of events from religious services to carnivals. During this week, Belize City feels like a carnival with parties everywhere. On the morning of September 10, the whole city parades through the streets and enjoys local cooking, spirits, and music with an upbeat atmosphere that continues well into the beginning of Independence Day on September 21.

National Independence Day

On September 21, 1981, Belize gained independence from Great Britain. Each year, Belizeans celebrate with carnivals on the main streets of downtown Belize City and district towns. Like giant county fairs, they include displays of local arts, crafts, and cultural activities, while happy Belizeans dance to a variety of exotic rhythms

from *punta* to *soka* to reggae. Again, don't miss the chance to sample local dishes from every ethnic group in the country. With this holiday back to back with the celebration of the Battle of St. George's Caye, Belize enjoys two weeks of riotous, cacophonous partying.

Baron Bliss Day

On March 9, this holiday is celebrated with various activities, mostly water sports. English sportsman Baron Henry Edward Ernest Victor Bliss, who remembered Belize with a generous legacy when he died, designated a day of sailing and fishing in his will. A formal ceremony is held at his tomb below the lighthouse in the Belize Harbor, where he died on his boat. Fishing and sailing regattas begin after the ceremony.

Ambergris Caye Celebration

If you're wandering around Belize near June 26–29, hop a boat or plane to San Pedro and join the locals in a festival they have celebrated for decades, **El Dia de San Pedro,** in honor of

NATIONAL HOLIDAYS IN BELIZE

January 1 – New Year's Day
March 9 – Baron Bliss Day
March or April – Good Friday
March or April – Easter Sunday
May 1 – Labour Day
May 25 – Commonwealth Day
September 10 – National Day
September 21 – Independence Day
October 12 – Columbus Day
November 19 – Garinagu (Garifuna) Settlement Day
December 25 – Christmas Day
December 26 – Boxing Day

SUNDAY: DAY OF REST

Belize is serious about its Sundays. Expect businesses in most parts of the country – even restaurants and cafés – to close on Sundays. The streets empty as well, giving a ghost-town feeling even to places like downtown Belize City. Usually, the only stores and eateries open are Chinese shops and maybe a few taco stands on the street.

the town's namesake, St. Peter. This is good fun; reservations are suggested. **Carnaval,** one week before Lent, is another popular holiday on the island. The locals walk in a procession through the streets to the church, celebrating the last hurrah (for devout Catholics) before Easter. There are lots of good dance competitions.

Maya Dances

If traveling in the latter part of September in San Antonio Village in the Toledo District, you have a good chance of seeing the **deer dance** performed by the Q'eqchi' Maya villagers. Dancing and celebrating begins around the middle of August, but the biggest celebration begins with a *novena,* nine days before the feast day of San Luis.

Actually, this festival was only recently revived. The costumes were burned in an accidental fire some years back at a time when (coincidentally) the locals had begun to lose interest in the ancient traditions. Thanks to the formation of the **Toledo Maya Cultural Council,** the Maya once again are realizing the importance of recapturing their past. Some dances are now performed during an annual Cacao Festival in Toledo District during the last weekend in May.

ESSENTIALS

Getting There

BY AIR

To Belizeans, flying in and out of Belize was a far-fetched idea when American hero Charles Lindbergh paid a dramatic visit to the small Caribbean nation as part of his ongoing effort to promote and develop commercial aviation. At the time (1927), Lindbergh had just completed his famous nonstop flight across the Atlantic. On his visit to Belize, the Barracks Green in Belize City served as his runway, and the sound of his well-known craft, *The Spirit of St. Louis,* attracted hundreds of curious spectators.

Today, there are dozens of daily flights in and out of the country, served by a growing number of major carriers. In general, airfares to Belize range from expensive to exorbitant, though rates occasionally dip throughout the year; Latin America travel specialists at **Exito Travel** (U.S. tel. 800/655-4054, www.exitotravel.com) are adept at finding special fares and "open jaw" flights (flying into one city in Central America and out of another).

Philip Goldson International Airport

Most travelers to Belize arrive at Philip Goldson International Airport (BZE), nine miles from Belize City, outside the community of Ladyville. The medium-size airport

© JOSHUA BERMAN

(by Central American standards) offers basic services like gift shops, currency exchange, and two restaurants; Internet is available in the **Sun Garden Restaurant** upstairs from the American terminal. Check out the "waving deck" upstairs by the other bar/restaurant for exciting farewell/hello energy. The airport is named after Phillip Stanley Wilberforce Goldson (1923–2001), a respected newspaper editor, activist, and politician. The airport's ongoing runway and apron expansion is being done to attract new air carriers from farther away, particularly the European market.

Arriving in Belize

After clearing customs, you'll be besieged by taxi drivers offering rides into town for a fixed US$25; split the cost with fellow travelers if you can. If you are not being picked up by a resort or tour company and you choose to rent a car, look for the 11 rental car offices, all together on the same little strip, across the parking lot from the arrival area.

If you're continuing to the cayes, you can choose to fly directly to Caye Caulker or San Pedro or take a taxi into town and get on a boat for about half the price and a few hours longer.

Don't forget to carry enough U.S. dollars for your US$36 departure fee (if it's not already included in your ticket).

BY BOAT

Daily boats to Punta Gorda travel back and forth from Puerto Barrios, Guatemala, and there are two boat services to Puerto Cortés, Honduras (one leaves from Placencia, the other from Dangriga). Boat owners should note that vessels traveling to the area must have permission from the Belize Embassy in Washington, D.C.

VIA MEXICO

Because airfares to Belize are so high, a few travelers choose to fly into the Mexican state of Quintana Roo on the Yucatán Peninsula, especially to Cancún, where discounted airfares are common. Others decide to drive all the

way from the States or Canada. By bus from Mexico is a cinch; many daily buses travel from the main terminal in Chetumal all the way to Belize City and back. You'll have to get out to wait in various customs and immigration lines, but just follow the crowd and you'll be fine. There are also several Mexican lines that run daily between Chetumal, Belize City, Cayo (Benque), and Guatemala.

Driving from Cancún

Yes, it is possible to rent a car in Cancún and continue south on a Belizean adventure, but it'll cost you both money and patience. Still, with the money you save with the cheaper airfare into Cancún, the mobility may be worth it. Cancún is 369 kilometers from the border at Santa Elena, roughly 4.5 hours in a car on Route 307. Corporate international rental companies will not let you take their vehicles across the border, so you'll have to find a more accommodating Mexican company, like **J.L. Vegas,** with one office near the airport and another in the Crystal Hotel. Next, you'll need to "make the papers," as the car guy will surely remind you.

Driving from the United States

The road from Brownsville, Texas, to the border of Belize is just under 1,400 miles. If you don't stop to smell the cacti, you can make the drive in three days, especially now that there is a toll-road bypass around Veracruz and the Tuxtla mountains (though you should consider stopping at these destinations). The all-weather roads are paved, and the shortest route through Mexico is by way of Tampico, Veracruz, Villahermosa, Escarcega, and Chetumal (check with Mexican authorities beforehand to find out the latest hoops you'll have to jump through). There often is construction on Mexican Highways 180 and 186. Lodging is available throughout the drive, although it is most highly concentrated in the cities and on the Costa Esmeralda, a beautiful strip of mostly deserted beach near Nautla (prices start at around US$20 for a very simple double). If attempting this trip, be sure you have a valid

TRAVELING SOUTH TO HONDURAS – AND BEYOND

A quick hop and a skip away, Honduras, the original banana republic, offers a wealth of less-trammeled destinations. By far, the two most-visited Honduran sites are the Copan ruins near the Guatemalan border and the Bay Islands, off the coast from La Ceiba. Either one can be reached in a day from Belize. Less known are the inland parks and treasures surrounding Lago de Yojoa, less than two hours south of the city of San Pedro Sula.

From Belize, you can fly to San Pedro Sula from Belize City (and from Savannah airstrip, near Placencia); or you can travel by boat from either Dangriga or Placencia, across the bay to Puerto Cortés, Honduras, a dirty port town which you'll want to leave as soon as possible. From Dangriga, the **Nesymein Neydy** (tel. 501/223-1235, 203-1128, or 203-4955, Honduras tel. 504/984-9544) makes the three-hour trip for US$50, leaving Saturdays at 9 A.M. and returning Tuesdays. **Gulf Cruza** (tel. 501/202-4506 or 603-7787, Honduras tel. 504/665-1200) departs from the main dock at Placencia every Friday at 9:30 A.M., returning Monday afternoon at 2 P.M. The trip costs US$50 and takes about four or five hours, stopping in Big Creek, Belize, for immigration purposes. Most travelers hook the trip into their own schedules, but at least one tour company in Belize City will book your seat on the Gulf Cruza boat *and* arrange for a shuttle to Placencia (US$15); Mundo Maya can even have the van pick you up at your hotel (call or visit them for details; they can book you on the Dangriga boat as well, but there's no shuttle).

Pick up *Moon Honduras* by Chris Humphrey and Amy E. Robertson for complete coverage of Honduras. Or keep heading south and pick up a copy of *Moon Nicaragua* by Randall Wood and yours truly. *¡Feliz viaje!*

credit card, Mexican liability insurance, a passport, and a driver's license—all original documents and one set of photocopies.

Driving Across the Border

The most crucial part of driving into Belize from Mexico is having a letter of permission from the car's owner; customs will scrutinize this document. Next, to avoid being turned back at the border, be sure to get the vehicle sprayed with insecticide from one of the roadside sprayers near the border—it's tough to pick them out, but look for a little white shack past the bridge after leaving Mexico and keep your receipt for when you reach customs/immigration (fumigation costs US$5). After passing through Mexican immigration (have your passport stamped and hand in your tourist card), you will cross a bridge welcoming you to Belize. On the righthand side, you will see two unsigned buildings where you must purchase insurance. The tire fumigation is near the fork in the road before the free zone. You will likely be greeted when you first pull over by men offering to help you through the stations, but their services are unnecessary. Still, it can be wise to befriend these touts, as many of them are related to the officers at the border. Give a small tip and ask them to clean your windows while you are getting insurance at the Atlantic house (you must have insurance before you enter immigration).

Although in Mexico proof of registration suffices as proof of ownership, in Belize you may be asked to show a title. You will not need a Temporary Vehicle Importation permit if entering for one month or less; for more time, you may need to post a bond on your vehicle (in greenbacks, to be refunded in Belizean dollars later). One very important detail when entering Mexico from the United States is to request a "doble entrada" on your passport to avoid steep fees. This should only cost 100 pesos, if it's available. Returning to Mexico from Belize, you'll pay a US$19 Belizean exit tax, per person.

Getting Around

BY AIR

Some Belizean airstrips are paved and somewhat official-looking (Belize City and San Pedro, for example); the rest are more like short abandoned roadways or strips of mown grass, but they work just fine. Because such small planes are used, you not only watch the pilot handling the craft, you may also get to sit next to him. Best of all, flying low and slow in these aircraft allows you to get a panoramic view of the Belize Barrier Reef, cayes, coast, and jungle (keep your camera handy).

Two airlines offer regularly scheduled flights to all districts in Belize, from both the international and municipal airports: **Tropic Air** (tel. 501/226-2012, U.S. tel. 800/422-3435, reservations@tropicair.com, www.tropicair.com) and **Maya Island Air** (tel. 501/223-1140, U.S. tel. 800/225-6732, mayair@btl.net, www.mayaislandair.com). Daily flights are available from Belize City to Caye Caulker, San Pedro, Dangriga, Placencia, Punta Gorda, and a handful of other tiny strips around the country. The Maya and Tropic flights usually combine several destinations in one route, so if you're traveling to PG, you may have to land and take off in Dangriga and Placencia first. Ditto for Caulker and San Pedro, the two of which are linked together. There are also regular flights to Flores, Guatemala, and you can fly between Corozal and San Pedro. If your scheduled flight is full, another will taxi up shortly and off you go.

Several charter flight companies will arrange trips to remote lodges like Lighthouse Reef Resort, Blancaneaux Lodge in the Mountain Pine Ridge, and Gallon Jug airstrip near Chan Chich. **Javier's Flying Service** (municipal airport, tel. 501/223-1029) is one such charter, offering local and international flights, air ambulance, and day tours.

Small planes fly throughout Belize.

© JOSHUA BERMAN

By Helicopter

Charter a chopper for a transfer, custom tour, filming/photography assignment, aerial property survey, search and rescue mission, or medevac with **Astrum Helicopters** (Mile 3½ on Western Highway, near Belize City, tel. 501/222-9462, www.astrumhelicopters.com); expect to pay around US$950 per hour (US$250 per person for most sightseeing tours). Astrum is a modern, professional outfit with new aircraft and a very skilled father-son pilot team.

BY BUS

The motley fleet of buses that serves the entire country ranges from your typical rundown, recycled yellow school bus to a handful of plush, air-conditioned luxury affairs. Belize buses are relatively reliable, on time, and less chaotic than the chicken-bus experience in other parts of Central America and Mexico. Still, most buses make a maddening number of stops, stretching seemingly short distances into long journeys that make Belize feel a lot bigger than it really is. For anyone who wants to meet Belizeans and see the countryside in an unrushed manner, this is the way to go. Most of these buses make frequent stops and will pick up anyone on the side of the road, anywhere—as long as space permits and even when it doesn't. The drivers will also drop you off wherever you wish.

Note that all buses between Belize City and points west and south—even expresses—stop in Belmopan for anywhere from 5 to 30 minutes. They'll do the same at any other city terminal that gets in their way, like Dangriga or Orange Walk; it's a good time for a bathroom break. Travel time from Belize City to Corozal or San Ignacio is about two hours, to Dangriga two to three hours, and to Punta Gorda five to six hours. Fares average about US$2–4 to most destinations, about US$7–12 for the longer routes.

The newest development in Belize's bus scene was the collapse of Novelo's, the government-backed monopoly which, um, overextended itself in a big national loan scandal in

ROAD DISTANCES FROM BELIZE CITY	
Belmopan	55 miles
Benque Viejo	81 miles
Corozal Town	96 miles
Dangriga	105 miles
Orange Walk Town	58 miles
Punta Gorda	210 miles
San Ignacio	72 miles

2004. The resulting scramble has left Belize's national bus system in the hands of no fewer than 12 small private companies. For the traveler, this may mean less reliable schedules and in some cities (Orange Walk, San Ignacio, and Punta Gorda) no actual bus station.

In Belize City, nearly all bus runs still begin and end at the main government-owned **Novelo's Terminal** (it's still called that even though the company no longer exists; tel. 501/207-4924, 207-3929, or 227-7146), located on West Collett Canal Street in one of Belize City's run-down areas; it is reached by walking west on King Street, across Collett Canal and into the terminal—definitely use a taxi at night. **James Bus** runs the most reliable daily Punta Gorda service, using the block in front of the Shell station on Vernon Street (two blocks north of the Novelo's) as its terminal.

Express direct bus service to Guatemala and Mexico leaves from the hectic intersection in front of the Water Taxi Terminal and Swing Bridge; this is the place to catch one of several private direct buses to Belize's borders and beyond. Boat-bus connections are convenient here, but it's all happening in the middle of one of Belize's busiest intersections, and at press time, city officials were reportedly about to prohibit buses from operating here. If they

DRIVING IN BELIZE

Rule number one about driving in Belize: Drive defensively! Expect everyone out there to make stupid passes and unexpected turns – they probably will and it's your job to stay out of their way (especially when they are bigger than you, like the buses and oil trucks that speed crazily around blind curves and over one-lane bridges).

Valid U.S. (or other nationality) driver's licenses and international driving permits are accepted in Belize for a period of three months after entering the country. Try not to drive at night if you can avoid it. Besides the additional hazards of night driving in general, some Belizean drivers overuse their high beams and many vehicles have no tail lights. Watch out for unmarked speed bumps. Driving rules are U.S.-style with one very strange exception: sometimes a vehicle making a left-hand turn is expected to pull over to the right, let traffic behind pass, and then execute the turn. This practice is being phased out, but you can still get a ticket – or rear-ended – so be careful.

Tires frequently get popped, so make sure you have a good spare to get you to the near-est used-tire dealer. New tires may be hard to come by, but Belizeans are geniuses with a patch kit. A decent used spare can be had for around US$30, a patch job about US$5. If you plan on traveling during the rainy season and/ or without a four-wheel drive vehicle, make sure you are prepared in the event you get stuck in the mud. In general, road conditions may dictate where you can and cannot go, and it is always best to ask around town if you plan to go off the beaten path. Watch out for speed bumps, even on the highways – no matter how slow you drive, on some, you may bottom out. If you're going to the cayes, be sure to seek out a secure pay parking lot in your city of departure, especially if it's Belize City (the municipal airport is probably the best choice).

Expect police checkpoints anywhere around the country: They'll check your seat belt (US$25 fine), car papers, driver's license, and, courtesy of the U.S. Drug Enforcement Agency, dogs will sniff for that dime bag of weed in your shaving kit (apparently, these small busts are as big a priority as the tons of cocaine flowing northward through the country).

succeed, these buses will be moved somewhere close by, but their various ticket counters will remain inside the Water Taxi Terminal.

Other small lines, which don't have phone numbers, are **Jex Buses,** which departs from 34 Regent Street and from the Pound Yard Bridge to Crooked Tree, and **Pooks** and **Russell's,** which go to Bermudian Landing.

BY RENTAL CAR

Driving Belize's handful of highways gives you the most independence when traveling throughout the country, but it is also the most expensive; rental fees were running US$75–125 per day and gasoline was approaching US$6 per gallon at press time—despite the discovery of oil in Belize. You'll also have to be adept at avoiding careless drivers and obstacles like pedestrians, farm animals, cyclists, iguanas, and moped-riding cruise ship passengers.

In some areas, like the Mountain Pine Ridge and other hinterlands, there is no public transportation, and a four-wheel drive rental car is a good way to go if you're into traveling on your own schedule. Alternatively, all jungle lodges arrange airport and town transfers for their guests (sometimes for free, sometimes for exorbitant amounts), and taxis can be chartered as well.

One of the first things you'll see upon walking out of the arrival lounge at the international airport is a strip of about a dozen car rental offices offering small, midsize, and large four-wheel drive vehicles. Vans and passenger cars are also available, some with air-conditioning—they cost more. Insurance is mandatory but (like taxes) not always included in the quoted rates. If you know exactly when you want the car, it's helpful (and often cheaper) to make reservations. Note the hour you pick up the car and try to return it before that time: a few minutes over could cost you another full day's rental fee. Also take the vehicle inspection seriously to make sure you don't get charged for someone else's dings.

Budget Rent a Car (tel. 501/223-2435, www.budget-belize.com) is reliable and offers new cars that are well maintained. You'll find a few other international rental agencies, like **Hertz** and **Avis,** as well as a number of locally owned agencies. **Jabiru Auto Rental** (tel. 501/224-4680, www.jabiruautorental.

bz) is very reliable and has low Internet rates. **Crystal Auto Rental** (tel. 501/223-1600, www.crystal-belize.com) is the only company that will allow you to drive across the border, but you won't be insured.

There are a few cheaper Cayo-based options as well, including **Cayo Rentals** (tel. 501/824-2153, abscomputer@btl.net), **Safe Tours Belize** (tel. 501/824-4262 or 614-4476, www.safetoursbelize.com) and **Matus Car Rentals** (tel. 501/663-4702 or 824-2089, matuscarrental@yahoo.com).

Visas and Officialdom

U.S. citizens must have a passport valid for the duration of their visit to Belize; U.S. citizens, British Commonwealth subjects, and citizens of Belgium, Denmark, Finland, Greece, Iceland, Italy, Liechtenstein, Luxembourg, Mexico, Spain, Switzerland, Tunisia, Turkey, and Uruguay do not need a visa. They are automatically granted a 30-day tourist pass and technically must have onward or return air tickets and proof of sufficient money (though I've never heard of anyone checking this). Visitors for purposes other than tourism, or who wish to stay longer than 30 days, need to visit an immigration office of the Government of Belize.

If you are planning on staying more than 30 days, you can ask for a new stamp at any immigration office in the country, or you can cross the border and return. The first few times are free, then there may be various fees to extend (the most I've been charged was US$12.50 for an extra 30 days).

U.S. citizens are strongly encouraged by the State Department to register their trip, no matter how short, online at www.travel.state.gov, so that the local embassy has emergency contact information on file.

FOREIGN EMBASSIES IN BELIZE

Only a handful of countries have embassies in Belize. The **United States Embassy**

(Floral Park Rd., Belmopan, tel. 501/822-4011 or 822-4012, embbelize@state.gov, http://belize.usembassy.gov) is open for U.S. citizen services from 8 A.M.–noon and 1 P.M.–4 P.M. Monday–Thursday and 8 A.M.–noon on Friday in its brand-new fortified US$50-million building. The after-hours emergency number for American citizens is 501/610-5030 (the U.S. Embassy moved from Belize City to Belmopan in late 2006). The **British High Commission** (Embassy Square, P.O. Box 91, Belmopan, tel. 501/822-2146, brithicom@btl.net, www.britishhighbze.com) is open 8 A.M.–noon and 1 P.M.–4 P.M. Monday–Thursday and 8 A.M.–2 P.M. Friday. El Salvador and India also have embassies in Belmopan.

Embassies in Belize City include China, Cuba, Mexico, Colombia, Holland, Sweden, and Taiwan.

MOVING TO BELIZE

It's a typical story—the gringo who vacationed in Belize and never left. There are a number of ways to do it, from starting a business, investing in land, retiring, or working online; there are a number of helpful resources as well. For more detailed information on joining the expat ranks, read *Living Abroad in Belize* by Lan Sluder (Avalon Travel).

EMBASSIES AND CONSULATES OF BELIZE

CANADA

Consulate of Belize in Ontario
c/o McMillan Binch, Suite 3800
South Tower, Royal Bank Plaza Toronto
Toronto, Ontario M5J 2JP, Canada
tel. 416/865-7000, fax 416/864-7048

Consulate of Belize in Quebec
1800 McGill College, Suite 2480
Montreal, Quebec H3A 3J6, Canada
tel. 514/288-1687, fax 514/288-4998
dbellemare@cmmtl.com

Consulate of Belize in Vancouver
2321 Trafalgar Street
Vancouver, British Columbia V6K 3T1, Canada
tel. 604/730-1224
dwsmiling@hotmail.com

COSTA RICA

Consulate of Belize in San José
Apartado Postal 11 121-1000
San José, Costa Rica
tel. 506/253-5598, fax 506/233-6394
gprisma@sol.racsa.co.cr

EUROPE

High Commission of Belize in London
22 Harcourt House 19, Cavendish Square
London, W1G 0PL, United Kingdom
tel. 44-20/7499-9728, fax 44-20/7491-4139
bzhc-lon@btconnect.com

Embassy of Belize and Mission of Belize to the
European Communities
Boulevard Brand Whitlock 136
1200 Brussels, Belgium
tel. 32-2/732-6204, fax 32-2/732-6246
embelize@skynet.be

Permanent Mission of Belize to the UNESCO
in France
1 Rue Miollis, Room M339
75015 Paris, France
tel. 33-1/45-68-32-11, fax 33-1/47-20-18-74
dl.belize@unesco.org

Permanent Mission of Belize to the United Nations in Geneva, Switzerland
7 Rue du Mont-blanc
CH 1201 Geneva, Switzerland
tel. 022/906-8420
mission.belize@ties.itu.int

JAPAN

Embassy of Belize in Tokyo
No. 38 Kowa Bldg., 4-12-24-907
Nishi-Azabu Minato-ku
Tokyo 106-00 31, Japan
tel. 81-3/3400-9106, fax 81-3/3400-9262
belize@mxd.mesh.ne.jp

MEXICO

Embassy of Belize in Mexico
215 Calle Bernardo de Galvez, Col. Lomas de Chapultepec
Mexico D.F. 11000
tel. 52-5/520-1274
embelize@prodigy.net.mx

Consulate of Belize in Cancún
Avenida Nader 34
Cancún, Quintana Roo, Mexico
tel. 52-9/887-8417
nel.bel@prodigy.net.mx

UNITED STATES

Consulate of Belize in Chicago
c/o Eztech Manufacturing, Inc.
1200 Howard Drive West
Chicago, IL 60185
tel. 630/293-0010
eztech@ameritech.net

Consulate of Belize in Florida
4173 S. Le Jeune Road
Coconut Grove, FL 33146
tel./fax 305/666-1121
bzconsulmi@mindspring.com

Consulate of Belize in Illinois
201 N. Church Street, Room 200
Belleville, Il 62223
tel. 618/234-4410

General Consulate of Belize in Los Angeles
5825 Sunset Boulevard, Suite 206
Hollywood, CA 90028
tel. 323/469-7343, fax 323/469-7346
belizeconsul@earthlink.net

Consulate of Belize in Louisiana
c/o Westbank Optical, Inc.
419 Lapalco Boulevard

Gretna, LA 70056
tel. 504/392-3655, fax 504/392-3809
jsbenard@hotmail.com

Consulate of Belize in Michigan
24984 Glen Orchard Drive
Farmington Hills, MI, 48336-1732

Permanent Mission of Belize to the United Nations in New York
885 Second Avenue
1 Dag Hammarskjöld Plaza, 20th Floor
New York, NY 10017
tel. 212/593-0999, fax 212/593-0932

Retiring

Any foreigner over the age of 45 with a monthly income of at least US$2,000 through a pension or annuity generated outside of Belize is eligible for **Qualified Retired Person** status. To learn more about becoming a **QRP** and receiving retirement incentives, go to www.belizeretirement.org or call 800/624-0686 (toll-free) from the United States or Canada.

Accommodations

Of the 624 licensed hotels in Belize, the vast majority (68 percent) are very small—only 10 rooms or less—and all but seven are considered boutique (50 rooms or less). Large foreign-owned hotel chains are few and far between in Belize. Most accommodations are simple, local affairs. Average room rates have been creeping up year after year; in 2007, the average rate was US$103. (If the descriptions in this book don't mention "tax included," it may be added on top of the advertised rate; it's worth asking about tax when booking your room.) I've selected the most well-kept, comfortable, friendly, family-run operations I could find throughout Belize. If you find any properties that deserve to be in these pages but aren't (or ones I've listed that you think should be removed), please let me know.

There are all types of accommodations in Belize.

BUDGET HOTELS

Budget accommodations are ample in Belize, as long as you have a flexible idea of what's "cheap." In this book, nightly rates under US$25 are reasonable, though value varies like anywhere else. In Belize, hostels and dormitories for under US$10 per person per night may mean a sacrifice in safety or cleanliness. At press time, US$10–15 is the bottom line for low-cost lodging, and it'll get you anything from a cramped concrete box to a generous wooden cabin like those found at the Trek Stop and other backpacker hot spots. Guesthouses and budget hotels sometimes offer a dormitory or bunkroom, shared among fellow travelers; this option is cheaper, but obviously you give up privacy and maybe security—and you'll enjoy shared bathrooms and cold water (assume that accommodations described in this book have hot water unless otherwise noted). Sometimes, nicer hotels offer a few "economy rooms," which are considerably cheaper than normal rates.

Great deals are abundant in the low season, when room rates plummet across the board, and walk-in specials can save you as much as 50 percent off normal winter (high-season) rates.

Some villages around the country are trying to emulate the guesthouse and homestay networks available in the southern Toledo villages. Sometimes calling themselves "bed-and-breakfasts," such options are usually primitive, often lacking electricity, running water, and flush toilets. Look for them along the Hummingbird Highway and in some outlying Cayo villages.

The Toucan Trail

Many budget travelers to Belize follow the **Toucan Trail** (www.toucantrail.com), a cooperative marketing effort of more than 100 small hotels with rooms for US$60 or less. The program is supported by the Belize Tourism Board in an effort to promote socially responsible, environmentally sound, sustainable tourism. The website is extremely useful in finding quality lodging.

UNDERSTANDING HOTEL RATES

Exact hotel rates are an elusive thing in Belize; seasonal pricing fluctuations are compounded by various hotel taxes and service charges, sometimes as much as 25-30 percent above the quoted rate. Using a credit card can add another 3-5 percent. Universal standards for presenting prices are absent in Belize's hotel industry. Always make sure the rate you read about or are quoted is actually the same amount you will be asked to pay.

The high season is loosely considered to be mid-December through the end of April, and it is marked by a rise in both the number of visitors and the price of most accommodations. Some places kick their rates up even higher during Christmas, New Year's, and Easter, calling these "holiday" or "peak" rates. A minority of hotels keep their rates the same year-round, but it's rarely that simple. *Moon Belize* quotes **high-season double occupancy** rates only! Expect lower rates (30-40 percent lower than what is quoted in this book) if traveling during the low/rainy season (May-November) and/or on your own. Occasionally walk-in discounts are given, when hotels are eager to avoid empty rooms and you stumble along at the right time.

UPSCALE

The sky's the limit when it comes to midrange and high-end accommodations in Belize. From business traveler standards to the chic lap of luxury, Belize has it all—if you've got the cash. A great many Belizean families and foreign investors have attempted to bring their personal visions of paradise to life throughout this class, and Belize's amazing selection of creative resorts and lodges has been featured in international travel magazines around the world. For the latest in luxe, click on "Belize" at Luxury Latin America (www.luxurylatinamerica.com).

Food and Drink

Throughout this book (and throughout Belize), you will find references to "Belizean" food, often preceded by words like "simple" and "cheap." It should be noted that the very idea of a national cuisine is as new as every other part of Belizean identity. Since the times of the Baymen, Belize has been an import economy, surviving mostly on canned meats like "bully beef" and imported grains and packaged goods. With independence, however, came renewed national pride, and with the arrival of tourists seeking "local" food, the word "Belizean" was increasingly applied to the varied diet of so many cultures. Anthropologist Richard Wilk, author of *Home Cooking in the Global Village: Caribbean Food from Buccaneers to Ecotourists,* writes, "The crucible of Belizean national cooking has been the *transnational* arena; the flow of migrants, sojourners, tourists, and media which increasingly links the Caribbean with the United States."

As for what's going to go in your belly when you get there, nobody will argue about the common denominator of Belizean food: **rice and beans.** The starchy staple is pronounced as one word with a heavy accent on the first syllable: *"RICE-n-beans!"* Belizeans speak of the dish with pride, as if they invented the concoction, and you can expect a massive mound of it with most midday meals. Actually, Belizean rice and beans *is* a bit unique: they use red beans, black pepper, and grated coconut, instead of the black beans and cilantro common in neighboring Latin countries. The rest of your plate will be occupied by something like **stew beef, fry chicken,** or a piece of fish, plus a small mound of either potato or cabbage salad. Be sure to take advantage of so much fresh fruit:

© JOSHUA BERMAN

standard Belizean plate: rice, stew beans, plantain, and chicken

oranges, watermelon, star fruit, mangoes, and papaya, to name a few.

The omnipresent **Chinese restaurants** are, in addition to being providers of authentic Chinese cuisine of varying quality, also famous for their cheap "fry chicken" and are just as Belizean as anyone else on the block. These are often your only meal options on Sundays and holidays.

For breakfast, try some **fry jacks** (fluffy fried-dough crescents) or **johnnycakes** (flattened biscuits) with your eggs, beans, and bacon. Unfortunately, most coffee served in the country is still instant or, if brewed, just plain horrible. This is changing, however, mostly because of demanding tourists like yourself who insist on a real mug o' Joe—or a soymilk, double-decaf latte, for that matter, which you'll find in finer restaurants and cafés.

One of the cheapest and quickest meal options, found nearly everywhere in Belize, is Mexican "fast-food" snacks, especially **taco stands,** which are everywhere you look, serving as many as five or six soft-shell chicken tacos for US$1. Also widely available are **salbutes,** a kind of hot, soggy taco dripping in oil; **panades,** little meat pies; and **garnaches,** which are crispy tortillas under a small mound of tomato, cabbage, cheese, and hot sauce.

Speaking of hot sauce, you'll definitely want to try to take home **Marie Sharp's** famous habanera sauces, jams, and other creative products. Marie Sharp is a classic independent Belizean success story, and many travelers visit her factory and store just outside Dangriga. (Her products are available on every single restaurant table and in every gift shop in the country.) Her sauce is good on pretty much everything.

Then, of course, there's the international cuisine, in the form of many excellent foreign-themed restaurants. San Pedro and Placencia, in particular, have burgeoning fine-dining scenes, and Cayo has excellent East Indian, Sri Lankan, and vegetarian fare.

Many restaurants in Belize have flexible hours of operation, and often close for a few hours between lunch and dinner.

Seafood

One of the favorite Belize specialties is fresh fish, especially along the coast and on the islands, but even inland Belize is never more than 60 miles from the ocean. There's lobster, shrimp, red snapper, sea bass, halibut, barracuda, conch, and lots more prepared in a variety of ways.

Conch (pronounced KAHNK) has been a staple in the diet of the Maya and Central American communities along the Caribbean coast for centuries. There are conch fritters, conch steak, and conch stew; it's also often used in *ceviche*—uncooked seafood marinated in lime juice with onions, peppers, tomatoes, and a host of spices. In another favorite, conch is pounded, dipped in egg and cracker crumbs, and sautéed quickly (like abalone steak in California) with a squirt of fresh lime. Caution: If it's cooked too long, it becomes tough and rubbery. Conch fritters are minced pieces of conch mixed into a flour batter and fried—delicious.

On many boat trips, the crew will catch a fish and some conch and prepare them for lunch, either as *ceviche,* cooked over an open beach fire, or in a "boil up," seasoned with onions, peppers, and *achiote,* a fragrant red spice grown locally since the time of the early Maya.

Don't order seafood out of season! Closed season for lobster is February 15–June 15, and conch season is closed July 1–September 30. The ocean is being overfished, due in large part to increasing demand from tourists. The once-prolific lobster is becoming scarce in Belizean waters. And conch is not nearly as easy to find as it once was. Most reputable restaurateurs follow the law and don't buy undersize or out-of-season seafood; however, a few have no scruples.

NON-ALCOHOLIC BEVERAGES

There are wonderful natural fruit drinks to be had throughout Belize. Take advantage of fresh lime, papaya, watermelon, orange, and other healthy juices during your travels—just be sure the drinks are made with purified water.

REDUCE, REUSE, RECYCLE

Consider the ecological footprint you leave in Belize after your vacation is over. Chances are that, after the jet fuel burned, your footprint's chief component is a huge pile of plastic water bottles. If you'd rather not contribute to Belize's volume of unnecessary solid waste (which, many agree, is the country's top environmental problem), think about ways to make that pile smaller. Do you order a new half-liter bottle with every meal instead of bringing your own larger one? Do you throw away every single bottle you buy, or do you refill them with purified water from the five-gallon jug in your hotel lobby? Consider bringing your own reusable water bottle to Belize and reduce that pile of trash to nothing but banana peels and mango pits. When reusing a plastic bottle, you'll want to disinfect it with a drop of bleach every couple of days (or ask your hosts to wash it with soap). Many health buffs say you should scrap the plastic altogether and only drink out of stainless steel water bottles.

Until 2000, beer and soda came in reusable glass bottles in Belize. That changed with the introduction of soft drinks in plastic bottles by the country's only major beverage distributor. Bowen & Bowen, Ltd. promised a recycling center to address the tonnage of plastic bottles bound to end up in landfills, along roads, and in the ocean, but have done little to make this happen. The small "Donated by Barry Bowen" trash containers found in Caye Caulker and other parts of Belize are nice, but could not accommodate a fraction of 1 percent of the plastic trash the company generates.

Reports of plastic collection points and a Belizean recycling program come and go, though it is possible that someone is sending scraps to Mexico. Keep an eye out and follow the folks in Belize City with feed bags of empties slung over their shoulders. Some businesses, especially in the Cayo District, refuse to sell plastic bottles at all until they can be properly disposed of or reused throughout Belize, as glass beer bottles still are. And no, drinking beer instead of water is not a sustainable solution.

Try to ease your plastic bottle consumption in Belize by refilling them.

© JOSHUA BERMAN

BITTERS: LOVE POTION NUMBER NINE

"It's good for your penis!" boomed Doctor Mac, extolling the wonders of bitters – that age-old Garinagu herbal tonic, aphrodisiac, and more. Mac poured a measured portion of yellowed liquid through a funnel into a recycled pint bottle. "It's good for making babies!" He laughed and clenched a fist atop an upraised forearm to emphasize his point – Central American sign language for "virility." **Bitters** are made by soaking herbs like *palo del hombre* (man-root) and jackass bitters in 80-proof white rum or gin. They are available under the counter of many a bar and corner store, a liquid baby-maker known in Garifuna as *"gifit."* Bitters are a cure-all used to treat everything from the common cold to cancer, sometimes taken as a daily shot to keep your system clean and your urine clear. And of course, bitters are a sure cure for impotency and infertility, according to any vendor of the stuff.

Belizean and Honduran Garinagu expats bring bitters back to the United States by the gallon (until the airlines' ban on liquids,

anyway). Until he moved to Chicago, the most famous bitters maker in the country was Doctor Mac, a formidable man, also known as "Big Mac," who was credited with the births of many local babies for the fertility juice he proffered. He used to make a version for women, the bottles labeled either "boy" or "gal."

Last time I was in the area, looking for the new king of the bitters crown, I was told "There's a new kid on the block," but not given any names. I did however, discover the bitters of "Kid B," a spry 76-year-old from Silk Grass Village, who spent 36 years as a welterweight prize fighter in Chicago. Find him at **Kid B's Cool Spot** in Silk Grass, just off the Southern Highway, north of the Hopkins turn-off.

Don't forget, in addition to curing what ails ya, bitters can get you really, really wasted. Be careful with long-term, regular use, both for your liver's sake and because some say the ingredients carry trace amounts of arsenic. Talk about a hangover.

ALCOHOLIC BEVERAGES
Beer

Perhaps the most important—or at least best-tasting—legacy left by nearly three centuries of British imperialism is a national affinity for dark beer. Nowhere else in Central America will you find ale as hearty and *morena* as you will in any bar, restaurant, or corner store in Belize, where beer is often advertised separately from stout, a good sign indeed for those who prefer more bite and body to their brew.

At the top of the heap are the slender, undersized (280 mL) bottles of **Guinness Foreign Extra Stout,** known affectionately by Belizeans as "short, dark, and love-lies." Yes, that's right, Guinness—brewed in Belize under license from behind the famous St. James's Gate in Dublin, Ireland, and packing a pleasant 7.5 percent punch of alcohol. No, this is not the same sweet nectar you'll find flowing from your favorite Irish pub's

draught handle at home, but c'mon, you're in Central America. Enjoy.

Next up is **Belikin Stout,** weighing in with a slightly larger bottle (342 mL) and distinguishable from a regular beer bottle by its blue bottle cap. Stouts run 6.5 percent alcohol and are a bit less bitter than Guinness, but still a delicious, meaty meal that goes down much quicker than its caloric equivalent of a loaf of bread. **Belikin Premium** (4.8 percent alcohol) boasts a well-balanced body and is brewed with four different types of foreign hops; demand often exceeds supply in many establishments, so order early.

Asking for a "beer" will get you a basic **Belikin,** which, when served cold, is no better or worse than any other regional draft. Lastly, the tiny green bottles belong to **Lighthouse Lager,** a healthy alternative to the heavies, but packing a lot less bang for the buck with only 4.2 percent alcohol and several ounces less beer (often for the same price).

All beer in Belize is brewed and distributed by the same company in Ladyville, just north of Belize City (Bowen and Bowen Ltd. also has the soft drink market cornered). Some batches are occasionally inconsistent in quality—if you get skunked, send back your mug and try again. You'll see most Belizeans vigorously wipe the rust and crud from the open bottle mouths with the napkin that comes wrapped around the top—you'd be smart to do the same. Beers in Belize cost anywhere from US$1.50–3 a bottle, depending on where you are.

Rum

Of all the national rums, **One Barrel** stands proudly above the rest. Smooth enough to enjoy on the rocks (add a bit of Coca-Cola for coloring if you need to), One Barrel has a sweet, butterscotchy aftertaste and costs about US$8 for a liter bottle, or US$3 per shot (or rum drink). Locals often stick to their favorite **Caribbean Rum,** fine if you're mixing it with punch, cola, or better yet, coconut water, *in* the coconut. Everything else is standard, white-rum gut rot.

Tips for Travelers

PAPERWORK

Make a photocopy of the pages in your passport that have your photo and information. When you get the passport stamped in the airport, it's a good idea to make a photocopy of that page as well, and store the copies somewhere other than with your passport. This will facilitate things if your passport ever gets lost or stolen. Also consider taking a small address book, credit cards, a travel insurance policy, and an international phone card for calling home. Be discreet when using a money belt—the best option is to buy one that looks like a regular belt, where you can zip the folded bills inside, and don't open it in public. A separate passport pouch can be used for documents, but make sure it's waterproof so it won't get soggy from your sweat.

ALTERNATIVE TRAVEL

By "alternative," I mean anyone traveling to Belize to teach, study, learn, volunteer, research, or work—instead of or in addition to traditional tourist activities. Following are a few options for alternative travel that I've come across—be sure to research more deeply on your own before committing. Some organizations offer full funding and support; others expect you to pay tuition to participate. For these, find out how much (if any) money you are expected to pay and, of that, how the

money is divided between the community where you'll be working and the organization's overhead costs. Look for specific opportunities that may suit your skills and experience; check **www.transitionsabroad.com.** There are numerous other websites, magazines, and books that specialize in volunteering and studying abroad, including the author's home page and blog, **www.joshuaberman.net.**

Field Research and Educational Travel

There are many opportunities to learn, teach, and volunteer at the **Belize Zoo and Tropical Education Center** (tel. 501/220-8004, www.belizezoo.org). The **Maya Mountain Lodge** in the Cayo District (tel. 501/824-2164, www.mayamountain.com) offers talks covering a range of subjects, including Maya ceramics. The **Oceanic Society** (U.S. tel. 800/326-7491, www.oceanic-society.org), a nonprofit conservation organization, maintains a field station in the Turneffe Island Atoll and invites curious travelers to participate in educational marine ecotourism activities, such as snorkel and kayak programs to learn about coral reef ecology and whale shark research projects (about US$2000 includes everything for eight-day trips). The family program includes interaction with Belizean and American researchers.

Global Vision International (www.gvi-usa.com) offers 4- to 12-week opportunities around the country—assisting wildlife rangers at Cockscomb Basin Wildlife Sanctuary, conducting marine surveys for dive masters at Blue Hole and Half Moon Caye Natural Monuments, and assisting Institute of Archaeology staff in site management of archaeological reserves, including at Caracol. Volunteer opportunities also exist from time to time at Wildtracks' Manatee Rehabilitation Center (tel. 501/614 8244, www.wildtracks-belize.org).

Do an "Expedition Search" with **Earthwatch Institute** (www.earthwatch.org) to find a menu of marine research opportunities in Belize. Due to budget cuts, it is uncertain whether Earthwatch will still run these tax-deductible "paying volunteer" programs in Belize; check the site for an update.

Budding marine biologists can join a research team to study manatees, dolphins, and marine habitat through lectures, literature review, and field research, including 30–40 hours on the water exploring mangrove islands, sea grass beds, and coral patches. This unique field course combines an overview of the ecology, behavior, and conservation of sirenians and cetaceans with hands-on manatee and dolphin research in the Drowned Cayes. You'll collect behavioral and environmental data and learn about photo ID techniques of tracking animals. University credit is available; the field course is led by **Caryn Self-Sullivan** of Sirenian International and Georgia Southern University (caryns@sirenian.org), and is taught by visiting professors during the summer, generally in June. The fee is US$2595 plus airfare.

In Toledo District, the **Belize Foundation for Research and Environmental Education** (BFREE; www.bfreebelize.net) offers student programs from one week to a whole semester, with lots of activities and cultural immersion programs available. BFREE has spearheaded amphibian research and monitoring in the Maya Mountains as a participant in the Maya Forest Anuran Monitoring Project, among other things. Also, the **Belize Rainforest Institute** (www.mayamountain.com) provides weeklong courses and workshops on such topics as rainforest ecology, butterflies, cultures of Belize, and ecotourism. You've also got the huge array of research and educational programs at **Monkey Bay Wildlife Sanctuary** (tel. 501/820-3032, www.monkeybaybelize. org), which specializes in groups and classes.

Look up the summer workshops and other educational trips offered by **International Zoological Expeditions** (U.S. tel. 800/548-5843, www.ize2belize.com); they've got bases and considerable experience in South Water Caye and Toledo District.

Programme for Belize (1 Eyre St., Belize City, tel. 501/227-5616, U.S. tel. 617/259-9500, www.pfbelize.org) is the group that manages the 260,000-acre Río Bravo Conservation Area and has a full menu of ecology and rainforest workshops.

For Mayaphiles and archaeology students, the **Belize Valley Archaeology Reconnaissance Project** (BVAR; www.bvar. org) conducts research and offers field schools at several sites in western Belize.

Two miles upriver from the village of San Pedro Columbia, in southern Belize, the **Maya Mountain Research Farm** (www.mmrfbz.org) is a registered NGO and working demonstration farm that promotes sustainable agriculture, appropriate technology, and food security using permacultural principles and applied biodiversity, and it offers hands-on coursework in all of the above.

Volunteer Opportunities

There are many opportunities for voluntourists to get their feet wet in the world of international development and resource conservation work throughout Belize. Some regional chapters throughout this book offer local volunteer opportunities or ways to help the community. For those interested in spending some time lending a hand, sharing their expertise, or supporting community efforts, there's plenty to choose from. Some of these programs cost money and some don't; be sure you know exactly what you're getting into when you sign

KEEPING THE "ECO" IN TOURISM

Belize is generally acknowledged as one of the world's freshest and most successful models of ecotourism. The word "ecotourism" was created in the 1980s with the best of intentions – ostensibly, to describe anything having to do with environmentally sound and culturally sustainable tourism. It was the "business" of preventing tourism from spoiling the environment and using tourism as an economic alternative to spoiling the environment for some other reason.

The success of the concept – and its marketing value – led to a worldwide surge in the usage of that prefix we know so well, even if its actual practice may sometimes fall short of original intentions. Indeed, "eco" has been used, abused, prostituted, and bastardized all over the world, and Belize is no exception. Some word-savvy tourism marketers have tried to freshen things up by using "alternative" or "adventure" tourism, but, when trying to describe an operation that practices the original definition of ecotourism mentioned above, I prefer "sustainable," "responsible," "ethical," or even "fair trade" tourism.

In 2009, Belize hosted the **Third Annual World Conference for Responsible Tourism.** The conference featured experts from around the world speaking on local economic development through tourism, the impact of mass tourism on local communities, and climate change.

The **Belize Eco-Tourism Association** (BETA; www.bzecotourism.org) and **Belize Audubon Society** (BAS; www.belizeaudubon.org) are two organizations concerned with keeping the "eco" in tourism – and in keeping pressure on the government of Belize to do the same. BETA was created on Earth Day in 1993 by a small group of members of the Belize Tourism Industry Association.

up. Also, be clear on what kind of work your position will entail, as well as your host organization's expectations and Belizean legal requirements. Speaking of which, Belizean immigration officially requires long-term volunteers to apply for special visas, a process which takes months and is not cheap. Some NGOs get around this (for short-term assignments, anyway) by calling their volunteers "interns."

The **Belize Audubon Society** (BAS; www.belizeaudubon.org) accepts qualified volunteers and interns for a variety of land and marine projects, with a three-month minimum (less for marine). Past skilled BAS volunteers have worked in community education; helped create trail signs, brochures, and management guidelines for protected areas and wardens; and analyzed the effectiveness of BAS gift shops. **Habitat for Humanity Belize** (tel. 501/227-6818), a world leader in providing low-income housing, operates in Belize City and beyond and accepts qualified volunteers and church groups to help erect home projects.

Cayo-based **Pro-Belize** (tel. 501/601-9121, www.myproworld.org) is part of ProWorld, an international placement organization that offers study and volunteer abroad experiences from two weeks to six months or longer. Your weekly tuition covers room, board, work placement, donation, and weekend excursions. The work in Belize can be in health, environment, micro-business, youth sports, fine arts, journalism, or women's issues. Semester-length courses are available.

In San Pedro, **Green Reef** (100 Coconut Dr., San Pedro Town, tel. 501/226-2833, www.greenreefbelize.org) is a nonprofit conservation organization that works to protect Belize's barrier reef and associated environment; they're always interested in hearing from potential volunteers, especially those who have skills in web design, photography, fund-raising, community outreach, and environmental education. Green Reef won an award from the Belize Tourism Board for Environmental Organization of the Year in 2003.

Itzamna Society (tel. 501/820-4023, www.epnp.org) is based in San Antonio, Cayo District, and was set up "for the protection and conservation of the environment and cultural patrimony" of the local Maya community and national park.

The Belize Botanic Garden (www.belizebotanic.org) sponsors a volunteer program where specialists pay US$500 for room and board while working on various garden projects.

The **Cornerstone Foundation** (tel. 501/824-2373, www.peacecorner.org/cornerstone.htm) is a humanitarian NGO based in the Cayo District, whose volunteer opportunities include HIV/AIDS education and awareness, special education, adult literacy, working with youth or women, and teaching business skills.

Teachers for a Better Belize (TFABB; www.tfabb.org) is a partnership of educators from North America and Belize who volunteer their time to improve the training of Belizean teachers and the education of children in rural Toledo villages. During summers, TFABB invites five to ten experienced North American K–8 teachers to Belize for one or two weeks to partner with Belizean teachers in presenting lessons at a teacher-training workshop in Punta Gorda. Every few years, they also need construction volunteers (no experience necessary). TFABB accepts donations of children's storybooks to ship to Belize.

Trekforce Belize (8 Saint Mark St., Belize City, tel. 501/223-1442, www.trekforce.org.uk) offers challenging conservation, community, and research trips from two weeks to five months long, including "jungle survival," Spanish school in Guatemala, and a teaching assignment in a rural Belizean school.

Aspiring organic farmers will want to check up on the few Belize listings for the **World Wide Opportunities on Organic Farms** (www.wwoof.org) network, which at last check had five independent host opportunities in Belize. You can often work on the farm in exchange for room and board, but conditions vary from site to site. Start with Barton Creek Outpost in Cayo (http://bartoncreekoutpost.com), which also offers other kinds of work/trade opportunities to stay in this backpacker's paradise.

Sustainable Harvest International's **Smaller World Program** (U.S. tel. 207/669-8254, shi@sustainableharvest.org, www.

sustainableharvest.org) has an office in Punta Gorda, where they coordinate sustainable agriculture projects with 100 area farmers. SHI offers service trips for groups, staying in rustic homestays or the relatively upscale Cotton Tree Lodge. Typical service trips for volunteers are 10 days long and include side trips to natural and cultural sites. Some projects they've done include organic gardens, multistory cacao and coffee plots, composting latrines, organic fertilizers and pesticides, biodigestors, and wood-conserving stoves. In Belize, the trips include sustainable chocolate tours and family volun-tourism trips.

U.S. Peace Corps

The Peace Corps (www.peacecorps.gov) is a U.S. government program created by John F. Kennedy in 1961, whose original goal was to improve America's image in the Third World by sending volunteers deep into the countryside of developing countries. Nearly fifty years later, some 8,000 volunteers are serving in more than 70 countries around the world. Accepted participants serve a two-year tour preceded by three months of intensive language and cultural training in the host country; they receive a bare-bones living allowance and earn a nominal "readjustment allowance" at the completion of their service.

The first group of Peace Corps volunteers arrived in Belize in 1962. Since that time, more than 1,700 volunteers have worked in Belize in a variety of projects. Currently, there are about 70 volunteers providing assistance in education, youth development, rural community development, environmental education, and HIV/AIDS prevention. Preservice training is conducted in rural Creole and mestizo villages and includes Spanish, Q'eqchi', and Garifuna language classes, depending on where the volunteer is being sent. Volunteers are placed throughout the country's six districts to work with government agencies and NGOs.

SPECIAL CONCERNS
Travelers with Children

Children love Belize and Belizeans love children. At least, this was my experience the last

© JOSHUA BERMAN

Family travel is full of adventure and possibility.

time I traveled with my family; the Belizeans we met couldn't get enough of my 9-month-old daughter, Shanti. For one, she was snatched away by every one of our restaurant servers, allowing us to eat in peace while Shanti and the restaurant staff entertained one another.

A select few romantic resorts do not allow children, but most do. Any place offering a special "family package" is a place to start your research. Always check in advance and tell the staff the ages of your children. You'll find most resorts are quite experienced at dealing with all ages.

For babies, be prepared with your own travel kit, but don't stress it too much if you forget something. There is a modern selection of jarred food, diapers, bottles, formula, and the like at Brodie's supermarkets in Belize City. If you're short on jars, or if baby wants more than breast milk, you'll find enough fresh fruit and fish to keep your baby growing the whole time you're in Belize. A few resorts can provide a crib in your room if you want one, but make sure you verify this in advance; otherwise bring

your own fold-up contraption, which can be great for the beach too, especially since you can easily drape a mosquito net over the top.

Once in Belize, a visit to the zoo is a must. There are a few kid-friendly cave trips and, of course, scrambling on the pyramids at any of the archaeological sites is heaven for young explorers. Just be extra careful about covering them up with loose, long clothing against the sun and mosquitoes, and make sure they stay hydrated while they rage through the jungle. Also, during the rainy season, it's best to steer clear of river activities like cave tubing, since rivers can be unpredictable when they swell with rain.

Women Travelers

For the independent woman, Belize is a great place for group or solo travel. Its size makes it easy to get around, English is spoken everywhere, and if you so desire, you won't be lacking for a temporary travel partner in any part of the country. You'll meet many fellow travelers at the small inexpensive inns and guesthouses.

GETTIN' HITCHED AND HONEYMOONIN'

Belize's reputation for romance is growing, and an increasing number of resorts cater to exotic weddings and honeymoon packages, including ceremonies conducted underwater, atop Maya pyramids, or in caves. Actually, I don't think anyone's been married in a cave yet, but someone's bound to do it. Most couples, however, are quite content with a barefoot beach ceremony.

For a US$50 marriage license, the couple must arrive in Belize three business days before submitting marriage paperwork to the Registrar General office on the fourth business day. A rush job costs US$250 and allows you to obtain your marriage license before arriving in Belize, in which case you can get married on your first day in country, if you so wish. For this service, you'll need a travel agent or wedding planner to act on your behalf in Belize.

The **Registrar General of Belize** (tel. 501/227-2053, www.belizelaw.org) handles marriage licenses. You'll need to show proof of citizenship (i.e., a valid passport), proof that you're over 18, and, where applicable, a certified copy of a divorce certificate or death decree to annul a previous marriage. Forms can be obtained at two locations: the General Registry, Supreme Court Building, Belize City and the Solicitor General's Office, East Block Building, Belmopan. No blood test is required.

A few select Belize wedding specialists can help you facilitate the paperwork, find ministers, and handle your party's flowers, accommodations, receptions, and everything else. Contact **Iraida Gonzales** on San Pedro (www.belizeweddings.com), **Lee Nyhus** in Placencia (www.secretgardenplacencia.com), and **Katie Valk,** who provides services anywhere in the country (www.belize-trips.com).

Belizeans are used to seeing all combinations of travelers; solo women are no exception.

That said, sexual harassment of females traveling alone or in small groups can be a problem, although most incidents are limited to no more than a few catcalls. Just keep on walking; usually, some minor acknowledgment that you have heard them will shut harassers up more quickly than totally ignoring them. Although violent sexual assault is not a common occurrence, it does occur (like anywhere in the world). Several American travelers were the victims of sexual assaults in recent years. At least one of these rapes occurred after the victim accepted a ride from a new acquaintance, while another occurred during an armed robbery at an isolated resort. Never give the name of your hotel or your room number to someone you don't know.

When away from the beach towns and cayes, know that revealing clothes *will* attract lots of gawking attention, possibly more than you want. Most of the small towns and villages are safe even at night, with the exception of Belize City—don't walk anywhere there at night, even with friends. The best protection to bring is common sense.

Feminine supplies are found everywhere, with the exception of the smallest outlying villages and some of the remote lodges.

A few international tour companies specialize in trips for independent, active women. For "uncommon advice for the independent woman traveler," pick up a copy of Thalia Zepatos's *A Journey of One's Own* (Eighth Mountain Press), a highly acclaimed women's travel resource.

Senior Travelers

Active seniors enjoy Belize. Some like the tranquility of the cayes, others the bird-watching in the Maya ruins. Many come to learn about the jungle and its creatures or about archaeology. **Elderhostel** (U.S. tel. 877/426-8056, www.elderhostel.org) has a number of tours to Belize, including dolphin and reef ecology projects.

Gay and Lesbian Travelers

Although there are plenty of out-and-about gay Belizean men (in Creole, "Batty-Men" or

TOUR COMPANIES AND TRAVEL AGENTS

International tour companies and travel specialists offer a huge variety of trips, from afternoon city tours to weeklong cruises and treks in the farthest reaches of the country, the logistics of which would be next to impossible for the solo traveler to arrange herself. These adventures cost money, and of course, as part of a group, you lose some independence. But then again, you are provided with security, freedom from planning, and, with some companies, downright luxury. In addition, booking through a travel agent may get you better hotel discounts than if you go it alone. Some of the following companies also help you plan independent trips for just you and your family.

Before choosing a tour company, research it well and ask lots of questions: Will you interact with the communities through which you'll be traveling? If so, are the people of those communities benefiting in some way other than the opportunity to watch you pass through their villages in air-conditioned vehicles with the windows rolled up? Will your tour operator create an environment that allows you to practice the tenets of ethical tourism as listed in this section?

BELIZE TRAVEL SPECIALISTS

More than either a travel agent or tour operator, "Belize specialists" are small, independent operations which work directly with their clients to arrange all kinds of niche, group, and solo travel within Belize. Here are two of the best:

Belize Trips (tel. 501/610-1923, U.S. tel. 561/210-7015, www.belize-trips.com) will make all your Belize dreams come true, helping you book mid- to upscale accommodations, active itineraries, weddings, and honeymoons. Owner Katie Valk finds out exactly what kind of experience her clients want and then, through her vast network of friends and colleagues across the country, makes that experience happen. Katie is a self-described "music business refugee from New York City" who has lived full time in Belize for twenty-odd years, and you'll often find her swinging a machete through the bush or paddling her kayak down some wildlife-choked river, as she seeks out and test-drives every adventure she promotes.

Barb's Belize (U.S. tel. 888/321-2272, www.barbsbelize.com) is another small operation that offers custom itineraries for any budget, from backpacker to decadently deluxe. Barb's specializes in unique interests such as traditional herbal medicine, jungle survival, and extreme adventure expeditions.

TOUR OPERATORS

For those interested in letting someone else do the driving (and planning, booking, etc.), various tour operators are reliable. In Belize City, Sarita and Lascelle Tillet of **S & L Travel and Tours** (91 N. Front St., tel. 501/227-7593 or 227-5145, www.sltravelbelize.com) operate as a husband/wife team. They drive late-model air-conditioned sedans or vans and travel throughout the country with airport pickup available. The Tillets have designed several great special-interest vacations and will custom design to your interests, whether they be the Maya archaeological zones (including Tikal), the cayes, or the caves and the countryside.

InnerQuest Adventures (www.innerquest.com) has over 14 years of experience leading wildlife-viewing trips with local guides around the country. They've been featured in dozens of magazines. Minnesota-based **Magnum Belize Tours** (U.S. tel. 800/447-2931, www.magnumbelize.com) is one of the biggest, most longstanding tour operators, with an extensive network of resorts across the country; the staff is very experienced and can customize every aspect of your trip.

Sea & Explore (U.S. tel. 800/345-9786, www.seaexplore.com) is run by owners Sue and Tony Castillo, native Belizeans who take pleasure and pride in sharing their country with visitors by the means of customized trips. They know every out-of-the-way destination and make every effort to match clients with the right areas of the country to suit their interests. Susan worked with the Belize Tourism Board before coming to the United States.

(continues on next page)

TOUR COMPANIES AND TRAVEL AGENTS (continued)

Mary Dell Lucas of **Far Horizons Archaeological and Cultural Trips** (U.S. tel. 800/552-4575, www.farhorizon.com) is known throughout the Maya world for her excellent archaeological knowledge and insight. Her company provides trips into the most fascinating Maya sites, regardless of location. Although Mary is an archaeologist herself, she often brings specialists along with her groups.

Also check **Jaguar Adventures Tours and Travel** (4 Fort St., tel. 501/223-6025, www.jaguarbelize.com), located in Belize City and offering night walks at the Belize Zoo, cave tubing trips, visits to Maya ruins, snorkeling the reef, and diving the atolls, to name a few adventures.

ADVENTURE TRAVEL

Dangriga- and Vancouver-based **Island Expeditions** (U.S. tel. 800/667-1630, www.islandexpeditions.com) has been leading exciting sea kayaking, rafting, ruins, nature, and snorkeling adventures in Belize since 1987. It's a very experienced and professional outfit, and they have a stunning island camp in Glover's Reef Atoll with canvas-wall tents on platforms, plus a new camp on Half Moon Caye.

Slickrock Adventures (U.S. tel. 800/390-5715, www.slickrock.com), based on their primitively plush camp on a private island in Glover's Reef Atoll, offers paddling trips of various lengths and specializes in sea kayaking, windsurfing, and inland activities like mountain biking.

With 17 years of experience as a premier land operator in Belize, **International Expeditions** (U.S. tel. 800/633-4734, belize@ietravel.com, www.ietravel.com) has a full-time office in Belize City. They offer group and independent nature travel in sturdy, comfortable vehicles and are staffed by travel and airline specialists, naturalists, and an archaeologist. Trips run 7-14 days with two- and three-day add-ons available.

You'll also find an interesting menu of tours offered by **Intrepid Travel** (tel. 1 800 970 7299, intrepidtravel.com), including a number of Maya-themed and regional trips.

"Benque Boys"), there is no established community or any gay clubs, per se. The foreign gay travelers we've seen were totally accepted by both their fellow lodge guests and Belizean hosts. Still, the act of "sodomy" (between men) is officially illegal in Belize, so a bit of discretion is advised.

Travelers with Disabilities

There are probably about as many wheelchair ramps in all of Belize as there are traffic lights (three); disabled travelers will generally be treated with respect, but expect logistics to be a bit challenging in places. Experience Belize Tours (tel. 501/225-2981, U.S. tel. 205/383-2921, www.experiencebelizetours.com) offers wheelchair-accessible tours for seniors, slow walkers, and disabled travelers. You can also try **Belize Special Tours** (tel. 501/600-4284 or 824-4748, belizeanlove@yahoo.com), catering specifically to travelers with disabilities,

which offers tours of the Belize Zoo, the lower flat of the museum, Belize City, and the Altun Ha ruins. Hok'ol K'in Guest House in Corozal and Red Jaguar Lodge in San José Succotz both have nice wheelchair-accessible suites and facilities. There is also a "Belize disabled travel holiday" listed on http://responsibletravel.com.

CAMERAS AND PHOTOGRAPHY
Film Processing

Most larger cities in Belize have one-hour photo labs, but technicians often know little about the processing machines, so print quality may be wanting. Most people shoot digital, anyway, these days, and print their images when they get home. Many Internet cafés have readers for your digital camera card, so you can make CD backups as you go. To be safe, travel with your own USB cable, so you can plug it in to a rented computer. You can also travel with a laptop and regularly upload your photos to clear your camera's memory card or travel with plenty of memory (an option which is increasingly affordable).

Photo Etiquette

Cameras can be a help or a hindrance when trying to get to know the locals. When traveling in the backcountry, you'll run into folks who don't want their pictures taken. Keep your camera put away until the right moment. *Always* ask permission first, and if someone doesn't want his or her picture taken, accept the refusal with a gracious smile and move on. Especially sensitive to this are Mennonites and Mayans, who usually specifically request that you not take their photos.

Underwater Photography

Most travelers use disposable underwater cameras, which may have depth limits, but if you're looking to publish something in *Dive Fever* magazine, you'll need a bit more under the hood. Some hotels, resorts, and shops in Belize rent underwater SRL cameras or housings for your own camera. Don't expect a large selection. Remember when buying film that the best for underwater is natural-, red-, or yellow-tint film; film such as Ektachrome with a bluish cast does not give the best results. A strobe or flash is a big help if shooting in deep water or into caves. Natural-light pictures are great if you're shooting in fairly shallow water. It's best to shoot on an eye-to-eye level when photographing fish. Be careful of stirring up silt from the bottom with your fins and try to hold very still when depressing the shutter; if you must stabilize yourself, *don't* grab onto any live coral—you will kill it and you may hurt yourself as well.

Health and Safety

BEFORE YOU GO
Resources

Staying Healthy in Asia, Africa, and Latin America, by Dirk G. Schroeder (Avalon Travel Publishing, 2000), is an excellent and concise guide to preventative medicine in the developing world and small enough to fit in your pack. Same goes for *The Pocket Doctor: A Passport to Healthy Travel* by Stephen Bezruchka (Mountaineers Books, 1999). A bit more unwieldy but a standard in the field is David Werner's *Where There Is No Doctor* (Hesperian Foundation, 1992).

For up-to-date health recommendations and advice, consult the "Mexico and Central America" page of the U.S. Centers for Disease Control and Prevention (CDC) at www.cdc.gov/travel/camerica.htm, or call their International Travelers Hotline at 404/332-4559 or 877/394-8747. Another excellent resource is the Belize page of www.mdtravelhealth.com. You can also call the Belizean embassy in your country for up-to-date information about outbreaks or other health problems.

STAYING HEALTHY

Ultimately, your health is dependent on the choices you make, and chief among these is what you decide to put in your mouth. Expect your digestive system to take some time getting accustomed to the new food and microorganisms in the Belizean diet. During this time (and after), use common sense: wash your hands with soap often; alcohol-based hand sanitizers are less effective at removing germs from your hands. Eat food that is well cooked and still hot when served. Be wary of uncooked foods, including shellfish and salads. That said, most restaurants in Belize are very careful and completely safe, especially (but not always) the fancier ones.

Most importantly, be aware of flies, the single worst transmitter of food-borne illnesses. Prevent flies from landing on your food, glass, or table setting. You'll notice Belizeans are meticulous about this, and you should be too. If you have to leave the table, cover your food with a napkin or have someone else wave a hand over it slowly. You can fold your drinking straw over and put the mouth end into the neck of your bottle to prevent flies from landing on it, and put napkins on top of the bottle neck and your glass, too. When you're finished with a dish, ask the waiter to clear it so you have fewer things to guard from the flies.

Drinking the Water

At least one well-meaning friend or relative told you not to drink the local water before you shipped off to Central America, and for the most part, we agree. Even though most municipal water systems are well treated and probably safe, there is not much reason to take the chance, especially when purified bottled water is so widely available and relatively cheap. Avoid ice cubes, unless you're confident they were made with boiled or purified water. Canned and bottled drinks without ice, including beer, are usually safe, but should never be used as a substitute for water when trying to stay hydrated, especially during a bout of diarrhea or when out in the sun.

If you plan on staying awhile in a rural area of Belize, check out camping catalogs for water filters that remove chemical as well as biological contamination. Alternately, six drops of liquid iodine (or three of bleach) will kill everything that needs to be killed in a liter of water—good in a pinch (or on a backcountry camping trip), but not something you'll find yourself practicing on a daily basis. Also, bringing any water to a full boil is 100 percent effective in killing bacteria.

Oral Rehydration Salts

Probably the single most effective preventative and curative medicine you can carry are packets of powdered salt and sugar which, when mixed with a liter of water (drink in small sips), is the best immediate treatment for dehydration due to diarrhea, sun exposure, fever, infection, or hangover. Particularly in

the case of diarrhea, rehydration salts are essential to your recovery. They replace the salts and minerals your body has lost due to liquid evacuation (be it from sweating, vomiting, or urinating), and they're essential to your body's most basic cellular transfer functions. Whether or not you like the taste (odds are you won't), consuming enough rehydration packets and water is very often the difference between being just a little sick and feeling really, really awful.

Sport drinks like Gatorade are super-concentrated mixtures and should be diluted *at least* 2:1 with water to make the most of the active ingredients. If you don't, you'll urinate out the majority of the electrolytes. Gatorade is common in most new gas stations and supermarkets, but rehydration packets are much, much cheaper and available from any drug store or health clinic. They can also be improvised even more cheaply, according to the following recipe: mix a half teaspoon of salt, a half teaspoon baking soda, and four tablespoons of sugar in one quart of boiled or carbonated water. Drink a full glass of the stuff after each time you use the bathroom. Add a few drops of lemon juice to make it more palatable.

Sun Exposure

Belize is located a scant 13–18 degrees of latitude from the equator, so the sun's rays strike the earth's surface at a more direct angle than in northern countries. The result is that you will burn faster and sweat up to twice as much as you are used to. Did we mention that you should drink lots of water?

Ideally, do like the majority of the locals do, and stay out of the sun between 10 A.M. and 2 P.M. It's a great time to take a nap anyway. Use sunscreen of at least SPF 30, and wear a hat and pants. Should you overdo it in the sun, make sure to drink lots of fluids—that means water, not beer—and try not to strain any muscles as you kick yourself for being so stupid. Treat sunburns with aloe gel, or better yet, find a fresh aloe plant to break open and rub over your skin.

DISEASES AND COMMON AILMENTS
Diarrhea and Dysentery

Generally, simple cases of diarrhea in the absence of other symptoms are nothing more serious than "traveler's diarrhca." If you do get a good case, your best bet is to let it pass naturally. Diarrhea is your body's way of flushing out the bad stuff, so constipating medicines like Imodium A-D are not recommended, as they keep the bacteria (or whatever is causing your intestinal distress) within your system. Save the Imodium (or any other liquid glue) for emergency situations like long bus rides or a hot date. Most importantly, drink lots of water! Not replacing the fluids and electrolytes you are losing will make you feel much worse than you need to. If the diarrhea persists for more than 48 hours, is bloody, or is accompanied by a fever, see a health professional immediately. That said, know that all bodies react differently to the changes in diet, schedule, and stress that go along with traveling, and many visitors to Belize stay entirely regular and solid throughout their trips.

Pay attention to your symptoms: Diarrhea can also be a sign of amoebic (parasitic) or bacillic (bacterial) dysentery, both caused by some form of fecal-oral contamination. Often accompanied by nausea, vomiting, and a mild fever, dysentery is easily confused with other diseases, so don't try to self-diagnose. Stool-sample examinations are cheap, can be performed at most clinics and hospitals, and are your first step to getting better. Bacillic dysentery is treatable with antibiotics; amoebic is treated with one of a variety of drugs that kill off all the flora in your intestinal tract. Of these, Flagyl is the best known, but other non-FDA-approved treatments like tinidazole are commonly available, cheap, and effective. Do not drink alcohol with these drugs, and eat something like yogurt or acidophilus pills to refoliate your tummy.

Malaria

By all official accounts, malaria is present in Belize, although you'll be hard-pressed to find anybody—Belizean or expat—who has actually experienced or even heard of a case of it. Still, many travelers choose to take a weekly prophylaxis of chloroquine or its equivalent. The CDC specifically recommends travelers to Belize to use brand-name Aralen pills (500 mg for adults), although you should ask your doctor for the latest drug on the market. Begin taking the pills two weeks before you arrive and continue taking them for four weeks after leaving the country. A small percentage of people have negative reactions to chloroquine, including nightmares, rashes, or hair loss. Alternative treatments are available, but the best method of all is to not get bit.

Dengue Fever

Dengue, or "bone-breaking fever," is a flulike, mosquito-carried illness that will put a stop to your fun in Central America like a baseball bat to the head. Dengue's occurrence is extremely low in Belize, but a couple dozen cases are still reported each year. There is no vaccine, but dengue's effects can be successfully minimized with plenty of rest, Tylenol (for the fever and aches), and as much water and *hydration salts* as you can possibly manage. Dengue itself is undetectable in a blood test, but a low platelet count indicates its presence. If you believe you have dengue, you should get a blood test as soon as possible, to make sure it's not the hemorrhagic variety, which can be fatal if untreated.

HIV/AIDS

HIV and AIDS are a growing problem in Belize. Thankfully, there is an impressive amount of international attention to the problem and awareness and education programs are common. The Peace Corps devotes an entire sector of its country program to this, and the Cornerstone Foundation is another active volunteer organization. When traveling in Belize, do not have unprotected sex, and say no to dirty needles and blood transfusions.

Ciguatera

This is a toxin occasionally found in large reef fish. It is not a common circumstance, but it is possible for grouper, snapper, and barracuda to carry this toxin. If after eating these fish you experience diarrhea, nausea, numbness, or heart arrhythmia, see a doctor immediately. The toxin is found in certain algae on reefs in all the tropical areas of the world. Fish do nibble on the coral, and if they happen to find this algae, over a period of time the toxin accumulates in their systems. The longer they live and the larger they get, the more probable it is they will carry the toxin, which is not destroyed when cooked.

Other Diseases

There is moderate incidence of hepatitis B in Belize. Avoid contact with bodily fluids or bodily waste. Get vaccinated if you anticipate close contact with the local population or plan to reside in Central America for an extended period of time.

Get a rabies vaccination if you intend to spend a long time in Belize. Should you be bitten by an infected dog, rodent, or bat, immediately cleanse the wound with lots of soap, and get prompt medical attention. In Belize, the chief risk is from rabid dogs near the Guatemalan border.

Tuberculosis is spread by sneezing or coughing, and the infected person may not know he or she is a carrier. If you are planning to spend more than four weeks in Belize (or plan on spending time in the Belize jail), consider having a tuberculin skin test performed before and after visiting. Tuberculosis is a serious and possibly fatal disease but can be treated with several medications.   No cases of cholera have been reported in Belize since 2000.

BITES AND STINGS
Mosquitoes and Sand Flies

Mosquitoes are most active during the rainy season (June–Nov.) and in areas with stagnant water, like marshes, puddles, and rice fields. They are more common in the lower, flatter regions of Belize than they are in the hills, though even in the highlands, old tires, cans, and roadside puddles can provide the habitat necessary to produce swarms of mosquitoes.

The mosquito that carries malaria is active during the evening and at night, while the dengue fever courier is active during the day, from dawn to dusk. They are both relatively simple to combat, and ensuring you don't get bitten is the best prophylaxis for preventing the diseases.

First and foremost, limit the amount of skin you expose—long sleeves, pants, and socks will do more to prevent bites than the strongest chemical repellant. Choose accommodations with good screens, and if this is not possible, use a fan to blow airborne insects away from your body as you sleep. Avoid being outside or unprotected in the hour before sunset, when mosquito activity is heaviest, and use a mosquito net tucked underneath your mattress when you sleep. Consider purchasing a lightweight backpackers' net, either freestanding or to hang from the ceiling, before you come south—mosquito nets are more expensive in Belize than at home. Some accommodations provide nets; others are truly free of biting bugs and don't need them. If you know where you're staying, ask before you arrive whether you'll need a net.

Once in Belize, you can purchase mosquito coils, which burn slowly, releasing a mosquito-repelling smoke; they're cheap and convenient, but try to place them so you're not breathing the toxic smoke yourself.

Sand flies don't carry any diseases that we know about, but, man, do they *suck!* Actually, these tiny midges, or no-see-ums, bite. Hard. They breed in wet, sandy areas and are only fought by the wind (or a well-screened room). Don't scratch those bites! For prevention, any thick oil is usually enough of a barrier—most people like baby oil or hempseed oil, and some swear that a hint of lavender scent in the oil keeps sand flies away too.

Scorpions, Spiders, and Snakes

Scorpions are common in Belize, especially in dark corners, at beaches, and in piles of wood. Belizean scorpions look nasty—black and big—but their stings are no more harmful than that of a bee and are described by some as what a cigarette burn feels like. Your lips and tongue may feel a little numb, but the venom is nothing compared to their smaller, translucent cousins in Mexico. Needless to say, to people who are prone to anaphylactic shock, it can be a more serious or life-threatening experience. Everyone has heard that when in a jungle, never put on your shoes without checking the insides—good advice—and always give your clothes a good visual going-over and a vigorous shake before putting them on. Scorpions occasionally drop out of thatch ceilings.

Don't worry, despite the prevalence of all kinds of arachnids, including big, hairy tarantulas, spiders do not aggressively seek out people to bite and do way more good than harm by eating things like Chagas bugs. If you'd rather the spiders didn't share your personal space, shake out your bedclothes before going to sleep and check your shoes before putting your feet in them.

Of the 59 species of snakes that have been identified in Belize, at least nine are venomous, most notably the infamous fer-de-lance (locally called a "Tommygoff") and the coral snake. The chances of the average tourist being bitten are slim. Reportedly, most snakebite victims are children. However, if you plan on extensive jungle exploration, check with your doctor before you leave home. Antivenin is available, doesn't require refrigeration, and keeps indefinitely. It's also wise to be prepared for an allergic reaction to the antivenin—bring an antihistamine and Adrenalin (epinephrine). The most important thing to remember if bitten: *Don't panic and don't run.* Physical exertion and panic cause the venom to travel through your body much faster. Lie down and stay calm; have someone carry you to a doctor. Do not cut the wound, use a tourniquet, or ingest alcoholic beverages.

Botfly

Ah, the lowly botfly! Also known as *torsalo,* screw-worm, or *Dermatobia hominis,* this insect looks like the common household fly. The big difference is that the botfly deposits its eggs on mosquitoes, which then implant them in an unsuspecting warm-blooded host. Burrowing quickly under the skin, the maggot sets up housekeeping. To breathe, it sticks a tiny tube through the skin, and there it stays until one of two things happen: you kill it, or it graduates and leaves home.

A botfly bite starts out looking like a mosquito bite, but if the bite gets red and tender instead of healing, get it checked out. Though uncomfortable and distasteful, it's not a serious health problem if it doesn't get infected. A tiny glob of petroleum jelly or tobacco over the air hole often works to draw out the varmint; just make sure you squeeze all of it out if it suffocates. For a gruesome close-up, Google "botfly removal," and meet some tourists who brought a little something extra home from their trip to Central America.

Marine Hazards

When you enter the marine world, you are a strange visitor among thousands of native critters. Most will only injure you if you somehow trigger their defense mechanisms—like if you step on them or grab them.

Anemones and sea urchins live in Belize waters. Some can be dangerous if touched or stepped on. The long-spined black sea urchin can inflict great pain, and its poison can cause an uncomfortable infection. Don't think that you're safe in a wetsuit, booties, and gloves. The spines easily slip through the rubber and the urchin is encountered at all depths. They are more abundant in some areas than in others; keep your eyes open. If you should run into one of the spines, remove it quickly and carefully, disinfect the wound, and apply antibiotic cream. If you have difficulty removing the spine, or if it breaks, see a doctor—*pronto!* Local remedies include urinating on the wound if nothing else is available.

Barracuda, moray eels, and sharks do not appreciate groping hands, and all have ample means to protect themselves. Enough said. As for your snorkel guide who picks up a nurse shark or ray and invites you to pet it, it's probably a better idea to look, not touch, and let him know your feelings before getting in the water—not necessarily because of the danger of attack, but more because we should let these animals alone.

Note that sharks are attracted to blood, certain low-frequency sounds (like those caused by an injured fish), electromagnetic disturbances, and certain shapes and color patterns. Avoid swimming with bleeding wounds. And while barracudas, like other predatory fish, can be excited by fish blood and jerky vibrations, they seem to be more visual hunters. They are likely to snap at something flashy, such as watches and bracelets, so leave your fancy jewelry at home.

A few seagoing critters resent being stepped on and can retaliate with a dangerous wound. The scorpion fish, hardly recognizable with its natural camouflage, lies hidden most of the time on a reef shelf or on the bottom of the sea. If you should step on or touch it you can expect a painful, dangerous sting. If this happens, see a doctor immediately.

If you leave them alone, stingrays are generally peaceful, but if stepped on they will zap you with a tail that carries a poisonous sting capable of causing anaphylactic shock. Symptoms include respiratory difficulties, fainting, and severe itching. Go quickly to the doctor and describe what caused the sting. One diver suggests a shuffling, dragging-of-the-feet gait when walking on the bottom of the ocean. If bumped, the ray will quickly escape, but if stepped on, it feels trapped and uses its tail for protection.

Tiny brown gel-encased globules called *pica-pica* produce a horrible rash; look for clouds of these guys around any coral patch before getting in. Avoid the bottom side of a moon jellyfish, as well as the Portuguese man-of-war (usually only in March). Sea wasps are tiny four-tentacled menaces that deliver a sting.

Fire worms (also known as bristle worms) will deposit tiny cactuslike bristles in your skin if touched. They can cause the same reaction as fire coral. *Carefully* scraping the skin with the edge of a sharp knife (as you would to remove a bee stinger) *might* remove the bristles. Any leftover bristles will ultimately work their way

out, but you might be very uncomfortable in the meantime. Cortisone cream helps to relieve the inflammation.

Several species of sponges have fine, sharp spicules (hard, minute, pointed calcareous or siliceous bodies that support the tissue) that should not be touched with the bare hand. The attractive red fire sponge can cause great pain; a mild solution of vinegar or ammonia (or urine, if there's nothing else) will help. The burning lasts a couple of days, and cortisone cream soothes. Don't be fooled by dull-colored sponges. Many have the same sharp spicules.

Coral

For the hundredth time, don't touch the coral! Many varieties of fire coral will make you wish you hadn't. Cuts from coral, even if just a scratch, will often become infected. Antibiotic cream or powder will usually take care of them. If you should get a deep cut, or if minute bits of coral are left in the wound, a serious and long-lived infection can ensue. See a doctor.

If you should get scraped on red or fire coral, you may feel a burning sensation for just a few minutes or up to five days. In some, it causes an allergic reaction and will raise large red welts. Cortisone cream will reduce inflammation and discomfort.

Don't Freak Out!

Don't let these what-ifs discourage you from an underwater or jungle adventure in Belize. Thousands of people dive in Belize's Caribbean and hike its forests every day of the year without incident. The above list is only to let you know what's out there, not to scare you into remaining in your room. Know what you're getting into and be sure your guide does as well, and then get into it!

MEDICAL CARE

Although there are hospitals and health clinics in most urban areas and towns, care is extremely limited compared with more developed countries. Serious injuries or illness may require evacuation to another country, and you should consider picking up cheap travel insurance that covers such a need—otherwise, you're looking at US$12,000 just for the medevac transport.

Many Belizean doctors and hospitals require immediate cash payment for health services, sometimes prior to providing treatment. Uninsured travelers or travelers whose insurance does not provide coverage in Belize may face extreme difficulties if serious medical treatment is needed. **International Medical Group** (www.imglobal.com) is one reliable provider that offers short-term insurance specifically for overseas travelers and expats for very reasonable rates.

Belize Medical Associates (5791 St. Thomas St., tel. 501/223-0302, 223-0303, or 223-0304, bzmedasso@btl.net, www.belizemedical.com) is the only private hospital in Belize City. They provide 24-hour assistance and a wide range of specialties. Look under "Hospitals" in the BTL yellow pages for an updated listing of other options. In San Ignacio, La Loma Luz Hospital (tel. 501/824-2087) offers primary care as well as 24-hour emergency services and is one of the best private hospitals in the country.

Medications and Prescriptions

Many medications are available in pharmacies in Belize, and some are more strict than others about requiring papers for prescription drugs. Definitely plan on the conservative side: Bring adequate supplies of all your prescribed medications in their original containers, clearly labeled and in date; in addition, carry a signed, dated letter from your physician describing all medical conditions and listing your medications, including their generic names. If carrying syringes or needles, carry a physician's letter documenting their medical necessity. Pack all medications in your carry-on bag and, if possible, put a duplicate supply in the checked luggage. If you wear glasses or contacts, bring an extra pair. If you have significant allergies or chronic medical problems, wear a medical alert bracelet.

Condoms are cheap and easy to find. Any corner pharmacy will have them, even in small towns of just a few thousand people. Female travelers taking contraceptives should know the generic name for the drug they use.

Bring a Small Medical Kit

At the very minimum, consider the following items for your first-aid kit: rehydration salt packets, sterile bandages/gauze, moleskin for blister prevention, antiseptic cream, strong sunblock (SPF 30), aloe gel for sunburns, some kind of general antibiotic for intestinal trouble, acetaminophen (Tylenol) for pain/fevers, eyedrops (for dust), birth control pills, condoms, and anti-fungal cream (clotrimazole).

NATURAL HEALING

In small rural villages, if you have a serious problem and no doctor is around, you can usually find a *curandero*. These healers practice the old, herb-based healing methods and may be helpful in a desperate situation away from modern technology. Locals who live in the dense, jungle areas inhabited by poisonous snakes go to the local "snake doctor," although many advise against it.

You may learn about the grapevine, which provides pure water to cleanse the navel of a newborn infant, or the bark of the negrito tree, also called dysentery bark, which treats severe dysentery (and which was sold for high prices by druggists in Europe when pirates discovered it many years back). Tea made from the China root is used for blood-building after an attack from parasites. Another tea made from *ki bix* acts as birth control by coating the lining of the uterus. This is just a tiny sampling of the information shared with visitors.

Due mainly to the influence of Rosita Arvigo, a healer based in the Cayo District, the Belizean government established **Terra Nova Medicinal Plant Reserve,** referred to in 1993 as the world's first medicinal plant reserve. The 6,000 acres are administrated by the **Belizean Association of Traditional Healers,** dedicated to the preservation of what might be important scientific help in future treatments of illnesses. Seedlings are brought here from threatened areas of the rainforest. A number of other "medicine trails" are found throughout Belize, including one at the Belize Botanic Garden in Cayo.

CRIME

Most of the crime in Belize (besides drug possession and trafficking) is petty theft and burglary. In the rare event that a stranger approaches you and demands your valuable items, remember that things can be replaced!

Staying Safe

It's best not to wear expensive jewelry when traveling. And don't carry large amounts of money, your passport, or your plane tickets if not necessary; if you must carry these things, wear a money belt under your clothes. Most hotels have safe-deposit boxes. Don't flaunt cameras and video equipment or leave them in sight in cars when sightseeing, especially in some parts of Belize City. Remember, this is a poor country and petty theft is its number-one crime—don't tempt fate.

It is generally not wise to wander around alone on foot late at night in Belize City. Go out with others if possible, and take a taxi. Most Belizeans are friendly, decent people, but, as in every community, a small percentage of unscrupulous crackheads will steal anything, given the opportunity. To many Belizeans, foreigners come off as "rich," whether they are or not. The local hustlers are quite creative when it comes to thinking of ways to con you out of some cash. Keep your wits about you, pull out of conversations that appear headed in that direction, don't give out your hotel name or room number freely or where they can be overheard by strangers, and remember—you're not on your own turf, so you're less familiar with everything around you.

In emergencies, dial 911 or 90 for police assistance. The number for fire and ambulance is also 90.

If You Are Robbed

If you are the victim of a crime while overseas, in addition to reporting it to local police, contact your embassy or consulate as soon as possible. The embassy or consulate staff can, for example, assist you in finding appropriate medical care and contacting family members or friends and will explain how funds can be transferred to you. Although the investigation and prosecution of the crime is solely the responsibility of local authorities, consular officers can help you to understand the local criminal justice process and to find an attorney if needed. From my experience, Belize police detectives respond quickly and take these matters—even near misses—seriously.

Police

Belizean police can hold somebody for 48 hours with no charges; one U.S. embassy warden called prison conditions in Belize "medieval," though this situation is improving rapidly. Some police officers have been arrested for rape and routinely beat and torture detainees (usually Belizeans). On the whole, though, most officers are good folks, making the best of a poorly paying job with very few resources. Don't try to bribe them if you're in trouble—you'll only contribute to a more corrupt system that does not need any encouragement.

Illegal Drugs

Belize's modern history began with law-breaking pirates hiding out among the hundreds of cayes, lagoons, and uninhabited coastlines of the territory. The same natural features have made Belize a fueling stopover for Colombian cocaine traffickers. The drug runners' practice of paying off their Belizean helpers with product (in addition to irresistible sums of cash) has created a national market for cocaine and crack with devastating effects, especially in Orange Walk Town and numerous coastal communities.

According to the U.S. State Department, traffickers increasingly use maritime operations in conjunction with aircraft "wet-drops" or off-loads from sea vessels to smuggle drug shipments into Belizean waters. Cocaine, air-dropped off the coast of Belize, is transported to the Belizean mainland or Mexico by small "go-fast" boats, stored, and then shipped onward to the United States. Occasionally, unintended recipients find this "sea lotto" (also known as "square grouper")—bales of uncut cocaine (also sometimes dumped overboard by traffickers who are about to get busted)—floating in the water.

The U.S. Drug Enforcement Agency (DEA) is active in Belize—as it is throughout Central America—to battle the flow of cocaine and other illegal drugs; the agency provides boat patrols, overflights, drug war technology and herbicides, and sniffing dogs at roadside checkpoints.

Marijuana, or ganja, grows naturally and quite well in the soils and climate of Belize, although the country is no longer the major producer it once was. In the early 1980s, "Belizean Breeze" was smuggled in massive enough quantities to make Belize the fourth-largest marijuana exporter to the United States. In the early 1980s, the DEA put an end to that with chemical-spraying programs, seizing and destroying 800 tons of marijuana in one year, mostly in the north of the country. Today, small-scale production continues, primarily for the domestic market. Some argue that the job vacuum created by marijuana suppression led directly to Belize's role in the trafficking of cocaine and the subsequent entrance of crack into Belizean communities.

Foreign, hip-looking tourists like yourself will most likely be offered pot (locally known as *"ta-boom-boom"*) at some point during your visit. Be careful: The proposal may be a harmless invitation to get high on the beach, or it may be coming from a hustler or stool pigeon who is about to rip you off and/or get you arrested. Marijuana prohibition is alive and well in Belize, despite widespread use of the herb throughout the population (not just among Rastas), and despite the herb's proven medical benefits. The controversial anti-ganja policy allows harsh penalties for possession of even tiny quantities of *cannabis sativa,* for both nationals and tourists alike. Tightly wrapped nuggets of buds, usually under two grams, are referred to as "bullets," and possessing even one of these can bring a fine of hundreds of dollars and possible incarceration. Also, watch out for guys selling prerolled joints called *serias,* as they may be laced with crumbled crack cocaine.

Prostitution

Although illegal in Belize, the sale of sex is alive and well at a handful of brothels throughout the country, usually on the highways outside major towns. Prostitutes are rarely Belizean and are often indentured sex slaves unwittingly recruited from Honduras, Guatemala, or El Salvador with false promises of legitimate employment. It is undeniable that foreign johns contribute to Belize's sex economy, especially on cruise days. Still, there is no tourist sex industry, per se, as there is in places like Cuba or Thailand.

Information and Services

MONEY

Automated teller machines (ATMs) are available in nearly all major Belizean towns, but they may operate on different card networks (Plus, Cirrus, etc.), so you may have to try a few to get your card to work. They're also often out of order.

Currency

The currency unit is the Belize dollar (BZE$), which has been steady at BZE$2 to US$1 for some years. While prices are given in U.S. dollars in this book, travelers should be prepared to pay in Belizean currency on the street, aboard boats, in cafés, and at other smaller establishments. Everyone accepts U.S. dollars though, as there is a continual shortage in the country, and folks with access to black-market changers, who sometimes give considerably more than 2:1, will be eager for your greens.

When you buy or sell currency at a bank, be sure to retain proof of sale. The following places are authorized to buy or sell foreign currency: Atlantic Bank Ltd., Bank of Nova Scotia, Barclays Bank, Belize Bank of Commerce and Industry, and Belize Global Travel Services Ltd. All are close together near the plaza in Belize City and in other cities. Hours are till 1 P.M. Monday–Friday, till 11 A.M. Saturday. You can also change money, sometimes at a rate a bit better than 2:1, at Casas de Cambio. But because Casas de Cambio must charge the official rate, many people still go to the black market, which gives a better rate.

At the Mexico-Belize border, you'll be approached by money changers (and you can bet they don't represent the banks). Many travelers buy just enough Belize dollars to get themselves into the city and to the banks. Depending on your mode of transport and destination, these money changers can be helpful. Strictly speaking, though, this is illegal—so suit yourself. The exchange rate is the same, but you'll have no receipt of sale. If selling a large quantity of Belize dollars back to the bank, you might be asked for that proof.

Credit Cards and Travelers Checks

Credit cards are taken at a growing number of business establishments, and travelers checks are increasingly obsolete, though still accepted at many places. You will find representatives of Visa, MasterCard, and American Express at the four commercial banks in Belize City and other towns; there you can make cash advances against your card.

Tipping

Most restaurants and hotels include a 10–15 percent service charge on the bill; if they don't, you should pay this amount yourself. It is not customary to tip taxi drivers unless they help you with your luggage. Always tip your tour guide if he or she has made your trip an enjoyable one.

Costs

Make no mistake: Belize vies with Costa Rica for being the most expensive country in Central America, and backpackers entering Belize from Mexico, Guatemala, and Honduras can expect some serious sticker shock after crossing the border. This was true even before the advent of tourism, because of the import-reliant economy and whatever other invisible market hands guide such things. Shoestring travelers squeaking by on US$25–35 per person per day in Belize are most likely stone sober and eating street tacos three times a day; they are not paying for tours or taxis, and they are surely not diving. They can still have a grand old time though, camped out in the bush (or in a US$10 room), doing lots of self-guided hiking, paddling, and cultural exploring. It's possible to travel on this little—but it depends on your comfort zone and definition of a good time.

If you've only got a seven-day vacation, you won't have to stretch your dollars over as many weeks or months as Susie Backpacker and her dog, Dreddie, and can thus spend more on lodging and activities. Figure at least US$100 per person per day if you want to pay for day trips and don't want to share a bathroom; serious divers or anglers should add a bit more. Weeklong packages at many dive and jungle resorts run between US$1,000 and US$1,600 and go up from there.

There are usually low-budget, decent quality exceptions to the rule across Belize, and I've tried to point all of those out in each region. In general though, prices are high and getting higher, and are especially sensitive to global petroleum fluctuations. Many mid- and upscale accommodations have raised their rates by as much as 20–40 percent since the last edition of *Moon Belize*—and not all have increased the quality of their service to match. Alcohol is always a good indicator: A bottle of One Barrel Rum is peaking at US$12 in most stores; a six-pack of Belikin beer can be a whopping US$10!

Be prepared for some additional taxes and service charges on your bill, which sometimes are and sometimes are not included in quoted rates:

• General Sales Tax (GST): 10 percent

• Hotel tax: 9 percent

• Service charge (often placed on bill): 10–15 percent

• Airport departure tax: US$20

If you use your credit card, it will cost you a little more at most businesses, sometimes 3–5 percent of the bill.

Incidentally, real estate prices are also shooting skyward, prompting many to predict that the bubble is soon due to burst. Compared to back home, rentals and lots may still be a bargain, but *caveat emptor*—and watch out for hidden costs on that condo. Owners' promises that your mortgage "will pay for itself" should be taken very carefully.

Bank Hours

Many banks are only open till 1 P.M. or 2 P.M. Monday–Thursday (staying open a bit later on Fridays), are often closed for lunch, and are always closed Saturday afternoons and Sundays.

TIME, WEIGHTS, AND MEASURES

The local time is Greenwich Mean Time minus six, the same as U.S. Central Time, year-round (there is no daylight saving time). The electricity is standard 110/220 volt, 60 cycles. Most distances are measured in inches, feet, yards, and miles, although there is some limited use of the metric system.

COMMUNICATIONS AND MEDIA

Mail

Posting a letter or postcard is easy and cheap, costing well under US$1, and the stamps are gorgeous. If you visit the outlying cities or cayes, bring your mail to Belize City to post—it's more apt to get to its destination quickly.

Post offices are located in the center of (or nearby) all villages and cities in Belize, although they usually don't look too post-officey from the outside. When writing letters to Belize, abbreviate Central America as "C.A." Be sure to

---

USEFUL NUMBERS

Police, fire, ambulance: 90 or 911

Directory assistance: 113 or 115

To report crimes: 0-800 922-TIPS

To report child abuse: 0-800-PROTECT

Operator assistance: 114 or 115

Date, time, and temperature: 121

---

include the periods; otherwise the U.S. Post Office will send your letters to California. You can receive mail in any town without getting a P.O. Box—just have the mail addressed to your name, care of "General Delivery," followed by the town, district, and "Belize."

FedEx, DHL, and other international couriers are widely available, and the Mailboxes, Etc. in Belize City (on Front St., just up from the Water Taxi Terminal) can take care of most of your mailing and package needs.

Sending mail within Belize, you can use either the post office system or the buses.

Public Telephones

Belize Telecommunications Limited's (BTL's) monopoly on Belizean telephones has been a big news item for years, and it was recently sold in a much-publicized stock transfer. How this will affect communications in the future is uncertain. As far as the traveler is concerned, there will always be a way to call home. The most common is to buy a prepaid BTL phone card and punch in the card's numbers every time you borrow a phone or use one of the many pay phones in the country. All towns also have a local BTL office, usually identified by a giant red and white radio tower somewhere very nearby; they can place calls anywhere in the country or world for you and will assign you to a semiprivate booth after they've dialed the number. They can also connect you to your homeland phone carrier. See www.btl.net for more information.

One reader gave the following warning: "*Do not* use the blue and yellow plastic hotel phones for international calls! I was charged US$42 for a one-minute phone call not once, but twice for the same call! After visiting BTL offices in Belize City, San Ignacio, and Punta Gorda, I could not get a refund, and the company claimed to have no record of the transaction (even though my credit-card company surely did)." According to a BTL employee, credit-card calls made through these phones are so expensive because the touch-tone "international operator" charges US$16 per minute. Even wilder, BTL will not disclose their phone rates to the institutions that house these phones.

Cell Phones

DigiCell (www.digicell.bz) offers prepaid temporary service to tourists. Get it at BTL's Airport Service Center, or bring your own GSM 1900 MHz handset and purchase a SIM pack from any DigiCell distributor nationwide. There are several local cellular services, both analog and digital, and coverage along roadways and in major towns is decent but still improving.

Smart Phones (Mile 1½ Northern Highway in Belize City, tel. 501/280-1010, www.smart-bz.com) is more user-friendly and cheaper than BTL and the rest, offering roaming service on your CDMA 800 MHz phone from home (including Verizon and Sprint). Activation fee is US$20, then you use prepaid cards available throughout the country.

International Calls and VOIPs

To call out of Belize, find a phone with international direct dialing service, then dial the international access code "00," followed by your country code, and then the city or area code and the number. The country code for Canada and the United States is "1" and England is "44." Australia is "61." BTL's telephone directory has a complete listing of country codes. An (often cheaper) alternative is to dial "10-10-199" instead of "00," followed by your country code, etc. Although they are not toll-free

from Belize, 800 numbers are dialed as they are written, preceded by the "00."

Belize's country code is "501." To receive a call in Belize from the United States, for example, tell the caller to dial "011" to tap into the international network, followed by "501" and your seven digit number. To call collect to Belize from other countries, dial the MCI operator at 1-800-COLLECT.

Some Internet cafés have found ways around BTL's illegal efforts to block VOIPs (voice over Internet protocols), some haven't, so VOIPing is still not 100 percent reliable in Belize. Free VOIPs (like Skype) offer dirt-cheap rates on international calls and are getting better to use by the day. If you have a laptop, be sure to install some sort of VPN (virtual private network) to encrypt the data coming in and out of your computer, thus bypassing BTL's VOIP jams. This is a hot topic that will surely evolve with the technology over the years.

Internet Access

Web access is widely available throughout the country and is improving all the time. Crappy dial-up connections are now the exception rather than the norm, and broadband (DSL, cable, and satellite) is springing up everywhere. If traveling with a laptop, you can usually find a landline to plug into your Ethernet dock at any of the more modern cafés—some have laptop docks already set up; some need to unplug a line from one of their computers. If you're in town for a while, many Internet businesses have monthly memberships that include unlimited access. You are welcome to sign up for a BTL account if you don't have your own ISP (Internet service provider), but that may lead to more headaches then you need, and there are many other options.

Wireless Internet (Wi-Fi) access is also increasingly available in Belize's accommodations, bars, and restaurants. I won't go so far as to tell you to *expect* wireless access yet, but if it's a concern of yours, definitely inquire whether your hotel has it or not. Most of these connections are free—with the exception of

You'll find an Internet connection in most places you travel in Belize.

BTL Hotspots, which are a ludicrous rip-off at US$15 per 24-hour period (plus tax!) and your only option at a handful of upscale hotels, including the Radisson and the Inn at Robert's Grove.

Local Newspapers and Magazines

Four weekly, highly politicized Belizean newspapers come out on Fridays, with occasional midweek editions, and you'll find many a Belizean conducting the weekly ritual of reading his favorite over a cup of instant coffee, and then going to happy hour to yap away about the latest scandal. *Amandala* and the *Reporter* seem to be the most objective and respected of these rags. The other two are *The Belize Times* and *The Guardian*. There are also publications in San Pedro and Placencia.

Definitely find a copy of *NICH Culture: A Magazine about Belize;* although it is published by a government body (NICH is the National Institute of Culture and History), this glossy, oversized quarterly is a brilliantly designed relief from the standard official line of brochure-like propaganda. Features about local customs and characters are illustrated with stunning photography and are ad-free (except for a few self-serving government bits). Look for it in the Image Factory in Belize City and in bookstores around the country.

In most gift shops, you'll find at least a few colorful Belizean history and picture books put out by **Cubola Productions,** a local publisher specializing in all things Belize, including maps, atlases, short stories, novels, and poems written by Belizeans. Cubola's publications give a great insight into the country.

Foreign News and Books

You will not find the *International Herald Tribune* on every newsstand like in other destinations. In fact, you may not find it at all. Check with the Radisson Hotel or Fort Street Guest House in Belize City, where you can sometimes find the *Miami Herald,* a relatively recent *Newsweek,* or if you're lucky, the *New York Times* or *London Times.* **Brodie's** and **The Book Center** also carry American magazines.

English-language novels (trashy and otherwise) are widely available in hotel gift shops, and many budget accommodations across the country have book exchanges.

Maps

The most readily available and up-to-date map to Belize is published by **International Travel Maps,** whose 1:250,000 map of Belize makes a useful addition to any guidebook (or wall), and was last updated in 2005. The best, biggest country map to hang on your wall at home (it's way too big to use as a travel guide) is a physical/political 1:265,000 scale, distributed by Cubola Productions and available at Angelus Press in Belize City for nearly US$40. The latest version was made in 2007, and there is also a folded version you can pack with you.

All of Belize's most heavily touristed areas create updated town maps, found most often at tourist information booths and car (or golf cart) rental places.

The **Government of Belize Land Department** in Belmopan has detailed topographic maps for the entire country—spendy at US$40 per quad, but vital if you're doing any serious backcountry travel. The British Army and United Kingdom Ordinance Survey have created a number of map series of various scales, but tracking them down will be a challenge.

More Information

The official government ministry is the **Belize Tourism Board** (BTB; tel. 501/227-2420, U.S. tel. 800/624-0686, 64 Regent St., www.travelbelize.org). The BTB offers a unique toll-free help line (800-SERVICE, 8 A.M.–5 P.M.), answered by real people in their marketing department. At the office (in Belize City, on the southside, near the Hotel Mopan), you'll find brochures on a number of reserves and national parks and information on various sections of the country. You'll usually find someone who's willing to talk to you and answer your questions.

The **Belize Tourism Industry Association** (BTIA, tel. 501/227-1144/5717, www.btia.org) is the industry-based association. These folks are also a source of good information about the country. BTIA sponsors a number of regional booths around the country with helpful maps and brochures.

You'll find more information at the **Embassy of Belize** in the United States (2535 Massachusetts Ave. NW, Washington, D.C. 20008, U.S. tel. 202/332-9636, www.embassyofbelize.org) and also the **Caribbean Tourism Association** (20 E. 46th St., New York, NY 10017, U.S. tel. 212/563-6011 or 800/624-0686, www.onecaribbean.org).

RESOURCES

Suggested Reading

Start with Belizean writers, particularly the novels of Zee Edgell, then continue with the catalog of **Cubola Productions** (www.cubola. com), a publishing company whose Belizean writers series includes six anthologies of short stories, poetry, drama, folktales, and works by women writers. Cubola also publishes sociology, anthropology, and education texts; seek them out at any bookstore or gift shop in Belize, or order a few titles before your trip. **Angelus Press** (www.angeluspress.com) is the other main publisher of Belizean writers. You'll also want to read a book—or six—by **Emory King** (www.emoryking.com); King arrived in Belize in 1953 when his yacht crashed on the reef at English Caye and has been talking and writing about his adopted country ever since. Following are a few more suggestions.

FICTION

Edgell, Zee. *Beka Lamb*. Portsmouth: Heinemann, 1982. The first internationally recognized Belizean novel, this story of a girl named Beka who is growing up with her country is required reading for all Belizean high schoolers and offers an excellent view of Belizean family life, history, and politics.

Highwater, Jamake. *Journey to the Sky: A Novel About the True Adventures of Two Men in Search of the Lost Maya Kingdom*. New York: Thomas Y. Crowell, 1978.

Lukowiak, Ken. *Marijuana Time*. Orion, 2000. Follow the author's experiences on a six-month "hardship posting" to Belize in 1983 with the British military: "The long days are palliated by a constant and increasingly compulsive supply of drugs and japes, until he starts using his position in the army postroom to send improbably large bundles of the stuff home—to his army flat in Aldershot."

Miller, Carlos Ledson. *Belize: A Novel*. Xlibris. com: 1999. This history-laden piece of fiction offers an impressively thorough snapshot of Belize over the last 40 years.

Westlake, Donald. *High Adventure*. Tor Books, 1986. Another marijuana-smuggling action thriller: "You are in the jungles of Belize. You pick your way carefully along the overgrown trail until you come to the clearing. There, above you, rest the ruins of a Mayan pyramid. Is that a stone whistle at your feet? An idol of the bat-god? Riches surround you and Kirby Galway will be more to happy to smuggle your finds to the United States in a bale of marijuana. Aren't you glad you met Kirby?"

HEALTH AND PRACTICAL

Arvigo, Rosita. *Sastun: One Woman's Apprenticeship with a Maya Healer and Their Efforts to Save the Vani*. San Francisco: Harper, 1995. One of the better-known books about Belize, which tells the story of the American-born author's training with 87-year-old Elijio Panti, the best-known Maya medicine man in Central America. It takes place in the remote, roadless expanse of Cayo District in western Belize.

Schroeder, Dirk. *Staying Healthy in Asia, Africa, and Latin America*. Emeryville, CA: Avalon Travel Publishing, 2000. An excellent resource that fits in your pocket for easy reference.

Sluder, Lan. *Living Abroad in Belize*. Emeryville, CA: Avalon Travel Publishing, 2005. The Living Abroad series helps readers realize their dreams of making a home in a foreign country; each Living Abroad title provides the tools necessary to find—and settle into—a new home.

Werner, David. *Where There Is No Doctor*. Palo Alto, CA: Hesperian Foundation, 1992.

Zepatos, Thalia. *A Journey of One's Own*. Portland, OR: Eighth Mountain Press, 2003. Offers "uncommon advice for the independent woman traveler."

NATURE AND FIELD GUIDES

As Belize is one of the most exhaustively studied tropical countries in the world, there are innumerable references that span every conceivable niche of flora, fauna, and geology. They come in massive, coffee-table sizes with color plates, as well as in pocket-size field guides: Tarantulas of Belize, Hummingbirds of Belize, Orchids of Belize, and so on. Following are a few titles that make up the tip of the iceberg for this category.

Arvigo, Rosita, and Michael Balick (foreword by Mickey Hart). *Rainforest Remedies: 100 Healing Herbs of Belize*. Wisconsin: Lotus Press, 1998.

Beletsky, Les. *Belize and Northern Guatemala: The Ecotravellers' Wildlife Guide*. San Diego, CA: Academic Press, 1999. One of the best reasonably-sized general nature guides to the area, with abundant color plates for all types of fauna.

Burgess, Robert. *Secret Languages of the Sea*. New York: Dodd, Mead, and Company, 1981. Burgess looks at the world of submarine communication.

Cousteau, Jacques-Yves. *Three Adventures: Galápagos, Titicaca, the Blue Holes*. Garden City, NY: Doubleday, 1973.

Jones, H. Lee, and Dana Gardener (illustrator). *Birds of Belize*. Christopher Helm Publishers Ltd., 2004. This is the long-awaited, much-acclaimed Bible of Belize birding (say *that* three times fast); it's a big book (445 pages, 56 color plates, 28 figures, 234 maps), prompting some birders I met to cut out all the plates and travel with those only.

Kuhlmann, Dietrick. *Living Coral Reefs of the World*. New York: Arco Publishing, 1985.

MacKinnon, Barbara. *100 Common Birds of the Yucatán Peninsula*. Cancún, Quintana Roo, Mexico: Amigos de Sian Ka'an, 1989.

Stevens, Katie. *Jungle Walk: Birds and Beasts of Belize, Central America*. Belize: Angelus Press, 1991. Order through International Expeditions, tel. 800/633-4734.

ARCHAEOLOGY

Carrasco, David. *Religions of Mesoamerica: Cosmovision and Ceremonial Centers*. San Francisco: Waveland Press, 1998. Carrasco details the dynamics of two important cultures—the Aztec and the Maya—and discusses the impact of the Spanish conquest and the continuity of native traditions.

Coe, Michael D. *The Maya, Seventh Edition*. New York: Thames and Hudson, 2005. A classic book, newly updated for anyone attempting to understand the Maya, the "most intellectually sophisticated and aesthetically refined pre-Columbian culture."

De Landa, Friar Diego. *Yucatán: Before and After the Conquest*. New York: Dover Publications, 1978 (translation of original manuscript written in 1566). The same man who provided some of the best, most lasting descriptions of ancient Maya also singlehandedly destroyed the most Maya artifacts and writings of anyone in history.

Schele, Linda, and David Freidel. *A Forest of Kings: The Untold Story of the Ancient Maya.* New York: William Morrow and Company, Inc., 1990.

Stephens, John L. *Incidents of Travel in Central America, Chiapas and Yucatán.* New York: Dover Publications, Inc., 1969 (originally Harper & Bros., New York, 1841). A classic 19th-century travelogue, Stephens's writing is wonderfully pompous, amusing, and incredibly astute—with historical and archaeological observations that still stand today. If you can, find a copy with the original set of illustrations by Stephens's expedition partner.

HISTORY, POLITICS, TOURISM, AND MEMOIR

Barcott, Bruce. *The Last Flight of the Scarlet Macaw: One Woman's Fight to Save the World's Most Beautiful Bird.* Random House, 2008. Fantastic nonfiction narrative about the Chalillo Dam in western Belize, a highly contentious construction project on the upper Macal River in Cayo. The author skillfully lays out the story and characters around the dam business, while providing a sweeping panoramic snapshot of a very unique country as it makes its debut in the new global economy.

Bolland, O. Nigel. *Belize: A New Nation in Central America.* Boulder, CO: Westview, 1986. This book is one of many socio-political analyses by this prolific author.

Duffy, Rosaleen. *A Trip Too Far: Ecotourism, Politics and Exploitation.* Earthscan, 2002. A critical look of the impacts of ecotourism, using Belize as a case study.

Fairweather, Stephen. *The Baymen of Belize.* London, 1992. May be out of print.

Fry, Joan. *How to Cook a Tapir: A Memoir of Belize.* University of Nebraska Press, 2009. The story of a young teacher's year abroad, living among the Maya in southern Belize nearly fifty years ago. The author offers an intimate glimpse at Maya village life in this heartfelt, oftentimes funny story of how she "painstakingly baked and boiled her way up the food chain" to gain acceptance among her neighbors and students.

Kerns, Virginia. *Women and the Ancestors: Black Carib Kinship and Ritual.* Urbana, IL: University of Illinois Press, 1983.

Pattullo, Polly. *Last Resorts: The Cost of Tourism in the Caribbean,* second edition. London: Latin America Bureau, 2005. Pattullo provides an interesting breakdown of how the Caribbean tourism industry is structured, as well as a hard-hitting commentary on who benefits and how, providing numerous examples from Belize.

Rabinowitz, Alan. *Jaguar: One Man's Struggle to Establish the World's First Jaguar Preserve.* Washington, D.C.: Island Press/Shearwater Books, 2000 (originally 1986). If you've only got time to read one book on Belize, I recommend this excellent eco-memoir. In addition to telling the true story of his jaguar work in Belize, Rabinowitz gives an alluring glance at Belize's wild post-independence, pre-tourism phase.

Roessingh, Carel. *Entrepreneurs in Tourism in the Caribbean Basin: Case Studies from Belize, the Dominican Republic, Jamaica, and Suriname.* Whitston Publishing Company, 2006.

Sawatzky, Harry. *They Sought a Country: Mennonite Colonization in Mexico. With an Appendix on Mennonite Colonization in British Honduras.* Berkeley, CA: University of California, 1971.

Shoman, Assad. *13 Chapters of a History of Belize.* Belize City: The Angelus Press, Ltd., 1994. A no-nonsense history of Belize from a fresh, Belizean perspective.

Sutherland, Anne. *The Making of Belize: Globalization in the Margins.* London: Bergin & Garvey Paperback, 1998. The British Bulletin of Publications calls this "an enjoyable mixture of academic research, anecdotal insights and strong, even controversial opinion. . . . This book deserves to be read by any visitor to Belize, whether arriving as a tourist or as a volunteer with one of the many international conservation organizations now operating there."

Wilk, Richard. *Home Cooking in the Global Village: Caribbean Food from Buccaneers to Ecotourists.* Palgrave Macmillan, 2006. Uses food to describe Belize's longtime struggle within "the great paradox of globalization." Wilk raises questions like "How can you stay local and relish your own home cooking, while tasting the delights of the global marketplace?" Includes menus, recipes, and "bad colonial poetry."

Internet Resources

The first page you bookmark should be **www.belizesearch.com,** the premier search engine for all things Belize, with access to more than 50,000 Belizean webpages and documents.

Ambergris Caye
www.ambergriscaye.com
Official site of Ambergris Caye and a lot more, with links to the whole country and a hugely popular user forum.

Belize Audubon Society
www.belizeaudubon.org
Lots of information on the parks BAS manages and general conservation efforts in Belize.

Belize First Magazine
www.belizefirst.com
The online exploits of Lan Sluder, a long-time travel writer on Belize with many books under his belt, including *San Pedro Cool,* which you can download.

The Belize Forums
www.belizeforum.com

Belize Kriol
www.kriol.org.bz
Official website of the National Kriol Council of Belize, promoting Kriol language and "kulcha."

Belize Tourism Board
www.travelbelize.org

Belize Zoo and Tropical Education Center
www.belizezoo.org

Caye Caulker Belize Tourism Industry Association
www.gocayecaulker.com

Diving in Belize
www.scubadivingbelize.com

Ecotourism
www.planeta.com
This is one of the premier ecotourism sites around; look up the Belize page for all kinds of current events and interesting tourism-related articles.

Government of Belize
www.belize.gov.bz

Immersion Travel
www.worldstogethertravel.com
An independent effort by passionate travelers who encourage everyone to go deep.

Lanic
www.lanic.utexas.edu/la/ca/belize
The University of Texas's Latin American Network Information Center is an acclaimed source of all kinds of information, with an extensive list of Belizean links.

Naturalight
www.belizenet.com
Portal to the vast Naturalight network.

San Pedro Sun
www.sanpedrosun.net
Lots of Belizean news and links from this island newspaper, in addition to the latest Ambergris scoop.

Toucan Trail
www.toucantrail.com
A network of budget hotels for independent travelers seeking affordable adventure and accommodation with "local flavor."

Transitions Abroad
www.transitionsabroad.com
Information on working, studying, and volunteering abroad, including updated listings of available positions.

Travel Health Concerns
www.cdc.gov
www.mdtravelhealth.com

United States Embassy in Belize
www.belize.usembassy.gov

Index

List of Maps

Acknowledgments

First and foremost, my sincerest thank you to Chicki Mallan, who wrote the first five editions of *Moon Belize*. This eighth editon would not have been possible without the hard work of my research assistants, Rosey Goodman and Joni Miller. If you go to Caye Caulker, say hi to Joni at the Ocean Academy and ask how you can help. Thanks also to so many new and old friends: Katie Valk, Richard Wilk, Tony Rath, Judy and Jan Wilson, Ian and Kate Morton, Juli Puryear, Rachel Graham, Polly Wood, Paul and Zoe Walker.

Special thank you to my birder friends who were gracious with their keen-eyed suggestions and corrections: Scott Schmidt, Delia Noble, and the rest of the Belize Audubon Society; Kevin Loughlin of Wildside Nature Tours; Nathan Forbes. I wish you all many "big days" ahead.

I enjoyed crossing paths with Paul "The Krazy African" Zway in the midst of his Central American luxury tent trade mission and Elsie the Automobile adventure (www.exclusivetents.com); he, Angelika, and I shared a hairy canoe ride down an engorged river, battled tiger's claw vines and face-sized spiders, tried to turn back, couldn't, and in the end, made it to the jungle lodge in time for sugar-coated cacao martinis. All in a day's work.

My wife, Sutay; daughter, Shanti; and mother-in-law, Louise, assisted in researching the southern chapters of this edition—an act of extreme patience, love, and flexibility, considering the hectic pace of guidebook research travel in 100 percent humidity.

Thanks also to my editors and colleagues at Avalon—Kevin McLain, Domini Dragoone, Albert Angulo, Jen Rios, Jodee Krainik, and the rest of the team. One of these days, we'll all go to Belize together, guys, I promise.

www.moon.com

DESTINATIONS | ACTIVITIES | BLOGS | MAPS | BOOKS

MOON.COM is ready to help plan your next trip! Filled with fresh trip ideas and strategies, author interviews, informative travel blogs, a detailed map library, and descriptions of all the Moon guidebooks, Moon.com is all you need to get out and explore the world—or even places in your own backyard. While at Moon.com, sign up for our monthly e-newsletter for updates on new releases, travel tips, and expert advice from our on-the-go Moon authors. As always, when you travel with Moon, expect an experience that is uncommon and truly unique.

MOON IS ON FACEBOOK—BECOME A FAN!
JOIN THE MOON PHOTO GROUP ON FLICKR

MAP SYMBOLS

▭▭▭ Expressway	**〖** Highlight	✗ Airfield	⚷ Golf Course
▭▭▭ Primary Road	○ City/Town	✈ Airport	🅿 Parking Area
▭▭▭ Secondary Road	◉ State Capital	▲ Mountain	▰ Archaeological Site
▭▭▭ Unpaved Road	✸ National Capital	✛ Unique Natural Feature	⚑ Church
- - - - - Trail	★ Point of Interest		
⋯⋯⋯ Ferry	• Accommodation	✎ Waterfall	⚲ Gas Station
◆─◆─ Railroad	▼ Restaurant/Bar	▲ Park	◔ Glacier
▭▭▭ Pedestrian Walkway	▪ Other Location	ⓣ Trailhead	▱ Mangrove
▥▥▥ Stairs	⋀ Campground	⛷ Skiing Area	▨ Reef
			▤ Swamp

CONVERSION TABLES

°C = (°F - 32) / 1.8
°F = (°C x 1.8) + 32
1 inch = 2.54 centimeters (cm)
1 foot = 0.304 meters (m)
1 yard = 0.914 meters
1 mile = 1.6093 kilometers (km)
1 km = 0.6214 miles
1 fathom = 1.8288 m
1 chain = 20.1168 m
1 furlong = 201.168 m
1 acre = 0.4047 hectares
1 sq km = 100 hectares
1 sq mile = 2.59 square km
1 ounce = 28.35 grams
1 pound = 0.4536 kilograms
1 short ton = 0.90718 metric ton
1 short ton = 2,000 pounds
1 long ton = 1.016 metric tons
1 long ton = 2,240 pounds
1 metric ton = 1,000 kilograms
1 quart = 0.94635 liters
1 US gallon = 3.7854 liters
1 Imperial gallon = 4.5459 liters
1 nautical mile = 1.852 km

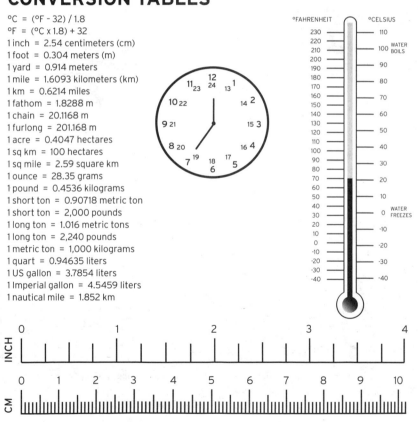

MOON BELIZE
Avalon Travel
a member of the Perseus Books Group
1700 Fourth Street
Berkeley, CA 94710, USA
www.moon.com

Editor: Kevin McLain
Series Manager: Kathryn Ettinger
Copy Editor: Teresa Elsey
Graphics and Production Coordinator:
   Domini Dragoone
Cover Designer: Domini Dragoone
Map Editor: Brice Ticen
Cartographers: Kat Bennett, Chris Markiewicz
Proofreader: Naomi Adler Dancis
Indexer: Rachel Kuhn

ISBN: 978-1-59880-210-8
ISSN: 1533-9130

Printing History
1st Edition – 1991
8th Edition – September 2009
5 4 3 2

Text © 2009 by Joshua Berman.
Maps © 2009 by Avalon Travel.
All rights reserved.

Some photos and illustrations are used by permission
and are the property of the original copyright
owners.

Front cover photo: Cushion Sea Star (Oreaster
reticulatus) in the clear Belizean waters, © Getty
Images/Stephen Frink.

Title page photo: flowers on the beach at Hopkins, ©
Joshua Berman.

Interior color photos: pages 4-6, 7 (top, and bottom
right), 9, 10 (top), 12, 14, 17, 18, 19 (bottom), 22, and
23: © Joshua Berman; page 7 (bird), 13, 20, and
24: Courtesy of the Belize Tourism Board/David
Humphreys; page 10 (bottom), 11, and 21: Courtesy
of the Belize Tourism Board/Tony Rath; page 16:
Courtesy of the Belize Tourism Board/David Solano;
page 19 (top): © 123rf.com/Darryl Brooks.

Printed in Canada by Friesens

Moon Handbooks and the Moon logo are the property
of Avalon Travel. All other marks and logos depicted
are the property of the original owners. All rights
reserved. No part of this book may be translated or
reproduced in any form, except brief extracts by a
reviewer for the purpose of a review, without written
permission of the copyright owner.

Although every effort was made to ensure that
the information was correct at the time of going
to press, the author and publisher do not assume
and hereby disclaim any liability to any party for any
loss or damage caused by errors, omissions, or any
potential travel disruption due to labor or financial
difficulty, whether such errors or omissions result
from negligence, accident, or any other cause.

KEEPING CURRENT

If you have a favorite gem you'd like to see included in the next edition, or see anything
that needs updating, clarification, or correction, please drop us a line. Send your
comments via email to feedback@moon.com, or use the address above.